The Theory of
Gambling and Statistical Logic

The Theory of Gambling

and Statistical Logic

RICHARD A. EPSTEIN

Aerospace Group, Space Systems Division
Hughes Aircraft Company, El Segundo, California

ACADEMIC PRESS

A Harcourt Science and Technology Company

San Diego   San Francisco   New York   Boston
London   Sydney   Tokyo

This book is printed on acid-free paper. ∞

Academic Press
A Harcourt Science and Technology Company
525 B Street, Suite 1900, San Diego, California 92101-4495, USA
http://www.academicpress.com

Academic Press
Harcourt Place, 32 Jamestown Road, London NW1 7BY, UK
http://www.academicpress.com

Library of Congress Cataloging-in-Publication Data

Epstein, Richard A.
    The theory of gambling and statistical logic.

    Includes bibliographies and indexes
    1. Games of chance (Mathematics)   2. Statistical
decision.   I. Title.
QA271.E67   1977   519   76-27440
ISBN 0-12-240761-X

PRINTED IN THE UNITED STATES OF AMERICA
        00 QW 9 8 7

*It is remarkable that a science which
began with the consideration of games
of chance should have become the most
important object of human knowledge. . . .
The most important questions of life are,
for the most part, really only problems
of probability.*

PIERRE SIMON, MARQUIS DE LAPLACE

Théorie Analytique des Probabilités, 1812

CONTENTS

PREFACE TO REVISED EDITION

Gambling being one of the few constants of the human condition, little change in its practice or basic theory could be expected over the decade since publication of the first edition of this book. Thus, most of the subject matter has retained, and will continue to retain, its currency.

Two areas alone can claim substantial progress. First, further analysis of security prices has supplied new insights into the mountainous jumble of quotations that spew forth from the stock exchanges. R. A. Levy at the University of Chicago Center for Research in Security Prices verified deviations from the random-walk theory. The Black–Scholes option model laid a concrete foundation for an edifice of investigations into warrant-hedging and commodity option-hedging. Edward O. Thorp, following "Beat the Dealer" with "Beat the Market," led the most practical, well-armed, and successful assault on the vaults of the securities and commodities markets.

Second, surprisingly, the game of Blackjack revealed a yet finer structure to mathematicians probing its intricacies. In particular, Peter Griffin of California State University, Sacramento, devised, analyzed, and evaluated card-counting systems in a comprehensive examination of memory-based strategies. Casino managements have reacted, thus far, by reducing the number of single-deck Blackjack games and emphasizing the play of four decks.

The discipline of computerized chess was predicted to produce a program competitive with master levels of skill. Embarrassingly, the best computer program compares with a B-rated human player. The prediction for the past decade is herein repeated—with less than full confidence—for the next decade.

Special appreciation is due to Dr. Thorp and Professor Griffin for their cooperation and contributions and to Julian Braun of the IBM Corporation for additional Blackjack data.

PREFACE TO FIRST EDITION

Gambling is a near universal pastime. Perhaps more people with less knowledge succumb to its lure than to any other sedentary avocation. As Balzac averred, "the gambling passion lurks at the bottom of every heart."

In our most puritan society, gambling—like other pleasures—is either taxed, restricted to certain hours, or forbidden altogether. Yet the impulse to gamble remains an eternal aspect of the apparent irrationality of man. It finds outlets in business, war, politics, in the formal overtures of the gambling casinos, and in the less ceremonious exchanges among individuals of differing opinions.

To some, the nature of gambling appears illusive, only dimly perceivable through a curtain of numbers. In others it inspires a quasi-religious emotion: true believers are governed by such mystical forces as "luck," "fate," and "chance." To yet others, gambling is the algorithmic Circe in whose embrace lies the road map to El Dorado: the "foolproof" system. Even mathematicians have fallen prey to the clever casuistry of gambling fallacies. Special wards in lunatic asylums could well be populated with mathematicians who have attempted to predict random events from finite data samples.

It is, then, the intent of this book to dissipate the mystery, myths, and misconceptions that abound in the realm of gambling and statistical phenomena.

The mathematical theory of gambling enjoys a distinguished pedigree. For several centuries, gamblers' pastimes provided both the impetus and the only concrete basis for the development of the concepts and methods of probability theory. Today, games of chance are used to isolate in pure form the logical structures underlying real-life systems while games of skill provide testing grounds for the study of multistage decision processes in practical contexts. We can readily confirm A. M. Turing's conviction that games constitute an ideal model system leading toward the development of machine intelligence.

It is also intended that a unified and complete theory be advanced. Thus it is necessary to establish formally the fundamental principles underlying the phenomena of gambling before citing examples illustrating their behavior. A majority of the requisite mathematical exposition for this goal has been elaborated and is available in the technical literature. Where deficiencies have prevented a comprehensive treatment, we have attempted to achieve the necessary developments. Mostly, however, this book constitutes a consolidation of knowledge found only in widely scattered sources.

The broad mathematical disciplines associated with the theory of gambling are probability theory and statistics, which are usually applied to those contests involving a statistical opponent ("nature"), and game theory, which is pertinent to games among "intelligent" contestants. To comprehend the operation of these disciplines normally requires only an understanding of the elementary mathematical tools—such as basic calculus. In a few isolated instances, rigorous proofs of certain fundamental statements dictate a descent into the pit of more abstract and esoteric mathematics (set theory, for example). When such instances arise, the reader not yet versed in advanced mathematical lore may gloss over the proofs with the assurance that their validity has been solidly substantiated.

If this book is successful, the reader previously susceptible to the extensive folklore of gambling will view the subject in a more rational light: the reader previously acquainted with the essentials of gambling theory will possess a more secure footing. The profits to be reaped from this knowledge are strongly dependent upon the individual. To any modestly intelligent person it is self-evident that the interests controlling operations of the gambling casinos are not, primarily, engaged in philanthropy. Furthermore, each of the principal games of chance or skill has been thoroughly analyzed by competent statisticians. Any inherent weakness, any obvious loophole, would have been uncovered long ago; and any of the multitude of miraculous "systems" which deserved its supernal reputation would have long since pauperized every gambling establishment in existence. The systems that promise something for nothing inevitably produce, instead, nothing for something.

It will also be self-evident to the reader that the laws of chance cannot be suspended despite all earnest supplications to the whim of Tyche or genuflections before the deities of the crap table. Such noumena cast small shadows on the real axis.

In the real world there is no "easy way" to assure a financial profit at the recognized games of chance or skill (if there were, the rules of play would soon be changed). An effort to understand the mathematics pertinent to each game, however, can produce a highly gratifying result. At least, it is gratifying to rationalize that we would rather lose intelligently than win ignorantly.

As with virtually all technical material, this book was not written in a vacuum. Much appreciation is due those who contributed both sympathetic ears and incisive criticism throughout that *annus mirabilis* required to complete the manuscript. In particular, we should like to award most honorable mention to the following individuals. Paul M. Cohen, of Litton Systems, is responsible for several shafts of light into the murky statistical depths. Dr. Douglas Anderson, of Purdue University, affixed his imprimatur of rigor to the corpus mathematica. Julian Braun, then of the Chicago IBM Datacenter, contributed gratuitously the programming effort underlying the Blackjack data presented in Chapter 7. And in a feat rivaling the decoding of the Knossos Linear B tablets, Mrs. Barbara Strouse, of Booz Allen Applied Research Inc., transcribed the original arcane chirographics into a legible text.

CHAPTER ONE

KUBEIAGENESIS

Shortly after *pithecanthropus erectus* gained the ascendency, he turned his attention to the higher-order abstractions. He invented a concept that has since been variously viewed as a vice, a crime, a business, a pleasure, a type of magic, a disease, a folly, a weakness, a form of sexual substitution, an expression of the human instinct. He invented gambling.

Archeologists rooting in prehistoric sites have uncovered large numbers of roughly dice-shaped bones, called astragalia, that were apparently used in games some thousands of years ago. Whether our Stone Age predecessors cast these objects for prophecy or amusement or simply to win their neighbors' stone axes, they began a custom that has survived both evolution and revolution.

Although virtually every primitive culture engaged in some form of dice play, many centuries elapsed before thought was directed to the "fairness" of throwing dice or to the equal probability with which each face falls or should fall. The link between mathematics and gambling remained long unsuspected.

Most early civilizations were entrapped by the deep-rooted emotional appeal of absolute truth; they demanded Olympian certitude and could neither conceive nor accept the inductive reliability sought by modern physics. "Arguments from probabilities are impostors" was the doctrine expressed in the dialogue *Phaedo*. Carneades, in the Second Century B.C., was the first to shift from the traditional Greek rationalist position by developing an embryonic probability theory which distinguished three types of probability, or degrees of certainty. However, this considerable accomplishment (against the native grain) advanced the position of empiricist philosophy more than the understanding of events of chance.

Throughout the entire history of man preceding the Renaissance, all efforts toward explaining the phenomena of chance were characterized by comprehensive ignorance of the nature of probability. Yet gambling flourished in various forms almost continuously from the time Paleolithic man cast his polished knucklebones and painted pebbles. Lack of knowledge has rarely inhibited anyone from taking a chance.

In the sixteenth century came the first reasoned considerations relating games of chance to a rudimentary theory of probability. Gerolamo Cardano (1501–1576), physician, philosopher, scientist, astrologer, religionist, gambler, murderer, was responsible for the initial attempt to organize the concept of chance events into a cohesive discipline. In *Liber de Ludo Aleae, the Book on Games of Chance* (published posthumously in 1663) he expressed a rough concept of mathematical expectation, derived power laws for the repetition of events, and conceived the definition of probability as a frequency ratio. Cardano described the "circuit" to be the totality of permissible outcomes of an event. The "circuit" was 6 for one die, 36 for two dice, 216 for three dice. He then defined the probability of occurrence of a particular outcome as the sum of possible ways of achieving that outcome divided by the "circuit." Cardano investigated the probabilities of casting astragals and undertook to explain the relative occurrence of card combinations, notably for the game of Primero (loosely similar to Poker). A century before de Méré he posed the problem of the number of throws of two dice necessary to obtain at least one roll of two aces with an even chance (he answered 18 rather than the correct value of 24.6). Of this brilliant but erratic Milanese, the English historian Henry Morley wrote, "He was a genius, a fool, and a charlatan who embraced and amplified all the superstition of his age, and all its learning." Cardano was imbued with a sense of mysticism; his undoing came through a pathological belief in astrology. In a publicized event he cast the horoscope of the frail fifteen-year-old Edward VI of England, including specific predictions for the fifty-fifth year, third month, and seventeenth day of the monarch's life. Edward was inconsiderate enough to expire the following year at the age of sixteen. Undismayed, Cardano then had the temerity to cast the horoscope of Jesus Christ, an act not viewed with levity by sixteenth century theologians. Finally, when the self-predicted day of his own death arrived, with his health showing no signs of faltering, he redeemed his reputation by an act of suicide.

Following Cardano, several desultory assaults were launched on the mysteries of gambling. Kepler issued a few words on the subject, and shortly after the turn of the seventeenth century Galileo wrote a small treatise titled, *Considerazione sopra il Giuoco dei Dadi.*[†] A group of gambling noblemen of the Florence court had consulted Galileo to determine why the total 10 appears more often than 9 in throws of 3 dice. The famous physicist showed that 27 cases out of 216 possible total the number 10, while the number 9 occurs 25 times out of 216.

Then, in 1654, came the most significant event in the theory of gambling as the discipline of mathematical probability emerged from its chrysalis. A noted gambler and roué, Antoine Gombauld, the Chevalier de Méré, Sieur de Baussay, posed to his friend the Parisian mathematician Blaise Pascal, the following problem: "Why do the odds differ in throwing a 6 in four rolls of one die as opposed to throwing two 6's in 24 rolls of two dice?" In subsequent correspondence with Pierre de Fermat (then a jurist in Toulouse) to answer this question, Pascal constructed the foundations on which the theory of probability rests today. In the discussion of various gambling problems, Pascal's conclusions and calculations were occasionally incorrect, while Fermat achieved greater accuracy by considering both dependent and independent probabilities. Deriving a solution to the "Problem of Points" (two players are lacking x and y points, respectively, to win a game; if the game is interrupted, how should the stakes be divided between them?), Pascal developed an approach similar to the calculus of finite differences. Pascal was an inexhaustible genius from childhood; much of his mathematical work was begun at the age of sixteen. At nineteen he invented and constructed the first calculating machine in history.[‡] He is also occasionally credited with the invention of the roulette wheel. Whoever of the two great mathematicians contributed more, Fermat and Pascal were first, based on considerations of games of chance, to place the theory of probability in a mathematical framework.

Curiously, the remaining half of the seventeenth century witnessed little interest in or extension of the work of Pascal and Fermat. In 1657 Christian Huygens published a treatise titled, *De Ratiociniis in Ludo Aleae* (Competition in Games of Chance), wherein he deals with the probability of certain dice combinations and originates the concept of "mathematical expectation." Leibnitz also produced work on probabilities, neither notable nor rigorous: he stated that the sums of 11 and 12, cast with

---

[†] Originally, "Sopra le Scoperte de i Dadi."

[‡] The first calculating machine based on modern principles must be credited, however, to Charles Babbage (1830).

two dice, have equal probabilities (*Dissertatio de Arte Combinatoria*, 1666). John Wallis contributed a brief work on combinations and permutations, as did the Jesuit John Caramuel. John Arbuthnot, Francis Roberts, and Craig were responsible for occasional pronouncements on combinatorial analysis, but without special distinction. A shallow debut of the discipline of statistics was launched by John Graunt in his book on population growth, *Natural and Political Observations Made Upon the Bills of Mortality*. John de Witt analyzed the problem of annuities, and Edmund Halley published the first complete mortality tables.[†] By mathematical standards, however, none of these works can qualify as first-class achievements.

More important for the advancement of probabilistic comprehension was the destructive scepticism that arose during the Renaissance and Reformation. The doctrine of certainty in science, philosophy, and theology was severely attacked. In England, William Chillingworth promoted the view that man is unable to find absolutely certain religious knowledge. Rather, he asserted, a limited certitude based on common sense should be accepted by all reasonable men. Chillingworth's theme was later applied to scientific theory and practice by Glanville, Boyle, and Newton, and given a philosophical exposition by Locke.

Turning into the eighteenth century, the "Age of Reason" irrupted and the appeal of probability theory again attracted qualified mathematicians. The *Ars Conjectandi* (Art of Guessing) of Jacob Bernoulli developed the theory of permutations and combinations. One-fourth of the work (published posthumously in 1713) consists of solutions of problems relating to games of chance. Bernoulli wrote other treatises on dice combinations and was the first to consider the problem of duration of play. He analyzed various card games (for example, Trijaques) popular in his time and contributed to probability theory the famous theorem that by sufficiently increasing the number of observations, any preassigned degree of accuracy is attainable. Bernoulli's theorem was the first to express frequency statements within the formal framework of the probability calculus. Bernoulli envisioned the subject of probability from the most general point of view to that date. He predicted applications for the theory of probability outside the narrow range of problems relating to games of chance; the classical definition of probability is essentially derived from his work.

In 1708 Remond de Montmort published his work on chance titled, *Essai d'Analyse sur les Jeux d'Hazards*. This treatise was largely concerned

---

[†] Life insurance per se is an ancient practice. The first crude table of life expectancies was drawn up by Domitius Ulpianus circa A.D. 200.

with combinatorial analysis and dice and card probabilities. In connection with the game of Treize, or Rencontres, de Montmort was first to solve the matching problem (the probability that the value of a card coincides with the number expressing the order in which it is drawn). He also calculated the mathematical expectation of several intricate dice games: for example, Quinquenove, Hazard, Esperance, Trois Dez, Passe-dix, and Rafle. Of particular interest is his analysis of the card games le Her and le Jeu des Tas. Following de Montmort, Abraham de Moivre issued his work, *Doctrine of Chances*, which extended the knowledge of dice combinations, permutation theory, and card game analysis (specifically, the distribution of Honors in the game of Whist), and, most important, which proposed the first limit theorem. In this and subsequent treatises, he developed further the concepts of matching problems, duration of play, probability of ruin, mathematical expectation, and the theory of recurring series, and increased the value of Bernoulli's theorem by the aid of Stirling's theorem. On the basis of his approximation to the sum of terms of a binomial expansion (1733), he is commonly credited with the invention of the normal distribution. De Moivre lived much of his life among the London coffeehouse gamblers.[†] It was likely this environment that led him to write the *Doctrine of Chances*, which is virtually a gambler's manual.

Miscellaneous contributors to gambling and probability theory in the first half of the eighteenth century include Nicolas Bernoulli, Barbeyrac, Mairan, Nicole, and Thomas Simpson. The latter was responsible for introducing the idea of continuity into probability (1756). In general, these mathematicians analyzed contemporary card games and solved intricate dice problems. Very little additional understanding of probability was furnished to the *orbis scientiarum*.

Daniel Bernoulli developed the concepts of risk and mathematical expectation by the use of differential calculus. He also deserves credit, with de Moivre, for indicating the significance of the limit theorem to probability theory. Leonard Euler, far more renowned for contributions to other branches of mathematics, worked for some time on questions of probabilities and developed the theory of partitions, a subject first broached in a letter from Leibnitz to Johann Bernoulli (1669). He published a memoir titled, *Calcul de la Probabilité dans le Jeu de Rencontre*, in 1751 and calculated various lottery sequences and ticket-drawing combinations. Jean le Rond d'Alembert was best known for his opinions contrary to the scientific theories of his time. His errors and paradoxes abound in eighteenth

[†] His mathematics classes were held at Slaughter's Coffee House in St. Martin's Lane; one successful student was Thomas Bayes.

century mathematical literature. According to d'Alembert, the result of tossing three coins differs from three tosses of one coin. He also believed that tails is more probable after a long run of heads, and promulgated the doctrine that a very small probability is practically equivalent to zero. This idea leads to the progression betting system that bears his name. His analyses of card and dice games were equally penetrating.

The Rev. Thomas Bayes (his revolutionary paper, "An Essay Towards Solving a Problem in the Doctrine of Chances," was published in 1763, two years after his death) contributed the theorem stating exactly how the probability of a certain "cause" changes as different events actually occur. Although the proof of his formula rests on an unsatisfactory postulate, he was the first to use mathematical probability inductively—that is, arguing from a sample of the population or from the particular to the general. Bayes's theorem has (with some hazard) been made the foundation of the theory of testing statistical hypotheses. Whereas Laplace later defined probability by means of the enumeration of discrete units, Bayes defined a continuous probability distribution by a formula for the probability between any pair of assigned limits. He did not, however, consider the metric of his continuum.

Lagrange added his contribution to probability theory and solved many of the problems previously posed by de Moivre. Beguelin, Buffon,[†] Johann Lambert, the later John Bernoulli, Mallet, and William Emerson wrote sundry articles on games of chance and the calculus of probability during the second half of the eighteenth century. The Marquis de Condorcet supplied the doctrine of credibility—that is, the statement that the mathematical measure of probability is an accurate measure of our degree of belief. Trembley, Malfatti, and E. Waring developed further the theory of combinations.

Quantitatively, the theory of probability is more indebted to Pierre Simon, Marquis de Laplace, than to any other mathematician. His great work, *Théorie Analytique des Probabilités*, was published in 1812 and was accompanied by a popular exposition, *Essai Philosophique sur les Probabilités*. These tomes represent an outstanding contribution to the subject, containing a multitude of new ideas, results, and analytic methods. Parts of a theory of equations in finite differences with one and two independent variables are proposed, the concomitant analysis being applied to problems of duration of play and random sampling. Laplace elaborated on the idea

---

[†] In his *Political Arithmetic*, Buffon considered the chance of the sun rising tomorrow. He calculated the probability as $1 - (\frac{1}{2})^x$, where x is the number of days the sun is known to have risen over past history. Another contribution from Buffon was the establishment of $1/10,000$ as the lowest practical probability.

of inverse probabilities first considered by Bayes. In subsequent memoirs, he investigated applications of generating functions, solutions and problems in birth statistics and the French lottery (a set of 90 numbers, five of which are drawn at a time), and generalized the matching problem of Montmort. Although he employed overly intricate analysis and not always lucid reasoning, he provided the greatest advance in probabilistic methodology in history. To Laplace is credited the first scientifically reasoned deterministic interpretation of the universe.

It was mid-eighteenth century when the empiricist David Hume studied the nature of probability and concluded that chance events are possessed of a subjective nature. Although he initiated development of the logical structure of the causality concept, Hume was unable to grasp fully the significance of inductive inference. He was not sufficiently endowed mathematically to exploit the theory of probability in a philosophic framework. By the early nineteenth century, the understanding of chance events had risen above the previous, naïve level; it was now accepted that probability statements could be offered with a high degree of certainty if they were transformed into statistical statements. The analysis of games of chance had led to the clarification of the meaning of probability and had provided its epistemological foundations.

Following Laplace, Denis Poisson was first to define probability as "the limit of a frequency" (*Rechercher sur le Probabilité des Jugements*, 1837), and the Austrian philosopher and mathematician Bernhard Bolzano expressed the view that probability represents a statistical concept of relative frequency. Like Laplace, Augustus de Morgan held that probability refers to a state of mind. Knowledge, he wrote, is never certain and the measure of the strength of our belief in any given proposition is referred to as its probability (Laplace had stated, "Chance is but the expression of man's ignorance."). The brilliant mathematician Karl Friedrich Gauss applied probability theory to astronomical research. After Gauss, most mathematicians chose to disregard a subject that had become virtually a stepchild in Victorian Europe. The English logician John Venn, the French economist Augustin Cournot, and the American logician Charles Sanders Peirce all expanded upon Bolzano's relative frequency concept. Henri Poincaré wrote an essay on chance, as did Peirce. In *The Doctrine of Chances*, Peirce in effect states that anything that can happen will happen: for example, insurance companies must eventually become bankrupt. This view, if taken literally, is a misleading signpost on a convoluted footpath.

Generally, the neglected orphan probability theory was fostered more by nonmathematicians. These men expanded the subject to include the modern statistical methods that may return far greater dividends in the long run. Among the major contributors are the Belgian demographer and anthropometrist Adolphe Quetelet[†]; Sir Francis Galton, who investigated correlations and placed the laws of heredity on a statistical basis (the initial concept of correlations is credited to the Frenchman Auguste Bravais, 1811–1863); W. F. R. Weldon; the American actuary Emory McClintock; Gregor Mendel; Clerk Maxwell; Ludwig Boltzmann; and Josiah Williard Gibbs, who contributed the foundations of statistical mechanics. One of the few pure statisticians of the era was Karl Pearson. Pearson is responsible for introducing the method of moments and defining the normal curve and standard deviation (1893). In 1900 he independently invented the "chi-square" test[‡] for goodness of fit. He is the author of a fascinating treatise titled, *The Scientific Aspect of Monte Carlo Roulette*. Few other qualified mathematicians were motivated toward applying the fruits of mathematical study to the naughty practice of gambling.

During the latter half of the nineteenth century, advances in probability theory were associated in great measure with Russian mathematicians. Victor Bunyakovsky promoted the application of probability theory to statistics, actuarial science, and demography. Pafnutii Tchebychev (1821–1894) generalized Bernoulli's theorem for the law of large numbers and founded the influential Russian school of mathematical probability. Two of his students were A. Liapounov (central limit theorem) and A. A. Markov, to whom is due the formulation of enchained probabilities. Tchebychev, Liapounov, and Markov together promulgated use of the vastly significant concept of a random variable.

Probability theory was carried into the twentieth century by two philosophers: Lord Bertrand Russell and John Maynard Keynes. In his *Principia Mathematica* (1903), Lord Russell combined formal logic with probability theory. Keynes was a successful gambler. He sharply attacked the frequency concept of probability and extended the procedures of inductive inference initiated by Bernoulli and Laplace. In related areas, the work of Vilfredo Pareto contributed to both mathematical economics (following Leon Walras) and sociology. The first decade of the century witnessed the connection, first adumbrated by Emile Borel, between the theory of probability and the measure-theoretic aspects of the functions of a real variable. In the 1920's, Borel's ideas were extended by Khintchine, Kolmogorov, Eugene Slutsky, Paul Lévy, and Anton Lomnitsky, among

---

[†] In discussing inductive reasoning, Quetelet avers that if an event (for example, the tide rising) has occurred m times, the probability that it will occur again is $(m + 1)/(m + 2)$. Note that the probability of unknown events ($m = 0$) is thereby defined as $1/2$. Possibly, Buffon's logic of the previous century gains by comparison.

[‡] The "chi-square" test was originated by Helmert in 1875.

others. Rigorous mathematical developments were supplied by Richard von Mises who, in a 1921 paper, introduced the notion of a sample space representing all conceivable outcomes of an experiment (the glass to contain the fluid of probability theory). With R. A. Fisher, von Mises advanced the idea of statistical probability with a definite operational meaning. It was his intent to replace all the doubtful metaphysics of probability "reasoning" by sound mathematics. Also in 1921, a mathematical theory of game strategy was first attempted by Borel, who was interested in gambling phenomena and subsequently applied some elementary probability calculations to the game of Contract Bridge. Beyond his real achievements, Borel convinced himself that he had proved the outstanding theorem that the human mind cannot imitate chance.

Game strategy as a mathematical discipline was firmly established by John von Neumann in 1928 when, in a creative mathematical paper on the strategy of Poker, he proved the minimax principle, the fundamental theorem of game theory. Later, in 1944, the concepts of game theory were expanded when von Neumann and Oskar Morgenstern published *The Theory of Games and Economic Behavior*.

Recent contributions to probability theory have become highly complex. The frontiers of the subject have advanced well beyond the earlier intimacy with games of chance. Fréchet, in the 1930's, generalized classical probability theory as an application of his abstract spaces. Kolmogorov and Khintchine, also in the 1930's, were largely responsible for the creation of the theory of stochastic processes. Other outstanding probability theorists—for example, Lindeberg, William Feller, and Serge Bernstein—and contemporary students of the subject now wield such weapons as infinite probability fields, abstract Lebesque integrals, and Borel sets, in addition to many specialized, esoteric, and formidable concepts applicable in formal analysis of the physical sciences. Probability theory and general mathematical developments have resumed the close coupling that existed from the mid-seventeenth century to Laplace's day, but which was disrupted for more than a hundred years.

With the analytic techniques and electronic computers available today, we can provide complete solutions to most of the conventional games of chance (card games such as Poker and Bridge are excluded because of the Herculean burden of calculations inherent in a realistic model). Probability theory, statistics, and game-theoretic techniques are being applied to genetics, economics, psychology, missile engineering, cat surgery, and prenatal conditioning. Mathematicians are closing in on the higher-order abstractions. As Aldous Huxley invented Riemann-surface tennis to fill the leisure hours of the denizens of his brave new world, so we might turn to such games as Minkowski Roulette, transfinite-cardinal Bingo, Kaluza craps, or quaternion lotteries to challenge our mathematically inclined gamblers.

Gamblers can rightfully claim to be the godfathers of probability theory, since they are responsible for provoking the stimulating interplay of gambling and mathematics that provided the impetus to the study of probability. For several centuries, games of chance constituted the only concrete field of application for probabilistic methods and concepts. Yet few gamblers are sufficiently knowledgeable of probability to accept their patrimony.

Psychology and the graduated income tax have largely outmoded the grandiose gesture in gambling. Freud suggested a sexual element in gambling,[†] and to emphasize the neurotic appeal, an organization called "Gamblers Anonymous" was organized in California in 1947, proffering sympathy to repentant, obsessive gamblers. The tax collector, hovering nearby, has discouraged the big winner from proudly publicizing his feat. "Bet-a-million" Gates and Arnold Rothstein no longer attract adulation. Most tales of recent great coups likely have been apocryphal ones. "Breaking the bank at Monte Carlo" is a euphemism for closing a single gaming table. It was last accomplished at the Casino Ste. des Bains de Mer during the final days of 1957, with a harvest of 180 million francs. As in so many other human pursuits, quantity has supplanted quality, and while today's wagers are smaller, it is the masses who are now gambling. Authorities estimate that each year in America alone, an excess of $30 billion is wagered. Tens of millions of gamblers contribute to this sum.

The ancient and universal practice 'of mankind has now become a modern and universal practice. Gambling casinos are spread over the earth: Las Vegas (first and foremost), Monte Carlo, Reno, Campione, Macao, the Casino d'Enghien, Geneva, Constanţa (for gambling Commissars), the Urca casino in Rio de Janeiro, Viña del Mar Kursaal, Quintandinha, Mar del Plata, Rhodes, Corfu, Marakech, San Juan, the Casino du Liban in Lebanon, Cannes, Nice, Deauville, Accra, Brighton, Estoril, Baden-Baden, Manila, and scores of others, glamorous and shoddy, legal and illegal.

To phrase it in the vulgate: You can lose your shirt anywhere in the world.

Suggested References

ASBURY, HERBERT, *Sucker's Progress, An Informal History of Gambling in America from the Colonies to Canfield*, Dodd, Mead, and Co., New York, 1938.

[†] Not surprisingly.

ASHTON, JOHN, *The History of Gambling in England*, Duckworth and Co., London, 1899.

BARBEYRAC, J., *Traité de Jeu*, 3 vols., Amsterdam, 1737.

CALCAGNINI, CELIO, "De Talorum Tesserarum ac et Calculorum Ludis ex More Veterum," in J. Gronovius, *Thesaurus Graecarum Antiquitatum*, Leyden, 1697–1702.

CANTOR, MORITZ, *Vorlesungen über Geschichte der Mathematik*, 4 vols., Leipzig, 1880–1908.

CARRUCCIO, ETTORE, *Mathematics and Logic in History and in Contemporary Thought*, Aldine Publishing Co., Chicago, 1964.

DAVID, FLORENCE NIGHTINGALE, *Games, Gods, and Gambling*, Hafner Publishing Co., New York, 1962.

DAVID, FLORENCE NIGHTINGALE, "Studies in the History of Probability and Statistics— 1. Dicing and Gaming (A Note on the History of Probability)," *Biometrika*, **42**, Part 1 (June, 1955), pp. 1–15.

DE MONTMORT, REMOND, *Essai d'Analyse sur les Jeux de Hazard*, Paris, 1708.

DICKSON, LEONARD E., *History of the Theory of Numbers*, 3 vols., Carnegie Institution, Washington, D.C., 1920.

HACKING, IAN, *The Emergence of Probability*, Cambridge University Press, London and New York, 1974.

HUYGENS, CHRISTIAN, *Tractatus de Ratiociniis in Ludo Aleae*, Amsterdam, 1657. French translation available in Martinus Nijhoff, *Oeuvres Complètes*, **14**, The Hague, 1920.

KING, AMY C., and CECIL B. READ, *Pathways to Probability*, Holt, Rinehart and Winston, Inc., New York, 1963.

LAPLACE, PIERRE SIMON, Marquis de, *A Philosophic Essay on Probabilities*, Dover Publications, New York, 1951 (translated by F. W. Truscott and F. L. Emory).

LUCAS, THEOPHILUS, *Memoirs of the Lives, Intrigues, and Comical Adventures of the Most Famous Gamesters and Celebrated Sharpers in the Reigns of Charles II, James II, William III, and Queen Anne*, London, 1714.

ORE, ØYSTEIN, *Cardano, the Gambling Scholar*, Princeton University Press, 1953. (Containing an English translation of Gerolomo Cardano, *The Book on Games of Chance*.)

TODHUNTER, ISAAC, *A History of the Mathematical Theory of Probability*, Chelsea Publishing Co., New York, 1949 (reprinted).

WESTERGAARD, H., *Contributions to the History of Statistics*, P. S. King & Son, London, 1932.

CHAPTER TWO

MATHEMATICAL PRELIMINARIES

The meaning of probability

The word "probability" stems from the Latin *probabilis*, meaning "truth-resembling"; thus the word itself literally invites semantic misinterpretation. Yet real concepts exist and are applicable in resolving or ordering certain questions. For our purpose, which is to categorize gambling phenomena, we shall confine ourselves to an operational definition of probability —one that avoids philosophic implications and Bergsonian vagueness and constrains the area of application. This restricted definition we term "rational probability."

> Rational probability is concerned only with mass phenomena or repetitive events that are subject to observation or to logical extrapolation from empirical experience.

That is, we must have, either in space or in time, a practically unlimited sequence of uniform observations or we must be able to adapt correlated past experience to the problem for it to merit the application of rational probability theory.

The extension of probability theory to encompass problems in the moral sciences, as attempted in the rampant rationalism of the eighteenth century, is not deemed invalid, but simply another field of endeavor. The views of de Morgan and Lord Keynes we classify as "philosophic probability." Questions of ethics, conduct, religious suppositions, moral attributes, unverifiable propositions, and the like are, in our assumed context, devoid of meaning.

Three principal concepts of probability theory have been expressed throughout the sensible history of the subject. First, the classical theory is founded upon the indefinable concept of equally likely events. Second, the limit-of-relative-frequency theory is founded upon an observational concept and a mathematical postulate. Third, the logical theory defines probability as the degree of confirmation of a hypothesis with respect to an evidence statement.

Our definition of rational probability theory is most consistent with and completed by the concept of a limiting relative frequency. If an experiment is performed whereby n trials of the experiment produce n_0 occurrences of a particular event, the ratio n_0/n is termed the relative frequence of the event. We then postulate the existence of a limiting value as the number of trials increases indefinitely. The probability of the particular event is defined as

$$P = \lim_{n \to \infty} \frac{n_0}{n} \qquad\qquad 2\text{-}1$$

The classical theory considers the mutually exclusive, exhaustive cases. The probability of an event is defined as the ratio of the number of favorable cases to the total number of possible cases. A weakness of the classical theory lies in its complete dependence upon a priori analysis. Analysis is feasible only for relatively unsophisticated situations wherein all possibilities can be assessed accurately; more often, various events cannot be assigned a probability a priori.

The logical theory is capable of dealing with some interesting hypotheses; however, its flexibility is academic and generally irrelevant to the solution of gambling problems. Logical probability, or the degree of confirmation, is not factual, but L-determinate—that is, analytic; an L concept refers to a logical procedure grounded only in the analysis of senses and without the necessity of observations in fact.

Notwithstanding this diversity of thought regarding the philosophical foundations of the theory of probability, there has been almost universal agreement as to the mathematical superstructure. And it is mathematics rather than philosophy or semantic artifacts that we summon to support statistical logic and the theory of gambling. Specifically in relation to gambling phenomena, our interpretation of probability is designed to accommodate the realities of the situation as these realities reflect accumulated experience. For example, a die has certain properties that can be determined by measurement. These properties include mass, specific heat, electrical resistance, and the probability that the up-face will exhibit a "3." Thus we view probability much as a physicist views mass or energy. Rational probability is concerned with the empirical relations existing between these types of physical quantities.

The calculus of probability

Mathematics, qua mathematics, is empty of real meaning. It consists merely of a set of statements: "if ..., then ..." As in Euclidean geometry, it is necessary only to establish a set of consistent axioms to qualify probability theory as a rigorous branch of pure mathematics. Treating probability theory, then, in a geometric sense, each possible outcome of an experiment is considered as the location of a point on a line. Each repetition of the experiment is the coordinate of the point in another dimension. Hence probability is a measure—like the geometric measure of volume. Problems in probability are thence treated as a geometric analysis of points in a multidimensional space. Kolmogorov has been largely responsible for providing this axiomatic basis.

AXIOMS AND COROLLARIES

A random event is an experiment whose outcome is not known a priori. We can state

> *Axiom I :* To every random event A there corresponds a number $P(A)$, referred to as the probability of A, which satisfies the inequality
>
> $$0 \leq P(A) \leq 1$$

Thus the measure of probability is a nonnegative real number in the range 0 to 1. Now consider an experiment whose outcome is certain or whose outcomes are indistinguishable (tossing a two-headed coin). To characterize such an experiment, we let E represent the collection of all possible outcomes; thence

> *Axiom II :* The probability of the certain event is unity. That is,
>
> $$P(E) = 1$$

The relative frequency of such events is (cf. Eq. 2-1) $n_0/n = 1$. Lastly, we require an axiom that characterizes the nature of mutually exclusive events (if a coin is thrown, the outcome heads excludes the outcome tails, and vice versa; thus, heads and tails are mutually exclusive). We formulate this axiom as follows:

> *Axiom III :* If the events $A_1, A_2, \ldots, A_n$ are mutually exclusive, the probability of the alternative of these events is equal to the sum of their

individual probabilities. Mathematically,

$$P(A_1 + A_2 + \cdots + A_n) = P(A_1) + P(A_2) + \cdots + P(A_n)$$

Axiom III expresses the additive property of probability. It can be extended to include events not mutually exclusive. If A_1 and A_2 are such events, the total probability (A_1 and/or A_2 occurs) is

$$P(A_1 + A_2) = P(A_1) + P(A_2) - P(A_1 A_2) \qquad 2\text{-}2$$

where $P(A_1 A_2)$ is defined as the *joint* or *compound probability* that both A_1 and A_2 occur.

From these axioms several logical corollaries follow.

Corollary I: The sum of the probabilities of any event A and its complement $\bar{A}$ is unity. That is,

$$P(A) + P(\bar{A}) = 1$$

The complement of an event is, of course, the nonoccurrence of that event.

Characterizing an impossible event O, we can state

Corollary II: The probability of an impossible event is zero, or

$$P(O) = 0$$

It is worth noting that the converse of Corollary II is not true. Given that the probability of some event equals zero, it does not follow that the event is impossible (there is a zero probability of selecting at random a pre-specified point on a line).

Another important concept is that of "conditional probability." The expression $P(A_2|A_1)$ refers to the probability of an event A_2, given (or conditional to) the occurrence of the event A_1. We can write, for $P(A_1) > 0$,

$$P(A_2|A_1) = \frac{P(A_1 A_2)}{P(A_1)} \qquad 2\text{-}3$$

By induction from Eq. 2-3 we can obtain the multiplication theorem (or the general law of compound probability):

Corollary III: The probability of the product of n events $A_1, A_2, \ldots, A_n$ is equal to the probability of the first event times the conditional probability of the second event, given the occurrence of the first event times the conditional occurrence of the third event given the joint occurrence of the first two events, and so forth. In mathematical form,

$$P(A_1 A_2 \cdots A_n) = P(A_1)P(A_2|A_1)P(A_3|A_1 A_2) \cdots P(A_n|A_1 A_2 \cdots A_{n-1})$$

$$2\text{-}4$$

It can be demonstrated that conditional probability satisfies Axioms I, II, and III. A special case of Corollary III occurs when the events $A_1, A_2, \ldots, A_n$ are independent; then the law of compound probability reduces to

$$P(A_1 A_2 \cdots A_n) = P(A_1)P(A_2) \cdots P(A_{n-1})P(A_n) \qquad \text{2-5}$$

Thus the necessary and sufficient condition for n events to be independent is that the probability of every n-fold combination that can be formed from the n events or their complements be factorable into the product of the probabilities of the n distinct components.

Finally, the concept of complete (or absolute) probability is expressed by

Corollary IV: If the random events A_1, A_2, $\ldots$, A_n are pairwise exclusive, then the probability $P(X)$ of any random event X occurring together with one of the events A_i is given by

$$P(X) = P(A_1)P(X|A_1) + P(A_2)P(X|A_2) + \cdots + P(A_n)P(X|A_n)$$

$$\text{2-6}$$

if $P(A_i) > 0$ for $i = 1, 2, \ldots, n$.

Combining the principles of complete and conditional probabilities leads us to the following statement.

Corollary IV(a): If the independent events $A_1, A_2, \ldots, A_n$ satisfy the assumptions of the complete probability theorem, then for an arbitrary event X associated with one of the events A_i, we have, for $P(X) > 0$,

$$P(A_i|X) = \frac{P(A_i)P(X|A_i)}{P(A_1)P(X|A_1) + P(A_2)P(X|A_2) + \cdots + P(A_n)P(X|A_n)}$$

$$i = 1, 2, 3, \ldots, n \qquad \text{2-7}$$

Equation 2-7 is known as Bayes's theorem, or the formula for a posteriori probability. It should be noted that no assumptions as to the probabilities of the respective A_i's are implied (a common error is to interpret Bayes's theorem as signifying that all A_i's are equal).

An example may aid in clarifying the preceding concepts. Given that the probability $P(K)$ of drawing at least one King in two tries from a conventional deck of 52 cards is $396/(52 \times 51) = 0.149$, that the probability $P(Q)$ of drawing a Queen in two tries is also 0.149, and that the joint probability (drawing both a King and a Queen) is $32/(52 \times 51) = 0.012$, what is the conditional probability $P(K|Q)$ that *one* of the two cards is a King, given that the other is a Queen?[†] What is the total probability $P(K + Q)$ that at least one card is either a King or a Queen? Are the two events—drawing a King and drawing a Queen—independent?

Applying Eq. 2-3 directly,

$$P(K|Q) = \frac{P(KQ)}{P(Q)} = \frac{32/(52 \times 51)}{396/(52 \times 51)} = \frac{8}{99} = 0.081$$

and, of course, the probability of one of the two cards being a Queen, given the other is a King, is also

$$P(Q|K) = \frac{P(KQ)}{P(K)} = \frac{32/(52 \times 51)}{396/(52 \times 51)} = \frac{8}{99} = 0.081$$

From Eq. 2-2 the total probability (drawing a King and/or a Queen) is given by

$$P(K + Q) = P(K) + P(Q) - P(KQ) = \frac{396 + 396 - 32}{52 \times 51} = 0.287$$

It is evident that the two events are not independent, since $P(KQ) \neq P(K)P(Q)$.

PERMUTATIONS AND COMBINATIONS

Gambling phenomena frequently require the direct extension of probability theory axioms and corollaries into the realm of permutational and combinatorial analysis. A *permutation* of a number of elements is any arrangement of these elements in a definite order. A *combination* is a selection of a number of elements from a population considered without regard to their order. Rigorous mathematical proofs of the theorems of permutations and combinations are available in many texts on probability theory. By conventional notation, the number of permutations of n distinct objects (or elements or *things*) considered r at a time without repetition is represented by P_n^r. Similarly, C_n^r represents the number of combinations of n distinct objects considered r at a time without regard to their order.

To derive the formula for P_n^r, consider that we have r spaces to fill and n objects from which to choose. The first space can be filled with any of the n objects (that is, in n ways). Subsequently, the second space can be filled from any of $n - 1$ objects ($n - 1$ ways). The third space can be filled

---

[†] Note that either of the two cards may be the postulated Queen. A variation asks the probability of one card being a King, given the other to be a non-King ($\bar{K}$). In this case, $P(K|\bar{K}) = 0.145$.

in $n - 2$ ways, etc., and the rth space can be filled in $n - (r - 1)$ ways. Thus

$$P_n^r = n(n - 1)(n - 2)\cdots(n - r + 1) \qquad \text{2-8}$$

For the case $r = n$, Eq. 2-8 becomes

$$P_n^n = n(n - 1)(n - 2)\cdots 1 \equiv n! \qquad \text{2-9}$$

that is, n factorial. Combining Eqs. 2-9 and 2-8, the latter can be re-written in the form

$$P_n^r = \frac{P_n^n}{P_{n-r}^{n-r}} = \frac{n!}{(n - r)!} \qquad \text{2-10}$$

It is also possible, from Eq. 2-8, to write the recurrence relation

$$P_n^r = P_{n-1}^r + rP_{n-1}^{r-1}$$

Similar considerations hold when we are concerned with permutations of n objects not all distinct. Specifically, let the n objects consist of m kinds of elements wherein there are n_1 elements of the first kind, n_2 elements of the second, etc., and $n = n_1 + n_2 + \cdots + n_m$. Then the number of permutations P_n of the n objects taken all together is given by

$$P_n = \frac{n!}{n_1!n_2!n_3!\cdots n_m!} \qquad \text{2-11}$$

Illustratively, the number of permutations of four cards selected from a 52-card deck is

$$P_{52}^4 = \frac{52!}{(52 - 4)!} = \frac{52!}{48!} = 52 \times 51 \times 50 \times 49 = 6,497,400$$

Note that the order is of consequence. That is, the A, 2, 3, 4 of spades differs from, say, the 2, A, 3, 4, of spades. If we ask the number of permutations of the deck, distinguishing the ranks but not the suits (that is, there are 13 distinct kinds of objects, each with four indistinct elements[†]), Eq. 2-11 states that

$$P_{52} = \frac{52!}{(4!)^{13}} = 9.203 \times 10^{49}$$

To this point we have allowed all elements of a population to be permuted into all possible positions. However, there arise certain instances wherein it is desired to enumerate solely those permutations that are

---

[†] Observe that if we distinguish the suits but not the ranks (4 distinct kinds of objects, each with 13 indistinct elements), we obtain a considerably smaller number of permutations— that is,

$$\frac{52!}{(13!)^4} = 5.3645 \times 10^{28}$$

constrained by prescribed sets of restrictions on the positions of the elements permuted. A simple example of a restricted-position situation is the "problème des ménages,"[†] which asks the number of ways of seating n married couples around a circular table, with men and women in alternate positions and with the proviso that no man be seated next to his spouse. Any problem of this type (permutations with restricted position) is reducible to an equivalent problem of placing k Rooks on a "chessboard" in such a way that no Rook attacks any other. The Rook is a Chess piece that moves along the rows and columns of a chessboard. For mathematicians, a "chessboard" is defined as an arbitrary array of cells arranged in rows and columns. Application of these concepts lies in the domain of combinatorial analysis. As we shall see briefly in Chapter 6, they are particularly useful and elegant in the solution of matching problems.

Turning to r combinations of n distinct objects, we observe that each combination of r distinct objects can be arranged in $r!$ ways—that is $r!$ permutations. Therefore, $r!$ permutations of each of the C_n^r combinations produce $r!C_n^r$ permutations. That is,

$$r!C_n^r = P_n^r = \frac{n!}{(n-r)!}$$

Dividing by $r!$, we obtain the expression for the number of combinations of n objects taken r at a time:

$$C_n^r \equiv \binom{n}{r} = \frac{n!}{r!(n-r)!} \qquad \qquad 2\text{-}12$$

where $\binom{n}{r}$ is the symbol used for binomial coefficients—that is, $\binom{n}{r}$ is the $(r+1)$st coefficient of the expansion of $(a+b)^n$. For values of r less than zero and greater than n, we define C_n^r to be equal to zero. (Equation 2-12 can also be extended to include negative values of n and r; however, in our context we shall not encounter such values.) It is also apparent that the number of combinations of n objects taken r at a time is identical to the number of combinations of the n objects taken $n-r$ at a time. That is,

$$\binom{n}{r} = \binom{n}{n-r} \quad \text{or} \quad C_n^r = C_n^{n-r}$$

We can also derive the number of combinations of n objects taken r at a time in the format

$$C_n^r = C_{n-1}^{r-1} + C_{n-1}^r \qquad \qquad 2\text{-}13$$

[†] So named by E. Lucas in *Théorie des Nombres*, Paris, 1891.

Equation 2-13 is known as Pascal's rule. By iteration it follows that

$$C_n^r = C_{n-1}^{r-1} + C_{n-2}^{r-1} + \cdots + C_{r-1}^{r-1} = C_{n-1}^r + C_{n-2}^{r-1} + \cdots + C_{n-1-r}^0$$

As an example, we might ask how many Bridge hands of 13 cards are possible from a 52-card population? Equation 2-12 provides the answer:

$$\binom{n}{r} = \binom{52}{13} = \frac{52!}{13!(52-13)!} = 635,013,559,600$$

Note that the ordering of the 13 cards is of no consequence. If it were, the resulting number of permutations would be greater by a factor of 13!

PROBABILITY DISTRIBUTIONS

When we are concerned with a nonhomogeneous population (n objects consisting of m kinds of elements with n_1 elements of the first kind, n_2 elements of the second kind, etc.), the number of permutations of the n objects taken all together is given by Eq. 2-11. We can also determine the number of combinations possible through selection of a group of r elements from the n objects. Thence it is feasible to ask the probability $P_{k_1,k_2,\ldots,k_m}$ that if a group of r elements is selected at random (without replacement and without ordering), the group will contain exactly $k_1 \leq n_1$ elements of the first kind, $k_2 \leq n_2$ elements of the second kind, etc., and $k_m \leq n_m$ elements of the mth kind. Specifically, it can be shown that

$$P_{k_1,k_2,\ldots,k_m} = \frac{\binom{n_1}{k_1}\binom{n_2}{k_2}\binom{n_3}{k_3}\cdots\binom{n_m}{k_m}}{\binom{n}{r}} \qquad \begin{array}{l} n = n_1 + n_2 + \cdots + n_m \\[1ex] r = k_1 + k_2 + \cdots + k_m \end{array} \qquad 2\text{-}14$$

Equation 2-14 represents the generalized *hypergeometric distribution*, the probability distribution for sampling from a finite population without replacement. It should be noted that in the limit (for arbitrarily large populations) sampling with or without replacement leads to the same results.

As an illustration of the hypergeometric distribution, we compute the probability that a Bridge hand of 13 cards consists of exactly 5 Spades, 4 Hearts, 3 Diamonds, and 1 Club. According to Eq. 2-14,

$$P_{5,4,3,1} = \frac{\binom{13}{5}\binom{13}{4}\binom{13}{3}\binom{13}{1}}{\binom{52}{13}} = 0.0054$$

since the order of the cards within the Bridge hand is of no consequence.

Another distribution of importance in practical applications of probability theory is the *binomial distribution*. If an event has two alternative results A_1 and A_2, so that $P(A_1) + P(A_2) = 1$, and the probability of occurrence for an individual trial is constant, the number of occurrences r of the result A_1 obtained over n independent trials is a discrete *random variable*, which may assume any of the possible values $0, 1, 2, \ldots, n$. A *random variable* is simply a variable quantity whose values depend on chance and for which there exists a distribution function. In this instance the number r is a *binomial variate* and its distribution $P(r)$ is known as the binomial distribution.[†] Letting $p = P(A_1)$ and $q = P(A_2) = 1 - p$, we can readily derive the expression

$$P(r) = \binom{n}{r} p^r q^{n-r}, \qquad r = 0, 1, 2, \ldots, n \qquad\qquad 2\text{-}15$$

Equation 2-15 is also frequently referred to as the *Bernoulli distribution*, since it was first derived by Jacob Bernoulli in *Ars Conjectandi*. If, instead of two possible outcomes of the experiment, there is an exhaustive set $A_1, A_2, \ldots, A_m$ of mutually exclusive results that occur with constant probabilities $p_1 = P(A_1)$, $p_2 = P(A_2), \ldots, p_m = P(A_m)$ for each individual trial, then the *multinomial distribution* specifies the compound or joint distribution of the number of results of each kind A_i. The probability of obtaining r_1 instances of A_1, r_2 instances of A_2, etc., and r_m instances of A_m with n independent trials is determined in a fashion similar to Eq. 2-15:

$$P(r_1, r_2, \ldots, r_m) = \frac{n!}{r_1! r_2! \cdots r_m!} p_1^{r_1} p_2^{r_2} \cdots p_m^{r_m} \qquad\qquad 2\text{-}16$$

where

$$p_1 + p_2 + \cdots + p_m = 1 \quad \text{and} \quad r_1 + r_2 + \cdots + r_m = n$$

If a chance event can occur with constant probability p on any given trial, then the number of trials r required for its first occurrence is a discrete random variable, which can assume any of the values $1, 2, 3 \cdots \infty$. The

---

[†] An interesting apparatus which generates the binomial distribution experimentally is the *Quincunx* (named after a Roman coin valued at five-twelfths of a lira), described by Sir Francis Galton in his book, *Natural Inheritance* (p. 63), 1889. The Quincunx consists of a board in which nails are arranged in rows, n nails in the nth row, the nails of each row being placed below the midpoints of the intervals between the nails in the row above. A glass plate covers the entire apparatus. When small steel balls (of diameter less than the horizontal intervals between nails) are poured into the Quincunx from a point directly above the single nail of the first row, the dispersion of the steel balls is such that the deviations from the center-line follow a binomial distribution.

distribution of this variable is termed the *geometric distribution*. If the first occurrence of the event is on the rth trial, the first $r - 1$ trials must encompass nonoccurrences of the event (the probability of nonoccurrence is $q = 1 - p$). The compound probability of $r - 1$ nonoccurrences is q^{r-1}; hence $r - 1$ nonoccurrences followed by the event has probability $q^{r-1}p$. Accordingly, the geometric distribution is defined by

$$p(r) = pq^{r-1}, \quad r = 1, 2, 3, \ldots \tag{2-17}$$

For the situation where events occur randomly in time, we can inquire as to the probability $P(r, T)$ that exactly r events occur in a specified time interval T. Defining α as the probability that one event occurs in the incremental interval ΔT (that is, there will occur α events per unit time and the *average* number of events in the interval T is αT), we can determine $P(r, T)$ as

$$P(r, T) = \frac{e^{-\alpha T}(\alpha T)^r}{r!} \tag{2-18}$$

Equation 2-18 defines the Poisson distribution; it serves as an approximation to the binomial distribution when the number of trials is large.

Applications of the probability distributions presented here are multifold. The following numerical example is representative. From a deck of 52 cards, 10 cards are dealt in a random fashion. The deck is then reshuffled and 15 cards selected at random. We ask the probability $P(r)$ that exactly r cards are common to both selections ($r = 0, 1, 2, \ldots, 10$). From the 52 cards, 15 can be selected in $\binom{52}{15}$ distinct ways. If r of these have been selected on the previous deal, then $15 - r$ are in the nonoccurring category. Obviously, there are $\binom{10}{r}$ distinct ways of choosing r of the cards from the first deal and $\binom{52-10}{15-r}$ ways of selecting the remaining cards. Thus, according to Eq. 2-14 for the hypergeometric distribution,

$$P(r) = \frac{\binom{10}{r}\binom{52-10}{15-r}}{\binom{52}{15}}$$

For no matching cards, $r = 0$, $P(0) = 0.022$; for $r = 5$, $P(5) = 0.083$; for $r = 10$, $P(10) = 1.9 \times 10^{-7}$.

MATHEMATICAL EXPECTATION

A quantity of great value in the evaluation of games of chance is the *mathematical expectation*. Its definition is straightforward: If a random variable X can assume any of n values, $x_1, x_2, \ldots, x_n$ with respective probabilities $p_1, p_2, \ldots, p_n$, the mathematical expectation of X, $E(X)$, is expressed by

$$E(X) = p_1 x_1 + p_2 x_2 + \cdots + p_n x_n = \sum_{i=1}^{n} p_i x_i \qquad 2\text{-}19$$

The mathematical expectation of the number showing on one die is accordingly

$$E(X) = \frac{1}{6}(1) + \frac{1}{6}(2) + \frac{1}{6}(3) + \frac{1}{6}(4) + \frac{1}{6}(5) + \frac{1}{6}(6) = 3.5 \qquad 2\text{-}20$$

since the possible values of X, the number showing, are 1, 2, 3, 4, 5, and 6, each with probability 1/6. For two dice, X can range between 2 and 12 with varying probabilities:

$$E(X) = \frac{1}{36}(2) + \frac{2}{36}(3) + \frac{3}{36}(4) + \frac{4}{36}(5) + \frac{5}{36}(6) + \frac{6}{36}(7) + \frac{5}{36}(8)$$

$$+ \frac{4}{36}(9) + \frac{3}{36}(10) + \frac{2}{36}(11) + \frac{1}{36}(12) = 7 \qquad 2\text{-}21$$

A useful theorem states that the mathematical expectation of the sum of several random variables $X_1, X_2, \ldots, X_n$ is equal to the sum of their mathematical expectations. That is,

$$E(X_1 + X_2 + \cdots + X_n) = E(X_1) + E(X_2) + \cdots + E(X_n) \qquad 2\text{-}22$$

Thus, if the mathematical expectation of the number showing on one die is 3.5 (according to Eq. 2-20), then the total number showing on n dice is $7n/2$, and the result of Eq. 2-21 is directly obtainable by letting $n = 2$. Similarly, the theorem can be proved that the mathematical expectation of the product of several independent variables $X_1, X_2, \ldots, X_n$ is equal to the product of their expectations. That is,

$$E(X_1 X_2 \cdots X_n) = E(X_1)E(X_2) \cdots E(X_n) \qquad 2\text{-}23$$

(Note that Eq. 2-23 appertains to independent variables, whereas Eq. 2-22 is valid for any random variables.) It can also be shown in simple fashion that

$$E(aX + b) = aE(X) + b$$

for any numerical constants a and b.

The condensed description of probability theory presented here cannot, of course, include all those tools required for the solution of gambling problems. However, it is hoped that most of the requisite information has been covered briefly and is of propaedeutic value; more comprehensive developments can be found by consulting the list of Suggested References at the end of the chapter.

Statistics

Between probability theory and statistics[†] there is not always a clear-cut distinction. In general, statistics can be considered as the offspring of the theory of probability; it builds on its parent and extends the area of patronymic jurisdiction. In this sense, probability theory enables us to deduce the probable composition of a sample, given the composition of the original population; by the use of statistics we can reverse this reasoning process so that it is possible to infer the composition of the original population from the composition of a properly selected sample. Frequently, however, the end objective of a statistical investigation is not of a purely descriptive nature. Rather, the descriptive characteristics are desired in order to compare different sets of data with the aid of the characteristics of each set. Similarly, we may wish to formulate estimates of the characteristics that might be found in related sets of data. In either case, it is evident that description is a preliminary stage, and further analysis is our principal goal.

As in the theory of probability, the meaning and end result of a statistical study are a set of conclusions. We do not predict the individual event, but consider all possible occurrences and calculate the frequency of occurrences of the individual events. Also, like probability theory, statistics is an invention of man rather than of nature. It, too, has a meaning ultimately based on empirical evidence and a calculus established on an axiomatic foundation. Attributing to statistics the inherent ability to describe universal laws leads to many prevalent and interesting fallacies.[‡] Following G. K. Chesterton, we caution against using statistics as a drunk uses a lamppost: for support rather than illumination.

MEAN AND VARIANCE

Analysis of the conventional games of chance involves only some of the

---

[†] The word "statistics" derives from the Latin *status*, meaning state (of affairs).

[‡] For a fascinating compendium of such fallacies, see Darrell Huff, *How to Lie with Statistics*, W. W. Norton and Co., New York, 1954.

more elementary aspects of statistical theory—primarily related to the concepts of variance, estimation, hypothesis testing, and confidence limits. Our treatment of the subject is therefore correspondingly limited.

The mathematical expectation of a random variable X is also known as the *mean* value of X. It is generally represented by the symbol μ; that is, $\mu = E(X)$. Thus $E(X - \mu) = 0$. Considering a constant c instead of the mean μ, the expected value of $X - c$ [that is, $E(X - c)$] is termed the *first moment* of X, taken about c. The mean (or center of mass of the probability function) depicts the long-run average result for an experiment performed an arbitrarily large number of times. This type of average refers to the arithmetical average of a distribution, defined according to Eq. 2-19. It should not be confused with the *mode* (that value of the distribution possessing the greatest frequency, and hence the most probable value of the distribution), the *weighted average* (wherein each value of the random variable X is multiplied by a weighting coefficient before the arithmetical averaging process), the *median* (the sum of the frequencies of occurrence of the values of X above and below the median are equal; for symmetrical distributions, the mean and the median are identical), the *geometric mean* (the positive nth root of the product of n random variables), or numerous others.[†]

In addition to the mean, another parameter is required to describe a distribution of values: a measure of spread or variability comparing various results of the experiment. The most convenient and commonly used measure of spread is the *variance*. Let X be a random variable assuming any of the m values x_i ($i = 1, 2, \ldots, m$) with corresponding probabilities $p(x_i)$ and with a mean $\mu = E(X)$. Then the variance, $\mathrm{Var}(X)$, is defined by

$$\mathrm{Var}(X) = E[(X - \mu)^2] = \sum_{i=1}^{m} (x_i - \mu)^2 p(x_i) \qquad \text{2-24}$$

Note that the units of $\mathrm{Var}(X)$ are squares of the units of x. Therefore, to recover the original units, the *standard deviation* of X, $\sigma(X)$, is defined as

$$\sigma(X) = \sqrt{\mathrm{Var}(X)} = \sqrt{E[(X - \mu)^2]} \qquad \text{2-25}$$

An invaluable theorem formulates the variance of X as the mean of the square of X minus the square of the mean of X. That is,

$$\sigma^2(X) = E(X^2) - [E(X)]^2 \qquad \text{2-26}$$

[†] Any type of average is known to statisticians as a "measure of central tendency." Its etymological ancestor is the Latin word *havaria*. Originally *havaria* referred to compensation funds paid to owners of cargo sacrificed to lighten ship during heavy storms. Those whose merchandise survived transit provided the indemnification to the losers. Thus the concept of "average" arises from a type of primitive insurance.

The mean value of the up-face of a die was calculated in Eq. 2-20 as 7/2. The mean of this value squared is

$$E(X^2) = \frac{1}{6}(1)^2 + \frac{1}{6}(2)^2 + \frac{1}{6}(3)^2 + \frac{1}{6}(4)^2 + \frac{1}{6}(5)^2 + \frac{1}{6}(6)^2 = \frac{91}{6}$$

Thus the variance of the number showing on the die is, according to Eq. 2-26,

$$\sigma^2(X) = \frac{91}{6} - \left(\frac{7}{2}\right)^2 = \frac{35}{12} \quad \text{and} \quad \sigma(X) = 1.71$$

For two dice, $E(X) = 7$ and $E(X^2) = 329/6$. Therefore the variance of the sum of numbers on two dice is

$$\sigma^2(X) = \frac{329}{6} - (7)^2 = \frac{35}{6} \quad \text{and} \quad \sigma(X) = 2.415$$

Occasionally the expected total showing on two dice is stated as 7 ± 2.415.

We can readily compute the mean and variance for each well-known probability distribution. The hypergeometric distribution (Eq. 2-14), with but two kinds of elements, simplifies to

$$P_k = \frac{\binom{n_1}{k}\binom{n - n_1}{r - k}}{\binom{n}{r}}, \quad k = 0, 1, 2, \ldots, r, \quad r \le n_1, \quad r \le n - n_1 \quad \text{2-27}$$

Consider an urn containing n balls of which n_1 are red and $n - n_1$ are black. Then if r balls are drawn *without replacement*, the probability that the number X of red balls drawn is exactly k is given by Eq. 2-27. The mean of X is expressed by

$$\mu = E(X) = \sum_{k=0}^{r} \frac{k\binom{n_1}{k}\binom{n - n_1}{r - k}}{\binom{n}{r}} = \frac{n_1 r}{n}$$

and the mean of X^2 can be shown to be

$$E(X^2) = \frac{n_1(n_1 - 1)r(r - 1)}{n(n - 1)} + \frac{n_1 r}{n}$$

Therefore, applying Eq. 2-26, the variance is

$$\sigma^2 = \frac{n_1 r(n - n_1)(n - r)}{n^2(n - 1)} \qquad \text{2-28}$$

For the binomial distribution (Eq. 2-15), we can compute the mean as

$$\mu = E(X) = np$$

and the mean of X^2 as

$$E(X^2) = np + n(n - 1)p^2$$

Thus the variance associated with the binomial distribution is

$$\sigma^2 = np + n(n - 1)p^2 - (np)^2 = np(1 - p) = npq \qquad 2\text{-}29$$

The Poisson distribution (Eq. 2-18) can be shown to possess a mean and a variance, both equal to the average number of events occurring in a specified time interval T. That is,

$$\mu = \sigma^2 = \alpha T$$

(α is the probability of the occurrence of one event during the time increment ΔT). Consequently, the Poisson distribution is often written in the form

$$P(r) = \frac{e^{-\mu}\mu^r}{r!} \qquad 2\text{-}30$$

THE LAW OF LARGE NUMBERS

Another highly significant theorem can be obtained from the definition of the variance by separating the values of the random variable X into those that lie within the interval $\mu - k\sigma$ to $\mu + k\sigma$ and those that lie without. The sum of the probabilities assigned to the values of X outside the interval $\mu \pm k\sigma$ is equal to the probability that X is greater than $k\sigma$ from the mean μ and is less than or equal to $1/k^2$.

$$\frac{1}{k^2} \geq P(|X - \mu| > k\sigma) \qquad 2\text{-}31$$

This expression is known as Tchebychev's theorem; it states that no more than the fraction $1/k^2$ of the total probability of a random variable deviates from the mean value by greater than k standard deviations.

A notable application of Tchebychev's inequality is determining the point of *stochastic convergence*; that is, the convergence of a sample probability to its expected value. If, in Eq. 2-31, we replace the random variable X by the sample probability p' (the ratio of the number of occurrences of an event to the number of trials attempted) and the mean μ by the single-trial probability of success p, Tchebychev's inequality becomes

$$P\left[|p' - p| > k\sqrt{\frac{pq}{n}}\right] \le \frac{1}{k^2} \qquad 2\text{-}32$$

since $\sigma = \sqrt{pq/n}$. Specifying the value of k as $k = \varepsilon/\sqrt{pq/n}$, where ε is some fraction greater than zero, Eq. 2-32 assumes the form

$$P[|p' - p| > \varepsilon] \le \frac{pq}{n\varepsilon^2} \qquad 2\text{-}33$$

which is the *law of large numbers*. It declares that no matter how small an ε is specified, the probability P that the sample probability differs from the single-trial probability of success by more than ε can be made arbitrarily small by sufficiently increasing the number of trials n. Thus, for an un-biased coin, the law of large numbers states that the probability of the sample probability differing from 1/2 by greater than a specified amount approaches zero as a limit. We conventionally express this fact by the statement that the sample probability converges stochastically to 1/2.

The law of large numbers has frequently been cited as the guarantor of an eventual head-tail balance. Actually, in colloquial form, the law pro-claims that the difference between the number of heads and the number of tails thrown may be expected to increase indefinitely as the number of trials increases, although by decreasing proportions. Its operating principle is "inundation" rather than "compensation" (cf. Theorems I and II of Chapter 3).

CONFIDENCE

In addition to a measure of the spread or variability of a repeated experi-ment, it is desirable to express the extent to which we have confidence that the pertinent parameter or specific experimental result will lie within certain limits. Let the random variable X possess a known distribution and let us take a sample of size $r(x_1, x_2, \ldots, x_r)$, with which we will estimate some parameter θ. Then, if θ_1 and θ_2 are two statistical estimations of θ, the probability ξ that θ lies within the interval θ_1 to θ_2 is called the *confidence level*. That is,

$$P(\theta_1 \le \theta \le \theta_2) = \xi$$

The parameter θ, it should be noted, is not a random variable. It represents a definite, albeit unknown, number. However, θ_1 and θ_2 are random variables, since their values depend on the random samples.

As an example, consider a random variable X that follows a normal distribution with a known standard deviation σ but with an unknown expectation μ. We ask the range of values of μ which admits of a 0.95 confidence level that μ lies within that range. From the definition of the normal distribution (Eq. 2-35), the probability that μ lies between

$$\theta_1 = \bar{x} - \frac{y\sigma}{\sqrt{r}} \quad \text{and} \quad \theta_2 = \bar{x} + \frac{y\sigma}{\sqrt{r}}$$

is given by

$$P\left(\bar{x} - \frac{y\sigma}{\sqrt{r}} \leq \mu \leq \bar{x} + \frac{y\sigma}{\sqrt{r}}\right) = \frac{1}{\sqrt{2\pi}} \int_{-y}^{y} e^{-x^2/2}\, dx \qquad \text{2-34}$$

From tables of the normal probability integral[†] we find that this probability is equal to 0.95 for $y = 1.96$. Thus, for an estimate $\bar{x}$ of μ from a small sample of size r, we can claim a 0.95 confidence that μ is included within the interval $\bar{x} \pm 1.96\sigma/\sqrt{r}$.

Let us postulate a Bridge player who receives ten successive Bridge hands, nine of which contain no Aces. He complains that this situation is attributable only to poor shuffling. What confidence level can be assigned to this statement? The probability that a hand of 13 cards randomly selected contains at least one Ace is

$$P(1 \text{ Ace}) = 1 - \frac{\binom{48}{13}}{\binom{52}{13}} = 0.696$$

The binomial distribution (Eq. 2-15) provides the probability that of ten hands, only one will contain at least one Ace:

$$P(1 \text{ Ace in 10 hands}) = \binom{10}{1}(0.696)^1(1 - 0.696)^9 = 0.00015$$

[†] Among many, M. Abramowitz and I. A. Stegun (eds.), *Handbook of Mathematical Functions*, U.S. Dept. of Commerce, National Bureau of Standards, June, 1964.

Thus, with a confidence level of 99.985 percent, the Bridge player can justly decry the lack of shuffling and maintain that as a consequence the null hypothesis [that $P(1 \text{ Ace}) = 0.696$] does not hold in this game.

ESTIMATION

In economic phenomena, one aspect of mathematical statistics widely applied is that of estimation from statistical data. Statistical inference is a method of inferring population characteristics on the basis of observed samples of information.[†] For example, we might be ignorant of the probability p that the throw of a particular coin will result in heads; rather we might know that in 100 coin-throwing trials 55 heads have been observed and wish to obtain from this result an estimate of p. In general, the parameters to be estimated can be any random variable: a probability, a mean, a variance, etc.

There are many "good" estimates of unknown parameters given by the discipline of statistics. A common procedure is that of the method of moments. To estimate k unknown parameters, the method of moments dictates that the first k sample moments be computed and equated to the first k moments of the distribution. Since the k moments of the distribution are expressible in terms of the k parameters, we can determine these parameters as functions of the sample moments, which are themselves functions of the sample values.

A particular type of estimate, which has proved to be useful, is the *maximum likelihood* estimate. It is obtained by expressing the joint distribution function of the sample observations in terms of the parameters to be estimated, and then maximizing the distribution function with respect to the unknown parameters. Solutions of the maximization equation yield the estimation functions as relations between the estimated parameters and the observations. Maximum likelihood estimates are those which assign values to the unknown parameters in a manner that maximizes the probability of the observed sample.

STATISTICAL DISTRIBUTIONS

Of the various distributions of value in statistical applications, two, perhaps, are utilized more frequently than others in general situations.

[†] The dangers of statistical inference are well known in certain commercial situations. Consider the proposition: "Statistics demonstrate that cancer-prone individuals tend toward cigarette smoking." Or: "By statistical correlation it can be established that baldness results from sitting in the front rows at burlesque shows."

Most important is the *normal* or *gaussian distribution*. In Eq. 2-15, $P(r)$ defines the binomial distribution—representing the probability of r successes in n independent trials when the single-trial probability of success is p. We can derive a smooth-curve approximation to the binomial distribution by replacing factorials with their Stirling approximations[†] and defining a continuous variable X:

$$X = \frac{r - np}{\sqrt{np(1 - p)}}$$

which is the deviation of the distribution measured in terms of the standard deviation (for the binomial distribution, $\sigma = \sqrt{npq}$ (cf. Eq. 2-29)). We then obtain

$$P(X) = \frac{1}{\sqrt{2\pi}} e^{-x^2/2} \qquad \qquad 2\text{-}35$$

for the normal distribution of the random variable X with zero mean and unit variance (x signifies the values assumed by X).

A distribution related to the normal, and readily derived therefrom, is the *chi-square* (χ^2) *distribution*, defined as the distribution of the sum of the squares of n independent unit normal variates. The χ^2 distribution is sometimes referred to as *Helmert's distribution*, after F. R. Helmert, its first investigator. For n degrees of freedom (that is, $\chi^2 = x_1^2 + x_2^2 + \cdots + x_n^2$), we can determine that

$$f(\chi^2) = \frac{1}{2^{n/2}\Gamma(n/2)} (\chi^2)^{(n/2)-1} e^{-\chi^2/2} \qquad \qquad 2\text{-}36$$

where $\Gamma(n)$ is the gamma function; $\Gamma(n) = (n - 1)!$ for integral values of n and $\Gamma(1/2) = \sqrt{\pi}$.[‡] Values of χ^2 are tabulated in mathematical handbooks.

In those instances where it is desired to measure the compatibility between observed and expected values of the frequency of occurrence of an event, the χ^2 statistic is highly useful. For n trials, let r_i represent the number

[†] $n! \approx \sqrt{2\pi n}\, n^n e^{-n}$.

[‡] Generally, $\Gamma(n) = \int_0^\infty x^{n-1} e^{-x} dx$ for all $n > 0$.

of times the event x_i is observed, and let s_i be the expected number of occurrences in n trials ($s_i = p_i n$, where p_i is the single-trial probability of x_i); then χ^2 is defined by

$$\chi^2 = \sum_{i=1}^{k} \frac{(r_i - s_i)^2}{s_i} \qquad\qquad 2\text{-}37$$

for the k events $x_1, x_2, \ldots, x_k$ (in actuality, Eq. 2-37 represents a limiting distribution valid for large n; empirically, we usually require $s_i > 5$ for all i). A value of zero for χ^2 corresponds to exact agreement with expectation. If the n-trial experiment is repeated an arbitrarily large number of times, we obtain a distribution of χ^2 that is identical to the χ^2 distribution (Eq. 2-36) with $m - 1$ degrees of freedom. The χ^2 test for goodness of fit is one of the most widely used methods capable of testing a hypothesis for the mathematical form of a single distribution, for a difference in the distribution of two or more random variables, and for the independence of certain random variables or attributes of variables. Its ready application to discrete distributions is not shared by other tests for goodness of fit, such as the Kolmogorov-Smirnov test (which applies as a criterion of fit the maximum deviation of the sample from the true distribution function).

Many other distributions can be derived by considering diverse functions of random variables. These distributions find widespread uses in statistical studies. As an example, if a situation arises such that only a small sample of the total population is available, the sample standard deviation is not an accurate estimate of the true standard deviation σ. This defect can be circumvented by introducing a new variable based on the sample standard deviation. The new variate is defined as the quotient of two independent variates, and the resulting distribution, an offshoot of the chi-square distribution, is *Student's t distribution*.[†] Its importance stems from the fact that it is functionally independent of any unknown population parameters, thus avoiding dubious estimates of these parameters.

In connection with elementary statistical logic and gambling theory, those distributions stated *ut supra* encompass the majority of significant developments. We shall introduce additional distributions only as they are required for special applications.

[†] The distribution of the quotient of two independent variates was first computed by the British statistician William Sealy Gosset who, in 1908, submitted it under the pseudonym "Student" (he was an employee of a Dublin brewery which did not encourage frivolous research).

Game theory

The theory of games, instituted by John von Neumann, is essentially a mathematical theory for the analysis of conflict among people or such groups of people as armies, corporations, or Bridge partnerships. It is applicable wherever a conflicting situation arises and possesses the capability of being resolved by some form of intelligence—as in the games of Chess, Bridge, Poker, capitalistic or oligopolistic economics, logistics, military operations, and certain aspects of social competition constrained by the necessity of rational behavior. Hence, the word "game" is defined as the course (playing) of a conflicting situation according to an a priori specified set of rules and conventions. Games are distinguished by the number of contending *interests*, by the value of the winning payment, by the number of moves required, and by the amount of information available to the interests.

Care should be exercised to avoid confusion with the colloquial meaning of the word "game." Tennis or Sumo wrestling are "games," but are not in the domain of game theory, since their resolution is a function of athletic prowess rather than intelligence (despite the fact that a minimum intelligence is requisite to understanding the rules). For social conflicts, game theory should be utilized with caution and reservation—in the courtship of the village belle, for example, the competing interests might not conform to the rules agreed upon; it is also difficult to evaluate the payoff by a single parameter; further, a reneging of the promised payoff is not unknown in such situations. Game theory demands a sacred character for rules of behavior which may not be observed in reality. The real world, with its emotional, ethical, and social suasions, is a far more muddled skein than the Hobbesian universe of the game theorist.

The number of players or competitors in a game are grouped into distinct decision-making units, or interests (Bridge involves four players, but two interests). With *n* interests, a game is referred to as an *n-person* game. It is assumed that the value of the game to each interest can be measured quantitatively by a number, called the *payoff*. In practice, the payoff is usually in monetary units, but may be counted in any type of exchange medium. If the payoff is transferred only among the *n* players participating, the game is designated a *zero-sum game*. Mathematically, if ρ_i is the payoff received by the *i*th player (when the *i*th player loses and must pay, ρ_i is negative), the zero-sum game is defined by the condition that the algebraic sum of all gains and losses equals zero:

$$\sum_{i-1}^{n} \rho_i = 0$$

Instances where wealth is created or destroyed or a percentage of the wealth is paid to a nonparticipant are examples of *nonzero-sum* games. Tic-tac-toe (which involves a maximum of 9 moves) and Chess (a maximum possible 5950 moves) describe a type of game wherein only a finite number of moves are possible, each of which is chosen from a finite number of alternatives. Such games are termed *finite* games, and obviously the converse situation comprises *infinite* games. The amount of information also characterizes a game. Competitions such as Chess, Checkers, or Shogi, where each player's move is exposed to his opponent, are games of *complete information*. A variant of Chess without complete information is Kriegspiel (precise knowledge of each player's move is withheld from his opponent). Bridge or Poker with all cards exposed would considerably alter the nature of that game. A variant of Blackjack with the dealt cards exposed is Zweikarten-spiel, proposed in Chapter 7.

STRATEGY

A system of divisions that selects each move from the totality of possible moves at prescribed instances is a *strategy*. A strategy may consist of personal moves (based solely on the player's judgment or his opponent's strategy, or both), chance moves (determined through some random Bernoulli-trial method with an assessment of the probability of the various results), or, as in the majority of games, by a combination of the two. If player A has a total of m possible strategies, $A_1, A_2, \ldots, A_m$, and player B has a total of n strategies, $B_1, B_2, \ldots, B_n$, the game is termed an $m \times n$ game. In such a game, for A's strategy A_i parried against B's strategy B_j, the payoff is designated by a_{ij} (by convention, A's gain is assigned a positive sign and B's profit a negative sign). The set of all values of a_{ij} is called the *payoff matrix* and is represented by $\|a_{ij}\|$ or, expressed as a paradigm,

Player B

	B_1	B_2	$\cdots$	B_n
A_1	a_{11}	a_{12}	$\cdots$	a_{1n}
A_2	a_{21}	a_{22}	$\cdots$	a_{2n}
.	.	.	$\cdots$	
.	.	.	$\cdots$	
.	.	.	$\cdots$	
A_m	a_{m1}	a_{m2}	$\cdots$	a_{mn}

Player A

Fig. 2-1   The general payoff matrix

As an elementary illustration, consider two players, A and B, selecting either heads or tails simultaneously; if the two selections match, player A wins one unit and conversely. The coin-matching payoff matrix is

	B_1 (Heads)	B_2 (Tails)
A_1 (Heads)	1	-1
A_2 (Tails)	-1	1

Fig. 2-2   Coin-matching payoff matrix

It is evident that if player A employs a *pure* strategy [for example, selecting A_1 (heads) continually] his opponent, player B, can gain the advantage by continually selecting tails. Intuitively, A's (and B's) best course of action is a *mixed* strategy—that is, alternating among the possible strategies according to some probability distribution. For the coin-matching payoff matrix, Fig. 2-2, A's optimal strategy S_A^* is to select A_1 or A_2 with probability 1/2. Stated mathematically,

$$S_A^* \equiv \begin{pmatrix} A_1 & A_2 \\ p_1^* & p_2^* \end{pmatrix} = \begin{pmatrix} A_1 & A_2 \\ \frac{1}{2} & \frac{1}{2} \end{pmatrix} \qquad\qquad 2\text{-}38$$

In general, the optimal strategy of player A for a given payoff matrix can be determined from the *minimax* principle, the quintessential statement of the theory of games (see Chapter 3). For each row of the matrix of Fig. 2-1, a_{ij} will have a minimum value α_i. That is, for all possible values of j (with a given i), α_i is the lowest value in the ith row of the matrix:

$$\alpha_i = \min_j a_{ij}$$

Player B can always prevent A from winning more than α_i. Thus, the best strategy of A is to select the maximum value of α_i. Denoting this maximum by α, we have

$$\alpha = \max_i \alpha_i$$

Combining these two equations,

$$\alpha = \max_i \min_j a_{ij} \qquad\qquad 2\text{-}39$$

which states that the maximum of the minimum yield (or *maximin*) is A's optimal strategy. The quantity α is the *lower value* of the game, since a profit of not less than α is assured to player A regardless of B's strategy. Considerations from the viewpoint of player B are similar. The maximum value of a_{ij} for each column in Fig. 2-1 is defined as

$$\beta_j = \max_i a_{ij}$$

and the minimum over all the β_j's is

$$\beta = \min_j \beta_j$$

so that β can be written in the form

$$\beta = \min_j \max_i a_{ij} \qquad\qquad 2\text{-}40$$

which states that the minimum of the maximum yield (or *minimax*) is B's optimal strategy. The quantity β is the *upper value* of the game, since a loss of not more than β is guaranteed to player B regardless of A's strategy.

SOLUTIONS OF GAMES WITH SADDLE POINTS

In the example of Fig. 2-2, $\alpha_1 = -1$, $\alpha_2 = -1$. Therefore the lower value of the game is $\alpha = -1$. Similarly, $\beta = +1$. Any strategy of player A is a maximum strategy, since A can never lose more than 1 unit, and similarly for player B. If both A and B adhere to a mixed strategy, the *average value* γ of the game is between the upper and lower values. Specifically,

$$\alpha \le \gamma \le \beta$$

For the case considered here, $\gamma = 0$ if the mixed strategies are unpredictable.

In some instances, the lower value of the game is equal to the upper value. That is,

$$\alpha = \beta = \gamma$$

and the game is said to possess a *saddle point*. Every game with a saddle point has a solution that defines the optimal strategies for all the players; the value of the game is simultaneously its lower and upper values. Further, if any player deviates from the indicated optimal strategy while the other players adhere to theirs, the outcome of the game for the deviating player can only be less than the average value. A proven theorem of game theory states that every game with complete information possesses a saddle point, and therefore a solution.

These considerations can be summarized as follows: For every finite game matrix $\|a_{ij}\|$, a necessary and sufficient condition that

$$\max_{i} \min_{j} a_{ij} = \min_{j} \max_{i} a_{ij} = \gamma \qquad\qquad 2\text{-}41$$

is that $\|a_{ij}\|$ possesses a saddle point. That is, there exists a pair of integers i_0 and j_0 such that $a_{i_0 j_0}$ is simultaneously the minimum of its row and the maximum of its column. Thus, if a game matrix possesses a saddle point, the solution of the game is evident and trivial.

A 2×2 game has a saddle point if and only if the two numbers of either diagonal are *not* both higher than either of the other two numbers. This situation occurs with a probability of 2/3. An unproven formula for the probability P_n that a randomly selected $n \times n$ game matrix exhibits a saddle point is

$$P_n = \frac{n}{2^{n-3} + n - 1}$$

For those instances where the matrix has no saddle point, recourse must be made to mathematical expectations, graphical methods of analysis, or other techniques.

SOLUTIONS OF GAMES WITHOUT SADDLE POINTS

In the heads and tails matching game of Fig. 2-2, let player A select his strategies from some random device that assigns a probability p to heads and $1 - p$ to tails. Further, let us assume that player B has secured knowledge of the nature of A's random device. Then the mathematical expectation of A, when B selects strategy B_1 (heads), is

$$E = (1)(p) + (-1)(1 - p) = 2p - 1$$

For B's choice of strategy B_2 (tails),

$$E = (-1)(p) + (1)(1 - p) = 1 - 2p$$

Clearly, if $p > 1/2$, player B will select strategy B_2 and A's expectation is negative. Conversely, for $p < 1/2$, B selects strategy B_1 and wins $1 - 2p$ units per game. It follows that if A selects A_1 and A_2 with equal probabilities $1/2$, the expectation of A and B is zero, regardless of B's strategy. Thus, A's optimal strategy is to let $p = 1/2$ (as indicated in Eq. 2-38).

In general, for $m \times n$ game matrices, let player A have a mixed strategy

$$S_A(m) = \begin{pmatrix} A_1 A_2 \cdots A_i \cdots A_m \\ p_1 p_2 \cdots p_i \cdots p_m \end{pmatrix}$$

which is interpreted to mean that strategy A_i is selected with probability p_i. The p_i's satisfy the condition

$$\sum_{i=1}^{m} p_i = 1 \quad.$$

Similarly, a mixed strategy for player B is designated by

$$S_B(n) = \begin{pmatrix} B_1 B_2 \cdots B_j \cdots B_n \\ q_1 q_2 \cdots q_j \cdots q_n \end{pmatrix}$$

where

$$\sum_{j=1}^{n} q_j = 1$$

When A and B employ the mixed strategies $S_A(m)$ and $S_B(n)$, respectively, the mathematical expectation of A is given by

$$E[S_A(m), S_B(n)] = \sum_{j=1}^{n} \sum_{i=1}^{m} a_{ij} p_i q_j$$

If it occurs that strategies $S_A^*(m)$ and $S_B^*(n)$ exist for players A and B, respectively, such that

$$E[S_A(m), S_B^*(n)] \leq E[S_A^*(m), S_B^*(n)] \leq E[S_A^*(m), S_B(n)]$$

then $S_A^*(m)$ and $S_B^*(n)$ are optimal strategies and $E[S_A^*(m), S_B^*(n)] = \gamma$ is the value of the game.

In solving games without saddle points, a preliminary step is to eliminate from the game matrix all duplicate strategies and those strategies that are totally unfavorable with respect to another strategy. If the remaining game generates an $m \times n$ matrix, the necessary and sufficient condition for γ to be the value of the game and for $S_A^*(m)$ and $S_B^*(n)$ to be the optimal strategies of A and B, respectively, is that

$$E[S_A(i), S_B^*(n)] \leq \gamma \leq E[S_A^*(m), S_B(j)]$$

for $1 \leq i \leq m$ and $1 \leq j \leq n$. Thus, for the solution of the game matrix $\|a_{ij}\|$, there must exist values of p_i, q_j, and γ which satisfy the conditions

$$a_{11}p_1 + a_{21}p_2 + \cdots + a_{m_1}p_m \geq \gamma$$

$$a_{12}p_1 + a_{22}p_2 + \cdots + a_{m_2}p_m \geq \gamma$$

$$\ldots\ldots\ldots\ldots\ldots\ldots\ldots\ldots\ldots\ldots\ldots$$

$$a_{1n}p_1 + a_{2n}p_2 + \cdots + a_{mn}p_m \geq \gamma$$

$$a_{11}q_1 + a_{12}q_2 + \cdots + a_{1n}q_n \leq \gamma \qquad \text{2-42}$$

$$a_{21}q_1 + a_{22}q_2 + \cdots + a_{2n}q_n \leq \gamma$$

$$\ldots\ldots\ldots\ldots\ldots\ldots\ldots\ldots\ldots\ldots\ldots$$

$$a_{m_1}q_1 + a_{m_2}q_2 + \cdots + a_{mn}q_n \leq \gamma$$

The preceding concepts are readily illustrated. Consider the 4×4 matrix

$$\|a_{ij}\| = \begin{Vmatrix} 1 & -1 & -1 & 2 \\ -1 & -1 & 3 & 0 \\ -1 & 2 & -1 & 1 \\ -2 & 0 & -2 & 0 \end{Vmatrix}$$

It is clear that player A would assign zero probability to strategy A_4, since, regardless of B's strategy, A's gain by selecting A_3 is always greater than the yield from A_4. Thus, A_3 *dominates* A_4 and we can eliminate A_4. Similarly, B_4 can be eliminated because it is dominated by B_1. The remaining game matrix is

$$\|a_{ij}\| = \begin{Vmatrix} 1 & -1 & -1 \\ -1 & -1 & 3 \\ -1 & 2 & -1 \end{Vmatrix}$$

Applying Eqs. 2-46 with the equality signs,

$$p_1 - p_2 - p_3 = \gamma$$
$$-p_1 - p_2 + 2p_3 = \gamma$$
$$-p_1 + 3p_2 - p_3 = \gamma$$
$$q_1 - q_2 - q_3 = \gamma$$
$$-q_1 - q_2 + 3q_3 = \gamma$$
$$-q_1 + 2q_2 - q_3 = \gamma$$

Combining these equations with the conditions $p_1 + p_2 + p_3 = 1$ and $q_1 + q_2 + q_3 = 1$, elementary algebraic methods provide the solution:

$$p_1^* = q_1^* = \frac{6}{13}$$

$$p_2^* = \frac{3}{13}; \quad q_2^* = \frac{4}{13}$$

$$p_3^* = \frac{4}{13}; \quad q_3^* = \frac{3}{13}$$

$$\gamma = -\frac{1}{13}$$

Thus, player A's optimal strategy is to select A_1, A_2, and A_3 with probabilities $\frac{6}{13}, \frac{4}{13}$, and $\frac{3}{13}$, respectively. Such a procedure would guarantee to A a loss of no more than $\frac{1}{13}$.

The preceding technique for solving game matrices without saddle points often involves computational complexities. In some instances, a geometrical interpretation is fruitful, particularly for $2 \times n$ games. In general, however, geometrical (or graphical) solutions of $m \times n$ game matrices pose exceptional mathematical difficulties. More advanced analytic techniques exist, but are unlikely to be required in connection with any of the conventional competitive games.

It is also possible to generalize (to multiperson games) the concept of the solution of a two-person, zero-sum game by introducing the notion of an *equilibrium point* (John Nash is responsible for this idea, although it had been previously applied in the field of economics under the terminology of Cournot's duopoly point). An *equilibrium point* is an *n*-tuple of mixed strategies such that each player's mixed strategy maximizes his payoff if the strategies of all other players are held invariant. For a two-person, zero-sum game, the set of equilibrium points simply defines the set of all pairs of opposing "best" strategies.

Finally, there is a large body of work developed to deal with infinite games, games with infinitely many strategies, and continuous games; however, these situations are beyond our scope of interest. Our presentation has attempted to outline only the basic mathematical tools useful for solving problems in applied gambling theory and statistical logic.

Suggested references

ARLEY, NIELS, and K. RANDER BUCH, *Introduction to the Theory of Probability and Statistics*, John Wiley & Sons, Inc., New York, 1950.

BIRNBAUM, ALLAN W., *Introduction to Probability and Mathematical Statistics*, Harper & Brothers, Publishers, New York, 1962.

BIRNBAUM, ALLAN W., "On the Foundations of Statistical Inference," *J. American Statistical Assoc.*, **57**, No. 298 (1962), pp. 269–326.

BOREL, ÉMILE, *Le Hasard*, Presses Universitaires de France, Paris, New Edition, 1948.

BROWN, G. SPENCER, *Probability and Scientific Inference*, Longmans, Green and Co., Ltd., London, 1957.

CARNAP, RUDOLF, *Logical Foundations of Probability*, Routledge and Kegan Paul, Ltd., London, 1950.

CHERNOFF, HERMAN, and LINCOLN E. MOSES, *Elementary Decision Theory*, John Wiley & Sons, Inc., New York, 1959.

CRAMÉR, HARALD, *The Elements of Probability Theory*, John Wiley & Sons, Inc., New York, 1955.

DE FINETTI, BRUNO, "Recent Suggestions for the Reconciliation of Theories of Probability," Proc. Second Berkeley Symposium on Mathematical Statistics and Probability, University of California Press, Berkeley, 1951, pp. 217–225.

FELLER, WILLIAM, *An Introduction to Probability Theory and Its Applications*, John Wiley & Sons, Inc., New York, 2nd ed., 1957.

FISHER, SIR RONALD A., *Statistical Methods and Scientific Inference*, Oliver and Boyd, Edinburgh 1956.

FISZ, MAREK, *Probability Theory and Mathematical Statistics*, John Wiley & Sons, Inc., New York, 1963.

FRY, THORTON C., *Probability and Its Engineering Uses*, D. Van Nostrand Company, Inc., New York, 1928.

GNEDENKO, B. V., *The Theory of Probability*, Chelsea Publishing Co., New York, 1962.

GOOD, I. J., *Probability and the Weighing of Evidence*, Charles Griffin and Co., Ltd., London, 1950.

GOODE, HARRY H., and ROBERT E. MACHOL, *System Engineering*, McGraw-Hill Book Co., Inc., New York, 1957.

HOEL, PAUL, *Introduction to Mathematical Statistics*, John Wiley & Sons, Inc., New York, 1947.

KENDALL, M. G., "On the Reconciliation of Theories of Probability," *Biometrika*, **36** (1949), pp. 101–106.

KOLMOGOROV, A. N., *Foundations of the Theory of Probability*, Chelsea Publishing Co., New York, 1956.

KYBURG, HENRY E., and HOWARD E. SMOKLER (eds.), *Studies in Subjective Probability*, John Wiley & Sons, Inc., New York, 1964.

LOÈVE, MICHEL, *Probability Theory*, D. Van Nostrand Company, Inc., New York, 1955.

MCKINSEY, J. C. C., *Introduction to the Theory of Games*, McGraw-Hill Book Company Inc., New York, 1952.

MOOD, ALEXANDER, *Introduction to the Theory of Statistics*, McGraw-Hill Book Company, Inc., New York, 1950.

MOSTELLER, FREDERICK, ROBERT ROURKE, GEORGE THOMAS, *Probability and Statistics*, Addison-Wesley Publishing Co., Reading, Mass., 1961.

NASH, JOHN, "Non-Cooperative Games," *Annals of Mathematics*, **54**, No. 2 (September, 1951), pp. 286–295.

PARZEN, EMANUEL, *Modern Probability Theory and Its Application*, John Wiley & Sons, Inc., New York, 1962.

RAMSEY, FRANK PLUMPTON, *The Foundation of Mathematics and Other Logical Essays*, Kegan Paul, London, 1931.

REICHENBACH, HANS, *The Theory of Probability*, Univ. of Calif. Press, Berkeley and L.A., 1949.

RIORDAN, JOHN, *An Introduction to Combinatorial Analysis*, John Wiley & Sons, Inc., New York, 1958.

SAVAGE, LEONARD J., "The Role of Personal Probability in Statistics," *Econometrica*, **18** (1950), pp. 183–184.

THRALL, R. M., C. H. COOMBS, and R. L. DAVIS (eds.), *Decision Processes*, John Wiley & Sons, Inc., New York, 1954.

USPENSKY, J. V., *Introduction to Mathematical Probability*, McGraw-Hill Book Company, Inc., New York, 1937.

VENN, JOHN, *The Logic of Chance*, Macmillan Company, London, 2nd ed., 1876.

VON MISES, RICHARD, *Probability, Statistics, and Truth*, George Allen and Unwin, Ltd., London, 1957.

VON NEUMANN, JOHN, and OSKAR MORGENSTERN, *Theory of Games and Economic Behavior*, Princeton University Press, Princeton, 1953.

WADSWORTH, G. P., and J. G. BRYAN, *Probability and Random Variables*, McGraw-Hill Book Company, Inc., New York, 1960.

WHITWORTH, WILLIAM, *Choice and Chance*, Hafner Publishing Company, New York (reprint), 1951.

WILLIAMS, J. D., *The Compleat Strategyst*, McGraw-Hill Book Company, Inc., New York, 1954.

CHAPTER THREE

FUNDAMENTAL PRINCIPLES OF A THEORY OF GAMBLING

Decision making and utility

The essence of the phenomenon of gambling is decision making. The act of making a decision consists of selecting one course of action, or strategy, from among the set of admissible strategies. A particular decision might indicate the card to be played, a horse to be backed, the fraction of a fortune to be hazarded over a given interval of play, or the time distribution of wagers. Associated with the decision-making process are questions of preference, utility, and evaluation criteria, *inter alia*. Together, these concepts constitute the *sine qua non* for a sound gambling-theory superstructure.

Decisions can be categorized according to the relationship between action and outcome. If each specific strategy leads invariably to a specific outcome, we are involved with decision making under *certainty*. Certain economic games exhibit this deterministic format, particularly those involving such factors as cost functions, production schedules, or time-and-motion considerations. If each specific strategy leads to one of a set of possible specific outcomes with a known probability distribution, we are in the realm of decision making under *risk*. Casino games and games of direct competition between conflicting interests encompass moves whose effects are subject to probabilistic control. Finally, if each specific strategy has as its consequence a set of possible specific outcomes whose a priori probability distribution is completely unknown or is meaningless, we are concerned with decision making under *uncertainty*.

Conditions of certainty are, clearly, special cases of risk conditions where the probability distribution is unity for one specific outcome and zero for all others. Thus a treatment of decision making under risk conditions subsumes the state of certainty conditions. There are no conventional games involving conditions of uncertainty[†] without risk. Often, however, a combination of uncertainty and risk arises; the techniques of statistical inference are valuable in such instances.

Gambling theory, then, is primarily concerned with decision making under conditions of risk. Furthermore, the making of a decision—that is, the process of selecting among n strategies—implies several logical avenues of development. One implication is the existence of an expression of preference or ordering of the strategies. Under some criterion, each strategy can be evaluated according to an individual's taste or desires, and assigned a *utility*. Thus utility defines a measure of the effectiveness of a strategy under a particular criterion. This notion of utility is fundamental and must be encompassed by a theory of gambling in order to define and analyze the decision process.

While we subject the concept of utility to mathematical discipline, the nonstochastic theory of preferences need not be cardinal in nature. It is often adequate if we express all quantities of interest and relevance in purely ordinal terms. The significant idea is that preference precedes characterization. Alternative A is preferred to alternative B; therefore A is assigned the higher (possibly numerical) utility; conversely, it is incorrect to assume that A is preferred to B because of A's higher utility.

THE AXIOMS OF UTILITY THEORY

Axiomatic treatments of utility have been given by von Neumann and Morgenstern, originally, and in modified form by Marschak, Milnor, Herstein, and Luce and Raiffa, among others. Von Neumann and Morgenstern have demonstrated that utility is a measurable quantity on the assumption that it is always possible to express a comparability—that is, a preference—of each *prize* (defined as the value of an outcome) with a probabilistic combination of other *prizes*. The von Neumann-Morgenstern formal axioms imply the existence of a numerical scale for a wide class of partially ordered utilities, and they permit a restricted specific utility of gambling.

[†] Bellman has shown that for decision making under conditions of uncertainty, one can approach an optimum moderately well by maximizing the ratio of the expected gain to the expected cost. Richard Bellman, "Decision Making in the Face of Uncertainty," I, II, *Naval Research Logistics Quarterly*, Vol. 1 (1954), pp. 230–232, 327–332.

Herein, we adopt four axioms that constrain our actions in a gambling situation. To facilitate formulation of the axioms, we define a lottery L as being composed of a set of *prizes* $A_1, A_2, \ldots, A_n$ obtainable with associated probabilities $p_1, p_2, \ldots, p_n$ (a prize can also be interpreted as the right to participate in another lottery). That is,

$$L = (p_1 A_1 ; p_2 A_2 ; \ldots ; p_n A_n)$$

And, for ease in expression, we introduce the notation **p** to mean "is preferred to," or "takes preference over"; **e** to mean "is equivalent to," or "is indifferent to"; and **q** to mean "is either preferred or is equivalent to." The set of axioms delineating utility theory can then be expressed as follows.

Axiom I(a). Complete Ordering: Given a set of alternatives $A_1, A_2,$ $\ldots, A_n$, a comparability exists between any two alternatives A_i and A_j. Either $A_i \mathbf{q} A_j$ or $A_j \mathbf{q} A_i$, or both.

Axiom I(b). Transitivity: If $A_i \mathbf{q} A_j$ and $A_j \mathbf{q} A_k$, then it is implied that $A_i \mathbf{q} A_k$. This axiom is requisite to consistency. Together, Axioms I(a) and I(b) constitute a complete ordering of the set of alternatives by **q**.

Axiom II(a). Continuity: If $A_i \mathbf{p} A_j \mathbf{p} A_k$, there exists a real, non-negative number r_j, $0 < r_j < 1$ such that the prize A_j is equivalent to a lottery wherein prize A_i is obtained with probability r_j and prize A_k is obtained with probability $1 - r_j$.

In our notation: $A_j \mathbf{e} [r_j A_i ; (1 - r_j) A_k]$. If the probability r of obtaining A_i is between 0 and r_j, we prefer A_j to the lottery, and contrariwise for $r_j < r \leq 1$. Thus r_j defines a point of inversion where a prize A_j obtained with certainty is equivalent to a lottery between a lesser prize A_i and a greater prize A_k whose outcome is determined with probabilities r_j and $(1 - r_j)$, respectively.

Axiom II(b). Substitutibility: In any lottery with an ordered value of prizes defined by $A_i \mathbf{p} A_j \mathbf{p} A_k$, $[r_j A_i ; (1 - r_j) A_k]$ is substitutible for the prize A_j with complete indifference.

Axiom III. Monotonicity: A lottery $[r A_i ; (1 - r) A_k] \mathbf{q} [r_j A_i ; (1 - r_j) A_k]$ if and only if $r \geq r_j$. That is, between two lotteries with the same outcome, we prefer that lottery which yields the greater probability of obtaining the preferred alternative.

Axiom IV. Independence: If among the sets of prizes (or lottery tickets) $A_1, A_2, \ldots, A_n$ and $B_1, B_2, \ldots, B_n, A_1 \, \mathbf{q} \, B_1, A_2 \, \mathbf{q} \, B_2$, etc., then an even chance of obtaining A_1 or A_2, etc., is preferred or equivalent to an even chance of obtaining B_1 or B_2, etc.

This axiom is essential for the maximization of expected cardinal utility.

Together, the four axioms encompass the principles of consistent behavior. Any decision maker who accepts them *can*, theoretically, solve any decision problem, no matter how complex, by merely expressing his basic preferences and judgments with regard to elementary problems and performing the necessary extrapolations.

UTILITY FUNCTIONS

With Axiom I as the foundation, we can assign a number $u(L)$ to each lottery L such that the magnitude of the values of $u(L)$ is in accordance with the preference relations of the lotteries. That is, $u(L_i) \geq u(L_j)$ if and only if $L_i \, \mathbf{q} \, L_j$. Thus we can assert that a utility function u exists over the lotteries.

Rational behavior relating to gambling or decision making under risk is now clearly defined; yet there are many cases of apparently rational behavior that violate one or more of the axioms. Common examples are those of the military hero or the mountain climber who willingly risks death and the "angel" who finances a potential Broadway play despite an obviously negative expected return. Postulating that the probability of fatal accidents in scaling Mt. Everest is 0.10 if a Sherpa guide is employed and 0.20 otherwise, the mountain climber appears to prefer a survival probability of 0.9 to that of 0.8, but also to that of 0.999 (depending on his age and health)—or he would forego the climb. Since his utility function has a maximum at 0.9, he would seem to violate the monotonicity axiom. The answer lies in the "total reward" to the climber—as well as the success in attaining the summit, the payoff includes exercise, scenery, subsequent publicity, the thrill due to the danger itself, and perhaps other forms of mental elation and ego satisfaction. In short, the utility function is still monotonic when the payoff matrix takes into account the climber's "gestalt." Similar considerations evidently apply for the Broadway "angel" and the subsidizer of unusual inventions, treasure-seeking expeditions, or world fairs.

Since utility is obviously a subjective concept, it is necessary to impose certain restrictions on the types of utility functions allowable. First and foremost, we postulate that our gambler be a *rational being*. By definition, the rational being is logical, mathematical, and consistent. Given that all *x*'s are *y*'s, he concludes that all non-*y*'s are non-*x*'s, but does not conclude that all *y*'s are *x*'s. When it is known that *U* follows from *V*, he concludes that non-*V* follows from non-*U*, but not that *V* follows from *U*. If he prefers alternative *A* to alternative *B*, and alternative *B* to alternative *C*, then he prefers alternative *A* to alternative *C*. The rational being exhibits no subjective probability preference. As initially hypothesized by Gabriel Cramer and Daniel Bernoulli as "typical" behavior, our rational being, when concerned with decision making under risk conditions (gambling), acts in such a manner as to maximize the expected value of his utility.

Numerous experiments have been conducted to relate probability preferences to utility.[†] The most representative utility function—illustrated by Fig. 3-1—is concave for small increases in wealth and then convex for larger gains. For decreases in wealth the typical utility function is first convex and then concave, with the point of inflection again proportional to the magnitude of present wealth. Generally, $u(W)$ falls faster with decreased wealth than it rises with increased wealth.

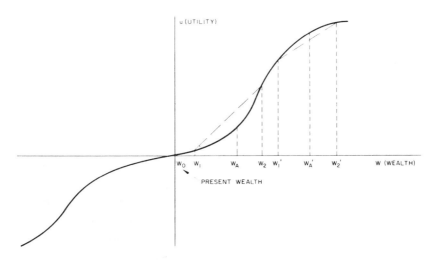

Fig. 3-1   Utility as a function of wealth

[†] Ward Edwards, "Probability-preferences in Gambling," *Am. J. Psychol.*, **66** (1953), pp. 349–364. Also, "Probability Preferences Among Bets With Differing Expected Values," *Am. J. Psychol.*, **67** (1954), pp. 56–67.

From Fig. 3-1, we can determine geometrically whether we would accept added assets W_a or prefer an even chance to obtain W_2 while risking a loss to W_1. Since the line $\overline{[W_2, u(W_2)], [W_1, u(W_1)]}$ passes above the point $[W_a, u(W_a)]$, the expected utility of the fair bet is greater than $u(W_a)$; the lottery is therefore preferred. However, when we are offered the option of accepting W'_a or the even chance of obtaining W'_2 or falling to W'_1, we draw the line $\overline{[W'_2, u(W'_2)], [W'_1, u(W'_1)]}$, which we observe passes below the point $u(W'_a)$. Clearly, we prefer W'_a with certainty to the even gamble indicated, since the utility function $u(W'_a)$ is greater than the expected utility of the gamble. This last example also indicates the justification for buying insurance. The difference between the utility of the specified wealth and the expected utility of the gamble is proportional to the amount of "unfairness" we would accept in a lottery or in an insurance situation.

The type of utility function described here implies that as present wealth decreases, there is a greater tendency to prefer gambles involving a large chance of small loss versus a small chance of large gain (the farthing "football" pools in England, for example, were patronized by the lower working classes, not the millionaires). Another implication is that a positive skewness of the frequency distribution of total gains and losses is desirable. That is, Fig. 3-1 suggests we tend to wager more conservatively when losing moderately, and more liberally when winning moderately. The term "moderate" refers to that portion of the utility function between the two outer inflection points.

THE OBJECTIVE UTILITY FUNCTION

From the preceding arguments it is clear that the particular utility function determines the decision-making process. Further, this utility function is frequently subjective in nature, differing among individuals and according to present wealth. However, to develop a simple theory of gambling, we must postulate a specific utility function and derive the laws that pertain thereto. Therefore we adopt the objective model of utility shown in Fig. 3-2, with the reservation that the theorems to be stated subsequently must be modified accordingly for each particular subjective model of utility.

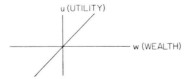

Fig. 3-2   The objective utility function

It has been stated that only misers and mathematicians truly act according to objective utilities. For them, each and every dollar maintains a constant value regardless of how many other dollars can be summoned in mutual support. For those readers who are members of neither profession, we recommend the study of such behavior as a sound prelude to the intromission of a personal, subjective utility function.

The objective model assumes that the utility of wealth is linear with wealth and that decision making is independent of nonprobabilistic considerations. It should also be noted that in the subjective model, the utility function does not depend on long-run effects; it is completely valid for single-trial operation. The objective model, on the other hand, rests (at least implicitly) on the results of an arbitrarily large number of repetitions of an experiment.

Finally, it must be appreciated that, within the definition of an objective model, there are several goals available to the gambler. He may, for example, wish to play indefinitely, gamble over a certain number of plays, or gamble until he has won or lost specified amounts of wealth. In general, the gambler's aim is not simply to increase wealth (a certainty of $1 million loses its attraction if a million years are entailed). Wealth per unit time or per unit play (income) is a better aim, but there are additional constraints. The gambler may well wish to maximize the expected wealth received per unit play, subject to a fixed probability of losing some specified sum. Or he may wish with a certain confidence level to reach a specified level of wealth. His goal dictates the amount of wealth that must be risked and the degree of risk. These variations lie within the objective model for utility functions.

DECISION-MAKING CRITERIA

Since gambling involves decision making, it is also necessary to inquire as to the "best" decision-making procedure. Again, there are many approaches to the definition of "best." For example, the Bayesian solution to the "best" decision proposes minimization with respect to average risk. The Bayes principle states that if the unknown parameter θ is a random variable distributed according to a known probability distribution f, and if $F_\Delta(\theta)$ denotes the risk function of the decision procedure Δ, we wish to minimize with respect to Δ the average risk

$$\int F_\Delta(\theta)\, df(\theta)$$

We could also minimize the average risk with respect to some assumed a priori distribution suggested by previous experience. This latter method, known as the restricted Bayes solution, is applicable in connection with decision processes wherein maximum risk does not exceed minimum risk by more than a specified amount. A serious objection to the use of the restricted Bayesian principle for gambling problems lies in its dependence upon subjective probability assignments. Whenever possible, we wish to avoid subjective weightings.

Another method of obtaining a "best" decision follows the principle of "minimization of regret." As proposed by Savage,[†] this procedure is designed for the player who desires to minimize the difference between the payoff actually achieved by a strategy and the payoff that could have been achieved if the opponent's intentions were known in advance and the appropriate strategy had been adopted. An obvious appeal is offered to the businessman whose motivation is to minimize the possible disappointment deriving from an economic transaction. The regret matrix is formed from the conventional payoff matrix by replacing each payoff a_{ij} with the difference between the column maximum and the payoff—that is, with $\max_i (a_{ij}) - a_{ij}$. For example, consider the payoff matrix

$$\|a_{ij}\| = \begin{array}{c|ccc} & B_1 & B_2 & B_3 \\ \hline A_1 & 3 & 4 & 5 \\ A_2 & 4 & 6 & 8 \\ A_3 & 3 & 6 & 9 \end{array}$$

which possesses a saddle point at (A_2, B_1) and a game value of 4 to player A under the minimax criterion. The regret matrix R engendered by these payoffs is

$$R = \begin{array}{c|ccc} & B_1 & B_2 & B_3 \\ \hline A_1 & 1 & 2 & 4 \\ A_2 & 0 & 0 & 1 \\ A_3 & 1 & 0 & 0 \end{array}$$

[†] Leonard J. Savage, "The Theory of Statistical Decision," *J. Am. Statistical Assoc.,* **46** (1951), pp. 55–67.

While there now exists no saddle point defined by two pure strategies, we can readily solve the matrix (observe that we are concerned with row maxima and column minima, since player A wishes to minimize the regret) to obtain the mixed strategies (0, 1/4, 3/4) for player A and (3/4, 0, 1/4) for his opponent B. The "regret value" to A is 3/4; the actual profit to A is

$$(3/4)[4(1/4) + 3(3/4)] + (1/4)[8(1/4) + 9(3/4)] = 4\frac{5}{8}$$

compared to a profit of 4 from application of the minimax principle.

Chernoff[†] has pointed out the several drawbacks of the "minimization of regret" principle: First, the "regret" is not necessarily proportional to losses in utility; second, there can arise instances whereby an arbitrarily small advantage in one state of nature outweighs a sizable advantage in another state; third, it is possible that the presence of an undesirable strategy might influence the selection of the "best" strategy. As an example of the last objection, assume that the criterion of "minimization of regret" dictates the selection of strategy A_3 from the set of strategies A_1, A_2, A_3, A_4; then it is possible that if A_4 is removed from the set, the same criterion might select A_2 as the "best" strategy from the set A_1, A_2, A_3.

Other criteria include the Hurwicz[‡] pessimism–optimism index, which emphasizes a weighted combination of the minimum and maximum utility numbers, and the "principle of insufficient reason," due to Jacob Bernoulli. This latter criterion assigns equal probabilities to all possible strategies of an opponent if no a priori knowledge is given. Such an assignment leads to patently nonsensical results.

For our objective model of utility we wish an objective definition of "best." To the greatest degree possible, we can achieve objectivity by adopting the minimax principle—that is, minimization with respect to maximum risk. We wish to minimize the decision procedure Δ with respect to the maximum risk $\sup_\theta F_\Delta(\theta)$—or, in terms of the discrete theory outlined in Chapter 2, $\min_\Delta \max_\theta F_\Delta(\theta)$. The chief criticism of the minimax (or maximin) criterion is that in concentrating on the worst outcome, it tends to be overly conservative. In the case of an intelligent opponent, the conservatism appears well-founded, since a directly conflicting interest is assumed. With "nature" as the opposition, it seems unlikely that the resolution of

[†] Herman Chernoff, "Rational Selection of Decision Functions," *Econometrica*, **22** (1954), pp. 422–443.

[‡] Leonid Hurwicz, "Optimality Criteria for Decision Making Under Ignorance," Cowles Commission Discussion Paper, *Statistics*, No. 370 (1951).

events exhibits such a diabolical character. This point can be illustrated (following Luce and Raiffa) by considering the matrix

$$
\|a_{ij}\| = \quad
\begin{array}{c|cc}
 & B_1 & B_2 \\
\hline
A_1 & 0 & \lambda \\
A_2 & 1 & 1 + \varepsilon
\end{array}
$$

We let λ be some number arbitrarily large and ε some positive number arbitrarily small. The minimax principle asserts that a saddle point exists at (A_2, B_1). Obviously an intelligent adversary would always select strategy B_1; "nature," however, might not be so inconsiderate and player A consequently would be foolish not to attempt strategy A_1 occasionally with the possibility of reaping the high profit λ.

While this fault of the minimax principle can entail serious consequences, we are unlikely to be concerned with such instances, for in the great preponderance of gambling situations we shall be facing either a skilled adversary or a "nature" whose behavior is known statistically. In the exceptional instance, for lack of a universally applicable criterion, we must stand accused of conservatism. Accordingly, we shall incorporate the minimax principle as one of the basic pillars of gambling theory.

The basic theorems

With an understanding of utility and the decision-making process, we are in a position to establish the theorems that constitute a comprehensive theory of gambling. While the theorems proposed are, in a sense, arbitrary, they are intended to be necessary and sufficient to encompass all possible courses of action arising from decision making under risk conditions. Ten theorems with associated corollaries are stated.[†] The restrictions to be noted are that our theorems are valid only for those phenomena whose statistics constitute a stationary time series and whose game-theoretic formulations are expressible as zero-sum games. Unless otherwise indicated, each theorem assumes that the sequence of plays constitutes successive independent events.

[†] Proofs of the theorems have been developed in the first edition of this book.

Theorem I: If a gambler risks a finite capital over a large number of plays in a game with constant single-trial probability of winning, losing, and tying, then any and all betting systems lead ultimately to the same value of mathematical expectation of gain per unit amount wagered.

A betting system is defined as some variation in the magnitude of the wager as a function of the outcome of previous plays. At the ith play of the game, the player wagers β_i units, winning the sum $k\beta_i$ with probability $0 \le p \le 1$ (k is a constant), losing β_i with probability $0 \le q \le 1$, and tying with probability $1 - p - q$.

It follows that a favorable (unfavorable) game remains favorable (unfavorable) and an equitable game ($pk = q$) remains equitable regardless of the variations in bets. It should be emphasized, however, that such parameters as game duration and the probability of success in achieving a specified increase in wealth subject to a specified probability of loss *are* distinct functions of the betting systems; these relations are considered shortly.

The number of "guaranteed" betting systems, the proliferation of myths and fallacies concerning such systems, and the countless people believing, propagating, venerating, protecting, and swearing by such systems are legion. Betting systems constitute one of the oldest delusions of gambling history. Betting system votaries are spiritually akin to the proponents of perpetual motion machines, butting their heads against the second law of thermodynamics.

The philosophic rationale of betting systems is usually entwined with the concepts of primitive justice—particularly the principle of retribution (*lex talionis*), which embodies the notion of balance. Accordingly, the universe is governed by an eminently equitable god of symmetry (the "Great C.P.A." in the sky) who ensures that for every head there is a tail. Confirmation of this idea is often distilled by a process of wishful thinking dignified by philosophic (or metaphysical) cant. The French philosopher Pierre-Hyacinthe Azaïs (1766–1845) formalized the statement that good and evil fortune are exactly balanced in that they produce for each person an equivalent result. Better known are such notions as Hegelian compensation, Marxian dialectics, and the Emersonian pronouncements on the divine or scriptural origin of earthly compensation. With less formal expression, the notion of head-tail balance extends back at least to the ancient Chinese doctrine of Yin-Yang polarity.

"Systems" generally can be categorized into multiplicative, additive, or linear betting systems. Each system is predicated upon wagering a sum of money determined by the outcome of the previous plays—thereby ignoring the implication of independency between plays. The sum β_i is bet on the ith play in a sequence of losses. In multiplicative systems,

$$\beta_i = K f(\beta_{i-1}, \beta_{i-2}, \ldots, \beta_1)$$

where K is a constant ≥ 1 and plays $i - 1, i - 2, \ldots, 1$ are immediately preceding (generally, if play $i - 1$ results in a win, β_i reverts to β_1). Perhaps the most popular of all systems is the "Martingale" or "doubling" or "geometric progression" system. Each stake is specified only by the previous one. In the event of a loss on the $i - 1$ play, $\beta_i = 2\beta_{i-1}$. In the event of a win occurring on the $i - 1$ play, $\beta_i = \beta_1$. Of course, with equal validity or equal misguided intent, we could select any value for K and any function of the preceding results.

Additive systems are characterized by functions that increase the stake by an additive factor (which may change with each play). A popular additive system is the "Labouchère," or "cancellation," system. A sequence of numbers $a_1, a_2, \ldots, a_n$ is established, the stake being the sum of a_1 and a_n. For a win, the numbers a_1 and a_n are removed from the sequence and the sum $a_2 + a_{n-1}$ is wagered; for a loss, the sum $a_1 + a_n$ constitutes the a_{n+1} term in a new sequence and $a_1 + a_{n+1}$ forms the subsequent wager. Since the additive constant is the first term in the sequence, the increase in wagers occurs at an arithmetic rate.

Linear betting systems involve a fixed additive constant. A well-known linear system is the "d'Alembert," or "simple progression," system, which is defined by

$$\beta_i = \beta_{i-1} \pm K \begin{cases} + & \text{if } i - 1 \text{ play results in loss} \\ - & \text{if } i - 1 \text{ play results in win} \end{cases}$$

It is obviously possible to invent other classes of systems. We might create an exponential system wherein each previous loss is squared, cubed, or, in general, raised to the nth power to determine the succeeding stake. For those transcendentally inclined, we might create a system that relates wagers by trigonometric functions. We could also invert the systems described here. The "anti-Martingale" system doubles the previous wager after a win and reverts to β_1 following a loss. The "anti-Labouchère" system adds a term to the sequence following a win and decreases the sequence by two terms after a loss. The "anti-d'Alembert" system employs the addition or subtraction of K according to a preceding win or loss, respectively. There are yet other systems designed to profit from the existence of imagined or undetermined biases. For example, in an even-bet head–tail sequence, the procedure of wagering on a repetition of the immediately preceding outcome of the sequence would be advantageous in the event of a constant bias; we dub this procedure the Epaminondas system in honor of the small boy (not the Theban general) who always did the right thing for the previous situation. Clearly, only the bounds of our imagination limit the number of systems we might conceive. And all these systems are equally valuable or not valuable. No one of them can affect the mathematical expectation of the game when successive plays are mutually independent.

The various systems do, however, affect the expected duration of play. Obviously a system that rapidly increases each wager from the previous one will change the pertinent fortune (bankroll) at a greater rate; the fortune will thereby fall to zero or reach a desired specified higher level more quickly than through a system that dictates a slower increase in wagers. The probability of successfully increasing the fortune to a specified level is also altered by the betting system for a given single-trial probability of success.

A multiplicative system, wherein the wager rises rapidly with increasing losses, offers a high probability of small gain with a small probability of large loss. The "Martingale" system, for example, used with an expendable fortune of 2^n units, provides a profit of 1 unit for all sequences of losses followed by a win when the number of consecutive losses does not exceed $n - 1$. Additive systems place more restrictions on the resulting sequence of wins and losses, but risk correspondingly less capital. For example, the "Labouchère" system concludes a betting sequence whenever the number of wins equals one-half the number of losses plus one-half the number of terms in the original sequence. At that time, the gambler has increased his fortune by $a_1 + a_2 + \cdots + a_n$ units. Similarly, a linear betting system requires almost equality between the number of wins and losses, but risks less in large wagers to recover early losses. In the "d'Alembert" system, for $2n$ plays involving n wins and n losses in any order, the gambler increases his fortune by $K/2$ units. Exactly contrary results are achieved for each of the "anti" systems mentioned (the "anti-d'Alembert" system decreases the gambler's fortune by $K/2$ units after n wins and n losses).

In general, for a game with single-trial probability of success p, a positive system offers a probability $p' > p$ of winning a specified amount at the conclusion of each sequence while risking a probability $1 - p'$ of losing a sum larger than $\beta_1 n$, where β_1 is the initial bet in a sequence and n is the number of plays of the sequence. A negative system provides a smaller probability $p' < p$ of losing a specified amount over each betting sequence, but contributes insurance against a large loss; over n plays the loss is always less than $\beta_1 n$. The "anti" systems described here are negative. Logarithmic ($\beta_i = \log \beta_{i-1}$ if the $i - 1$ play results in a loss) or fractional [$\beta_i = (\beta_{i-1})/K$ if the $i - 1$ play is a loss] betting systems are typical of the negative variety. For the fractional system, the gambler's fortune X_{2n} after $2n$ plays of n wins and n losses in any order is

$$X_{2n} = X_0 \left(1 - \frac{1}{K^2}\right)^n$$

The gambler's fortune is reduced, but the insurance premium against large losses has been paid. Positive systems are inhibited by the extent of the gambler's initial fortune and normal limitations imposed on the magnitude of each wager. Negative systems have questionable utility in a gambling context and are generally preferred by insurance companies. Neither type of system, of course, can budge the mathematical expectation from its fixed and immovable value.

Another category of "system" involves wagering only on selected members of a sequence of plays (again, we are discussing mutually independent events). The decision to bet or not to bet on the outcome of the nth trial is made to be a function of the preceding trials. Illustratively, we might bet only on the odd-numbered trials, the prime-numbered trials, or those trials immediately preceded by a sequence of ten "would have been" losses. To describe this situation, we formulate the following theorem.

Theorem II: No advantage accrues to the process of betting only on some subsequence of a number of independent repeated trials forming a complete sequence.

This statement in mathematical form is best couched in terms of measure theory. We establish a sequence of functions $\Delta_1, \Delta_2(\zeta_1), \Delta_3(\zeta_1, \zeta_2), \ldots$, where Δ_i assumes a value of either 1 or zero, depending only on the outcomes $\zeta_1, \zeta_2, \ldots, \zeta_{i-1}$ of the $i - 1$ previous trials. Let $\omega:(\zeta_1, \zeta_2, \ldots)$ be a point of the infinite-dimensional Cartesian space Ω_∞ (allowing for an infinite number of trials); let $F(n, \omega)$ be the nth value of i for which $\Delta_i = 1$;

and let $\zeta'_n = \zeta_F$. Then $(\zeta'_1, \zeta'_2, \ldots)$ is the subsequence of trials on which the gambler wagers. We wish to show that the probability relations valid for the space of points $(\zeta'_1, \zeta'_2, \ldots)$ are equivalent to those pertaining to the points $(\zeta_1, \zeta_2, \ldots)$ and that the gambler therefore cannot distinguish between the subsequence and the complete sequence.

The most prevalent and fallacious of the system philosophies that ignores the precept of Theorem II is known as "maturity of the chances." According to this doctrine, we wager on the nth trial of a sequence only if the preceding $n - 1$ trials have produced a result opposite to that which we desire as the outcome of the nth trial. In Roulette, we would be advised, for example, to await a sequence of nine consecutive "reds," say, before betting on "black." Presumably, this doctrine arose from some misunderstanding of the law of large numbers. Its effect is to assign a memory to a phenomenon that, by definition, exhibits no correlation between events.

One final aspect of disingenuous betting systems remains to be mentioned. It is expressible in the following form.

Corollary: No advantage in terms of mathematical expectation accrues to the gambler who possesses the option of discontinuing the game after each play.[†]

The question of whether or not an advantage exists with this option was first raised by John Venn, the English logician, who postulated a coin-tossing game between opponents A and B; the game was equitable except that only A was permitted to stop or continue the game after each play. Since Venn's logic granted infinite credit to each player, he concluded that A indeed has an advantage. Lord Rayleigh subsequently pointed out that the situation of finite fortunes alters the conclusion, so that no advantage exists.

Having established that no class of betting system can alter the mathematical expectation of a game, we proceed to determine the expectation and variance of a series of plays. The definition of each play is that there exists a probability $p, 0 \leq p \leq 1$, that the gambler's fortune is increased by α units, a probability $q, 0 \leq q \leq 1$, that the fortune is decreased by β units, and a probability $r = 1 - p - q$ that no change in the fortune occurs (designated a "tie"). The bet at each play, then, is β units of wealth.

Theorem III: For n plays of the general game, the mean or mathematical expectation is $n(\alpha p - \beta q)$ and the variance is $n[\alpha^2 p + \beta^2 q - (\alpha p - \beta q)^2]$.

[†] In French, the privilege of terminating play arbitrarily while winning has been accorded the status of an idiom: *le droit de faire Charlemagne.*

This expression for the mathematical expectation leads directly to a definition of a *fair* or *equitable* game. It is self-evident that the condition for no inherent advantage to any player is that

$$E(X_n) = 0$$

For the general case, a fair game signifies

$$\alpha p = \beta q \qquad\qquad 3\text{-}1$$

To complete the definition we can refer to all games wherein $E(X_n) > 0$ (that is, $\alpha p > \beta q$) as positive games; similarly, negative games are described by $E(X_n) < 0$ (or $\alpha p < \beta q$).

Comparing the expectation and the variance of the general game, we note that as the expectation deviates from zero, the variance decreases and approaches zero as p or q approaches unity. Conversely, the variance is maximal for a fair game. It is the resulting fluctuations that may cause a gambler to lose a small capital even though his mathematical expectation is positive. The variance of a game is one of our principal concerns in deciding if and how to play. For example, a game that offers a positive single-play mathematical expectation may or may not have a strong appeal, depending upon the variance as well as upon other factors such as the game's utility. A game characterized by $p = 0.505$, $q = 0.495$, $r = 0$, $\alpha = \beta = 1$, has a single-play expectation of $E(X) = 0.01$. We might be interested in this game, contingent upon our circumstances. A game characterized by $p = 0.01$, $q = 0$, $r = 0.99$, $\alpha = \beta = 1$, also exhibits an expectation of 0.01. However, our interest in this latter game is not casual—it is highly intense. We would likely mortgage our wife and total possessions to wager the maximum stake. The absence of negative fluctuations clearly has a profound effect upon the gambler's actions.

These considerations lead to the following two theorems, the first of which is known as "the gambler's ruin." (The ruin probability and the number of plays before ruin are classical problems that have been studied by James Bernoulli, De Moivre, Lagrange, Laplace, and many others.)

> *Theorem IV :* In the general game (where a gambler bets β units at each play to win α units with single-trial probability p, lose β with probability q, or remain at the same wealth level with probability $r = 1 - p - q$) begun by a gambler with wealth z and continued until the gambler's capital either increases to $a \geq z + \beta$ or decreases to less than β (the ruin point), the probability of ruin P_z is bounded by

$$\lambda^z \frac{\lambda^{a-z-(\alpha-1)} - 1}{\lambda^{a-(\alpha-1)} - 1} \leq P_z \leq \lambda^{z-(\beta-1)} \frac{\lambda^{a-z} - 1}{\lambda^{a-(\beta-1)} - 1} \qquad\qquad 3\text{-}2$$

where λ is a root of a particular exponential equation.

For values of a and z large with respect to α and β, the bounds are extremely close.

If the game is equitable—a mathematical expectation equal to zero—we can derive the bounds on P_z as

$$\frac{a - z - (\alpha - 1)}{a - (\alpha - 1)} \leq P_z \leq \frac{a - z}{a - (\beta - 1)} \qquad \text{3-3}$$

With the further simplification that $\alpha = \beta = 1$, as is the case in many conventional games of chance, the probability of ruin reduces to the form

$$P_z = \frac{(q/p)^a - (q/p)^z}{(q/p)^a - 1} \qquad \text{3-4}$$

And the probability, $\bar{P}_z$, of the gambler successfully increasing his capital from z to a is

$$\bar{P}_z = 1 - P_z = \frac{(q/p)^z - 1}{(q/p)^a - 1} \qquad \text{3-5}$$

For a fair game, $p = q$, and we obtain

$$P_z = \frac{a - z}{a} \qquad \text{3-6}$$

and

$$\bar{P}_z = \frac{z}{a} \qquad \text{3-7}$$

It is interesting to note the probabilities of ruin and success when the gambler ventures against an infinitely rich adversary. Letting $a \to \infty$ in the fair game represented by Eq. 3-3, we again observe that $P_z \to 1$. Therefore, whenever $\alpha p \leq \beta q$, the gambler must eventually lose his fortune z. However, in a favorable game as $(a - z) \to \infty$, $\lambda < 1$, and the probability of ruin approaches

$$P_z \to \lambda^z$$

With the simplification of $\alpha = \beta = 1$, Eq. 3-4, as $a \to \infty$, becomes

$$P_z \to \left(\frac{q}{p}\right)^z \qquad \text{3-8}$$

for $p > q$. Thus, in a favorable game, the gambler can continue playing indefinitely against an infinite bank and, with arbitrarily large capital z, can make his probability of ruin as close to zero as desired. We can conclude that with large initial capital, there is a high probability of winning a small amount even in games that are slightly unfavorable; with smaller capital a favorable game is required for a high probability of increasing the wealth by an appreciable amount.

These considerations lead directly to the formulation of the following theorem.

> *Theorem V :* A gambler with initial fortune z, playing a game with the fixed objective of increasing his fortune by the amount $a - z$, has an expected gain that is a function of his probability of ruin (or success). Moreover, the probability of ruin is a function of the betting system. For equitable or unfair games, a "maximum boldness" strategy is optimal—that is, the gambler should wager the maximum amount permissible consistent with his objective and current fortune. For favorable games, a "minimal boldness" or "prudence" strategy is optimal—the gambler should wager the minimum sum permitted under the game rules.

The "maximum boldness" strategy coincides with the Martingale, or doubling, betting system, with the particular conditions imposed on the range of z that $0 \leq z < a$. (Caveat: If a limit is placed on the number of plays allowed the gambler, the "maximum boldness" strategy is not then necessarily optimal.) For equitable games, the stakes or variations thereof are immaterial; in this case, the probability of success (winning the capital $a - z$) is given simply by the ratio of the initial bankroll to the specified goal, as per Eq. 3-7.

In the first part of this chapter the concept of goal utility was discussed. Maximizing the probability of success in attaining a specified increase in wealth without regard to the number of plays, as in the preceding theorem, is but one of many criteria. It is also feasible to specify the desired increase in wealth $a - z$ and determine the betting strategy that minimizes the number of plays required to achieve the increase. Another criterion is to specify the number of plays n and maximize the magnitude of the gambler's fortune after the n plays. Yet another is to maximize the rate of increase in the gambler's capital. In general, any function of the gambler's fortune, the desired increase therein, the number of plays, etc., can be established as a criterion and maximized or minimized to achieve a particular goal.

An interesting criterion proposed by J. L. Kelly concerns the maximization of the exponential rate of growth G of the gambler's capital in favorable games ($p > q$), G being defined as

$$G = \lim_{n \to \infty} \frac{1}{n} \log \frac{x_n}{x_0}$$

where x_0 is initial fortune and x_n the fortune after n plays. If the gambler bets a fraction f of his capital at each play, after n plays the fortune has the value

$$x_n = (1 + f)^w (1 - f)^{n-w} x_0$$

for w wins in the n wagers. The exponential rate of growth is therefore

$$G = \lim_{n \to \infty} \left[\frac{w}{n} \log(1 + f) + \frac{n - w}{n} \log(1 - f) \right]$$

$$= \frac{p}{(1 - r)} \log(1 + f) + \frac{q}{(1 - r)} \log(1 - f)$$

Maximizing G with respect to f, it can be shown that

$$G_{max} = \frac{1 - r + p \log p + q \log q - 2(1 - r) \log(1 - r)}{1 - r}$$

which, for $r = 0$ (no ties), reduces to $1 + p \log p + q \log q$, the Shannon rate of transmission of information over a noisy communication channel.

Kelly's betting system is an example of a large class of utility functions of the form

$$U_\alpha(x) = \frac{x^\alpha - 1}{\alpha}$$

with $\alpha = 0$. Breiman has shown that Kelly's system is asymptotically optimal under two criteria: (1) minimal expected time to achieve a fixed level of resources and (2) maximal rate of increase of wealth.

Contrary to the types of "systems" discussed in connection with Theorem I, Kelly's fractional (or logarithmic or proportional) gambling system is not a function of previous history. Generally, a betting system for which each wager depends only on present resources and present probability of success is known as a *Markov betting system* (the sequence of values of the gambler's fortune form a Markov process). It is heuristically evident that, for all sensible criteria and utilities, a gambler can restrict himself to Markov betting systems.

While Kelly's system is particularly interesting (it is an example of the rate of transmission of information formula applied to uncoded messages), it implies an infinite divisibility of the gambler's fortune, which is impractical by virtue of a lower limit imposed on the minimum bet β in realistic situations. There also exists a practical upper limit on β, which would inhibit the logarithmic gambler, and allowable wagers are necessarily quantized. We can observe that fractional betting constitutes a negative system (see the discussion following Theorem I). Disregarding its impracticability, a fractional betting system therefore provides positive insurance against loss of the gambler's entire fortune and yields a unity probability of eventually achieving any specified increase in wealth.

For favorable games replicated indefinitely in time against an infinitely rich adversary, a better criterion is to optimize the "return on investment"— that is, the net gain per unit time divided by the total capital required to undertake the betting process. In this circumstance we would increase the individual wager $\beta(t)$ as our bankroll $z(t)$ increased, maintaining a constant "return on investment" R, according to the definition

$$R = \frac{(p - q)\beta(t)}{z(t)}$$

A more realistic procedure for favorable games is to establish a confidence level in achieving a certain gain in wealth and then inquire as to what magnitude wager results in that confidence level for the particular value of $p > q$. This question is answered as follows.

Theorem VI: In games favorable to the gambler, there exists a wager β defined by

$$\beta \simeq \left[\frac{-z}{\log(1 - \bar{P}_z)} - \frac{\bar{P}_z(1 - \bar{P}_z)^{a/z} z^2}{a[\log(1 - \bar{P}_z)]^2(1 - \bar{P}_z)^{a/z}\bar{P}_z - z(1 - \bar{P}_z)[\log(1 - \bar{P}_z)]^2} \right] \log\left(\frac{q}{p}\right)^{-1}$$

$$\simeq \frac{-z}{\log(1 - \bar{P}_z)} \log\left(\frac{q}{p}\right)^{-1} \quad \text{for} \quad \bar{P}_z > 0.5, \quad a \gg z \qquad 3\text{-}9$$

such that continually betting β units or less at each play yields a confidence level of $\bar{P}_z$ or greater of increasing the gambler's fortune from an initial value z to a final value a.

In Fig. 3-3, Eq. 3-9 is illustrated for $z = 100$, $a = 1000$. and various values of the confidence level $\bar{P}_z$. For a given confidence in achieving the wealth of 1000 units, higher bets cannot be hazarded until the game is quite favorable. A game characterized by $(q/p) = 0.63$ ($p = 0.61, q = 0.39, r = 0$), for example, is required before 10 units of the 100 initial fortune can be wagered under a 0.99 confidence of attaining 1000. Note that for $a \gg z$, the optimal bets become virtually independent of the goal a. This feature, of course, is characteristic of favorable games.

Generally, with an objective utility function, the purpose of increasing the magnitude of the wagers in a favorable game (thereby decreasing the

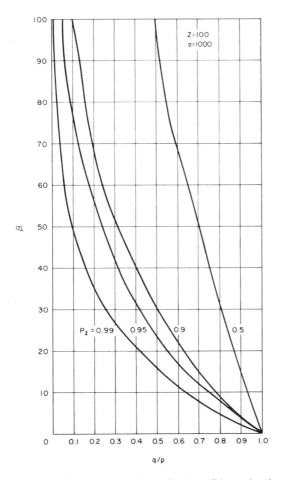

Fig. 3-3 Optimal wager for a fixed confidence level

probability of success) is to decrease the number of plays required to achieve this goal. We can also calculate the probability of ruin and success for a specific number of plays of a game.

Theorem VII: In the course of n plays of a game, a gambler with capital z playing unit wagers against an opponent with capital $a - z$ has a probability of ruin given by

$$P_{z,n} = \frac{(q/p)^a - (q/p)^z}{(q/p)^a - 1} - \frac{[2\sqrt{pq}/(1 - r)]^{n+1}(q/p)^{z/2}}{a}$$

$$\sum_{i=1}^{a-1} \frac{\sin(\pi j/a)\sin(\pi z j/a)[\cos(\pi j/a)]^n}{1 - [2\sqrt{pq}/(1 - r)]\cos(\pi j/a)}$$

3-10

where p, q, and r are the gambler's single-trial probability of winning, losing, and tying, respectively.

As the number of plays $n \to \infty$, the expression for $P_{z,n}$ approaches the P_z of Eq. 3-4. Equation 3-10 is illustrated in Fig. 3-4, which depicts $P_{z,n}$ versus n for an initial gambler's fortune of $z = 10$ and an adversary's fortune $a - z = 10$; several values for the single-trial probabilities of winning and losing p and q, respectively, are given.

An obvious extension of Theorem VII ensues from considering an adversary either infinitely rich or possessing a fortune such that n plays with unit wagers cannot lead to his ruin. This situation is stated as follows.

Corollary: In the course of n plays of a game characterized by probabilities p, q, and r of winning, losing, or tying, respectively, at each play, a gambler with capital z, wagering unit bets against an (effectively) infinitely rich adversary, has a probability of ruin given by

$$P_{z,n} = \frac{q^z}{(1 - r)^{z + 2k}} \left[(1 - r)^{2k} + zpq(1 - r)^{2k - 2} + \frac{z(z + 3)}{2!} \right.$$

$$\left. \cdot (pq)^2(1 - r)^{2k - 4} + \cdots + \frac{z(z + k + 1)\cdots(z + 2k - 1)(pq)^k}{k!} \right]$$

3-11

where

$$k = \frac{n - z}{2} \quad \text{or} \quad \frac{n - z - 1}{2}, \quad \text{according as } |n - z| \text{ is even or odd}$$

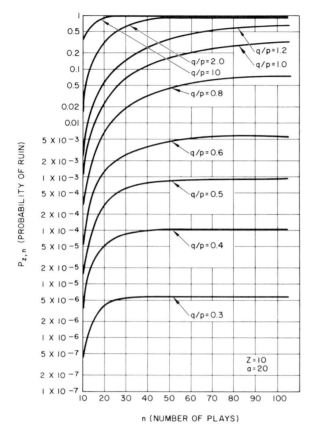

Fig. 3-4   Ruin probability in the course of n plays

Figure 3-5 illustrates Eq. 3-11 for $z = 10$, $p = q = 1/2$, and $r = 0$. For a large number of plays of an equitable game against an infinitely rich adversary, it is possible to derive the approximation

$$P_{z,n} \simeq 1 - \frac{2}{\sqrt{\pi}} \int_0^{z\sqrt{3/(6n+4)}} e^{-\zeta^2} \, d\zeta \qquad 3\text{-}12$$

which is available in numerical form from tables of probability integrals. Equation 3-12 indicates, as expected, that the probability of ruin approaches unity asymptotically with increasing values of n.

Equations 3-11 and 3-10 are attributable to Lagrange. A relatively simpler expression results if, instead of the probability of ruin over the

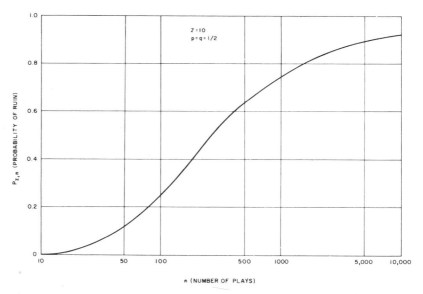

Fig. 3-5   Ruin probability in the course of n plays of a "fair" game against an infinitely rich adversary

course of n plays, we ask the expected number of plays $E(n)_z$ before ruin of a gambler with initial capital z:

$$E(n)_z = \frac{z}{(q-p)(1-r)} - \frac{a[1-(q/p)^z]}{(q-p)(1-r)[1-(q/p)^a]}, \qquad p \neq q \qquad 3\text{-}13$$

For equitable games, $p = q$, and the expected duration simplifies to

$$E(n)_z = \frac{z(a-z)}{1-r}$$

For example, in a game characterized by $p = q = 1/2, r = 0$, a gambler with 100 units of wealth, wagering unit bets against an opponent with 1000 units, can expect the game to last for 90,000 plays. Against an infinitely rich opponent, Eq. 3-13 becomes, as $a \to \infty$,

$$E(n)_z \to \frac{z}{(q-p)(1-r)}$$

for $p < q$. In the case $p > q$, the expected game duration versus an infinity of Croesuses is a meaningless concept. For $p = q, E(n)_z \to \infty$.

We have previously defined a favorable game as one wherein the single-trial probability of success p is greater than the single-trial probability of loss q. A game can also be favorable if it comprises an ensemble of sub-games, one or more of which is favorable. Such an ensemble is herewith termed a *compound game*. The rules of a compound game require the player to wager a minimum of one unit on each subgame; further, the relative frequency of occurrence of each subgame is known to the player and he is informed immediately in advance of the particular subgame about to be played (selected at random from the pertinent probability distribution). Blackjack (Chapter 7) provides the most common example of a compound game.

Clearly, given the option of bet size variation, the player of a compound game can obtain any positive mathematical expectation desired. He has only to wager a sufficiently large sum on the favorable subgame(s) to overcome the negative expectations accruing from unit bets on the un-favorable subgames. However, such a policy entails a high probability of ruin. It is more reasonable to establish the criterion of minimizing the probability of ruin while achieving an overall positive expectation—that is, a criterion of survival. A betting system in accord with this criterion is described by Theorem VIII.

> *Theorem VIII :* In compound games there exists a critical single-trial probability of success $p^* > 1/2$ such that the optimal wager for each subgame $\beta^*(p)$, under the criterion of survival, is specified by

$$\beta^*(p) = \begin{cases} 1, & \text{if } p < p^* \\ \dfrac{\log[(1-p)/p]}{\log[(1-p^*)/p^*]}, & \text{if } p \geq p^* \end{cases} \qquad 3\text{-}14$$

As a numerical illustration of this theorem, we consider a compound game wherein two-thirds of the time the single-trial probability of success takes a value of 0.45 and the remaining one-third of the time a value of 0.55: Equation 3-14 gives the optimal wager for this compound game as

$$\beta^* = \begin{cases} 1, & \text{for } p = 0.45 \\ \dfrac{\log(0.45/0.55)}{2 \log 0.9777} = 4.45, & \text{for } p = 0.55 \end{cases}$$

Thus the gambler who wagers the minimum one-unit bet when $p = 0.45$ and 4.45 units when $p = 0.55$ achieves an overall expectation of

$$\frac{2}{3}(0.45 - 0.55) + \frac{1}{3} \cdot 4.45(0.55 - 0.45) = +0.82$$

while maximizing his probability of survival (it is assumed that the gambler initially possesses a large but finite capital pitted against essentially infinite resources).

Much of the preceding discussion in this chapter has been devoted to proving that no betting system constructed upon past history can affect the expected gain of a game. With certain goals and utilities it is more important to optimize probability of success, number of plays, or some other pertinent factor. However, strictly objective utilities are concerned with the mathematical expectation of a game. There are two quantities that relate directly to mathematical expectation: strategy and information. The relationship of strategy and expectation is a consequence of the fundamental theorem of game theory, the von Neumann minimax principle (discussed in Chapter 2). This relationship can be stated as follows.

Theorem IX : For any two-person rectangular game characterized by the payoff matrix $\|a_{ij}\|$, where player A has m strategies $A_1, A_2, \ldots, A_m$ selected with probabilities $p_1, p_2, \ldots, p_m$, respectively, and player B has n strategies $B_1, B_2, \ldots, B_n$ selected with probabilities $q_1, q_2, \ldots, q_n$, respectively ($\sum_i p_i = \sum_j q_j = 1$), the mathematical expectation $E[S_A(m),$ $S_B(n)]$ for any strategy $S_A(m)$ and any strategy $S_B(n)$ is defined by

$$E[S_A(m), S_B(n)] = \sum_{i=1}^{m} \sum_{j=1}^{n} a_{ij} p_i q_j$$

Then, if the $m \times n$ game has a value γ, a necessary and sufficient condition that $S_A^*(m)$ be an optimal strategy for player A is that

$$E[S_A^*(m), S_B(n)] \geq \gamma \qquad\qquad 3\text{-}15$$

for all possible strategies $S_B(n)$. Similarly, a necessary and sufficient condition that $S_B^*(n)$ be an optimal strategy for player B is that

$$E[S_A(m), S_B^*(n)] \leq \gamma \qquad\qquad 3\text{-}16$$

Some of the properties of two-person rectangular games are discussed in Chapter 2. If it is our objective to minimize our maximum loss or maximize our minimum gain, the von Neumann minimax theorem and its associated corollaries enable us to determine the optimal strategies for any two-person rectangular game. However, further considerations arise from the introduction of information into the system. The nature and amount of information available to each player affect the mathematical expectation of the game. In Chess, Checkers, or Shogi, for example, complete information is given; each player is fully aware of his opponent's moves. In Bridge, the composition of each player's hand is clearly secret information, to be disclosed gradually, first by imperfect communication and then by sequential exposure of the cards. In Poker, the withholding of knowledge of each player's hand is critical to the outcome. We shall relate, at least qualitatively, the general relationship between information and expectation.

In the coin-matching game matrix of Fig. 2-2, wherein each player selects heads or tails with probability $p = 1/2$, the mathematical expectation of the game is obviously zero. But now consider the situation where player A has in his employ a spy capable of ferreting out the selected strategies of player B and communicating them to player A. If the spy is imperfect in applying his espionage techniques or the communication channel is susceptible to error, player A has only a probability knowledge of B's strategy. Specifically, if p is the degree of knowledge, the game matrix is that shown in Fig. 3-6, where (i, j) represents that strategy of A that selects i when A is informed that B's choice is H (heads) and j when A is informed that B has selected T (tails). For $p > \frac{1}{2}$, the strategy A_2 dominates the others; selecting A_2 consistently yields an expectation for A of

$$E = \tfrac{1}{2}(2p - 1) + \tfrac{1}{2}(2p - 1) = 2p - 1$$

With perfect spying, $p = 1$ and A's expectation is unity at each play; with $p = \frac{1}{2}$, the spying provides no information and the expectation is, of course, zero.

If, in this example, player B also has recourse to undercover sleuthing, the game outcome is clearly more difficult to specify. In general, we can construct a payoff curve for player A's optimal strategy S_A^* as a function of B's strategy. Figure 3-7 illustrates the payoff curve for A's optimal strategy

	$B_1(H)$	$B_2(T)$
$A_1(H,H)$	1	-1
$A_2(H,T)$	$2p - 1$	$2p - 1$
$A_3(T,H)$	$1 - 2p$	$1 - 2p$
$A_4(T,T)$	-1	1

Fig. 3-6 Coin-matching payoff with spying

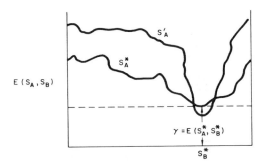

PLAYER B's STRATEGY DOMAIN

Fig. 3-7   Optimal and hypothetical payoff curves

S_A^* and a hypothetical strategy S_A'. With both A and B resolutely playing their optimal strategies S_A^* and S_B^*, respectively, the game has value γ. However, if A has information that B intends to deviate from his optimal strategy, there may exist counterstrategies, such as S_A', which exploit such deviation better than A's maximin strategy. Such a strategy, by definition, is constrained to yield a smaller payoff against B's optimal strategy (otherwise S_A' would dominate S_A^* and the latter would not be optimal); hence A risks the chance that B does not deviate appreciably from S_B^*. Player B may have the option of providing false information or "bluffing" and may attempt to lure A into selecting a nonoptimal strategy by such means. We have thus encountered a *circulus in probando*.

It is difficult to establish a precise quantitative relationship between the information available to one player and the concomitant effect upon his expectation. We can, however, state the following qualitative theorem.

> *Theorem X :* If a player is accorded information regarding his opponent's strategy, a decision rule for selecting strategies based on that information will perform at least as well as one neglecting the information.

ADDITIONAL THEOREMS

It is possible, of course, to enumerate more theorems than the ten advanced herein. Such additional theorems do not, we believe, warrant the status accruing from a fundamental character or extensive application in gambling situations. Further, as individual examples requiring specialized game-theoretic tenets arise in subsequent chapters, they will be either proved or assumed as axiomatic.

A "theorem of information" might illustrate the difficulty of developing general principles applicable to games with communication. Certain games, such as Poker, can involve actions that are motivated by the intent to suppress information. As an example, a player at Draw Poker might draw two cards rather than three to an original holding of a single pair in order to imply a better holding or to avoid the adoption of a pure strategy (thereby posing only trivial analysis to his opponents). In partnership games such as Bridge, the communication process often has a twofold intent: to maximize the information transmitted between the partnership while minimizing the usefulness of the information to the opponents. Generally, the first of these two motivations predominates.

Without regard to the effect on the communication process produced by the structure of the individual game, we can state a general desideratum that, however modified, must be considered in games comprising an element of communication:

> In games involving partnership communication, one objective is to transmit as much information as possible over the permissible communication channel of limited capacity. Without constraints on the message set, this state of maximum information occurs under a condition of minimum redundancy and maximum information entropy.

Proofs of this theorem are given in many texts on communication theory.[†] The condition of maximum information entropy holds when, from a set of n possible messages, each message is selected with probability $1/n$. Although no conventional game consists solely of communication, there are games—such as "Guess It" (Chapter 6)—where communication is the prime ingredient and the principle of this theorem is invoked. In most games, such as Bridge, communication occurs under conditions of constraints and cost functions. Specifically in Bridge, minimum redundancy or maximum entropy occurs if every permissible bid is weighted with identical probabilities. However, further weighting is obviously indicated, since certain bids are assigned greater values and an ordering to the sequence of bids is also imposed.

There are also theorems reflecting a general nature, although not of sufficient importance to demand rigorous proof. Illustrative of this category is the "theorem of pooled resources":

[†] For example, Arthur E. Laemmel, *General Theory of Communication*, Polytechnic Institute of Brooklyn, 1949.

If m contending players compete (against the "house") in one or more concurrent games, each player with an initial bankroll z_i, $i = 1, 2, \ldots m$, and if the total resources are pooled in a common fund available equally to all players, then each player possesses an effective initial bankroll z_{eff} given by

$$z_{\text{eff}} = \sum_i^m z_i - \varepsilon \qquad\qquad 3\text{-}17$$

under the assumption that the win–loss–tie sequences of players i and j are uncorrelated.

The small quantity ε is the quantization error—that is, with uncorrelated outcomes for the players, the m different wagers can be considered as occurring sequentially in time with the proviso that each initial bankroll z_i can be replenished only once every mth play. This time restriction on withdrawing funds from the pool is a quantization error, preventing full access to the total resources. As the correlation between the players' outcomes increases to unity, the value of z_{eff} approaches $\Sigma z_i/m$. (Other theorems of this type will be incorporated in the ensuing text.)

Finally, there are several other types of game theorems that have not been considered, although they illustrate basic principles within the domain of the theory of games. Most of these principles arise from games not feasible as practical gambling contests. For example, games with infinite strategies, games allowing variable coalitions, generalized n-person games, etc., are beyond the scope undertaken herein and are rarely of concrete interest.

In summation, the preceding ten theorems and associated discussions have established a rudimentary outline for the theory of gambling. A definitive theory depends, first and foremost, upon utility goals—that is, upon certain restricted forms of subjective preference. Within the model of strictly objective goals, we have shown that no betting system can alter the mathematical expectation of a game; however, probability of ruin (or success) and expected duration of a game are functions of the betting system employed. We have, in each instance, assumed that the plays of a game are statistically independent and that no bias exists in the game mechanism. It follows that a time-dependent bias permits application of a valid betting system and any bias (fixed or varying) enables an improved strategy.

Statistical dependence between plays also suggests the derivation of a corresponding betting system to increase the mathematical expectation. In Chapter 6 we shall outline the theory of Markov chains, which relates statistical dependence and prediction.

Prima facie evidence of the validity of the concepts presented herein is displayed by the major gambling establishments of the world. Since the "house" is always engaged in favorable games, it wishes to make a large number of small wagers. This goal is accomplished by limiting the maximum individual wager; further, a limit on the lowest wager permitted inhibits negative betting systems. In general, casino games involve a redistribution of wealth among the players at each play while the "house" removes a certain percentage, either directly or statistically. In the occasional game where all players contend against the "house" (as in Bingo), the payoff is fixed per unit play. The "house," of course, has one of the most objective evaluations of wealth that can be postulated. No casino has ever been accused of subjective utility goals.

Suggested references

ANSCOMBE, F. J., and R. J. AUMANN, "A Definition of Subjective Probability," *Ann. Mathematical Statistics*, **34**, No. 1 (March, 1963), pp. 199–205.

BLACKWELL, DAVID, "On Optimal Systems," *Ann. Mathematical Statistics*, **25**, No. 2 (June, 1954), pp. 394–397.

BLACKWELL, DAVID, and M. A. GIRSHICK, *Theory of Games and Statistical Decisions*, John Wiley & Sons, Inc., New York, 1954.

BOREL, EMILE, "On Games That Involve Chance And The Skill Of The Players," *Econometrica*, **21** (1953), pp. 97–117.

BREIMAN, LEO, "Optimal Gambling Systems For Favorable Games," Proc. Fourth Berkeley Symposium on Mathematical Statistics and Probability, University of California Press, Berkeley, 1961, pp. 65–78.

BREIMAN, LEO, "On Random Walks With An Absorbing Barrier and Gambling Systems," Western Management Science Institute, Working Paper No. 71, UCLA., Los Angeles, Calif., March, 1965.

CHOW, Y. S., and H. ROBBINS, "On Optimal Stopping in a Class of Uniform Games," Mimeograph Series No. 42, Department of Statistics, Columbia University, June, 1965.

COOLIDGE, J. L., "The Gambler's Ruin," *Ann. Mathematics*, Second Series, **10**, No. 1 (1908–1909), pp. 181–192.

COVER, T. M., "Partially Controllable Random Walk," The RAND Corporation, Report P-2450, Santa Monica, California, September, 1961.

DOOB, J. L., "Note on Probability," *Ann. Mathematics*, **37**, No. 2 (April, 1936).

DOOB, J. L., "What is a Martingale?" *Am. Math. Monthly*, **78**, No. 5, (May, 1971), pp. 451–463.

DE FINETTI, BRUNO, "La Teoria del Rischio e il Problema della 'Rovina dei Giocatori,'" Giornale dell' Istituto Italiano degli Attuari, **10** (1939), pp. 41–51.

DUBINS, LESTER E., and LEONARD J. SAVAGE, "Optimal Gambling Systems," *Proc. Nat. Acad. Sci. U.S.*, (Oct. 19, 1960), p. 1597.

DUBINS, LESTER E., and LEONARD J. SAVAGE, *How to Gamble If You Must*, McGraw-Hill Book Company Inc., New York, N.Y., 1965.

EPSTEIN, RICHARD A., "An Optimal Gambling System For Favorable Games," Hughes Aircraft Co., Report TP-64-19-26, OP-61, July, 1964.

EPSTEIN, RICHARD A., "The Effect of Information on Mathematical Expectation," Hughes Aircraft Co., Report TP-64-19-27, OP-62, July, 1964.

EPSTEIN, RICHARD A., "Expectation and Variance of a Simple Gamble," Hughes Aircraft Co., Report TP-64-19-30, OP-65, July, 1964.

FELLER, WILLIAM, *An Introduction to Probability Theory and Its Applications*, John Wiley & Sons, Inc., New York, 2nd ed., 1957.

FERGUSON, THOMAS S., "Betting Systems Which Minimize the Probability of Ruin," Working Paper No. 41, U.C.L.A. Western Management Science Institute, Los Angeles, California, October, 1963.

HALMOS, PAUL R., "Invariants of Certain Stochastic Transformations: The Mathematical Theory of Gambling Systems," *Duke Mathematical J.*, **5**, No. 2 (June, 1939), pp. 461–478.

KELLY, JOHN L. JR., "A New Interpretation of Information Rate," *Bell System Technical J.*, **35**, No. 4 (July, 1956), pp. 917–926.

KUHN, HAROLD W., "Extensive Games and the Problem of Information," *Contributions to the Theory of Games*, Vol. 2, Study No. 28, Princeton University Press, Princeton, New Jersey, 1953, pp. 193–216.

LEVINSON, HORACE C., *The Science of Chance*, Rinehart & Company, Inc., New York, 1956.

LUCE, R. DUNCAN, and HOWARD RAIFFA, *Games and Decisions*, John Wiley & Sons, Inc., New York, 1957.

MARCUS, MICHAEL B., "The Utility of a Communication Channel and Applications to Suboptimal Information Handling Procedures," *I.R.E. Trans. Professional Group on Information Theory*, Vol. IT-4, No. 4 (December, 1958), pp. 147–151.

MORGENSTERN, OSKAR, "The Theory of Games," *Scientific American*, **180** (May, 1949), pp. 22–25.

PRATT, JOHN W., HOWARD RAIFFA, and ROBERT SCHLAIFER, "The Foundations of Decision Under Uncertainty: An Elementary Exposition," *J. American Statistical Assoc.*, **59**, No. 306 (June, 1964), pp. 353–375.

RAYLEIGH, LORD, "On Mr. Venn's Explanation of a Gambling Paradox," *Scientific Papers of Lord Rayleigh*, Art. 50, **1**, 1869–1881, Cambridge University Press, 1899.

SAKAGUCHI, MINORU, "Information and Learning," *Papers of the Committee on Information Theory Research*, Electrical Communication Institute of Japan, June 21, 1963.

SAMUELSON, P. A., "Probability, Utility, and the Independence Axiom," *Econometrica*, **20** (1952), pp. 670–678.

SAVAGE, LEONARD J., *The Foundations of Statistics*, John Wiley & Sons, Inc., New York, 1954.

SAVAGE, LEONARD J., "The Casino That Takes a Percentage and What You Can Do About It," The RAND Corporation, Report P-1132, Santa Monica, California, October 17, 1957.

SNELL, J. L., "Application of Martingale System Theorems," *Trans. Amer. Mathematical Society*, **73**, No. 1 (July, 1952), pp. 293–312.

VON NEUMANN, JOHN, and OSKAR MORGENSTERN, *Theory of Games and Economic Behavior*, Princeton University Press, Princeton, 1953.

CHAPTER FOUR

COINS, WHEELS, AND ODDMENTS

Coin matching and finger flashing were among the first formal games to arise in the history of gambling. The class of Morra games extends back to the pre-Christian era, although not until comparatively recent times have game-theoretic solutions been derived. While records do not indicate the nature of ancient coin games, even the first crude metal currency was fashioned with its two sides distinguishable. With a form of heads and tails presenting itself in the medium of exchange, only a small degree of sophistication is required to propose a simple class of wagers.

Biased coins

The first hand-hewn coins were markedly unsymmetrical, likely exhibiting a significant deviation from equiprobability of heads and tails. Applying statistical techniques, possible bias in a coin is examined by the Tchebychev inequality in the form

$$P[|p' - p| > \varepsilon] \le \frac{pq}{\varepsilon^2 n} \qquad \textit{4-1}$$

(cf. Eq. 2-33). That is, the probability P that the success ratio p' taken over n trials differs from the single-trial probability p by more than any small amount $\varepsilon > 0$ is given by Eq. 4-1. This probability can be made arbitrarily small by adjusting ε and n, and with any stated accuracy we can calculate the values of stochastic convergence of the probabilities of heads and tails.

An interesting application of Bayes's theorem arises in connection with a possibly biased coin. Consider, for example, that 50 throws of a coin have been observed wherein heads appeared only five times. If the coin were true, we know the probability of such an occurrence to be

$$P = \binom{50}{5}(1/2)^5(1/2)^{45} = 1.88 \times 10^{-9}$$

Let P_b be the extent of our a priori knowledge that the coin may be biased and P_t be the complementary probability that the coin is true. If the coin is indeed biased in favor of tails, the event of five heads in 50 trials has occurred with some probability P_1. Then, according to Bayes's theorem, the probability P_e that the coin is biased in view of the experimental evidence is

$$P_e = \frac{P_b \cdot P_1}{P_b \cdot P_1 + P_t(1.88 \times 10^{-9})} = \frac{P_1}{P_1 + (P_t/P_b)(1.88 \times 10^{-9})}$$

If the coin were selected from a conventional sample and if our suspicion as to its bias were quite small (P_t/P_b quite large), then P_e (which is greater than P_b) corrects our estimate of the coin. If, initially, we had suspected the coin with greater conviction, then P_e approaches unity and the evidence implies near-certainty of bias. Postulating that the coin is biased toward tails by a 9:1 ratio, we can compute P_1 as

$$P_1 = \binom{50}{5}(0.1)^5(0.9)^{45} = 0.185$$

A more pragmatic interpretation of the problem might state "in the neighborhood of" rather than "exactly" five heads in 50 trials. In this case, the probability P_e of a biased coin is correspondingly greater.

When a coin used to generate a head–tail sequence is under suspicion of entertaining a bias, a logical betting procedure (the Epaminondas system suggested in Chapter 3) consists of wagering that the immediately preceding outcome will be repeated. If p and q represent the true probabilities of obtaining heads and tails, respectively, this system yields a single-trial winning probability of $p^2 + q^2$. The mathematical expectation of gain is, accordingly, $(2p - 1)^2$.

The question of the behavior of a typical coin was at one time of sufficient interest to generate some rather boring experiments. The naturalist Buffon performed 4040 throws of a coin which resulted in 2048 heads and 1992 tails; the deviation of 28 from a perfect balance falls within one standard deviation of 31.8, assuming probabilities of 1/2 for both heads and tails ($\sigma = \sqrt{pqn} = \sqrt{4040/4} = 31.8$). In the past century, the Belgian

Quetelet performed an equally tedious analogous experiment. From an urn containing 40 black balls and 40 white balls, he made 4095 draws, replacing each time the ball drawn. A white ball was selected 2065 times and a black ball 2030 times; the deviation from a perfect balance is 17.5, compared to a standard deviation of 32. More recently, J. E. Kerrich, while interned during World War II, recorded ten series of coin throws, each consisting of 1000 throws. No series produced less than 476 nor more than 529 heads. The coin-tossing record is probably held by the statistician Karl Pearson who, in 24,000 tosses, obtained 12,012 heads. In view of these experiments and other empirical evidence, and in light of modern numismatic techniques, we can assume that a coin selected at random from the population in circulation has a vanishingly small probability of significant bias.

Statistical properties of coins

PROBABILITY DISTRIBUTION OF HEADS AND TAILS

As a historical aside, we note that Roberval (a mathematician contemporary to Pascal and Fermat) argued for the probability of obtaining at least one head in two throws of an unbiased symmetric coin to be 2/3 (instead of 3/4). Rather than considering four cases (HH, HT, TH, and TT), Roberval admitted only three (H, TH, and TT), since, he maintained, that if H occurs on the first trial, it is unnecessary to throw the coin again. D'Alembert advanced similar arguments at a later date, claiming that in two throws of a coin, the three possible outcomes are two heads, one head and one tail, and two tails. This type of "reasoning" illustrates a weakness of the classical definition of probability theory.

$$
\begin{array}{ccccccccc}
& & & & 1_1 & 1_{-1} & & & \\
& & & 1_2 & 2_0 & 1_{-2} & & & \\
& & 1_3 & 3_1 & 3_{-1} & 1_{-3} & & & \\
& 1_4 & 4_2 & 6_0 & 4_{-2} & 1_{-4} & & & \\
1_5 & 5_3 & 10_1 & 10_{-1} & 5_{-3} & 1_{-5} & & & \\
1_6 & 6_4 & 15_2 & 20_0 & 15_{-2} & 6_{-4} & 1_{-6} & & \\
1_7 & 7_5 & 21_3 & 35_1 & 35_{-1} & 21_{-3} & 7_{-5} & 1_{-7} & \\
1_8 & 8_6 & 28_4 & 56_2 & 70_0 & 56_{-2} & 28_{-4} & 8_{-6} & 1_{-8}
\end{array}
$$

Fig. 4-1   Pascal's triangle

For n throws of a coin, the probability distribution of the number of heads and tails is described by the binomial expression of Eq. 2-15. The binomial coefficients are represented in tabular form by Pascal's triangle, Fig. 4-1. In the format shown, a_b states that in n throws of a fair coin, a gambler betting one unit on heads can expect a gain of b units a times out of the 2^n possible outcomes. Illustratively, for $n = 5$ throws, out of every 32 such trials the gambler can expect to win 5 units once, 3 units five times, 1 unit ten times, and to lose 1 unit ten times, 3 units five times, and 5 units once. Pascal's triangle is readily extended by noting that each a term is the sum of the two a terms above it.

RUNS OF HEADS AND TAILS

In addition to the probability distribution of the number of heads (or tails) in n throws of a coin, the statistical properties of a random sequence of heads (or tails) also embrace the number of runs of various lengths. By definition, a run of length m comprises a sequence of m consecutive heads (tails) immediately preceded and followed by the occurrence of tails (heads). (A definition that contains the initial and concluding throws would alter slightly the pertinent formulas.) We are interested both in the probability $P_n^m(k)$ of observing a specified number k of runs of length m and the expected value of k (the mean number of runs) as

$$\bar{k} = E(k) = \sum_{k=0}^{\infty} k P_n^m(k) \qquad\qquad 4\text{-}2$$

(cf. Eq. 2-19). The summation consists of a finite number of terms, since $P_n^m(k) = 0$ for $k > (n - 2)/m$. The probability that a sequence commences with a run of m heads or tails (framed by tails or heads, respectively) is clearly $q^2 p^m + p^2 q^m$, where p represents the probability of throwing heads at each trial and $q = 1 - p$ the probability of throwing tails. There are $n - m - 1$ ways of positioning the run of m heads or tails within the entire sequence of length n, and the events of a sequence containing a run of m heads or tails beginning at each of the $n - m - 1$ positions are not mutually exclusive. Rather, the probability of each such event is weighted according to the number of runs occurring in the sequence. This weighting conforms to that of Eq. 4-2, which can then be written explicitly as

$$\bar{k} = (n - m - 1)(p^2 q^m + q^2 p^m) \qquad\qquad 4\text{-}3$$

As the number of throws becomes large, the number of runs of length m becomes approximately normally distributed. For $n \gg m$ and $p = q = 1/2$, we can write

$$\bar{k} \simeq \frac{n}{2^{m+1}}$$

as the expected number of runs of length m in a sequence of n throws of a fair coin.

Arbitrarily accurate determination of the probability $P_n^m(k)$ can be achieved by computing its higher moments. First, we derive the expression for the variance σ_m^2 of $P_n^m(k)$. We observe that the probability for a sequence to include two distinct runs of length m at two specified positions in the sequence is $(p^2 q^m + q^2 p^m)^2$. Further, for $n \gg m$, there are $n(n-1)/2$ ways of situating the two runs among the n positions in the sequence so that $[n(n-1)/2](p^2 q^m + q^2 p^m)^2$ represents the sum of the probabilities of all sequences containing at least two runs of length m. Similar to the reasoning leading to Eq. 4-3, each of these probabilities is to be weighted according to the number of ways a group of two runs can be selected from k runs—that is, $k(k-1)/2$. Therefore,

$$\frac{1}{2} \sum_{k=0}^{\infty} k(k-1) P_n^m(k) = \frac{n(n-1)}{2}(p^2 q^m + q^2 p^m)^2 \qquad 4\text{-}4$$

The left-hand side of Eq. 4-4 can be rewritten in the form

$$\sum_{k=0}^{\infty} k(k-1) P_n^m(k) = \sum_{k=0}^{\infty} k^2 P_n^m(k) - \sum_{k=0}^{\infty} k P_n^m(k) \qquad 4\text{-}5$$

The first term of the right-hand side of Eq. 4-5 is equivalent to $\sigma_m^2 + \bar{k}^2$ (cf. Eq. 2-26). Thence, combining Eqs. 4-2, 4-3, 4-4, and 4-5,

$$\sigma_m^2 = \bar{k} = n(p^2 q^m + q^2 p^m)$$

for $n \gg m$.

By extending the procedure used to determine the variance, higher-order moments of $P_n^m(k)$ can also be derived. In general, for large n, the rth moment can be developed from the expression

$$\sum_{k=0}^{\infty} \binom{k}{r} P_n^m(k) = \binom{n}{r}(p^2 q^m + q^2 p^m)^r$$

R. von Mises has shown that since the moments remain finite as $n \to \infty$, the probability $P_n^m(k)$ asymptotically approaches a Poisson distribution. Specifically, in this instance,

$$P_n^m(k) \to \left(\frac{\bar{k}^k}{k!}\right) e^{-k} \equiv \varphi(k) \qquad 4\text{-}6$$

where

$$K = \lim_{n \to \infty} n(p^2 q^m + q^2 p^m) \qquad\qquad 4\text{-}7$$

That is, the probability that n trials will exhibit k runs of length m approaches $\varphi(k)$ for large values of n where K is the expected value of k.

Over fifty years ago the German philosopher K. Marbe developed a theory of probability based on the concept that long runs contradict the premise of independent trials. Searching for runs in the sequences of new-born males and females, he investigated the birth records of four cities, each record covering 49,152 parturitions. The longest run he discovered consisted of 17 consecutive occurrences of the same sex. Marbe concluded that as a run of girls (say) continues, the probability of the next birth being another girl decreases from its initial value (of about $\frac{1}{2}$).[†]

From Eqs. 4-6 and 4-7 we can obtain an assessment of Marbe's conclusions. With $m = 18$, $n = 49{,}152$, and $p = q = 1/2$, we have

$$K = 0.09375 \qquad \text{and} \qquad \varphi(0) = 0.9105$$

Hence, in each of his four sequences, Marbe observed an event that had a probability of 0.9105—a situation hardly so unusual as to warrant revising established theories.

LEADS OF HEADS OR TAILS

Other questions that arise in connection with a sequence of coin throws concern the probability of one player (betting, say, on heads) remaining ahead of his opponent and the number of times during a sequence that the players are even. This type of problem is best viewed by considering the number of ways or paths by which a particular proportion of heads and tails can be obtained. A path from the origin to a point (n, s)—for any integer s and any positive integer n—is a polygonal line whose vertices have abscissas $0, 1, \ldots, n$ and ordinates $s_0, s_1, s_2, \ldots, s_n$ such that $s_i - s_{i-1} = \pm 1$. The quantity $\{s_1, s_2, \ldots, s_n\}$ is therefore the representation of a path. In the illustration of Fig. 4-2, n increases one unit with each coin toss, and s increases one unit with each throw of heads and decreases one unit with each occurrence of tails. The path shown indicates a sequence of THHHTHTTHHH; the point (11, 3) relates that the sequence of length 11 has resulted in a net gain of 3 for heads. In general, the number of paths

---

[†] Modern statisticians, confronted with the birth of 17 consecutive girls, might conclude that the probability of the next birth being a girl is greater than $1/2$, and would search for some nonprobabilistic factor such as the town's drinking water.

$N(n, s)$ by which we can arrive at a point (n, s) is given by

$$N(n, s) = \binom{n}{(n + s)/2} \qquad\qquad 4\text{-}8$$

which is valid for all values of n and s, since $n + s$ is always even.

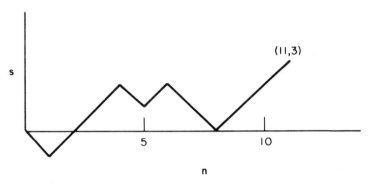

Fig. 4-2   One-dimensional random-walk path

For $s = 0$, we can rewrite Eq. 4-8 in the more convenient form

$$N(2n, 0) = \binom{2n}{n}$$

which designates the number of paths from the origin to a point $2n$ on the abscissa. Then, if $P_{2t,2n}$ is the probability that in the interval from 0 to $2n$ along the abscissa, the path has $2t$ vertices on the positive side (including zero) and $2n - 2t$ vertices on the negative side, it can be shown that

$$P_{2t,2n} = \binom{2t}{t}\binom{2n - 2t}{n - t}2^{-2n} \qquad\qquad 4\text{-}9$$

That is, Eq. 4-9 defines the probability that the player betting on heads, say, leads during exactly $2t$ out of the $2n$ trials. For large values of n, we can apply Stirling's formula to derive the approximation

$$P_{2t,2n} \simeq \frac{1}{\pi\sqrt{t(n - t)}}$$

The ratio $2t:2n$ describes the fraction of the time spent on the positive side and the probability that this fraction lies between $1/2$ and k, $1/2 < k < 1$, is

$$\sum_{(n/2)<t<kn} P_{2t,2n} \simeq \frac{1}{\pi}\sum_{(n/2)<t<kn}\frac{1}{\sqrt{t(n - t)}}$$

The quantity $1/\sqrt{t(n-t)}$ can be written in the form

$$\frac{1}{n}\left[\frac{t}{n}\left(1-\frac{t}{n}\right)\right]^{-1/2}$$

whence the summation of the expression in the brackets is the Riemann sum approximating the integral

$$\frac{1}{\pi}\int_{\frac{1}{2}}^{k}\frac{d\xi}{\sqrt{\xi(1-\xi)}} = \frac{2}{\pi}\arcsin k^{1/2} - \frac{1}{2} \qquad\qquad 4\text{-}10$$

Or, since the probability that $t/n \le 1/2$ approaches $1/2$ as n approaches infinity,

$$\frac{1}{\pi}\int_{0}^{k}\frac{d\xi}{\sqrt{\xi(1-\xi)}} = \frac{2}{\pi}\arcsin k^{1/2} \qquad\qquad 4\text{-}11$$

Equation 4-11 constitutes the first arc sine law. It states that for a given value of k, $0 < k < 1$, and for very large values of the sequence length n, the probability that the fraction of time spent on the positive side t/n is less than k approaches $(2/\pi)\arcsin k^{1/2}$.

Values of t/n near $1/2$ are least probable; t/n is most likely to assume values close to zero or unity. For example, we can observe (from Eq. 4-9) that in $2n = 10$ throws of a coin, the less fortunate player has a probability of $2P_{0,10} = 0.492$ of never being in the lead. The probability that the player betting on heads in a sequence of 10 throws leads throughout is 0.246; the probability that heads leads throughout 20 throws is 0.176; and over a trial of 30 throws, the probability of heads being continually in the lead is 0.144. By contrast, the probability that heads leads 6 times out of 10 throws is 0.117; the probability that heads leads 10 times out of 20 throws is 0.061; and the probability of heads leading 16 times out of 30 is only 0.041. Figure 4-3 illustrates the arc sine law for large values of n. We can observe that with probability 0.05, the more fortunate player will be in the lead 99.89 percent of the time, and with probability 0.5 he will lead 85.36 percent of the time. It is evident that the lead changes sides much less frequently than one would expect intuitively.

A rephrasing of the arc sine law implies that an increasingly large number of coin throws are required before the path from the origin crosses the abscissa (see Fig. 4-2). Defining a "tie" as the condition that n heads and n tails have occurred out of $2n$ throws, the number of ties is proportional to

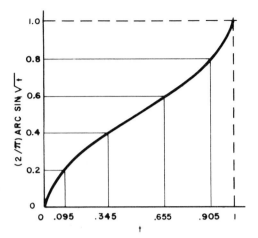

Fig. 4-3   The arc sine law

$\sqrt{2n}$. Specifically, if P_{2n}^u is the probability that the sequence of heads and tails reaches a tie exactly u times in $2n$ throws, we can show that

$$P_{2n}^u = \binom{2n - u}{n} 2^{u - 2n} \qquad\qquad 4\text{-}12$$

and as n becomes extremely large, the use of Stirling's formula leads to the approximation

$$P_{2n}^u \simeq \sqrt{n\pi}\, e^{-u^2/4n} \qquad\qquad 4\text{-}13$$

Note that the number of ties, given by Eqs. 4-12 and 4-13, is stochastically twice the number of times the lead changes sides.

According to Eq. 4-12, P_{2n}^u is a monotonically decreasing function of n except for the equal values P_{2n}^0 and P_{2n}^1 (that is, $P_{2n}^0 = P_{2n}^1 > P_{2n}^2 > P_{2n}^3 > \cdots$). Thus, the most probable number of ties in a sequence of heads and tails of any length is 0 or 1. On the other hand, the expected number of ties in a sequence of length $2n$ is given by

$$E(u) = \binom{2n}{n}(2n + 1)2^{-2n} - 1$$

and, from Stirling's formula for large values of n,

$$E(u) \simeq 2\sqrt{\frac{n}{\pi}} \qquad\qquad 4\text{-}14$$

Hence, in a sequence of $2n = 20$ throws, the expected number of ties is 2.7, while for a sequence of a million throws, the expected number of ties is less than 800; the most probable number of ties remains 0 or 1.

Also, we can sum Eq. 4-14 over k values of $u(u = 0, 1, 2, \ldots, k - 1)$ obtaining, similarly to Eq. 4-10, the integral (from the Riemann sum)

$$P(k) = \sqrt{\frac{2}{\pi}} \int_0^k e^{-\zeta^2/2} d\zeta \qquad \qquad 4\text{-}15$$

That is, for a given value of k, $0 < k < \sqrt{2n}$, the probability that over a sequence of length $2n$ the number of ties is less than $k\sqrt{2n}$ is formulated by Eq. 4-15 as n becomes large. Illustratively, the probability that less than $\sqrt{2n}$ ties occur in a sequence of length $2n$ (n large) is 0.683; the probability that the number of ties is less than $2\sqrt{2n}$ is 0.9545; and the probability of less than $4\sqrt{2n}$ ties occurring is 0.999936.

Postulating a coin-tossing game concluded at the appearance of the first tie, we can compute the expected game duration. From Eq. 4-12, the probability that the first tie occurs at play $2n$ is equal to

$$P^0_{2n-2} - P^0_{2n} = \binom{2n-2}{n-1} 2^{-2n+2} - \binom{2n}{n} 2^{-2n}$$

$$= \frac{1}{2n} \binom{2n-2}{n-1} 2^{-2n+2}$$

The expected duration $E(N)$ is therefore

$$E(N) = \sum_{n=1}^{\infty} 2n[P^0_{2n-2} - P^0_{2n}] = \sum_{n=1}^{\infty} \binom{2n-2}{n-1} 2^{-2n+2} = \infty$$

as can be verified by the use of Stirling's formula. It should be noted that although $E(N)$, the expected duration before the occurrence of a tie, is infinite, the duration N is finite (a tie will occur in a finite number of plays with unity probability).

Finally, we can inquire as to the probability distribution of the maximum value assumed by the path between the origin and the point $(2n, s)$. It can be shown that over a sequence of length $2n$, the player betting on heads has probability $_\eta P_{2n}$ of reaching his first maximum lead at the ηth play, where

$$_\eta P_{2n} = \binom{2t}{t} \binom{2n-2t}{n-t} 2^{-2n-1}, \text{ for } \begin{cases} \eta = 2t, & t = 1, 2, \ldots, n \\ \eta = 2t + 1, & t = 0, 1, 2, \ldots, n-1 \end{cases} \qquad 4\text{-}16$$

Quite remarkably, Eq. 4-16 displays values exactly $\frac{1}{2}$ of those generated by Eq. 4-9. Thus the probability that heads has its first maximum lead at either $2t$ or $2t + 1$ is identical to the probability that heads leads by the fraction t/n of the time over a sequence of length $2n$. Therefore, the approximation of the arc sine law applies, so that the maxima for heads tend to occur near the beginning or the end of a sequence independent of its length.

BALLOT PROBLEMS

A historical foreshadowing of the arc sine laws was contained in a lemma of the French mathematician J. L. F. Bertrand (1887). The first of a series of statements on the "ballot problem," Bertrand's lemma stated: "If in a ballot, candidate A scores α votes and candidate B scores $\beta < \alpha$ votes, then the probability that throughout the counting there are always more votes for A than for B equals $(\alpha - \beta)/(\alpha + \beta)$." An interesting generalization was subsequently contributed by Dvoretzky and Motzkin: "If ω is an integer satisfying $0 < \omega < \alpha/\beta$, then the probability that throughout the counting the number r of votes registered for A is always greater than ω times the number s of votes registered for B equals $(\alpha - \omega\beta)/(\alpha + \beta)$; and the probability that always $r \geq \omega s$ equals $(\alpha + 1 - \omega\beta)/(\alpha + 1)$."

It is implied that the counting procedure selects each ballot from a homogeneous mixture of all ballots. Thus, application of the theorems to the eccentric ritual that occurs on election nights in the United States is likely to lead to erroneous conclusions in those (frequent) cases where the ballots are not counted in a random order—urban and rural units, for example, are tallied in blocks and do not always contribute similar voting proportions for candidates A and B.

Coin matching

The simplest game of coin matching consists of two players simultaneously selecting heads or tails and comparing their choices. If the choices agree, player A wins one unit; otherwise, player B wins one unit. As we have seen previously (Fig. 2-2), the appropriate payoff matrix is

	B_1 (Heads)	B_2 (Tails)
A_1 (Heads)	1	-1
A_2 (Tails)	-1	1

Optimal strategies for both A and B consist of selecting their two pure strategies, each with probability $\frac{1}{2}$; the mathematical expectation of the game then obviously equals zero.

Opportunity for profit occurs if the payoff matrix is unsymmetrical or one player secures an a priori knowledge of his opponent's strategy. We shall illustrate two schemes for contriving an unbalance that, with only superficial analysis, appears rather deceptive. First, consider a variation of the simple coin-matching game wherein player A pays $1\frac{1}{2}$ units to B if the coins match at heads and 1/2 unit if the match occurs at tails; nonmatches result in B paying one unit to A. The payoff matrix then becomes

$$
\begin{array}{cc}
 & \begin{array}{cc} B_1 & B_2 \\ (\text{Heads}) & (\text{Tails}) \end{array} \\
\begin{array}{c} A_1 \\ (\text{Heads}) \\ A_2 \\ (\text{Tails}) \end{array} &
\left\|\begin{array}{cc} -1\frac{1}{2} & 1 \\ 1 & -\frac{1}{2} \end{array}\right\|
\end{array}
$$

Applying Eqs. 2-42 for the 2 × 2 game where A selects strategy A_1 with frequency p_1 and A_2 with frequency $1 - p_1$,

$$a_{11}p_1 + a_{21}(1 - p_1) = \gamma$$

$$a_{12}p_1 + a_{22}(1 - p_1) = \gamma$$

Solving for p_1,

$$p_1 = \frac{a_{22} - a_{21}}{a_{11} + a_{22} - a_{12} - a_{21}} = \frac{-\frac{1}{2} - 1}{-1\frac{1}{2} + (-\frac{1}{2}) - 1 - 1} = \frac{3}{8} \qquad 4\text{-}17$$

Thus A's optimal strategy is specified as

$$S_A^* = \begin{pmatrix} A_1 & A_2 \\ \dfrac{3}{8} & \dfrac{5}{8} \end{pmatrix}$$

The value of the game is $\gamma = 1/16$ (the game is favorable to player A by 1/16 unit per play) regardless of B's strategy. B can insure his loss of not more than an average of 1/16 unit by playing his optimal mixed strategy

$$S_B^* = \begin{pmatrix} B_1 & B_2 \\ \dfrac{3}{8} & \dfrac{5}{8} \end{pmatrix}$$

(Note that if each strategy for both players is selected with a probability of 1/2, the value of the game reverts to 0.) For the game to be equitable, A must pay 1/16 unit per play to B.

A second, more sophisticated coin-throwing game with an unsymmetrical payoff matrix can be represented as follows: Player A throws a coin, the outcome of the throw being withheld from player B. According to the rules of this game, if the outcome is heads, A must declare "heads" and demand payment of one unit from B. If the outcome is tails, A is permitted two choices—he may declare "heads" and demand one unit from B, or he may declare "tails" and pay one unit to B. For each play wherein A declares "heads," B has two pure strategies—he may believe A's declaration of "heads" and pay one unit or he may demand verification of the outcome. A is then compelled to reveal the coin to B; if the outcome is indeed heads, B must pay two units. However, if it develops that A is bluffing and the coin shows tails, B receives two units from A.

To determine the payoff matrix $\|a_{ij}\|$, we consider the four possible combinations of A's being truthful or bluffing and B's believing or demanding verification. If A bluffs and B believes (a_{11}), A receives one unit whether the coin shows heads ($p = 1/2$) or tails ($p = 1/2$).

Therefore

$$a_{11} = \frac{1}{2}(1) + \frac{1}{2}(1) = 1$$

If A bluffs and B demands verification (a_{12}), A receives two units when the coin shows heads and pays two units when it discloses tails.

Thus

$$a_{12} = \frac{1}{2}(2) + \frac{1}{2}(-2) = 0$$

For the pure strategy of A's being truthful and B's believing (a_{21}), A receives one unit in the case of heads and pays one unit in the case of tails. That is,

$$a_{21} = \frac{1}{2}(1) + \frac{1}{2}(-1) = 0$$

Finally, when A is truthful and B demands verification (a_{22}), A receives two units for heads and pays one unit for tails.

Thus

$$a_{22} = \frac{1}{2}(2) + \frac{1}{2}(-1) = \frac{1}{2}$$

The payoff matrix of the game is therefore represented by

	B_1 (Believe)	B_2 (Disbelieve)
A_1 (Bluff)	1	0
A_2 (Truthful)	0	$\frac{1}{2}$

From Eq. 4-17 we can compute A's selection frequency for A_1 as

$$p_1 = \frac{a_{22} - a_{21}}{a_{11} + a_{22} - a_{12} - a_{21}} = \frac{1/2}{1 + (1/2)} = \frac{1}{3}$$

Hence A's optimal strategy is given by

$$S_A^* = \begin{pmatrix} A_1 & A_2 \\ \dfrac{1}{3} & \dfrac{2}{3} \end{pmatrix}$$

and the value of the game is $\gamma = 1/3$. Both A_1 and A_2 are maximin strategies. If A uses either one as a pure strategy, his average yield is zero. The mixed strategy provides the positive yield of 1/3 unit per play. Similar considerations to ascertain B's optimal strategy show that

$$S_B^* = \begin{pmatrix} B_1 & B_2 \\ \dfrac{1}{3} & \dfrac{2}{3} \end{pmatrix}$$

If B selects either B_1 or B_2 as a pure minimax strategy, his average yield is $-\frac{1}{2}$ instead of $-\frac{1}{3}$. To arrange for an equitable game, A must pay 1/3 unit per play to B.

A second method of increasing the expected gain consists of an analysis of the opponent's mechanism for selecting his mixed strategies. Of course, if a set of mixed strategies is derived from a truly random device, further analysis is of no avail. However, if the opponent is generating a sequence of heads and tails from the depths of his mind, there exists almost always a pattern, however complex.[†] To reveal such a pattern, Fourier analysis, individual symbol correlation, pair correlation, etc., might prove advantageous. Generally, we attempt to predict the probability of heads (tails)

† In Edgar Allan Poe's *The Purloined Letter*, C. Auguste Dupin describes a boy who could analyze his opponent's facial expression to predict the guessing of odd or even.

occurring as the $(n + 1)$st term of a sequence, given the previous n terms. A tentative step toward this goal is shown in Fig. 4-4.

The point Q is determined by the proportion of correct calls to date and the proportion of heads to date. If Q falls in the left or right triangles of Fig. 4-4, we select the pure strategies "always tails" or "always heads," respectively. If Q falls in the upper triangle, a mixed strategy is followed, with heads and tails equally likely to be chosen. If Q falls into the lower triangle, a mixed strategy is determined as follows: A line between the diagram center C and the point Q intercepts the abscissa at a point X.

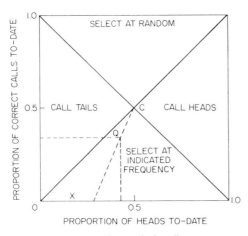

Fig. 4-4   Heads-tails predictive diagram

The proper frequency ratio of heads and tails is then $X/(1 - X)$. For example, if $X = 0.2$, correct strategy dictates selecting heads with probability 0.2 and tails with probability 0.8.

On a more complex level, several individuals have constructed machines that analyze the sequence chosen by their human opponents and thereby achieve positive mathematical expectations in matching games. One of the more interesting of such machines is the SEER (SEquence Extrapolating Robot) built at Bell Telephone Laboratories by D. W. Hagelbarger (a simpler version was constructed previously by C. E. Shannon). The machine can recognize any of the four periodic sequences:

HHHH···

TTTT ···

HTHTHT ···

HHTTHHTT···

A certain number of plays is required for the machine to acknowledge each sequence when it occurs and a lesser number to assimilate any phase change in the sequence instigated by its opponent. Against human opposition the machine usually emerges victorious, since individual patterns tend to be not random but a function of emotions and previous training and experience. To increase its competitive élan, the machine selects a correlated output only when it is winning; when losing, it plays randomly. It is, of course, possible to outwit the machine from a knowledge of its analytic procedure.[†]

Coin games

THE ST. PETERSBURG PARADOX

There exists a probably mythical tradition that the high-class gambling casinos of the eighteenth century employed a resident statistician for the purpose of establishing odds and entrance fees for any game whatsoever that a customer might wish to propose. From this tradition arose the apocryphal tale of the mathematics student who entered the casino in St. Petersburg and suggested a game renowned to date as the St. Petersburg paradox.[‡] The student offered to pay a fixed fee for each trial consisting of a sequence of coin tosses until heads appears. Another trial and another fee might be instituted following each occurrence of heads. The student was to receive 2^n rubles for each trial, where n is the throw defining the first occurrence of heads following a run of $n - 1$ tails. According to the tale, the casino's statistician quoted some particular entrance fee per trial and the student proceeded to break the bank, since the game possesses an infinite expected gain. (Actually, the game was originally proposed by Nicolas Bernoulli[§] and used by his cousin Daniel to formulate the concept of moral expectation; see Chapter 11.)

The probability of throwing $n - 1$ tails followed by heads is $(1/2)^n$. With the appearance of heads at the nth throw, the trial concludes and the

[†] Inevitably, an umpire machine was constructed, which linked the Shannon machine and the Hagelbarger machine, pitting them together in a Wellsian struggle. The Shannon machine triumphed with a ratio of 55 wins to 45 losses.

[‡] Inquiries among Russian mathematicians have elicited the intelligence that this game is *not* currently referred to in the Soviet Union as the Leningrad paradox.

[§] D'Alembert, Condorcet, Bertrand, and Poisson, among many, undertook explanations of the game. D'Alembert wrote to Lagrange: "Your memoir on games makes me very eager that you should give us a solution of the Petersburg problem, which seems to me insoluble on the basis of known principles."

student receives 2^n rubles. Thus the student's expectation is

$$E = \sum_n \left(\frac{1}{2}\right)^n \cdot 2^n = 1 + 1 + 1 + \cdots$$

that is, infinite. Therefore, the only "fair" entrance fee would be an infinite amount of rubles.

Yet, back in his classes at the university, the same logic would result in the student's receiving a failing grade. Firstly, the expectation is infinite in a real sense only if the casino had infinite wealth; otherwise—if the casino's fortune were N rubles, for example—the student's expectation of winning a sum in excess of N rubles would be zero. Secondly, the casino's finite wealth implies a finite "fair" entrance fee. Thirdly, with a finite sum for his own fortune, the student would have a high probability of ruin before achieving any extremely large gain.

There are two approaches to resolve the "paradox" of infinite expectation. First, the game can be turned "fair" in the classical sense by imposing an entrance fee that is not constant per trial, but rather is a function of the number of trials (Bertrand's solution). If we let e_n be the accumulated entrance fee and S_n the accumulated gain after n trials, then the game is equitable if, for every $\varepsilon > 0$,

$$P\left[\left|\frac{S_n}{e_n} - 1\right| > \varepsilon\right] \to 0 \qquad\qquad 4\text{-}18$$

Equation 4-18 is the analog of the law of large numbers. From this expression it can be shown that

$$e_n = n \log_2 n$$

Thus, if the student had 64 rubles, he would fairly be allowed 16 trials. Note the implication that two students each with 64 rubles (representing a total purchasing power of 32 trials) would differ from one student with 128 rubles (representing a purchasing power of 26.94 trials).

Variable entrance fees are, for several reasons, undesirable and unfeasible in gambling operations. A better approach is to consider a casino with finite capital N. The probability p_n that heads first appears on the nth throw of a sequence remains $(1/2)^n$. However, the payoff a_n at the nth throw is now constrained by

$$a_n = 2^n \qquad \text{if } 2^n \le N$$

$$a_n = N \qquad \text{if } 2^n > N$$

Therefore, if $[n_0]$ is the highest value of n such that $2^n \le N$, the mathematical expectation of the game is

$$E = \sum_{n=1}^{[n_0]} (\tfrac{1}{2})^n 2^n + \sum_{n=[n_0]+1}^{\infty} (\tfrac{1}{2})^n N \qquad 4\text{-}19$$

The second term in Eq. 4-19 is a geometric series whose sum is $N/(2)^{[n_0]}$. If the casino possesses a million rubles, $[n_0] = 19$ and

$$E = \sum_{n=1}^{19} (1) + \frac{1,000,000}{2^{19}} = 19 + 1.90 = 20.90$$

Hence the casino should demand 20.90 rubles from the student as an entrance fee. For a billion-ruble bank, the "fair" entrance fee is 30.86 rubles, and for a trillion-ruble bank, 40.82 rubles. If the game is contested between two poor students, the one acting as banker exacts a "fair" entrance fee of 7.656 rubles if holding a fortune of 100 rubles. With a capitalization of only 10 rubles, the payment per trial should be 4.25 rubles.

The expected duration $E(n)$ of one trial of the St. Petersburg game is readily seen to be

$$E(n) = \sum_{i=0}^{\infty} \frac{i+1}{2^i} = 2 \text{ throws}$$

Thus, on the average, every third toss of the coin initiates a new trial and decrees a fresh payment. Consequently, the player can avoid a high-ruin probability only with a large bankroll.

ST. PETERSBURG REVISITED

If the mythical student had been enrolled in one of our better universities, he might have proposed the more subtle game of being paid n rubles, where n is now the first play of the sequence when the number of heads exceeds the number of tails. Here, too, an infinite-expectation game arises if the casino is granted infinite wealth. Since heads can first exceed tails only on an odd value of n, let $n = 2k + 1$. The probability that heads first exceeds tails at the nth throw of the coin (that is, that over $n - 1$ throws the s versus n path of Fig. 4-2 contains $n - 1$ vertices on or below the abscissa) is given by

$$p_{2k+1} = \frac{\binom{2k-1}{k} \dfrac{2}{k+1}}{2^{2k+1}}, \qquad k > 0$$

$$p_1 = \frac{1}{2}$$

and the payoff is $2k + 1$ rubles. Therefore, the expectation is expressed as

$$E = \frac{1}{2} + \sum_{k=1}^{\infty} \frac{\binom{2k-1}{k}(2k+1)}{(k+1)2^{2k}} = \sum_{k=0}^{\infty} \frac{\binom{2k+1}{k}}{2^{2k+1}} = \sum_k f(k)$$

The ratio of the kth term and the $(k + 1)$st term is

$$\frac{f(k)}{f(k+1)} = \frac{\binom{2k+1}{k}2^{2k+3}}{\binom{2k+3}{k+1}2^{2k+1}} = \frac{2k+4}{2k+3}$$

Thus

$$\lim_{k \to \infty} \frac{f(k)}{f(k+1)} \to 1$$

and the expectation is a divergent series.

As in the St. Petersburg game, we could erroneously conclude that the "fair" entrance fee is infinite. However, for a finite capital N possessed by the casino, the payoff a_n is, in reality,

$$a_n = n = 2k + 1, \quad \text{if } N \geq 2k + 1$$

$$a_n = N, \quad \text{if } N < 2k + 1$$

Similarly to Eq. 4-19, we can write the true expectation as

$$E = \sum_{k=0}^{[k_0]} \frac{\binom{2k+1}{k}}{2^{2k+1}} + \sum_{k=[k_0]+1}^{\infty} \frac{\binom{2k-1}{k}N}{(k+1)2^{2k}} \qquad \text{4-20}$$

where $[k_0]$ is the greatest value of k for which $2k + 1 \leq N$.

Equation 4-20 can be evaluated by the application of Stirling's formula. The second term of Eq. 4-20 is expressible in the form

$$\frac{\binom{2k-1}{k}}{(k+1)2^{2k}} = \frac{(2k-1)!}{(k+1)!(k-1)!2^{2k}}$$

$$\simeq \frac{\sqrt{2\pi}\left(\frac{2k-1}{e}\right)^{2k-1+1/2}}{\sqrt{2\pi}\left(\frac{k+1}{e}\right)^{k+1+1/2}\sqrt{2\pi}\left(\frac{k-1}{e}\right)^{k-1+1/2}2^{2k}}$$

$$\simeq \left(\frac{e}{4\pi}\right)^{1/2} k^{-3/2}$$

the latter expression arising from use of the further approximation

$$\left(1 + \frac{1}{x}\right)^x = \exp\left[x \ln\left(1 + \frac{1}{x}\right)\right] \simeq e$$

and, since the sum of $k^{-3/2}$ from $[k_0] + 1$ to ∞ is bounded by

$$\int_{[k_0]+1}^{\infty} k^{-3/2}\, dk = \frac{2}{\{[k_0] + 1\}^{1/2}} \leq \sum_{k=[k_0]+1}^{\infty} k^{-3/2}$$

$$\leq \int_{[k_0]+1}^{\infty} (k - 1)^{-3/2}\, dk = \frac{2}{[k_0]^{1/2}}$$

we can write

$$\sum_{k=[k_0]+1}^{\infty} \frac{\binom{2k-1}{k}}{(k+1)2^{2k}} \simeq \left\{\frac{e}{\pi[k_0]}\right\}^{1/2}$$

Similarly, for the first term of Eq. 4-20 we can show that

$$\sum_{k=0}^{[k_0]} \frac{\binom{2k+1}{k}}{2^{2k+1}} \simeq \sum_{k=0}^{[k']} \frac{\binom{2k+1}{k}}{2^{2k+1}} + 2\{\sqrt{[k_0]} + \sqrt{[k']}\}$$

where $[k']$ is an integer (greater than 10) selected to reduce the error of the approximation to less than 1 percent. For values of k less than $[k']$, exact numerical calculations are required. When played against another poor student with a limited fortune of $N = 10$ rubles, the fair entrance fee becomes, by these approximations, 6.36 rubles per trial. For $N = 100$ rubles, the first student should pay 23.3 rubles to begin a sequence of plays. Against casino bankrolls of one million rubles and one billion rubles, respectively, fair entrance payments are 2580 rubles and 81,500 rubles.

PROBABILITY OF AN EVEN NUMBER OF HEADS

A great number of other games and puzzles can be formulated through a sequence of coin throws. As one example, we ask the probability P_n that an even number of heads is observed in n tosses of a coin. We let p equal the probability that the coin falls heads, q equal the probability of obtaining tails, and note that the distribution of the number of heads is binomial. Thence,

$$P_n = \sum_i \binom{n}{2i} p^{2i} q^{n-2i} = \frac{1}{2}[(p + q)^n + (q - p)^n] = \frac{1}{2}[1 + (q - p)^n]$$

For a fair coin, $p = q = 1/2$, and the probability of obtaining an even number of heads in n tosses is evidently $1/2$ (independent of n). A coin biased completely toward tails ($q = 1$, $p = 0$) yields a unity probability for P_n (there will always be zero heads in any sequence of throws). Over n throws of a coin biased completely toward heads ($p = 1$, $q = 0$), the number of heads obtained is obviously even or odd as n is even or odd.

PROBABILITY OF NO SUCCESSIVE HEADS

The probability of tossing a fair coin n times without realizing two successive throws of heads forms the basis of a simple coin game. To formulate this probability, we note that f_n, the number of ways of tossing the coin n times without the appearance of successive heads, can be decomposed into two mutually exclusive terms: f_{n-1}, those in which the nth throw is tails and the previous $n - 1$ throws have exhibited no successive heads, and f_{n-2}, those in which the nth throw is heads, the $(n - 1)$th throw is tails, and the previous $n - 2$ throws occurred without successive heads. Thus

$$f_n = f_{n-1} + f_{n-2} \qquad\qquad 4\text{-}21$$

Equation 4-21 is readily identified as the Fibonacci sequence, the nth term of which corresponds to $n - 2$ throws of the coin. Since all 2^n sequences of n throws are equiprobable, the probability P_n that two or more successive heads do not appear in n throws is simply

$$P_n = \frac{f_{n+2}}{2^n}$$

or, expressed as a summation,

$$P_n = 1 - \sum_{i=0}^{n-1} 2^{-(i+1)} f_i$$

where f_i is the ith term of the Fibonacci sequence $f_0 = 0, f_1 = 1, f_2 = 1, f_3 = 2, \ldots$.

For $n = 10$, $P_n = 144/2^{10} = 0.141$, the probability that in ten throws of a fair coin, no successive heads appear. By $n = 20$, $P_n^{\cdot}$ has fallen off to $17{,}711/2^{20} = 0.017$.

THROWING DIFFERENT NUMBERS OF COINS

Another facet of coin problems with unexpected ramifications arises in the situation where two players A and B, possessed of $n + 1$ and n coins, respectively, each throw their coins simultaneously, observing the number that turn up heads. We seek the probability P_A that A, owning the additional coin, has obtained more heads than B. This probability can be formulated by the double sum

$$P_A = \frac{1}{2^{2n+1}} \sum_{i=1}^{n+1} \sum_{j=0}^{n} \binom{n+1}{i+j} \binom{n}{j} \qquad\qquad 4\text{-}22$$

A readily verifiable relationship for binomial coefficients is

$$\sum_{j=0}^{n} \binom{n+1}{i+j} \binom{n}{j} = \binom{2n+1}{n+i}$$

Applying this equivalence to Eq. 4-22, the probability that A achieves more heads than B is determined explicitly to be

$$P_A = \frac{1}{2^{2n+1}} \sum_{i=0}^{n+1} \binom{2n+1}{n+i} = \frac{2^{2n}}{2^{2n+1}} = \frac{1}{2} \qquad\qquad 4\text{-}23$$

Surprisingly, P_A is not a function of the number of coins n. However, the probability P_B that B achieves more heads than A *is* a function of n. Letting P_e be the probability that A and B throw the same number of heads, we can evaluate P_e as

$$P_e = \frac{1}{2^{2n+1}} \sum_{j=0}^{n} \binom{n+1}{j} \binom{n}{j} = \binom{2n+1}{n} 2^{-2n-1} \qquad\qquad 4\text{-}24$$

The difference between unity and the sum of Eqs. 4-23 and 4-24 defines the probability P_B:

$$P_B = \left[2^{2n} - \binom{2n+1}{n} \right] 2^{2n+1}$$

As a first generalization, we can let player A be accorded m more coins than the n possessed by player B. For the probability that A obtains more heads with $n + m$ coins than B with n coins, we can state the recursive relationship.

$$P_A(n, m) = P_A(n, m-1) + \frac{1}{2^{2n+m}} \binom{2n+m-1}{n}, \qquad m \geq 1$$

$$P_A(n, 0) = \frac{1}{2} - \frac{1}{2^{2n+1}}$$

or, expressed as a summation,

$$P_A(n, m) = \frac{1}{2} + \frac{1}{2^{2n+m}} \sum_{i=1}^{m-1} 2^{m-1-i} \binom{2n+i}{n}, \qquad m \geq 2 \qquad\qquad 4\text{-}25$$

Only the value $P_A(n, 1)$ is not a function of n. The probability that A and B produce the same number of heads is, in the general instance,

$$P_e(n, m) = \frac{1}{2^{2n+m}} \sum_{i=0}^{n} \binom{n+m}{i}\binom{n}{i} = \frac{1}{2^{2n+m}} \binom{2n+m}{n}$$

The probability that B obtains more heads than A, although throwing fewer coins, is given by $1 - P_A(n, m) - P_e(n, m)$.

A further generalization consists of characterizing A's coins by a probability p_a of turning up heads and a probability $q_a = 1 - p_a$ of turning up tails, and B's coins by probabilities p_b and $q_b = 1 - p_b$ of showing heads and tails, respectively. The probability that A achieves the greater number of heads can then be formulated by the double sum

$$P_A(n, m) = \sum_{j=0}^{n} \sum_{i=j+1}^{n+m} \binom{n}{j}\binom{m+n}{i} p_a^i p_b^j q_a^{n+m-i} q_b^{n-j}$$

which reduces to Eq. 4-25 for $p_a = p_b = 1/2$ (that is, for conventional coins).

Our final generalization is described by requiring player A to select his $m + n$ coins at random from a box containing an infinite variety of coins covering the spectrum from $p_a = 0$ to $p_a = 1$. The distribution of coins for A is specified by $f_a(p_a)$. Similarly, player B selects his coins from a source distributed according to the density function $f_b(p_b)$. Then the probability that A counts more heads than B is expressible in the form

$$P_A(n, m) = \sum_{j=0}^{n} \sum_{i=j+1}^{n+m} \int_0^1 f_a(p_a) \binom{n+m}{i} p_a^i q_a^{n+m-i} dp_a \int_0^1 f_b(p_b) \binom{n}{j} p_b^j q_b^{n-j} dp_b$$

A COIN WITH UNKNOWN PROBABILITIES

An interesting category of problems involving coins is that concerning sequential decisions with a limited memory. Consider a coin such that the probabilities p and $q = 1 - p$ of turning up heads or tails, respectively, are unknown. If we guess correctly the outcome of a throw, we receive one unit payment; conversely, we must pay one unit. Of course we wish to maximize our expected return over a sequence of coin throws; thus if $p > q$, we adopt the strategy of calling heads at every throw (or tails if $p < q$). Since the relative magnitudes of p and q are unknown, however, we are constrained to utilize the memory of the preceding r events to maximize our percentage of correct guesses. One strategy, due to Marcus, suggests that we begin by calling heads and continue steadfastly unless the first k ($1 \leq k \leq r$) consecutive throws are not heads or until r consecutive tails occur. Thence, tails is called according to the same rule. The key facet to the problem of selecting a value of k that maximizes the mathematical expectation is that the value is a function of p. It follows that it is impossible to determine the optimal strategy for unknown characteristics p and q of the coin.

THE TWO-ARMED BANDIT

A coin problem in the domain of sampling statistics is that of the "Two-armed Bandit" (so-called because it can be formulated as a slot machine with two levers). There are given two coins, A and B, which possess probabilities p_a and p_b, respectively, of exhibiting heads. The player is accorded no knowledge whatsoever of the values p_a and p_b; yet, at each step in a sequence of coin tosses, he must select one of the two coins and wager that its outcome is heads. Over the sequence of n tosses he receives one unit payment for each heads and loses one unit for each tails. We wish to determine a judicious rule for the coin-selection procedure.

While no rigorous proof of an optimal strategy has been achieved, Robbins has proposed the principle of "staying on a winner" and has shown it to be uniformly better than a strategy of random selection. According to this principle, the player chooses coin A or B at random for the first toss and thereafter switches coins only upon the occurrence of tails. That is, for $j = 1, 2, \ldots, n$, if the jth toss results in heads, the same coin is thrown at the $(j + 1)$st trial; otherwise, the alternate coin is thrown. Accordingly, the probability P_j of obtaining heads at this jth toss can be expressed by the recursive relationship

$$P_{j+1} = P_j(p_a + p_b - 1) + p_a + p_b - 2p_ap_b$$

and we can derive the limiting expression for P_j explicitly as

$$\lim_{j \to \infty} P_j = \frac{p_a + p_b - 2p_ap_b}{2 - (p_a + p_b)} = q_a + \frac{q_b^2}{1 - q_a} \qquad \text{4-26}$$

where

$$q_a = \frac{p_a + p_b}{2} \qquad \text{4-27}$$

and

$$q_b = \frac{|p_a - p_b|}{2} \qquad \text{4-28}$$

Over the n tosses he is permitted, the player wishes to achieve the greatest possible expected value of the sum $S_n = x_1 + x_2 + \cdots + x_n$, where $x_j = 1$ or -1 according as heads or tails occurs at the jth toss. Hence, the expectation per toss received by the player in following the "staying on a winner" rule is, applying Eqs. 4-26, 4-27, and 4-28.

$$\lim_{n \to \infty} E\left(\frac{S_n}{n}\right) = 2\left(\frac{q_a - p_a p_b}{1 - q_a}\right) - 1 \qquad\qquad 4\text{-}29$$

Now if the player knew the greater of the two probabilities p_a and p_b, he would achieve the expectation

$$E\left(\frac{S_n}{n}\right) = 2 \max(p_a, p_b) - 1 = 2(q_a + q_b) - 1 \qquad\qquad 4\text{-}30$$

Robbins has suggested the difference in these expectations as a measure of the asymptotic loss per toss due to ignorance of the true probabilities. Thence, the loss $L_1(A, B)$, associated with the "staying on a winner" rule is given by Eq. 4-30 minus Eq. 4-29, or

$$L_1(A, B) = 2q_b\left(1 - \frac{q_b}{1 - q_a}\right) \geq 0$$

It can be shown that $L_1(A, B)$ assumes a maximum value of $2(3 - 2^{3/2}) \simeq 0.344$ when $p_a = 0$ and $p_b = 2 - 2^{\frac{1}{2}} \simeq 0.586$ (or vice versa). Consequently, use of the "staying on a winner" rule entails an average loss per toss of 0.344 unit due to ignorance of the true state of "nature."

By adopting the rule of selecting a coin at random for each throw, or selecting a coin at random and continuing to use it, or alternating between coins, the player obtains an average loss per toss of

$$L_2(A, B) = 2q_b = |p_a - p_b| \qquad\qquad 4\text{-}31$$

Equation 4-31 exhibits a maximum value of 1 when $p_a = 0$ and $p_b = 1$ (or vice versa). We can also prove that $L_1(A, B) \leq L_2(A, B)$ for all values of p_a and p_b. Further, no other strategy proposed will yield a loss function less than $L_1(A, B)$.

For the special case where it is given that $p_a = 1 - p_b$, the "Two-armed Bandit" problem reduces to one of sequential decisions with a memory including all known history of the coin. The obvious strategy in this instance is to wager on heads or tails as either owns a majority of the previous tosses.

More extensive developments of the nature of adaptive competitive decisions have been published by J. L. Rosenfeld.

Diverse recreations

ODD MAN OUT

A common game among friendly competitors is that of "Odd Man Out." It consists of an odd number m of players, each throwing a single coin; if, among the m players, there is one whose coin shows an outcome different from all others, that player is declared "Odd Man Out." Defining p as the single-trial probability of heads, the probability $P(H_1)$ of exactly one heads appearing among m coins is

$$P(H_1) = \binom{m}{1} p q^{m-1}$$

and the probability $P(T_1)$ of exactly one tails among m coins is

$$P(T_1) = \binom{m}{m-1} p^{m-1} q$$

Thus, the probability P that exactly one heads or exactly one tails appears is equal to

$$P = m(p^{m-1}q + pq^{m-1}) \qquad\qquad 4\text{-}32$$

For a fair coin, $p = q = 1/2$ and Eq. 4-32 simplifies to

$$P = \frac{m}{2^{m-1}}$$

With $m = 3$, the probability that one player is "Odd Man Out" is 3/4 and with $m = 5$, the probability falls off to 5/16.

Letting $Q = 1 - P$, the probability that no player becomes "Odd Man Out" until the nth play is $Q^{N-1}P$. And since n is a random variable that follows a geometric distribution with the parameter P, we can observe that the mean of n is equal to the mean of the geometric distribution, so that the expected duration of the game is defined by

$$E(n) = \frac{1}{P} = \frac{2^{m-1}}{m}$$

The expected game duration is 1.33 plays for $m = 3$ and 3.2 plays for $m = 5$. Similarly, the variance has the form

$$\sigma^2(n) = \frac{Q}{P^2}$$

Hence, for $m = 3$, the standard deviation is 2/3 of a play, while for $m = 5$, the standard deviation is 2.65 plays.

ROTATION

With three players, a variation of the "Odd Man Out" theme is the game of "Rotation." Designating the three players as A, B, and C, we match A versus B, with the winner advancing to a contest with C. The winner of this second match then plays the loser of the first match and the players continue to rotate according to this procedure until one player has triumphed twice in succession. If each match is a fair contest, the probabilities P_A, P_B, and P_C of players A, B, and C, respectively, winning the game are determined by simple algebraic methods. Let p_w represent the probability of a player's winning the game immediately following the winning of a match and p_l be the probability of ultimately winning the game following the loss of a match. Then

$$P_A = P_B = \frac{1}{2}p_w + \frac{1}{2}p_l \qquad P_C = \frac{1}{2}p_w$$

and

$$p_w = \frac{1}{2} + \frac{1}{2}p_l$$

Eliminating p_w and p_l,

$$P_A = P_B = \frac{5}{14} \qquad P_C = \frac{2}{7}$$

Player C obviously is handicapped by not participating in the first match. The expected duration $E(n)$ of the "Rotation" game is computable as

$$E(n) = \sum_{i=1}^{\infty} (i + 1)2^{-i} = 3 \text{ matches}$$

THREE-FINGERED MORRA

The game of Three-fingered Morra is an ancient pastime of notable simplicity. It provides an example where the optimal strategy was unknown for centuries, owing to the ignorance of elementary game theory. Each of two players (in the simplified version) simultaneously exhibits one, two, or three fingers while guessing at the number of fingers that his opponent will show. If just one player guesses correctly, he wins an amount equal to the sum of the fingers displayed by himself and his opponent. Otherwise, the trial results in a draw. Letting (i, j) be the strategy of showing i fingers while guessing j, $(i, j = 1, 2, 3)$, the 9×9 payoff matrix can be evolved as illustrated in Fig. 4-5.

Player A	Player B								
	B_1 (1, 1)	B_2 (1, 2)	B_3 (1, 3)	B_4 (2, 1)	B_5 (2, 2)	B_6 (2, 3)	B_7 (3, 1)	B_8 (3, 2)	B_9 (3, 3)
A_1 (1, 1)	0	2	2	−3	0	0	−4	0	0
A_2 (1, 2)	−2	0	0	0	3	3	−4	0	0
A_3 (1, 3)	−2	0	0	−3	0	0	0	4	4
A_4 (2, 1)	3	0	3	0	−4	0	0	−5	0
A_5 (2, 2)	0	−3	0	4	0	4	0	−5	0
A_6 (2, 3)	0	−3	0	0	−4	0	5	0	5
A_7 (3, 1)	4	4	0	0	0	−5	0	0	−6
A_8 (3, 2)	0	0	−4	5	5	0	0	0	−6
A_9 (3, 3)	0	0	−4	0	0	−5	6	6	0

Fig. 4-5   Payoff matrix for three-fingered Morra

Applying a system of equations, as in Eq. 2-42, to determine the optimal strategies, we can demonstrate that there are four basic mixed strategies for each player:

$$S_A^* = S_B^* = \begin{cases} S_1: & (0, \quad 0, \quad 5/12, \quad 0, \quad 4/12, \quad 0, \quad 3/12, \quad 0, \quad 0) \\ S_2: & (0, \quad 0, \quad 16/37, \quad 0, \quad 12/37, \quad 0, \quad 9/37, \quad 0, \quad 0) \\ S_3: & (0, \quad 0, \quad 20/47, \quad 0, \quad 15/47, \quad 0, \quad 12/47, \quad 0, \quad 0) \\ S_4: & (0, \quad 0, \quad 25/61, \quad 0, \quad 20/61, \quad 0, \quad 16/61, \quad 0, \quad 0) \end{cases}$$

Actually, Three-fingered Morra has an infinite number of optimal mixed strategies, since each convex linear combination of these four mixed strategies is also optimal. That is, for an arbitrary parameter λ, $0 < \lambda < 1$, the mixed strategy $[\lambda S_1 + (1 - \lambda)S_2]$, which is a convex linear combination of S_1 and S_2, constitutes an optimal mixed strategy. Since the game matrix is symmetrical, the value γ of the game is zero.

Among a set of optimal mixed strategies, there may exist one or more that are preferable in the event of an opponent's departure from optimality. In selecting such a particular mixed strategy, we assume that player B commits an error, the consequences of which he attempts to minimize, while player A acts to maximize his advantage. The procedure employed by player A to determine his selection is developed as follows:

In the payoff matrix, Fig. 4-5, A's nine pure strategies (i, j) are replaced by his four optimal mixed strategies, resulting in the 4×9 matrix of Fig. 4-6.

	(1, 1)	(1, 2)	(1, 3)	(2, 1)	(2, 2)	(2, 3)	(3, 1)	(3, 2)	(3, 3)
S_1	2/12	0	0	1/12	0	1/12	0	0	2/12
S_2	4/37	0	0	0	0	3/37	0	4/37	10/37
S_3	8/47	3/47	0	0	0	0	0	5/47	8/47
S_4	14/61	4/61	0	5/61	0	0	0	0	4/61

Fig. 4-6   Reduced Morra payoff matrix

Removing from this matrix those pure strategies of player B [namely, (1, 3), (2, 2), and (3, 1)] that yield the value of the game (0) against every optimal mixed strategy of A, we are left with the further reduced 4×6 matrix R:

$$R = \begin{Vmatrix} 2/12 & 0 & 1/12 & 1/12 & 0 & 2/12 \\ 4/37 & 0 & 0 & 3/37 & 4/37 & 10/37 \\ 8/47 & 3/47 & 0 & 0 & 5/47 & 8/47 \\ 14/61 & 4/61 & 5/61 & 0 & 0 & 4/61 \end{Vmatrix}$$

Again applying Eq. 2-42 to determine the solutions of R, we find two mixed strategies:

$$S_A'^* = \begin{cases} S_1': & (120/275, \quad 0, \quad 94/275, 61/275) \\ S_2': & (12/110, 37/110, \quad 0, \quad 61/110) \end{cases}$$

or, in terms of A's nine pure strategies, S_1' and S_2' each translates to the same solution of the original payoff matrix. Specifically,

$$S_A^* = (0, 0, 23/55, 0, 18/55, 0, 14/55, 0, 0) \qquad \textit{4-33}$$

The value of the game to A with payoff matrix R is 2/55. Thus, if player A employs the particular optimal mixed strategy of Eq. 4-33, he maximizes his minimum gain accruing from any deviation of B from an optimal strategy, winning at least 2/55 units in the event.

TREIZE OR RENCONTRES; HATS AND BIRTHDAYS

Another matching game of considerable age was proposed by Montmort in his treatise (printed in 1708) concerning the analysis of games of chance. An urn contains n balls numbered $1, 2, 3, \ldots, n$, which are thoroughly mixed and drawn out one at a time without replacement. Montmort asked the probability that no ball would be drawn in the order indicated by its number—that is, that the ith ball would never coincide with the ith drawing.

Since the urn originally was assigned 13 balls, the game was called Treize; another name commonly applied is Rencontres (coincidences).

We denote by u_n the number of ways of drawing n balls without a match between ball number and drawing order. Let ball j appear at the first draw and ball 1 at the ith draw. For $i = j$, $n - 2$ balls remain to be selected in u_{n-2} ways; there are $(n - 1)u_{n-2}$ such cases, since i may range from 2 to n. For $i \neq j$, the $n - 1$ balls other than the jth must be associated with $n - 1$ numbers other than the first, with ball 1 not appearing at the jth draw. This situation is identical to the original problem with $n - 1$ balls—that is, u_{n-1} ways remain to select the $n - 1$ balls with a total of $(n - 1)u_{n-1}$ cases. Thus we can write the recursion formula

$$u_n = (n - 1)u_{n-2} + (n - 1)u_{n-1}$$

which, by induction, is equivalent to

$$u_n = nu_{n-1} + (-1)^n \qquad\qquad 4\text{-}34$$

To solve Eq. 4-34, we substitute $u_i = i!p_i$, where p_i signifies the probability that i balls are drawn without a match:

$$p_i - p_{i-1} = \frac{(-1)^i}{i!}$$

Summing from $i = 2$ to $i = n$ and observing that $p_1 = 0$, we have

$$p_n = \sum_{i=2}^{n} \frac{(-1)^i}{i!} = \frac{1}{2!} - \frac{1}{3!} + \cdots + \frac{(-1)^n}{n!} \qquad\qquad 4\text{-}35$$

for the probability that none of the n balls corresponds in number to the drawing order.

Equation 4-35 evidently coincides with the first $n + 1$ terms of the expansion of e^{-x} with $x = -1$. Hence, for large n, $p_n \to e^{-1} = 0.368\ldots$; the probability P_1 of at least one match occurring is $P_1 = 1 - p_n \simeq 0.632$. Surprisingly, this probability is practically independent of n for all but small values of n.

In general, it can shown that among n events $A_1, A_2, \ldots, A_n$, the probability $P[m]$ that exactly m of these events are matched with any other specified ordering of the A_i's is given by

$$P[m] = \frac{1}{m!} - \binom{m + 1}{m}\frac{1}{(m + 1)!} + \binom{m + 2}{m}\frac{1}{(m + 2)!} - \cdots$$

$$\pm \binom{n}{m}\frac{1}{n!} \qquad\qquad 4\text{-}36$$

where $1 \le m \le n$. For large values of n, Eq. 4-36 becomes

$$P[m] \to \frac{1}{m!} \cdot \frac{1}{e}$$

Other classical variations of Montmort's game include the problem of mixed-up hats and the probability of identical birthdays. If n gentlemen check their hats with a checkroom attendant who, subsequently, dispenses the hats at random, the probability that no one recovers his own hat is given by Eq. 4-35. We can complicate the problem by requiring the n gentlemen each to deposit r articles of apparel with the incompetent checkroom attendant. Thence, the probability that no one regains a single correct article is p_n^r. If we ask the probability $_r p_n$ that each gentleman receives at least one incorrect article, we can show that

$$_r p_n = 1 - n^{1-r} + \frac{[n(n-1)]^{1-r}}{2!} - \cdots$$

A more difficult (and apparently unsolved) variation concerns the probability that each gentleman, having checked a hat and a coat, subsequently is given a wrong hat and coat belonging to two *different* persons (empirically, the probability is approximately 0.04 for $n \ge 5$).

The simplest statement of the birthday problem asks the probability P that in a gathering of n persons, at least two celebrate the same birthday. It is evident that

$$P = 1 - \left(1 - \frac{1}{365}\right)\left(1 - \frac{2}{365}\right) \cdots \left(1 - \frac{n-1}{365}\right) = 1 - \frac{365!}{(365-n)! \, 365^n}$$

for $n < 365$. With $n = 23$ persons, the probability of at least one matching set of birthdays is greater than $\frac{1}{2}$ ($P = 0.507$). For 50 persons, the probability of at least one match is 0.965, and for 100 persons, the probability that no two persons have the same birthday is 1.28×10^{-6}.

More generally, we can select people at random until we find k with identical birthdays. The expected number of people sampled, $E(365, k)$, for the occurrence of this event is

$$E(365, k) = \int_0^\infty \left[S_k\left(\frac{x}{365}\right) \right]^{365} e^{-x} \, dx \simeq (k!)^{1/k} \, \Gamma\left(1 + \frac{1}{k}\right) 365^{(1-1/h)}$$

$$(4\text{-}37)$$

where $S_k(x)$ is the kth partial sum of x—that is, $S_k(x) = \sum_{i<k} x^i/i!$. Evaluating the asymptotic relationship of Eq. 4-37 for several values of k:

$$E(365, 2) \simeq 24 \qquad E(365, 5) \simeq 263$$

$$E(365, 3) \simeq 83 \qquad E(365, 10) \simeq 872$$

$$E(365, 4) \simeq 167 \qquad E(365, 20) \simeq 2196$$

It is assumed that all birthdays are independently and uniformly distributed over the year. Since birthdays are not strictly uniformly distributed, the expression for the probability of coincident birthdays represents a lower bound—and the values of $E(365, k)$ given represent upper bounds.

URNS AND BALLS

Likely an infinite number of games can be invented with urns and balls. One of the earliest is due to Daniel Bernoulli, who posed the problem of three urns, the first containing n white balls, the second n black balls, and the third n red balls. A ball is selected at random from urn 1 and placed in urn 2; a ball is then selected at random from urn 2 and placed in urn 3; finally, a ball is selected at random from urn 3 and placed in urn 1. This process is thence repeated m times. Bernoulli inquired as to the expected numbers of the various colors of balls in each of three urns after the m complete mixings. The solution is determined from second-order equations in finite differences. Let W, B, and R refer to the numbers of white, black, and red balls, respectively, and the subscripts to the urn numbers. Then, after m complete mixings, the expected number of balls residing in their "home" urns is

$$E_1(W) = E_2(B) = E_3(R)$$
$$= \frac{n}{3}\left[\left(1 - \frac{1}{n} + \frac{a}{n}\right)^m + \left(1 - \frac{1}{n} + \frac{b}{n}\right)^m + \left(1 - \frac{1}{n} + \frac{c}{n}\right)^m\right]$$

where a, b, and c are the three cube roots of unity. To a good approximation

$$E_1(W) = E_2(B) = E_3(R)$$
$$\simeq n\left[\left(\frac{n-1}{n}\right)^m + \frac{m(m-1)(m-2)}{3!n^3}\left(\frac{n-1}{n}\right)^{m-3}\right]$$

Thus, if each urn originally contained 50 balls of a given color and the mixing process is continued for 10 rounds, we would expect from this equation to find less than 41 (actually 40.9) white balls still in the first urn, etc. The mixing process appears to occur rapidly, with $E_1(W)$ obviously approaching $n/3$ as m increases.

Similarly, we can show

$$E_2(W) = E_3(B) = E_1(R)$$

$$= \frac{n}{3}\left[a^2\left(1 - \frac{1}{n} + \frac{a}{n}\right)^m + b^2\left(1 - \frac{1}{n} + \frac{b}{n}\right)^m + c^2\left(1 - \frac{1}{n} + \frac{c}{n}\right)^m\right]$$

$$\simeq n\left[\frac{m}{n}\left(\frac{n-1}{n}\right)^{m-1} + \frac{m(m-1)(m-2)(m-3)}{4!n^4}\left(\frac{n-1}{n}\right)^{m-4}\right]$$

Hence, for $n = 50$ and $m = 10$, we would expect to find 8.3 white balls in the second urn. Finally, we can also derive the expression

$$E_3(W) = E_1(B) = E_2(R)$$

$$= \frac{n}{3}\left[a\left(1 - \frac{1}{n} + \frac{a}{n}\right)^m + b\left(1 - \frac{1}{n} + \frac{b}{n}\right)^m + c\left(1 - \frac{1}{n} + \frac{c}{n}\right)^m\right]$$

$$\simeq n\left[\frac{m(m-1)}{2!n^2}\left(\frac{n-1}{n}\right)^{m-2}\right.$$

$$\left. + \frac{m(m-1)(m-2)(m-3)(m-4)}{5!n^5}\left(\frac{n-1}{n}\right)^{m-5}\right]$$

For $n = 50$ and $m = 10$, the expected number of white balls in the third urn is 0.8. The diffusion rate is apparent from these figures.

An urn problem due to Polya concerns n_1 white balls and n_2 black balls mixed in the same container. A single ball is selected at random, its color noted, and replaced in the urn together with N additional balls of the same color. After repeating this procedure r times, we inquire as to the probability $P(k, r)$ that exactly k white balls have been noted. First we observe that, at the initial trial, there is a choice of $n = n_1 + n_2$ balls; the second trial offers a choice of $n + N$ balls, etc.; and at the rth trial, a selection is performed from $n + (r - 1)N$ balls. The total number of arrangements $A(n, r)$ is therefore

$$A(n, r) = n(n + N)\cdots[n + (r - 1)N] = \frac{N^r(r + n/N)}{\Gamma(n/N)}$$

where Γ is the complete gamma function. Thence, the total number of ways $C(k, n)$ of obtaining k white balls in r trials is, accordingly,

$$C(k, r) = \frac{\binom{r}{k}N^r\Gamma(r + n_1/N)\Gamma(r - k + n_2/N)}{\Gamma(n_1/N)\Gamma(n_2/N)}$$

The quotient of these two expressions produces the probability of obtaining exactly k white balls throughout the r trials:

$$P(k, r) = \frac{C(k, r)}{A(n, r)} = \frac{\Gamma(k + n_1/N)\Gamma(r - k + n_2/N)\Gamma(r + 1)\Gamma(n/N)}{\Gamma(k + 1)\Gamma(r - k - 1)\Gamma(r + n/N)\Gamma(n_1/N)\Gamma(n_2/N)}$$

$$4\text{-}38$$

With $N = 0$, we have the usual problem of sampling with replacement; in this instance Eq. 4-38 reduces to

$$P(k, r) = \binom{r}{k}\left(\frac{n_1}{n}\right)^k\left(\frac{n_2}{n}\right)^{r-k}$$

which is, alternatively, directly obtainable from the binomial distribution. With $N = -1$, we are confronted with the problem arising from sampling without replacement.

An urn of similar design contains n balls, all of different colors. A ball is drawn at random and replaced, its color noted. The process is repeated until a color appears for the second time (for the general problem, we would repeat the sampling until a color appears for the mth time). We can derive the expression for the expected number of drawings for the reappearance of a color as

$$E(n) = \sum_{k=1}^{n} \frac{k(k + 1)n!n^{-(k+1)}}{(n - k)!} \sim \sqrt{\frac{\pi n}{2}} + \frac{2}{3} + \frac{1}{12}\sqrt{\frac{\pi}{2n}} + \cdots$$

For large values of n, the first term of the expansion is paramount. With $n = 52$, $E(52) \sim 10$.

One class of urn problem involves unspecified comparisons of one or more urns and requires a definite quantity of information to be resolved. For example, consider a configuration of s urns, a certain number t of which contain only black balls while the remaining $s - t$ hold only white balls. A ball is selected from an arbitrary urn. In order to determine the outcome (black or white) uniquely, we must acquire the knowledge of which category includes the chosen urn. The amount of information I necessary to resolve the problem is specified by

$$I = \frac{-t}{s}\log\left(\frac{t}{s}\right) - \frac{s - t}{s}\log\left[\frac{s - t}{s}\right]$$

THE PROBLEM OF POINTS

Another classic problem is the second of the two queries that the Chevalier de Méré posed to his friend Pascal: to wit, the problem of points. In its general form, the problem concerns a game between two players who have interrupted their play before the game is concluded. While k points are required to win the stakes, the interruption occurs when player A has won $m < k$ points and player B, $n < k$ points. If A's probability of winning a single point is p and B's single-trial probability of winning is q (p and q can be a measure of the players' relative skills), the question to be answered is how the stakes should be divided at the time of the game's interruption. Pascal provided a solution for p and q; however, to Montmort is credited the generalized solution. Player A's probability of winning the game, P_A, can be derived in the form

$$P_A = p^{k-m}\left[1 + q(k-m) + \frac{q^2(k-m)(k-m+1)}{2!}\right.$$
$$\left. + \cdots + \frac{q^{k-n-1}(2k-m-n-1)!}{(k-m-1)!(k-n-1)!}\right]$$

Similarly, player B's probability of winning the game, P_B, is given by

$$P_B = q^{k-n}\left[1 + p(k-n) + \frac{q^2(k-n)(k-n+1)}{2!}\right.$$
$$\left. + \cdots + \frac{p^{k-m-1}(2k-m-n-1)!}{(k-m-1)!(k-n-1)!}\right]$$

If $p + q < 1$, the remaining probability $(1 - p - q)$ represents a drawn contest. In either case, the stakes should be divided equitably in the ratio $P_A : P_B$.

Casino games

While many ingenious games could be invented based on coin tossing, or its equivalent, or on drawing balls from urns, the gambling emporia of the world have generally ignored these possibilities. Rather, there has been emphasis on games that offer high odds—that is, a large payoff against a small wager (with correspondingly low probability of winning). Roulette, slot machines, Bingo, lotteries, sweepstakes, pools, and raffles constitute the great majority of the high-payoff games; all are linked by a common characteristic: No nontrivial optimal strategy exists or has a meaning. That is, in these games, once having selected that category of wager which maximizes the mathematical expectation (invariably negative under normal circumstances), any further refinements, such as a process to select a number for betting, is irrelevant unless, of course, the player is guided by some peculiar subjective utility function. Thus, these games are relatively unimaginative and uninteresting, since they are completely described by the most trivial aspects of gambling theory.

ROULETTE

Roulette is the oldest casino game still in operation and, to many, the most glamorous. Its invention has been attributed to Pascal, to the ancient Chinese, to a French monk, and to an Italian mathematician imprecisely referred to as Don Pasquale, who posed the question of the probabilities of selecting numbers from a set of 36 (to the children of a family where he was employed as a tutor). In any event, the game was introduced into Paris in the year 1765 by Gabriel de Sartine, a police lieutenant, who had been searching for a new gambling device that would not be readily subject to the tricks of the countless sharpers then abounding in Paris. Its popularity was immediate and overwhelming. When the Monte Carlo casino was inaugurated in 1863, Roulette was the most widely played game, proving a particular favorite of the upper classes. The men who "broke the bank" at Monte Carlo almost inevitably performed that feat at Roulette.

The American Roulette mechanism and the betting layout are illustrated in Fig. 4-7. The arrangement of the numbers 1 through 36 plus 0 and 00 is not selected at random, but represents an attempt to alternate high–low and odd–even numbers as well as red–black colors. In Europe and South America the wheels are constructed with but one zero (green); the arrangement of the numbers along these wheels differs from that of American Roulette, although each number retains the same color (also, the European wheel is generally smaller than the American).

A ball is spun in a direction counter to that of the wheel's motion. The winning number is that compartment in which the ball comes to rest. Thirteen types of wagers are offered by the Roulette layout. Table 4-1 summarizes these wagers with the associated payoffs. The split or *à cheval* bet is effected by placing the wager on any line separating any two numbers.

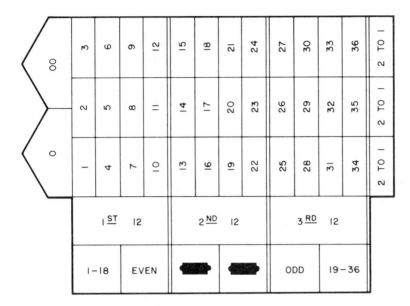

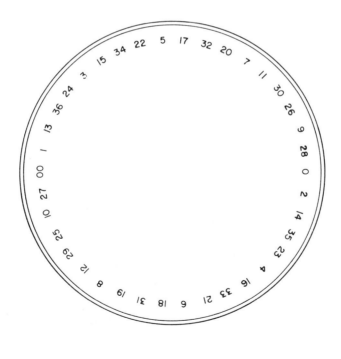

Fig. 4-7 The American Roulette wheel and layout

TABLE 4-1   Roulette Payoffs and Probabilities

Type of Bet	Payoff	Single-trial Probability of Success (American Roulette)	Single-trial Probability of Success (European Roulette)
Single-number (*en plein*)	35–1	0.4737	0.4865
Two-number, or split (*à cheval*)	17–1	0.4737	0.4865
Three-number, or "street" (*transversale*)	11–1	0.4737	0.4865
Four-number, or square (*carré*)	8–1	0.4737	0.4865
Five-number, or line	6–1	0.4605	
Six-number, or "line" (*sixain*)	5–1	0.4737	0.4865
Twelve-number, or column	2–1	0.4737	0.4865
Twelve-number, or dozen	2–1	0.4737	0.4865
Low or high (*Manque,* or *passe*)	Even	0.4737	0.4931
Odd or even (*Impair,* or *pair*)	Even	0.4737	0.4931
Red or black (*rouge* or *noir*)	Even	0.4737	0.4931
Split, or *a cheval* between red–black and odd–even	2–1	0.4737	0.4865
Split, or *a cheval* between two columns or two dozens	1–2	0.4737	0.4865

To bet on three numbers, the stake is placed on the side line of the layout—only three consecutive numbers $[(n/3) - 2, (n/3) - 1,$ and $n/3]$ are permitted. For a bet on four numbers, the stake is placed on the intersection of the lines between any four numbers according to the arrangement of the layout. The five-number bet is available only for the numbers 1, 2, 3, 0, 00. For six numbers, the wager is placed on the intersection of the side lines and a cross line. The method of betting on columns, dozens, high–low, odd–even, and red–black is self-evident from Fig. 4-7. A bet placed on the line between red and even (or black and odd) wins only if the number at which the ball comes to rest is both red and even (this bet is not admissible in many casinos). Similarly, a split bet between two columns or two dozens is placed on the line between the columns or dozens, thereby giving the player 24 numbers out of 38 (or 37).

In the case of American Roulette, the single-trial probability of success (defined as the probability of occurrence renormalized with respect to an even payoff) of 0.4737 (a "house take" of 5.263 percent) holds for all classes of wagers except the five-number bet, which is inferior. For European Roulette, the "house take" on the number bets is 2.703 percent; a bet on high–low, odd–even, or red–black does not lose if the ball drops into the 0 slot. In that event, the stake is declared "in prison" and may be recovered if the succeeding outcome matches that of the bet. Thus, the even-payoff bets offer a higher probability of success (a "house take" of only 1.388 percent). In any case, the mathematical expectation of all Roulette wagers is negative, and the game is therefore always unfavorable to those players possessing an objective utility function.

For inexplicable reasons, Roulette has attracted more people with "systems" than any other casino game.[†] The most common approach is based on recording the numbers appearing in play in the hope of detecting a favored one or group. Some then bet on the least favored, following the compensation principle. Others, with more reason, wager on the most favored. To aid this practice, there are many small boutiques in Monte Carlo, for example, that sell Roulette numbers recorded on previous days (one can purchase the Monte Carlo *Revue Scientifique*, containing a month's log of Roulette numbers). As indicated by Theorem I of Chapter 3, no system can alter the expected gain, which, for Roulette, is quite negative. The hope of a positive expected gain lies in detecting a wheel with sufficient bias. Since the numbered compartments along the circumference of the rotating cylinder are separated by thin metal partitions, or frets, it is possible for one or more of these partitions to become weakened or bent, thus creating a bias (a completely flexible fret would double the expected return

[†] A hypnotically idiot "system" was offered by a 1959 issue of *Bohemia*, a Cuban magazine. The "system" depends on the fact that the third column of the betting layout has 8 red numbers and only 4 black numbers. One is advised to wager, consequently, one unit on black and simultaneously one unit on the third column. The "reasoning" then suggests that on the average out of 38 plays, the zero and double-zero each appear once, causing a loss of 4 units; red appears 18 times, of which 8 are in the third column, so that the player will lose the 2 units ten times and win 2 units eight times for a net loss of 4 units in these 18 plays; finally, black appears 18 times, 14 times in the first and second columns, which loses one bet but wins the other for an even break, and four times in the third column, whereupon both bets win for a net gain of 12 units (the column bet pays 2 to 1) over these 18 plays. Overall, the gain is −4 on 0 and 00, −4 on the 18 red numbers, and +12 on the 18 black, thereby netting 4 units for every 38 plays. While the fallacy is evident, the gullibility of the users is beyond comment.

Equally incredible, there have been many well-known personalities, who, specializing in Roulette systems, have devoted countless hours to the subject. Sir Arthur Sullivan, for example, devised 30 different "systems," none of which bore fruit.

from 0.9474 to 1.8948). Irregular bearings and other mechanical imperfections might also create a small bias.[†]

A method that proffers a positive mathematical expectation regardless of the precision of the Roulette mechanism can be exercised with the aid of a small computer. Approximately 20 seconds elapse from the time the Roulette *tourneur* spins the ball along the outer rim of the wheel until the deadline for placing wagers. During this time, the angular velocity of the ball relative to the cylinder can be measured; a moderately simple procedure consists of generating a timing pulse whenever the ball passes the green zero (for example). From the increasing interval between pulses, a small special-purpose computer can readily determine the time-decreasing function of angular velocity. When this function reaches a standard minimum value, predetermined by calibration of the wheel, the ball will separate from the outer rim, fall onto the rotating cylinder, and eventually come to rest in one of the numbered compartments. The average angular rotation of the cylinder over the time required for the ball to drop from the rim into a compartment is also predetermined by calibration. With the addition of a reference phase for the rotating cylinder (which can be determined at any ball velocity), it is thence feasible to predict the final resting position of the ball. It should be noted that the method is independent of the initial momentum (assuming some sensible minimum) imparted to the ball. Operational tests have indicated an expectation of +35 percent.

Another method, due to Thorp,[‡] for developing a positive expectation relies upon the observation that the Roulette apparatus is often aligned with a slight tilt from the horizontal. In such a configuration, the ball will not drop from that sector of the outer rim on the "high" side. A tilt of 0.2°

[†] In 1947, Albert R. Hibbs and Roy Walford, then students at the California Institute of Technology, invaded the Palace and Harold's Club in Reno, Nevada, in search of biased Roulette apparatus. Using a Poisson approximation to the normal distribution, they established confidence limits for distinguishing biased from unbiased wheels. With their criterion, approximately one wheel in four exhibited an unbalance sufficient to overcome the "house take." Significant financial success was achieved at the Reno clubs and subsequently, in 1948, at the Golden Nugget in Las Vegas. To eliminate the labor of recording numbers generated·by the Roulette game, a stroboscope might be applied to detect any appreciable distortion in the frets between compartments. One could also apply the chi-square test to investigate the possibility of bias.

Hibbs and Walford were preceded in their exploitation of biased wheels by an English engineer named William Jaggers who, at the end of the nineteenth century, won 1,500,000 francs from the Monte Carlo casino following a frequency analysis of Roulette history. The record for stamina in Roulette recording is likely held by Allan Wilson, with a tally of 80,000 continuous plays (100,000 in all).

[‡] Thorp, Edward O., "Optimal Gambling Systems for Favorable Games," *Rev. Inst. Internat. Statist.* 37, No. 3 (1969).

creates a forbidden zone of about 30 percent of the wheel. The ball's motion on the rim is described by the nonlinear differential equation for a pendulum that at first revolves completely around its point, but gradually loses momentum until it oscillates through a narrower angle.

The forbidden zone partially quantizes the angle at which the ball can leave the rim, and therefore quantizes the final angular position of the ball on the inner cylinder (as a function of initial conditions). This quantization is exceptionally narrow: the greater velocity (and longer path to the inner cylinder) of a ball leaving the rim beyond the low point of the tilted wheel balances almost precisely the lower velocity (and shorter path) of a ball leaving at the low point. Thorp has designed and constructed a hand-held computer capable of predicting up to eight revolutions of the ball in advance of its leaving the rim. He reports an expectation of +44 percent.

DOUBLE ROULETTE

In February, 1936, the game of Double Roulette was installed at the Monte Carlo casino. The mechanism consisted of two concentric cylinders, independent and adjoining, each containing 37 numbers. At each play two numbers were selected by spinning two balls independently; to win, the player was required to have wagered upon both winning numbers (separate betting layouts were provided for the inner and outer wheels)—otherwise he lost the two wagers. If both numbers appeared, the player was paid off at odds of 1200 to 1 (a "house take" of 12.272 percent). The player could also bet two numbers (*à cheval*) on each wheel, and if both pairs were represented by the two winning numbers, the payoff was 280 to 1 (a "house take" of 17.896 percent). Betting three numbers on each wheel won at odds of 120 to 1 if the two winning numbers represented both triplets (a "house take" of 20.453 percent). Winning combinations from bets of four numbers on each wheel paid 64 to 1 (a "house take" of 24.032 percent). Finally, the player could wager on combinations of six numbers on each wheel, with a payoff of 25 to 1 (a "house take" of 31.629 percent). These odds involved too great a "house take" even for the carriage grade of Monte Carlo and the game of Double Roulette was soon consigned to oblivion.

MULTICOLORE

The game of Multicolore was introduced at Monte Carlo in the mid-1950's. It consists of a spinning wheel divided into 25 compartments. A billiard ball is rolled, at random, onto the wheel, settling into a shallow cup corresponding to one of the 25 divisions. The divisions are distinguished

Fig. 4-8   Multicolore

by five colors: six greens, reds, whites, and yellows, and a single blue. Each set of colors is numbered 4-3-3-3-2-2 and the single blue division is numbered 24. A player places his stake according to the colors; if the ball comes to rest at the color selected, the player is paid the odds of 2 to 1, 3 to 1, 4 to 1, or 24 to 1, as indicated by the number of the winning compartment. A sketch of the Multicolore apparatus is shown in Fig. 4-8. Evidently, a wager on green, red, white, or yellow yields a mathematical expectation of −0.08 (a "house take" of 8 percent), whereas a wager on blue offers even odds for a zero mathematical expectation.

LA BOULE

Another wheel game, similar to Roulette and Multicolore, is La Boule, played in most European casinos. The wheel and betting layout are illustrated in Fig. 4-9. Wagers can be placed on any of the nine numbers, on

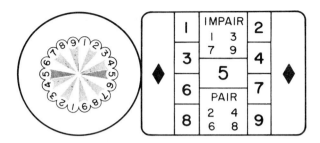

Fig. 4-9   La Boule

noir (1, 3, 6, 8) or *rouge* (2, 4, 7, 9), on *impair* (1, 3, 7, 9) or *pair* (2, 4, 6, 8), and on *manque* (1, 2, 3, 4) or *passe* (6, 7, 8, 9). Single-number bets are assigned a payoff of 7 to 1 (many casinos pay only 6 to 1, compared to equitable odds of 8 to 1) for an expected return of 0.889. The other, multiple, bets offer an even payoff (compared to equitable odds of 1.25 to 1); since the number 5 is excluded,[†] each wager has four chances out of nine of winning—that is, a single-trial probability of success of 0.444 (a "house take" of 11.11 percent).

The same principle of La Boule, based on a total of nine numbers, can be applied to other numbers. For example, the game of Avions (which rated a brief appearance at Monte Carlo) is based on 17. *Pair–impair*, *manque–passe*, and *rouge–noir* pay even odds, while single-number bets offer 15 to 1. Wagers on groups of four numbers are available at odds of 3 to 1 (the number 9 is omitted from all but the single-number bets). The "house take" in the game of Avions is 5.88 percent.

SLOT MACHINES

Such games as Bingo, Keno, lotteries, pools, raffles, punchboards, slot machines, etc., differ only in superficial mechanical aspects from the basic wheel games. Since the player has no inexpensive means of confirming the mathematical expectation, it is usually quite low. Slot machines,[‡] for example, range from an expected return of about 0.9 in the more liberal

---

[†] For obvious reasons, the 5 is sometimes referred to in France as *l'ami de la maison*.

[‡] The ancestors of the modern slot machines were called "Buffaloes;" they were constructed similar to wheels of fortune in an upright box. Ninety spaces were partitioned around the circumference of the wheel: 30 red, 30 black, 16 green, 8 yellow, 4 white, and 2 blue spaces. A coin was inserted into a slot representing a particular color and the wheel spun. If the pointer stopped on a red space and the red slot contained a coin, the payoff was 2 to 1. Blue yielded a payoff of 39 to 1 (correct odds: 44 to 1).

The first practical slot machine, the classic Liberty Bell, was invented in 1895 by Charles Fey, a San Francisco mechanic. Return of the money inserted was reportedly set at 60 percent. Generally, slot machines consist of three independent reels, each with 20 decals.

casinos to virtually zero in the "crooked" ones. There is no way of establishing a priori the "house take" of the esurient "one-armed bandits" (on the dubious assumption that each decal on each reel appears equiprobably, the composition of the reels can be determined in a few plays; given the payoffs, the expected return is thence computable). For those who feel that the expected odds are insufficiently inequitable, some casinos feature two, three, or four slot machines joined together and operated by a single lever; the payoff is normally increased arithmetically (with the number of linked machines), while the probability of success drops exponentially. Despite the "take," slot machines usually predominate in most casinos; in Las Vegas they outnumber all other forms of gambling by more than 10 to 1.

The only legitimate methods of increasing the slot machine expected return to a value greater than unity are based upon mechanical imperfections. One example is the celebrated "rhythm method." Discovered in 1949 by an Idaho farmer who had aided a friend in repairing slot machines, this method rested on the fact that certain symbols would reappear after a certain number of seconds if they had previously stopped near the pay line. A player could insert a coin, pull the handle, pause for the correct time interval, and pull the handle a second time. The concomitant payoff was approximately 120 percent of the funds invested. By 1951 the slot machine manufacturers had installed a "variator," which caused the symbols to appear at varying intervals, thereby destroying the effectiveness of the "rhythm method." Subsequently, the mechanical speed regulator was replaced by a hydraulic oil-filled cylinder with a piston at one end.

Another example of profiting from imperfections of the slot machines is the so-called Sydney system, discovered by an Australian named George Clampett. The method of play is based on slight differences in release times of the three reels when the handle is pulled. Specifically, it is possible through skillful pressuring of the handle to lock the left-hand reel in place while spinning the second and third reels until a paying combination of symbols is obtained. The high degree of skill required to exploit the "Sydney system" has apparently discouraged most slot machine enthusiasts.

POOLS, LOTTERIES, AND SWEEPSTAKES

Many pools, notably those based on European football (soccer), have proved enormously popular. In the case of the government-sponsored English pool, the expected return is 0.5, since 30 percent of the gross sales is returned to the government and 20 percent to the promoters. However, at the time of this writing, winnings are tax-free in England, thereby assuaging some who are repelled by highly unfavorable games. The largest prize in the history of the English football pools is $947,400, garnered by a Lincolnshire factory worker (September, 1966) on a 52-cent bet. The greatest winning odds to date have been achieved by an unidentified man who, on October 11, 1960, won $493,515 for a one-farthing (7/24 cent) bet, the payoff occurring at odds greater than 169 million to 1. In the United States, baseball and basketball pools frequently offer smaller expected returns (often about 0.4). Lotteries are slightly better. The Italian, French, and English national lotteries offer an expected return on investment on the order of 0.6. The Swedish national lottery (the "penning-lotteriet") has an 0.5 value and the Puerto Rican lottery offers about 0.68. In Latin America, the return is often much less, as lotteries are traditionally devoted to financing everything from soccer stadiums to revolutions. As a numerical example, the French National Lottery awards, out of sales of about 100 million francs, one prize of 3 million francs, five prizes of 1 million francs, five of 500,000 francs, 100 of 100,000 francs, 100 of 50,000 francs, 200 of 25,000 francs, 1000 of 10,000 francs, 10,000 of 1000 francs, and 100,000 consolation prizes of 100 francs (old francs, that is). Thus, the expected return of a 100-franc ticket is 60.5 francs.

Similar figures apply to sweepstakes. The principle herein is to associate the lottery with a prominent horse race. A number of winning tickets are selected at random, proportional to the number of horses entered in the particular event; each ticket is then matched to a specific horse. In the French sweepstakes, the "Win, Place, and Show" horses contribute a payoff of 3 million francs, $1\frac{1}{2}$ million francs, and 1 million francs, respectively, with the other tickets drawn receiving consolation prizes. The expected return of a French sweepstakes ticket is approximately 0.57. The more popular Irish sweepstakes bestows a smaller return of about 0.4. A peculiarly Italian institution is the Totopapa, a lottery based on the outcome of a papal election. It offers an expected return of about 0.5.

Lotteries were prevalent in Roman times and were exploited for both public and private profit. The first-known public lottery was sponsored by Augustus Caesar to raise funds for repairing the city of Rome; the first public lottery awarding money prizes, the Lotto de Firenze, was established in Florence in 1530. In the United States, lotteries and raffles were once considered indispensable to the nation's growth. In fact, the American colonies were floated on lotteries—the Virginia colonization company was organized through the permission of King James I in 1612 to conduct a revenue-raising lottery. By a resolution of 18 Nov., 1776, the Continental Congress established a $10 million lottery, "for carrying on the present most just and necessary war in defence of the lives, liberties, and property of the inhabitants of these United States." It was intended that $8,500,000 be returned to the ticket holders, leaving $1,500,000 for expenses and profit. However, the lottery was undersold and accounted for less than one-third of the anticipated gain. In April, 1963, New Hampshire became the first state to sanction lotteries since Louisiana rescinded its lottery law in 1894, following congressional action to prohibit the sending of lottery tickets through the mail. Within eight years, New York and New Jersey joined the gambling fraternity.

KENO

Such games as Bingo (probably descended from the Italian parlor game, Lotto) and Keno have expectations varying with entrance fees and value of the prizes. Bingo normally consists of a card imprinted with a 5×5 array of numbers selected from the set 1 to 75 (except for the center position, which is marked "free"), which are matched against a sequence of numbers generated by a wheel or some other random device. "Bingo" is attained with the matching of five colinear numbers.

The game of Keno has become formalized with its adoption by many of the Las Vegas casinos. Twenty numbers are selected at random by the "house" from the set of numbers 1 through 80. The player can select from 1 to 15 numbers of the set; a win occurs if some fraction of the player's subset matches with any of the 20 numbers drawn by the "house." In general, if the player selects n numbers, the probability $P(k)$ that $k \leq n$ will be among the 20 selected from the set 1 through 80 is

$$P(k) = \frac{\binom{20}{k}\binom{80-20}{n-k}}{\binom{80}{n}} \qquad 4\text{-}39$$

When the player selects but one number, $n = k = 1$ and $P(k) = 0.25$. Equitable odds, therefore, are 3 to 1; the "house," however, offers 2.2 to 1 for an expected return of 0.8. For $n = 2$, both numbers are required to be among the 20 selected to qualify as a win: thus, from Eq. 4-39, with $n = k = 2$, $P(k) = 0.06$, "House" odds are 12 to 1, yielding an expected return of 0.7816.

A more typical wager at Keno consists of selecting 10 numbers. In this case, the "house" offers a payoff if 5 or more of the 10 are among the 20 called. Table 4-2 shows the probability of matching k numbers ($0 \leq k \leq$

10) for $n = 10$ and the associated "house" payoffs. The "house" pays the indicated return for values of k from 5 through 10, thereby proffering an expected return of 0.7942—a "house take" in excess of 20 percent. Other admissible bets allow the player to select any n between 0 and 15; the payoffs are generally awarded for values of k greater than about $n/2$. Overall, the "house take" varies from about 20 percent for the smaller values of n to more than 30 percent for $n = 15$.

TABLE 4-2   Keno Payoffs and Probabilities

k Matches	$P(k)$	"House" Odds	Expected Value
0	0.0458		
1	0.1796		
2	0.2952		
3	0.2674		
4	0.1473		
5	0.0514	Even	0.1029
6	0.0115	17–1	0.2066
7	0.0016	179–1	0.2900
8	1.35×10^{-4}	1299–1	0.1760
9	6.12×10^{-6}	2599–1	0.0159
10	1.12×10^{-7}	24,999–1	0.0028
			Total = 0.7942

The rationale used by most players (subconsciously) in betting on Keno games (or any game with negative mathematical expectation) is that the utility of m dollars is greater than m times the utility of one dollar (perhaps the technical term "utility" should be replaced in this context by the more descriptive word "lure"). It is strange that the casinos do not cater to this taste by increasing the expected value for the less probable events. For example, in the Keno game where $n = 10$, the payoff for ten matches could be increased to 1,000,000 to 1 while yet leaving a "house take" of almost 10 percent.

The more eclectic devotee of gambling theory will tend to avoid such games as Keno, Bingo, Roulette, and the like, since no significant decision-making process is involved and their mathematical expectations remain stubbornly negative. Only the imposition of an urgent, subjective utility function would entice such a player to these games of "pure chance."

Problems

The following miscellaneous games are raised as a challenge to the dedicated reader.

1. *The Jai-Alai Contest.* In a Jai-Alai game, two players from a group of n compete for a point while the remaining $n - 2$ players form a waiting line. The loser between each contending pair takes his place at the end of the line while the winner is then matched with the first waiting player. That player who first accumulates $n - 1$ points is declared the game winner. Letting p_{ij} represent the single-trial probability of success for the ith player when matched against player j, what is the probability P_i that the ith player becomes the first to garner the required $n - 1$ points?

2. *Increasing Opportunities.* An event occurs with constant probability p. Player A is awarded the first opportunity to achieve that event. If he fails, player B is given two opportunities. Thence, in the event of no success, player A is offered three tries, etc. (each player receives one more opportunity than given his opponent on the previous play), until the event occurs. For what value of p is the game fair? That is, solve

$$\frac{1}{2} = p + (1 - p)^3[1 - (1 - p)^3]$$

$$+ (1 - p)^{10}[1 - (1 - p)^5] + (1 - p)^{21}[1 - (1 - p)^7] + \cdots$$

$$= \sum_{j=0}^{\infty} q^{2j^2 + j} - q \sum_{j=0}^{\infty} q^{2j^2 + 3j}$$

where $q = 1 - p$.

3. *A Sampling Game.* Of three urns, one contains 75 white balls and 25 black balls, a second urn contains 50 white and 50 black balls, and a third urn contains 25 white and 75 black balls. The player may sample (without replacement) as many balls as desired from each urn at the cost of one unit per ball drawn. Whenever he wishes, he may attempt to identify the three urns (according to their contents), winning $a > 1$ units if correct and losing $b > 1$ units if incorrect. What sample should be taken and from what urns? This problem can also be posed using replacement of each sampled ball.

4. *The Variable Payoff Matrix.* Each of two players is given four markers. Player A's markers are labeled $+4$, $+3$, $+2$, and $+1$, while B's are labeled -4, -3, -2, and -1. Beginning with A, the players alternately place a personal marker on any empty square of a 3×3 checkerboard

whose center square is marked with a 0. When all nine squares of the board are filled, the players then execute the game matrix that has been constructed by the previous moves. Compute the optimum strategies available to each player.

For a more complex version of this game, let A select his four markers from the set $+1, +2, \ldots, +n$, and B select his from the set $-1, -2, \ldots, -n$. Yet another variant might allow both players to choose markers from a common set.

5. *Extreme-Value Roulette.* Consider the wager—available with a conventional Roulette apparatus—that the highest outcome of the first n plays is a number that exceeds all those numbers obtained over the subsequent m plays (the 0 and 00 can be ranked low). What values of m and n and what corresponding payoff would reasonably be acceptable to the management of a casino? Show that as the set of numbers on the wheel becomes arbitrarily large, the probability that the highest of the first n numbers exceeds the subsequent m numbers approaches $n/(n + m)$. *Note:* The general problem of exceedances lies in the domain of extreme-value statistics; see Emil J. Gumbel, *Statistics of Extremes*, Columbia University Press, 1958.

Suggested references

BERTRAND, JOSEPH, "Calcul des Probabilités. Solution d'un Problème," *Comptes Rendus de l'Académie des Sciences*, Paris, **105** (1887), pp. 437–439.

BOLL, MARCELL, *La Chance et les Jeux de Hazard*, Librairie Larousse, Paris, 1936.

BRADT, R. N., S. M. JOHNSON, and S. KARLIN, "On Sequential Designs for Maximizing the Sum of n Observations," *Ann. Math. Statistics*, **27**, No. 4 (December, 1956), pp. 1060–1074.

DRESHER, MELVIN, *Games of Strategy—Theory and Application*, Prentice-Hall, Inc., New Jersey, 1961.

DVORETZKY, ARYEH, and TH. MOTZKIN, "A Problem of Arrangements," *Duke Mathematical J.*, **14**, No. 2 (June, 1947), pp. 305–313.

FELDMAN, DORIAN, "Contributions to the 'Two-Armed Bandit' Problem," *Ann. Math. Statistics*, **33**, No. 3 (September, 1962), pp. 847–856.

FELLER, WILLIAM, *An Introduction to Probability Theory and Its Applications*, John Wiley & Sons, Inc., New York, 2d. ed., 1957.

HAGELBARGER, D. W., "SEER, A SEquence Extrapolation Robot," *I.R.E. Trans. on Electronic Computers*, Vol. EC-5, No. 1 (March, 1956).

LESSING, RONALD, "The Duration of Bingo Games," *J. Recreational Math.* 7, No. 1 (Winter 1974), pp. 56–59.

LEVY, PAUL, "Sur Certains Processus Stochastiques Homogènes," *Compositio Mathematica*, **7**, (1939), pp. 283–339.

MARBE, K., *Die Gleichförmigkeit in der Welt*, Munich, 1916.

MARCUS, MICHAEL B., "Sequential Decision Problems With a Limited Memory," The RAND Corporation, Report P-1201, Santa Monica, Calif., October 17, 1957.

MIDAS, *How To Win At This And That*, Fontana Books, London, 1964.

PEARSON, KARL, "Scientific Aspects of Monte Carlo Roulette," *Fortnightly Review*, February, 1894.

PHILLIPS, HUBERT, *Pools and the Punter*, Watts, London, 1955.

RIORDAN, JOHN, "The Enumeration of Election Returns by Number of Lead Positions," *Ann. Mathematical Statistics*, **35**, No. 1 (March, 1964), pp. 369–379.

ROBBINS, HERBERT, "A Sequential Decision Problem With a Finite Memory," *Proc. Nat. Acad Sci. U.S.*, **42** (December, 1956), pp. 920–923.

SCARNE, JOHN, *Scarne's Complete Guide to Gambling*, Simon and Shuster, Inc., New York, 1961.

TAKACS, LAJOS, "A Generalization of the Ballot Problem and Its Application in the Theory of Queues," *J. Am. Statistical Assoc.*, **57**, No. 298 (June, 1962), 327–337.

USPENSKY, J. V., *Introduction to Mathematical Probability*, McGraw-Hill Book Company, Inc., New York, 1937.

VON MISES, RICHARD, *Mathematical Theory of Probability and Statistics*, Academic Press, Inc., New York, 1964.

WHITE, GERALD M., "Penny Matching Machines," *Information and Control*, Vol. 2 (December, 1959), pp. 349–363.

CHAPTER FIVE

COUPS AND GAMES WITH DICE

A brief chronicle

The casting of knuckle bones for amusement, profit, or divination dates from the dawn of civilization. As knucklebones were marked and evolved into dice, cleromancy (divination by dice) and gambling became intimately intermingled—the gods of old shaped human destiny by rolling dice and then used the same dice in games among themselves. One of the oldest mythological fables tells of Mercury playing at dice with Selene and winning from her the five days of the epact (thus totalling the 365 days of the year and harmonizing the lunar and solar calendars). In the same vein, it was reported by Herodotus that the Egyptian Pharaoh Rhamsinitus regularly rolled dice with the goddess Ceres. The entire world in the great Sanskrit epic, the Mahābhārata,[†] is treated as a game of dice in which Siva (god of a thousand names) plays with his queen, the fortunes of the dice thrown determining the fate of mankind.

Both the Greeks[‡] and the Romans were enthusiastic dice devotees, casting the tessera (cube) and talus (elongated cube) in their games (in the Far East, the teetotum, or spinning die, was more common); the talus was

---

[†] One tale from the Mahābhārata tells of the pious and righteous King Yudhishthira, gambling with Sakuni, an expert with false dice. Yudhishthira lost all.

[‡] According to post-Homeric legend, the invention of dice is attributed to Palamedes during the Trojan war. On the other hand, according to Herodotus, the Lydians claimed to be the originators of dice.

occasionally numbered 1, 3, 4, 6, leaving the ends unassigned. Regal and passionate dice players of fame in ancient Rome included Nero, Augustus, Caligula, Claudius I,[†] Domitian, and Julius Caesar. Dice were still requisitioned for sortilege, divination, or judicial decision, the most renowned example being the episode of Julius Caesar tossing a die to resolve his indecision over a crossing of the Rubicon. During the Middle Ages, dice playing was one of the favorite pastimes of the knights and ladies. Dicing schools and guilds of dicers prospered—all despite repeated interdiction. Charles V of France in 1369 forbade the play of certain games of chance, and an edict of the provost of Paris in 1397 prohibited the labor classes from playing at "tennis, bowls, dice, cards, or nine-pins on working days."

It was known by the Greek geometers that five regular polyhedra exist. The tetrahedron, with four equilateral triangles as faces, does not roll well nor does it offer great variety; the hexahedron, or cube, with six square faces, appears to satisfy both the desired motion and number requirements; the octahedron, with eight faces in the form of equilateral triangles, has greater variety, but rolls a bit too readily; the dodecahedron, with 12 pentagons as faces, and the icosahedron, with 20 equilateral triangles as faces, roll far too fluidly for control in a restricted area and have more possibilities than can be comprehended by the unsophisticated mind. Hence, the adoption of the hexahedron as a die appears to be a natural selective process. It is strange, however, that the octahedron has not been pressed into service by some enterprising modern casino. For more sophisticated gamblers, the use of irregular polyhedra might provide a provocative challenge.

Earliest dice were imprinted with consecutive numbers on opposite faces: 1 opposite 2, 3 opposite 4, and 5 opposite 6. However, as far back as the eighteenth dynasty of Egypt (*ca.* 1370 B.C.), the present standardized format was introduced whereby the two-partitions of 7 are ensconced on opposing faces. Under this constraint there are two topologically distinct constructions for a die (the 3 two-partitions of 7 define three axes; a well-known geometric theorem states that there exist 2 three-dimensional coordinate systems—left-handed and right-handed—which remain distinct under rotation). Most casinos employ right-handed dice—the values 1, 2, and 3 progress counterclockwise around their common corner—although the left-handed variety are occasionally seen.

[†] Claudius (10 B.C.–A.D. 54), the grandson of Mark Antony (who had whiled away odd moments at Alexandria engaging in dice games), was the author of a book, *How to Win at Dice*, which, unfortunately, has not survived.

The word "die" retains an obscure provenance. The French scholar DuCange suggested that the expression *jeu de dé* is derived by corruption from *juis de dé = judicium dei* (judgement of God). Scheler (*Dictionnaire Étymologique*) argued, however, that *dé* = die stems not from *deus*, but from *datum*, which first signified chance—that is, that which is given or thrown.

Detection of Bias

It was dice problems that contributed the initial impetus to the development of probability theory. Cardano, Pascal, and Fermat enunciated the concept of equally likely outcomes for the six sides of the die to face upward; thus, by definition, the probability that any one side will face upward is 1/6 (more rigorously, one must establish the necessary and sufficient conditions for the applicability of the limiting ratio of the entire aggregate of possible future throws as the probability of any one particular throw). Many experimenters have attempted to confirm (or dispute) this figure empirically. The most widely published dice data were compiled by the English biologist W. F. R. Weldon, who recorded 26,306 throws of 12 dice, and the Swiss scientist, Rudolf Wolf, who performed 100,000 throws (!) of a single die.

Wolf's experiment produced a *1*, 16,632 times; a *2*, 17,700 times; a *3*, 15,183 times; a *4*, 14,393 times; a *5*, 17,707 times; and a *6*, 18,385 times. The validity of the hypothesis that the probability of each side appearing up is 1/6 may be checked by the χ^2 test (Eq. 2-37):

$$\chi^2 = \sum_{i=1}^{k} \frac{(r_i - s_i)^2}{s_i}$$

where r_i is the actual number of times the ith side appears, s_i the predicted number, and k the number of possible outcomes. If $\chi^2 = 0$, exact agreement is evidenced. As χ^2 increases for a given number of trials, the probability of bias increases. Applying the χ^2 test to Wolf's data, we obtain

$$\chi^2 = \frac{12,474,769}{16,667} = 748.5$$

To comprehend the significance of this value, we note from Eq. 2-36 that repeating this experiment theoretically should yield a distribution of χ^2 given by

$$f(\chi^2) = \frac{(\chi^2)^{(k-3)/2} e^{-\chi^2/2}}{2^{(k-1)/2} \Gamma[(k-1)/2]} \qquad 5\text{-}1$$

with $n = k - 1$ degrees of freedom. A die obviously exhibits 5 degrees of freedom. We now wish to designate a value of χ_0^2 such that the probability of χ^2 exceeding χ_0^2 represents the significance level of the experimental results. Selecting a significance level of 0.01, we can, from Eq. 5-1, find a value χ_0^2 such that

$$P[\chi^2 > \chi_0^2] = \int_{\chi_0^2}^{\infty} p_n(x)\, dx = 0.01$$

where p_n is the probability density function. It can be established[†] that $\chi_0^2 = 15.1$ appertains for the case under consideration. That is, if the die were perfect, rolling it repeatedly 100,000 times would result less than 1 percent of the time in a value of χ^2 greater than 15.1. Since $\chi^2 = 748.5$, we may conclude that the probability of Wolf's die being unbiased is vanishingly small. We might have suspected this fact, since all faces of the die except the 1 differ by considerably more than the standard deviation, $\sigma = 117.8$, from the expected value of 16,667.

Weldon's data recorded the event that of $12 \times 26{,}306 = 315{,}672$ possibilities, the numbers 5 or 6 appeared on the dice 106,602 times—which yield a one-degree-of-freedom χ^2 value of 27.1 (the equivalent figure from Wolf's data is 342.5). A reasonable conclusion is that a die of poor quality (such as those manufactured in the nineteenth century) is likely to develop a bias when thrown a large number of times. The dice employed by the major gambling casinos are generally machined to tolerances of 1/2000 inch, are of hard homogeneous material, and are rolled only a few hundred times on a soft green felt surface before being retired. Thus, the probability of finding an unintentionally biased die—and determining wherein lies the bias—in a casino is quite small.

A final question concerning biased dice relates to the number of throws of a die necessary to ascertain the existence of a bias (we assume throughout that the rolls of a die comprise a stationary statistic—that is, the bias is not altered with time). A bound to the number of throws required is given by Bernoulli's form of the law of large numbers. Let S be the number of successes in n throws of the die with probabilities p and $q = 1 - p$ for success and failure, respectively, of a given alternative, and let $f_n = S/n$ be the relative frequency of successes. Then, for any number $\varepsilon > 0$ and any number $\eta (0 < \eta < 1)$, we have

$$P(|f_n - p| < \varepsilon) \geq 1 - \eta \qquad \text{for any integer } n \geq pq/\varepsilon^2\eta \qquad 5\text{-}2$$

Illustratively, we can ask how many throws of a die are required to ensure

---

[†] χ_0^2 is obtained most readily from tables of the χ^2 distribution; for example, R. A. Fisher, *Statistical Methods for Research Workers*, Oliver and Boyd, Edinburgh.

a probability of 0.95 ($\eta = 0.05$) that the relative frequency of the outcome 6 differs from the results expected of a perfect die ($p = 1/6$, $q = 5/6$) by not more than $\varepsilon = 0.01$. Substituting into Eq. 5-2:

$$P\left(\left|f_n - \frac{1}{6}\right| < 0.01\right) \geq 0.95 \qquad \text{for } n \geq \frac{(1/6)(5/6)}{(0.01)^2(0.05)} = 27{,}778$$

Therefore, 27,778 throws of a perfect die will ensure a relative frequency of $1/6 \pm 0.01$, with at least a 0.95 confidence. If we suspect the die of bias, we obtain a bound on the number of throws to determine p by observing that the maximum value of $pq = p(1 - p)$ is $1/4$. Therefore,

$$n \geq \frac{1/4}{\varepsilon^2 \eta}$$

and for $\varepsilon = 0.01$ and $\eta = 0.05$, $n \geq 50{,}000$. Thus, 50,000 throws of a suspected die are sufficient to determine p to an accuracy of 0.01 with a confidence of 0.95.

Bernoulli's rule, since it is applicable to any distribution, yields a value for n which, in this instance, is extremely conservative. When dealing with a binomial distribution, a better estimate of the requisite number of throws to ascertain a bias is provided by the Laplace–Gauss theorem (a special case of the central limit theorem). The probability that the outcome 6 occurs between np_1 and np_2 times in n throws of a die, where p is the estimated single-trial probability of a 6, is given approximately as

$$P(np_1 \leq np \leq np_2) \simeq \frac{1}{\sqrt{2\pi}} \int_{\frac{n(p_1 - p)}{\sqrt{npq}}}^{\frac{n(p_2 - p)}{\sqrt{npq}}} e^{-x^2/2}\, dx = \Phi\left[\frac{n(p_2 - p)}{\sqrt{npq}}\right]$$

$$- \Phi\left[\frac{n(p_1 - p)}{\sqrt{npq}}\right] \qquad \text{5-3}$$

where $\Phi(x)$ is the cumulative probability function. Thus, the probability that, for a perfect die, p differs from $1/6$ by not more than 0.01 with 0.95 confidence is expressed by

$$P\left(-0.01 \leq p - \frac{1}{6} \leq 0.01\right) \geq 0.95 = P\left\{-0.01\left[\frac{n}{(1/6)(5/6)}\right]^{1/2}\right.$$

$$\leq \left[\frac{n}{(1/6)(5/6)}\right]^{1/2} [p - (1/6)] \leq 0.01\left[\frac{n}{(1/6)(5/6)}\right]^{1/2}\right\}$$

$$\leq \frac{1}{\sqrt{2\pi}} \int_{-0.01\left[\frac{n}{(1/6)(5/6)}\right]^{1/2}}^{0.01\left[\frac{n}{(1/6)(5/6)}\right]^{1/2}} e^{-x^2/2} \, dx = 2\Phi\left(0.06\sqrt{\frac{n}{5}}\right) - 1$$

since $\Phi(-x) = 1 - \Phi(x)$. Hence, the requirement on the number of throws n is governed by the relation

$$\Phi\left(0.06\sqrt{\frac{n}{5}}\right) \geq \frac{0.95 + 1}{2} = 0.975$$

and, from tables of the cumulative probability function, we find that $n = 5335$ throws of the die suffice to obtain a relative frequency of $1/6$ ± 0.01 with a confidence level of 0.95—considerably less than the 27,778 throws suggested by Bernoulli's rule.

Similarly, if we suspect the die of bias and assign an unknown value p to the probability of an outcome, we wish to find the number of throws n sufficient to determine p within a tolerance of 0.01 with 0.95 confidence. The Laplace–Gauss theorem states that

$$P\left[\frac{-0.01n}{\sqrt{npq}} \leq \frac{n(f_n - p)}{\sqrt{npq}} \leq \frac{0.01n}{\sqrt{npq}}\right] \simeq 2\Phi\left(\frac{0.01n}{\sqrt{npq}}\right) - 1 \geq 0.95$$

or

$$\Phi\left(\frac{0.01n}{\sqrt{npq}}\right) \geq 0.975 \tag{5-4}$$

From tables of the cumulative probability function, the condition of Eq. 5-4 is fulfilled for

$$\frac{0.01n}{\sqrt{npq}} \geq 1.96 \tag{5-5}$$

and, since the maximum value of pq is $1/4$, Eq. 5-5 indicates that a bound occurs at $n \geq 9604$. Therefore, 9604 throws of a suspect die can test for bias to within 1 percent with 0.95 confidence; this value, it should be noted, is less than one-fifth that suggested by the Bernoulli rule.

As in the case of coins in the preceding chapter, we now proceed under the assumption that the dice referred to are "fair" and that successive throws of a die are independent. "Fairness" implies that the possible outcomes are equiprobable. The statement of independent successive events signifies that if the events $A_1, A_2, \ldots, A_n$ are independent, the probability of their joint occurrence is the product of the probabilities of their individual occurrences—that is,

$$\text{prob}\{A_1 + A_2 + \cdots A_n\} = \text{prob}\{A_1\} \cdot \text{prob}\{A_2\} \cdots \text{prob}\{A_n\}$$

Finally, it follows that successive dice throws constitute an ergodic process: n throws of one die are equivalent to one throw of n dice.

Probability problems with dice

DE MÉRÉ'S PROBLEM

Dice problems are generally quite susceptible to straightforward analysis. A few simple formulas encompass virtually all forms of dice play. De Méré's problem, which triggered the inception of probability theory, is readily solved by consideration of simple repetitions. If a chance event has a constant probability p of occurrence on any given trial, then the number of trials n required for its first occurrence is a discrete random variable that can assume any of the infinitely many positive integral values $n = 1$, $2, 3, \ldots$. The distribution of n is the geometric distribution (cf. Eq. 2-17)

$$f(n) = q^{n-1}p$$

and the cumulative distribution function $F(n)$ is given by

$$F(n) = \sum_{t=1}^{n} f(t) = 1 - q^n$$

Therefore the probability P_n that the event occurs in n trials is expressed by

$$P_n = F(n) = 1 - (1 - p)^n \qquad\qquad 5\text{-}6$$

De Méré had raised the question of the probability of obtaining at least one 6 in one roll of four dice as compared to the probability of obtaining at least one outcome of double 6 in 24 rolls of two dice. His "reason" indicated that the two probabilities should be identical, but his experience insisted that the former dice game offered a positive expected gain and the latter a negative expected gain. The single-trial probability of rolling a 6 with one die is defined as $p = 1/6$ and that of throwing a double 6 with two dice is $p = (1/6)^2 = 1/36$. Thus the probability P_4 of obtaining at least one 6 in one roll of four dice (or four rolls of one die) is, from Eq. 5-6,

$$P_4 = 1 - \left(1 - \frac{1}{6}\right)^4 = 0.5177$$

and the probability P_{24} of obtaining at least one double 6 in 24 rolls of two dice has the value

$$P_{24} = 1 - \left(1 - \frac{1}{36}\right)^{24} = 0.4914$$

De Méré also inquired as to the number of rolls necessary to ensure a probability greater than 0.5 of achieving the 6 or double 6, respectively. Solving Eq. 5-6 for n,

$$n = \frac{\log(1 - P_n)}{\log(1 - p)}$$

For $p = 1/6$ and $P_n > 1/2$,

$$n > \frac{\log 2}{\log 6 - \log 5} = 3.81$$

Hence, four rolls of a die are required to obtain a probability greater than $1/2$ of rolling a 6. For $p = 1/36$ and $P_n > 1/2$,

$$n > \frac{\log 2}{\log 36 - \log 35} = 24.61$$

Therefore, 25 is the smallest integral number of rolls of two dice which offers a probability greater than $1/2$ of achieving a double 6.

PROBABILITY OF A PARTICULAR OUTCOME

Analogous reasoning to that leading to the formula for simple repetition will conclude that the probability of achieving a particular outcome exactly m times in n throws is the binomial expression

$$P_n^m = \binom{n}{m} p^m q^{n-m} \qquad\qquad 5\text{-}7$$

Thus, the probability P_4^1 of exactly one 6 in four rolls of a die is computed to be

$$P_4^1 = \binom{4}{1}(1/6)(5/6)^3 = 0.386$$

and for the probability P_{24}^1 of obtaining exactly one double 6 in 24 rolls of two dice,

$$P_{24}^1 = \binom{24}{1}(1/36)(35/36)^{23} = 0.349$$

Similarly, if a chance event has constant single-trial probability p, and n

denotes the number of trials up to and including the rth success, the distribution of n has the form

$$f(n) = \binom{n-1}{r-1} p^r q^{n-r}, \qquad n = r, r+1, \ldots \qquad \qquad 5\text{-}8$$

which is recognizable as Pascal's distribution.

In 6000 rolls of a die, we know from Eq. 5-7 that the probability of obtaining the outcome 6 exactly m times is given by

$$P^m_{6000} = \binom{6000}{m} (1/6)^m (5/6)^{6000-m}$$

By extension, the probability that m lies between 950 and 1050 inclusive is then

$$P_{6000}(950 \leq m \leq 1050) = \sum_{m=950}^{1050} \binom{6000}{m} (1/6)^m (5/6)^{6000-m} \qquad 5\text{-}9$$

To evaluate Eq. 5-9, we can apply the normal approximation to the binomial distribution:

$$\sum_{m=a}^{b} \binom{n}{m} p^m q^{n-m} \simeq \frac{1}{\sqrt{2\pi}} \int_{\frac{a-np-(1/2)}{\sqrt{npq}}}^{\frac{b-np+(1/2)}{\sqrt{npq}}} e^{-x^2/2} \, dx$$

$$= \Phi\left(\frac{b-np+(1/2)}{\sqrt{npq}}\right) - \Phi\left(\frac{a-np-(1/2)}{\sqrt{npq}}\right) \qquad 5\text{-}10$$

similar to Eq. 5-3. With this approximation, the probability that in 6000 throws of a die the outcome 6 occurs between 950 and 1050 times is computed as

$$P_{6000}(950 \leq m \leq 1050) \simeq \Phi\left(\frac{1050 - 1000 + 1/2}{\sqrt{6000(1/6)(5/6)}}\right)$$

$$- \Phi\left(\frac{950 - 1000 - 1/2}{\sqrt{6000(1/6)(5/6)}}\right)$$

$$= 2\Phi(1.7494) - 1$$

$$= 0.919$$

from tables of the cumulative probability function for the normal distribution. A perfect die, then, will produce a particular outcome 1000 ± 50 times 91.9 percent of the time over 6000 trials.

A general formula, useful for the solution of many dice games, is that which states the probability $P(s)$ of obtaining a given sum s of the outcomes of n dice (or n throws of one die). Of the 6^n different configurations of n dice, the number of configurations whereby the n outcomes sum to a number s is equivalent to the number of solutions of the equation

$$a_1 + a_2 + \cdots + a_n = s \qquad\qquad 5\text{-}11$$

where each of the a_i's are integers between 1 and 6. A theorem of the discipline of number theory states that the number of solutions of Eq. 5-11 for any n corresponds to the coefficient of x^s in the expansion of the polynomial

$$(x + x^2 + x^3 + x^4 + x^5 + x^6)^n = \left[\frac{x(1 - x^6)}{1 - x}\right]^n$$

Applying the binomial theorem,

$$x^n(1 - x^6)^n = \sum_{j=0}^{n} (-1)^j \binom{n}{j} x^{n+6j} \qquad\qquad 5\text{-}12$$

and

$$(1 - x)^{-n} = \sum_{k=0}^{\infty} \binom{n + k - 1}{n - 1} x^k \qquad\qquad 5\text{-}13$$

Multiplying the two series of Eqs. 5-12 and 5-13 and dividing by 6^n, the total number of configurations, we obtain

$$P(s) = \text{coeff}(x^s) = 6^{-n} \sum_{j=0}^{[(s-n)/6]} (-1)^j \binom{n}{j} \binom{s - 6j - 1}{n - 1} \qquad\qquad 5\text{-}14$$

for the probability of a total of s points on n dice, where $[(s - n)/6]$ is the largest integer contained in $(s - n)/6$. As a numerical example, the game of "Razzle-Dazzle" is played (in Havana) with eight dice. If we were interested, say, in the probability that a throw of these eight dice totals 30, Eq. 5-14 indicates that

$$P(30) = 6^{-8} \sum_{j=0}^{3} (-1)^j \binom{8}{j} \binom{29 - 6j}{7} = 0.0748$$

PROBABILITY OF ALL POSSIBLE OUTCOMES

We can also inquire as to the probability that one throw of n dice ($n \geq 6$) will produce each of the outcomes, $1, 2, \ldots, 6$ at least once. We know from the theorem of total probability (Eq. 2-2) that the probability of events $A_1, A_2, \ldots, A_m$ occurring simultaneously is

$$P(A_1 + A_2 + \cdots + A_m) = \sum_i P(A_i) - \sum_{i,j} P(A_i A_j)$$

$$+ \sum_{i,j,k} P(A_i A_j A_k) - \cdots \qquad 5\text{-}15$$

For the $m = 6$ events possible from the throw of a die, we can show that Eq. 5-15 leads to

$$P_n = \sum_{k=0}^{5} (-1)^k \binom{6}{k} \left(1 - \frac{k}{6}\right)^n$$

for the probability that all possible outcomes of a die are represented in a throw of n dice. Numerically, for $n = 8$,

$$P_8 = 0.114$$

With ten dice, $P_{10} = 0.272$, and with the minimum of six dice, P_6 has the value 0.0154 (P_6 is equivalent to $6!/6^6$). Thirteen dice are required to obtain a probability greater than $1/2$ for the occurrence of all six outcomes ($P_{13} = 0.514$).

A related question concerns the probability P_{6n} that in one throw of $6n$ dice (or $6n$ throws of a single die), all six outcomes are equally represented. It can be readily shown that

$$P_{6n} = (6n)!(n!)^{-6} 6^{-6n}$$

By the aid of Stirling's formula, we can determine that $P_{6n} \simeq n^{-5/2}(2\pi)^{-2}$.

Formal dice games

ODD—EVEN

One of the oldest formalized dice games, extending back several centuries, is the Oriental version of odd–even (Japanese: *cho-han*). A single die is thrown until an odd-numbered outcome appears for the first time. A variation of this game involves wagering on the number of throws of the die for the odd-numbered outcome to appear twice or three times. If p is the single-trial probability of an odd-numbered outcome, and n the number of throws of the die until this outcome occurs for the rth time, the parameter $n - r$ obeys the negative binomial distribution,[†]

$$P(n) = \binom{n-1}{n-r} p^r q^{N-r}, \qquad N = r, r + 1, \dots \qquad 5\text{-}16$$

which, of course, is equivalent to the Pascal distribution of Eq. 5-8. With $p = 1/2$ and $r = 1$,

$$P(n) = (1/2)^n$$

specifying the equitable odds for a wager on n—the event occurs on the first throw with a probability of 0.5. For $r = 2$,

$$P(N) = (n - 1)(1/2)^n$$

and it is an even bet that the event occurs by the third throw. In general, a probability of 0.5 holds that the event occurs by the $(2r - 1)$st throw of the die. A slightly more interesting game consists of wagering on the number of throws to obtain a 6, say, r times. As an example, for $r = 3$ and $p = 1/6$, Eq. 5-16 indicates a probability greater than 0.5 (specifically, 0.513) that the third 6 appears by the sixteenth throw.

NICOLAS BERNOULLI'S GAME—EXPECTED NUMBER OF THROWS TO ACHIEVE A PARTICULAR OUTCOME

A similar but more elementary problem was posed by Nicolas Bernoulli and can be considered the forerunner of the St. Petersburg game. Bernoulli inquired as to the expected value of n in a game consisting of rolling a die until a 6 appears for the first time at the nth throw, the payoff being n units. From Eq. 5-16, the probability of 6 first appearing at the nth throw is seen to be

$$P(n) = (1/6)(5/6)^{n-1} \qquad 5\text{-}17$$

Evidently, the largest value of $P(n)$ in Eq. 5-17 occurs for $n = 1$. Therefore the most probable number of throws to obtain a 6 is 1. The expected number is expressed by

$$E(n) = \frac{1}{6} \sum_{n=1}^{\infty} n(5/6)^{n-1} \qquad 5\text{-}18$$

[†] For an interesting application of the negative binomial distribution, see R. A. Epstein and Lloyd Welch, "A Generalization of the Banach Match-box Problem," Hughes Aircraft Co., Communications Division Report OP-56, September, 1963.

Using the identity $1 + 2x + 3x^2 + \cdots = (1 - x)^{-2}$, Eq. 5-18 becomes

$$E(n) = \frac{1}{6}[1 - (5/6)]^{-2} = 6 \qquad\qquad 5\text{-}19$$

and as we would have anticipated, six throws are expected for obtaining one particular outcome of the die. This value should be clearly distinguished from the number of throws (four) required to obtain a 6 with probability greater than $1/2$.

The specific example of Eq. 5-19 can be generalized by the following theorem.

In any series of trials where the probability of occurrence of a particular event X is constantly p, the expected number of trials to achieve that event $E(X)$ is the reciprocal of the probability of its occurrence.

We can prove this statement by noting that if p is constant, the probability of X first occurring at the ith trial follows the geometric distribution (Eq. 2-17)

$$X(i) = p(1 - p)^{i-1}$$

The expected number of trials is then defined by

$$E(X) = \sum_{i=1}^{\infty} ip(1 - p)^{i-1} = p + \sum_{i=2}^{\infty} ip(1 - p)^{i-1} \qquad\qquad 5\text{-}20$$

With the substitution $j = i - 1$, Eq. 5-20 is rewritten in the form

$$E(X) = p + (1 - p) \sum_{j=1}^{\infty} (j + 1)p(1 - p)^{j-1}$$

Therefore

$$E(X) = p + (1 - p)[E(X) + 1]$$

and

$$E(X) = \frac{1}{p} \qquad\qquad 5\text{-}21$$

As an example, since the probability of rolling the sum of 9 with two dice is $4/36$, the expected number of rolls of two dice to achieve a 9 is nine.

MULTIPLAYER DICE PROBABILITIES

Another dice problem relates to those games wherein the players attempt, in order, to obtain a particular outcome. Let p represent the probability of the outcome with any number of dice and $q = 1 - p$. Player A begins the game, and if he fails to achieve the desired result, he passes the dice to player B, who then essays the goal. The two players continue their turns at the dice until one wins by obtaining the desired result. We can readily show that player A enjoys probability P_A of winning, where

$$P_A = \frac{p}{1 - q^2}$$

while player B is bequeathed the smaller probability P_B of winning:

$$P_B = \frac{pq}{1 - q^2}$$

In general, with m players, the dice being rotated from players 1 to 2 to ... to $m - 1$ to m to 1 to 2 to ... etc., until one player wins, the probability P_k that the kth player wins the game is

$$P_k = \frac{q^{k-1}p}{1 - q^m}$$

We can observe that P_k approaches the limit of $1/m$ (an equitable game for all the players, since it is not a function of k) as $p \to 0$.

JAMES BERNOULLI'S GAME

To illustrate one of the pitfalls inherent in skewed distributions, we consider the following dice game initially propounded by James Bernoulli. Let a solitary player perform one throw of a single die, securing the result i (one of the values 1 through 6). He then selects i dice from a set of six and throws them once (or throws the single die i times), obtaining the sum s_i. If $s_i > 12$, the player receives one unit payment; if $s_i < 12$, he loses one unit; and if $s_i = 12$, the game is declared a tie. The total number of outcomes is 6×6^6, and if we enumerate those contributing a sum greater than, equal to, or less than 12, we conclude that

$$P(s_i > 12) = \frac{130{,}914}{6 \times 6^6} = 0.468$$

$$P(s_i = 12) = \frac{13{,}482}{6 \times 6^6} = 0.048$$

$$P(s_i < 12) = \frac{135{,}540}{6 \times 6^6} = 0.484$$

Comparing these equations, it is apparent that the player is burdened with a negative mathematical expectation [specifically, $0.468(1) - 0.484(-1) = -0.016$]. Yet, the expected sum obtained from throwing i dice according to the game rules is

$$E(s_i) = [E(i)]^2 = (3.5)^2 = 12.25$$

which is greater than the sum specifying a tie. Were the distribution about 12.25 symmetrical rather than skewed, the game would be favorable to the player.

A MAXIMIZATION GAME

A dice game popular for some time, especially among military personnel, consists of throwing five dice simultaneously, declaring one or more of the dice to be "frozen," and repeating the process with the remaining dice until all five dice are "frozen" (in five or less throws). The game's objective is to maximize the sum of the points on the five "frozen" dice. By obtaining a total of s points, a player receives $s - 24$ units from each of the other players ($24 - s$ units are paid to each other player if $s < 24$). We wish to determine an optimal strategy and its corresponding mathematical expectation. The expected sum arising from a throw of one die is, as we have seen in Chapter 2 (Eq. 2-20),

$$E(s_1) = \frac{1}{6}(1 + 2 + 3 + 4 + 5 + 6) = 3\tfrac{1}{2}$$

Therefore, with the option of rethrowing one die and declaring it "frozen," we would rethrow it if its outcome were less than the expected value—that is, 1, 2, or 3. With two dice plus the option of rethrowing one, the mathematical expectation of the sum of the points on the two dice is given by

$$E(s_2) = \frac{1}{36}(6 + 6) + \frac{2}{36}(6 + 5) + \frac{2}{36}(6 + 4) + \frac{2}{36}[6 + E(s_1)] + \cdots$$

$$= 8.236$$

With three dice plus the option of rethrowing two, one of which may be thrown for the third time, the expectation of the sum is

$$E(s_3) = \frac{1}{216}(6 + 6 + 6) + \frac{3}{216}(6 + 6 + 5) + \cdots$$

$$= 13.425$$

Similarly, throwing four dice with rethrow options according to the stated rule produces an expectation of the sum of

$$E(s_4) = \frac{1}{6^4}(6 + 6 + 6 + 6) + \frac{4}{6^4}(6 + 6 + 6 + 5) + \cdots$$

$$= 18.844$$

and with five dice, according to the game rules, the mathematical expectation of the sum has the value

$$E(s_5) = \frac{1}{6^5}(6 + 6 + 6 + 6 + 6) + \frac{5}{6^5}(6 + 6 + 6 + 6 + 5) + \cdots$$

$$= 24.442$$

The optimal strategy is indicated by these expectations. Thus, the option of rethrowing one die should be exercised if its outcome is 3 or less, since the expectation of the rethrow is higher (3.5). With the option of rethrowing two dice, combinations totaling 9 or less should be (at least partially) rethrown. For example, 4-4 is rethrown and 5-4 declared "frozen"; with the combination 5-3, only the 3 should be rethrown, resulting in an expectation of $5 + 3\frac{1}{2} = 8.5$ [rethrowing the 5 and the 3 results, of course, in an expectation of $E(s_2) = 8.236$]. With the option of rethrowing three dice, all combinations totaling 15 or less should be examined to determine whether rethrowing one, two, or three dice maximizes the expectation. As examples, with 5-5-3, we "freeze" the two 5's and rethrow the 3 [$10 + E(s_1)$ is the maximum value], and with 5-4-4 we rethrow all three dice [$E(s_3)$ is maximum]. Following the first roll of the game we have the option of rethrowing four dice. Here we examine all combinations totaling 21 or less, to determine whether rethrowing one, two, three, or four dice maximizes the expectation. Illustratively, with 5-5-5-3 we would rethrow all four dice [resulting in $E(s_4)$] and with 6-5-4-4 we would rethrow the 5-4-4 [resulting in $6 + E(s_3)$]. Clearly, a 6 is never rethrown; 5 and 4 are rethrown or not, depending on the number of dice remaining with rethrow options; and 3, 2, and 1 are always rethrown whenever permitted by the rules. The expected gain $E(G)$ of the game is the sum of the products of each possible payoff by its corresponding probability,

$$E(G) = \sum_{s=5}^{30} (s - 24)P(s) \qquad\qquad 5\text{-}22$$

where the values of s can range from 5 (all 1's on the five dice) to 30 (all 6's on the five dice). The values of $P(s)$ are computed by delineating the various combinations of dice that total each value of s; the results are presented

TABLE 5-1   Maximization Game Probabilities

s	P(s)	s	P(s)	s	P(s)	s	P(s)	s	P(s)
30	0.0109	25	0.1410	20	0.0397	15	0.0015	10	—
29	0.0383	24	0.1291	19	0.0250	14	0.0005	9	—
28	0.0809	23	0.1076	18	0.0145	13	0.0001	8	—
27	0.1193	22	0.0817	17	0.0076	12	—	7	—
26	0.1401	21	0.0586	16	0.0036	11	—	6	—
								5	—

in Table 5-1.[†] Substituting the appropriate numerical values into Eq. 5-22, we obtain

$$E(G) = 0.438$$

Thus, 25 is the most probable sum achieved by optimal play and the game is highly favorable to the player rolling the dice. The prevailing opinion that the game is nearly equitable is, perhaps, founded on the assumption of nonoptimal strategies.

ALL SIXES

A game similar in its mechanics, although not in the computations, consists of rolling n (usually 5) dice, attempting to achieve the outcome 6 on all dice. Following each throw of the dice, those showing a 6 are set aside and the remainder rethrown; this process is then continued indefinitely until all n dice exhibit a 6. We wish to determine the expected number of throws $E_n(N)$ to obtain all 6's on the n dice according to these rules. The classical method of solving this problem proceeds by computing $P_n(N)$, the probability of achieving the goal with n dice by the Nth throw, and then summing the product $NP_n(N)$ over all values of N and n (from 1 to ∞). This method involves a large number of tedious calculations; fortunately, there exists a clever insight leading to a direct solution of this problem.

The probability of throwing at least one 6 in a roll of n dice is $1 - (5/6)^n$; hence, the expected number of rolls to obtain at least one 6 is $6^n/(6^n - 5^n)$. If the throw that achieves the first 6 contains no other 6's, the probability of which is $n5^{n-1}/(6^n - 5^n)$, the problem reduces to one with $n - 1$ dice. If the throw achieving the first 6 contains exactly one additional 6, the probability of which is

$$\frac{n(n-1)5^{n-2}}{2(6^n - 5^n)}$$

[†] For this problem and others in this book concerned with an enormous number of combinations, an IBM 7090 was used to perform the requisite calculations.

the problem reduces to one with $n - 2$ dice. Proceeding by induction, we are subsequently led to the expression

$$E_n(N) = \frac{6^n + \sum_{k=0}^{n-1} 5^k \binom{n}{k} E_k(N)}{6^n - 5^n}$$

5-23

where $E_0(N) = 0$. For $n = 5$ dice, Eq. 5-23 is evaluated as

$$E_5(N) = 13.024$$

Thus, slightly more than 13 throws are expected to obtain all 6's on five dice with repeated throws of those dice exhibiting non-6's.

TURN THE DIE

A simple strategic dice game suggested by Martin Gardner involves a single die that is given a quarter-turn at each move, recording a running sum of the up-faces exhibited. Player A initially throws the die and then follows player B sequentially in moving the die a quarter-turn. The object of the game is to maneuver the cumulative sum of the up-faces exactly to a specified goal.

Strategy for either player dictates the attempt to force the running sum to a value equal to the residue of the goal, mod 9, or to prevent the opponent from achieving that value. For example, if the goal is set at 31 ($= 4$, mod 9) and player A throws a 4, he strives to include the totals 4-13-22-31 in the running series. Thus, if B plays 6 or 5, A counters with 3 or 4, respectively (totaling 13); if B plays 1 or 2, A shows 4 or 3, respectively, which totals 9 and prevents B from reaching 13 (the 4 is not available). In general, letting r be the residue of the goal, mod 9, one should play to $r - 5$ leaving the 5 on the top or bottom of the die and to $r - 3$, $r - 4$, or $r + 1$ leaving the 4 unavailable.

Except for $r = 0$, a win for player A exists for at least one roll of the die. Table 5-2 indicates the winning rolls for each residue of the goal, mod 9. Clearly, if the first player is afforded the option, he chooses a goal with residue 7, mod 9, thereby obtaining a fair game.

TABLE 5-2   Winning Numbers for Turn-the-Die Game

r	0	1	2	3	4	5	6	7	8
Winning first roll of die		1, 5	2, 3	3, 4	4	5	3, 6	2, 3, 4	4

PIG

A game presenting several unusual facets in terms of strategic concepts is that commonly referred to as Pig. Two dice are thrown in this game and the sum of the points obtained at each roll is recorded and added to the sum achieved on the previous throws. The game's objective is to obtain a cumulative total exceeding 100. Each player is permitted to continue throwing the two dice until (1) the outcome 1 appears on one or both dice, or (2) the player voluntarily relinquishes the dice. The next player then casts the dice a number of times, restricted in the same manner. When a player stops voluntarily, his accumulated sum is designated a "plateau." Subsequently, the appearance of a 1 on either die reverts that player's sum to the previous plateau.

Optimal strategy (when to declare a plateau and surrender the dice) is a function of the previous plateau, the current score, the opponents' plateaus, and the number of opponents. Evidently, the generalized form of Pig entails enormous complexities in the formulation of a strategy. We can approach a quantitative strategy by simplifying the game to a solitaire event wherein the object is to achieve a cumulative total of 24 or more. In this elementary case, the player pays one unit for each turn at the dice—that is, whenever a 1 appears on either die or a plateau is declared. We wish to determine the strategy that minimizes the expected number of units paid (the payoff, upon reaching 24 or more, is presumably some fixed sum). Let (a, b) represent the position of the player with current score a and plateau b. We shall prove that the optimal strategy for this game is never to declare a plateau; it is sufficient to examine this strategy for the case of $a = 23$ and $b = 0$.

Let V be the expected additional cost under a strategy of declaring a plateau at $(23, 0)$ and paying one unit. Two events can subsequently occur: The player can throw a 1 on either die, remaining at $(23, 23)$, or he can obtain an outcome without a 1 on either die, in which case the game is concluded. The conditional expectation of a throw of two dice, given that neither exhibits a 1, is

$$E = \frac{2(2 + 3 + 4 + 5 + 6)}{5} = 8$$

and the probability of the nonappearance of a 1 on either of two dice is 25/36. In the (23, 23) case, the expected cost is then $1/(25/36) = 36/25$; as a consequence we can write for V,

$$V = 1 + \frac{11}{36} \cdot \frac{36}{25} = \frac{36}{25} \qquad\qquad 5\text{-}24$$

Now, if we let W be the expected number of units paid in the $(0, 0)$ case under a strategy of never declaring a plateau, and V_1 be the expected cost at $(23, 0)$ under this strategy, we have

$$V_1 = \frac{11}{36}(1 + W) \qquad\qquad 5\text{-}25$$

To prove that the optimal strategy is never to declare a plateau, we must show that $V_1 < V$; that is, from Eqs. 5-24 and 5-25, that

$$W < \frac{36^2}{11 \times 25} - 1 = 3.71$$

The quantity W is the expected number of times a 1 is thrown on either die before achieving a continuous run (without 1's) adding up to 24 or greater. Let P be the probability of accumulating a score of 24 or more without the appearance of a 1. Then

$$W = \frac{1}{P}$$

Enumerating all possible combinations, we can calculate the probabilities, p_i, of reaching 24 or more with i rolls of two dice without a 1 appearing; i can assume the values 2, 3, 4, 5, 6. Numerically, $p_2 = 7.7 \times 10^{-4}$, $p_3 = 0.186$, $p_4 = 0.100$; $p_5 = 2.5 \times 10^{-3}$; and $p_6 = 3.3 \times 10^{-6}$. Thus, $P = 0.289$ and

$$W = 3.465$$

which is less than the critical value of 3.71. Hence, no plateau should be declared in this game. If the solitaire version of Pig is played with a goal of 100, it appears that the first plateau should be declared at about the level of 25.

In the generalized solitaire case, where the player is currently at $(a, 0)$ and has a goal of d points, thereby requiring an additional $d - a$ points, we can give an indication of his strategy (taking 0 as the previous plateau implies no loss of generality). Let $W(d)$ be the expected further cost in the $(0, 0)$ situation and $W(d - a)$ the expected further cost under a strategy of declaring a plateau at $(a, 0)$; $W(d - a)$ can ultimately be obtained by induction from $W(d)$. Also, let $V(a + \alpha, d)$ be the expected cost if the two dice exhibit the sum of α (given that α is obtained without a 1 on either die). Then, if a plateau is not declared at $(a, 0)$, needing $d - a$ additional points, the expected cost $C(a, d)$ is formulated as

$$C(a, d) = \frac{11}{36}[1 + W(d)] + \frac{1}{(25/36)}$$
$$\cdot \left[\frac{1}{25} V(a + 4, d) + \frac{2}{25} V(a + 5, d) + \cdots + \frac{1}{25} V(a + 12, d) \right]$$

If a plateau is declared at $(a, 0)$, the expected cost $C'(a, d)$ is then

$$C'(a, d) = 1 + W(d - a)$$

Therefore, we can write

$$V(a, d) = \min[1 + W(d - a), C(a, d)]$$

To evaluate this function requires the enumeration of all possible branchings of the cumulative dice totals to d, a prodigious arithmetical task.

Qualitatively, there will be less plateaus declared when the game is played against an opponent and yet less plateaus as the number of opponents increases and as one or more opponents obtain plateaus closer to the goal. Delineating a general strategy entails excessive machine computations.

Casino games

CRAPS

Of the various dice games adopted by the gambling casinos, the most prevalent, by far, is Craps. The direct ancestor of Craps is the game of Hazard, reputedly (according to William of Tyre, d. 1190) invented by twelfth-century English Crusaders during the siege of an Arabian castle.[†] Montmort established formal rules for Hazard (originally: "Hazart") and it subsequently became highly popular in early nineteenth-century England and France. In the British clubs the casts of 2, 3, or 12 were referred to as "Crabs." Presumably, the French adaptation involved a Gallic mispronunciation, which contributed the word "Craps," and since the game immigrated to America with the French colony of New Orleans, its currency became firmly established.[‡] Adopted by the American Negro (the

---

[†] Jean Bodel's play, "Le Jeu de Saint Nicolas," *ca.* A.D. 1200, features a scene involving thieves gambling at Le Hasard in a tavern.

[‡] Another plausible legend credits Count Bernard Mandeville Marigny with introducing the game to New Orleansites. Marigny was a Creole and as such was known as Johnny Crapeaud (French for "toad," the term was originally applied to Frenchmen by Nostradamus in allusion to the fleur-de-lis pattern of the French national standard which, as altered by Charles VI in 1365, resembled three toadlike flowers; Guillim, in *Display of Heraldrie*, 1611, refers to the device as "three toads, erect, saltant"—the modern pejorative is "frog"). Thus the game was referred to as Crapeaud's, or finally, Craps.

phrase "African dominoes" is often a synonym for dice), Craps spread from New Orleans, up the Mississippi, and thence out across the country. A rather disreputable aura surrounded the game during the latter half of the nineteenth century, owing to its manipulation by professional crooks traveling the steamboats and pullman cars of the era. However, its huge popularity among the soldiers of World War I gained for Craps a veneer of social respectability. It was subsequently enshrined into the salons of Monte Carlo and on the green baize table tops of Las Vegas; today the cabalistic signs of the Craps layout can be seen in every major gambling casino of the world.

Craps is played with two dice. A player throws both dice, winning unconditionally if he produces the outcomes 7 or 11 (as the sum of the numbers showing on the two dice), which are designated as "naturals." If the player casts the outcomes 2, 3, or 12—referred to as "craps"—he loses unconditionally. If he produces the outcomes 4, 5, 6, 8, 9, or 10, each of these outcomes being known as a "point," he continues the sequence of throws until either the same outcome (point) is repeated or the outcome 7 occurs. Repetition of the particular "point" is a win, while the appearance of a 7 now signifies a loss.

TABLE 5-3   Two-Dice Probabilities

Outcome	2	3	4	5	6	7	8	9	10	11	12
Probability	$\frac{1}{36}$	$\frac{2}{36}$	$\frac{3}{36}$	$\frac{4}{36}$	$\frac{5}{36}$	$\frac{6}{36}$	$\frac{5}{36}$	$\frac{4}{36}$	$\frac{3}{36}$	$\frac{2}{36}$	$\frac{1}{36}$

The types of wagers are illustrated by the conventional betting layout shown in Fig. 5-1. There are several bets allowable on this layout. The most common bet, the pass line, wagers on a simple win for the player. Its probability is stated as

$$P = p(7) + p(11) + p(\text{"point"} + \text{"point" preceding 7})$$

The probabilities of the outcomes 2 through 12 of a throw of two dice are obtainable directly from Eq. 5-14 and are tabulated in Table 5-3. Thence the probability of throwing a 7 is 6/36 and of throwing an 11 is 2/36. The probability of throwing a "point" is 24/36; of this probability, one-fourth comprises a 4 or 10, which recurs before a 7 with probability 1/3; one-third comprises a 5 or 9, which recurs before a 7 with probability 2/5; and five-twelfths comprises a 6 or 8, which recurs before a 7 with probability

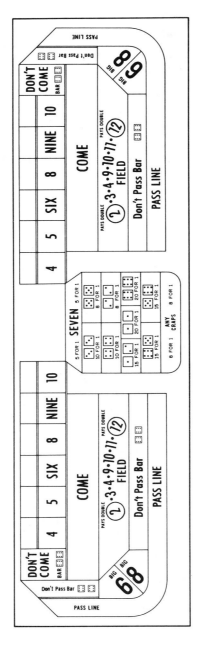

Fig. 5-1   Craps layout

5/11. Thus, the probability of "making a pass" is

$$p = \frac{6}{36} + \frac{2}{36} + \frac{24}{36}\left(\frac{1}{4} \cdot \frac{1}{3} + \frac{1}{3} \cdot \frac{2}{5} + \frac{5}{12} \cdot \frac{5}{11}\right) = \frac{244}{495} = 0.492929\cdots$$

Generally, in casino Craps, the opposite of the "pass line" bet is the "don't pass, bar twelve" bet—that is, the throw of 12 on the first roll of a sequence is considered a tie for the player wagering on the "don't pass" result. Hence the probability of winning a "don't pass, bar twelve" bet is

$$P = 1 - p(\text{"pass"}) - \frac{1}{2}p(12) = 1 - \frac{244}{495} - \frac{1}{2}\left(\frac{1}{36}\right) = \frac{217}{440}$$

$$= 0.4931818\cdots$$

The "come" and "don't come" bets are identical to "pass" and "don't pass," respectively, except that they may be initiated at any time rather than on the first roll of a particular player's sequence. A "field" bet wagers that the succeeding outcome of the dice is a 2, 3, 4, 9, 10, 11, or 12. Thus, the "field" bet wins with probability 16/36; however, odds of 2 to 1 are offered if the 2 or 12 appears, thereby decreasing the "house take." Betting the "big six" or "big eight" constitutes wagering that that outcome will appear before a 7; the probability of this event is obviously $(5/36)/[(5/36) + (6/36)] = 5/11$. Betting a "seven", "eleven," "two," "twelve," and "three" are self-evident wagers that the next roll will produce that particular outcome. A "hard way" bet defines the wager that a specified even-numbered outcome (4, 6, 8, or 10) will occur with the same number of points showing on each die (defined as a double number, or "hard way") before the same outcome with different points showing on each die (the "easy way") or the outcome 7 occurs. Finally, an "odds" bet is permitted following the establishment of a "point" during a "pass," "don't pass," "come," or "don't come" wager. A sum smaller or equal to the original stake may be wagered that the "point" will reappear before the outcome 7 (or, the contrary wager is acceptable). The "house" odds constitute a "fair" bet in this circumstance. Accepting the "odds" bet whenever available increases the expected gain of the "pass" and "come" bets to -0.0085 and of the "don't pass" and "don't come" bets to -0.0083. A tabulation of the various wagers with associated probabilities and expected gains is given in Table 5-4.

Despite the great popularity of Craps, its participants are offered no significant strategy other than selection of the wager with the least unfavorable odds. Because of its rapid pace, however, the game has attracted

TABLE 5-4   Table of Odds at Craps

Bet	Payoff Odds	Winning Probability	Expected Gain
Pass line	1–1	0.493	−0.014
Don't pass, bar twelve	1–1	0.493	−0.014
Come	1–1	0.493	−0.014
Don't come	1–1	0.493	−0.014
Field	1–1 plus 2–1 on 2 and 12	0.472	−0.056
Big six or eight	1–1	0.455	−0.091
Seven	4–1[†]	0.417	−0.167
Hard way	9–1 on 6 and 8	0.455	−0.091
	7–1 on 4 and 10	0.444	−0.111
Any craps	7–1	0.444	−0.111
"Two" or "twelve"	29–1	0.417	−0.167
"Eleven"	14–1	0.417	−0.167
"Three"	14–1	0.417	−0.167
Odds	2–1 on 10 and 4	0.500	0.000
(not an independent wager)	3–2 on 5 and 9	0.500	0.000
	6–5 on 8 and 6	0.500	0.000

[†] In many casinos, the inferiority of this bet (and others similar) is camouflaged by stating the odds as 5 *for* 1, since the original stake is returned with the winning sum. This intent of this wording is not altogether above suspicion.

a plethora of "systems" and has developed a small thesaurus of esoteric machinations and mumbled incantations ("Baby needs a new pair of shoes"). Like the Roulette ball, the dice possess "neither conscience nor memory"[†] and are democratic to a fault.

Of those determined experimenters who have tested the probabilities of Craps, perhaps the greatest stamina was demonstrated by B. H. Brown,[‡] who conducted a series of 9900 Craps games. Brown obtained 4871 successes and 5029 failures compared with the theoretically expected values of 4880 successes and 5020 failures. The discrepancy is well within one standard deviation. Although the major gambling casinos do not maintain statistical records on the results of games of Craps, one event has been recorded—that wherein a young man achieved 28 consecutive "passes" at the Desert Inn Casino, Las Vegas, Nevada (June 10, 1950). Odds against such an event are 400 million to 1.

[†] Joseph Bertrand.

[‡] Bancroft H. Brown, "Probabilities in the Game of 'Shooting Craps'," *Am. Math. Monthly*, **26** (1919), p. 351.

Associated with Craps are a number of so-called proposition bets. These wagers generally entail the probability of a specified outcome occurring in a specified number of throws or before another particular outcome occurs. A typical example is the proposition that a player will obtain both the outcomes 6 and 8 (with two dice) before the outcome 7 occurs twice —an event of probability 0.56. A more interesting variation on a "proposition bet" concerns two players A and B alternately throwing the two dice. Player A begins the game and wins if he casts the outcome 6 before B casts the outcome 7. Player B's successful outcome has probability 6/36 compared to 5/36 for that of player A; however, since A casts first, the game is more equitable than would first appear. Specifically, we can readily show that if the game is limited to n throws, A's probability p_n of winning is

$$p_n = \frac{30}{61}\left[1 - \left(\frac{155}{216}\right)^{(n+\delta)/2}\right] \quad \text{for } \delta = 0 \text{ or } 1 \text{ as } n \text{ is even or odd}$$

Similarly, B has probability q_n of winning, expressed by

$$q_n = \frac{31}{61}\left[1 - \left(\frac{155}{216}\right)^{(n-\delta)/2}\right]$$

and the probability r_n of a tie (no winner after n throws) is

$$r_n = \left(\frac{155}{216}\right)^{(n-\delta)/2}$$

As n increases indefinitely, the probability of a tie declines to zero, and p_n and q_n approach 30/61 and 31/61, respectively. Hence, the game favors player B.

CHUCK-A-LUCK

Another game with dice is Chuck-A-Luck (originally known as "Sweat-Cloth," it has long been played illegally in British pubs under the name Crown and Anchor—the six sides of the dice are inscribed Clubs, Diamonds, Hearts, Spades, Crown, and Anchor), which was exported from the British Isles to the United States about 1800. Three dice are agitated inside a double-ended, rotatable cage with an hourglass cross section (the "Bird Cage"). A player may wager upon any of the outcomes 1 through 6. If one (and only one) die exhibits that outcome ($p = 75/216$), the player wins at even odds; if two dice exhibit that outcome ($p = 15/216$), the payoff is 2 to 1; if all three dice show the player's choice ($p = 1/216$), the payoff is 3 to 1; otherwise

Fig. 5-2   The Monte Carlo dice game

(that is, if the specified outcome appears on none of the three dice) the player loses. Elementary calculations indicate a probability of success of 0.461. An equitable game would offer odds of 1 to 1, 2 to 1, and 20 to 1, or of 1 to 1, 3 to 1, and 5 to 1 for the specified outcome occurring once, twice, or three times on the three dice.

THE MONTE CARLO DICE GAME

A three-dice game previously popular at European gambling resorts is the Monte Carlo Dice Game, evidently named after the casino that first promulgated its play. The betting layout is illustrated in Fig. 5-2. The term *priles* refers to triplets—that is, the instance of all three dice exhibiting the identical outcome. An equitable payoff for an individual *prile* is 215 to 1 and for all *priles* is 35 to 1. The probabilities of obtaining the outcomes 4 through 17 are given immediately by Eq. 5-14. Table 5-5 tabulates the "house take" for these wagers. Betting on "high" wins for the player if the outcome of the dice is 11 or higher, except for the occurrence of *priles*, which constitute the "house take." Similarly, the "low" bet comprises the outcomes 10 or lower. Odd or even wagers are also inequitable by the percentage of the priles. The bottom row of numbers on the betting layout

TABLE 5-5   Three-Dice Game Probabilities

Outcome	Payoff Odds	Equitable Odds	Expected Gain
4	60–1	71–1	−0.153
5	30–1	35–1	−0.139
6	18–1	20.6–1	−0.120
7	12–1	13.4–1	−0.097
8	8–1	$9\frac{2}{7}$–1	−0.125
9	6–1	7.64–1	−0.190
10	6–1	7–1	−0.125
11	6–1	7–1	−0.125
12	6–1	7.64–1	−0.190
13	8–1	$9\frac{2}{7}$–1	−0.125
14	12–1	13.4–1	−0.097
15	18–1	20.6–1	−0.120
16	30–1	35–1	−0.139
17	60–1	71–1	−0.153

functions as a Chuck-A-Luck game. Likely, the high "house take" of the Monte Carlo Dice Game has contributed to its demise.

BARBOTTE, COUNTER DICE, TWENTY-SIX, AND OTHERS

Many hundreds, if not thousands, of dice games have evolved over the years. It is obviously feasible to mention only a few of these. Barbotte is a Canadian version of Craps wherein the player wins if the two dice produce 3-3, 5-5, 6-6, or 6-5. He loses with the outcomes 1-1, 2-2, 4-4, and 2-1. The remaining values are not registered. In this form, Barbotte is a fair game. Counter Dice is a game played occasionally in taverns. The player selects a number 1 through 6 and thence rolls ten dice from a cup ten times in all (equivalent to throwing 100 dice). If the player's selected number occurs 20 times, he is paid at odds of 2 to 1; if the number appears 25 times, the payoff is 4 to 1; and if the number occurs 30 or more times, the payoff is 20 to 1. The expected number of times a particular outcome appears is $16\frac{2}{3}$. A version of Counter Dice, well known in Chicago bars, is "Twenty-six." A player selects a particular outcome of a die as his "point"; he then rolls ten dice 13 times, recording the total number of occurrences of his "point." The expected number is evidently $130/6 = 21\frac{2}{3}$. There is no "standard" payoff; however, most establishments pay 4 to 1 for 26 occurrences of the "point," with increasing odds (usually to about 8 to 1) for 33 or more occurrences of the "point." The probability of obtaining 26 particular outcomes in 13 throws of ten dice (equivalent to 130 throws of a single die) is given directly by Eq. 5-7:

$$P_{130}^{26} = \binom{130}{26}(1/6)^{26}(5/6)^{104} \simeq 5.33 \times 10^{-2}$$

The probability of obtaining 26 or more occurrences of the "point" is, from Eq. 5-10,

$$P_{130}(26 \le m \le 130) \simeq \Phi\left(\frac{130 - (130/6) + (1/2)}{\sqrt{130(1/6)(5/6)}}\right)$$

$$- \Phi\left(\frac{26 - (130/6) - (1/2)}{\sqrt{130(1/6)(5/6)}}\right)$$

$$= 1.0000 - 0.8164 = 0.1836$$

and the probability of achieving 33 or more occurrences of the "point" is, similarly,

$$P_{130}(33 \le m \le 130) \simeq 1.0000 - \Phi\left(\frac{33 - (130/6) - (1/2)}{\sqrt{130(1/6)(5/6)}}\right)$$

$$= 1.0000 - 0.9845 = 0.0155$$

The game of Seven was once played in minor European gambling casinos. Throwing two dice, the player could bet on *manque* or *passe* according to Fig. 5-3. The outcome 7 was always won by the house.

2 3 4 MANQUE 5 6	8 9 10 PASSE 11 12

Fig. 5-3

Probability of success on either wager is $15/36 = 0.4167$, resulting in a "house take" of $16\frac{2}{3}$ percent. Zanzibar, a game with three dice, was also played occasionally in Europe, as was the game of *Passe-dix* (past ten). The latter is an ancient game that fell into disuse until, in the seventeenth century, it attracted the attention of Galileo. Three dice are thrown and the player can wager on *manque* (the outcome 10 or lower) or *passe* (the outcome over 10—whence the name *Passe-dix*). Other dice games that have attained a fleeting popularity in gambling casinos are Razzle-Dazzle (played in Havana casinos with eight dice), Cusek (a type of Roulette played with dice in Macao), In-and-In, and Carabino.

POKER DICE

Analysis of any of these dice games and determination of an optimum fixed strategy are conceptually trivial. However, there are certain games whose solutions involve an overwhelming amount of calculation, even for a high-speed electronic computer. Liars Dice (where the application of judicious prevarication is the essential ingredient) and Poker Dice (equivalent to conventional Poker played with an infinite number of card decks) are two such examples. Poker Dice (each die shows the six outcomes: Nine, Ten, Jack, Queen, King, and Ace) invokes the theory of partitions. The occupancy problem posed is that of five dice occupying six cells; we therefore consider a partition of the six cells into six subpopulations (0 through 5). A throw of five dice, from the viewpoint of Poker Dice, can yield one of seven results: no two alike, one pair, two pairs, three of a kind, four of a kind, five of a kind, and a "full house." The respective probabilities are obtained by counting the partitions for each case:

$$P \text{ (no two alike)} = 6! \cdot 6^{-5} \qquad\qquad = 0.0926$$

$$P \text{ (one pair)} \quad = \left(\frac{6!}{2!3!} \cdot \frac{5!}{2!}\right) 6^{-5} \quad = 0.4630$$

$$P \text{ (two pairs)} \quad = \left(\frac{6!}{3!2!} \cdot \frac{5!}{2!2!}\right) 6^{-5} = 0.2315$$

$$P \text{ (three alike)} \quad = \left(\frac{6!}{2!3!} \cdot \frac{5!}{3!}\right) 6^{-5} \quad = 0.1543$$

$$P \text{ ("full house")} = \left(\frac{6!}{4!} \cdot \frac{5!}{3!2!}\right) 6^{-5} \quad = 0.0386$$

$$P \text{ (four alike)} \quad = \left(\frac{6!}{4!} \cdot \frac{5!}{4!}\right) 6^{-5} \qquad = 0.0193$$

$$P \text{ (five alike)} \quad = \left(\frac{6!}{5!} \cdot \frac{5!}{5!}\right) 6^{-5} \qquad = 0.0008$$

These seven results are further subdivided by the ranking of the paired dice, etc. The laborious calculations required to compute the strategy and probabilities for the second and third rolls are vastly greater than the minimal amount of mathematical interest derivable therefrom.

Related games

BACKGAMMON

Backgammon constitutes one of the oldest games known, extending back to the third millenium B.C. It offers a combination of nontrivial strategies with the chance outcomes of dice throwing. However, the several artificial rules governing the movement of the pieces again dictate an astronomical amount of computation for any realistic model. Contrary to the case for many card games, a mathematically tractable model provides no particular insight into the general strategy. Analyses of certain end-game positions have been achieved and have indicated superior mid-game strategies. By employing positional evaluation functions, it appears feasible to program existing computers for a level of competence well above that of human players.

DOMINOES

The game of dominoes bears obvious resemblance to a dicing pastime— each domino displays the specific outcome of a throw of two dice, including the possibility of a zero (hypothesizing a seven-sided die). Thus, a set of dominoes consists of 28 unique pieces (in general, if each half-domino exhibits up to n pips, then $(n + 1)(n + 2)/2$ pieces comprise a complete set, and each number from 0 to n occurs $n + 2$ times on the faces of the dominoes). After partitioning the dominoes, face down, in random fashion among two, three, or four players, each player, in turn, attempts to extend an open-ended chain of dominoes by matching the value of the open half-domino with an equal-value half-domino selected from his "hand." The game is concluded when a player has eliminated all the dominoes in his hand (thereby winning) or when no player can add to the domino chain; in the latter case the winner is that player holding the least number of dominoes. Usually, scoring consists of awarding the winner points equal to the total value of the dominoes remaining in the opponents' hands.

As a game with incomplete information, the optimal strategy at Dominoes must be based on a probabilistic assessment of each unseen hand. An algorithm for optimum selection of the domino to be played at each step has been evolved by Iu. A. Pervin and programmed for the computer "Strela." Initial probabilities are assigned to each of the unseen dominoes being held by a particular opponent. Then, as the game progresses, information on the dominoes held by the participants increases, and the probabilities for the undisclosed dominoes are recomputed. Two additional stages of learning are delineated: that occurring over several games with no change in opponents so that any systematic preferences of play might be determined, and that occurring over any large number of games so that an accumulated experience is recorded, statistically analyzed, and applied toward the improvement of the logical branches of the algorithm. A contest among the machine "Strela" and three "expert" players ended with the victory of the former.

Generally, dice games, like Roulette, embody trivial structures and involve only simple probabilities and negative expectations. Their outcomes depend entirely upon chance and cannot therefore be influenced by the decisions of the players. Even the rare exceptions, such as Pig, admit only of pure strategies. For more intellectually enjoyable games, it is necessary to investigate those situations concerned with memory, mixed strategies, or specialized skills.

Dice divertissements

Fanciers of dice idiosyncrasies may wish to grapple with the following problems.

1. *Weighted Dice.* Consider a set of n dice weighted according to a probability distribution $p_i, i = 1, 2, \ldots, 6, \sum_{i=1}^{6} p_i = 1$. Throwing these n dice results in an outcome (the sum of the numbers showing on the up-faces) ranging from n to $6n$. Prove that it is impossible to effect a weighting such that all possible outcomes are equiprobable.

2. *Morra Dice.* Each of two players simultaneously (and privately) selects from one to three dice and records a number from 2 to 36. The dice selected by the players are then thrown and their outcome compared to the recorded numbers. That player whose number is closer to the outcome of the (2, 3, 4, 5, or 6) dice wins one unit from his opponent; if no one is closer, the game is a draw. Compute the payoff matrix and optimal strategies.

3. *Distinct Dice.* Invent a simple dice game whereby interchange of the two topologically distinct dice alters the playing strategies.

Suggested references

EPSTEIN, RICHARD A., "Solution of a Simple Dice Game," Hughes Aircraft Co., Report OP-63, Communications Division, July, 1964.

EPSTEIN, RICHARD A., "Optimal Strategy For a Game With Dice," Hughes Aircraft Co., Report OP-64, Communications Division, July, 1964.

FELLER, WILLIAM, *An Introduction to Probability Theory and Its Applications*, John Wiley & Sons, Inc., New York, 2d ed., 1957.

GARDNER, MARTIN, "Mathematical Games," *Scientific American*, **199**, No. 1 (July, 1958), pp. 102–106.

JACOBY, OSWALD, *How To Figure the Odds*, Doubleday and Co., Inc., Garden City, New York, 1947.

JACOBY, OSWALD, and CRAWFORD, JOHN R., *The Backgammon Book*, The Viking Press, New York, 1970.

KEELER, EMMETT B., and SPENCER, JOEL, "Proper Raising Points in a Generalization of Backgammon," The Rand Corporation, P-4078, May, 1969.

PERVIN, IU. A., "On Algorithms and Programming for Playing at Dominoes," *Doklady Akademii Nauk. SSSR*, Vol. 124, No. 1 (January, 1959), pp. 31–33. Translated in *Automation Express* (April, 1959), pp. 26–28.

PHILPOTT, WADE E., "Domino and Superdomino Recreations," *J. Recreational Math.*; Part 1:,Vol. 4, No. 1 (Jan. 1971), pp. 2–18: Part 2: Vol. 4, No. 2 (April, 1971), pp. 79–87; Part 3: Vol. 4, No. 4, (Oct. 1971), pp.229–243; Part 4: Vol. 5, No. 2 (April, 1972), pp. 102–122; Part 5: Vol, 5. No. 3 (July, 1972), pp. 177–196; Part 6: Vol. 6, No. 1 (Winter, 1973), pp. 10–34.

SCARNE, JOHN, and CLAYTON RAWSON, *Scarne On Dice*, The Military Service Publishing Co., Harrisburg, Pennsylvania, 1945.

THORP, EDWARD O., "Backgammon: Part I, The Optimal Strategy for the Pure Running Game," Second Annual Conference on Gambling, South Lake Tahoe, Nevada, June, 1975.

CHAPTER SIX

THE PLAY OF THE CARDS

Origins and species

The invention of playing cards has been variously credited to the Indians, Arabs, and Egyptians. Chinese records claim that the first modern pack was shuffled in the reign of Sèun-ho,[†] about A.D. 1120, and that cards became commonplace by the reign of Kaou-tsung, who ascended the throne in 1131; however, card games per se date back more than two millenia, preceding the invention of paper.[‡]

Card playing was introduced into Europe through the Crusades (the Arabs endured lengthy sieges with cards and other gambling paraphernalia) and became widespread in Western society during the fourteenth century. In 1423, the Franciscan friar St. Bernardino of Siena preached a celebrated sermon against cards (*Contra Alearum Ludos*) at Bologna, attributing their invention to the devil. Despite such ecclesiastic interdiction, Johannes Gutenberg printed playing cards the same year as his famous Bible (1440). The cards from Gutenberg's press were Tarot cards, from which the modern deck is derived. The Tarot pack consisted of 78 cards—22 high-ranking cards known as "atouts" (literally: "above all"; later, these cards were called "triumph" or "trump"), which included a Joker (*le Fou*), and

---

[†] According to the Chinese dictionary, Ching-tsze-tung, compiled by Eul-koung and first published in 1678.

[‡] The word "card" stems from the Greek word for paper, $\chi \acute{\alpha} \rho \tau \eta \varsigma$. Similarly, the Hebrew term for playing card, *qlaf*, is equivalent to "parchment."

four denominations of 14 cards each, the ranks comprising ten numbered cards plus a King, Queen, Cavalier or Knight, and a Valet or Knave. The four denominations, or suits, represented the four major divisions of medieval society: Swords symbolized the nobility; Coins, the merchant class; Batons or Clubs, the peasants; and Cups or Chalices, the Church. These suits can still be seen in the contemporary playing cards of Italy, Spain, Andorra, and Portugal.

About 1500, the French dropped the 22 "atouts" and eliminated the Knight, leaving $4 \times 13 = 52$ cards comprising the deck. They also transformed Swords, Coins, Batons, and Cups into Piques (soldiers' pikes), Carreaux (building tiles, lozenge- or diamond-shaped), Trèfles (trefoils or clover leaves), and Coeurs (hearts). In sixteenth-century Spain, Swords were Espados; Coins were square pieces of currency, Dineros; Batons, Clubs, or Cudgels were Bastos; and Cups or Chalices were Copas. Hence, we have adopted the French symbols, translated the names of two (Hearts and Diamonds) into English and applied to the other two English translations of Spanish names for different symbols. Such is the illogic of language.

Despite a number of coincidences, no firm connection has been found between the structure of the deck and the calendar. It seems palpable to link the four suits with the seasons and the 13 ranks with the lunar months (corresponding to one card per week of the year). Further, if we assign a weight of 13 to the Kings, 12 to the Queens, 11 to the Jacks, etc., the 52-card pack totals 364; adding 1 for the Joker equals the number of days in a (nonbissextile) year. Such is the treachery of numerology.

Initially, the court cards[†] were designed as portraits of actual personages, and stylistic vestiges of the individuals remain today. The four original kings of fourteenth-century Europe were Charlemagne (Hearts), the biblical David (Spades), Julius Caesar (Diamonds), and Alexander the Great (Clubs). Distaff royalty included Helen of Troy as the Queen of Hearts, Pallas Athena as the Queen of Spades, and the biblical Rachel as the Queen of Diamonds. Regal ladies passingly honored as card monarchs were Joan of Arc, Elizabeth I, Elizabeth of York (wife of Henry VII), Roxane, Judith, Hecuba, Florimel, and Fausta, among many. Famous Jacks were frequently renowned warriors, such as Hogier La Danois, one of Charlemagne's lieutenants (Spades); Etienne de Vignoles, a soldier under Charles VII of France (Hearts); Ogier the Dane (Spades); Roland,

---

[†] A corruption of *coat* cards, so called because they bear the representation of a clothed or *coated* figure (not because the King, Queen, and Knave may be considered as members of a royal court).

Charlemagne's nephew (Diamonds); and the gallant knight Sir Lancelot (Clubs).

Many cultures have evolved decks partitioned in other ways. The Hindus, for example, employ a deck with ten denominations, representing the ten incarnations of Vishnu. The Italians use, generally, a 40-card deck and the Spanish a 48-card deck. The French play games with both the 52-card pack and the 32-card Piquet pack (omitting twos through sixes). Clearly, the number of cards comprising a deck is arbitrary and could be selected to satisfy the needs of a particular game. However, we shall consider, unless otherwise specified, the 52-card pack partitioned into 4 denominations and 13 ranks.

Randomness and shuffling

BIAS

The question of the "fairness" of a deck of cards is distinct from questions of bias relating to coins, dice, or roulette. Intuitively, a deck of cards is "fair" if each outcome is enumerated and is represented identically as all others. Experimenters have conducted tests to establish the veracity of this intuition. Most notably, the statistician C. V. L. Charlier performed 10,000 drawings (with replacement) from a conventional 52-card deck. He recorded draws of 4933 black cards and 5067 red cards for a deviation of 67 from the expected value. The standard deviation is

$$\sigma = \sqrt{10,000 \times \tfrac{1}{2} \times \tfrac{1}{2}} = 50$$

assuming red and black cards to be equiprobable. A result with a 1.34σ deviation is certainly not unusual.

CUT AND SHUFFLE OPERATIONS

Rather than bias, a far more significant parameter for cards is randomness. Since the ordering of a deck of cards is neither random nor nonrandom in itself (every possible ordering is equiprobable a priori), we must adopt a dynamic concept of randomness. That is, the question of randomness is meaningful only when the ordering is being changed by some process such as shuffling. We will consider five types of processes that transform one ordering of a deck into another.

A *simple cut c* translates the top card of the deck to the bottom; thus the power c^i of this operation separates the deck after the ith card and is merely a phase shift transforming the order $1, 2, 3, \ldots i, j, k, \ldots 2n$ into the order $j, k, \ldots 2n, 1, 2, 3, \ldots i$. The *perfect shuffle operation* s on a $2n$-card deck separates the top n cards from the bottom n cards and precisely interleaves them, the top and bottom cards remaining unchanged in position. Functionally,

$$s(1, 2, 3, \ldots, n - 1, n, n + 1, \ldots, 2n - 1, 2n)$$

$$= (1, n + 1, 2, n + 2, \ldots, n, 2n)$$

From this equation it follows that if the card in position a_0 is moved to position a_1 by the perfect shuffle s, then

$$a_1 \equiv 2a_0 - 1, \qquad \mathrm{mod}\,(2n - 1)$$

noting that $a_1 = 1$ for $a_0 = 1$ and $a_1 = 2n$ for $a_0 = 2n$. After k iterations of s, the card originally in position a_0 has moved to position a_k. Thus,

$$a_k \equiv 2^k a_0 - (2^k - 1), \qquad \mathrm{mod}\,(2n - 1)$$

The *modified perfect shuffle* s' constitutes the same operation, but with the $(n + 1)$st card moving to the top and the nth card to the bottom. Defining this operation:

$$s'(1, 2, 3, \ldots, n - 1, n, n + 1, \ldots, 2n - 1, 2n)$$

$$= (n + 1, 1, n + 2, 2, \ldots 2n, n)$$

and if the card in position b_0 is moved to position b_1 by the modified perfect shuffle s',

$$b_1 \equiv 2b_0, \qquad \mathrm{mod}\,(2n + 1)$$

In general, after k iterations of s',

$$b_k \equiv 2^k b_0, \qquad \mathrm{mod}\,(2n + 1)$$

The *amateur shuffle operation* s_a divides the deck approximately into two groups of n cards and interleaves them singly or in clusters of 2, 3, or 4 according to some probability distribution. Finally, we define the *random shuffle* s_r as an operation equivalent to scattering the deck in a high wind and having the cards retrieved by a blindfolded inebriate.

Since the random shuffle renders equiprobable all possible orderings of the 52 cards, it is associated with the greatest amount of information. Specifically, $\log_2 52! = 225.7$ bits of information are required for description of a random shuffle operation. A perfect shuffle is completely deterministic and hence is not accompanied by an information parameter.

An amateur shuffle operation, wherein the probability of the ith card in the final sequence originating in either half of the deck is $1/2$, provides 2^{52} possible sequences. Hence, the maximum amount of information associated with this shuffling process is $\log_2 2^{52} = 52$ bits. With a known probability distribution constraining the s_a operator, the information required to specify s_a is evidently less than 52 bits.

RANDOMNESS AND CYCLING

It can be shown that to randomize the deck, the amateur shuffle operation must be repeated *at least* five times. Typical forms of s_a dictate 20 to 30 replications to achieve randomization.

TABLE 6-1   Deck Cycles with Perfect Shuffles

$2n$	f	$2n$	f
2	1	32	5
4	2	34	10
6	4	36	12
8	3	38	36
10	6	40	12
12	10	42	20
14	12	44	14
16	4	46	12
18	8	48	23
20	18	50	21
22	6	52	8
24	11	54	52
26	20	56	20
28	18	58	18
30	28	60	58

$2n$ = deck length
f = shuffles to cycle the deck

If the perfect shuffle operation s is iterated f times on a $2n$-card deck, where f is the exponent of 2, mod $(2n - 1)$, the deck is restored to its original ordering. Specifically, eight perfect shuffles cycle the 52-card pack to its original ordering,[†] since $2^8 = 1$, mod 51. Table 6-1 tabulates the value of f for decks up to $2n = 60$ cards.

[†] It is worthwhile to note that two perfect shuffles of a "fresh" deck (arranged, conventionally, by suits in ascending ranks) followed by simple cuts order the cards for a deal of four "perfect" hands at bridge (all 13 cards of a suit comprising each hand). This fact may account partially for the astounding number of "perfect" hands reported each year.

For the modified perfect shuffle operation s', 52 iterations are necessary to cycle the deck, since 2 is "primitive," mod 53—that is, $f' = 52$ is the lowest solution to $2^{f'} = 1$, mod 53. Thus, f and f' are the orders of s and s', respectively. The operation c has order $2n$, since c is a "primitive" cyclic permutation on $2n$ cards. It can be shown that the operations c and s together (cut and shuffle) generate the entire symmetric group S_{2n} of permutations on the $2n$ cards (the operations c and s' also generate an entire symmetric group of permutations). The order of the product operation cs assumes one of two values. If the deck size is such that $2n - 1$ is a power p^m of a prime p, where n is any positive integer, and 2 is primitive, mod p^m—that is, $f = \phi(p^m) = p^{m-1}(p - 1)$, where ϕ is Euler's function —then the order of cs, $O(cs)$, is

$$O(cs) = (f + 1)\, \phi(p^{m-1})$$

If, on the other hand, either $2n - 1$ has two or more distinct prime factors or, although $2n - 1$ is a power of a prime, 2 is not primitive, mod $(2n - 1)$, then the order of cs is given by

$$O(c\hat{s}) = f(f + 1)$$

as is the case for the conventional deck, $n = 26$.

A proof of the theorem that the operations c and s (or c and s') applied to a deck of $2n$ cards generate the entire symmetric group S_{2n} of permutations on the $2n$ cards has been published by S. W. Golomb. This theorem expresses the equivalence between the operations $c^i s^k$ and s_r. That is, the perfect shuffle and single-cut operations sufficiently iterated can produce complete randomness.

For decks of $2n - 1$ cards, we can define the perfect shuffle $\bar{s}$ as an operation that separates the bottom n cards from the top $n - 1$ cards and precisely interleaves the two sets, the bottom card remaining invariant and the nth card emerging on the top. The operation $\bar{s}$ has order f |the exponent of 2, mod $(2n - 1)$| and the simple-cut operation $\bar{c}$ is definable as with an even-numbered deck and has order $2n - 1$. A theorem due to Golomb states that the operations $\bar{c}$ and $\bar{s}$ applied iteratively to a deck of $2n - 1$ cards generate a subgroup of the symmetric group S_{2n-1} of order

$$O(\bar{c}\bar{s}) = (2n - 1)f \le (2n - 1)(2n - 2)$$

This subgroup is proper for $n > 2$. Therefore the operation $c^i s^k$ can never be made equivalent to the random shuffle operation s_r, since not all permutations of odd-sized decks are obtained by the cutting and perfect shuffling operations.

CHARACTERISTICS OF THE AMATEUR SHUFFLE

Of more practical concern is the amateur shuffle operation s_a. Experiments undertaken by the author indicate that neophyte shufflers tend to interleave cards in clusters at the beginning and end of each shuffle; intermediate positions are generally alternated singly or by twos. More proficient shufflers appear to overcome the clustering tendency, which is caused by the first and final cards of the new sequence adhering to the fingers. Indeed, post-graduate shufflers, such as dealers at Las Vegas, exhibit a uniform type of card interleaving with quite small variances. The nature of the s_a operator was investigated by recording the sound waves produced by shuffling a deck of cards (a flat-response microphone and sharp-skirted high-pass filters were used with a fast-response sonograph). Duration of a beginner's shuffle is about 700 milliseconds, while virtuoso shufflers average about 1/2 second for a shuffle.

It was found that highly expert shufflers create sequences with single-card interlacings approximately eight times as frequent as two-card interlacings; a group of three cards appears less than once per shuffle. Thus, to an excellent approximation, the geometric distribution

$$P(\eta) = \left(\frac{8}{9}\right) \left(\frac{1}{9}\right)^{\eta - 1}, \qquad \eta = 1, 2, 3, \dots \qquad \qquad 6\text{-}1$$

represents the probability that a sequence consists of η cards. It is evident from this equation that a large measure of orderliness is preserved for a small number of shuffles. This fact suggests the feasibility of predicting the position of a card following the s_a operation. However, the problem of prediction is subsequent to the question of the correlation between successive card sequences.

CORRELATION OF CARD SEQUENCES; MARKOV CHAINS; ENTROPY

The shuffling operation evidently is not a function of the order of the deck of cards on which it operates nor of the past history of the deck. Hence, successive operations correspond to independent trials with fixed transition probabilities. The sequence of cards is therefore said to form a *Markov chain* and the matrix of transition probabilities is *doubly stochastic* (both the row sums and the column sums are unity).

Illustratively, consider a four-card deck in its initial state: $S = 1, 2, 3, 4$. There are 4! possible states for the entire deck (numbering of the states is arbitrary):

S_1: 1, 2, 3, 4	S_7: 1, 2, 4, 3	S_{13}: 2, 1, 3, 4	S_{19}: 4, 1, 2, 3
S_2: 1, 3, 2, 4	S_8: 1, 4, 2, 3	S_{14}: 2, 1, 4, 3	S_{20}: 4, 1, 3, 2
S_3: 1, 3, 4, 2	S_9: 1, 4, 3, 2	S_{15}: 2, 3, 1, 4	S_{21}: 4, 2, 1, 3
S_4: 3, 1, 2, 4	S_{10}: 3, 4, 2, 1	S_{16}: 2, 3, 4, 1	S_{22}: 4, 2, 3, 1
S_5: 3, 1, 4, 2	S_{11}: 3, 2, 1, 4	S_{17}: 2, 4, 1, 3	S_{23}: 4, 3, 1, 2
S_6: 3, 4, 1, 2	S_{12}: 3, 2, 4, 1	S_{18}: 2, 4, 3, 1	S_{24}: 4, 3, 2, 1

Letting $p_{j,k}$ be the transition probability of transforming the deck from state S_j to state S_k, the matrix P of transition probabilities is

$$P = \begin{Vmatrix} p_{1,1} & p_{1,2} & p_{1,3} & \cdots & p_{1,24} \\ p_{2,1} & p_{2,2} & p_{2,3} & \cdots & p_{2,24} \\ \cdot & \cdot & \cdot & \cdot & \cdot \\ \cdot & \cdot & \cdot & \cdot & \cdot \\ \cdot & \cdot & \cdot & \cdot & \cdot \\ p_{24,1} & p_{24,2} & p_{24,3} & \cdots & p_{24,24} \end{Vmatrix} \qquad 6\text{-}2$$

If the transformation between successive states of the deck is performed by a shuffling process that divides the deck in half and then interlaces the two halves, the orderings of 1, 2, and 3, 4, are preserved. That is, only the first six states are possible after a single such shuffle operation performed on state S_1. Similarly, from state S_2 only the states S_1, S_2, S_7, S_{13}, S_{14}, and S_{17} are possible with a single shuffle as prescribed. Considering all the forbidden transformations, the matrix P of Eq. 6-2 reduces to the form

$$P = \begin{Vmatrix} P_{1,1} & P_{1,2} & P_{1,3} & \cdots & 0 & 0 \\ P_{2,1} & P_{2,2} & 0 & \cdots & 0 & 0 \\ \cdot & \cdot & \cdot & \cdot & \cdot & \cdot \\ \cdot & \cdot & \cdot & \cdot & \cdot & \cdot \\ \cdot & \cdot & \cdot & \cdot & \cdot & \cdot \\ 0 & 0 & 0 & \cdots & 0 & P_{24,24} \end{Vmatrix} \qquad 6\text{-}3$$

which completely defines a Markov chain with states $S_1, S_{21}, \ldots, S_{24}$.

It is also possible to consider a transition from state S_j to state S_k that occurs in more than a single step. With n steps the transition can be described as $S_j \to S_{j_1} \to S_{j_2} \to \ldots \to S_{j_{n-1}} \to S_k$. Iterating the shuffle operation n times is equivalent to a matrix P^n of transition probabilities. Denoting by $p_{j,k}^{(n)}$ the probability of finding the system in state S_k at step $t + n$, given that at step t it was in state S_j, we can readily prove

$$p_{j,k}^{(2)} = \sum_m p_{j,m}\, p_{m,k}$$

and, by induction,

$$p_{j,k}^{(n)} = \sum_m p_{j,m}\, p_{m,k}^{(n-1)}$$

This recursion formula implies the nature of matrix multiplication:

$$P^n = P P^{n-1} \qquad\qquad 6\text{-}4$$

Applying the principle of Eq. 6-4 to the transition probability matrix of Eq. 6-3, we have, for two shuffle operations,

$$
P^2 =
\begin{Vmatrix}
(p_{1,1}^2 + p_{1,2}p_{2,1} + p_{1,6}p_{6,1}) & \cdots & (p_{1,5}p_{5,24}) \\
(p_{1,1}p_{2,1} + p_{2,1}p_{2,2} + p_{17,1}p_{2,17}) & \cdots & (p_{2,14}p_{14,24}) \\
(p_{8,1}p_{3,8}) & \cdots & (p_{3,20}p_{20,24}) \\
\cdot & \cdot & \cdot \\
\cdot & \cdot & \cdot \\
\cdot & \cdot & \cdot \\
(p_{17,1}p_{24,17}) & \cdots & (p_{24,14}p_{14,24} + p_{24,22}p_{22,24} + p_{24,24}^2)
\end{Vmatrix}
\qquad 6\text{-}5
$$

After two shuffles, all 24 states acquire nonzero probabilities. Thus, with only the restriction of equipartition on the shuffling operator, the deck ordering becomes randomized very quickly for this simplified deck. The transition matrix for a three-shuffle process is defined by the product of the matrices P (Eq. 6-3) and P^2 (Eq. 6-5). The procedure is continued, according to Eq. 6-4, for additional shuffles.

As a measure of the relationship between the initial state S_j and the state S_k that results after n shuffles, the concept of entropy logically suggests itself, since we are concerned with a Markov process. In statistical mechanics, the concept of entropy generally arises through Boltzmann's hypothesis, which relates it to probability. Therein, p_1 is defined as the probability of a system being in cell (or state) i of its phase space. The entropy H of the set of probabilities $p_1, p_2, \ldots, p_n$ is

$$H = -K \sum_i p_i \log p_i$$

Entropy, then, is a measure of uncertainty or of disorder; the greater the entropy, the less is the preservation of order. The constant K simply specifies the unit of measure; it is expedient to set $K = 1$.

Applying the entropy concept to the phenomenon of card shuffling, we define

$$H_{j,k} = -\sum p_{j,k}^{(n)} \log p_{j,k}^{(n)}$$

as the measure of the relationship between an initial state S_j of the deck and a state S_k following an n-shuffle process.

To compute numerical values of entropy for a nontrivial deck length requires an excessive amount of arithmetical labor. The transition probabilities for a 52-card deck form a 52! × 52! matrix ($52! \simeq 10^{68}$); evaluations of P^n and $H_{j,k}$ in such a case are far beyond the reach of any practical high-speed digital computer. Fortunately, since the ultimate goal is to develop a useful prediction function, there exists a pragmatic simplification that dispenses with the computational chores.

PREDICTION

We can state the problem of prediction as follows: Given the deck of cards in state S_j, and following n shuffles, given the first m cards of the new sequence represented by state S_k, what predictions can be made concerning the $(m + 1)$st card? Note that since we are applying the prediction to the goal of increasing the probability of success at some game, we wish a probability distribution of this $(m + 1)$st card; that is, we wish to obtain a maximum expectancy decision rather than a maximum likelihood prediction. Rigorously, we should now examine all those states reachable from state S_j after n shuffles whose sequences begin with the m cards specified. The corresponding transition probabilities for each allowable state are then tabulated according to the possible cards that can occur in the $(m + 1)$st position. Then the probability distribution of the $(m + 1)$st card is obtained. However, we now invoke our pragmatic observation that

> given the original sequence and the first m cards of the final sequence, the $(m + 1)$st card must be one of 2^n cards, n shuffles having transformed one sequence into the other.

To apply this observation usefully, we consider only those transition processes comprising one, two, or three shuffles; for n equal to six or more shuffles, the statement is virtually useless with a conventional deck. First, we must specify for the shuffling process a probability distribution that is applicable to a finite-length deck (Eq. 6-1 implies an infinite deck). From experience, an expert shuffling operation interleaves alternate packets of cards where each packet consists of one, two, or three cards (with amateur shuffling the packets may comprise four or more cards). Accordingly, we let r_1, r_2, and r_3 represent the probabilities that a packet selected at random is composed of one, two, or three, cards, respectively, where

$$r_1 + r_2 + r_3 = 1$$

Or, equivalently, we can define p_1 as the probability that a packet ends with the first card. Given that the packet does not end with the first card, the (conditional) probability that it ends with the second card is designated by p_2. And, given that the packet does not end with the second card, the (conditional) probability that it ends with the third card is $p_3 = 1$. Evidently,

$$r_1 = p_1, \quad r_2 = (1 - p_1)p_2, \quad r_3 = (1 - p_1)(1 - p_2)$$

If three consecutive cards of the new sequence are observed, one of four patterns must occur: A A A, A A B, A B A, or A B B, where A represents a card from one section of the divided deck and B represents a card from the other section. The probability of occurrence of each of these four patterns is readily calculated to be

$$P(AAA) = \frac{r_3}{R}$$

$$P(AAB) = \frac{1 - r_1}{R}$$

$$P(ABA) = \frac{r_1}{R}$$

$$P(ABB) = \frac{1 - r_1}{R}$$

where

$$R = r_1 + 2r_2 + 3r_3$$

We can now compute the transition probabilities between packets after observing one of the four allowable patterns. Let $P_t(X)$ be the probability of a transition, given the event X, and let $Q_t(X)$ be the probability of no transition. Then it is elementary to demonstrate that

$$P_t(AAA) = 1 \qquad\qquad\qquad\qquad\text{6-6}$$

$$P_t(AAB) = p_1 = r_1 \qquad\qquad\qquad\text{6-7}$$

$$P_t(ABA) = p_1 = r_1 \qquad\qquad\qquad\text{6-8}$$

$$P_t(ABB) = p_2 = \frac{r_2}{1 - r_1} \qquad\qquad\qquad\text{6-9}$$

$$Q_t(AAA) = 0 \qquad\qquad\qquad\qquad\text{6-10}$$

$$Q_t(AAB) = 1 - p_1 = 1 - r_1 \qquad\qquad\text{6-11}$$

$$Q_t(ABA) = 1 - p_1 = 1 - r_1 \qquad\qquad\text{6-12}$$

$$Q_t(ABB) = 1 - p_2 = \frac{r_3}{1 - r_1} \qquad\qquad\text{6-13}$$

For a second shuffle, consider the A cards to be divided into C and E cards and the B cards to be divided into D and F cards, depending on the deck partitioning. The first test is to apply Eqs. 6-6 through 6-13 for transition probabilities between members of the CD set and the EF set. Secondly, we apply the same equations to determine the conditional transition probabilities for the C set versus the D set and the E set versus the F set. The next card in sequence within each set occurs with the probability accorded that set. This procedure can evidently be generalized to three or more shuffles; for n shuffles, there are 2^n sets of cards.

A numerical example will clarify the above concepts. Observation of professional card dealers indicates a shuffling operation described by

$$P(\eta) = \begin{cases} (8/9)(1/9)^{n-1} & \text{for } \eta = 1, 2 \\ (1/9)^{n-1} & \text{for } \eta = 3 \\ 0 & \text{for } \eta \geq 4 \end{cases} \qquad\qquad\text{6-14}$$

(which approximates Eq. 6-1). That is, in terms of packet lengths, $r_1 = 8/9$, $r_2 = 8/81$, and $r_3 = 1/81$. Thus, assuming an equipartition of the deck, the probability of successive cards of the post-shuffle sequence alternating between members of the opposing halves of the original sequence is 8/9; at any point in the new sequence, the probability of obtaining two consecutive members of the original sequence is 8/81; and the probability of obtaining, at any point, three consecutive members of the original sequence is 1/81.

With this probability distribution for the shuffling process, the prediction function for the $(m + 1)$st card is readily obtained. Consider the initial state S_j defining the sequence of cards $c_1, c_2, c_3, \ldots, c_{51}, c_{52}$. A single shuffle is performed according to Eq. 6-14 (with equipartition of the deck and the first card remaining invariant). The first m cards forming the new state are then composed of α cards of one half and $m - \alpha$ cards of the other half. Thus, the $(m + 1)$st card is either the $(\alpha + 1)$st card of the first half (the A set) or the $(m - \alpha + 1)$st card of the second half (the B set) with respective probabilities corresponding to Eq. 6-14 as a function of the $(m - 2)$nd, $(m - 1)$st, and mth cards. As an example, let $m = 10$ and let the first ten cards of the new sequence following one shuffle be $c_1, c_2, c_{27}, c_3, c_{28}, c_4, c_{29}, c_5, c_{30}, c_{31}$. The eleventh card must be either c_{32} or c_6 with probabilities 1/9 and 8/9, respectively, as seen from Eqs. 6-13 and 6-9.

Continuing the example: After two shuffles (we assume now that results of the first shuffle are not disclosed) with the first ten cards of the new state forming the sequence $c_1, c_{27}, c_{13}, c_2, c_{39}, c_{40}, c_{28}, c_{14}, c_{15}, c_3$, the eleventh card must be c_4, c_{29}, c_{16}, or c_{41}. Let the A set initially encompass cards $c_1, c_2, \ldots, c_{26}$ and the B set cards $c_{27}, c_{28}, \ldots, c_{52}$. Then, following two shuffles, the classification of the first ten cards of the new sequence is

C set : c_1, c_2, c_3

D set : c_{27}, c_{28}

E set : c_{13}, c_{14}, c_{15}

F set : c_{39}, c_{40}

The first test, as described above, is to distinguish between the CD and EF sets. Referring to the new sequence, the last three cards form an AAB pattern; then, from Eqs. 6-7 and 6-11,

$$P\{EF\} = r_1 = \frac{8}{9} \qquad\qquad 6\text{-}15$$

and

$$P\{CD\} = 1 - r_1 = \frac{1}{9} \qquad\qquad 6\text{-}16$$

Equations 6-15 and 6-16 represent the probabilities that the eleventh card is a member of the EF or CD set, respectively. Now, given that the eleventh card belongs to the EF set, we test for E versus F by noting that the last three cards of the EF set (c_{40}, c_{14}, c_{15}) form an ABB pattern. Hence, applying Eqs. 6-9 and 6-13,

$$P\{F|EF\} = \frac{r_2}{1 - r_1} = \frac{8}{9} \qquad\qquad 6\text{-}17$$

and

$$P\{E|EF\} = \frac{r_3}{1 - r} = \frac{1}{9} \qquad\qquad 6\text{-}18$$

Similarly, in testing for C versus D, we note that the last three cards of the CD set (c_2, c_{28}, c_3) form an ABA pattern. Thence, from Eqs. 6-8 and 6-12,

$$P\{D|CD\} = r_1 = \frac{8}{9} \qquad\qquad 6\text{-}19$$

and

$$P\{C|CD\} = 1 - r_1 = \frac{1}{9} \qquad\qquad 6\text{-}20$$

The probability that the eleventh card is c_4, c_{29}, c_{11}, or c_{41} is then determined by Eqs. 6-15 through 6-20 in the following manner:

$$P\{c_4\} = P\{C|CD\} \cdot P\{CD\} = (1 - r_1)^2 = \frac{1}{81}$$

$$P\{c_{29}\} = P\{D|CD\} \cdot P\{CD\} = r_1(1 - r_1) = \frac{8}{81}$$

$$P\{c_{16}\} = P\{E|EF\} \cdot P\{EF\} = \frac{r_1 r_3}{1 - r_1} = \frac{8}{81}$$

$$P\{c_{41}\} = P\{F|EF\} \cdot P\{EF\} = \frac{r_1 r_2}{1 - r_1} = \frac{64}{81}$$

Continuation of this procedure for three shuffles is straightforward, albeit hampered by arithmetical drudgery. Practical applications of card prediction, even with our pragmatic theorem, invite the aid of a small computer.

MONGE'S SHUFFLE

There are many methods of card shuffling other than the alternate interleaving of card packets.[†] Each method might be associated with one or

[†] For more esoteric studies of shuffling phenomena, the reader is referred to the works of Henri Poincaré and Jacques Hadamard on probability chains.

more convenient theorems for card prediction, depending on the regularities involved in the shuffling procedure. As one example, consider a pack of cards arranged in the order $c_1, c_2, c_3, \ldots$; we shuffle this pack by placing c_2 above c_1, c_3 under c_1, c_4 above c_2, c_5 under c_3, etc.; this operation is known as Monge's shuffle. Then, illustratively, if the pack contains $6n - 2$ cards, the $2n$th card always retains its original position. With 22 cards ($n = 4$) shuffled repeatedly by this process, the eighth card never changes place; the fifth and sixteenth cards oscillate, exchanging positions at each shuffle; and the third, thirteenth, and eighteenth cards circulate in an independent cycle, regaining their original positions every third shuffle. Cyclic periods of the full deck are generally longer with Monge's method as compared with the perfect shuffle (interleaving alternate cards).

There exists a theorem stating that the cyclic period ρ resulting from Monge's shuffle on a $2n$-card deck is equal to the smallest root of the congruence

$$2^\rho \equiv -1, \quad \mod(4n + 1)$$

and if this congruence possesses no solutions, ρ equals the smallest root of the congruence:

$$2^\rho \equiv 1, \quad \mod(4n + 1)$$

With 52 cards ($n = 26$), Monge's shuffle operations cycle the deck after 12 shuffles ($2^{12} \equiv 1$, mod 105), compared to 8 for the perfect shuffle. For a 16-card deck, the original order returns after 5 of Monge's shuffles, compared to 4 perfect shuffles needed for cycling.

Card probabilities

SAMPLING WITHOUT REPLACEMENT

Combinations and permutations of cards generally involve the hypergeometric distribution (Eq. 2-14)—as opposed to dice or coin combinations, which are governed by the binomial distribution. That is, card statistics involve the principle of sampling without replacement. An elementary illustration of this principle, which demonstrates the considerable difference from sampling with replacement, is that of drawing two cards at random from a complete deck. The probability of both cards being Aces (say) is $(4/52) \cdot (3/51) = 0.0045$, whereas if the first card is replaced before drawing the second, the probability of obtaining two Aces is $(4/52)^2 = 0.0059$. Another example supplies greater emphasis: A single red card is removed from the 52-card pack. Then 13 cards are drawn and found to be the same color; the (conditional) probability that they are black is

$$\frac{26!/13!}{26!/13! + 25!/12!} = \frac{2}{3}$$

a greater difference than might be expected from the corresponding probability of 1/2 for sampling with replacement. Of course, if the population size (52, initially) is large compared with the sample size (4, for the example of the card ranks), the binomial and hypergeometric distributions produce approximately the same results. The striking differences occur as cards are withdrawn from the deck. If we consider the number of cards m drawn without replacement until a Spade appears (at the mth draw), it is simple to show that

$$P(m) = \frac{13\binom{39}{m-1}}{(53-m)\binom{52}{m-1}}, \qquad m = 1, 2, \ldots, 40$$

constitutes the probability distribution over m. Clearly, $P(m)$ becomes quite small as more cards are withdrawn without a Spade appearing. For $m = 11$, $P(m)$ has decreased to 0.0124 from its value of 0.25 at $m = 1$. For $m = 40$, $P(40) = 1.575 \times 10^{-12}$. Similarly, the number of cards drawn without replacement until an Ace appears is

$$P(m) = \frac{4\binom{48}{m-1}}{(53-m)\binom{52}{m-1}}, \qquad m = 1, 2, \ldots, 49$$

For $m = 11$, $P(m)$ is 0.0394 as compared with $P(1) = 1/13$. For $m = 49$, $P(49) = 3.694 \times 10^{-6}$.

An example demanding careful distinction between a priori and a posteriori probabilities in sampling without replacement concerns a pack of cards from which one card has been removed. Two cards are drawn at random and found to be Spades. We wish to determine the probability that the missing card is also a Spade. A priori, this probability is 1/4. The joint probability that the missing card and the two drawn are Spades is

$$p_1 = \frac{1}{4} \times \frac{12}{51} \times \frac{11}{50} = \frac{11}{850}$$

while the joint probability that the missing card is a non-Spade and two

Spades are drawn is

$$P_2 = \frac{3}{4} \times \frac{13}{51} \times \frac{12}{50} = \frac{39}{850}$$

Hence, applying Bayes's theorem, Eq. 2-7, to determine the a posteriori probability of the missing card being a Spade, we obtain

$$P(\text{Spade}|\text{two Spades drawn}) = \frac{P(\text{Spade}) \, P(\text{two Spades drawn}|\text{Spade})}{P(\text{two Spades drawn})}$$

$$= \frac{P_1}{P_1 + P_2} = \frac{11}{50}$$

EXPECTED NUMBER OF CARDS TO ACHIEVE SUCCESS

An important consideration in card probabilities is the expected number of cards drawn without replacement to achieve a particular success. We could ask, for example, the expected number of cards drawn to uncover the first Ace, or the first Spade, etc. The solution of this type of problem is obtained from the discrete analog to the nonparametric technique used in order statistics. An equivalent to the density function of ordered observations can be derived directly. With a deck composed of a kinds of cards and b of each kind (there are, then, $n = ab$ total cards), the probability $P_i(r)$, $i < a$, that none of the i kinds is represented in a random sample of r cards is given by

$$P_i(r) = \frac{\binom{n - ib}{r}}{\binom{n}{r}} = \frac{(n - r)_{ib}}{(n)_{ib}}, \qquad r = 1, 2, \ldots, n - ib + 1$$

Now, if we define $p_i(r)$ as the probability of failure through the first $r - 1$ cards times the probability of success on the rth card, we have

$$p_i(r) = \frac{ibP_i(r - 1)}{n - r + 1} = \frac{ib(n - r)_{ib-1}}{(n)_{ib}}, \qquad \begin{cases} r = 1, 2, \ldots, n - ib + 1 \\ i < a \end{cases} \qquad 6\text{-}21$$

For $i = a$, $p_a(1) = 1$.

The expected number of cards to achieve the event specified by the probability $p_i(r)$ is defined by

$$E_i(r) = \sum_{n=1}^{n-b+1} rp_i(r) = \sum \frac{rib(n - r)_{ib-1}}{(n)_{ib}} = \frac{n + 1}{ib + 1} \qquad 6\text{-}22$$

with the expression for $p_i(r)$ substituted from Eq. 6-21. By extension, the expected number of cards $E_i^m(r)$ to uncover the mth number of one of i groups of b cards is

$$E_i^m(r) = \frac{n+1}{ib+1}\, m, \qquad m \leq ib \qquad\qquad 6\text{-}23$$

(If the cards are drawn with replacement, $E_i^m(r)$ is easily shown to be nm/ib.)

We can now answer the questions posed. The expected number of cards to uncover the first Ace is, from Eq. 6-22 with $n = 52$, $i = 1$, and $b = 4$,

$$E_1(r) = \frac{53}{5} = 10.6$$

The expected number of cards until the appearance of the first Spade is also given by Eq. 6-22, with $i = 1$ and $b = 13$:

$$E_1(r) = \frac{53}{14} = 3.786$$

And, according to Eq. 6-23, it is expected that

$$E_1^{13}(r) = 49.214$$

cards are required to expose all Spades in the deck. It also follows that the expected number of cards between successive Spades are equal. That is, if player A deals from the pack until a Spade appears, then passes the remainder of the deck to player B, who deals until a second Spade appears and then passes the remainder of the deck to player C, who deals cards until the appearance of the third Spade, the expectations of the number of cards dealt by A, B, and C are identical.

From Eq. 6-22 we can also answer the following question: What is the expected number of cards drawn without replacement until at least one card of each suit is exposed? With four suits, S, H, D, and C, we can write this expectation in the form

$$
\begin{aligned}
E(S \cup H \cup D \cup C) = {}& E(S) + E(H) + E(D) + E(C) - E(S \cap H) \\
& - E(S \cap D) - \cdots - E(D \cap C) \\
& + E(S \cap H \cap D) + E(S \cap H \cap C) + \cdots \\
& + E(H \cap D \cap C) - \cdots \\
& - E(S \cap H \cap D \cap C)
\end{aligned}
$$

After appropriate substitutions,

$$E(S \cup H \cup D \cup C) = (n + 1) \left[\frac{\binom{a}{1}}{b + 1} - \frac{\binom{a}{2}}{2b + 1} \right.$$

$$\left. + \frac{\binom{a}{3}}{3b + 1} - \cdots \pm \frac{\binom{a}{a}}{ab + 1} \right]$$

For the conventional deck, $a = 4$, $b = 13$ (and $n = 52$); thus

$$E(S \cup H \cup D \cup C) = 53 \left(\frac{4}{14} - \frac{6}{27} + \frac{4}{40} - \frac{1}{53} \right) = 7.665 \qquad \textit{6-24}$$

Interestingly, replacement of the cards creates a problem easier to solve. Drawing until each suit is exposed at least once represents four exclusively ordered events. The probability of obtaining the first suit at the first card is $p_1 = 1$. The probability that the second card is a suit other than the first is $p_2 = 3/4$. Subsequently, $p_3 = 1/2$ and $p_4 = 1/4$ by the same reasoning. Thus, by applying Eq. 5-21, we have

$$E_1(r) = 1, \quad E_2(r) = \frac{4}{3}, \quad E_3(r) = 2, \quad E_4(r) = 4$$

The sum of these expectations produces

$$E(S \cup H \cup D \cup C) - 8\tfrac{1}{3}$$

which, as might well be anticipated, is greater than the value (Eq. 6-24) obtained by sampling without replacement.

COMBINATIONS

The number of combinations of n objects taken r at a time is given by Eq. 2-14 as $\binom{n}{r}$. Thus, the number of distinct Poker hands totals

$$\binom{52}{5} = 2,598,960 \qquad \textit{6-25}$$

and the number of different hands possible at cribbage is $\binom{52}{6} = 20,358,520$.

An extension of this combinatorial formula considers the probability P that, in a random sample of size r selected without replacement from a population of n elements, all of N given elements are contained in the sample. It is simple to prove that

$$P = \frac{\binom{n-N}{r-N}}{\binom{n}{r}}$$

Illustratively, the probability that a Poker hand contains all four Aces is

$$P = \frac{\binom{52-4}{5-4}}{\binom{52}{5}} = 1.847 \times 10^{-5}$$

Similar combinatorial formulas can answer most of the elementary probability questions that arise in games of cards.

Simple card games

In addition to the conventional card games that have evolved throughout the centuries, many rudimentary games can be invented spontaneously to illustrate certain principles.

FIRST ACE WINS

Consider the simple game wherein two players, A and B, alternately draw cards from a deck, the winner being the player who first draws an Ace. If player A draws the first card, he wins the game immediately with probability

$$p_1 = \frac{a}{n}$$

(where a is the number of aces and n the total number of cards). Player A also wins on his second try if the first two cards are non-Aces and the third is an Ace. The probability p_2 of this occurrence, by the theorem of compound probabilities, is expressed in the form

$$p_2 = \frac{a(n-a)(n-a-1)}{n(n-1)(n-2)}$$

Similarly, the probability p_3 of A winning on his third try (the first four cards drawn being non-Aces and the fifth an Ace) is

$$p_3 = \frac{a(n-a)(n-a-1)(n-a-2)(n-a-3)}{n(n-1)(n-2)(n-3)(n-4)}$$

Hence, the probability P_A that player A wins the game is the sum $p_1 + p_2 + p_3 + \cdots + p_{(n-a)/2}$:

$$P_A = \frac{a}{n}\left[1 + \sum_{i=1}^{(n-a)/2} \frac{(n-a)_{2i}}{(n-1)_{2i}}\right]$$

Analogously, player B's probability P_B of winning the game is

$$P_B = \frac{a}{n}\sum_{i=0}^{[(n-a)/2]-1} \frac{(n-a)_{2i+1}}{(n-1)_{2i+1}}$$

For $a = 4$ and $n = 52$, we have, numerically,

$$P_A = 0.52 \quad \text{and} \quad P_B = 0.48$$

Thus, player A gains a 4-percent advantage by being first to draw.

With three players A, B, and C attempting, in order, to draw the first Ace, we can readily derive the expressions

$$P_A = \frac{a}{n}\left[1 + \sum_{i=1}^{(n-a)/3} \frac{(n-a)_{3i}}{(n-1)_{3i}}\right]$$

$$P_B = \frac{a}{n}\sum_{i=0}^{[(n-a)/3]-1} \frac{(n-a)_{3i+1}}{(n-1)_{3i+1}}$$

$$P_C = \frac{a}{n}\sum_{i=0}^{[(n-a)/3]-1} \frac{(n-a)_{3i+2}}{(n-1)_{3i+2}}$$

For $a = 4$ and $n = 52$, these equations are evaluated numerically as

$$P_A = 0.360 \qquad P_B = 0.333 \qquad P_C = 0.307$$

Obviously, as the number of players increases, the greater is the advantage of drawing first.

HIGHEST RANK IN A SAMPLE

It is also informative to consider a game wherein the cards of a pack are exposed one by one until all four suits are represented, with the first-drawn card of each suit set aside. Of the four cards so collected, we inquire as to the probability P_m that m is the highest rank (Ace = 1, Jack = 11, Queen = 12, King = 13). Clearly, the probability P that the greatest rank does not exceed m is $P = P_1 + P_2 + \cdots + P_m$, which is equivalent to $(m/13)^4$, since the probability that each suit contributes a rank m or less is $m/13$. Therefore, replacing m by $m - 1$, we can write

$$P - P_m = P_1 + P_2 + \cdots + P_{m-1} = \left(\frac{m-1}{13}\right)^4$$

Combining the expressions for P and $P - P_m$,

$$P_m = \frac{m^4 - (m-1)^4}{13^4}$$

which is monotonically increasing with m. For $m = 13$ (King), $P_{13} = 0.274$.

INFORMATION: THE EXPOSED ACE

It is enlightening to consider an example that illustrates the effect of information on card probabilities. Suppose that in a random sample of five cards, one is known to be an Ace. Then the probability P that the remaining four cards comprise at least one more Ace is

$$P = \frac{\binom{4}{2}\binom{48}{3} + \binom{4}{3}\binom{48}{2} + \binom{4}{4}\binom{48}{1}}{\binom{4}{1}\binom{48}{4} + \binom{4}{2}\binom{48}{3} + \binom{4}{3}\binom{48}{2} + \binom{4}{4}\binom{48}{1}} = 0.1222$$

Now suppose that of the five-card sample, one is known to be the Ace of Spades. The probability P' that the remaining four cards include at least one more Ace is then determined to be

$$P' = \frac{\binom{3}{1}\binom{48}{3} + \binom{3}{2}\binom{48}{2} + \binom{3}{3}\binom{48}{1}}{\binom{51}{4}} = 0.2214$$

In this instance the knowledge of the specific Ace has increased the probability of one or more additional Aces in the sample. Knowledge of the color only results in an intermediate value of the probability for additional Aces. Specifically, the probability P'' of the four unknown cards comprising one or more Aces, given the first card to be a red Ace, is

$$P'' = \frac{\binom{2}{2}\binom{2}{0}\binom{48}{3} + \binom{2}{1}\binom{2}{1}\binom{48}{3} + 2\binom{2}{2}\binom{2}{1}\binom{48}{2} + \binom{2}{2}\binom{2}{2}\binom{48}{1}}{\binom{2}{1}\binom{48}{4} + \binom{2}{2}\binom{2}{0}\binom{48}{3} + \binom{2}{1}\binom{2}{1}\binom{48}{3} + 2\binom{2}{2}\binom{2}{1}\binom{48}{2} + \binom{2}{2}\binom{2}{2}\binom{48}{1}} = 0.1896$$

This probability is closer to the specified-Ace value than to the value for the case of an unspecified Ace. In order to avoid semantic confusion, each case should be considered as a distinct dichotomy—the particular condition (red Ace, for example) is either specified or not; alternations between color and suit produce equal probabilities for all cases.

The simplest model reduces the deck to two cards, marked Hi and Lo, randomly dispensed, one to each of two players. Player A looks at his card and may either pass or bet. If he passes, he pays player B an amount $a > 0$. If he bets, player B, without looking, has the option of (1) passing, whereby he pays a units to A, or (2) calling, whereby A or B receives an amount $b > a$ from his opponent according as A's card is Hi or Lo. It is elementary to show that if A's card is Hi, he bets with unity probability, whereas if he draws the Lo card, he should bet with probability P_1:

$$P_1 = \frac{b - a}{b + a}$$

B's strategy is to call with probability P_2:

$$P_2 = 1 - P_1 = \frac{2a}{b + a}$$

and the value γ of the game is

$$\gamma = aP_1 = \frac{a(b - a)}{b + a}$$

Matching problems

Problems of card matching, or rencontres, are often resolved most elegantly through the application of combinatorial analysis. The simplest form of card matching consists of exposing in sequence the cards from two n-card decks and noting how often a match occurs (decks are assumed to consist of n distinct cards numbered $1, 2, \ldots, n$); a solution is given by Eq. 4-36. We can also consider the problem as equivalent to determining the number of permutations of n distinct elements such that the number of times i that element k is in the kth position corresponds to the number of matches, $i \leq k = 1, 2, \ldots, n$. This view situates the problem in the domain of permutations with restricted position (see Chapter 2); the application of hit and rook polynomials is thereby suggested. A *rook polynomial* $R(x)$ is an ordinary generating function of the number of ways of placing non-mutually attacking rooks on a chessboard. Thus, to formulate the rook polynomial, we envision the equivalent $n \times n$ chessboard as containing n rooks, no two in the same row or column; i rooks on the negatively sloped diagonal correspond to i matches.

The rook polynomial is then expressible as

$$[R(x)]^n = (1 + x)^n$$

Further, we define a *hit* as the occurrence of an element of a permutation in a forbidden position. Thus the *hit polynomial* $N_n(t)$ engenders the permutations by enumerating the number of hits. That is,

$$N_n(t) = \sum N_i^i$$

where N_i is the number of permutations of n distinct elements, i of which are in restricted positions. Clearly, the rook polynomial determines the hit polynomial, and vice versa. For the simple card-matching problem, the hit polynomial is given by

$$N_n(t) = [1 + (t - 1)E^{-1}]^n n! = (E - 1 + t)^n 0! \qquad 6\text{-}26$$

where E is a shift operator, so that $(n - k)! = E^{-k} n!$ Equation 6-26 is recognizable as a form of the *Appell polynomial* $D_n(t)$. By definition,

$$D_n(t) = n! \sum_{k=0}^{n} \frac{(t - 1)^k}{k!}$$

and the recursion formula for Appell polynomials is

$$D_n(t) = nD_{n-1}(t) + (t - 1)^n \qquad 6\text{-}27$$

Setting $t = 0$ is equivalent to allowing no matches to occur among all permutations of the n elements. Equation 6-27 then simplifies to

$$D_n(0) = nD_{n-1}(0) + (-1)^n$$

And, by iteration of this equation, we can derive the expression

$$D_n(0) = \sum_{k=0}^{n} \binom{n}{k} (-1)^k (n - k)! = (E - 1)^n 0!$$

as the applicable hit polynomial. Since $n!$ is the total number of permutations, $D_n(0)/n!$ is the probability of no matches occurring, and the probability

P of at least one match is

$$P = 1 - \frac{D_n(0)}{n!} = 1 - \sum_{k=0}^{n} \binom{n}{k} (-1)^k (n-k)!$$

$$= 1 - \sum_{k=0}^{n} \frac{1}{k!} (-1)^k$$

$$= 1 - \frac{1}{2!} + \frac{1}{3!} - \cdots + \frac{(-1)^{n-1}}{n!}$$

For large values of *n* (conventionally, $n = 52$), a close approximation for *P* is given by

$$P \to 1 - \frac{1}{e} = 0.632$$

identical to Montmort's urn problem discussed in Chapter 4.

A more difficult matching problem, not readily handled by conventional means, is the matching of two *n*-card decks, each of which comprises *a* suits and *b* cards in each suit. A match is now defined as the coincidence of two cards of the same rank without regard to suit (we could, obviously, interchange rank and suit and inquire as to the matching by suits). To determine the rook polynomial for $a = 4$ and $b = 13$, consider a 4×4 chessboard. There are $4^2 = 16$ ways of placing a single Rook on such a board; two mutually nonattacking Rooks can be placed in

$$\frac{4^2 \times 3^2}{2!} = 72 \text{ ways}$$

three nonattacking Rooks can be placed on this board in

$$\frac{4^2 \times 3^2 \times 2^2}{3!} = 96 \text{ ways}$$

and four Rooks allow

$$\frac{4^2 \times 3^2 \times 2^2 \times 1^2}{4!} = 24 \text{ ways.}$$

It is clearly impossible to place five or more nonattacking Rooks on a 4×4 chessboard. The Rook polynomial is therefore written as

$$R(x) = 1 + 16x + 72x^2 + 96x^2 + 24x^4$$

We are specifically concerned with the polynomial $[R(x)]^{13}$ arising from the 13 cards in each suit. The corresponding hit polynomial assumes the form

$$N_n(t) = 52! + 13 \cdot 16 \cdot 51!(t-1) + \cdots + (24)^{13}(t-1)^{52} \qquad 6\text{-}28$$

and the quantity $N_n(0)/n!$ is the probability of no matches. While straight-forward, the calculations attendant to Eq. 6-28 are formidable in number.

By recourse to a high-speed digital computer, the values of $P(i)$, the probabilities of exactly i matches (disregarding suits), are obtained as

$P(0) = .01623$	$P(6) = .10576$
$P(1) = .06890$	$P(7) = .05855$
$P(2) = .14416$	$\cdots$
$P(3) = .19819$	$\cdots$
$P(4) = .20132$	$P(51) = 0$
$P(5) = .16111$	$P(52) = 1.087 \times 10^{-50}$

Hence the probability of at least one match is $1 - P(0) = 0.984$, somewhat higher than might be expected intuitively. It is also of interest to calculate the expected number of matches as

$$E(i) = \sum_{i=0}^{52} iP(i) = 4$$

which is also the most probable number. The standard deviation is $8/\sqrt{17}$. While the probabilities of obtaining i matches with distinct decks closely conform to a Poisson distribution, approximations for the case of structured decks are somewhat inaccurate. A method (due to Riordan) of estimating $P(i)$ by the expansion of binomial moments produces errors on the order of 5 percent. Another approximation (suggested by R. E. Greenwood) is that of a Gram-Charlier series of type B. For a four-fold deck with a large number of cards ($n \gg 52$), a good approximation is $P(0) \simeq e^{-4} = .0183$.

We can also construct rook polynomials for other than square chess-boards; for example, rectangular, triangular, or trapezoidal chessboards have been utilized to solve problems in combinatorics. Simon Newcomb's problem offers a classical illustration involving polynomials corresponding to a triangular board. First posed by that eminent American astronomer, the problem relates to a deck of cards that are dealt out onto a single pile as long as the cards are in nondescending order (consecutive cards of the same rank become members of the same pile); a new pile is begun with each occurrence of a card of lesser rank than its predecessor. It is desired to determine the number of ways in which k piles appear. The hit poly-nomial is expressed by $A(1^{n_1}2^{n_2} \cdots s^{n_s})$ for a deck composed of n_1 single elements, n_2 pairs, n_3 triplets, etc. A conventional deck, specified by 4^{13}, generates the hit polynomial

$$A(4^{13}) = [A(A + 1 - t)(A + 2 - 2t)(A + 3 - 3t)]^{13}$$

where the A's are triangular permutation polynomials. Similar to Simon Newcomb's problem is the question of the number of ways of placing k bishops on an $n \times n$ chessboard so that no bishop is attacked by another. In general, it is difficult to obtain explicit solutions to problems of this nature.

A simplified version of a matching problem due to Levene consists of shuffling together the Hearts and Spades of a conventional deck. The 26 cards are then divided into two piles of 13 cards each and matched against each other; a match is recorded if the ith of Spades and the ith of Hearts occur at the same position in the two piles. We wish to determine the probability of exactly r matches. The problem is attacked most readily by deriving the moments of the number of matches as

$$\mu(i) = \left(\frac{1}{2}\right)^i \frac{(N)_i}{[N - (1/2)]_i}, \qquad i = 1, 2, \ldots$$

where N is the number of cards in each pile. The probability distribution of the number of matches r is accordingly determined to be

$$p(r) = \binom{n}{r} \frac{i}{2^r [N - (1/2)]_r} \sum_{j=0}^{N-r} \frac{(N - r)_j (-1)^j}{[N - r - (1/2)]_j 2^j j!}$$

The probability of no matches is, for $N = 13$, 0.5948. For $r = 1$, $p(1) = 0.3088$; also $p(2) = 0.0804$ and $p(3) = 0.0140$. As $N \to \infty$, the number of matches assumes a Poisson distribution and $p(r)$ approaches the values 0.6065, 0.3033, 0.0758, and 0.0126 for $r = 0, 1, 2, 3$, respectively.

Oddly, the above problem assumes a simpler form (suggested by Kullback) if the compositions of the two piles are determined by random, independent drawings from two populations. Let the first pile be composed by drawing cards from a population containing a_i cards of the ith kind, $i = 1, 2, \ldots, k$, where p_i is the constant probability that a card of the ith kind is drawn. Similarly, let the second pile be formed by drawing cards from a second population containing b_i cards of the ith kind, $i = 1, 2, \ldots, k$, and let p_i' be the constant probability of drawing a card of the ith kind from this population. Each pair of cards in the same position in the two piles constitutes an independent event; thus the probability p of a match is simply

$$p = \sum_{i=1}^{k} p_i p_i'$$

The probability of r matches therefore forms a binomial distribution

$$p(r) = \binom{N}{r} p^r (1 - p)^{N-r}$$

As N and k both increase indefinitely, $p(r)$ becomes Poisson-distributed.

A PERMUTATION PROBLEM

Many card problems pose difficulties not readily surmounted by even the incisive technique of permutations with restricted positions. Consider a random permutation on an ordered n-card deck, which is characterized as follows: The pack of cards is sampled randomly, without replacement, until card 1 is obtained. At this point the cards exposed, $a_1, a_2, \ldots, a_{m_1-1}, 1$, are said to form the *first cycle*, of length m_1. Let x be the lowest-numbered card remaining unexposed in the deck (not in the first cycle); from these $n - m_1$ cards we again sample without replacement until x is obtained. The cards newly exposed, $b_1, b_2, \ldots, b_{m_2-1}, x$, are said to form the *second cycle*. This process is continued until all n cards are categorized into cycles. We thence inquire as to the length and expected number of the cycles arising from this permutation process. Golomb, Welch, and Goldstein have proved several theorems for this problem in connection with cycles from nonlinear shift registers.[†] The distribution of the lengths m_1 of the first cycle is flat; that is, all values of m_1 from 1 to n are equiprobable (at $1/n$). Consequently, the expected length $\bar{m}_1$ of the first cycle is

$$\bar{m}_1 = \frac{n + 1}{2}$$

with a standard deviation of

$$\sigma = \frac{\sqrt{3(N^2 - 1)}}{6}$$

The expected length of the second cycle has the value

$$\bar{m}_2 = \frac{1}{2}\left[n - \frac{(n + 1)}{2} + 1 \right] = \frac{n + 1}{4}$$

and, in general, the expected length of the ith cycle is given by

$$\bar{m}_i = \frac{n + 1}{2^i}$$

[†] Solomon W. Golomb, Lloyd R. Welch, and Richard M. Goldstein, "Cycles from Nonlinear Shift Registers," PR No. 20-389, Jet Propulsion Laboratory, California Institute of Technology, Pasadena, Calif., Aug. 30, 1959.

The expected number of cycles $\bar{c}$ obtained from the n-card deck is defined as

$$\bar{c} = \sum_{i=1}^{n} i^{-1}$$

which, for $n = 52$, equals 6.83. The standard deviation about this mean is given by

$$\sigma = \left[\sum_{i=1}^{n} \frac{n-i}{(n-i-1)^2} \right]^{1/2}$$

which evaluates to 2.91 for $n = 52$.

Letting L_n be the expected length of the longest cycle, the probability that the first cycle is longest is evidently equal to the relative expected length L_n/n of the longest cycle. It is then possible to demonstrate the existence of the constant λ, defined as

$$\lambda = \lim_{n \to \infty} \frac{L_n}{n}$$

The longest cycle thus has an expected length of λn; the second longest cycle has an expected length of approximately $\lambda(1 - \lambda)n$; and, with progressively decreasing accuracy, the kth longest cycle has an expected length of $\lambda(1 - \lambda)^{k-1}n$. Golomb, Welch, and Goldstein have determined the upper and lower bounds on λ to be

$$\lambda \geq \frac{2}{3} + \frac{1}{3} \ln \frac{27}{32} = 0.61003 \cdots$$

and

$$\lambda \leq 1 + \frac{1}{3} \ln \frac{27}{32} - \frac{1}{e \ln (32e/27)} = 0.62891 \cdots$$

A digital computer program has produced the value $\lambda = 0.62432965\ldots$. No algebraic relationship between λ and other mathematical constants has yet been established.

Formal card games

Literally tens of thousands of formalized card games have evolved or have been invented over the past few centuries. The majority of them have disappeared into a well-deserved oblivion. Of the remainder, only a very few entail greater complexity than a pure strategy or simple mixed strategy. Many games possess only rudimentary structure, but have strategies involving selection among an astronomical number of alternatives. Bridge (which we shall consider in a separate chapter) and Poker are generally nominated as the two card games demanding the highest level of skill —particularly the former, which is recognized by international competition (the level of Poker skills is subject to some debate).

A partial enumeration of the more popular card games might include Bézique, with its variations of Pinochle, Rubicon Bézique, and Chinese Bézique; Hearts, with its variations of Black Lady, Cancellation Hearts, Omnibus Hearts, Polignac, and Slobberhannes; the diverse forms of Poker; Conquian (a corruption of the Spanish *con quien*?), the direct ancestor of all Rummy games, which bred the Canasta family (including Samba, Bolivia, and Oklahoma) and the Gin Rummy family (including Seven-Card Rummy, Kings and Queens, Five-Hundred Rummy, Persian Rummy, Contract Rummy, Continental Rummy, Brelan—a fifteenth-century French rummy game—and Panguingue or "Pan"); All Fours, with its derivatives of Seven Up, Auction Pitch, and Cinch; Skat (which has inspired a World Congress of Skat players) with its variations of Schafkopf, Calabrasella, and Six Bid Solo; Klaberjass or Kalabriasz (among many spellings); Cribbage, which represents the rare case of having been invented by one man, Sir John Suckling (1609–1642), who based it on the contemporarily popular game of Noddy; the Cassino family; the Whist family, with its offshoots of Black Maria, Mort, Cayenne, Boston, Preference, and Vint; Whist's successors: Auction Bridge, Contract Bridge, Brint, Calypso, and Towie (originated by J. Leonard Replogle), *inter alia*; the many Solitaire games, including Klondike, Canfield, Spider, Forty Thieves, Golf, and the varieties of Patience; Bassette (a predecessor of Faro invented by Pietro Cellini at the end of the sixteenth century); Primero (Cardano's favorite game); Primero's descendants: Brag and Loo; Gilet, a French version of Primero; Michigan; the varieties of Euchre; Handicap; Muggins; Gleek; Ecarté; Belote (a relative of this French game, Jo-Jotte, was created by Ely Culbertson in 1937); Monte and its many variations; Svoyi Kozin; Durachki; Tresillo; Quadrille (or Cuartillo); Ombre; "66"; Tablanette; Hasenpfeffer; Spoil Five (the national game of Ireland); Manilla; Quinze; Angel-beast; and innumerable others. The procedures for these games can be found in the rule books for card games, such as those listed at the end of this chapter.

Recently, a number of card games have been devised with the intent of embedding more sophisticated analytic techniques than those required by games surviving the evolutionary filter. For example, the game of "Eleusis," invented by Robert Abbott, involves principles of pattern recognition similar to those discussed (Chapter 4) for coin-matching phenomena. Each of $n - 1$ players attempts to analyze a card-acceptance rule established by the nth player, thus permitting the successful analyzer to contribute the most cards from his hand in accordance with that rule. The appeal of "Eleusis" and its siblings has been confined, thus far, to an eclectic minority of game fanciers. Yet more intricate card games (directly related to reality) are designed and produced by Abt Associates, Cambridge, Mass.

Casino games

Despite their proliferation, card games have not generally flourished in the major gambling emporia. Trente et Quarante, Baccarat Chemin de Fer, Blackjack, Faro, and Poker comprise the contemporary card games available to the public. American casinos generally limit themselves to Faro, Blackjack, and Poker, with Chemin de Fer having been recently installed in several of the Las Vegas gambling mansions. The game of Blackjack offers sufficient interest that it will be considered separately in the next chapter.

FARO

Although declining in popularity, the game of Faro is still played in a few casinos in the western United States. It was derived by French gamblers from the Venetian game of Bassette and the Italian Hocca, which in turn were adapted from the German Landsquenet. The latter is known to have been played in the camps of Teutonic foot soldiers as early as the year 1400. Initially named Pharaoh or Pharoo, the game was highly popular in mid-seventeenth century France; it was subsequently brought to the United States by French colonists in New Orleans, early in the eighteenth century. If Faro disappears from the gambling casinos, it will be remembered from Pushkin's classic short story, "The Queen of Spades."

In Faro the suits have no significance, only the ranking of the cards being pertinent. A dealer representing the "house" conducts the game for any number of players up to six with a single deck. The first card drawn, called a "soda," is not used, nor are the last three cards. After the "soda" is exposed two cards are dealt face up from a Faro box at each round. The first card designates a losing and the second card a winning rank. A player may wager on any rank becoming winning or losing as that rank occurs in the second or first position (the player can also bet the reverse situation, which is referred to as "coppering" the bet). The process continues until 24 pairs of cards have been played. All exposed cards are recorded by a casekeeper, providing a convenient memory display.

If a player bets one unit on a specified rank to win (say Q), then he wins a payoff at odds of one to one if the next two cards dealt are (X, Q) in that order, where X is any card not of rank Q. He loses the bet when the cards are (Q, X). In the event of a tie, (Q, Q), the player loses one-half his wager. If (X, X) occurs, the game continues with the player afforded the option of altering or removing his bet.

The player can also place bets on odd or even and high or low. Odd or even wagers that the winning (or losing) card is odd or even as the player designates; if the two cards are both odd or even, the bet is a tie; if the two cards are of the same rank, the "house" again pockets one-half the wager. High or low wagers that the winning (or losing) card is the higher (or lower) of the two; if the two cards are of equal rank, the bet is considered a tie. Analysis of these options is equivalent to that for wagering on a given rank.

We assume a unit wager is placed on rank Q and allowed to remain until the bet is either won or lost or until $j \leq 24$ rounds have occurred, all with outcomes of (X, X). The analysis depends on whether or not rank Q is the "soda" and on the betting policy (as a function of the number of Q's left in the deck).

Case I: Q is not the "soda."

Play begins with 4 Q's and 47 X's. A decision (win, lose, or tie) must occur in the 24 rounds possible. The probability $R(j)$ that a decision has not occurred before round j is the probability that no Q appears in the first $2(j - 1)$ cards. That is,

$$R(j) = \binom{47}{2[j-1]} \bigg/ \binom{51}{2[j-1]}$$

Entering round j, we have reduced the 47 X's by $2(j - 1)$, so that $47 - (2j - 2) = 49 - 2j$ X's remain. Thence the probability $T(j)$ that round j produces a tie, (Q, Q), is

$$T(j) = \binom{4}{2} \bigg/ \binom{53 - 2j}{2}$$

And the probability of a tie, $P(T)$, for all 24 rounds is the product of these quantities:

$$P(T) = \sum_{j=1}^{24} T(j)R(j) = 0.0404$$

The player's expectation E_x, given the "soda" to be an X, is

$$E_x = -\tfrac{1}{2}P(T) = -0.0202$$

Case II: Q is the "soda."

Play begins with 3 Q's and 48 X's. In the 24 rounds possible a decision does not occur only if the final three cards are all Q's. This probability is expressed by

$$P(\text{no decision}) = \binom{48}{0}\binom{3}{3}\Big/\binom{51}{3} = 4.8 \times 10^{-5}$$

As above, the probability $R(j)$ that no Q occurs in the first $j - 1$ rounds is the probability that no Q occurs in the first $2(j - 1)$ cards:

$$R(j) = \binom{48}{2[j-1]}\Big/\binom{51}{2[j-1]}$$

Entering round j we have reduced the 48 X's by $2(j - 1)$, so that $48 - 2(j - 2) = 50 - 2j$ X's remain. The probability of a tie on round j is

$$T(j) = \binom{3}{2}\Big/\binom{53-2j}{2}$$

Thus, for all 24 rounds, the probability of a tie is given by

$$P(T) = \sum_{j=1}^{24} T(j)(Rj) = 0.0300$$

And the player's expectation E_Q, given the "soda" to be a Q, is

$$E_Q = \tfrac{1}{2}P(T) = -0.0150$$

More appropriately, we are interested in the conditional expectation per unit wager, given that (X, X) does not occur on all 24 rounds. This figure is obtained by dividing E_Q by $[1 - P\text{ (no decision)}]$. In this instance, the difference is insignificant.

Other betting policies consist of waiting until one, two, or three Q's have been exposed and then wagering on Q. Expectations are, accordingly, improved. With but a single Q remaining in the deck, the bet on Q yields a zero expectation. Most casinos prohibit zero expectation wagers without a prior wager at a negative expectation.

A thorough analysis of Faro mathematics has been accomplished by Thorp.[†] He has shown that removing the unit wager placed on the first round (Q is not the "soda") if (X, X) occurs maximizes the conditional expectation of this case, resulting in $E_x = -0.0156$. A maximum conditional expectation of -0.0102 can be obtained if, under the policy of betting only when three Q's remain in the deck, the player bets only when Q is the "soda" and allows the bet to remain for one round only. Under the policy of betting only with two Q's remaining in the deck, optimum strategy dictates a wager only on round two—when the first round and the "soda" contain two Q's—and yields the maximum conditional expectation of -0.0053. This expectation represents an upper bound for any strategy limited to negative expectation bets.

Perhaps the small (and zero) expectations obtainable from Faro account for its declining popularity, at least among casino owners.

TRENTE ET QUARANTE

Trente et Quarante is another game of pure chance found in virtually all French casinos (there are more than 170 recognized gambling establishments in the Gallic republic). It is played with six packs of cards shuffled together, forming a total deck of 312 cards. Suits are not of basic significance and each card is assigned a value equal to its rank (Ace is 1) with Jacks, Queens, and Kings set equal to 10. A dealer representing the "house" deals two rows of cards, the first row corresponding to Noire and the second to Rouge. Cards are dealt in each row until the cumulative total of their points reaches or exceeds 31. Thus, Noire and Rouge are each associated with a number that ranges between 31 and 40. Each of several players may place wagers according to the diagram of Fig. 6-1. A bet on Rouge wins if the cumulative total of the second row is lower (closer to 31) than that of the first row (Noire). If the two totals are equal, the bet is a tie unless the equality exists at 31, in which case the "house" pockets one-half of all stakes. Similarly, a wager on Noire wins if the first-row total is the lesser. The payoff for a winning bet is at even odds. Couleur is determined by the first card dealt. If Rouge (Noire) wins and the first card is red (black), the Couleur wins; otherwise, Inverse wins. A player betting on Couleur or Inverse also ties if the two totals are equal at 32 through 40 and loses one-half the stake if the two totals are 31.

[†] THORP, EDWARD O., "Nonrandom Shuffling with Applications to the Game of Faro," *J. Am. Statist. Assoc.* **68**, No. 344 (Dec., 1973), pp. 842–847.

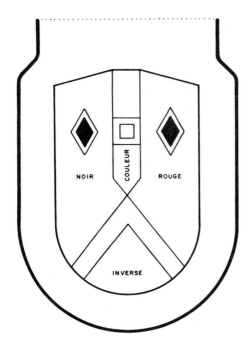

Fig. 6-1   The Trente et Quarante layout

Probabilities for the totals 31 through 40 were first computed by Denis Poisson and subsequently by Joseph Bertrand with the assumption of sampling with replacement (equivalent to an infinite deck); the concomitant error is extremely small with a pack of six conventional decks. Table 6-2 summarizes the pertinent probabilities. From this table it is readily calculated that the game of Trente et Quarante offers the player an expected return of 0.989 (a "house take" of 1.1 percent) since the probability of a

TABLE 6-2   Trente et Quarante Probabilities

Total	Probability
31	0.148
32	0.138
33	0.128
34	0.117
35	0.106
36	0.095
37	0.084
38	0.072
39	0.061
40	0.052

tie at 31 is $(0.148)^2 = 0.0219$. Other ties (at 32 through 40) occur with a frequency of 8.783 percent. A reduction to a "house take" of 0.90 percent is available through an "insurance" bet, permitting the player to wager an additional 1-percent stake (quantized to the higher 5-franc level) that cancels the loss in event of a tie at 31; the "insurance" bet is garnered by the "house" in all instances except ties at 32 through 40.

BACCARAT CHEMIN DE FER

A game offering a simple mixed strategy at one of its decision points is Baccarat. Introduced into France from Italy during the reign of Charles VIII (*ca.* 1490), the game was apparently devised by a gambler named Felix Falguiere who based it on the old Etruscan ritualism of the "Nine Gods."[†] According to legend, twenty-six centuries ago in "The Temple of Gold Hair" in Etruscan Rome, the "Nine Gods" prayed standing on their toes to a golden-tressed virgin who cast a *novem dare* (nine-sided die) at their feet. If her throw was 8 or 9, she was crowned a priestess. If she threw a 6 or 7, she was disqualified from further religious office and her vestal status summarily transmuted. And if her cast was 5 or under, she walked gracefully into the sea. Baccarat was designed with similar partitions (albeit less dramatic payoffs) of the numbers, modulo 10.

Two versions of the game have evolved: Baccarat Banque and Baccarat Chemin de Fer. In the former version, the banker or "house" opposes all players; in the latter, the contention is between one player who assumes the role of banker and another player—the "house" acts as a referee and charges 5 percent of all wagers on the banker. Hence, Chemin de Fer is a two-person game and affords the greater interest. It is this form of Baccarat that has been played in the United States since 1920 and is currently featured in several Las Vegas casinos.

Chemin de Fer is usually played with eight (sometimes six) conventional 52-card decks; thus, most probability calculations can be performed under the assumption of independence (sampling with replacement) with very small error. Each card from Ace through Nine is assigned the face value of its rank; the Tens, Jacks, Queens, and Kings contribute nothing. A hand consists of two or three cards, the value of the hand being the sum of the individual card values, mod 10. A sum of 9 ranks highest, 8 second highest, and so forth. The banker and the player each are dealt two cards. If either pair totals 8 or 9, it is announced and the two hands are compared, the higher count winning the equal wagers; equal counts are declared a tie.

[†] Macaulay, *Horatius at the Bridge*: "Lars Porsena of Clusium/By the Nine Gods he swore/...".

If neither the player nor banker possesses a total of 8 or 9, the player is given the option of receiving one additional exposed card. The banker then may also exercise an option to take an additional card, face up. Since other persons are permitted to bet on the player's hand, rules are established to restrict his strategies. He must draw the additional card with a count of 4 or less and cannot draw with a count of 6 or 7; a free choice is permissible only on a total of 5. The banker is responsible for his own decision. Subsequently, the two hands are compared, the higher count winning.

While the player enjoys but two strategies (draw or stay if dealt a 5), the banker faces 88 possible situations requiring a draw or stay decision (the banker's hand may show a total from 0 through 7 and the player may have drawn no card or a card of value 0 through 9) and, consequently, 2^{88} strategies. Chemin de Fer generates, therefore, a 2×2^{88} game matrix. Fortunately, from a computational standpoint, most of the banker's strategies are dominated. Against the two strategies of the player, the dominating choices of the banker can be readily computed and are shown in Table 6-3. Inspection of this table reveals that all but four of the banker's alternatives constitute the better choice against either player strategy. These four alternatives, the only ones of significance, are

1. The player does not draw and the banker has a total of 6.
2. The player draws a 1 and the banker has a total of 4.
3. The player draws a 4 and the banker has a total of 5.
4. The player draws a 9 and the banker has a total of 3.

Thus, we have reduced the game to a 2×2^4 matrix, the matrix originally computed by Kemeny and Snell.[†]

Denoting the banker's strategies over his four alternatives by DDDD, DDDS, etc., where D indicates draw and S stay, we find that there exist further dominances among the 16 strategies. Specifically, strategy SSDD dominates strategies SDSS, SDSD, and SDDS; DSDD dominates DDSS, DDSD, and DDDS; a mixture of SSDD and DSDD dominates SDDD, DSSS, DSSD, and DSDS; and a mixture of SSSS and SSDD dominates SSSD. Thus the game is reduced to a 2×5 matrix. From a theorem of game theory, we know that there exists at least one 2×2 subgame (a kernel) whose solution is equivalent to that of the 2×5 game. For Chemin de Fer, there is a unique kernel: that game defined by the banker's strategies SSDD and DSDD. Alternatives (2),(3), .and (4) are

[†] John G. Kemeny and J. L. Snell. "Game-Theoretic Solution of Baccarat," *Am. Math. Monthly,* **64** (September, 1957), pp. 465–469.

TABLE 6-3   Chemin de Fer Dominating Strategies

PLAYER

Banker's Total	Draws on 5		Stays on 5	
	Banker Draws when Player Receives	Banker Stays when Player Receives	Banker Draws when Player Receives	Banker Stays when Player Receives
0, 1, 2	No card, 1, 2, 3, 4, 5 6, 7, 8, 9, 10		No card, 1, 2, 3, 4, 5, 6, 7, 8, 9, 10	
3	No card, 1, 2, 3, 4, 5, 6, 7, 9, 10	8	No card, 1, 2, 3, 4, 5, 6, 7, 10	8, 9
4	No card, 1, 2, 3, 4, 5, 6, 7	8, 9, 10	No card, 2, 3, 4, 5, 6, 7	1, 8, 9, 10
5	No card, 4, 5, 6, 7	1, 2, 3, 8, 9, 10	No card, 5, 6, 7	1, 2, 3, 4, 8, 9, 10
6	No card, 6, 7	1, 2, 3, 4, 5, 8, 9, 10	6, 7	No card, 1, 2, 3, 4, 5, 8, 9, 10
7		No card, 1, 2, 3, 4, 5, 6, 7, 8, 9, 10		No card, 1, 2, 3, 4, 5, 6, 7, 8, 9, 10

thus resolved: in case (2) the banker should stay; in cases (3) and (4) the banker should always draw.

Solution of the remaining 2×2 game matrix indicates that the player's optimal mixed strategy is $(2/11, 9/11)$; that is, when his count is 5 he should stay with probability $2/11$ and draw with probability $9/11$. The banker's optimal mixed strategy is $(1429/2288, 859/2288)$; when his count is 6 and the player has not drawn |alternative (1)|, he stays with probability $1429/2288$ and draws with probability $859/2288$. Finally, the value of the game is evaluated as $-679{,}568/53{,}094{,}899 = -0.0128$, the minus sign indicating that the game favors the banker.

In modern casinos the banker is often not allowed discretionary play, but is obligated to follow the strategy indicated by Table 6-3 plus SSDD for the four nondefined cases. This fixed strategy is optimal against the mixed strategy $(1/2, 1/2)$ for the player. The value of the game with these restrictions is -0.0137 (a "house take" of 1.37 percent for a bet on the player). For a bet on the banker, a charge of 5 percent of the net winning sum is levied, entailing a "house take" of 1.16 percent.

Baccarat rules often permit a side bet at odds of 9 to 1 that the banker's (or player's) two cards will total 9 (or 8). A knowledge of the remaining 9's and non-9's in the eight decks thus enables occasional positive-expectation wagers. Thorp has calculated that for a deck composition of n cards remaining, t of which are 9's, the probability of the banker receiving a two-card total of 9 is

$$P_{n,t} = \frac{2(n - t)(32n + 351t - 32)}{1149n(n - 1)}$$

The side bet yields a positive expectation whenever $P_{n,t} > 0.1$.

Card games with skill

LE HER

Unlike Faro, Trente et Quarante, or Chemin de Fer, several card games involve a degree of rudimentary skill—that is, a choice among simple but significant strategies is available. Examples of such games are Cribbage, L'écarté, La Belote, and Hana Fuda. Yet other games exist which, although not satisfying the requirements for popular appeal, offer greater insight into the structure of card play. An example in this category is the strategic game Le Her, an eighteenth-century card game whose solution was first sought by N. Bernoulli and de Montmort.

Le Her is played between two persons, a dealer and a receiver, with the standard 52-card pack. The dealer gives one card to the receiver and one card to himself. If the receiver is dissatisfied with his card, he may exchange cards with the dealer—unless the dealer has a King, in which case he is permitted to retain it. If the dealer is then dissatisfied with his original card or that obtained in exchange from the receiver, he may replace it with a third card selected from the deck; however, if the new (third) card is a King, the replacement is canceled and the dealer must retain his undesired card. The object of the game is to conclude with the higher card, each card having the value of its rank (Ace equals 1); in the event of a tie (equally ranked cards), the dealer is the winner.

Three moves comprise the game: a chance move, which selects the first two cards from the population of 52; a personal move by the receiver; and a personal move by the dealer. Since cards of 13 ranks can be either held or exchanged, there are 2^{13} strategies available to each player. However, it is simple to demonstrate that two strategies dominate the other $2^{13} - 2$. Obviously, if the receiver obtains an 8 or greater, he will retain it and will exchange his card if its value is 6 or lower. His decision relates to the rank 7. As a consequence, the dealer's decision relates to the rank 8.

Dealer's Strategies	Receiver's Strategies	
	Hold 7 and over	Change 7 and under
Hold 8 and over	$\dfrac{16,182}{33,150}$	$\dfrac{16,122}{33,150}$
Change 8 and under	$\dfrac{16,146}{33,150}$	$\dfrac{16,182}{33,150}$

Fig. 6-2   Le Her payoff matrix

The payoff matrix of Le Her is therefore a 2×2 matrix; its elements are displayed in Fig. 6-2. Applying the minimax principle, we can determine that optimal strategy for the dealer dictates mixing his two strategies in the ratio of 3:5. The receiver's optimal strategy is (5/8, 3/8). Probability of success for the dealer is 0.487 and therefore 0.513 for the receiver; that is, the game's expectation for the dealer is -0.026. Although it appears at first that the advantage lies with the dealer, since he wins the ties, the reverse is true—owing to the greater ability of the receiver to influence the game's outcome.

GUESS IT

A much cleverer game is "Guess It," invented by Rufus Isaacs of the RAND Corporation.[†] A deck of n consecutively numbered cards is randomly dealt out to two players, with the last card remaining unassigned and undisclosed. The objective of the game is to identify this last card. Each player, in turn, either *calls* or *asks*. A call consists of specifying the undisclosed card; if correct, the caller wins; otherwise he loses. An ask consists of an inquiry to the player's opponent as to whether his hand contains a particular named card. The opponent must reply truthfully—a response of "yes" locates that card for both players; it is then exposed and may not be subsequently involved in a query. A response of "no" implies that either the asking player is bluffing (the particular card is in his own hand) or the undisclosed card is that asked. This dilemma is resolved automatically within two further moves. To illustrate the point, player A asks player B about card x and is given the answer "no." For his part, player B wishes to ascertain whether or not A is bluffing. If he decides affirmatively, he calls x as the undisclosed card and either wins or loses the game immediately as

---

[†] Rufus Isaacs, "A Card Game with Bluffing," *Am. Math. Monthly*, **42** (February, 1955), pp. 99–108.

his appraisal of A's strategy is right or wrong; if he decides negatively, he asks A about some other card. The move then reverting to A, if A does not call x but asks another query of B, it is known by both players that x is contained in A's hand and it is therefore exposed. Thus the art of the game centers on the acquisition of information with as little disbursement of it as possible until sufficient knowledge is gained to warrant a call.

We wish to determine the optimal strategies. Let $P(a, b)$ be the win probability for player A (A moves first) where initially he holds a cards and his opponent holds b cards (the deck contains $a + b + 1$ cards). Selecting the payoff as 1 or 0, according as A wins or loses, $P(a, b)$ also represents the value of the game to A. Further, let $P_1(a, b)$ be A's win probability under the restriction that his first move must be an ask. Since a call on the first move has a probability of success of $1/(b + 1)$, we have

$$P(a, b) = \max\left[\frac{1}{b + 1}, P_1(a, b)\right]$$

with the boundary conditions

$$P(a, 0) = 1 \qquad\qquad\qquad 6\text{-}29$$

and

$$P(0, b) = \frac{1}{b + 1} \qquad\qquad\qquad 6\text{-}30$$

We can also write

$$P_1(a, 0) = \frac{a}{a + 1}$$

since a player can always ask without betraying information by selecting his asking card equiprobably from the entire deck; such a process is termed a *safe move*.

For $a > 0$ and $b > 0$, let player A's first move be an ask and let p be the probability that A bluffs on that move. If the reply to A's ask is "no," then player B's options, for his contiguous move, are (1) to call the particular card asked about, with probability ρ_1; (2) to call some other card, with probability ρ_2; or (3) to ask, with probability $1 - \rho_1 - \rho_2$. If A is bluffing, response (1) results in a win for A—that is, an outcome of 1; response (2) affords B a probability of $1/a$ of calling correctly—hence the outcome is $(a - 1)/a$; response (3) is predicated on A's bluffing—if it is wrong, the game concludes with A's next move. If A is not bluffing, he has then determined the undisclosed card (having received a "no" answer), the probability of this situation being $(1 - p)/(b - 1)$. For this case, (1) results in a win for B, and the outcome is 0; response (2) is a loss for B, with outcome 1; and response (3) also loses for B because A will call on the following move; thus the outcome is again 1.

The probability that A's ask receives a "yes" reply is $b(1 - p)/(b + 1)$. In this event, the outcome is equivalent to a new game with B awarded the first move and a hand of $b - 1$ cards—that is, $1 - P(b - 1, a)$. We can write, therefore,

$$P_1(a, b) = \max_p \min_{\rho_1 \rho_2} \left\{ p \left[\rho_1 + \frac{\rho_2(a - 1)}{a} + (1 - \rho_1 - \rho_2)(1 - P_1') \right] \right.$$
$$\left. + \frac{(1 - p)(1 - \rho_1)}{b + 1} + \frac{b(1 - p)}{b + 1}[1 - P(b - 1, a)] \right\} \qquad 6\text{-}31$$

where

$$P_1' = P_1(b, a - 1)$$

Equation 6-31 uniquely determines $P(a, b)$ for all a and b if, in addition, we assume that either player always calls when he knows the undisclosed card with certainty, that he never deliberately calls incorrectly, and that his asking card is selected in a safe manner (if the player bluffs, for example, the asking card is chosen equiprobably from those in his own hand).

The minimax solution need be evaluated only for two cases:

$$a = 1 \quad \text{and} \quad P_1' \geq \frac{1}{a}, \quad P_1' \geq \frac{b \cdot P(b - 1, a)}{b + 1}$$

We can show that for $a = 1$, Eq. 6-31 leads to

$$p = \frac{1}{b + 2} \qquad 6\text{-}32$$

which is a safe move in choosing whether or not to bluff. For the second case,

$$p = \frac{1}{1 + (b + 1)P_1'} \qquad 6\text{-}33$$

Equations 6-32 and 6-33 provide optimal strategies for bluffing or asking. Also, from Eq. 6-31, we can derive the probabilities governing B's responses. For the first case ($a = 1$),

$$\rho_1 = \frac{(b + 1) - b \cdot P(b - 1, 1)}{b + 2}$$

and

$$\rho_2 = \frac{1 + b \cdot P(b - 1, 1)}{b + 2}$$

while for the second case,

$$\rho_1 = \frac{(b + 1)P'_1 - b \cdot P(b - 1, 1)}{1 + (b + 1)P'_1}$$

and

$$\rho_2 = 0$$

The win probability $P(a, b)$ is determined completely by the boundary conditions of Eqs. 6-29 and 6-30 and by

$$P(1, b) = \frac{1 + b[1 - P(b - 1, 1)]}{b + 2}, \qquad b \geq 1$$

$$P(a, 1) = \frac{1 + \dfrac{a \cdot P(1, a - 1)}{a + 1}}{1 + 2P(1, a - 1)}, \qquad a \geq 1$$

and

$$P(a, b) = \frac{1 + b \cdot P(b, a - 1)[1 - P(b - 1, a)]}{1 + (b + 1)P(b, a - 1)}, \qquad a > 1, \quad b > 1$$

A table of $P(a, b)$ given by Isaacs encompasses values of a and b up to 5. This table is repeated in Table 6-4.

TABLE 6-4   "Guess It" Win Probabilities

			a		
b	1	2	3	4	5
1	0.500	0.667	0.688	0.733	0.750
2	0.500	0.556	0.625	0.648	0.680
3	0.400	0.512	0.548	0.597	0.619
4	0.375	0.450	0.513	0.543	0.581
5	0.333	0.423	0.467	0.512	0.538

Reprinted by permission of the RAND Corporation.

The game converges quickly to a decision. Consider the situation where player B has one card remaining and player A asks. If the reply is "yes," A has ascertained the undisclosed card and B must call in self-defense; if the reply is "no," B should call with probability ρ_1.

POKER

Of all the multitude of card games invented, possibly the most popular among Americans is that of Poker. Derived from the ancient Persian pursuit called *$\bar{A}$s N$\hat{a}$s* or *Dsands*, the game was played with 20 cards[†] during its popularity in eighteenth-century Paris. A descendant of *$\bar{A}$s N$\hat{a}$s*, known as *Poque* in French, came to the United States with the French colonists of New Orleans, whence arose the word "Poker" from the American mispronunciation of *Poque*. An English version of the game is Brag and another French offshoot is named Ambigu. The full 52-card deck was adapted to Poker around 1830, although the form of the game remained essentially that of straight Poker. Draw Poker was not introduced until the early 1860's, during the American Civil War. There are few games that better illustrate elementary probability theory and, consequently, many works have calculated the probabilities of Poker hands and draws. Deriving an optimal strategy, however, is beyond the scope of current game theory, owing to the large number of strategic alternatives that exist in Poker. It is the usual practice to set up a simplified version of the real game and attempt to gain an insight from game-theoretic analysis of the model.

Elementary combinatorial formulae enable us to calculate the probabilities of all significant subdivisions of the 2,598,960 five-card hands (Eq. 6-25) at Poker. Ten categories are defined, and within each category the winning hand of two is that composed of the higher rank or suit. In descending order of value, the ten categories are: Royal Flush, Straight Flush, Four of a Kind, Full House, Flush, Straight, Three of a Kind, Two Pairs, One Pair, and High Card (it is assumed that the nature of each category is known or is self-explanatory). Consider the probability of obtaining a hand consisting of exactly one pair. The rank of the pair can occur in $\binom{13}{1}$ ways, and for any rank the two cards forming the pair can be selected in $\binom{4}{2}$ ways. The three other ranks can occur in $\binom{12}{3}$ ways and a card of each rank can be selected in $\binom{4}{1}$ ways. Hence,

---

[†] The deck consisted of four suits, each of five ranks: Lion, King, Lady, Soldier, and Dancing Girl.

$$P(\text{one pair}) = \frac{\binom{13}{1}\binom{4}{2}\binom{12}{3}\binom{4}{1}^3}{\binom{52}{5}} = 0.4226$$

Similar arguments hold in determining the following probabilities:

$$P(\text{two pairs}) = \frac{\binom{13}{2}\binom{4}{2}^2\binom{11}{1}\binom{4}{1}}{\binom{52}{5}} = 0.0475$$

$$P(\text{three of a kind}) = \frac{\binom{13}{1}\binom{4}{3}\binom{12}{2}\binom{4}{1}^2}{\binom{52}{5}} = 0.0211$$

$$P(\text{straight})^\dagger = \frac{10\binom{4}{1}^5 - 10\binom{4}{1}}{\binom{52}{5}} = 0.0039$$

$$P(\text{flush}) = \frac{\binom{4}{1}\binom{13}{5}}{\binom{52}{5}} = 0.0020$$

$$P(\text{full house}) = \frac{\binom{13}{1}\binom{4}{3}\binom{12}{1}\binom{4}{2}}{\binom{52}{5}} = 0.0014$$

$$P(\text{four of a kind}) = \frac{\binom{13}{1}\binom{4}{4}\binom{12}{1}\binom{4}{1}}{\binom{52}{5}} = 0.25 \times 10^{-3}$$

$$P(\text{all straight-flushes})^\dagger = \frac{10\binom{4}{1}}{\binom{52}{5}} = 0.15 \times 10^{-4}$$

† For straights and straight-flushes, the Ace is permitted to rank either high or low.

These results are summarized in Table 6-5. The relative values of the hands are, of course, ordered inversely to the probabilities. Their "real" values in the course of a game are functions of the number of competing players.

TABLE 6-5   Poker-Hand Probabilities

Hand	Probability
High card	0.5012
One pair	0.4226
Two pairs	0.0475
Three of a kind	0.0211
Straight	0.0039
Flush	0.0020
Full house	0.0014
Four of a kind	0.24×10^{-3}
Straight-flush (single)	0.14×10^{-4}
Royal flush	0.15×10^{-5}
Four flush	0.043
Four straight (open)	0.035
Four straight (middle)	0.123
Four straight (end)	0.0087
Four straight-flush	0.123×10^{-3}

Each probability shown in Table 6-5 is strictly applicable only to independent hands. As an illustration of the change in probability associated with a second, dependent, hand, we can compute the probability of obtaining a straight, given another hand composed of A, 2, 3, 4, 5. For this case, $P = 137/32,637 = 0.0042$ compared with $P = 0.0039$ for the probability of a straight in an independent hand.

In certain forms of Poker, the player is permitted to replace one, two, or three cards in his hand with an equivalent number from the remainder of the pack. The probabilities of achieving certain improvements are readily computed and are enumerated in Table 6-6. It does not follow that optimal play can be derived directly from the probabilities given in Tables 6-5 and 6-6. There exist strategies such as "bluff" or "inverse bluff" that, in certain circumstances, might create an advantage to drawing two cards rather than three to a pair, as an example, although the former allows an improvement of 0.260 compared with 0.287.

The next logical computation is that which provides the probable ranking of all possible hands, before and after the draw, as a function of the number of players contending (and of the number of cards each opponent

TABLE 6-6   Draw Possibilities

Original Hand	Cards Drawn	Improved Hand	Probability
One pair	3	Two pairs	0.160
	3	Three of a kind	0.114
	3	Full house	0.0102
	3	Four of a kind	0.0028
	3	Any improvement	0.287
	2	Two pairs	0.172
	2	Three of a kind	0.078
	2	Full house	0.0083
	2	Four of a kind	0.0009
	2	Any improvement	0.260
Two pairs	1	Full house	0.085
Three of a kind	2	Full house	0.061
	2	Four of a kind	0.043
	2	Any improvement	0.104
	1	Full house	0.064
	1	Four of a kind	0.021
	1	Any improvement	0.085
Four straight (open)	1	Straight	0.170
Four straight (gap)	1	Straight	0.085
Four flush	1	Flush	0.191
Three flush	2	Flush	0.042
Two flush	3	Flush	0.0102
Four straight-flush (open)	1	Straight-flush	0.043
	1	Any straight or flush	0.319
Four straight-flush (gap)	1	Straight-flush	0.021
	1	Any straight or flush	0.256

has drawn). Knowing the wager risked on each hand, it is then possible to calculate the expectation and devise an optimum strategy. However, because of the formidable computational labor attendant to the large number of hands, such a description is rendered inaccessible to mathematical treatment. Since the advent of von Neumann's theory of games, we can achieve a systematic theoretical execution of any two-person, zero-sum game. We therefore select an analog to Poker, which is amenable to the peculiar restrictions of the present status of game theory, and content ourselves with analyses of simple models that resemble many aspects of the realistic Poker game.

POKER MODELS; THE THREE-CARD DECK; CONTINUOUS RED DOG

Poker models rank as a favorite pastime with many game theorists, perhaps because simplified Poker presents the right degree of challenge—neither impossibly difficult as many real games nor trivial as many games of pure chance. Also attractive to applied mathematicians are the many elements (probabilistic analysis, risk, psychology, bluffing, etc.) common to Poker and business, war, and politics. Poker models have been analyzed by Borel, von Neumann, H. W. Kuhn, Bellman and Blackwell, and Goldman and Stone, among others. Borel's analysis was primarily probabilistic rather than game-theoretic; von Neumann's model involves two persons, a player who is permitted a choice of two bets, high or low, and a dealer who is permitted to "call" or "fold." No "ante" is considered. A symmetric Poker game, one stage more complicated than the von Neumann model, has been considered by Goldman and Stone. Both the von Neumann and the Goldman and Stone games are *continuous*—that is, an infinite continuum of possible hands is assumed, thereby avoiding the difficulties due to the enormous but finite number of hands in the real game.

The model due to H. W. Kuhn requires an ante of one unit from each of two players, A and B. A's hand consists of a single card drawn from a deck of three cards, numbered 1, 2, 3. Beginning with A, the players choose alternately either to bet one unit or to pass without betting. Two successive bets or passes terminate a play; the hands are then compared and the player holding the higher card wins. A player passing after a bet by his opponent also ends the play and loses the ante.

With the three cards and two players there are six possible deals. For each deal, five possible courses of action may ensue: A passes, B passes (payoff is one unit to the high-card holder); A passes, B bets, A passes (payoff is one unit to B); A passes, B bets, A bets (payoff is two units to high-card holder); A bets, B passes (payoff is one unit to A); and A bets, B bets (payoff is two units to high-card holder). Thus, 30 possible plays can be enumerated. Player A selects from 3^3 pure strategies, while player B has 4^3 pure strategies. Fortunately, many of these strategies are completely dominated and can therefore be eliminated without altering the value of the game. For example, no player would bet on a 1 or pass with a 3 when confronted by a bet. Such strategies are immediately eliminated through the application of "Poker sense."

We adopt the binary notation of the ordered triplet $(\_\_, \_\_, \_\_)$, where each space is filled by a p (pass) or a b (bet), the ordering being by opportunity and by card. Thus (pp, pb, bb) means the player should pass at both his first and second opportunities when holding a 1 card, should pass at the first opportunity and bet at the second when holding a 2, and should bet at both opportunities when holding a 3. With this symbolism, the game matrix is illustrated in Fig. 6-3. The matrix consists of eight undominated pure strategies for player A and four undominated pure strategies for

Player A	Player B			
	(pp, pp, bb)	(pp, pb, bb)	(bp, pp, bb)	(bp, pb, bb)
(pp, pp, pb)	0	0	$-1/6$	$-1/6$
(pp, pp, bp)	0	$1/6$	$-1/3$	$-1/6$
(pp, pb, pb)	$-1/6$	$-1/6$	$1/6$	$1/6$
(pp, pb, bp)	$-1/6$	0	0	$1/6$
(bp, pp, pb)	$1/6$	$-1/3$	0	$-1/2$
(bp, pp, bp)	$1/6$	$-1/6$	$-1/6$	$-1/2$
(bp, pb, pb)	0	$-1/2$	$1/3$	$-1/6$
(bp, pb, bp)	0	$-1/3$	$1/6$	$-1/6$

Fig. 6-3   Payoff matrix for a three-card Poker model

player B. A positive payoff is defined as favorable to player A (the payoffs are fractional, since each number is averaged over the six possible deals).

Kuhn gives the following 12 mixed strategies optimal for player A:

$(2/3)(pp, pp, pb) + (1/3)(pp, pb, pb)$

$(1/3)(pp, pp, pb) + (1/2)(pp, pb, bp) + (1/6)(bp, pp, pb)$

$(5/9)(pp, pp, pb) + (1/3)(pp, pb, bp) + (1/9)(bp, pb, pb)$

$(1/2)(pp, pp, pb) + (1/3)(pp, pb, bp) + (1/6)(bp, pb, bp)$

$(2/5)(pp, pp, bp) + (7/15)(pp, pb, pb) + (2/15)(bp, pp, pb)$

$(1/3)(pp, pp, bp) + (1/2)(pp, pb, pb) + (1/6)(bp, pp, bp)$

$(1/2)(pp, pp, bp) + (1/3)(pp, pb, pb) + (1/6)(bp, pb, pb)$

$(4/9)(pp, pp, bp) + (1/3)(pp, pb, pb) + (2/9)(bp, pb, bp)$

$(1/6)(pp, pp, bp) + (7/12)(pp, pb, bp) + (1/4)(bp, pp, pb)$

$(5/12)(pp, pp, bp) + (1/3)(pp, pb, bp) + (1/4)(bp, pb, pb)$

$(1/3)(pp, pp, bp) + (1/3)(pp, pb, bp) + (1/3)(bp, pb, bp)$

$(2/3)(pp, pb, bp) + (1/3)(bp, pp, bp)$

Player B enjoys two optimal mixed strategies:

$(1/3)(pp, pp, bb) + (1/3)(pp, pb, bb) + (1/3)(bp, pp, bb)$

$(2/3)(pp, pp, bb) + (1/3)(bp, pb, bb)$

With these mixed strategies the game matrix has a value of $-1/18$.

Two psychological factors present in this Poker model are forms of bluffing and underbidding or cautious strategies. In general, there are four such strategic policies, which can be mixed as the occasion demands: bold play (bet on every hand), cautious play (bet low or pass initially on every hand), normal play (bet on high-valued hands and pass on low-valued hands), and bluff play (bet on low-valued hands and pass on high-valued hands).

Many other models of simplified Poker can be concocted. Usually, a detailed analysis of these models furthers the understanding of certain mathematical concepts rather than providing any insight into the real game of Poker. One exception—a simplified version of Red Dog, originated by Bellman and Blackwell, offers several features of interest. This model propounds a two-person game played with a continuous deck of cards representing all values from 0 to 1. Each player antes one unit; then player A deals a card x_1, $0 \le x_1 \le 1$, to his opponent, player B, and a card y_1, $0 \le y_1 \le 1$, to himself. B is then afforded the option of betting an amount $f(x_1)$, $1 \le f(x_1) \le M$, or of folding. If B folds, A wins the ante; if B bets, A must cover the wager. The cards are then exposed, and if $x \ge y$, B wins $f(x) + 1$; if $x \le y$, A wins $f(x) + 1$. We wish to determine B's strategy and the mathematical expectation of the game.

Let x and y have the distribution functions $F(x)$ and $G(y)$, respectively, subject to the usual normalization

$$\int_0^1 dF(x) = \int_0^1 dG(y) = 1$$

Also, let a_1 be some number in the unit interval such that B folds if $x \le a_1$ and bets $f(x)$ if $x \ge a_1$. Then B's expectation can be expressed by

$$E_B = \int_{a_1}^1 \int_0^x [1 + f(x)] \, dF(x) \, dG(y)$$

$$- \int_{a_1}^1 \int_x^1 [1 + f(x)] \, dF(x) \, dG(y) - \int_0^{a_1} dF(x)$$

$$= \int_{a_1}^1 [1 + f(x)][2G(x) - 1] \, dF(x) - \int_0^{a_1} dF(x) \qquad 6\text{-}34$$

and B wishes to select a_1 and $f(x)$ so as to maximize E_B. Rewriting Eq. 6-34 in the form

$$E_B = \int_{a_1}^1 [2G(x) - 1] f(x) \, dF(x) + \int_{a_1}^1 2G(x) \, dF(x) - 1 \qquad 6\text{-}35$$

we can observe that the first integral is negative for all values of $2G(x) - 1 < 0$ if x is less than a certain value x_0 and is positive for $2G(x) - 1 > 0$ if $x > x_0 | 2G(x) - 1$ is a nondecreasing function of x and thus the integral is a nonincreasing function of a_2, given $a_1 \le \chi_0 |$. Therefore, for any value of a_1, $f(x)$ is selected as

$$f(x) = 1, \qquad a_1 < x \le x_0$$
$$f(x) = M, \qquad x_0 < x \le 1 \qquad\qquad 6\text{-}36$$
$$f(x) = 0 \text{ (B folds)}, \qquad 0 \le x \le a_1$$

For the unit minimum bet, the mathematical expectation is negative in the region $a_1 \leq x < x_0$; M units constitute the maximum bet, the expectation being positive in the region $x_0 < x \leq 1$. Substituting these values of $f(x)$ into Eq. 6-35 and rearranging terms, we have for the expectation of player B,

$$E_B = \int_{a_1}^{x_0} [4G(x) - 1] \, dF(x)$$

$$+ (M + 1) \int_{x_0}^{1} [2G(x) - 1] \, dF(x) - 1 + \int_{x_0}^{1} dF(x)$$

from which it follows that a_1 is selected by the condition

$$a_1 = \min[x, 4G(x) - 1 \geq 0] \qquad\qquad 6\text{-}37$$

As an illustration, consider x and y to be uniformly distributed over the unit interval—that is, $F(x) = x$ and $G(y) = y$. Then Eq. 6-37 gives a value of $1/4$ for a_1, x_0 takes the value $1/2$, and Eq. 6-36 indicates that

$$f(x) = 1, \qquad 1/4 < x \leq 1/2$$
$$f(x) = M, \qquad 1/2 < x \leq 1$$
$$f(x) = 0 \text{ (B folds)}, \quad x \leq 1/4$$

Substituting these values into Eq. 6-35, we have

$$E_B = \int_{1/4}^{1/2} (4x - 1) \, dx + (M + 1) \int_{1/2}^{1} (2x - 1) \, dx - 1 + \int_{1/2}^{1} dx$$

$$= \frac{M}{4} - \frac{1}{8}$$

for B's expectation (the game offers B a distinct advantage). For a discrete version, let the game be played with a deck of cards ranked $1, 2, \ldots, 52$. Then player B bets the maximum amount M if his card is in the top half of the deck or the minimum of one unit if his card is in the third quarter of the deck; he folds when drawing a card valued in the lowest quarter.

RED DOG IN PROPRIO

The actual game of Red Dog (or High Card Deal) is played with the conventional pack of 4 suits and 13 ranks. Each of N players receives a hand of five cards (or four as N exceeds 8). Following an ante of one unit, each player in turn may either fold or bet an amount ranging from one unit to the size of the "pot" that his hand contains a card of greater value *in the same suit* than one to be drawn from the remainder of the pack.

An analysis of this game, using a model similar to that for continuous Red Dog, results in a strategy which dictates that the player should wager the maximum stake (the entire "pot") when his hand falls in the region

$$\sum_{i=1}^{4} x_i \geq 2$$

where x_i is the relative ranking in the ith suit of the highest card in that suit (we have assumed that the cards are uniformly distributed). A minimum bet should be risked when the hand is described by

$$2 \geq \sum_{i=1}^{4} x_i \geq 1$$

and the folding region is defined by

$$\sum_{i=1}^{4} x_i \leq 1$$

As an illustration, consider a hand consisting of the Ace of Spades, the Queen and Three of Hearts, the Four of Diamonds, and the Nine of Clubs (Ace is ranked high). For the Ace of Spades, $x_1 = 13/13$; for the Queen of Hearts, $x_2 = 11/13$; the Four of Diamonds contributes $x_3 = 3/13$; and the Nine of Clubs is ranked by $x_4 = 8/13$. Therefore, in this example,

$$\sum_{i=1}^{4} x_i = \frac{13 + 11 + 3 + 8}{13} = \frac{35}{13}$$

and we should bet the maximum that a card in this hand can exceed, in its suit, the rank of any card exposed from the remainder of the deck.

SINGLE HIGH CARD

Related to Red Dog is the game of Single High Card. Although trivial in format, solution of this game entails a lengthy and involved procedure. We furnish, therefore, the optimal strategies, leaving their derivation to the determined reader. Each of two players antes one unit and receives a single card from a standard deck. Player A is then given the option of passing, thereby forfeiting the ante, or betting an amount $a > 1$. If A bets, player B may pass or call. In the latter event the two single-card hands are compared and the player with the higher hand collects the wager of $a + 1$ units (it is assumed that the 52 cards are individually ranked).

Letting p_i be the probability that A bets on card i and q_j the probability that B bets on card j, $i, j, = 1, 2, \ldots, 52$, optimal strategy is expressed as follows: If $2 \cdot 51/(a + 1)$ is an integer, then

$$p_i = q_j = 1 \qquad \text{for all } i, j \geq 53 - \frac{2 \cdot 51}{a + 1}$$

player B also plays

$$q_j = 0 \qquad \text{for all } j < 53 - \frac{2 \cdot 51}{a + 1}$$

and player A selects

$$p_i, \qquad i < 53 - \frac{2 \cdot 51}{a + 1}$$

in an arbitrary manner subject only to the constraints

$$\sum_{i=1}^{52 - [2 \cdot 51/(a+1)]} p_i \geq \frac{a - 1}{a + 1} \left(\frac{2 \cdot 51}{a + 1} - 1 \right) \qquad \text{6-38}$$

and

$$\sum_{i=1}^{51 - [2 \cdot 51/(a+1)]} p_i \leq \frac{2 \cdot 51(a - 1)}{(a + 1)^2} \qquad \text{6-39}$$

If the quantity $2 \cdot 51/(a + 1)$ is not an integer, B's strategy changes only for

$$j = \left[53 - \frac{2 \cdot 51}{a + 1} \right]$$

where $[x]$ represents the largest integer not exceeding x; with this value of j, B plays $q_j = 2 \cdot 51/(a + 1)$, mod 1. A's strategy is altered for values of

$$i < 53 - \frac{2 \cdot 51}{a + 1}$$

which are now chosen arbitrarily under the constraint

$$\sum_{i=1}^{52 - [2 \cdot 51/(a+1)]} p_i = \frac{a - 1}{a + 1} \left[\frac{2 \cdot 51}{a + 1} - 1 \right] \qquad \text{6-40}$$

The value γ of the game is given by

$$\gamma = \frac{1}{51 \cdot 52} \sum_{i \neq j} [p_i(1 - q_j) - (1 - p_i) + a\delta_{ij}p_iq_j] \qquad \text{6-41}$$

where

$$\delta_{ij} = \begin{cases} 1, & i > j \\ -1, & i < j \end{cases}$$

To illustrate, let a, the amount wagered beyond the ante, be equal to two units. Then A's optimal strategy consists of betting on all cards of rank 19 or higher and passing or betting with the first 18 cards according to any probability distribution restricted by

$$\sum_{i=1}^{18} p_i \geq 11 \quad \text{and} \quad \sum_{i=1}^{17} p_i \leq \frac{34}{3}$$

as indicated by Eqs. 6-38 and 6-39. Player B calls with a card of rank 19 or higher and passes otherwise. If we play the game described by $a = 10$, A's optimal strategy commands a bet on cards of rank 43 or higher and selects any wagering probability distribution over the lower 42 cards that conforms to the constraint of Eq. 6-40:

$$\sum_{i=1}^{42} p_i = \frac{9 \cdot 2 \cdot 51}{11^2} = \frac{918}{121}$$

Player B calls with cards of rank 44 or higher, passes with cards of rank 42 or less, and plays $q_{43} = 3/11$. Value of this game, from Eq. 6-41, is -0.46; the game thus favors player B.

Countless varieties of poker have evolved over the years and more will inevitably be invented. Some, such as Stud Poker (five cards per hand, one hidden and four exposed successively, no draw) or Seven-Card Stud,[†] are tight games, almost purely strategical. Others, such as those with certain cards or groups of cards declared "wild" (allowed to assume any value desired), tend to increase the variance and decrease the strategic content of the basic game. Although more ingenious and challenging card games may be proposed by gamblers or mathematicians, it is improbable that any game will so inspire game theorists and analysts or will achieve the public success and addiction as that gained by the pastime of Poker.

[†] Featured by "The Thanatopsis Literary and Inside Straight Club," Seven-Card Stud was highly popular but little understood during the 1920's. It was also celebrated previously at Charles Steinmetz's famed Poker gathering, "The Society for the Equalization and Distribution of Wealth."

Poker problems

The following Poker-like games are elementary in their formulation, but pose considerable difficulties in their solution.

1. *A Three-Person Money Game.* Three players simultaneously expose either a $1.00, a $5.00, a $10, or a $20 bill. If all three expose the same value, the game is a draw. If the three bills are all different, that player with the middle value wins the money shown by the other two. If two of the bills exposed are equal, that player with the different value wins from the other two. What is the optimal (mixed) strategy? *Note:* For a simpler version, the problem can be stated with $1.00 and $5.00 bills only, deleting the middle-man-wins possibility.

2. M-*Level Poker.* Each player is dealt a random integer $\leq N$. Bids of from 1 to M are entered simultaneously by the players by wagering a stake equal to the bid. The highest bidder (highest stake) wins the pot. If one or more players tie with highest bids, their cards are exposed and the pot taken by that player with the highest-value card (greatest integer). Compute the optimal strategy.

3. *Two-Level, Two-Person Poker.* Each of two players is dealt a random integer $\leq N$ and then bids a or b $(a > b > 0)$ with a stake equal to the bid. If both players bid alike, "high hand" resolves the issue. Otherwise, the bidder of b is given the option of folding (and losing b) or calling by raising his stake to a, whence the player holding the higher integer takes the pot. Compute the optimal strategy.

4. *Hi-Lo Forehead Poker.* Three players ante one unit apiece and each receives a random integer $\leq N$. Without looking at the integer, it is exposed on the forehead for the other two players to observe. Simultaneously, each player announces for either "Hi" or "Lo." The pot is split between the two winners of Hi and Lo. If all declare for Hi (Lo), a single winner is determined by the highest (lowest) integer. Compute the optimal strategy. A modification of this game permits the players to draw lots to determine the order of announcing for Hi, Lo, or Hi and Lo.

5. *Mental Poker.* Each of n players antes one unit and mentally selects an integer $\leq N$, recording it privately. All n integers chosen are then exposed; that player owning the highest *unique* integer wins the pot. Compute the optimal strategy and show that only the n highest integers need be considered by each player.

Suggested references

ABBOTT, ROBERT, *Abbott's New Card Games*, Stein and Day, New York, 1963.

BATTIN, I. L., "On the Problem of Multiple Matching," *Ann. of Math. Statistics*, **13**, No. 3 (Sept., 1942), pp. 294–305.

BELLMAN, RICHARD, *Introduction to Matrix Analysis*, McGraw-Hill Book Company Inc., New York, 1960.

BELLMAN, RICHARD, "On Games Involving Bluffing," *Rendiconti del Circolo Matematico di Palermo*, Series 2, Vol. 1 (May-August, 1952), pp. 139–156.

BELLMAN, RICHARD, and D. BLACKWELL, "Some Two-Person Games Involving Bluffing," *Proc. Nat. Acad. Sci. U.S.*, Vol. 35 (1949), pp. 600–605.

BHARUCHA-REID, A. T., *Introduction to the Theory of Markov Processes and Their Applications*, McGraw-Hill Book Company Inc., New York, 1960.

BOLLE, *Das Knocheispiel der Alten*, Wismar, 1886.

BOREL, E., *et al.*, *Traité du Calcul des Probabilités et de ses Applications*, Vol. 4, Part 2, Paris, 1938.

BREITKOPF, J. G. L., *Versuch den Ursprung der Spielkarten, die Einführung des Keinenpapiers und den Anfang der Holzschneidekunst in Europa zu Erforschen*, Leipzig, 1784.

CHATTO, WILLIAM, *Facts and Speculations on the Origin and History of Playing Cards*, J. R. Smith, London, 1848.

CUTLER, W. H., "An Optimal Strategy for Pot-Limit Poker, *Am. Math. Monthly*, **82**, No. 4 (April, 1975), pp. 368–376.

EPSTEIN, RICHARD A., "Card Prediction for A Shuffled Deck," Hughes Aircraft Co., Report TP-64-19-11, OP-68, July, 1964.

FINDLER, NICHOLAS V. *et al.*, *Studies on Decision Making Using the Game of Poker, Information Processing*, **71**, North Holland Publ. Co., 1972.

FRÉCHET, M., *Traité du Calcul des Probabilités*, tome 1, fasc. 3, 2ᵉ livre, Gauthiers-Villars and Cie., Paris, 1936.

GILLIES, D. B., J. P. MAYBERRY, and J. VON NEUMANN, "Two Variants of Poker," Study 28, *Contributions to the Theory of Games*, Princeton University Press, Princeton, New Jersey, Vol. 2, 1953, pp. 13–50.

GOLDMAN, A. J., and J. J. STONE, "A Symmetric Continuous Poker Model," *J. Research Nat. Bur. Standards*, **64B**, No. 1 (Jan.-Mar., 1960), pp. 35–40.

GOLOMB, SOLOMON W., "Permutations by Cutting and Shuffling," Jet Propulsion Laboratory Technical Release No. 34-3, California Institute of Technology, Pasadena, Calif., Feb. 25, 1960.

GREENWOOD, ROBERT E., "Probabilities of Certain Solitaire Card Games," *J. Amer. Statistical Assoc.*, **48**, No. 261 (March, 1953), pp. 88–93.

HERVEY, GEORGE F., *A Handbook of Card Games*, Paul Hamlyn, London, 1963.

JOHNSON, PAUL B., "Congruences and Card Shuffling," *Am. Math. Monthly*, Vol. 63 (December, 1956).

JOSEPH, A. W., and M. T. L. BIZLEY, "The Two-Pack Matching Problem," *J. Royal Statistical Soc.*, **22**, Series B (1960), pp. 114–130.

KARLIN, SAMUEL, and RODRIGO RESTREPO, "Multistage Poker Models," Study 39, *Contributions to the Theory of Games*, Princeton University Press, Princeton, New Jersey, Vol. 3, 1957, pp. 337–363.

KENDALL, M. G., and J. D. MURCHLAND, "Statistical Aspects of the Legality of Gambling," *J. Royal Statistical Soc.*, **127**, Pt. 3, Series A (1964), pp. 359–391.

KUHN, H. W., "A Simplified Two-Person Poker," Study 24, *Contributions to the Theory of Games*, Princeton University Press, Princeton, New Jersey, Vol. 1, 1950, pp. 97–103.

LEMYRE, G., *Le Baccara*, Hermann and Compagnie, Paris, 1935.

MOREHEAD, ALBERT H., and GEOFFREY MOTT-SMITH, *Hoyle's Rules of Games*, A Signet Key Book, New American Library, 1946.

NASH, JOHN F., and LLOYD S. SHAPLEY, "A Simple Three-Person Poker Game," Study 24, *Contributions to the Theory of Games*, Princeton University Press, Princeton, New Jersey, Vol. 1, 1950, pp. 105–116.

PHILLIPS, HUBERT, *The Pan Book of Card Games*, Pan Books Ltd., London, 1960.

POISSON, DENIS, "Mémoire sur L'Avantage du Banquier au Jeu de Trente et Quarant," *Ann. Mat. Pures Appl.* **xvi**, N. vi (Decembre, 1825) pp. 173–208.

PRUITT, WILLIAM E., "A Class of Dynamic Games," Technical Report No. 19, Stanford University Applied Mathematics and Statistics Laboratories, Stanford, California, Dec. 4, 1959.

RIORDAN, JOHN, *An Introduction to Combinatorial Analysis*, John Wiley & Sons, Inc., New York, 1958.

RIVE, L'ABBE, *Eclaircissements sur l'Invention des Cartes a Jouer*, Paris, 1780.

THORP, EDWARD O., and WALDEN, WILLIAM E., "The Fundamental Theorem of Card Counting with Applications to Trente-et-Quarante and Baccarat," *Internat. J. Game Theory*, **2**, Issue 2, 1973.

THORP, EDWARD O., "Solution of a Poker Variant," *Informat. Sci.* **2**, No. 3 (July, 1970), pp. 299–301.

USPENSKY, J. V., and M. A. HEASLAT, *Elementary Number Theory*, McGraw-Hill Book Company, Inc., New York, 1939.

VAN RENSSELAER, MRS. J. K., *The Devil's Picture Books*, Dodd, Mead, and Co., New York, 1890.

WATANABE, SATOSI, "Information Theoretical Analysis of Multivariate Correlation," *IBM J. Research and Development*, Vol. 4, No. 1 (January, 1960), pp. 66–82.

WILDE, EDWIN F., and TOMANDL, DANIEL A., "On Shuffling Cards," *Math. Mag.*, **42**, No. 3 (May, 1969), pp. 139–142.

YARDLEY, HERBERT C., *The Education of a Poker Player*, Simon and Schuster, New York, 1957.

CHAPTER SEVEN

BLACKJACK

Memorabilia

The exact origin of the game of Blackjack is rather murky; it was not invented by a single person, but apparently evolved from related card games sometime in the past century and gained currency during World War I. Blackjack (or "21," or Vingt-et-Un) exhibits structural similarities to Baccarat, "$7\frac{1}{2}$," Quinze, and also to Trente et Quarante. However, the connection with these games remains historically tenuous.

The name "Blackjack" stems from the practice of paying 3 to 2 for a total of "21" achieved with two cards, plus a special bonus if the two cards comprise the Ace of Spades and the Jack of Spades or Clubs. While the bonus generally has been discontinued in gambling casinos, the name remains—although "21" would be a more logical appellation.

Blackjack does not constitute a game in the usual game-theoretic sense, since one player's strategy is fixed—the dealer cannot exercise independent judgment or intelligence (we might refer to it as a "one-person game"). Its interest lies in its property of being the only form of public gambling available where the player is able to obtain a mathematical expectation greater than zero. Unlike Craps and Roulette, Blackjack does possess a memory (the interdependence of the cards) and a conscience (inferior play will inevitably be penalized) and is not democratic (the mental agility and retentiveness of the player are significant factors). These facts have been realized in a qualitative sense by many professional gamblers

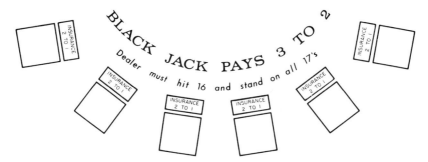

Fig. 7-1   The Blackjack layout

for several decades. In the 1950s, numerical analyses of the Blackjack strategy were performed concurrently by engineers and mathematicians at various engineering laboratories across the United States. Quantitative results achieved by electronic computer programming (a Remington Rand 1103) were reported by the author in talks at UCLA, Princeton, and other universities in 1955. The first published strategy (Baldwin *et al.*) appeared in 1956. Dr. Allan Wilson of San Diego State University conducted a machine simulation of several hundred thousand hands of Blackjack in 1957, obtaining the most accurate results to that date. For the present chapter, the numerical calculations were obtained with the assistance of an IBM 7044 computer. Programming and many contributions regarding variations in Blackjack strategies are due to Julian Braun of IBM.

Blackjack is a favored pastime in the Nevada gambling emporia and in the resort casinos of the Caribbean area. In Europe, the game is largely ignored at most casinos (such as those in Nice, Cannes, and Monte Carlo), but is featured at the Casino Municipale di Venezia (under a sign announcing "Gioco del Blak Jak o 21"). Inevitably, there are variations in the rules of the game as played in different cities, in different casinos of the same city, and even in a single casino from time to time, at the whim of a gaming manager. In general, however, these various rules are in accord on the principal points and differ only in minutiae. We shall adopt, therefore, a set of rules that, to the greatest extent possible, reflects the degree of commonality that exists; for the fine-structured regulations, we shall follow those prevailing along the "strip" of Las Vegas.

Rules

An illustration of the Blackjack layout is shown in Fig. 7-1. A single, conventional 52-card pack of cards is used in the game of Blackjack, although certain casinos employ two or more packs, shuffled together. Each card is assigned a numerical value corresponding to its rank, except for the court (or picture) cards, which have a value of 10, and the Aces, which are evaluated as 1 or 11, at the discretion of the player. A dealer representing the "house" and N players (usually N is from 1 to 6) participate in the game. All wagers are placed by the players prior to the deal; minimum and maximum bets are established by the "house"—a $1.00 minimum and a $500 maximum are customary in the "strip" casinos.

Each player and the dealer receive two cards initially. Of the dealer's two cards, one is exposed and the other remains face down; the player's two cards are commonly dealt face down, although their exposure is irrelevant to the dealer, who conforms to a mechanistic, predetermined strategy. The player may request additional cards as long as the numerical total of his hand is less than 21; these cards are dealt face up. Following the decisions of each player to draw cards or to "stick," the dealer exposes his hidden card. If the value of his cards totals 16 or less, he must "hit" (deal to his hand another card). If his hand totals 17 through 21, he must "stick." When the dealer's cards include an Ace, it must be counted as 11 if his total is thereby brought to 17 or more without exceeding 21; otherwise, the Ace is given the value of 1.

If the player "busts" (exceeds 21), he automatically loses his bet. If he does not exceed 21, but the dealer subsequently busts, the player automatically wins. If neither player nor dealer "busts," the hand closer to 21 is the winning one. In the case where the dealer and player conclude with hands of the same total, the play is a tie (or "standoff" or "push") and the bet is canceled. A win for the player receives a payoff at even odds.

An Ace and a face card or Ten comprising the first two cards dealt to either player or dealer constitute a two-card total of 21, called a "natural" or "Blackjack." Such a combination wins over all others. If the player receives a "Blackjack" and the dealer does not, the payoff to the player is 1.5 times his wager. The dealer wins only the amount wagered when he has a "Blackjack" and the player does not. "Blackjack" occurring in both the player and dealer hands constitutes a tie. When the dealer's face-up card is an Ace, he offers the option of an "insurance" wager—that is, the player may bet an amount equal to one-half his original stake that the dealer's face-down card is a Ten (or face card). If the player accepts, he is paid at 2 to 1 for a winning "insurance" bet and, of course, loses his initial bet, so that no money changes hands thereby. When the "insurance" bet loses, the half-bet is taken by the dealer and the play proceeds normally with the addition of the knowledge that the dealer's down-card is a non-Ten. For the case where the dealer's up-card is a Ten, he checks his down-card for the event of its being an Ace,[†] whereupon his hand constitutes a "Blackjack"; otherwise the play proceeds with the knowledge that the dealer's down-card is a non-Ace.

An Ace combined with one or more non-Tens comprise a *soft* (or double-valued) total, the Ace nominally being accorded the value of 11. The player may consider such a hand as soft or *hard* (single-valued) at his discretion; the dealer, however, must count the Ace as 11 if the total thereby falls into the 17 to 21 bracket, and as 1 otherwise. When the player's initial two cards are of the same rank (a pair), he is afforded the option of splitting them. This procedure permits each card to be treated as a separate hand. A second bet, equal to the original, is required and the player then draws additional cards as desired to his two hands, in sequence (all the cards are face up for this situation). If the split pair is Aces, only a single additional card is allowed to be drawn to each Ace; further, if a 10-valued card is drawn to either split Ace, the resultant numerical total is considered as a normal 21 rather than as a "Blackjack." Finally, a player splitting a pair and drawing a third card of the same rank may split the second pair (and the third pair, if it occurs) at the risk of another wager equal to the original bet (pairs of Aces, of course, may not be split more than once).

The player is also given the option of "doubling down" with the initial two cards of his hand.[‡] This procedure entails doubling the original bet while exposing the two cards and drawing one and only one additional card (this third card is, conventionally, dealt face down). A player splitting a pair (except Aces) may, after receiving a second card to the split card, double down on that two-card combination.

Pertinent mathematics

As successive rounds of Blackjack are dealt from a deck, the process entails sampling without replacement and dependent trials (see Chapter 2). Both optimal player strategy and optimal bet size are, therefore, functions of the remaining deck composition. Further, because of nonrandom shuffling, it is possible to predict with some accuracy the arrangement of the deck, in which instance the strategy encompasses the predictive function.

[†] Some casinos offer an "insurance" bet when the dealer's up-card is a Ten. The bet is at odds of 10 to 1 against the down-card's being an Ace.

[‡] Occasionally, certain casinos have, in moments of uncontrolled generosity, permitted doubling down with three or more cards.

The first step, however, is to calculate the *zero-memory strategy*—that is a strategy based only upon initial information (the two cards dealt to the player and the dealer's exposed card). We assume that a single player competes against the dealer and that all orderings of the deck are equiprobable.

Under the rules of Blackjack there are 55 distinct two-card hands admissible for the player. The dealer's up-card may assume one of ten values. Hence the player's zero-memory strategy must be defined over 550 possible cases; in every case he will either draw, stick, split, or double down, and in some cases he will draw more than one additional card. The zero-memory strategy is a function of the dealer's probabilities of obtaining 17, 18, 19, 20, 21, or exceeding 21 ("busting") and the player's probabilities of obtaining various totals as a result of drawing or sticking (or splitting or doubling down) with a particular two-card combination. These probabilities are encompassed in the player's mathematical expectations from drawing and not drawing. Defining the random variable t_0 as the tw ͻ-card total dealt to the player and the random variable τ as the final total obtained by the dealer (according to his rule of drawing to 16 and below and sticking with 17 and above), then, sticking with t_0, the player's single-play probability of winning P_W is determined by

$$P_W = P(t_0 > \tau) + P(\tau > 21)$$

The player's single-play probability of tying P_T is

$$P_T = P(t_0 = \tau)$$

and the single-play probability P_L of a loss for the player is given by

$$P_L = P(t_0 < \tau \le 21)$$

where

$$P_W + P_T + P_L = 1$$

Thus, the player's mathematical expectation as a function of his total t_0 can be expressed as

$$E(t_0) = P_W - P_L = 2P_W + P_T - 1$$
$$= 2P(t_0 > \tau) + 2P(\tau > 21) + P(t_0 = \tau) - 1 \qquad 7\text{-}1$$

We now define another random variable t_1 to be the total obtained by the player upon drawing one card; if t_1 is double-valued not exceeding 21 (that is, a soft hand), it is taken to represent the larger total. The player's single-play probability of winning following a draw is then

$$P_W = P(21 \geq t_1 > \tau) + P(\tau > 21)P(t_1 \leq 21)$$

and the single-play probability of tying is

$$P_T = P(t_1 = \tau \leq 21)$$

The player's single-play probability of loss in the event of drawing a card is given by

$$P_L = P(t_1 < \tau \leq 21) + P(t_1 > 21)$$

Similar to Eq. 7-1, the mathematical expectation as the result of drawing a card and obtaining the total t_1 is expressed as

$$E(t_1) = 2P_W + P_T - 1$$
$$= 2P(21 \geq t_1 > \tau) + 2P(\tau > 21)P(t_1 \leq 21)$$
$$+ P(t_1 = \tau \leq 21) - 1 \qquad \qquad 7\text{-}2$$

For every value of t_0 the player has the option of sticking or drawing an additional card to increase his total to t_1, where t_1 can be determined as a probability distribution. Clearly, it is to the player's advantage to draw if $E(t_1)$ is greater than $E(t_0)$. Thus, the basic decision equation is the difference between Eqs. 7-2 and 7-1. That is, rearranging terms,

$$E(t_1) - E(t_0) = 2P(21 \geq t_1 > \tau) - 2P(t_0 > \tau)$$
$$- 2P(t_1 > 21)P(\tau > 21)$$
$$+ P(t_1 = \tau \leq 21) - P(t_0 = \tau) \qquad \qquad 7\text{-}3$$

Evidently, the player draws an additional card or sticks as $E(t_1) - E(t_0)$ is positive or negative, respectively. Following a drawn card, if it develops that $t_1 < 21$, the player is again faced with the decision to stick with t_1 or draw a second additional card to obtain the total t_2. Iteration of Eq. 7-3, with t_1 replacing t_0 and t_2 replacing t_1, yields the value of $E(t_2) - E(t_1)$. Continued iterations eventually produce the state $E(t_{i+1}) - E(t_i) < 0$, and the player sticks on his total of $t_i \leq 21$. The maximum value of t_i for which $E(t_{i+1}) - E(t_i) > 0$ is designated as t^* and represents the maximum drawing total for a particular set of known cards (the dealer's up-card plus other disclosed cards).

Having established the values of t^* for the various relevant situations, we can evaluate the basic decision equation for soft totals of the player's hand. If t_{s_0} is the player's original two-card soft total and $\bar{t}_1$ represents the total obtained by drawing one additional card to t_{s_0}, then $\bar{t}_1$ may be equivalent either to a new soft total t_{s_1} or to a hard total t_1. In the latter instance, a draw is indicated for the condition $E(\bar{t}_1) - E(t_{s_0}) > 0$. If the new total is also soft, then the difference of the mathematical expectations is iterated, with t_{s_1} replacing t_{s_0} and t_{s_2} replacing t_{s_1}. Continued iteration eventually produces the condition $E(\bar{t}_{i+1}) - E(t_{s_i}) < 0$, at which point the player should stick on the soft total t_{s_i}. The maximum value of t_{s_i} for which $E(\bar{t}_{i+1}) - E(t_{s_i}) > 0$ is designated as t_s^*, the maximum soft drawing total.

Similar reasoning leads to the basic decision equation for exercising the option of doubling down on the original two-card total of t_0 or t_{s_0}. Clearly, the player should double down only if twice the mathematical expectation received from accepting the single double-down card is greater than the expectation obtained by following the normal drawing strategy.

Another option available to the player is that of splitting an original holding of a pair into two distinct wagers. The basic decision equation for splitting pairs is expressed more readily by defining $E^*(t_0)$ as the mathematical expectation obtained by following the optimum strategy, including the option of doubling down, beginning with a hard total of t_0. Then the player should split his pair if

$$2E^*\left(\frac{t_0}{2}\right) - E^*(t_0) > 0 \qquad\qquad 7\text{-}4$$

For the special case wherein the initial two cards form a pair of Aces, only a single additional card may be drawn to each Ace, and doubling down with the split hands is not permitted.

The decisions regarding doubling down and splitting pairs should not —at least for those players with finite fortunes—be resolved strictly by mathematical expectation since the additional sum required for the double down or split wager alters the probability of attaining a specific increase in wealth. However, we assume here that the bet size is always small with respect to the current fortune.

Finally, whenever the dealer's up-card is an Ace, the player is offered the option of buying "insurance." In this case the basic decision equation is evaluated directly (without extensive computation) from the exposed cards. If m is the total number of exposed cards (including the player's hand, the dealer's up-card, and any other cards previously observed) and $Q(10)$ designates the number of Tens remaining, the player should accept the "insurance" bet if

$$\frac{Q(10)}{52 - m} > \frac{1}{3}$$

Thus, the decision to buy "insurance" is independent of the total (although not the composition) of the player's hand; the "insurance" bet is properly viewed as a side wager, not directly related to the course of the game.[†]

It should be noted that it is in the probability of exceeding 21 that the dealer's advantage resides; that is, *all* ties are not distinguished by a nullification of the wager, for the player must, perforce, conduct his play first. If he busts and the dealer busts subsequently, the game is not a tie, but a win for the dealer. Offsetting this advantage of the dealer is the greater flexibility and additional options offered to the player. The advantage to the "house" of compelling the player to perform the first decisions is emphasized by the game of Zweikartenspiel, considered later in this chapter.

ASSUMPTIONS

In programming an electronic computer to evaluate the calculations of the expectation equations, it is necessary to assume certain simplifications: First, if a player stands on a total t_i, he stands on any total t_{i+1} greater than t_i (the exceptions to this rule are noted in the strategy); second, if a player draws on a total t_i, he draws to all totals t_{i-1} less than t_i. These assumptions, while almost always valid, do not hold for certain "pathological" cases that occur in drawing cards from a severely depleted deck.[‡] It is further assumed that all configurations of the undisclosed cards are equiprobable (thereby disregarding nonrandom shuffling procedures) and the effect of other participants on the deck composition integrates to zero (a consequence of the assumption of equiprobability).

Another premise is that of a strictly objective utility function. The mathematical expectation of an event that has probability of success p and probability of failure q is defined as $p - q$. If, in addition, the event has probability r of remaining unresolved (a tie), only the objective utility function permits the retention of $p - q$ as defining the mathematical expectation. Specifically, in the game of Blackjack it is frequently necessary to select between one event, characterized by (p', q'), and another, characterized by (p, q, r); for example, sticking with a total of 16 or less (which

---

[†] Appropriation of the word "insurance" to describe this wager must be classed as a stroke of genius. The word implies that high-total hands, such as those comprised of two Tens, should be "insured" to protect their value, whereas low-total hands are not worthy of being "insured." It is apparent from Eq. 7-5 that this "reasoning," contrary to a correct appraisal, leads the susceptible player into increasing the "house take."

[‡] For example, if the remaining portion of the deck consists of two Fives, two Sixes, and a Ten, the appropriate strategy dictates sticking with a total of 10 and drawing to a total of 11 when the dealer's up-card is a Ten.

excludes the possibility of a tie) must be compared with the action of drawing a card, the latter strategy including the possibility of a tie. According to the objective utility function, time is irrelevant and the significant probabilities are calculated on a per-play basis; thus the ties are resolved by sharing the probability r equally between the probabilities p and q. That is,

$$p' = p + \frac{r}{2} \quad \text{and} \quad q' = q + \frac{r}{2}$$

so that the game (p, q, r) still exhibits a mathematical expectation of $p - q$. Another utility function might emphasize time (that is, the number of plays to achieve a given goal), but consider the variance to be irrelevant (perhaps because of an excessively large initial fortune). In that instance, the game (p, q, r) would be resolved by renormalizing the probabilities p and q. Thus,

$$p' = \frac{p}{1 - r} \quad \text{and} \quad q' = \frac{q}{1 - r}$$

Other subjective utility functions could produce all possible values of p' and q'.

Generally, in numerical evaluations of the equations for the mathematical expectation, it is hypothesized that the dealer's and player's probabilities of obtaining the respective totals τ and t_i by subsequent drawing of cards are independent. Since the cards are drawn sequentially without replacement from the same deck, a dependency obviously exists. However, the assumption of independence introduces only a minute error. The use of Monte Carlo techniques in the enumeration of over four million hands of Blackjack by a high-speed electronic computer provides a good approximation of this error: The assumption of independence creates a pessimistic evaluation of the game expectation by 0.003. An exact program compatible with any computer with a Fortran IV compiler (courtesy of Julian Braun of IBM Corp.) has been used to generate the data for this chapter. By virtue of this program, it is possible to forego the usual reliance upon independence between player's and dealer's draws and to derive a precisely optimal strategy.

THE COMPUTER PROGRAM

The essence of the computer program for the determination of Blackjack strategies is an algorithm permitting the cycling through every possible card combination (obtained by successive drawings, without replacement, from the original deck) until a specified total is reached and with the exclusion of specified subtotals. For each allowable combination of cards, the probability of occurrence is computed and registered in an appropriate counter. Thus the probability of reaching any number ≤ 21 or exceeding 21 by any drawing strategy is obtainable. In order to limit the magnitude of the computation, the algorithm contains a provision limiting the maximum number of cards in any specific combination (hand) to seven. This restriction imparts a maximum error of 0.00005 to each numerical probability (that is, accuracy to four decimal places is ensured). Accuracy is increased somewhat above this figure by distributing the probabilities of 7-or-more-card combinations proportionately among the allowable totals. Separate computations are performed for each of the 550 initial situations of the game of Blackjack (the dealer's up-card may be one of 10 values and the player may hold one of 55 two-card hands).

A TEN OR ACE UP-CARD

When the dealer's up-card is an Ace (or Ten) and it is announced that his hole-card is not a Ten (or Ace), the probability $P(x)$, $x = 1, 2, \ldots, 10$, of the player subsequently drawing a card of rank x (Ace $= 1$) must be normalized to account for the non-Ten (or non-Ace) held by the dealer. Let $Q(x)$ be the number of x-value cards remaining in the deck and let the dealer's hole-card be designated by x_1. Then, defining

$$n = \sum_{x=1}^{10} Q(x)$$

we can state that if the player draws an additional card, given that the dealer's cards are an exposed Ace paired with a non-Ten down-card, the probability $P(x)$ of his obtaining an x-ranked card is

$$P(x) = P(x_1 = x)\left[\frac{Q(x) - 1}{n - 1}\right] + P(x_1 \neq x)\left[\frac{Q(x)}{n - 1}\right]$$

$$= \frac{Q(x)}{n - Q(10)}\left[\frac{Q(x) - 1}{n - 1}\right] + \frac{n - Q(x) - Q(10)}{n - Q(10)}\left[\frac{Q(x)}{n - 1}\right]$$

$$= \frac{Q(x)|n - Q(10) - 1|}{(n - 1)|n - Q(10)|}, \qquad x \neq 10$$

and

$$P(10) = \frac{Q(10)}{n - 1} \qquad \text{for } x = 10$$

Similarly, given that the dealer's up-card is a Ten and his hole-card a non-Ace, the player's probability of drawing a card of rank x is given by

$$P(1) = \frac{Q(1)}{n-1} \qquad \text{for } x = 1$$

and

$$P(x) = \frac{Q(x)|n - Q(1) - 1|}{(n-1)[n - Q(1)]}, \qquad x \neq 1$$

(For rapid approximations, these computations can be simplified by assuming that $P(x) = Q(x)/n$ for the player's probability of obtaining an x-ranked card. The dealer's probability of achieving a specified total is then readily adjusted for a Ten or Ace up-card by multiplying the unconditional probability of obtaining that total by $|1 - Q(1)/n|^{-1}$ or $|1 - Q(10)/n|^{-1}$, respectively.)

Optimal strategies

THE ZERO-MEMORY STRATEGY

With the preceding considerations, the player's expectations by sticking or drawing a card in each of the 550 initial situations are calculated. The difference in expectations $E(t_1) - E(t_0)$ is iterated until t^*, the maximum value of t_i for which $E(t_{i+1}) - E(t_i)$ becomes positive, is determined. By following the strategy of drawing to all totals t^* and below, and sticking with all totals $t^* + 1$ and above, the player maximizes his mathematical expectation for each case. This maximal expectation is enumerated in App. Tables A(1)–A(10). Similarly, for soft totals t_s^*, the maximum soft drawing number is computed and the corresponding maximal expectations given in the tables. Finally, $2E(t_1)$ and $2E(\bar{t}_1)$, the expectations from doubling down on hard and soft totals, respectively, and $2E^*(t_0/2)$, the expectation by splitting an original pair and following an optimal strategy with each new total $t_0/2$, are enumerated. The situations where doubling down and pair splitting are favored are emphasized by bold-face type. In those cases where the optimal strategy indicates drawing, the maximum drawing numbers t^* for hard totals and t_s^* for soft totals are indicated.

Tables A(1) through A(10) delineate the optimal *zero-memory* strategy; that is, no memory other than that of the player's initial two cards and the dealer's up-card is required. Addition of the properly weighted individual expectations arising from this strategy yields a mathematical expectation for the game of Blackjack of 0.0010. It constitutes, thereby, the only positive-expectation game offered by the public gambling casinos.

The optimal zero-memory strategy is summarized, in simplified form, in Table 7-1. With the six exceptions noted, each hand of the player can be considered as constituting a specific total (rather than individual cards). This convenient simplification is a mnemonic aid for quick recollection of each division point. Using abstract totals (calculations based on a 51-card deck rather than a 49-card deck as above), Table 7-2 presents the difference in expectations between drawing and standing. It is evidently advisable to draw whenever this difference is positive. In order to obtain a feeling for the magnitude of the numerical approximation concomitant to the use of abstract totals for the player's hands, a comparison can be made with the corresponding probabilities of Tables A(1) through A(10) showing the difference in expectations between drawing and standing for exact composition of the player's cards. The expectation differences are based on the possibility of drawing a single additional card at each decision point. Table 7-3 depicts the player's expectations when standing on an abstract total of 16 or less, 17, 18, 19, 20, and 21. Also of interest are the dealer's probabilities of obtaining 17, 18, 19, 20, 21, BJ, and busting according to his fixed method of play. These probabilities are illustrated in Table 7-4.

In addition to the exact strategy for the 49-card deck, we might compute the optimal strategy for hands containing three or more cards, particularly for those decision points where the difference in expectations between drawing and standing is small. App. Table B shows the partitioning of hands totaling 16 into two-, three-, and four-card combinations when the dealer's up-card is a Ten. The expectations given are conditional to the dealer's hole card being a non-Ace. We can, from this table, construct the following rule: Against a Ten, draw with two-card 16's; draw with three- and four-card 16's that include two Sixes or one Six with a Seven, Eight, or Nine, or holding 2, 2, 2, 10; otherwise, stand.

Complete analyses of all multiple-card hands are contrary to the law of diminishing returns, since some hundreds of thousands of such hands exist. It is worth while only to mention a few cases. For example, against a dealer's up-card of Seven, it can be demonstrated that the player should stand with a four-card 16 if the highest-value card is 5 or less (the Ace ranked as 1). There are five such hands, the average disadvantage from drawing in this situation being 2.2 percent. The same rule is applicable to five-card 16's; in this instance there are ten such hands, and the average disadvantage due to drawing is 4.8 percent. Against a dealer's up-card of Eight, it is advisable to stand with four-card 16's, the highest-value card being a Five or less. The disadvantage from drawing in this situation averages 1.5 percent. For five-card 16's with the highest-value card equal to

5 or less, the average loss due to drawing is 3.4 percent. Against a dealer's up-card of Nine, the player should stand on 2 three-card 16's: (3, 5, 8) and (4, 4, 8). Of the 30 possible four-card 16's, there are 13 that dictate a standing strategy, and of the 34 possible five-card 16's, the player is advised to stand in 23 instances.

TABLE 7-1   Summary of Optimal Zero-Memory Strategy[†]

		Dealer's Up-Card									
		2	3	4	5	6	7	8	9	10	A
Player's Hard Total	17										
	16						x	x	x	x	x
	15						x	x	x	x	x
	14						x	x	x	x[f]	x
	13	a					x	x	x	x	x
	12	x	x[b]	c			x	x	x	x	x
	11	D	D	D	D	D	D	D	D	D	D
	10	D	D	D	D	D	D	D	D	x	x
	9	D	D	D	D	D	x	x	x	x	x
	8	x	x	x	x[d]	D[e]	x	x	x	x	x
	7	x	x	x	x	x	x	x	x	x	x
Player's Soft Total	19										
	18		D	D	D	D			x	x	
	17	D	D	D	D	D	x	x	x	x	x
	16	x	x	D	D	D	x	x	x	x	x
	15	x	x	D	D	D	x	x	x	x	x
	14	x	x	D	D	D	x	x	x	x	x
	13	x	x	D	D	D	x	x	x	x	x
Player's Pair	2's	S	S	S	S	S	S				
	3's	S	S	S	S	S	S				
	4's				S						
	5's										
	6's	S	S	S	S	S	S				
	7's	S	S	S	S	S	S	S			
	8's	S	S	S	S	S	S	S	S	S	S
	9's	S	S	S	S	S			S	S	
	10's										
	A's	S	S	S	S	S	S	S	S	S	S

[†] Symbolism: x = draw, D = double down, S = split.
EXCEPTIONS:

    a. Draw with hand (3, 10) vs. a 2

    b. Stand with hands (3, 9), (4, 8), and (5, 7) vs. a 3

    c. Draw with hand (2, 10) vs. a 4

    d. Double down with hand (3, 5) vs. a 5

    e. Do not double with hand (2, 6) vs. a 6

    f. Stand with hand (7, 7) vs. a 10

TABLE 7-2   Expectation by Drawing Minus Expectation by Standing (Abstract Totals)

Player's Hard Total	Dealer's Up-Card									
	A	2	3	4	5	6	7	8	9	10
12	0.2476	0.0393	0.0149	-0.0139	-0.0404	-0.0230	0.2089	0.1885	0.1415	0.1537
13	0.2212	-0.0161	-0.0440	-0.0796	-0.1124	-0.0932	0.1651	0.1483	0.1429	0.1173
14	0.1948	-0.0714	-0.1055	-0.1476	-0.1844	-0.1633	0.1214	0.1487	0.1063	0.0809
15	0.1684	-0.1295	-0.1695	-0.2154	-0.2560	-0.2332	0.1184	0.1113	0.0696	0.0445
16	0.1384	-0.1902	-0.2334	-0.2833	-0.3274	-0.2619	0.0776	0.0739	0.0330	0.0083
17	-0.0933	-0.4006	-0.4377	-0.4922	-0.4867	-0.5079	-0.3647	-0.1047	-0.1351	-0.1616
18	-0.5452	-0.7639	-0.7933	-0.7931	-0.8256	-0.8819	-0.9856	-0.6850	-0.4248	-0.4732
19	-1.0314	-1.1404	-1.1207	-1.1390	-1.1805	-1.2128	-1.3285	-1.3024	-0.9861	-0.8041
20	-1.5458	-1.4875	-1.4968	-1.5057	-1.5341	-1.5544	-1.6240	-1.6407	-1.6035	-1.4072
Player's Soft Total										
17	0.2869	0.1417	0.1318	0.1150	0.1375	0.1190	0.1578	0.3150	0.2644	0.2254
18	-0.0091	-0.0742	-0.0764	-0.0544	-0.0521	-0.0931	-0.2345	-0.0683	0.0830	0.0295
19	-0.3118	-0.2845	-0.2526	-0.2377	-0.2393	-0.2596	-0.4029	-0.4496	-0.2838	-0.1742
20	-0.6075	-0.4611	-0.4448	-0.4224	-0.4119	-0.4216	-0.5292	-0.6112	-0.6599	-0.5559

TABLE 7-3   Player's Expectations

Player's Total	Dealer's Up-Card									
	A	2	3	4	5	6	7	8	9	10
≤16	-0.6604	-0.2941	-0.2489	-0.1944	-0.1422	-0.1584	-0.4803	-0.5228	-0.5331	-0.5350
17	-0.4766	-0.1551	-0.1185	-0.0634	0.0225	0.0086	-0.1080	-0.3919	-0.4112	-0.4109
18	-0.1019	0.1156	0.1427	0.1817	0.2207	0.2820	0.4030	0.1020	-0.1854	-0.1642
19	0.2766	0.3792	0.3974	0.4165	0.4611	0.4956	0.6189	0.5944	0.2759	0.0827
20	0.6580	0.6349	0.6445	0.6535	0.6827	0.7035	0.7751	0.7921	0.7555	0.5640
21	0.9248	0.8794	0.8839	0.8849	0.8937	0.9021	0.9270	0.9302	0.9389	0.9604

TABLE 7-4   Dealer's Probabilities

Dealer's Total	Dealer's Up-Card									
	A	2	3	4	5	6	7	8	9	10
17	0.1261	0.1390	0.1303	0.1310	0.1197	0.1670	0.3723	0.1309	0.1219	0.1144
18	0.1310	0.1318	0.1310	0.1142	0.1235	0.1065	0.1386	0.3630	0.1039	0.1129
19	0.1295	0.1318	0.1238	0.1207	0.1169	0.1072	0.0773	0.1294	0.3574	0.1147
20	0.1316	0.1240	0.1233	0.1163	0.1047	0.1007	0.0789	0.0683	0.1223	0.3289
21	0.0516	0.1205	0.1161	0.1151	0.1063	0.0979	0.0730	0.0698	0.0611	0.0365
>21	0.1165	0.3530	0.3758	0.4028	0.4289	0.4208	0.2599	0.2386	0.2334	0.2143
BJ	0.3137									0.0784

TABLE 7-5 Player's Expectation for Various Types of Decks

Type of Deck	Player's Overall Expectation	A†	A‡	Dealer's Up-Card								
				2	3	4	5	6	7	8	9	10‡	10†
Full Deck	0.0009	−0.085	−0.360	0.099	0.135	0.183	0.236	0.241	0.145	0.054	−0.043	−0.169	−0.102
Q(A) = 0	−0.0242			0.036	0.071	0.118	0.162	0.210	0.061	−0.022	−0.106	−0.205	−0.205
Q(2) = 0	0.0174	−0.065	−0.368		0.154	0.201	0.297	0.315	0.186	0.104	0.004	−0.171	−0.098
Q(3) = 0	0.0213	−0.062	−0.367	0.125		0.240	0.320	0.345	0.199	0.108	−0.034	−0.170	−0.097
Q(4) = 0	0.0263	−0.065	−0.369	0.132	0.201		0.367	0.384	0.218	0.073	−0.026	−0.167	−0.093
Q(5) = 0	0.0357	−0.057	−0.363	0.190	0.248	0.324		0.414	0.185	0.079	−0.016	−0.158	−0.084
Q(6) = 0	0.0234	−0.076	−0.376	0.185	0.248	0.323	0.378		0.162	0.064	−0.044	−0.165	−0.091
Q(7) = 0	0.0203	−0.052	−0.360	0.178	0.243	0.297	0.240	0.237		0.084	−0.027	−0.162	−0.088
Q(8) = 0	0.0028	−0.042	−0.353	0.166	0.213	0.154	0.202	0.219	0.141		−0.046	−0.166	−0.092
Q(9) = 0	−0.0043	−0.023	−0.341	0.141	0.074	0.137	0.187	0.191	0.141	0.030		−0.153	−0.078
Q(10) = 0	0.0163	−0.078	−0.078	0.003	−0.010	−0.012	0.001	0.073	0.056	0.063	0.053		
Q(10) = 5	−0.0264	−0.116	−0.224	−0.030	−0.026	−0.013	0.006	0.059	0.068	0.033	−0.017	−0.101	−0.003
Q(10) = 6	−0.0299	−0.118	−0.244	−0.029	−0.023	−0.008	0.016	0.062	0.074	0.032	−0.024	−0.113	−0.019
Q(10) = 8	−0.0313	−0.120	−0.279	−0.023	−0.010	0.014	0.053	0.084	0.085	0.031	−0.036	−0.131	−0.044
Q(10) = 10	−0.0266	−0.119	−0.308	−0.004	0.018	0.051	0.095	0.117	0.100	0.031	−0.043	−0.145	−0.065
Q(10) = 12	−0.0185	−0.112	−0.330	0.026	0.054	0.093	0.143	0.158	0.117	0.037	−0.048	−0.157	−0.081
Q(10) = 20	0.0189	−0.050	−0.381	0.181	0.218	0.266	0.317	0.319	0.170	0.071	−0.032	−0.173	−0.111
Q(10) = 24	0.0351	−0.015	−0.399	0.255	0.291	0.344	0.398	0.396	0.193	0.090	−0.017	−0.171	−0.113
Q(10) = 30	0.0582	0.051	−0.414	0.369	0.408	0.459	0.509	0.503	0.225	0.119	0.012	−0.164	−0.112
Q(10) = 36	0.0766	0.121	−0.425	0.477	0.513	0.561	0.607	0.598	0.256	0.148	0.044	−0.155	−0.108

† Conditional probability that the dealer's hole card excludes a Blackjack.
‡ Includes the probability that the dealer's hole card completes a Blackjack.

THE SURRENDER RULE

Of the many variations in the basic (Las Vegas) rules useful to the player, one of the most interesting is the "surrender" option. Under this rule the player may "surrender"—that is, relinquish—any hand (not exceeding 21) at a cost of one-half the sum wagered if the dealer's up-card is any value other than an Ace.[†] A partial "surrender" is also permitted, whereby the player may reduce his bet from β_1 to β_2 with a penalty payment of $(\beta_1 - \beta_2)/2$ units. With objective utility functions, the partial "surrender" option is never accepted. Full "surrender" $(\beta_2 = 0)$ should be opted for whenever $[E(t)]$, the player's expectation using optimal strategy with a total t, is less than -0.5. From Tables A(1) through A(10), the two-card player holdings that should be "surrendered" are $(10, 6)$, $(10, 5)$, $(9, 7)$, $(9, 6)$, and $(7, 7)$, all versus a Ten as the dealer's up-card. Evaluation of three-or-more-card holdings is more complex because the order of occurrence of the cards is significant. Detailed analysis indicates that, overall, the "surrender" option offers the player a gain in expectation of 0.0015 for zero-memory play.

STRATEGIES WITH MEMORY

Because of the fluctuations in the composition of the deck as it is depleted over successive (and *dependent*) trials, it is intuitively apparent that altering decisions or the magnitude of the wager or both in accordance with the fluctuations should prove advantageous to the player.

At the onset of each round, there is a probability distribution F_c that describes the player's expectation given a knowledge of c cards. A theorem, proven by Thorp, states that as c increases, F_c spreads out; therefore increasing the bet size for positive expectations and betting the minimum sum for negative expectations improve the player's overall expectation, $E(F_c)$. When a decision strategy computed on the basis of $52-c$ cards is used, $E(F_c)$ increases as c increases. Card-counting systems yielding expectations of 0.02 and greater have been devised.

It should be noted that the F_c are dependent—when a deck enters into a favorable composition, it tends to remain favorable.

Q(X) STRATEGIES

To compute strategies for each of the astronomical number of significant partial deck compositions is a patent impossibility. A pragmatic approach is to consider certain easily recognizable features of the depleted deck and analyze the strategy for these characteristics.

[†] This concept was first displayed publicly in 1958 by the Continental casino in Manila and is currently in force in other Far East gambling houses such as the Casino de Macao.

The most simple characteristic is that situation wherein all cards of a particular value are absent from the remaining deck structure. Letting $Q(x) = y$ represent a deck that contains y cards of value x, we can calculate the changes in strategy and the mathematical expectation associated with that deck. Table 7-5 illustrates the player's overall expectations for these types of decks as a function of the dealer's up-card. From the table it is apparent that $Q(5) = 0$ (the absence of all four Fives) is the most advantageous of the single-rank deletions, the player's expectation being 0.0357. For a single player competing against the dealer, almost the entire deck being utilized, the absence of the four Fives will occur 9.8 percent of the time. With additional players, the gain per unit time decreases. From Table 7-5 we can also deduce that a shortage of Twos through Eights is advantageous to the player, whereas a shortage of Nines, Tens, and Aces is advantageous to the dealer. Strategies can evidently be devised which conform to these observations.

Optimal strategies (to achieve the expectations shown in Table 7-5) for the $Q(x) = 0$ decks are depicted in App. Tables C(1), C(2), C(3). For the case $Q(5) = 0$, the optimal strategy is quite similar to the zero-memory strategy summarized in Table 7-1, differing only in a few particulars. For $Q(10) = 0$, on the other hand, a marked deviation in basic strategy is evidenced: A maximum hard drawing number of 17 is indicated regardless of the dealer's up-card; further, no double-down combination exhibits a positive expectation.

ANOMALOUS DECISION POINTS

With certain types of depleted decks there occasionally arise two distinct maximum hard-drawing numbers for a particular dealer's up-card. As an example, with all four sixes removed from the deck, the optimal strategy in the instance where the dealer's up-card is a Ten proves to be $t^* = 14$ *and* $t^* = 16$. That is, the player is advised to draw when holding a total of 14 or less, stick on a total of 15, and draw to a total of 16! Such an apparent eccentricity is due to the discrete and constrained combinations of cards comprising each sum. Table 7-6 tabulates ten instances of anomalous behavior where the optimal strategy leads to two values of t^*. The "better" maximum drawing number (that is, that value providing the greater mathematical expectation, were it necessary to restrict the basic strategy to single-valued representations of t^*) is bold-face type in each case.

COUNTING TENS; THE *T*-RATIO STRATEGY

A far more effective strategy than that offered by $Q(5) = 0$ consists of maintaining a continuing record (as the deck is dealt out) of the ratio of

TABLE 7-6   Two-Valued Drawing Numbers

Type of Deck	Dealer's Up-Card	t^*	
$Q(6) = 0$	10	**14**	16
	9	14	**16**
	A	**14**	16
$Q(7) = 0$	10	**12**	15
$Q(8) = 0$	10	12	**16**
	9	12	**16**
$Q(9) = 0$	6	**11**	13
	4	**11**	13
	3	**11**	13
	2	**11**	13

non-Tens to Tens remaining in the deck. This number was first used extensively by Dr. Edward O. Thorp, who calculated the various decision changes and bet-size variations as a function of the remaining non-Tens to Tens ratio. For convenience, we designate this parameter as the "T ratio." Initially, since there are 36 non-Tens and 16 Tens in the full deck, the T ratio is $36/16 = 2.25$. As the deck is dealt through, the player's mathematical expectation varies inversely as the T ratio; that is, as a general rule, the greater the percentage of Tens remaining in the deck, the greater the player's expectation. Fig. 7-2 presents the player's expectation as a function of the T ratio when the player employs the zero-memory strategy and when he employs a strategy adapted to the running count of Tens and non-Tens.

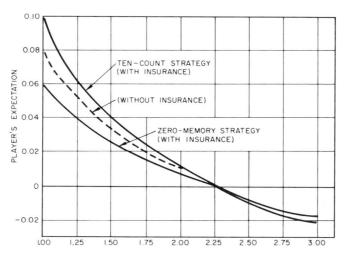

Fig. 7-2   Player's expectation as a function of the T ratio (*Permission—Edward O. Thorp.*)

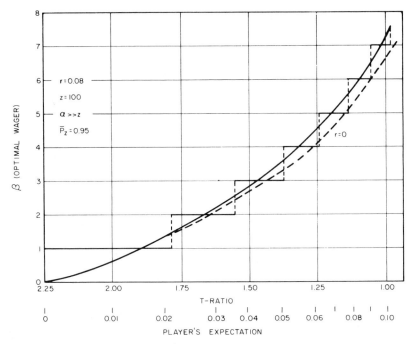

Fig. 7-3   Optimal wager as a function of the *T* ratio

For a particular initial fortune z, the optimal wager β^* to reach a level of resources a with a fixed confidence level $\bar{P}_z$ is specified by Eq. 3-9 as a function of (q/p). We can readily compute β^* as a function of the mathematical expectation, given the probability r of tying (for the game of Blackjack, $r \simeq 0.083$). Letting $z = 100$, $\bar{P}_z = 0.95$ (allowing a probability of ruin equal to 0.05), and establishing the goal of a final fortune a greatly in excess of z, we illustrate in Fig. 7-3 the optimal wager at Blackjack as the game expectation (and hence the T ratio) varies. As a comparison, the dotted line in the figure presents the optimal wager for a game with $r = 0$. Since gambling casinos generally do not permit fractional-unit bets, we quantize the betting scale as indicated by the steps in Fig. 7-3 (a one-unit minimum wager is assumed to be mandatory). Table 7-7 lists the ranges of the T ratio for each bet β^*. Obviously, if a higher confidence level is desired, the betting scale will be more conservative, and vice versa. Also, it should be noted that, according to established rules, the wager is placed at the beginning of each deal; therefore, the T ratio specifying the bet and that specifying the strategy may be different, since the latter includes the more recent cards dealt to the dealer and player(s).

Since Blackjack constitutes a compound game, we can also compute the optimal wager under a criterion of survival according to Eq. 3-14. For

TABLE 7-7   Quantized Wagers for *T* Ratios

T Ratio	β^* (in units)
≥ 1.78	1 (minimum)
Between	
1.78 and 1.51	2
1.51 and 1.38	3
1.38 and 1.23	4
1.23 and 1.14	5
1.14 and 1.05	6
1.05 and 1.02	7

this computation a knowledge of the relative frequency of the *T* ratios is required; we shall set forth the relative frequency, following a description of the optimal strategy arising through use of the Ten-count method.

The variation in strategy as a function of the running *T* ratio is indicated by Table 7-8. Each number on the chart is a *critical ratio* and is defined as that value of the *T* ratio for which the mathematical expectations of two opposing decisions (draw and stand, for example) are equal. In each drawing-versus-standing situation (defined by the player's total and the dealer's up-card), the player should draw *if and only if the T ratio is greater or equal to the critical ratio* for that situation. Otherwise his preferred strategy is to stand. That is, the hand total corresponding to t^* occurs in that position whose critical value is immediately below the running *T* ratio. For each doubling-down or splitting situation, the player should double down or split *if and only if the T ratio is less than or equal to the critical ratio* for that situation. Otherwise the zero-memory strategy should be followed (the several exceptions in the pair-splitting strategy are noted in the table).

The critical ratios are calculated from a computer program using Eqs. 7-3 and 7-4, but with an appropriate number of Tens added to or deleted from the deck in order to effect a particular *T* ratio.

To determine the approximate magnitude of the error arising from the use of abstract totals for the player's hands, we compute the critical ratios for several specific hands versus a dealer's up-card of Ten. These computations are compiled in Table 7-9. Comparison with Table 7-8 reveals an average error of about 10 percent in the critical ratio, due to describing the player's hands by abstract totals. The accuracy of the Ten-count system is consistent with this degree of approximation.

In Table 7-10 we illustrate several specific hands totaling 16 versus a 6 and versus a 3. Inspection of this figure will convey some understanding of the sensitivity of the Ten-count system. The variation of mathematical expectation as a single Ten is added to or deleted from the deck is seen to be

TABLE 7-8 Optimal Strategy as a Function of Critical Ratios

Player's Hard Total	Cards	Dealer's Up-Card									
		2	3	4	5	6	7	8	9	10	A
for Doubling Down											
5	2,3			1.0	1.1	1.1					
6	2,4	0.9	1.1	1.0	1.2	1.3					0.9
7	3,4	1.2	1.1	1.3	1.5	1.5	1.1				0.9
7	2,5	1.3		1.2	1.4	1.4	1.0				1.0
8	4,4	1.4	1.5	1.8	2.1	2.2	1.1	1.5			
8	3,5		1.5	1.7	2.0	2.2	1.0	1.6			
8	2,6					2.0	1.0	1.6			
9	4,5	2.2	2.4	2.8	3.4	3.6	2.0	1.5			
9	3,6	2.2	2.4	2.8	3.3	3.3	2.0	1.6			
9	2,7	2.3	2.5	2.8	3.1	3.3	2.0	1.6			
10	5,5	4.0	4.3	5.1	6.3	6.6	4.2	3.2	2.6	1.9	1.8
10	4,6	3.8	4.3	5.0	6.0	6.1	4.1	3.1	2.5	1.9	1.8
10	3,7	3.7	4.2	4.8	5.5	5.6	3.8	3.0	2.4	2.0	1.8
10	2,8	3.6	4.0	4.4	5.1	5.2	3.5	2.7	2.5	1.9	1.8
11	5,6	4.2	4.5	5.4	6.3	6.1	4.0	3.2	2.7	2.9	2.3
11	4,7	4.0	4.3	5.0	5.6	5.6	3.8	3.0	2.6	2.9	2.2
11	3,8	3.8	4.1	4.6	5.2	5.2	3.6	2.9	2.6	2.8	2.1
11	2,9	3.7	4.0	4.3	5.0	5.0	3.4	2.9	2.5	2.7	2.1
for Drawing											
12		2.0	2.1	2.2	2.4	2.3				1.1	1.0
13		2.3	2.5	2.6	3.0	2.7				1.3	1.1
14		2.7	2.9	3.3	3.7	3.4			1.1	1.6	1.2
15		3.2	3.6	4.1	4.8	4.3			1.4	1.9	1.3
16		3.9	4.5	5.3	6.5	4.6		1.2	1.7	2.2	1.4
17											3.1
18											

TABLE 7-8   *Continued*

	2	3	4	5	6	7	8	9	10	A
Player's Soft Total for Doubling Down										
13	1.5	1.7	2.1	2.6	2.7					
14	1.5	1.8	2.3	2.9	3.0					
15	1.6	1.9	2.4	3.0	3.2					
16	1.6	1.9	2.5	3.1	4.0					
17	2.1	2.5	3.2	4.8	4.8	1.1				
18	2.0	2.2	3.3	3.8	3.5					
19	1.4	1.7	1.8	2.0	2.0					
20	1.3	1.3	1.5	1.6	1.6					
Player's Pair										
2's	3.1	3.8	S	S	S	$\overline{1.1}$	$\overline{3.8}$	$\overline{4.2}$	$\overline{5.3}$	
3's	S	S	S	S	S	1.1	2.4			
4's	1.3	1.6	1.9	2.4						
5's										
6's	2.4	2.6	3.0	3.6	4.1	3.4				1.3
7's	S	S	S	S	S	S	S			4.8
8's	S	S	S	S	S	S	S	S		1.5
9's	2.4	2.8	3.1	3.7	3.2	1.6	S	4.2	$\overline{1.6}$	
10's	1.4	1.5	1.7	1.9	1.8					
A's	4.0	4.1	4.5	4.9	5.0	3.8	3.3	3.1	3.2	2.6

$\overline{X}$ signifies that the indicated action is for values of the T ratio *greater than or equal to* the critical ratio. X.

The player's soft drawing strategy t_s^* is equivalent to the zero-memory strategy except that soft 18 vs. an A has a critical ratio of 2.2.

TABLE 7-9   Critical Ratios for Some Specific Hands†

	Player's Hand	Critical Ratio	Player's Hand	Critical Ratio	Player's Hand	Critical Ratio	Player's Hand	Critical Ratio	Player's Hand	Critical Ratio
12:	2, 10	1.08	3, 9	1.23	4, 8	1.19	5, 7	1.16	6, 6	1.05
13:	3, 10	1.26	4, 9	1.21	5, 8	1.52	6, 7	1.49		
14:	4, 10	1.54	5, 9	1.48	6, 8	1.58	7, 7	2.35		
15:	5, 10	2.01	6, 9	1.95	7, 8	1.84				
16:	6, 10	2.04	7, 9	2.20						

† Dealer's up-card = 10.

TABLE 7-10   Critical Ratios and T Ratios for Some Hands of Total 16

Situation	Q(10)	$E(t_1)$	$E(t_1) - E(t_0)$	T-Ratio	Q(10)	$E(t_1)$	$E(t_1) - E(t_0)$	T-Ratio	Critical Ratio
(6, 10) vs. 6	9	-0.3262	0.0061	4.250	10	-0.3022	-0.0299	3.778	4.17
(7, 9) vs. 6	9	-0.3279	0.0062	3.667	10	-0.3037	-0.0300	3.300	3.60
(2, 6, 8) vs. 6	8	-0.3267	0.0082	4.000	9	-0.3016	-0.0297	3.556	3.90
(2, 4, 10) vs. 6	7	-0.3512	0.0026	5.550	8	-0.3224	-0.0377	4.714	5.45
(4, 5, 7) vs. 6	6	-0.3500	0.0104	5.333	7	-0.3215	-0.0298	4.571	5.14
(6, 10) vs. 3	9	-0.4024	0.0010	4.250	10	-0.3783	-0.0326	3.778	4.24
(7, 9) vs. 3	9	-0.4000	0.0019	3.667	10	-0.3764	-0.0314	3.300	3.65
(2, 6, 8) vs. 3	8	-0.3996	0.0050	4.000	9	-0.3742	-0.0303	3.556	3.94
(2, 4, 10) vs. 3	7	-0.4548	0.0168	5.500	8	-0.4290	-0.0188	4.714	5.13
(4, 5, 7) vs. 3	6	-0.4302	-0.0077	5.333	7	-0.4021	-0.0450	4.571	5.44

relatively small. More extensive and exact calculations for the Ten-count system are evidently not warranted.

Maintaining an up-to-date knowledge of the T ratio automatically provides us with a decision when the option of the "insurance" wager arises. Given the dealer's up-card to be an Ace, the probability that his hole-card is a Ten is simply a function of the percentage of Tens in the remaining portion of the deck. Since 2 to 1 odds are offered (a maximum wager of one-half the original bet is permitted) against the hole-card being a Ten, the offer should be accepted for all values of the T ratio less than 2.0, independent of the numerical total of the player's hand.

The expectation of gain accrued through use of the Ten-count strategy is a function of that percentage of the 52-card deck dealt before reshuffling. If, for example, the deck is reshuffled following the conclusion of each play (the average number of cards required per play is 5.36 with a single player opposing the dealer), the Ten-count strategy yields a mathematical expectation of $+0.0025$. If the deck is reshuffled only after at least 32 cards have been dealt and at the end of a play, $E = 0.0050$, including the gain from the "insurance" wager (in the preceding example, "insurance" is never accepted, since the T ratio never falls below 2.0). When the deck is reshuffled after at least 39 cards dealt and the completion of a play, $E = 0.0080$, including the gain from "insurance." Reshuffling when at least 46 cards have been dealt at the end of a play, or reshuffling in midplay if 50 cards have been used and an additional card requested, results in a game expectation of $E = 0.0123$, including the gain from "insurance." These figures, which are calculated on the basis of constant wagers, indicate the greater importance of the last few cards remaining in the deck when a memory system is employed (the average yield on the last play of each deck prior to reshuffling is in excess of 0.03).

App. Table D presents the frequency of occurrence of each T ratio at 0.1 intervals from 0.0 to over 6.8. Relative frequencies of doubling down and splitting are also shown. "Insurance" wagers at T ratios greater than 2.0 occur, since the actual bet is placed prior to the play when the T ratio has a value less than 2.0. When a betting system ($\bar{P}_z = 0.95$, $z = 100$, $a \gg z$) such as that illustrated in Fig. 7-3 is applied, the game expectation is increased to 0.035. Over seven million hands of Blackjack were machine-simulated to obtain these figures (exact calculations involve a prodigious number of Markov chains) with at least 46 cards of each deck dealt before reshuffling, mandatory shuffling occurring after 50 cards have been turned. A smoothed curve, using a least mean squares polynomial fit, of the relative frequencies of the T ratios is drawn in Fig. 7-4.

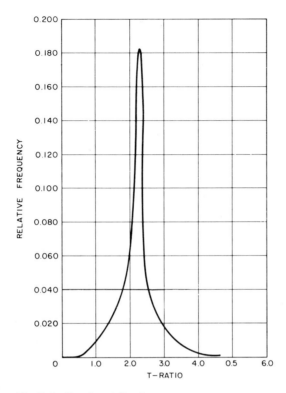

Fig. 7-4   *T*-ratio relative frequency

Another, more conservative, betting system is applicable to Blackjack owing to its character as a compound game. The survival criterion discussed in Theorem VIII of Chapter 3 indicates a critical expectation of +0.021. Table D or Fig. 7-4 then enables us to calculate the optimal wager β^* as a function of expectation (or T ratio). Specifically, from Eq. 3-14,

$$\beta^* = \begin{cases} 1, & p < 0.5105 \\ \dfrac{\log[(1-p)/p]}{\log[(1-0.5105)/0.5105]}, & p \geq 0.5105 \end{cases} \qquad 7\text{-}5$$

corresponding to a critical expectation of 0.021 (a critical single-trial probability of success of 0.5105). We have assumed a zero probability of tying, thereby injecting an additional element of conservatism into the betting scheme; with a tie probability of 0.08, the statistical fluctuations

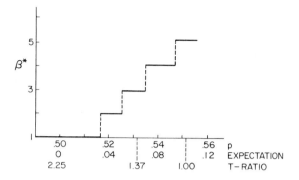

Fig. 7-5   Optimal wager under the survival criterion

are reduced from those implied in the development of Eq. 3-14. Equation 7-5 is plotted in Fig. 7-5 for the usual values of T ratios and expectations. Over the small range of expectations encountered in Blackjack, the conservative optimal wager varies almost linearly with expectation (for $p \geq 0.5105$).

MULTIDIGIT MEMORY SYSTEMS

Further improvements over the Ten-count strategy involve finer-structured memory systems. The next logical step consists of classifying the card ranks as Aces, Tens, and non-Tens. A simple adjustment to the bet size as a function of the number of Aces remaining in the deck can be effected without undue strain on the memory. From Table 7-5 we can observe that removal of all four Aces results in a game expectation of $E[Q(1) = 0] = -0.0242$. And, with the Aces removed, the T ratio becomes $32/16 = 2.00$, which denotes an expectation of $E = +0.0100$ (see Fig. 7-2). Thus, the four Aces control an expectation differential $\Delta E = 0.0342$. Consequently, an Ace-correction factor F can be applied to that expectation signified by the T ratio. A simple expression, suggested by E. O. Thorp and derived by considering deviations from the expected number of Aces remaining at any instant, is

$$F = 0.0342 \left[\frac{13Q(1)}{n} - 1 \right]$$

7-6

where n is the number of cards remaining. The expectation revised to include the numerical value of F then determines the magnitude of the wager β^* according to the specified confidence level, objective, and initial fortune.

Memory systems can be developed further by incorporating cards of other ranks. For example, a four-digit memory, suggested by the "natural" structure of the game, consists of classifying cards according to Tens, Aces, Twos through Fives, and Sixes through Nines. The deck, at any instant, is described by $| Q(10), Q(1), Q(2-5), Q(6-9) |$, where $Q(10)$ can take on values 1 through 16, $Q(1)$ values 1 through 4, and $Q(2-5)$ and $Q(6-9)$ values 1 through 20. Use of this four-digit parameter to determine bet size and strategic decisions is operationally burdensome. A format for computing the correct decisions for any arbitrary subset of the 52-card deck can be derived from the exact program described earlier. It is possible thereby to ascertain the optimal strategy corresponding to any desired memory system.

POINT-COUNT SYSTEMS

Another approach, which avoids the excessive calculations inherent in a fine-structured memory system, is exemplified by the "point-count" method. In this scheme a point value is assigned each rank and the optimal strategy and bet size are determined as functions of the running point count. By convention, the point value for a rank is chosen to be positive if removing a card of that rank from the deck favors the player and negative if it favors the house. Ideally, the magnitude of the point value (restricted to a small integer for tractability) reflects both the rank's influence on expectation and its influence on strategic determinants. The running point count should correspond roughly to the player's running expectation, thus regulating the bet size, and it should provide a measure of the deck's composition, thus regulating strategy. An operative point-count also begins at zero for the full deck and satisfies the condition

$$\sum_{i=1}^{10} q_i = 0$$

where q_i is the point value of the ith rank (Ace = rank 1).

Table 7-11 shows the effect on player expectation E of removing a card of rank i from a complete 52-card deck—an effect calculated by eliminating the gain that accrues from varying the zero-memory strategies for the $Q(i) = 0$ depletions of the deck (Table 7-5). The relative changes in expectation, Δr_i, are computed by subtracting from each ΔE_i the amount of gain accruing from the appropriate change of strategy when that card is removed (this gain is approximately—but not precisely—the normalized weighted sum of the ΔE_i's). If the point value assigned to rank i is proportional to Δr_i, then the system is ideal for bet variations. Unfortunately, such a system proves inadequate in propounding strategy variations. Compromise in betting correlation is indicated to obtain a system with a high strategic efficiency.

Table 7-11   Effect on Player Expectation of Removing One Card of Specified Rank[a]

Card of rank i removed	Full-deck expectation $E = 0.10\%$									
	A	2	3	4	5	6	7	8	9	10
Expectation E_i (%)	−0.48	0.50	0.56	0.70	0.86	0.56	0.41	0.12	−0.06	−0.39
Change in expectation (%)	−0.58	0.40	0.46	0.60	0.76	0.46	0.31	0.02	−0.16	−0.49
Δr_i	−0.591	0.388	0.463	0.610	0.786	0.457	0.298	−0.004	−0.193	−0.494

[a] Courtesy of J. Braun

Some of the more practical and efficient point-count systems are listed in Table 7-12. The first consideration in selecting a system for operational use is the level of complexity—determined by the magnitude of the largest point assigned. As a practical matter in maintaining a running point count, higher levels of complexity demand extreme feats of mental agility.

Since optimal strategy is only slightly affected by changes in density of Aces in the deck, it appears reasonable to assign a point value of 0 to the Ace. However, the player's expectation is strongly affected by the Ace (Table 7-11); systems with $q_1 = 0$ are often supplemented, therefore, with a separate Ace count used to determine the bet size (proportional to positive expectation).

Strategic efficiency constitutes the prime criterion within a given level of complexity. For any counting system, its strategic or playing efficiency is defined as the quotient of the expected gain it engenders and the total expected gain possible. Griffin has shown that the total expected gain $E(n)$ resulting from appropriate departures from the zero-memory strategy with n cards remaining in the deck is approximated by

$$E(n) \sim \frac{\sigma_n}{\sqrt{2\pi}} e^{-\mu^2/2\sigma_n{}^2} - \frac{\mu}{\sqrt{2\pi}} \int_{\mu/\sigma_n}^{\infty} e^{-x^2/2} \, dx \qquad \text{7-7}$$

where μ is the full-deck expectation from the zero-memory strategy,

$$\sigma_n^2 = \frac{\sigma^2}{n} \left(\frac{51 - n}{50} \right),$$

and σ^2 is the variance of the full-deck payoffs (a bivariate normal density is assumed for the average payoff). It should be noted from Eq. 7-7 that $E(n)$ increases as n decreases, and also as σ increases and as μ decreases. To derive the similar expression for a point-count system, it is assumed that the average point value for the system and the average payoff for the n-card

Table 7-12   Point-Count Systems

| System | Point values | | | | | | | | | | Strategic efficiency | Betting correlation | Player's expectation | |
	A	2	3	4	5	6	7	8	9	10			1-Unit bet	1,4-Units bet
First level														
Braun +−	−1	1	1	1	1	1	0	0	0	−1	0.510	0.96	0.007	0.020
E. Gordon	0	1	1	1	1	0	0	0	0	−1	0.574	0.86	0.007	0.020
Einstein, Hi-Opt	0	0	1	1	1	1	0	0	0	−1	0.615	0.88	0.008	0.022
Griffin-1	0	0	0	1	1	1	1	0	0	−1	0.637	0.86	0.008	0.022
Second level														
Revere	−2	1	2	2	2	2	1	0	0	−2	0.527	0.96	0.006	0.021
Stepine	0	1	1	2	2	1	1	0	0	−2	0.671	0.92	0.009	0.025
Griffin-2	0	1	1	2	2	2	1	0	−1	−2	0.672	0.92	0.009	0.024
Third level														
Griffin-3	0	1	2	2	3	2	2	1	−1	−3	0.690	0.92	0.009	0.025
Fourth level														
Revere Adv. (71)	−4	2	3	3	4	3	2	0	−1	−3	0.523	0.995	0.006	0.020
Revere Adv. (73)	0	2	2	3	4	2	1	0	−2	−3	0.657	0.92	0.008	0.022
Griffin-4	0	1	2	3	4	3	3	1	−1	−4	0.6913	0.91	0.009	0.025
Fifth level														
Griffin-5	0	2	2	4	5	4	3	1	−1	−5	0.6909	0.91	0.009	0.025
Other														
Thorp Ultimate	−9	5	6	8	11	6	4	0	−3	−7	0.525	0.996	0.007	0.025
Ten-Count	4	4	4	4	4	4	4	4	4	−9	0.621	0.74	0.007	0.019

subset of the deck are bivariate normally distributed with correlation coefficient ρ. Then the expected gain $F(\rho)$ for the point-count system is approximated by

$$F(\rho) \sim \frac{\rho\sigma_c}{\sqrt{2\pi}} \, e^{-\mu_c{}^2/2\rho^2\sigma_c{}^2} - \frac{\mu_c}{\sqrt{2\pi}} \int_{\mu_c/\rho\sigma_c}^{\infty} e^{-x^2/2} \, dx$$

where μ_c and σ_c^2 are the expectation and variance resulting from the point-count application. Strategic efficiency is thus given by $F(\rho)/E(n)$ and increases with decreasing n (as the deck is depleted). For values of $\rho < 1$ and $\mu_c \neq 0$, efficiency is less than ρ; for $\mu_c = 0$, efficiency $= \rho$.

Table 7-12 evaluates various point-count systems with respect to efficiency, betting correlation, and expected gain. Calculations were performed with $n = 20$ cards remaining; results vary only slightly from $n = 10$ to $n = 40$. Griffin has computed the optimal (maximum efficiency) system for each level of complexity (independent of betting correlation and excluding the insurance wager; Griffin-2, although slightly superior to Stepine in strategic efficiency, shows a slight inferiority when insurance is included). With $q_1 = 0$, no appreciable improvement in efficiency exists from point counts beyond the third level of complexity—where the maximum possible efficiency of about 70 percent (for single-parameter systems) is nearly attained. Betting correlation, however, does generally improve with an increase in the level of complexity. Expected gains from the various point-count systems are surprisingly similar (from 0.006 to 0.009). Increasing the bet to 4 units whenever the single-trial expectation exceeds 0.01 (about 21 percent of the time) also yields similar gains (on the order of 0.022).

If the bet is increased with all favorable decks (about 40 percent of the time), the Griffin-1 system appreciates in utility above the others—particularly against the dealer's 10 and Ace. (Against the dealer's 7, 8, and 9, Griffin-1's efficiency is low, as is that of most point-count systems.) An empirical formula for the average profits given by a point-count system as a function of its strategic efficiency η and betting correlation ρ has been derived by Griffin as

$$S = 0.008(\beta - 1)\rho + 0.005(\beta + 1)\eta \qquad\qquad 7\text{-}8$$

where β units are bet on all favorable decks and 1 unit is bet otherwise. Eq. 7-8 suggests that strategic efficiency and betting correlation are accorded approximately equal importance for $\beta = 4$. Substituting $\eta = 0.637$ and $\rho = 0.86$ for the Griffin-1 system, we then have

$$S = 0.037$$

as the average profit per hand, betting either 1 or 4 units (exclusive of the insurance wager). Note that S is not expressed as a fraction of the bet and therefore does not conform to the criterion of minimizing the gambler's probability of ruin (see Chapter 3).

To compute concomitant strategy change parameters for a point-count system, we define the running index I as

$$I = \text{point-count} \times 100/\text{no. of cards remaining}$$

and the critical index I_c as that value of I for which the draw, stand, double-down, or split decision changes from that of the zero-memory strategy. Table 7-13 presents the critical indices for the Griffin-1 system (the calculations presume the dealer to hit soft 17). If the running index is greater than the corresponding critical index for totals of 12 through 16, the player should stand. If the running index is less than or equal to the critical index, the player should draw. When the player's total is 11 or less and $I > I_c$, optimal strategy is to double-down; for $I \leqslant I_c$, optimal strategy dictates drawing only. Similarly for pairs, the player is advised to split when $I > I_c$. The insurance bet is accepted for $I > 4$.

A count system also enables greater acceptance of the surrender option in those casinos where it is available. Table 7-13 provides critical surrender indices whereby $I > I_c$ prescribes the hand to be discarded for one-half the wager.

Thorp's T ratios are translatable to a point-count system by assigning a value of -9 to the 10 rank and a value of 4 to all other ranks. The relation between T, the non-tens to tens ratio, and the running point count R is identified by

$$R = (9 - 4T)n/(1 + T)$$

where n is the number of cards remaining. The low betting correlation of the ten-count system (Table 7-12) recommends a supplemental means of regulating the bet size—such as the Ace-correction factor (Eq. 7-6).

Thorp's ultimate point-count system, aside from its high level of complexity, offers the greatest betting correlation. It should be applied for determining the bet size while using the ten-count for determining playing strategies.

A drawback inherent in all point-count systems stems from the necessary condition that a large number of deck configurations can correspond to a particular count. The procedure for determining critical indices consists of maintaining the expected density for zero-valued ranks and varying the weights of other ranks in proportion to their assigned point values.

Table 7-13   Critical Indices for Griffin-1 System[a]

	Dealer's up-card									
	2	3	4	5	6	7	8	9	10	A
Player's hard total										
16	−18	−20	−23	−26	−31	30	23	12	1	6
15	−12	−13	−16	−19	−22	23	27	16	6	9
14	−6	−7	−10	−13	−15			20	11	11
13	−2	−4	−6	−8	−12				23	17
12	4	2	−1	−4	−6					25
11 (Double down)	−19	−21	−22	−26	−28	−20	−14	−9	−6	−2
10 (Double down)	−16	−17	−19	−22	−25	−15	−10	−3	10	7
9 (Double down)	2	0	−4	−10	−13	7				
8 (Double down)	24	17	10	8	5	32				
7 (Double down)	38	29	22	19	18					
Player's soft total										
20	19	17	14	11	11	32				
19	13	7	6	3	3	27				
18	2	−2	−7	−11	−12	28				
17	2	−3	−7	−16	−19	20				
16	12	4	−1	−10	−18					
15	16	6	−1	−9	−16					
14	15	12	4	−8	−12					
13	13	11	5	−3	−6					
Player's pair										
2's	12	2		−12	−15					
3's	13	7		−4	−8					
4's										
5's										
6's	4	0	−2	−8	−9					
7's	−20	−20	−25							
8's						12		20[b]	12[b]	
9's	−2	−3	−5	−10	−10					
10's	20	16	13	10	10					
A's										
Indices for surrender player's hard total										
17								22	23	
16						33	13	2	−4	
15						32	15	4	0	
14						20	14	7	5	
13						24	20	15	11	
12								25	20	

[a] Courtesy of Peter Griffin.   [b] Do *not* split pair when running index exceeds critical index.   [c] Use zero-memory strategy when no critical index is given.

Each critical index then represents an "average" deck configuration; it is not apparent that a particular configuration solicits the same strategy as does this "average," although both share the same point count. Griffin has shown that the player's conditional expectation is a nonlinear function of the difference between the computed critical index and its "correct" value.

THE HI-LO SYSTEM

A variation of the point-count method is the "Hi-Lo" system, first developed by Harvey Dubner of Simmond's Precision Products, Incorporated. The procedure here consists of defining the Tens and Aces as "highs," the Twos through Sixes as "lows," and ignoring the Sevens through Nines. A Hi-Lo index I is thence defined as

$$I = \frac{Q(10, \ 1) - Q(2\text{--}6)}{n}$$

that is, the difference between the number of Twos through Sixes remaining and the number of Tens and Aces remaining divided by the total number of cards remaining in the deck. The concomitant strategy changes (from the zero-memory strategy) due to utilization of the Hi-Lo system are very few. As I assumes a value between 0.05 and 0.20, t^* decreases to 11 against a dealer's up-card of Two through Six and to 14 against a dealer's up-card of Ten or Ace. For values of I greater than 0.20, t^* decreases to 11 against a dealer's up-card of Two through Nine and to 13 against a Ten or Ace.

Dubner's system—equivalent to a running index for the Braun $+ -$ point count—has been developed and redefined by Thorp as $-100I$ (so that a positive index correlates with favorable deck compositions). Proper bet size is one-half the Thorp Hi-Lo index for positive values of $-100I \geq 4$ and 1 unit for all other values.

Possible improvements

To increase the expectation appreciably above that attainable from a point-count system requires an immediate-access, high-speed computer. With the exact strategy calculated at each instant for any arbitrary subset of the deck, it is estimated that an expectation of 0.05 would be achieved with constant wagers. Following a "conservative" bet-variation scheme ($\bar{P}_z = 0.95$, $z = 100$) in addition, an overall game expectation of about 0.13 ensues.

Greater positive expectations can be effected by applying predictive functions for the dealer's hole-card and the next card to be dealt based on statistical knowledge of the shuffling procedure (see Chapter 6). The probability that a particular undisclosed card is of value x is then $P_{ij}^{(N)}$ rather than $Q(x)/n$, where $P_{ij}^{(N)}$ is the transition probability between states i and j over the course of n shuffles. Obviously, the game expectation depends on the accuracy of the predictive function. With perfect prediction, the expectation reaches a value of close to 0.40.

In Blackjack, only a modest advantage attends the pooling of resources among the m players opposing the dealer. The win–lose correlation coefficient between any two players in the same game is about 0.5; that is, discounting ties, two players will incur the same result (win or lose) 75 percent of the time and opposite results 25 percent of the time. Thus, the effective bankroll z_{eff}, for m cooperating players, is approximately (cf. Eq. 3-17) given by

$$z_{\text{eff}} < \left(\frac{m+1}{2}\right)^{-1/2} \sum_{i=1}^{m} z_i$$

where z_i is the initial fortune of the ith player.

Blackjack variations

ALL CARDS EXPOSED

As an illustration of the efficacy of the knowledge of undisclosed cards, we consider the game of Blackjack played under the rule that *both* of the dealer's cards are exposed to view. The optimal zero-memory strategy, displayed in App. Table E, changes markedly from that applicable under the conventional rules. Applying this strategy, the resulting mathematical expectation is 0.099. Appendix Table G details the individual expectations for each of the dealer's 55 possible hands. This game might well have the appeal for a trial in the gambling casinos. The "house," of course, would levy a 10 percent charge on all wagers.

ZWEIKARTENSPIEL

Another variation of the basic Blackjack game is that which we have named "Zweikartenspiel." In this instance, both of the dealer's cards are exposed and, as a compensating factor, the dealer wins the wager in the event of a tie. The optimal zero-memory strategy for Zweikartenspiel is given in App. Table F. Pursuing this strategy results in a game expectation of 0.021. Mathematical expectations for each of the dealer's 55 hands are presented in App. Table H. Unfortunately, with respect to its adoption by the public gambling casinos, the options of doubling down and splitting would have to be restricted to render Zweikartenspiel a fair or slightly unfavorable game. The ensuing version would possess a rather dull, simplified structure (levying a tax of 2.5 percent is somewhat cumbersome). Thus, the game does not appear destined for popular acclaim.

GRAYJACK

Lastly, we have contrived a simplified version of Blackjack, which is commended as offering an insight into the structure of the conventional game. For this version, termed "Grayjack," the deck is comprised of but 13 cards: 1 Ace, 2 Twos, 2 Threes, 2 Fours, 2 Fives, and 4 Sixes. Each card is accorded its face value except for the Ace, which is valued as 1 or 7, at the player's discretion. Object of the game for the player is to obtain a numerical total greater than the dealer's and less than or equal to 13. A sum exceeding 13 automatically loses. Doubling down with any original two-card hand is permitted, as is splitting of any initial pair. Grayjack is defined by the Ace and a Six, and when dealt to the player, is paid 3 to 2 (when the dealer's up-card is the Ace, the option of "insurance" is offered against the hole-card's being a Six with a payoff of 2 to 1). The dealer is constrained to draw with totals of 10 and less and to stand with 11, 12, and 13. For the dealer, the Ace must be valued as 7 if thereby his hand totals 11 through 13, but not 14 or above. The player may draw or stand at each instant (with totals of 13 or less) at his discretion.

Optimal strategy and game expectation are readily computed owing to the reduced size of the deck. These calculations are left as an exercise for the interested reader.

Suggested references

BALDWIN, ROGER R., WILBERT E. CANTEY, HERBERT MAISEL, JAMES P. MCDERMOTT, "The Optimum Strategy in Blackjack," *J. Am. Statistical Assoc.*, **51**, No. 275 (September, 1956), pp. 429 439.

BRAUN, JULIAN H., "Comparing the Top Blackjack Systems," *Gambling Quarterly*, Toronto, Fall/Winter, 1974.

GORDON, EDWARD, "Optimum Strategy in Blackjack—A New Analysis," Claremont Economic Papers, No. 52, The Claremont Colleges, Claremont, California, January, 1973.

GRIFFIN, PETER, "The Rate of Gain in Player Expectation for Card Games Characterized by Sampling without Replacement and an Evaluation of Card Counting Systems," Chapter 25 in *Gambling and Society*, Charles Thomas Publ. Co., Springfield, Illinois, 1975.

GRIFFIN, PETER, "Use of Bivariate Normal Approximations to Evaluate Single Parameter Card Counting Systems in Blackjack," Second Annual Conference on Gambling, Lake Tahoe, Nevada, June, 1974.

GRIFFIN, PETER, "On the Likely Consequences of Errors in Card Counting Systems," Mathematics Dept., Sacramento State Univ., Sacramento, California, 1976.

HANSON, JAMES N. "Nonlinear Programming, Simulation, and Gambling Theory Applied to Blackjack," Computer and Information Science Department, Cleveland State University, Cleveland, Ohio, June, 1974.

THORP, EDWARD, "A Favorable Strategy for Twenty-One," *Proc. Natl. Acad. Sci.* **47**, No. 1 (January, 1961), pp. 110–112.

THORP, EDWARD, *Beat the Dealer*, Blaisdell Publishing Co., New York, 1962, Revised: Random House, New York, 1966.

THORP, EDWARD O., and WALDEN, W. E., "The Fundamental Theorem of Card Counting," *Internat. J. Game Theory*, **2**, No. 2 (1973).

WILSON, ALLAN, *The Casino Gambler's Guide*. Harper and Row, Publishers, New York, 1965.

CHAPTER EIGHT

CONTRACT BRIDGE

The family tree

As an exemplifier of strategic concepts arising both from probability considerations and the exchange of information, Contract Bridge is likely the most challenging card game extant; it is certainly the most obsessive for its ranks of zealous followers. The initial progenitor of all Bridge forms is the game of Triumph, which gained currency about A.D. 1500. In the mid-seventeenth century, Triumph evolved into Whist,[†] a partnership game for four players. The change from Whist to Bridge occurred about 1886 with the publication in London of a small pamphlet, titled *Biritch, or Russian Whist.* This title created the fallacy that Bridge is of Russian origin.[‡] In actuality, while the precise etymology cannot be traced with assurance, the word has likely evolved from a Levantine source.

Whist and Bridge possess similar structures. However, in Whist, the trump suit is established arbitrarily by the last card dealt, whereas in Bridge, the trump suit is selected by the dealer. Further, Bridge introduces the idea of a "dummy" hand.

[†] The English lawyer Edmond Hoyle produced a work titled, *A Short Treatise on Whist,* which led to his position as the panjandrum of game rules.

[‡] The word "Biritch" is not a recognized Russian word, however liberal be the retransliteration to Cyrillic. The Russians did play a card game named "Ieralashch" resembling short Whist without a trump suit. From this game are derived "Siberia" and "Preference," which share certain characteristics with Bridge.

The game of Auction Bridge originated at the turn of the twentieth century in India when three members of the Indian Civil Service stationed at an isolated community designed a three-handed form of Bridge to compensate for the lack of a fourth player. Their key contribution was the concept of competitive bidding for the declaration. Another innovation due to this trio is the type of scoring whereby failure to fulfill the contract will credit points "above the line" to the adversaries rather than contributing toward game (previously in Bridge, no distinction was made between points won by gaining a contract or by defeating the opposition's contract). The game was shortly modified (by card-playing members of Britain's Bath Club) from the original format, acquiring a four-handed form. No exact date has been recorded for the birth of Auction Bridge; however, Oswald Crawfurd, upon his return from India, published a letter in the *London Times*, 16 January, 1903, outlining the new rules. Mr. Crawfurd was also responsible for promoting the game to a wide circle in England.

Contract Bridge came into existence in November, 1925, on a steamship en route from Los Angeles to Hawaii.[†] Harold S. Vanderbilt, one of the participants of the first game played, introduced the invention to the New York clubs, in which it supplanted Auction Bridge in remarkably short time. The distinctive feature of Contract Bridge ordains that a team cannot score "below the line" the tricks it gains unless it previously has contracted to win those tricks. A variant of Auction Bridge known as Plafond (French slang for "intelligence"), developed in France about 1922, had previously introduced this feature; however, Mr. Vanderbilt and his cronies added the concept of vulnerability, the slam bonuses, and the scoring format which is essentially that in force at present.

This brief sketch of the family tree of Bridge indicates the marked trend to eliminate elements of pure chance and to emphasize the importance of skillful bidding and play. Legal recognition of this fact was first expressed in 1962 by the California State Supreme Court, which, in a five to two ruling, declared that Contract Bridge is a game of skill and not of chance.

Assumptions

It is presumed herein that the reader is intimately familiar with the format, terminology, rules of play, and the scoring numeration of Contract Bridge. From the game-theoretic viewpoint, Bridge constitutes a two-person game (each "person" or "team" is composed of two players) with incomplete

---

[†] Legend persists in placing the event on a Caribbean cruise to Havana.

information. The communication process occurs under certain sequential restraints and with a limited vocabulary. There are 15 words in the bidding dictionary: One, Two, Three, Four, Five, Six, Seven, Clubs, Diamonds, Hearts, Spades, No-Trump, Pass, Double, and Redouble.[†] Combinations of these words within the bidding regulations permit a set of 38 possible messages.[‡]

In partitioning the deck of 52 cards among the four players, we assume that all 52! states of the deck are equiprobable, so that no bias exists in the distributions of the hand compositions. It has been shown by Emile Borel that the effect of nonrandom shuffling on hand compositions is generally not appreciable, since the order of cards within each hand is irrelevant. If the shuffling procedure is sufficient to ensure a high probability that two initially consecutive cards become divorced, prediction of the location of a card proves to be quite difficult. In general, we assume that the initial ordering of the deck is not known by any of the players, as is the case in Duplicate Bridge. (For informal Bridge games, biases are introduced by a proclivity of the cards to coalesce in quaternary patterns of the same suit— due to the manner of collecting tricks—or in ascending ranks within a suit; the consecutive K, A combination, for example, is probable and, during the subsequent deal, tends to favor the player holding the Ace.)

Distributional probabilities

SUIT DISTRIBUTIONS

The first problem to be attacked in an analysis of Contract Bridge is concerned with the nature or composition of the hand. The total number of different situations possible among four Bridge hands is astronomical. Specifically,

$$\frac{52!}{(13!)^4} = 53,644,737,765,488,792,839,237,440,000$$

constitute the number of distinct ways the deck can be partitioned into four hands. For one hand in particular, there are

$$\binom{52}{13} = 635,013,559,600$$

distinct combinations of 13 cards; playing ten hands per hour around the

[†] For Duplicate Bridge tournaments, an essential sixteenth word is the call, "Director."
[‡] Variations in inflection and intensity of sound permit (unethically) additional messages.

clock, one could theoretically play for over seven million years without receiving the same hand twice. Each of these hands may be classified according to the distribution of suits comprising it. If the hand is specified by $(a$-b-c-$d)$, where a is the number of Spades, b the number of Hearts, c the number of Diamonds, and d the number of Clubs, and $a + b + c + d = 13$, there are 560 distinguishable hands (by suits), the probability P_s of each being given by (cf. Eq. 2-14)

$$P_s(a\text{-}b\text{-}c\text{-}d) = \frac{\binom{13}{a}\binom{13}{b}\binom{13}{c}\binom{13}{d}}{\binom{52}{13}} \qquad 8\text{-}1$$

If the suit distribution is not specified by the number of cards in each particular suit, but rather as four numbers relating to suit lengths in any order, the probability distribution P_u is expressed by

$$P_u(a\text{-}b\text{-}c\text{-}d) = kP_s(a\text{-}b\text{-}c\text{-}d)\begin{cases} k = 24 & \text{if } a \neq b \neq c \neq d \\ k = 12 & \text{if } a = b \neq c \neq d \\ k = 4 & \text{if } a = b = c \neq d \end{cases} \qquad 8\text{-}2$$

There are 39 possible classes of hands with the suits unspecified. It should be noted that Eqs. 8-1 and 8-2 may also be interpreted as yielding the distribution of four suits (specified or unspecified) in one hand or one suit among four hands. For example, $P_u(a\text{-}b\text{-}c\text{-}d)$ also represents the probability that *some* player receives a Spades, another b Spades, a third c Spades, and the last player d Spades, while $P_s(a\text{-}b\text{-}c\text{-}d)$ can represent the probability that South, West, North, and East have, respectively, $a, b, c,$ and d cards of a particular suit.

Other combinatorial formulae for suit distributions of Bridge hands are readily derived from the principles expounded in Chapter 2. For example, the probability $P(m, n)$ that a player's hand contains exactly m cards of a particular suit while his partner (or one opponent) has exactly n cards of that suit can be derived as

$$P(m, n) = \frac{\binom{13}{m}\binom{39}{13-m}\binom{13-m}{n}\binom{26+m}{13-n}}{\binom{52}{13}\binom{39}{13}}$$

The parameter $P(m, n)$ is equivalent to the probability of selecting two hands at random from the deck, the first containing m cards and the second n cards of a particular suit.

The 39 distributions of the four suits in a single hand of 13 cards (or of one particular suit among the four players) are enumerated in Table 8-1,

TABLE 8-1   Probability Distributions of the Suits in a Hand

Distribution (a-b-c-d)	Probability of Occurrence P_u (Suits Unspecified)	Probability of Occurrence P_s (Suits Specified)
4-4-3-2	0.21551	0.01796
5-3-3-2	0.15517	0.01293
5-4-3-1	0.12931	0.00539
5-4-2-2	0.10580	0.00882
4-3-3-3	0.10536	0.02634
6-3-2-2	0.05642	0.00470
6-4-2-1	0.04702	0.00196
6-3-3-1	0.03448	0.00287
5-5-2-1	0.03174	0.00265
4-4-4-1	0.02993	0.00748
7-3-2-1	0.01881	0.00078
6-4-3-0	0.01326	0.00055
5-4-4-0	0.01243	0.00104
5-5-3-0	0.00895	0.00075
6-5-1-1	0.00705	0.00059
6-5-2-0	0.00651	0.00027
7-2-2-2	0.00513	0.00128
7-4-1-1	0.00392	0.00033
7-4-2-0	0.00362	0.00015
7-3-3-0	0.00265	0.00022
8-2-2-1	0.00192	0.00016
8-3-1-1	0.00118	0.00010
7-5-1-0	0.00109	0.00005
8-3-2-0	0.00109	0.00005
6-6-1-0	0.00072	0.00006
8-4-1-0	0.00045	0.00002
9-2-1-1	0.00018	0.00002
9-3-1-0	0.00010	4.2×10^{-6}
9-2-2-0	0.00008	6.9×10^{-6}
7-6-0-0	0.00006	4.6×10^{-6}
8-5-0-0	0.00003	2.6×10^{-6}
10-2-1-0	1.1×10^{-5}	4.6×10^{-7}
9-4-0-0	9.6×10^{-6}	8.1×10^{-7}
10-1-1-1	4.0×10^{-6}	9.9×10^{-7}
10-3-0-0	1.5×10^{-6}	1.3×10^{-7}
11-1-1-0	2.5×10^{-7}	2.1×10^{-8}
11-2-0-0	1.2×10^{-7}	9.6×10^{-9}
12-1-0-0	3.2×10^{-9}	2.7×10^{-10}
13-0-0-0	6.3×10^{-12}	1.6×10^{-12}

TABLE 8-2   Probability of the Length of the Longest
Suit in a Hand

Length of Longest Suit	Probability of Occurrence
4	0.35081
5	0.44340
6	0.16548
7	0.03527
8	0.00467
9	0.00037
10	1.65×10^{-5}
11	3.64×10^{-7}
12	3.19×10^{-9}
13	6.30×10^{-12}

according to Eqs. 8-1 and 8-2, in order of probability of occurrence. Table 8-2 details the probability distribution of the length of the longest suit in a hand selected at random.

From Table 8-1 we can determine the probability that a hand contains, for example, a void in one suit. We can also compute this probability from the expression

$$P(\text{void}) = \sum_{i=1}^{4} (-1)^{i-1} \binom{4}{i} \frac{(52 - 13i)_{13}}{(52)_{13}} = 0.051$$

Similarly, the probability of obtaining a singleton (with no void) is readily calculated as 0.306 and the probability of a doubleton (with no singleton or void) as 0.538. Additional information that we might extract from Table 8-1 is the probability of a void in a specific suit as 0.013, the probability of obtaining a two-suited hand as 10^{-4} (the probability that the hand contains only two specific suits is 2×10^{-5}), and the probability that all four suits are represented in the hand as 0.949.

The distribution of suits among a two-hand coalition of 26 cards is computed in the same manner as the one-hand distribution. Letting $e, f, g,$ and h represent the number of Spades, Hearts, Diamonds, and Clubs, respectively, in the 26-card coalition, the probability of a specific distribution is, analogous to Eq. 8-1,

$$P_s(e\text{-}f\text{-}g\text{-}h) = \frac{\binom{26}{e}\binom{26}{f}\binom{26}{g}\binom{26}{h}}{\binom{52}{26}}$$

8-3

And for the distribution with the suits unspecified, we have, analogous to Eq. 8-2,

$$P_u(e\text{-}f\text{-}g\text{-}h) = kP_s(e\text{-}f\text{-}g\text{-}h)\begin{cases} k = 24 & \text{if } e \neq f \neq g \neq h \\ k = 12 & \text{if } e = f \neq g \neq h \\ k = 4 & \text{if } e = f = g \neq h \\ k = 6 & \text{if } e = f \neq g = h \end{cases} \qquad 8\text{-}4$$

There are 104 coalition hands with the suits unspecified and 1834 distinct hands ordered by the particular suits. The more probable distributions are listed in App. Table I in order of probability (by unspecified suits) according to Eqs. 8-3 and 8-4. Among the 104 classes, 28 form their own complements; for example, if one team has an 8-7-6-5 distribution, the other team must have 5-6-7-8. These distributions are marked, in Table I, with an asterisk. It should also be noted that two distributions (such as 7-7-7-5 and 8-6-6-6) that constitute a complementary pair occur with the same probability; there are 28 such pairs in the 104 possible distributions of the coalition hand.

In Table 8-3, the lengths of the longest suit and the corresponding probabilities of occurrence are enumerated for the 26-card coalition. Also, we can collate the probabilities that a hand or a coalition selected at random contains a specified number of cards in a specified suit. Table 8-4 illustrates these data.

RANK DISTRIBUTIONS

In order to obtain a complete picture of the a priori probability distributions of Bridge hands, it remains to describe the distribution of cards by rank. A simple derivation leads to the expression for the probability $P(k)$

TABLE 8-3   Probability of Length of Longest Suit in a Coalition

Length of Longest Suit	Probability of Occurrence
7	0.15736
8	0.45745
9	0.28100
10	0.08673
11	0.01582
12	0.00158
13	0.00006

TABLE 8-4 Probability Distributions of Suit Lengths

No. of Cards in a Specified Suit	Probability of Occurrence 13-Card Hand	Probability of Occurrence 26-Card Coalition
0	0.01279	1.6×10^{-5}
1	0.08006	0.00040
2	0.20587	0.00395
3	0.28633	0.02175
4	0.23861	0.07356
5	0.12469	0.16183
6	0.04156	0.23849
7	0.00882	0.23849
8	0.00117	0.16183
9	9.3×10^{-5}	0.07356
10	4.1×10^{-6}	0.02175
11	9.1×10^{-8}	0.00395
12	8.0×10^{-10}	0.00040
13	1.6×10^{-12}	1.6×10^{-5}

that a random Bridge hand contains exactly k cards, $k = 0, 1, 2, 3, 4$, of a particular rank:

$$P(k) = \frac{\binom{4}{k}\binom{48}{13-k}}{\binom{52}{13}} \qquad 8\text{-}5$$

Analogously, the probability $P_c(k)$ that a 26-card coalition hand contains exactly k Aces (for example) is

$$P_c(k) = \frac{\binom{4}{k}\binom{48}{26-k}}{\binom{52}{26}} \qquad 8\text{-}6$$

Equations 8-5 and 8-6 are displayed in Table 8-5. It is worth noting that, for the coalition hands, $P_c(0) = P_c(4)$ and $P_c(1) = P_c(3)$.

The distribution of a particular rank among the four hands is determined from considerations concerning the number of permutations of n objects taken all together (cf. Eq. 2-13). If the four Aces (or any other rank) are so distributed that South, West, North, and East have A_1, A_2, A_3, and A_4 Aces, respectively, where $A_1 + A_2 + A_3 + A_4 = 4$, we can derive

TABLE 8-5   Probability of Obtaining k Cards of a Specific Rank

No. of Cards in a Specific Rank	Probability of Occurrence in 13 Cards $P(k)$	Probability of Occurrence in 26 Cards $P_c(k)$
0	0.30382	0.05522
1	0.43885	0.24970
2	0.21349	0.39016
3	0.04120	0.24970
4	0.00264	0.05522

the corresponding probability $P_s(A_1\text{-}A_2\text{-}A_3\text{-}A_4)$ of the event as

$$P_s(A_1\text{-}A_2\text{-}A_3\text{-}A_4)$$

$$= \frac{4!(13!)^4}{A_1!A_2!A_3!A_4!(13-A_1)!(13-A_2)!(13-A_3)!(13-A_4)!(52)_4}$$

$$8\text{-}7$$

And, if we ask the probability $P_u(A_1\text{-}A_2\text{-}A_3\text{-}A_4)$ that one player's hand contains A_1 Aces, another A_2 Aces, another A_3 Aces, and a final hand A_4 Aces, we have

$$P_u(A_1\text{-}A_2\text{-}A_3\text{-}A_4)$$

$$= kP_s(A_1\text{-}A_2\text{-}A_3\text{-}A_4) \begin{cases} k=1 & \text{if } A_1 = A_2 = A_3 = A_4 \\ k=4 & \text{if } A_1 \neq A_2 = A_3 = A_4 \\ k=6 & \text{if } A_1 = A_2 \neq A_3 = A_4 \\ k=12 & \text{if } A_1 = A_2 \neq A_3 \neq A_4 \end{cases} \quad 8\text{-}8$$

The five possible distributions of the four Aces and their probabilities of occurrence, according to Eqs. 8-7 and 8-8, are tabulated in Table 8-6.

TABLE 8-6   Probability Distribution of Any Specific Rank

$(A_1\text{-}A_2\text{-}A_3\text{-}A_4)$	Probability of Occurrence P_u (Players Unspecified)	Probability of Occurrence P_s (Players Specified)
2-1-1-0	0.58430	0.04869
3-1-0-0	0.16480	0.01373
2-2-0-0	0.13484	0.02247
1-1-1-1	0.10550	0.10550
4-0-0-0	0.01056	0.00264

There are 35 distinct distributions of the Aces when the ordering (by players) is considered.

To determine the probability $P_n(0)$ that a Bridge hand contains no cards of any of n specified ranks, we can rederive Eq. 8-5 in the form

$$P_n(0) = \frac{\binom{52 - 4n}{13}}{\binom{52}{13}} = \frac{(39)_{4n}}{(52)_{4n}} \qquad\qquad 8\text{-}9$$

Another related problem is the probability that a specified rank is the highest to appear in a Bridge hand. This probability, $P_m(\bar{0})$, is given by

$$P_m(\bar{0}) = \frac{(39)_{4n}}{(52)_{4n}} \left[1 - \frac{(39 - 4n)_4}{(52 - 4n)_4} \right] \qquad\qquad 8\text{-}10$$

where there are n different ranks higher than the mth, the latter being the highest appearing in the particular hand. Equations 8-9 and 8-10 are evaluated in Table 8-7; the ranks are considered in descending order.

TABLE 8-7   Probability of Occurrence of Cards by Rank

n	Event	Probability of Occurrence $P_n(0)$	Highest Card m	Probability of Occurrence $P_m(\bar{0})$
1	No A	0.30382	K	0.22207
2	No A or K	0.08175	Q	0.06280
3	No A, K, Q	0.01895	J	0.01531
4	No A, K, Q, J	0.00364	10	0.00309
5[†]	No A, K, Q, J, 10	0.00055	9	0.00049
6	No A, K, Q, J, 10, 9	5.9×10^{-5}	8	5.5×10^{-5}
7	No A, K, Q, J, 10, 9, 8	3.9×10^{-6}	7	3.8×10^{-6}
8	No A, K, Q, J, 10, 9, 8, 7	1.2×10^{-7}	6	1.2×10^{-7}
9	No A, K, Q, J, 10, 9, 8, 7, 6	8.8×10^{-10}	5	8.8×10^{-10}

† This hand has been awarded the appellation of "Yarborough" owing to the habit of Lord Yarborough of England (over a century ago) to offer £1000 to £1 against its occurrence. His Lordship likely showed an excellent profit, since £1827 for £1 would constitute a fair wager.

Similarly, the probability $P_n(0)_c$ that a 26-card coalition contains no cards of any of n different ranks can be shown to be

$$P_n(0)_c = \frac{\binom{52 - 4n}{26}}{\binom{52}{26}} = \frac{(26)_{4n}}{(52)_{4n}} \qquad \qquad 8\text{-}11$$

And the probability $P_m(\bar{0})_c$ that a specified rank is the highest appearing in the coalition is

$$P_m(\bar{0})_c = \frac{(26)_{4n}}{(52)_{4n}}\left[1 - \frac{(26 - 4n)_4}{(52 - 4n)_4}\right] \qquad \qquad 8\text{-}12$$

where the n highest ranks (above the mth) are absent. Table 8-8 tabulates Eqs. 8-11 and 8-12 for the ranks considered in descending order.

TABLE 8-8   Probability of Occurrence of Cards by Rank in a Coalition

n	Event	Probability of Occurrence $P_n(0)_c$	Highest Card m	Probability of Occurrence $P_m(\bar{0})_c$
1	No A	0.05522	K	0.05314
2	No A, K	0.00208	Q	0.00203
3	No A, K, Q	4.7×10^{-5}	J	4.6×10^{-5}
4	No A, K, Q, J	5.1×10^{-7}	10	5.1×10^{-7}
5[†]	No A, K, Q, J, 10	1.8×10^{-9}	9	1.8×10^{-9}
6	No A, K, Q, J, 10, 9	7.6×10^{-13}	8	7.6×10^{-13}

[†] When a Bridge player and his partner both receive hands void of all cards Ten or higher, we might term the circumstance a "double-Yarborough." The odds against its occurrence are 546 million to 1.

Residual probabilities

Having determined the significant a priori distributions of the cards both by suit and by rank, we can proceed to the processes that follow the partitioning of the deck among the four players. The first problem encountered by the player is that of evaluating his hand quantitatively so that the various bidding decisions can be resolved. By virtue of the game structure and objective, a complete evaluation must include both the offensive and defensive potential of the hand in terms of the rank and denominational content. Further, the scale of evaluation must be sufficiently simple that it can be readily utilized by the player without recourse to a high-speed digital computer; thus, an evaluation system that, for example, lends more weight to the Seven of Spades than to the Six of Spades, while technically correct, is obviously cumbersome.

Since Bridge is a game involving imperfect information, a player's strategy is dependent upon the probability distribution of cards in the other players' hands, given the composition of his own hand. Bidding (and opening lead) strategy is a function of the probability distribution of 39 cards in the three unknown hands, while playing strategy is a function of the cards comprising the opponents' hands. We shall consider first the residual probabilities of cards in three hands. Focusing our attention upon the South player, we inquire as to the probability that, given a cards of a particular suit in the South hand, the remaining $13 - a$ cards of that suit are distributed with b cards in the West hand, c in the North hand, and d in the East hand ($b + c + d = 13 - a$). (Obviously, any other specific order of the remaining three players is equivalent.) Applying the theorem of conditional probability (Eq. 2-3) to Eq. 8-1, we have

$$P_s[(b\text{-}c\text{-}d)|a] = \frac{\binom{13}{a}\binom{13}{b}\binom{13}{c}\binom{13}{d}}{P(a)\binom{52}{13}} \qquad 8\text{-}13$$

where the values of $P(a)$, the probability that South has a cards of the particular suit, are given in Table 8-4. Equation 8-13 enumerates the residues in each suit, depending on the number of cards of that suit in the South hand. Appendix Table J tabulates each residual distribution for $a = 0, 1, 2, \ldots, 13$. The probability distribution of the residues without regard to order is computed from the expression

$$P_u[(b\text{-}c\text{-}d)|a] = kP_s[(b\text{-}c\text{-}d)|a] \begin{cases} k = 6, & b \neq c \neq d \\ k = 3, & b = c \neq d \\ k = 1, & b = c = d \end{cases} \qquad 8\text{-}14$$

Clearly, the unspecified residue probabilities total unity for each value of a.

A large number of residual distributions of interest can be calculated by means of Eqs. 8-13 and 8-14. For example, Table 8-9 indicates the probabilities that at least one opponent (East or West) possesses a void,

TABLE 8-9   Residual Suit Probabilities

Cards of a Particular Suit in the South Hand	At Least One Opponent's Hand Contains (in that suit):		
	Void	Void or Singleton	Void or Singleton or Doubleton
0	0.003	0.033	0.181
1	0.005	0.056	0.266
2	0.009	0.092	0.375
3	0.017	0.144	0.505
4	0.029	0.220	0.649
5	0.051	0.323	0.790
6	0.085	0.458	0.904
7	0.141	0.618	0.975
8	0.226	0.785	1.000
9	0.355	0.926	1.000
10	0.538	1.000	1.000
11	0.772	1.000	1.000
12	1.000	1.000	1.000
13	1.000	1.000	1.000

a void or singleton, and a singleton or doubleton in the particular suit of which the South hand contains a cards.

Another concern is the probability that a player other than South has been dealt a hand containing a specific number of cards of a particular suit or of a particular rank, given the number of pertinent cards in the South hand. Table 8-10 presents a table of these probabilities. Illustratively, if South has five Spades, there are eight remaining among the other three players; the probability that the North hand (say) contains exactly four Spades is, from Table 8-10, 0.174 (the probability that North has four or more Spades is $0.174 + 0.054 + 0.009 + 0.001 + 2 \times 10^{-5} = 0.238$). Or, if South observes one Ace in his hand, there are three remaining among the other players; from Table 8-10 we can read the probability that West (say) owns exactly two of these three Aces as 0.222.

Evaluation systems

The various evaluation systems extant are designed primarily as guides toward forming optimal bid sequences; they are not derived, except in a primitive sense, from considerations of probability distributions of the unknown cards or of probabilistic trick-taking potentials of the hand.

TABLE 8-10   General Residual Probabilities

No. of Cards of Interest Remaining Among Three Hands	Number of Cards of Interest in a Specified Hand													
	0	1	2	3	4	5	6	7	8	9	10	11	12	13
1	0.667	0.333												
2	0.439	0.456	0.105											
3	0.285	0.462	0.222	0.031										
4	0.182	0.411	0.308	0.090	0.009									
5	0.114	0.338	0.352	0.161	0.032	0.002								
6	0.071	0.262	0.357	0.228	0.071	0.010	0.001							
7	0.043	0.195	0.334	0.278	0.121	0.027	0.003	1.1×10^{-4}						
8	0.025	0.139	0.292	0.306	0.174	0.054	0.009	0.001	2.1×10^{-5}					
9	0.015	0.096	0.242	0.311	0.222	0.091	0.021	0.003	1.6×10^{-4}	3.4×10^{-6}				
10	0.008	0.064	0.192	0.296	0.259	0.133	0.040	0.007	6.6×10^{-4}	2.9×10^{-5}	4.5×10^{-7}			
11	0.005	0.041	0.145	0.267	0.281	0.177	0.067	0.015	2.0×10^{-3}	1.4×10^{-4}	4.4×10^{-6}	4.7×10^{-8}		
12	0.002	0.026	0.106	0.229	0.286	0.216	0.101	0.029	4.9×10^{-3}	4.8×10^{-4}	2.4×10^{-5}	5.2×10^{-7}	3.3×10^{-9}	
13	0.001	0.015	0.074	0.187	0.275	0.248	0.139	0.049	0.010	1.3×10^{-3}	9.2×10^{-5}	3.1×10^{-6}	4.2×10^{-8}	1.2×10^{-10}

Currently, the most popular of these systems is that advanced by Charles Goren, wherein each Ace in a hand is accorded four points, each King three points, each Queen two points, and each Jack one point[†]; cards of rank Ten and lower are not rated (except that a Ten when occurring with a Jack of the same suit may be counted as one-half a point). Card distributions conducive to sluffing, ruffing, coups, squeezes, end plays, and duplication of values are recognized in the Goren system by adding three points per void, two points per singleton, and one point per doubleton, short-suit points and high-card points in a given suit being mutually exclusive. A hand containing all four Aces is awarded one bonus point, and one point is deducted for an Ace-less hand. Empirical data have indicated that team assets of approximately 26 points are needed for successfully fulfilling a game contract in No-Trump or in a major suit; a successful minor-suit game contract generally requires about 29 points.

The probability that a Bridge hand is composed of A Aces, K Kings, Q Queens, and J Jacks is given by

$$P(A-K-Q-J) = \frac{\binom{4}{A}\binom{4}{K}\binom{4}{Q}\binom{4}{J}\binom{36}{13-A-K-Q-J}}{\binom{52}{13}}$$

To determine the probability of occurrence of a particular number of high-card points in a hand, we total the various partitions of the four highest ranks that constitute that number of points. Figure 8-1 delineates the probability distribution of high-card points in the Goren point-count system. It should be noted that the curve is unimodal and relatively smooth. The standard deviation has a value of 4 points about the mean of 10 points.

Other point-count systems that have gained transient popularity in. scattered European communities are those assigning relative values 7-5-3-1, 6-4-2-1, and 7-4-2-1. The probability distribution curves for these systems are more irregular and more skewed than that of the 4-3-2-1 system. One attribute of the Goren system is the smallest standard deviation relative to the magnitude of the mean; it should be noted that since the point distribution curve is not binomial, the limits of $\pm 1\sigma$ about the mean do not encompass 68 percent of the probabilities, but in this instance somewhat more.

[†] The 4-3-2-1 point-count system was originally suggested by Milton C. Work.

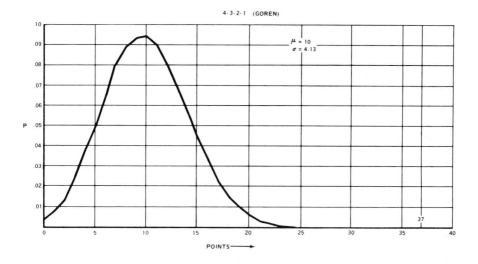

Fig. 8-1   Point-count probabilities; the Goren system (4-3-2-1)

Point-count systems in general suffer two principal failings. First, the points awarded to each high card (Honor) are not correlated with other Honors in the same suit (the now little-used Culbertson system provided this correlation, but with a point structure too coarse for precise application). Second, it is not credible that the relative numerical ranking of the Ace, King, Queen, and Jack corresponds to reality nor, indeed, that it is possible to specify relative values that are even approximately valid for most situations. An attempt to determine, for example, if an Ace can be equivalently replaced by two Queens—in the Goren scale—would require that the substitution be made over millions of Bridge games with a distribution of the two Queens by suit and with a further distribution of the card displaced by the second Queen. It seems unlikely that the results of the second set of games would be similar to the first.

Before delineating a point-count system free of these defects, it may be illuminating to restate the purpose of any point-count system. The criterion controlling the decision to pass or bid a given hand (and what bid to call) is established by the mathematical expectation of that hand resulting from the pass or bid (and subsequent probable bids). Determination of the expectation of all hands of distinguishable significance is unfeasible because of the astronomical number of such hands. It is necessary, therefore, to construct a measure of the hands and to act on the expectation of the measure. A point-count system must provide this measure and, additionally, must possess a sufficiently simple structure to be of practical utility at the Bridge table.

The distinguishable features of the hands, as measured by a point-count system, are enumerated by the number of ranks considered (these ranks define the Honors) and the suit-length distribution. With n ranks designated as Honors, there are 2^n combinations of Honors possible in each suit. As a compromise between simplicity and precision, we shall consider the three ranks: Ace, King, and Queen. The remaining ten ranks are all classified as indistinguishable x's. Thus, there are 88 combinations of the three Honors and zero through ten of the x's in each suit. The offensive and defensive trick-taking potential of each combination is calculated by proper permutations of the residual probabilities shown in App. Table J. Adding together the trick-taking potential of each suit defines the probabilistic measure of the hand. Determination of the trick-taking potential of the hand in this fashion inherently accounts for the distribution of the suit lengths. Offensive and defensive trick-taking potentials are listed to the nearest tenth of a trick in Table 8-11.

It would be convenient if it were now possible to determine that the expectation as a result of bidding initially with a particular hand is positive, given r offensive and s defensive probabilistic tricks. However, as has been demonstrated by H. W. Kuhn, a necessary and sufficient condition for a game structure to be essentially determinate is that the player be accorded essentially perfect information. Thus, there is likely no "best" way of playing Bridge. Further, because of this lack of perfect information, the player is constrained to act on the basis of probabilistic considerations and inferences drawn from the partner's or opponents' bidding or lack of bidding. Such inference based on partial knowledge renders it difficult to devise a program format for playing Bridge with a digital computer.

Hence, without an extensive computer program, it is impossible to specify the precise requirements for an opening bid. However, we estimate, subjectively, that a hand containing a total of twelve or more combined offensive and defensive probabilistic tricks qualifies for an opening bid and thereby results in a positive expectation. To proceed further and attempt to define a bidding scale as a function of the probabilistic trick-taking potential of the hand plus the reevaluation requisite following every bid or pass necessitates a complete book devoted to the subject. Such a detailed investigation is beyond the scope of this chapter. Here, we can present only the probability distributions that enter into the bidding and playing decisions.

Bidding

Two principles dominate the construction of any feasible (or "quasi-optimal") bidding system. First, the bids should be functions of the probabilistic potential of the hand and should be reevaluated as further inferential information (from the other players' bidding) is received. Second, the bidding format must be constrained by consideration of the game's objective, the scale of scoring, and the subgoals of conveying maximal information to one's partner while revealing minimal significant information to the opponents. Since private signaling (either in the bidding or in lead-directing play) is disallowed by the rules of Bridge—only pure signaling strategies, publically announced, are permitted—the game cannot be solved by means of characteristic functions[†] [of course, both direct signaling

TABLE 8-11   Offensive and Defensive Trick-taking Potentials

Honors	Potential Offensive Tricks *x's*										
	0	1	2	3	4	5	6	7	8	9	10
AKQ	3.6	3.6	4.9	5.9	7.0	8.0	9.0	10.0	11.0	12.0	13.0
AK	2.9	2.9	3.0	3.8	5.1	6.5	7.5	8.8	10.0	11.0	12.0
AQ	2.6	2.6	2.7	3.7	4.9	6.0	7.2	8.3	9.6	10.8	12.0
KQ	2.3	2.5	2.6	3.5	4.7	5.6	7.0	8.2	9.3	10.3	11.3
A	2.1	2.1	2.1	2.2	3.1	4.4	5.7	6.8	7.5	9.5	10.8
K	1.8	1.8	1.8	1.9	2.8	4.1	5.3	6.4	7.3	8.9	10.1
Q	1.6	1.6	1.6	1.7	2.6	3.8	5.1	6.2	6.9	8.8	10.1
—	1.1	1.2	1.2	1.2	1.3	2.2	3.5	4.8	6.0	6.8	8.8

Honors	Potential Defensive Tricks *x's*										
	0	1	2	3	4	5	6	7	8	9	10
AKQ	2.4	2.1	1.8	1.5	1.3	1.0	0.7	0.5	0.2	0.0	0.0
AK	2.1	1.9	1.8	1.7	1.5	1.3	1.0	0.7	0.5	0.2	0.0
AQ	1.8	1.7	1.6	1.5	1.3	1.2	0.9	0.7	0.5	0.2	0.0
KQ	1.5	1.5	1.3	1.1	0.8	0.6	0.5	0.3	0.1	0.0	0.0
A	1.5	1.4	1.3	1.3	1.2	1.1	1.0	0.8	0.6	0.5	0.2
K	1.1	1.1	1.0	1.0	0.8	0.7	0.5	0.4	0.3	0.1	0.0
Q	1.0	0.9	0.8	0.7	0.5	0.4	0.4	0.3	0.2	0.1	0.0
—	0.7	0.6	0.6	0.6	0.6	0.5	0.4	0.3	0.2	0.2	0.1

[†] A characteristic function is the numerical set function defined as the value of a play for all players belonging to a specified coalition.

(between partners) and inverted signaling (deception or bluffing against opponents) occur in Bridge].

From an information-theoretic viewpoint, the information conveyed per bid (under the constraint of an ascending sequence of bids) is maximized if the probability of any particular bid's occurring (as dictated by the measure applied to the hand) is twice the probability of the next highest bid; thus an opening bid of one Club would occur twice as frequently as an opening of one Diamond, which in turn would exhibit twice the frequency of one Heart, etc. The bid selected, then, is that one giving rise to the maximum mathematical expectation. A bidding system conforming to this principle is not feasible, owing to the artificial scale of scoring established for Bridge and the agreed-upon game objectives. However, certain restrictions or conventions in the bidding format can approximate this system; for example, not opening with a bid of a major suit unless that suit is composed of five or more cards tends to augment the frequency of one Club and one Diamond openings.

With a single partnership conducting the auction, there are $2^{36} - 1$ distinct bidding sequences possible. With all four players participating in the bidding, $(4 \times 22^{35} - 1)/3$ different sequences may result. An attempt to correlate the bidding sequences with the probability distributions of the hands is therefore arithmetically unfeasible. Several simplified Bridge models have been devised (most notable is that due to G. L. Thompson of Princeton University) with a decreased deck size (an eight-card deck composed of two denominations, four of each kind, admits of $8!/2!6! = 28$ different hands and $8!/(2!)^4 = 2520$ distinct deals) and a reduced bidding scale. However, no model yet proposed offers any practical insight to the serious Bridge player.

The play

TWO-HAND RESIDUES

Immediately as the dummy is exposed, each player is cognizant of 26 cards: the 13 of his hand and the 13 in dummy (technically, declarer and his right-hand opponent can account for a twenty-seventh card: the opening lead). There are, therefore, 26 undisclosed cards and each of the three remaining players is interested in the residual probability distributions of the two hidden hands. The probability $P_n(k; r)$ that one particular closed hand contains exactly $k \leq r$ cards of a specified suit when there are r residual cards of that suit outstanding (that is, that the player's hand combined with the dummy's hand contains $13 - r$ cards of the suit) is expressed by

$$P_n(k; r) = \frac{\binom{n}{k}\binom{n}{r-k}}{\binom{2n}{r}}$$ 8-15

where each player's hand consists of a total of n cards. At the opening lead, $n = 13$; App. Table K(1) tabulates Eq. 8-15 for this initial case with all the partitions of each residue, $1, 2, 3, \ldots, 13$. As stated previously, these probabilities are not adjusted for any inferential information transmitted during the auction phase.

From Table K(1) we can observe the general rule that when the residue is odd, the most probable partition is that closest to symmetry, and when the residue is even, the least unbalanced unsymmetrical partition is most probable; equipartition is next most probable. The sole exception occurs with a residue of two cards, in which case the equipartition 1–1 is most probable.

As each trick is played, the number of cards comprising each hand is reduced by one and the partition probabilities for each residue are altered. App. Tables K(2)—K(12) present these probabilities for hands of 12 cards, 11 cards, ..., to hands of 2 cards. Clearly, as the total number of cards in a hand decreases, the probability of equipartition or nearly equal partition increases.

FURTHER PARTITIONING

We can, of course, utilize Tables K(1) through K(12) to determine partition probabilities for Honors or specific ranks as well as for suits.

There are several variations of interest involving the partitioning of cards of different kinds among the undisclosed hands. Consider, for example, the group of pertinent cards to be divided into two distinct classes: H and X. Then the residue of r cards is composed of h cards of class H and x cards of class X, where

$$r = h + x$$

The probability $P_n(h, x; i, y; r)$ that a hand of n cards contains $i \leq h$ cards of class H and $y \leq x$ cards of class X, where

$$k = i + y,$$ 8-16

is given by

$$P_n(h, x; i, y; r) = P_n(k, r)\frac{k!(r-k)!h!x!}{r!y!(x-y)!i!(h-i)!}$$ 8-17

for the case of two undisclosed hands, $P_n(k; r)$ being specified by Eq. 8-15. As a numerical illustration, let the outstanding cards in a particular suit (between the two hands of East-West) be the A, Q, J, x, x, x with ten cards remaining in each hand. We are interested in the probability that West's hand contains two Honors and one small x. In this instance, $r = 6$, $h = 3$ (the three Honors), $x = 3$ (the three x's), $i = 2$, and $y = 1$. Thus, by Eqs. 8-17, 8-16, and 8-15,

$$P_{10}(3, 3; 2, 1; 6) = P_{10}(3, 6)\frac{3!\,3!\,3!\,3!}{6!\,1!\,2!\,2!\,1!}$$

$$= \frac{9}{20}P_{10}(3, 6)$$

$$= \frac{9}{20}\cdot\frac{120}{323} = 0.16718$$

When we are interested in the probability $P_n(i, y; r)$ that a hand contains k cards of a particular suit, the k cards being divided into i specific honors and y small indistinguishable cards ($k = i + y$), combinatorial considerations lead to the expression

$$P_n(i, y; r) = P_n(k; r)\frac{k!(r-i)!}{r!y!}$$ 8-18

If, in the example immediately preceding, we ask the probability that West has the A, the Q, and one x, Eqs. 8-18 and 8-15, for $r = 6$, $k = 3$, $i = 2$, and $y = 1$, yield

$$P_{10}(2, 1; 6) = P_{10}(3, 6)\frac{3!\,(6-2)!}{6!\,1!} = \frac{1}{5}P_{10}(3, 6) = 0.09000$$

We could also inquire as to the probability $P_n(k - j; r)$ that, of the r residual cards in a suit, West (say) has k cards, with $j < k$ specific cards being excluded from his hand. The appropriate formula is readily derived as

$$P_n(k, -j; r) = P_n(k; r)\frac{(r-k)!(r-j)!}{r!(r-k-j)!}$$

In the illustration above, we ask the probability that West has three cards of the six remaining, but with the A excluded from his hand. In this case, $r = 6$, $k = 3$, $j = 1$, and

$$P_{10}(3, -1; 6) = P_{10}(3, 6)\frac{(6 - 3)!(6 - 1)!}{6!(6 - 3 - 1)!} = \frac{1}{2}P_{10}(3, 6) = 0.18576$$

Other, similar, classifications of the partitions among the hidden hands can also be analyzed by recourse to elementary combinatoric methods (these combinatorics are equally applicable for the case of three closed hands). Joint partitions of two, three, or four suits can be analyzed by extension of the methods presented here; however, the number of combinations are too great for a book not devoted exclusively to Bridge.

PROBABILITY OF QUEEN DROP

The specific location of a particular card in a residue of r cards is associated with a probability proportional to the number of cards in the individual partition. Such probabilities can be obtained quickly from Tables K(1) through K(12). Perhaps the most common question of this type posed is with respect to the location of the Queen of a suit. Table 8-12 enumerates the probability that with residues of four and five cards in a suit and a hand of n cards, the Queen of that suit will drop from a defensive hand with two plays; that is, the probability that the Queen is partitioned alone or with a single other card of its suit. It should be noted that, for this situation, the probability of successfully dropping the Queen does not increase appreciably until more than half of the tricks have been played.

TABLE 8-12   Probability of Queen Drop for Residues 4 and 5

n Cards in Hand	Probability of Queen Drop Residue = 4	Probability of Queen Drop Residue = 5
13	0.53131	0.32783
12	0.53416	0.32919
11	0.53759	0.33083
10	0.54180	0.33282
9	0.54706	0.33529
8	0.55385	0.33847
7	0.56294	0.34266
6	0.57576	0.34849
5	0.59524	0.35714
4	0.62858	0.37143
3	0.70000	0.40000
2	1.00000	

INVERSE PROBABILITIES

Since only a pragmatic approach to bridge probabilities is immediately feasible, the calculations presented in this chapter are based on the assumption of a random distribution of the cards. Yet each bid or play on the part of an opponent (or partner) may infer a holding not heavily regarded by the a priori probabilities. Specifically, each possible holding of an opponent can be classified into one of m exhaustive and mutually exclusive groups, $h_1, h_2, \ldots, h_m$. If H_i represents the number of possible partitions belonging to the ith group, then

$$\sum_{i=1}^{m} H_i = \binom{r}{k}$$

is the total number of possible partitions for a residue of r cards, $k \le r$ of which belong to the opponent in question.

We designate by E the event of a particular series of bids and plays entered by the opponents; thence $P(E|H_i)$ specifies the conditional probabilities that would occur if the particular opponent's holding belongs to h_i. From Bayes theorem we can express the inverse probability $P(H_j|E)$ that the opponent's holding belongs to h_j, given that the event E has occurred, as

$$P(H_j|E) = \frac{H_j P(E|H_j)}{\sum_i H_i P(E|H_i)}$$

The conditional probabilities $P(E|H_j)$ are estimated on the basis of observation of the behavior of the particular opponents or of the normal strategies followed by Bridge players of a certain caliber.

Qualitative inferences are used constantly by Bridge players and can be said to express the essence of the game. The lead of a Queen often infers possession of the Jack of that suit; the failure to lead a suit can infer possession of the King; etc. Quantitative inferences, although difficult to apply during the play, could obviously provide considerable aid in assessing an opponent's holding, thereby indicating the optimum course of action.

Expectations

In general, the decisions leading to a certain line of play (or bidding) are resolved (if only subjectively) by computing the corresponding mathematical expectations and selecting that line resulting in the maximum expectation. For example, the Bridge player is often confronted with a choice between a play that yields m points with (virtual) certainty and one that yields $a > m$ points with probability p or $b < m$ points with probability $q = 1 - p$. The expectation E_1 of the first play is

$$E_1 = m$$

while the second play has an expectation E_2 given by

$$E_2 = pa + qb$$

Clearly, the player elects to accept the m points if $m > pa + qb$, and conversely.

We can apply the comparison of expectations, as an example, to calculate the probability of success desired before bidding a game contract— as opposed to a partial game contract. If P is the probability of success, the expectation E_g from fulfilling a bid game contract is

$$E_g = P(T + B) - (1 - P)C \qquad \text{8-19}$$

where T is the trick value of a game (100 points for No-Trump or a minor suit and 120 for a major suit), B is the game bonus (300 points when non-vulnerable, 500 when both teams are vulnerable, and 700 when the declarer's team alone is vulnerable), and C is the penalty for being set one trick (50 points when nonvulnerable and 100 points when vulnerable). The expectation E_p accruing from a partial game contract is

$$E_p = P(T + B_p) + (1 - P)(T - T_1 + B_p) \qquad \text{8-20}$$

where $B_p = 50$ is the point bonus for achieving a partial game and T is the number of points per trick (20 in a minor suit and 30 in No-Trump or a major suit). Comparing Eqs. 8-19 and 8-20, a necessary criterion for bidding a game contract is that

$$P > \frac{T - T_1 + C + B_p}{T - T_1 + C + B}$$

To place constraints of necessity and sufficiency on the probability of success, we observe that the opponents should double a game contract whenever

$$P < \frac{C}{T + C}$$

TABLE 8-13   Conditions Constraining Game Contract Bids

Game Contract	Not Vulnerable	Lone Vulnerable	Both Vulnerable
Major Suit	0.393	0.306	0.374
Minor Suit	0.397	0.306	0.375
No-Trump	0.386	0.299	0.368

Thus, the necessary and sufficient condition for bidding a game contract is that

$$P > \frac{T - T_1 + 2C + B_p}{2T - T_1 + 2C + B} \qquad \text{8-21}$$

The various cases encompassed by Eq. 8-21 are enumerated in Table 8-13. Numerical values of the game bonuses are according to the rules of rubber Bridge. For duplicate Bridge the expectation is measured not in points, but in terms of relative position among the contending teams; corresponding values of P for duplicate Bridge are somewhat higher. We can observe that at rubber Bridge the condition of vulnerability permits an attempt at a game contract with a smaller probability of success than required when nonvulnerable; the reverse situation holds for duplicate Bridge.

The principal problem in attempting to reduce Bridge to strictly mathematical formulation is the difficulty of assigning to each situation an appropriate value of P. Not only are there Herculean computational chores from the immense number of combinations, but there are the necessarily subjective weighting functions that must be assigned to the inferential information of the bidding and playing and also the psychological behavior of the players. For these reasons, an attempt to obtain an "optimal" solution for Bridge play soon encounters prohibitive complexity. One of the great charms of Bridge is its relative immunity from exhaustive game-theoretic analysis.

Bridge-playing computers

Notwithstanding the obstacles to a mathematical theory of Bridge, several heuristic computer programs have been written attempting to develop a competitive format for machine play. Generally, heuristic programs exhibit a jejune nature. Playing logic is based on sketchy rules of thumb—or clichés—such as "second-hand plays low, third-hand high," "cover an Honor with an Honor," and "lead initially fourth card in the longest suit with strength." Adhering to such generalities, no computer is likely to win a duplicate Bridge tournament. However, a program devised by G. L.

Carley for the IBM 7090 has demonstrated an ability beyond that of a Bridge neophyte.

A more sophisticated Bridge program has been written by E. R. Berlekamp for the solution of double-dummy problems. Berlekamp's program first attempts to locate some branch of the solution; when it succeeds, a proof-checking routine examines the heuristic line to ascertain the correctness of the proposed solution. This proof-checking routine generates sets of constraints under which the specific line of play succeeds in fulfilling the contract and thence constructs rigorous proofs by nonexhaustive methods. When it finds that the heuristic line is not successful against all defensive strategies, it plays a new defensive line and changes the heuristic to another line of play to reply to the new defense. When the heuristic ultimately fails in fulfilling the contract, the proof-checking routine generates negative sets of constraints and endeavors to prove the contract unmakable. Eventually, the routine must construct either a positive or a negative proof.

For miniature problems and most 13-card hands, Berlekamp's program requires about one minute to converge to a complete solution. For the more difficult full hands, the computer time without helpful hints runs considerably longer. Although the program is designed for No-Trump play only, extension to trump contracts is straightforward.

Bridge mutants

There have been several suggested variations of the basic game of Contract Bridge, none successful. An attempt was made in 1938 to introduce a five-suit Bridge game. The fifth suit, Royals, symbolized by a Crown and ranked between Spades and No-Trump, enlarged the deck to 65 cards. With each deal a player received 16 cards for his hand, the remaining card being placed, face up, on the table. It could be exchanged by the declarer for any card in his own hand. Five-suit Bridge perished, almost stillborn.

Another form of Bridge, popular in several European clubs, equates overtricks with undertricks. Thus, declarer's goal during the play is to fulfill *exactly* the number of tricks contracted. Otherwise, the contract is considered unfulfilled and he is penalized for tricks taken in excess of the contract. Precision defensive play, in particular, is more difficult in this game.

A more interesting variation, found mostly in Spain, is "Bridge with Nulos." The bid of Nulos is ranked between Spades and No-Trump. A contract at Nulos signifies the intent of taking $13 - x$ tricks, *or less*, where x is the number of tricks called for by a non-Nulos contract. There is no trump suit during the play of a Nulos contract and its scoring is identical to No-Trump. A bid of three Nulos constitutes a game contract (with the objective of taking four tricks or less); six Nulos (taking one trick or less) is a small slam and seven Nulos (no tricks taken by declarer) is a grand slam. The player who is the partner of the first Nulos bidder is designated as declarer.

Bridge with Nulos offers the advantage that even exceptionally poor hands may participate in the bidding, the auction being thereby more competitive. And the possibility of a Nulos bid (as a "sacrifice," for example) may influence an otherwise conventional bidding sequence. The play of a contract at Nulos is not simply the reverse of a No-Trump process, since the high cards in the declarer's or dummy's hand represent the possibility of taking unwanted tricks. Rather, the Nulos game demands a distinct, unique strategy.

Finally, there are many versions of two-handed Bridge (colloquially known as "Honeymoon Bridge"). Most possess strategic deficiencies that have prevented widespread popularity. We can recommend one particular two-handed game, which we call Psychic Bridge,[†] that exhibits some Bridge-like characteristics. In this game each player is dealt 26 cards from which he selects 13, discarding the remaining 13. Bidding is initiated by the dealer and thence continues until a pass is entered; the bidding format and scoring are identical to that of the conventional game. In the play, the nondeclarer leads the first trick, the play proceeding along the lines drawn by Contract Bridge (except that two cards constitute a trick). The interesting aspects of Psychic Bridge concern selection of the 13-card playing hand from the 26 cards received (essentially a choice between defensive and offensive strategics), estimation of the opponent's selection philosophy, and the extent to which bluffing elements are introduced into the bidding.

Another form of two-handed Bridge is engaged in by players with a large degree of mutual trust. For this version, 13 cards are dealt to each of the two players, the remaining 26 cards being placed face down on the table. The dealer and his opponent alternate in bidding, with the dealer having the option of making the first bid. Bidding continues until a call is followed by a pass (two initial passes cancels the deal). The final bidder is designated as declarer and the opponent is charged with the opening lead. Declarer plays a card on this lead, the opponent plays a second card, and then declarer also plays a second card. Thus, four cards, two from each player, constitute a trick. Following each trick, the players draw two cards each from the remaining face-down cards of the deck, thus rebuilding the hands to 13

---

† Suggested by David L. Silverman.

cards. Winner of the previous trick then leads. The final replenishment from the deck comprises only one card apiece; play then continues until the hands are exhausted. Scoring is identical to that of Contract Bridge.

An element of trust enters into this game, since a player can renege deliberately (he might lead a presumed singleton and trump with his second card of that trick). He can claim later that additional cards in that suit were subsequently added to his hand by drawing from the remaining deck. Thus, it is likely that this game will retain its popularity only among those couples maintaining a "honeymoon" status.

Suggested references

BERLEKAMP, ELWYN R., and HWANG, F. K., "Constructions for Balanced Howell Rotations for Bridge Tournaments," *J. Combinat. Theory*, **12**, No. 2 (March, 1972), pp. 159–166.

BOREL, EMILE, and ANDRÉ CHERON, *Theorie Mathematique du Bridge a la Portee de Tous*, Gauthier-Villars, Paris, 1955.

CARLEY, GAY LOREN, "Program for Contract Bridge," M.S. Thesis, Massachusetts Institute of Technology, 1962.

CULBERTSON, ELY, *The New Gold Book of Bidding and Play*, The John Winston Co., Philadelphia, 1949.

DALKEY, NORMAN, "Equivalence of Information Patterns and Essentially Determinate Games," *Contributions to the Theory of Games*, Vol. 2, Princeton University Press, Princeton, New Jersey, 1953, pp. 217–243.

FREY, RICHARD L., and ALAN F. TRUSCOTT, eds., *The Official Encyclopaedia of Bridge*, Crown Publishers, Inc., New York, 1964.

GOREN, CHARLES H., *Contract Bridge Complete*, Doubleday and Co., Inc., Garden City, New York, 1952.

KARPIN, FRED L., *Psychological Strategy in Contract Bridge*, Harper & Row, New York, 1960.

KUHN, H. W., "Extensive Games and the Problem of Information," *Contributions to the Theory of Games*, Vol. 2, Princeton University Press, Princeton, New Jersey, 1953 pp. 193–216.

MACKEY, REX, *The Walk of the Oysters*, W. H. Allen, London, 1964.

THOMPSON, GERALD L., "Bridge and Signalling," *Contributions to the Theory of Games*, Vol. 2, Princeton University Press, Princeton, New Jersey, 1953, pp. 279–289.

THOMPSON, GERALD L., "Signalling Strategies in *n*-Person Games," *Contributions to the Theory of Games*, Vol. 2, Princeton University Press, Princeton, New Jersey, 1953, pp. 267–277.

WATSON, LOUIS H., *Watson's Classic Book on the Play of the Hand at Bridge*, Barnes and Noble, Inc., New York, rev. ed., 1958.

WAUGH, DAN F., and FREDERICK V. WAUGH, "On Probabilities in Bridge," *J. Amer. Statistical Assoc.*, **48**, No. 261 (March, 1953), pp. 79–87.

CHAPTER NINE

WEIGHTED STATISTICAL LOGIC AND STATISTICAL GAMES

Strategic selection

There are certain phenomena, such as weather and ocean wave movements, whose statistics are pseudostationary—in the sense that they would be statistically predictable if we possessed sufficiently microscopic information regarding their nature. Since such information may never be practically available, they are treated as nonstationary. On the other hand, games whose outcomes depend to a large extent on human, animal, or psychological factors are truly nonstationary in nature. Statistics of horse-racing events, for example, clearly change with improved training methods and breeding controls. Stock market activity, as another example, causes different people to react differently, and the same person may well react differently to the same stimulus applied at different times. Forty years ago if J. P. Morgan advised, "Buy!", almost everyone bought (while J. P. Morgan likely sold short). At present, no financier could influence investment behavior to the same extent.

In games of (essentially) pure skill, such as Chess, Go, football, Tic-Tac-Toe, and three-cushion billiards, the psychological elements enter in a subtle manner. The *dernier cri* strategy (whether the latest T-formation variation or a new Chess gambit) and the players' conformity to it, the players' mental and physical health, or their esthetic sensibilities may be significant factors.

Many of those professionally concerned with more serious games such as warfare, both military and economic, have long been accustomed to regard problems of strategy, where nonstationary statistics are involved, as too enigmatic to be subjected to intellectual analysis. Such problems were considered the exclusive province of men who had crystallized long experience into a set of heuristic rules of play. Mathematical models were viewed merely as exercises in fantasy; the usual approach was that precarious system of trial and error referred to by its adherents as pragmatism and by its opponents as willful bungling. More recently, the rise in respectability of such disciplines as Operations Research has instituted an incisive, analytic approach to the previously arcane regions of war strategy and weapons development. One consequence of the newer approach, on the national level, is a posture of greater political sophistication.

Yet, any effort to reduce human behavior to precise mathematical formulae must be less than convincing in light of the present state of conceptual analysis techniques. We await the development of better conceptual tools and more refined use of strategic language. Until then it may be impossible to achieve a completely intelligent choice among alternative courses of action. We attempt, rather, to determine a "best" decision constrained by the limitations of our model and its underlying assumptions.

The choice of a probable "best" course of action from two or more alternatives based on statistical inference as to their relative merits defines a process of strategic selection by weighted statistical logic. There are four basic steps leading to an ultimate decision:

1. Determination and evaluation of the individual factors pertinent to the final decision.

2. Expression of the alternate courses of action in terms of the weighting assigned each of the individual pertinent factors.

3. Derivation of a composite ranking, representing the overall relative merit of each alternate course of action.

4. Recognition and designation of the highest ranking alternative as the optimum course of action.

The key to this approach is the judicious choice and proper manipulation of the pertinent factors affecting the selective decision. In attempting to predict the outcome of a football contest, for example, we might list such factors as weather, field conditions, home team, and the number of disabled players. Our prediction is a function of these parameters. Were we to include the color of the fullback's eyes, it is evident that our prediction would rest on a rather shaky foundation. Following our choice of the significant ingredients, we examine each for its probable contribution to the outcome. Thus, the space of permissible outcomes is described in a probabilistic sense. If our assessment of the relative importance of each factor is erroneous, our final ranking may well be incorrect. For example, if our football model emphasized the disabled star passer, adverse weather conditions might prove more responsible for shifting the probabilities. Finally, the optimum prediction lies impotent in the face of a "blocked kick," or a "fumble," or some other unforeseen catastrophic departure from planned behavior.

An expression ordaining the choice of a "best" course of action from a number of alternatives can be fashioned as a simple summation of the values representing the individual factors involved in each of the alternate plans. We then examine the composite score attained by each alternate and select that yielding the highest numerical quantity. That is, letting Q_{ji} be the numerical value of the jth individual strategic factor of n such factors as it affects the ith course of action out of m possible plans, we can write

$$R_i = Q_{ai} + Q_{bi} + \cdots + Q_{ji} + \cdots + Q_{ni}, \qquad i = 1, 2, \ldots, m \qquad 9\text{-}1$$

where R_i is the composite score representing the relative merit of the ith course of action.

The factors $Q_{j1}, Q_{j2}, \ldots, Q_{ji}, \ldots, Q_{jm}$ are obviously all related quantities in that they stem from the same strategic element. Their numerical values vary in accordance with the contribution of that element to the particular course of action under consideration. It is therefore useful to define $Q_a, Q_b, \ldots, Q_j, \ldots, Q_n$ as representing the constant numerical value (quality level) of individual strategic elements and define W_{ij} as the weighting factor that modifies the jth strategic element in accordance with its relative contribution to the ith course of action. Thus,

$$Q_{ji} = W_{ij}Q_j$$

and Eq. 9-1 becomes

$$R_i = W_{ia}Q_a + W_{ib}Q_b + \cdots + W_{ij}Q_j + \cdots + W_{in}Q_n = \sum_{j=a}^{n} W_{ij}Q_j$$

which constitutes the general form for the equation describing a decision based on weighted logic.

We now examine the composite numbers R_i and select that with the highest numerical value. The corresponding course of action can then be credited with the greatest relative merit, and the parameters R_i can be described as *figures of merit*.

The election of the particular symbolic representation and definition of terms used here are purely arbitrary. They are designed for a type of decision-making logic wherein the strategic elements are known or measured quantities whose individual values are constant for all courses of action. Only their weight varies relative to the different actions. There exist other decision-making situations wherein the strategic elements vary in value while the weighting factors remain constant for all actions. For example, in the judging of beauty contests, the strategic elements might be figure, poise, and personality. While the score achieved by the contestants on each of these points might vary considerably, the relative weight assigned to each attribute would be identical for all contestants. The basic mathematical model is not changed, but merely the definition of which symbols represent constant and which represent variable quantities for the considerations leading to a final decision. Summation of the individual weighted factors still yields a valid figure of merit, and selection of the highest figure of merit from the group still constitutes a strategic decision.

Usually, the various parameters or strategic elements that comprise a particular plan are expressed in unrelated terms or dimensions. Mathematical expressions for deriving figure-of-merit numbers and the logic circuitry for reaching a strategic decision cannot encompass a summation of unrelated units such as degrees, inches, and dollars. It becomes necessary, therefore, to translate the measured values of the strategic elements into quantized form; a common scaling factor is adopted providing relative

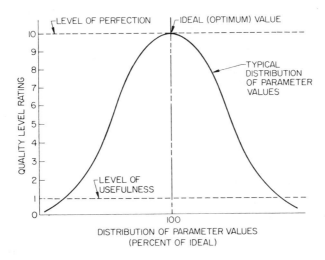

Fig. 9-1   Common scaling of unrelated quantities

quality level ratings for each parameter. Accordingly, the entire range of possible values that each parameter of a particular family of specimens could exhibit are arranged in the form of a statistical distribution. As illustrated in Fig. 9-1, two arbitrary levels are established, defining a "minimum level of usefulness" and a "level of perfection." The "level of perfection" is fixed by the ideal or optimum value specified; the "minimum level of usefulness" is specified by the minimum value that any unit of that type can exhibit and still serve usefully in its most general application. A quality level rating of 1.0 is assigned at the "minimum level of usefulness" and the "level of perfection" is assigned a rating of 10. The interval between these two levels is then divided into nine equal increments and assigned appropriate quality level ratings. All quantities can now be measured and compared against a common scale and their relative quality expressed quantitatively. With each of the significant parameter values similarly translated, all expressions regarding the courses of action are in quantized form and can be combined to designate a strategic decision.

Obviously, the spectrum of possible parameter values does not necessarily conform to a normal distribution pattern. Certain types of parameters follow a continuously increasing (positive slope) distribution, while others exhibit a continuously decreasing (negative slope) characteristic. The assignment of relative quality levels in the first case is exemplified in Fig. 9-2. Here, the "level of perfection" is established by the specified or rated value of the parameter and a quality rating of 10 is assigned. Although the actual measured value of a parameter may exceed its rated value, the quality rating saturates at 10. The "minimum level of usefulness" is established in the same manner as for the normal distribution except that in the case of a negative slope distribution, it becomes the maximum useful value.

In certain situations it may be found that the simple system described above yields insufficient resolution of quality ratings. Measurements of parameters may result in such small deviations from the ideal value that no differentiation in quality ratings is observable, owing to a lack of fine graduations. One solution to this problem is the use of decimal subdivisions of the primary quality-rating increments; another is an increase in the span between minimum usefulness and perfection. Both methods could be utilized to provide an exceptional degree of resolution.

Assignment of weighting factors that ensure a valid basis for strategic trade-offs and decisions is quite similar to the problem of establishing quantized quality ratings. The paramount objective is creation of a system maintaining a constant proportionality of relative values throughout the course of a single decision and throughout a series of strategic decisions.

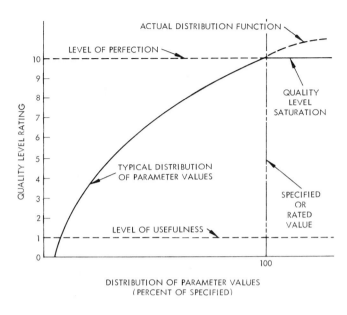

Fig. 9-2   Relative quality levels for an increasing distribution

During a sequence of events that produces a single decision, it is necessary that identical weighting factors carry equal significance when assigned to different applications; otherwise, the resultant figure-of-merit numbers cannot be compared on an equal basis. Also, from decision to decision it is vital that the assigned weighting factors retain an identical relationship of relative importance; otherwise, intercomparisons of different parameters from the same family on the basis of figure-of-merit achievement for identical applications are not valid. A weighting factor of 5, assigned to a particular parameter, for instance, must imply exactly the same degree of importance for one application as for another and must represent precisely the same degree of bias when applied to one test sample or another. A method that satisfies both criteria and possesses further advantage as an instinctive mental process is the assignment of weighting factors on a percentile basis. That is, the sum of the individual weighting factors is normalized to 1.0 (or 100 percent).

As an example of the concepts discussed above, the simple mechanics of decision by weighted strategy are demonstrated in Table 9-1. Two test samples are shown, each having four significant parameters (a, b, c, d). The measured values of the parameters (Q_a, Q_b, Q_c, Q_d) are given in quantized form (a number between 1 and 10 describing the relative quality of each parameter). Percentile weighting factors representing three possible applications for each test sample are tabulated as W_1, W_2, and W_3. The figure-of-merit equations are

$$R_i = W_{ia}Q_a + W_{ib}Q_b + W_{ic}Q_c + W_{id}Q_d, \qquad \sum_{j=a}^{d} W_{ij} = 1, \qquad i = 1, 2, 3$$

Comparison of test samples I and II illustrates the usual case of individual items with different parameter characteristics that are under consideration for use in a number of identical applications. From an examination of the figure-of-merit numbers, we can draw the following specific conclusions: I is best suited for application 1; II is best suited for application 3; and I and II are equally suited for application 2.

TABLE 9-1   Two Examples of Decision by Weighted Strategy

	TEST SAMPLE I				Merit Index	TEST SAMPLE II				Merit Index
	Parameters					Parameters				
	a	b	c	d	R	a	b	c	d	R
Q_j	6	2	4	3		3	5	2	7	
W_1	0.5	0.3	0.1	0.1	4.3[†]	0.5	0.3	0.1	0.1	3.9
W_2	0.3	0.1	0.3	0.3	4.1	0.3	0.1	0.3	0.3	4.1
W_3	0.1	0.2	0.1	0.6	3.2	0.1	0.2	0.1	0.6	5.7[†]

[†] Best strategic application of test sample.

The matrix model used here as a descriptive example, consisting of four parameters and three applications, appears deceptively simple. Yet, even this elementary situation involves 10,000 possible parameter-value permutations and 84 different weighting-factor combinations for each parameter. A total of 91 different figure-of-merit numbers are possible, ranging in value from 1.0 to 10.0. To adapt this system for use in an actual situation, it is quite likely that the matrix would be expanded to include additional parameters and applications, or that additional resolution of parameter- and weighting-factor values would be required. Expansion of the matrix to five parameters increases the number of possible parameter-value combinations to 100,000. Retaining the 4 × 3 matrix, but adding one decade resolution to each of the parameter scales, also produces 100,000 combinations. The mathematical manipulation, storage, and comparison of this number of quantities immediately suggests high-speed electronic computers. The simplicity of the individual computations involved in achieving a strategic decision by weighted statistical logic permits the use of straight-forward computer programs.

Horse racing

Of the various games with formalized wagering, perhaps none so embodies the concept of subjective evaluation as horse racing, the "Sport of Kings." Betting on comparative speeds of horses apparently originated among the Hittites in the second millenium B.C.—archeologists have uncovered a lengthy treatise on the breeding and training of horses written for a Hittite king about 1500 B.C. The earliest full-length account of a chariot race appears in Book xxiii of the *Iliad*. Competitive rules for prescribed distances were instituted for the Thirty-third Olympiad of Greece, *circa* 624 B.C. The Romans refined the idea by adding handicapping and the concept of "betting against the house" for their chariot races. Thence, racing declined with the onset of the Middle Ages and was not renewed until early in the seventeenth century when James I sponsored its establishment at Epsom and Newmarket; his grandson Charles II was such an avid racing addict that he became known as the "father of the British turf." The succeeding 300 years have seen undiminished interest in the sport.

Three major types of horse racing prosper in the United States (distributed over 28 major race tracks plus some hundreds of smaller tracks). Recognized and embellished by legalized (on-track) betting are thoroughbred, standard bred (harness), and quarterhorse racing. By definition, a thoroughbred horse is lineally descended from one of three Near East progenitors (the Byerly Turk, the Darley Arabian, and the Godolphin Barb) bred to English mares about the turn of the eighteenth century. Competition generally is among six to twelve horses and occurs over certain standard distances measured counterclockwise[†] about an oval track: six furlongs, seven furlongs, one mile, $1\frac{1}{8}$ miles, $1\frac{1}{4}$ miles, and $1\frac{1}{2}$ miles. Races are also categorized according to prize, sex (three sexual classes are recognized: stallions, mares, and geldings), age of the contending horses (all equine birthdays are celebrated on January 1st of each year by decree of the Thoroughbred Racing Association), and the horse "rating" or quality. The general divisions are Handicap and Stakes races, Claiming and Optional Claiming races, Allowance and Classified Allowance races, and Maiden races.

[†] French and Japanese horses, among others, race in clockwise fashion.

For any and all data regarding the history, breeding, or racing of horses, the reader is referred to the library on the grounds of the Keeneland (Kentucky) racetrack. Devoted exclusively to hippology, its volumes of racing literature and turf records date from the eighteenth century.

Predicting the outcome of a horse race is an activity that exerts continuing appeal to the extraordinarily opulent. It is intellectually lucrative albeit fiscally ruinous. So many factors can affect the outcome that a strategic decision by weighted statistical logic without the use of a high-speed computer for each application is unfeasible. An enumeration of the pertinent factors might include considerations of post position, track condition, weather, weight carried, previous performances, appearance or condition of the horse, earnings, jockey, owner, trainer, class of race, equipment changes, and numerous others. Many of these factors comprise statistical phenomena of a nonstationary nature. For this reason, data samples gathered over a few seasons of racing at several tracks offer little predictive value, although copious records of past races have been sifted in the search for significant patterns. Any finite data sample, if analyzed sufficiently, can be shown to exhibit patterns of regularity. A simple prediction, however, cannot sensibly be constructed on the shifting sands of nonstationary processes.

PARI-MUTUEL BETTING

The betting procedure for horse racing is based upon the consensus of subjective probabilities assigned to the contending horses by the aggregation of bettors. This procedure is termed the *pari-mutuel* method and determines the payoff odds on each horse inversely proportional to the amount of money wagered on that horse. Invented in France by Pierre Oller in 1865, the pari-mutuel form of betting essentially ensures a fixed profit to the track operator independent of the winning horses (pari-mutuel wagering is also applied for Jai Alai contests). In 1933 the first completely electrical totalizator, automatically computing odds and issuing tickets, was introduced at Arlington Park, Chicago, and subsequently installed at all major racing establishments.[†] Generally (depending on the country or the state within the United States) the track operators remove about 15 percent of the total wagered on each race and redistribute the remainder among those bettors selecting the winning horses. Additionally, an approximately 2-percent loss is sustained by each bettor due to the

---

[†] Totalizators are normally limited to the issuance of 12 different wager tickets. With 13 or more horses going to the post, two or more are coupled together as a betting unit, either because they share common ownership or because they are labeled as "field horses" (a group defined by their long odds).

"breakage" rule—that is, the payoff is quantized to the lower 10-cent level (based on the conventional minimum wager of $2.00). Allowable bets are Win, Place (the horse to finish first or second), Show (the horse to finish first, second, or third), Across the Board (a minimum $6.00 wager divided equally among Win, Place, and Show), Daily Double (two horses in different races, usually the first and second, both to win), and, at certain tracks, Quinella (two horses in the same race to finish first and second, without regard to order). In France the Quinella bet (of Canadian origin) is known as a *couplé*; most French tracks also permit a *place couplé*, whereby the bettor selects two horses to occupy any two of the first three places. A once-a-week opportunity at French tracks is the Pari Tiercé bet: The bettor selects three horses to finish first, second, and third, without regard to order. The legal minimum return on a $2.00 winning ticket is normally $2.10; when the totalizator indicates a smaller payoff (after deducting the 15 percent "house take"), the situation is termed a "minus pool" and the difference to $2.10 is supplied by the track operators.

To describe mathematically the pari-mutuel model, we postulate n bettors $B_1, B_2, \ldots, B_n$ concerned with a race involving m horses $H_1, H_2, \ldots, H_m$. Each bettor B_i applies his weighted statistical logic to what he deems to be the pertinent factors and thereby achieves an estimate of the relative merits of each horse H_j, expressed in quantitative terms—that is, a subjective probability distribution over the m horses. Specifically, we have an $n \times m$ subjective probability matrix $\{p_{ij}\}$, where p_{ij} designates the probability, in the opinion of B_i, that H_j will win the race. A sum $b_i > 0$ is then wagered by B_i in a manner that maximizes his subjective mathematical expectation. That is, B_i observes the pari-mutuel probabilities $\pi_1, \pi_2, \ldots, \pi_m$, as indicated by the track tote board, that horses $H_1, H_2, \ldots, H_m$, respectively, might win the race; he then follows a strategy of distributing the amount b_i among those horses H_j for which the ratio p_{ij}/π_j is a maximum.

We assume that the sum b_i is small with respect to the total amount wagered by the n bettors on the race and therefore does not appreciably influence the pari-mutuel probabilities. We further assume that each column of the matrix $\{p_{ij}\}$ contains at least one entry; otherwise, if the jth column consists of all zeros, no bettor has selected horse H_j and it can theoretically be eliminated from consideration.

The pari-mutuel system is described by three conditions. First, if β_{ij} is the sum wagered by B_i on H_j, we have

$$\sum_{j=1}^{m} \beta_{ij} = b_i \qquad\qquad 9\text{-}2$$

Second, the pari-mutuel format imposes the relation

$$\sum_{i=1}^{n} \beta_{ij} = k\pi_j \qquad\qquad 9\text{-}3$$

where k is the constant of proportionality relating the amount bet on each horse to its pari-mutuel probability. Third, each B_i bets so as to maximize his subjective expectation E_i—that is, when

$$E_i = \frac{p_{ij}}{\pi_j} > 1 \qquad\qquad 9\text{-}4$$

and he bets only on horses for which the inequality holds. Nonnegative numbers π_j and B_{ij} that satisfy Eqs. 9-2, 9-3, and 9-4 are termed *equilibrium probabilities* and *equilibrium bets*, respectively. Their existence is readily proved by means of fixed-point theorems (a clever, elementary proof has been given by Eisenberg and Gale).

Pari-mutuel probabilities for the Win position are determined by the proportionality constant

$$k = (1 - K) \sum_{i=1}^{n} b_i$$

where K is the "house take," so that

$$\pi_j = \frac{\displaystyle\sum_{i=1}^{n} \beta_{ij}}{(1 - K) \displaystyle\sum_{i=1}^{n} b_i} \qquad\qquad 9\text{-}5$$

The odds on each horse are quoted as $(1 - \pi_j)/\pi_j$ to 1. The pari-mutuel probabilities for the Place position are slightly more complicated. The total amount wagered for Place is decreased by the "house take" and then divided into two parts, one-half being distributed among bettors on the winning horse and the other half among bettors on the placing horse. Similarly, pari-mutuel probabilities for the Show position are computed by dividing the total amount bet for Show less the "house take" into three equal parts, one-third being distributed among bettors on the winning horse, one-third among bettors on the placing horse, and one-third among bettors on the showing horse. Thus, it can be observed that the payoffs for a particular horse finishing in the Place or Show position are a function of the other winning horses. The payoff will be higher, the greater the odds on the other horses sharing the mutuel pool.

"REAL" PROBABILITIES FOR A RACE

There are diligent hippophiles who profess the ability to analyze competitive horses so as to determine the objective odds of a given horse in a race. That is, these excellent dopesters can, presumably, assess the "real" probability ρ_j (as opposed to the subjective, pari-mutuel probability π_j) that horse H_j will finish first in a particular gymkhana. It is of interest to derive the optimal betting strategy for a race, given the distribution of "real" probabilities for the contenders.

Let the total wealth bet on the jth horse, $k\pi_j$ (Eq. 9-3), be partitioned into the sum s_j wagered by the subjective "crowd" and the amount t_j contributed by our knowledgeable dopester. The dopester's profit $F(t_1, t_2, \ldots, t_m)$ from an investment spread over the m horses is defined by

$$F(t_1, t_2, \ldots, t_m) = (1 - K) \left[\sum_{j=1}^{m} (s_j + t_j) \right] \sum_{j=1}^{m} \frac{\rho_j t_j}{s_j + t_j} - \sum_{j=1}^{m} t_j$$

It is desired to select a value of $t_j \geq 0$ so as to maximize $F(t_1, t_2, \ldots, t_m)$, where the maximal F possesses a positive magnitude. Rufus Isaacs of the RAND Corporation, in his original statement of the problem, showed that F has a positive maximum if

$$\max_{1 \leq j \leq m} \frac{\rho_j}{s_j} > \frac{1}{(1 - K) \sum_i s_i}$$

Consequently, for a solution $\bar{t} = (\bar{t}_1, \bar{t}_2, \ldots, \bar{t}_m)$, we can write

$$\frac{\partial F}{\partial t_i} = (1 - K) \sum_{j=1}^{m} \frac{\rho_j t_j}{s_j + t_j} + (1 - K) \frac{\rho_i s_i}{(s_i + t_i)^2} \sum_{j=1}^{m} (s_j + t_j) - 1 = 0$$

Then the quantity $\rho_i s_i / (s_i + \bar{t}_i)^2$ exhibits the same value for all i such that $\bar{t}_i > 0$; defining this value by $1/\lambda^2$, we have

$$\bar{t}_i = \lambda \sqrt{\rho_i s_i} - s_i$$

A maximal form of F never occurs for all $\bar{t}_i > 0$ (that is, the dopester never bets on all the horses). Rather, there may exist some number of horses k whose "real" expectation is greater than the subjective expectation realized from the actual wealth invested on their behalf by the "crowd." Then

$$\bar{t}_1 = \bar{t}_2 = \cdots = \bar{t}_{k-1} = 0$$

$$\bar{t}_k > 0, \quad \bar{t}_{k+1} > 0, \ldots, \quad \bar{t}_m > 0$$

where $\bar{t}$ is uniquely determined by k:

$$\bar{t}_i = \lambda_k \sqrt{\rho_i s_i} - s_i, \qquad \text{for } i = k, k + 1, \ldots, m \qquad \text{9-6}$$

and

$$\lambda_k^2 = (1 - K) \sum_{j=1}^{k-1} s_j \left[1 - (1 - K) \sum_{j=k}^{m} \rho_j \right]^{-1} \qquad \text{9-7}$$

As a numerical example, consider the horse-race data given in Table 9-2. Horse H_7 offers the soundest investment, since it returns 75 times the wager, less the "house take," yet possesses a win probability of 0.05. However, if the statistically minded dopester plunges heavily on H_7, the pari-mutuel reaction will alter the odds appreciably.[†] To maximize his

TABLE 9-2   Hypothetical Horse Race

Horse	"Real" Probability of Winning	Amount Wagered by the "Crowd"
H_1	0.40	$35,000
H_2	0.18	10,000
H_3	0.12	9,000
H_4	0.10	8,000
H_5	0.10	7,000
H_6	0.05	5,000
H_7	0.05	1,000
		$75,000

expected profit, the dopester should examine the subset (possibly null) of horses whose "real" expectation is greater than their subjective expectation. The subset for the race illustrated here is composed of horses H_2, H_5, and H_7. Thus, from Eq. 9-7 with $K = 0.15$ (15 percent "house take"),

$$\lambda_k = \left[\frac{0.85(35,000 + 9000 + 8000 + 5000)}{1 - 0.85(0.18 + 0.10 + 0.05)}\right]^{1/2} = 259.5$$

[†] An illustration of the sensitivity of the pari-mutuel system is supplied by the so-called builder play, a betting coup whereby a group of bettors monopolize the mutuel windows at a track, placing small wagers on unlikely winners while confederates are placing large wagers with off-track bookmakers on the more probable winners. Notable builder plays include the 1964 coup at the Dagenham (East London) Greyhound Stadium and a 1932 feat staged at the Aqua Caliente (Mexico) racetrack. In the latter instance, odds on the winning horse (Linden Tree) were increased from a logical 7 to 10 to almost 10 to 1. The Dagenham coup was better organized, allowing only a single on-track ticket to be sold on the winning combination (Buckwheat and Handsome Lass), causing pari-mutuel payoff odds of 9872 to 1.

And, from Eq. 9-6, the optimal wager on horse H_2 is computed as

$$\bar{t}_2 = 259.5\sqrt{0.18 \times 10,000} - 10,000 = \$1018.98$$

No wager should be placed on horse H_5, since the "house take" of 15 percent leads to a negative value of $\bar{t}_5$:

$$\bar{t}_5 = 259.5\sqrt{0.05 \times 7000} - 7000 < 0$$

Horse H_7 should receive a bet of magnitude

$$\bar{t}_7 = 259.5\sqrt{0.05 \times 1000} - 1000 = \$837.68$$

In this discussion we have deliberately avoided pursuing the conceptual connotations of "real" probabilities as applied to a horse race. However, it is intuitively apparent that any individual who can assess the probability of a given horse winning a race more accurately than the ensemble of other bettors can apply this profit maximization method.

PSYCHOLOGICAL BETTING SYSTEMS

Because of the inherently subjective nature of the pari-mutuel betting format, it may be feasible to devise methods of horse selection based solely on the psychological behavior of the bettors. For example, one "system" consists of wagering on the favorite (shortest odds) horse in the last race of a day's program. While favorite horses are not more prone to win the last race than any other, the payoff is frequently greater than it would be in earlier races, since there apparently exists a tendency to place a larger percentage of the total wagers on the longer-odds horses. This tendency possibly arises from the losers' attempts to regain their losses and the winners' inclinations to leave prior to the last race. Another "system" advises wagering on the favorite horse if the previous two or more races have been won by favorites, and conversely. The rationale in this instance suggests that many bettors are susceptible to a "maturity of the chances" doctrine and therefore tend to avoid wagering on a favorite horse when preceding races have produced winning favorites; thus the favorite offers higher odds than would arise from independent considerations. Both "systems" have been tested by examination of a limited data sample. The results indicate an increase in expectation of approximately 15 percent over a random selection of horses. Presumably, as bettors gain additional mathematical sophistication, this figure would decrease.

More cyclopedic means exist for utilizing the relatively invariant psychological behavior of horse-racing bettors as reflected by the pari-mutuel probabilities. A logical method involves a statistical classification of races according to the subjective probability distribution of each horse's winning chances and a comparison of the mathematical expectation with previous data.[†] Each race can be distinguished by a distribution of the probabilities π_j, as specified by Eq. 9-5. One of several parameters might be chosen as a measure of this distribution; for simplicity, we select the natural and convenient measure of entropy. Thus we categorize all races according to the entropy H of that race:

$$H = - \sum_{j=1}^{m} \pi_j \log \pi_j$$

A maximum entropy race is one wherein all horses are accorded identical pari-mutuel probabilities (that is, identical sums are wagered on each horse). A uniform distribution of π_j over the interval 0 to 1 constitutes a minimum-entropy race. By examining records of past races, we can obtain a frequency distribution $f(H)$ (actually a histogram) of pari-mutuel entropies.

For every race, we can then compute the frequency distribution $g(\pi_j)$ of the pari-mutuel probabilities and therefore the distribution

$$F(E) = \pi_j \left[\frac{g(\pi_j)}{\pi_j} - 1 \right]$$

of expectations. Performing this computation over all possible entropies, we can construct a surface of expectation density as a function of entropy. To determine whether to bet on a particular race, and on which horses, we first calculate the entropy of the race just prior to its running. For a particular entropy we have a pari-mutuel expectation density profile $F_1(E)$ available from past data. A typical example is illustrated in Fig. 9-3. The m pari-mutuel probabilities associated with the m horses are compared with this profile; if one or more values of π_j leads to a positive expectation, we may wager on the corresponding horses.

Compilation of data over a limited period of time at several tracks has indicated that a positive mathematical expectation usually occurs in races of relatively high entropy. For these situations, horses with odds of 6 to 1, 7 to 1, and 8 to 1 have most often exhibited the positive payoff probability.

Other than lotteries or football pools, horse racing constitutes one of the poorest forms of betting available to the average gambler, owing to the

---

† For this suggestion we are indebted to Frank Paulsen of the Jet Propulsion Laboratory.

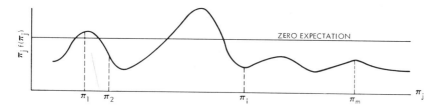

Fig. 9-3   Expectation density profile of a particular entropy

15 percent "house take" plus "breakage." Overcoming the highly negative mathematical expectation of horse racing poses virtually insurmountable obstacles in terms of acquiring the requisite knowledge, constructing an appropriate model, and performing the attendant computations. Records of the published handicappers indicate a lack of success for all methods based solely on subjective evaluations.

The stock market

Another game comprising weighted subjective judgments and nonstationary statistics is that offered by the stock market[†] (or commodity markets). Constituting a gigantic decision-making phenomenon, the stock market— with its codified folklore and certified respectability—offers a broad appeal to the gambler (euphemistically referred to as a "speculator"). Like horse-race handicappers, stock market analysts frequently attempt to predict the future on the basis of past performances and, like horse racing, the market has successfully withstood all nostrums for financial success; the pot of gold exists, but the labyrinthine path to its den has not yet been charted.

Rigorous technical analysis of the stock market encounters a vertiginous array of factors, some real, some imagined, to which security prices respond with varying sensitivities. Treatment of the apparently whimsical fluctuations of the stock quotations as truly nonstationary processes requires a model of such complexity that its practical value is likely to be limited. An additional complication, not encompassed by most stock market models, arises from the manifestation of the market as a nonzero-sum game. The theory of games has shown that consideration of nonzero-

---

[†] So called from the custom of English brokers of recording transactions by duplicating notches in two wooden stocks (the customer retained one stock and the broker the other; a matching of the notches evidently ensured honesty).

sum games immediately injects questions of cooperation, bargaining, and other types of player interaction before and during the course of the game. Also, considerations of subjective utility functions arise—for nonzero-sum games we are generally concerned with equilibrium point-preserving vectors of utility functions. Even when treated as a zero-sum game, the stock market implies utility functions that are *nonstrategy-preserving* (by definition, if a player's strategy is independent of his fortune at the time of the play, his utility function is *strategy-preserving*; it can be shown that such utility functions must be either linear or exponential).

A further peculiarity of the stock market arises from the time duration of a complete play (a buy-and-sell transaction, in either order). What constitutes a profit over an extended period of time is complicated by the time-varying purchasing power of money, taxation rates, availability of merchandise, inventions, war, government changes, political upheavals, and shifts in mass psychology influencing the mores of investors. Reflecting an amalgam of economic, monetary, and psychological factors, the stock market represents possibly the most subtly intricate game invented by man.

DESCRIPTIVE MODELS

According to tradition, the New York Stock Exchange was established in Wall Street in 1792 under the shade of a buttonwood tree. By 1815 it had moved indoors and was offering 24 issues for trade. In 1870 the number of securities listed reached 278, and at present over 1400 stocks are available on this one exchange.[†] Throughout these 175 years, multitudinous models have been proposed as descriptive of the behavior of security prices. Classically, efforts are directed toward relating the values of securities with industrial production levels or other measures of economic health. Yet industrial stocks and industrial production have moved together but 51 percent of the time since mid-nineteenth century (36 percent of the time both have risen, while 15 percent of the time both have fallen; rising industrial production has seen a falling market 25 percent of the time, and stocks have risen despite falling production 24 percent of the time). The industrial cycle itself is exhibiting markedly changing characteristics. "Boom" and "bust" periods are apparently less frequent and violent under the constraints of government controls. From 1854 through 1933, the United States experienced 21 economic depressions, an average of one

---

[†] In addition to the New York exchange, there are 10 registered exchanges in the United States plus 3 Canadian exchanges.

every 45 months; between 1933 and 1965, six depressions resulted in an average of one every 64 months.

Of those models that deal directly with security prices—short-circuiting economic and monetary analysis—the great majority are of an interpretive nature. The Dow theory and its host of relatives typify those models based on crude measurements with such ambiguous formulation as to require interpreters, most of whom disagree among themselves. We can only note the remarkably contradictory conclusions that have evolved from a single collection of data.

Other models are predicated upon assumed (or imagined) correlations between stock price fluctuations and various fluctuating phenomena in and out of the world. Sunspot activity, astrological events, ionic content of the air, and Jovian radio signals are but some of the supposed correlated events; one enterprising individual ran, for a time, a fairly successful investment service based on his "readings" of comic strips in the *New York Sun*. Not surprising to the statistician, good correlations can be found over discretely chosen limited data samples *in the past*. Their failure to survive the transition from past to future can surprise only the irrepressible optimist.

Although the first serious study of a stock market (Vienna) was conducted prior to 1871 by Carl Menger (as a background for his theory of prices and the concept of marginal utility), it was not until 1900 that a competent mathematician began a scientific and empirical investigation into the nature of security prices. In that year, Louis Bachelier, a student of Poincaré, completed his doctoral dissertation, "Théorie de la Spéculation." Bachelier developed an elaborate mathematical theory of speculative prices and tested it against government securities (*rentes*) on the Paris Bourse. His pioneer studies launched the theory of stochastic processes, established the probability law for diffusion in the presence of an absorbing barrier, and foreshadowed many other areas of interest to probability theorists. Because his work relied on heuristic rather than rigorous reasoning, it was largely ignored by mathematicians and remained unrecognized for decades. It was also ignored by economists until, following the debacle of 1929, aroused interest in the mysteries of the market led to its rediscovery. Holbrook Working (1934) was principally responsible for reviving the mathematical approach and, subsequently, Alfred Cowles focused his research on the ability of the publicized forecasters to predict stock prices, finding that no success beyond that due to chance could be attributed to their prognostications. In 1938, with the publication of *Common Stock Indexes*, the Cowles Foundation presented the first major organized collection of statistical data on the U.S. stock market.

Statistical analysis of the process of price formation gained momentum during the 1950's. Maurice Kendall investigated the independence of price changes (1953) and M. F. M. Osborne undertook to describe the form of the limiting distribution of prices. Osborne was also the first to probe into and publish the relationship between the behavior of individual stocks and the general market. More recently, mathematicians and economists have combined in joint efforts to understand the principles of trading securities.

Under a grant from the brokerage firm of Merrill Lynch, Pierce, Fenner and Smith Inc., the University of Chicago established, in 1960, a Center for Research in Security Prices, to conduct research into the behavior of stocks, individually and collectively. Monthly closing prices of all common stocks listed on the New York Exchange from January, 1926, to December, 1960, have been placed on tape. Buying and selling at various intervals over this period have been programmed for an IBM 7094 computer. Another computer program was written to determine the performance of a "random" investor (the particular security and the buying and selling moments were selected at random); over the 35-year period covered by the program, the "random" investor obtained a median gain of 10 percent per annum on his capital.

From Bachelier to the Chicago Research Center, virtually all academic investigators agree upon one point: To a good approximation, price changes in speculative markets, such as commodities and securities, behave like independent, identically distributed random variables with finite variances. It then follows, according to the central limit theorem, that price changes over a small interval of time are normally distributed. (Actually, the log-normal distribution provides a better fit.) The model thus depicted is referred to by statisticians as a random walk, and by physicists as Brownian motion. It asserts that *a history of past prices alone is of no substantial value in the prediction of future prices*. No gambling rule exists which can produce a profit (assuming truly independent price increments—see Theorem I of Chapter 3). Except for appreciation due to earnings retention, the conditional expectation of tomorrow's price, given today's price, is today's price.

The random-walk model is consistent with the postulate of stock exchanges as "perfect" markets. That is, if a substantial group of investors believed that prices were too low, they would enter buying bids, thereby forcing prices higher, and vice versa, quickly forcing prices into conformity with the "intrinsic value" of the securities. Data supporting the random-walk model have been processed with considerable statistical sophistication by a large number of academic investigators (M. G. Kendall, A. Moore, *inter alia*). C. W. J. Granger and O. Morgenstern have applied the technique of spectral analysis to time series of stock prices. A spectrum of a time series represents completely the autocorrelation function for any stationary stochastic process with finite variance and also determines the best linear predictor for that time series. The technique is utilized with reservation in connection with economic data, since the basic phenomenon is nonstationary. However, if the underlying structure of the time series is not a fast-changing function of time, spectral analysis can prove useful. In virtually every case examined by Granger and Morgenstern, the first differences of various stock aggregates exhibited a spectrum quite flat over the entire frequency range, thus providing additional support to the random-walk thesis.

Analyses of security prices are characterized by two distinct approaches. Fundamental analysis relies upon evaluation of economic and financial data to ascertain the "intrinsic value" of a corporate security. Technical analysis, on the other hand, is concerned solely with market price trends and patterns —price histories are examined in search of patterns that portend future prices. The "technician" or "chartist" then speaks in terms of "head and shoulders," "double tops," "support levels," "resistance points," etc., referring to structures delineated by a chart of price versus time. (In practice, most investment counselors combine fundamental and technical principles in appraising securities.) But if the random-walk model is valid, then all technical analysis is unavailing; historical price patterns are merely statistical fossils.

A weakness of the random-walk model lies in its assumption of instantaneous adjustment, whereas the information impelling a stock toward its "intrinsic value" gradually becomes disseminated throughout the market place. Further, technical analysts maintain that assigning an "intrinsic value" to a stock is futile since price changes result from the interaction of supply and demand rather than from absolute economic valuations. The countervailing view holds that actions of the technicians themselves tend to create the trends and patterns they have predicted. Random stock selection, studies showed, performed as well (on the average) as did the most expertly managed funds.

Slight departures from randomness have often been observed, but of insufficient degree to overcome brokerage commissions. A study by V. Niederhoffer has indicated a tendency for stock prices to cluster at integer values. Empirical evidence for this type of price congestion was first presented by M. F. M. Osborne. The clustering effect apparently stems from buy-limit and sell-limit bids (as opposed to market orders and stop orders), which tend to be placed at integer values, combined with the reluctance of specialists to trade for their own accounts. Intelligent trading of floor traders and specialists evidently causes the ratio of highs to lows to be greater than unity at 7/8 and less than unity at 1/8 fractions.

A modification of the normality model, due to P. H. Cootner, proposes that market investors be categorized either as amateurs or specialists. Actions of the amateurs in buying and selling create random price fluctuations. Specialists, on the other hand, act to counteract price deviations that they consider unduly large. Thus the specialists behave as reflecting barriers tending toward a more stable market.

Cootner also investigated moving-average trend indicators. This strategy suggests that if a stock penetrates its own moving average—defined, conventionally, over a 200-day period—on the upside, it should be bought (or covered if in a short position). If the penetration occurs on the downside, the stock should be shorted (or sold if in a long position). Following this strategy produced profits only before commissions were assessed.

A model contributed by S. S. Alexander conjectures that stock prices are statistically described by a random walk in time with persistence in direction. That is, if a stock price has increased by a certain percentage, · then it exhibits a tendency to increase yet further before turning downward. The same tendency is observable in the reverse sense. The obvious decision rule dictates buying when the market rises by x percent, holding until it declines by x percent, then selling and going short until it again rises x percent, etc. Such a system is referred to as an x percent filter rule. Ignoring brokerage commissions, Alexander found that the smallest filter (1 percent) yielded the greatest profits; larger filters also proved superior to the equivalent buy-and-hold strategy. With commissions, however, the small filters furnished net losses.

Alexander's filter technique requires that prices change substantially before a transaction is signalled. Cootner's moving-average policy permits more rapid response since price changes are interpreted relative to some trend. Neither system is capable of profitably exploiting minor departures from normality and neither can detect nonlinear mechanisms in the price fluctuations if they exist.

The first circumvention of the random-walk model was achieved by Robert A. Levy who postulated that co-movements of stock prices could conceal existing dependencies in successive price changes. Using a relative measure of strength for a stock rather than an absolute measure filters out co-movements—that is, the effects of the "general market." Accordingly, Levy proposed, the strength of a stock should be measured in relation to a market average. Those stocks that have historically evidenced a strong price trend *compared to other securities* (not in terms of absolute price changes) should continue to evince superior performance. (The random-walk model is based on logarithmic, percentage, or arithmetic changes in price.) Data indicate that relative strength persists over half-year intervals.

Levy further subclassified his relative-strength ranks by historical volatility rankings and by historical market rankings (that is, rating the strength of the general market at a given time period). He obtained a return on investment considerably greater than that from equivalent random selection investments and with less risk than that associated with random selection. Historical relative strength is therefore confirmed as a valid stock-selection criterion.

WARRANT HEDGING

The practice of warrant hedging (simultaneously buying a security and shorting its associated warrant) has been recognized for several decades. Its effectiveness, its anatomy, and its operation, however, were not analyzed until the 1960s, when Edward O. Thorp and Sheen T. Kassouf performed a thorough autopsy.

A warrant is defined as an option to buy a share of common stock at a fixed price—referred to as the exercise price. Warrants themselves are bought and sold in essentially the same manner as common securities although, unlike stocks, they are (usually) issued with an expiration date, beyond which the warrant retains no value. Adroit hedging of the warrant against the stock largely cancels the risk attendant to each separately while still offering a substantial return on investment.

The specifics of a warrant-hedging transaction involves shorting m warrants at selling price w and exercise price e for every share of stock bought at price s (m is known as the mix). If, at or before the expiration date of the warrant, the stock is selling at price S and the warrant at price W, the percentage profit return R from concluding the transaction is

$$R = \frac{S - s + m(w - W)}{mw + s\mu} \qquad\qquad 9\text{-}8$$

where μ is the margin required for stock purchase and $mw + s\mu \equiv I$ is the initial investment capital. As its expiration date approaches, the warrant will have a price approaching zero if the stock price is at or below the exercise price; if the stock price exceeds the exercise price, the warrant will sell for about the difference between the stock and exercise prices. That is,

$$W \sim \begin{cases} S - e, & S > e \\ 0, & S \le e \end{cases}$$

Equation 9-8 can then be written in the form

$$R \sim \begin{cases} \dfrac{(1-m)S + m(w+e) - s}{I}, & S > e \\[3mm] \dfrac{S + mw - s}{I}, & S \le e \end{cases} \qquad 9\text{-}9$$

R remains positive throughout the range

$$(s - mw) < S < \left[\frac{s - m(w + e)}{1 - m}\right]$$

and assumes its maximum value when $S = e$ (disregarding commissions). According to the random-walk model, the mean value of S is s; Eq. 9-9 for this case shows a profit of $R = mw/I$.

Thorp and Kassouf restrict the hedging system to those warrants whose expiration date is four years or less and whose stock is selling at less than 120 percent of the exercise price. For each transaction they select a mix that provides a conservative balance between potential risk and potential profit. Often the mix is chosen so that the zone of potential profit is distributed logarithmically equal above and below the stock price. Applying these guidelines, they report consistent profits of about 25 percent per year on invested capital.

As a numerical illustration, consider a stock selling at 20 with a warrant selling at 5 and an exercise price of 25. A mix of 2 provides equal logarithmic safety against stock fluctuations. Then, if we buy 100 shares of the stock and short 200 warrants, the invested capital with 50 percent margin is $I = 200(5) + 100(20)(0.5) = \$2000$. The safety zone ranges throughout $10 < S < 40$ with its maximum value at $S = 25$, whence (from Eq. 9-9)

$$R = \frac{1500}{2000} = 75 \text{ percent.}$$

Examples of warrants suitable for hedging appear with decreasing frequency as the hedging system has become increasingly applied in the marketplace. A different market with further profit potential was initiated in April, 1973, when the Chicago Board of Options Exchange (CBOE) permitted public buying and selling of call options on selected stocks. Since a call can be treated identically to a warrant, a system of option-hedging (selling calls while buying the associated stock) is mathematically equivalent to warrant-hedging. The classic construct in this field is the Black–Scholes option model, which demonstrates that hedging options short and common stock long and continuously adjusting the mix lead to a riskless rate of profit return.

War games

Various simplified games have been postulated for simulations of political and economic processes. Corporation games, in particular, exhibit a strong appeal to game theorists and voting games of the "oceanic" type (wherein a few powerful players compete with a sea of infinitesimal minor players) are extensively described in the technical literature. The connection of these games with real situations is often tenuous.

Games of warfare have also commanded considerable attention. War games have been cultivated by military men at least since military Chess in the seventeenth century and K. Venturini's map exercises at the end of the eighteenth. Contests between two players (armies) are generally predicated upon certain arbitrary rules for resolving conflict, the resolution occurring frequently under subjective criteria. One of the first attempts, and perhaps the most well-known, to obtain quantitative results for prediction of outcome and effectiveness of two opposing sides in a military situation originated with F. W. Lanchester. Formulated in 1916, Lanchester's laws state that the strength of a given force should be considered as proportional to the average effectiveness of each unit of force and to the first or second power of the number of units employed, provided each unit is able to fire on any or all units of the opposing force. By definition, the effectiveness of a unit is measured by the number of opposing units that it is capable of destroying per unit time. Mathematically, if a force of n units is engaged in combat against a force of m units (replacement of incapacitated units is precluded), the probability $P(n, m)$ that the first force wins the engagement (defined as reducing the opposing force to zero) is formulated by the linear partial difference equation

$$P(n, m) = Q(n, m)P(n, m - 1) + 1 - Q(n, m)P(n - 1, m) \qquad 9\text{-}10$$

where $Q(n, m)$ is the probability that the next casualty is incurred by the second force. With $Q(n, m)$ equated to a constant p, we have Lanchester's linear law. The square law is obtained by setting $Q(n, m) = rn/(rn + m)$, where r is the ratio of the relative effectiveness of a unit of the first force to that for a unit of the second force.

The natural boundary conditions are

$$P(n, 0) = 1, \quad P(0, m) = 0 \qquad 9\text{-}11$$

for all values of n and m. Subject to these conditions, Eq. 9-10, for $Q(n, m) = p$ and $q = 1 - p$, exhibits the solution

$$P(n, m) = \sum_{i=0}^{n-1} \binom{m-1+i}{i} p^m q^i$$

R. H. Brown has shown that a good approximation for Lanchester's linear law is given by the normal probability function

$$P(n, m) = \frac{1}{\sqrt{2\pi}} \int_{-\infty}^{w} e^{-x^2/2} \, dx \qquad \qquad 9\text{-}12$$

where

$$w = \frac{np - mq}{\sqrt{(n + m)pq}} \qquad \qquad 9\text{-}13$$

(as a consequence of the DeMoivre–Laplace theorem).

Lanchester's square law, subject to the boundary conditions of Eq. 9-11, is satisfied by

$$P(n, m) = r^m \sum_{i=1}^{n} \binom{n}{i} (-1)^{n-i} i^{n+m} \frac{\Gamma(ri + 1)}{\Gamma(m + ri + 1)n!} \qquad \qquad 9\text{-}14$$

When the two opposing forces are equally effective, so that $r = 1$, Eq. 9-14 reduces to the simpler form:

$$P(n, m) = \sum_{i=1}^{n} \binom{n+m}{n-i} \frac{(-1)^{n-i} i^{n+m}}{(n+m)!}$$

R. H. Brown has demonstrated that Eq. 9-12 is also valid as an approximation to the square law with

$$w = \frac{\sqrt{3}\,(n\sqrt{r} - m)}{\sqrt{(n + m)r^{1/2}}} \qquad \qquad 9\text{-}15$$

Letting $p = \sqrt{r}/(1 + \sqrt{r})$, Eq. 9-15 can be written in the form

$$w = \frac{\sqrt{3}\,(np - qm)}{\sqrt{(n + m)pq}}$$

so that the linear and square laws differ (under this interpretation of p) only by a factor of the square root of 3 along the probability integral curve. Following Lanchester's laws, the victor is consequently able to minimize his losses by committing only sufficient units to ensure a desired probability of victory.

According to the linear law, two opposing forces are equally balanced if the ratio of their initial numbers is equal to the inverse ratio of their effectiveness—that is, if $n/m = q/p$. In that instance, $w = 0$ (Eq. 9-13) and $P(n, m) = 1/2$. The square law illustrates the advantages of concentration of forces. It is apparent that the effective strength of a force is proportional to the first power of its effectiveness and to the square of the number of units entering the engagement. Thus, two forces are equally matched when the relative effectiveness ratio r is equal to the square of the inverse ratio of the number of units; that is, $r = m^2/n^2$, for which $w = 0$ (Eq. 9-15) and $P(n, m) = 1/2$. Accordingly, it is more profitable to increase the number of units in an engagement than to increase (by the same percentage) the effectiveness of the combatants. It would appear from Lanchester's square law that a tactical or strategical use of concentration can counterbalance a moderate advantage in weapon efficiency.

Although not usually classed as a war game, a strategic model originated by David Blackwell reflects certain characteristics of warfare by assigning a limited supply of commodities to the two players. At each move the players commit one of their commodities (without replacement), which are then compared, the higher-valued commodity winning the move; the victory is awarded to that player who has won the greater number of moves when the supply of commodities is exhausted. An interesting case arises when the commodities are cyclically ordered. Consider that player A is provided with an initial supply of a women and b cats; B's initial resources consist of c men and d mice. The winner of a move is resolved under the rule that women defeat men who defeat cats who defeat mice who defeat women. An equitable game is defined by the condition $ab = cd$; if $ab > cd$, the game is favorable to player A.

Another form of warfare simulation is the Colonel Blotto game, a tactical military deployment problem initiated in Caliban's *Weekend Problems Book*. Typically, Colonel Blotto is faced with the task of allocating his forces on one or more battlefields without knowledge of the opposing deployment. With few exceptions, this type of problem is readily solved through application of the minimax principle.

For more complex analyses of military and social conflicts, the reader is referred to the work of Lewis Richardson and Anatol Rapoport.

Games with information lag

Other prototypes of those real conflicts that encompass probabilistic elements in their resolution are games with information lag, games of pursuit, and games of timing. In these situations, game-theoretic considerations generally dictate use of mixed strategies. Since models distinguished by their realism are often excessively complex, we usually impose constraints departing considerably from reality. An illustration of this condition occurs in the classic military problem of a marksman aiming at a mobile target with a time lag in the information of the target's position as available to the marksman. This type of game with an information lag is generally unsolvable. However, a model proposed by Rufus Isaacs of the RAND Corporation introduces certain interesting concepts.

THE BOMBER AND THE SHIP

Let the marksman P be an airplane with a single bomb and unerring aim, and let the evading target E be a ship with no offensive capability, but with the sole objective of avoiding the bomb—that is, reducing the hit probability to a minimum. A time lag Δt occurs between release of the bomb from the plane and its detonation; hence, the bomber must aim at an anticipated position of the ship. Assuming that the ship travels with constant speed v, but in an arbitrary direction, it can, following release of the bomb, be anywhere within a circle of radius $v \Delta t$ at the time the bomb strikes the ocean surface. To minimize the probability of a hit, the ship should appear at all points of the circle with equal probability. However, to achieve this equiprobability, the ship's mixed strategy must assign heavy weighting to straight-line paths, since there is but a single path (a straight line) by which the ship can reach a point on the circumference of the circle and many paths by which it can reach an interior point. Thus an attempt at achieving equiprobability compromises future position, for the high probability of straight-line paths enables the bomber to defer his action until, observing the linear behavior of the ship, he can extrapolate and obtain a hit with virtual certainty. It is apparent, therefore, that by attempting equiprobability at one instant, the ship becomes vulnerable at other instants; rather, it should seek a probability distribution that, albeit only approximately uniform, is stationary (that is, independent of time so that the ship can maintain a strategy without reference to the plane's action).

Derivation of a strategy yielding an optimal stationary probability distribution is extremely difficult. To simplify the situation, we postulate a one-dimensional discrete ocean. The ship is consequently constrained to be located on one of a row of points, and at each unit of time moves left or right to a contiguous point or remains at rest (Isaac's model does not permit the nonmoving option). The time lag between bomb release and detonation is an integral number n of time units (or moves). An equivalent statement is that the bomber knows all positions of the ship which precede its present position by n moves or more. For $n = 1$, the bomber knows the past history except for its most recent position; the ship must therefore be one space to the left, one space to the right, or exactly at the last observed point. A strategy for the case $n = 1$ is trivial: The ship decides to move left, right, or remain at rest with equiprobabilities of $1/3$. The airplane can release its bomb at any time, and regardless of its strategy, the hit probability (value of the game) remains constant at $1/3$.

The situation for $n = 2$ is considerably more complex. Beginning at point 0, the ship, following two moves, can be at any one of five points: $-2, -1, 0, +1, +2$. A diagram of the possible paths is shown in Fig. 9-4. If the game is played only for the instant that P releases the bomb when E is at point 0, then clearly the best strategy for E is to arrange for equal probability of arriving at any of the five points at $t = 2$. One method of achieving this uniform probability is illustrated by the initial path probabilities indicated in Fig. 9-4. If, however, P is afforded the option of releasing the bomb at a time of his own choosing, this arrangement of the path probabilities cannot be extended to ensure probabilities of $1/5$ for all five points two units ahead in time. For example, if P moves to point -1 at $t = 1$, he cannot reach points $-3, -2, -1, 0$, and $+1$ at $t = 3$ with equal probabilities. Since the probability of moving to point 0 at $t = 2$ from point -1 at $t = 1$ is less than $1/5$, it is impossible to reach point $+1$ at $t = 3$ with a probability of $1/5$, given the starting position of point -1 at $t = 1$.

To derive a stationary strategy, we must surrender the ideal of achieving equiprobability at all five points two time units in the future. It is logical to select a strategy for E dependent only on the previous move. We let E move in the same direction as his last active move with probability p_1, change direction with probability p_2, and remain at rest with probability $1 - p_1 - p_2$. The consequent path probabilities are shown in Fig. 9-5 (a previous move at $t = -1$ is postulated with no loss of generality). From this diagram it is evident that the probabilities of E reaching the five points $-2, -1, 0, +1, +2$ at time $t = 2$ are, respectively,

$$P(-2) = p_1^2$$

$$P(-1) = 2p_1(1 - p_1 - p_2)$$

$$P(0) = p_2(p_1 + p_2) + (1 - p_1 - p_2)^2$$

$$P(+1) = 2p_2(1 - p_1 - p_2)$$

$$P(+2) = p_1 p_2$$

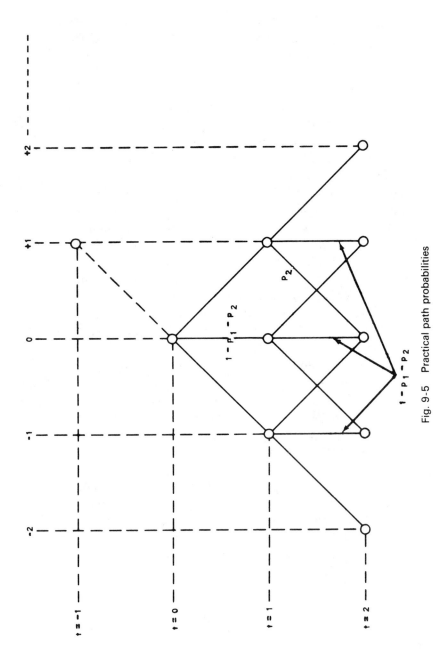

Fig. 9-5   Practical path probabilities

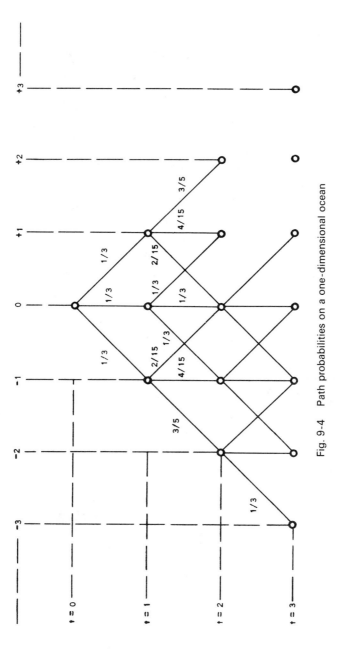

Fig. 9-4   Path probabilities on a one-dimensional ocean

In accordance with the dictates of game theory, we assume that since P will aim at that point associated with the highest probability, it is E's objective to minimize the maximum of these five polynomials.

Thus, we wish to determine those values of p_1 and p_2 for which $\max_{p_1 p_2} P(i)$, $i = -2, -1, 0, +1, +2$, is a minimum. In Fig. 9-6 we sketch the regions in the $p_1 p_2$ plane where the four polynomials $P(-2)$, $P(-1)$, $P(+1)$, and $P(+2)$ possess maximal values. Specifically, $P(-1)$ dominates in region I, $P(-2)$ in region II, $P(+1)$ in region III, and $P(+2)$ in region IV. Each of these four regions is then examined along the projection of the curve of intersection of the dominating polynomial with the fifth polynomial $P(0)$. The four intersection curves are determined by solution of the simultaneous equations

$$\frac{dP(0)}{dp_1} + \frac{dP(0)}{dp_2}\frac{dp_2}{dp_1} = 0$$

9-16

$$\frac{d[P(0) - P(i)]}{dp_1} + \frac{d[P(0) - P(i)]}{dp_2}\frac{dp_2}{dp_1} = 0, \qquad i = -2, -1, +1, +2$$

which are also sketched in Fig. 9-6. The minimax point must be located along a curve of intersection, either at a boundary point or at a zero derivative point. Solution of Eqs. 9-16 and $P(0) - P(i)$ with the boundary lines yields the minimax solution $p_1 = \frac{1}{2}$, $p_2 = \frac{1}{4}$, which defines the unique

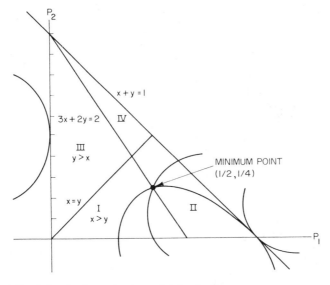

Fig. 9-6   Regions of polynomial domination

optimal strategy for E. The five polynomials are then evaluated as

$$P(-2) = 1/4$$

$$P(-1) = 1/4$$

$$P(0) = 1/4$$

$$P(+1) = 1/8$$

$$P(+2) = 1/8$$

Thus the probability that E arrives at points -2, -1, or 0 at time $t = 2$ is $1/4$; the value of the game is also $1/4$.

We can simplify the case $n = 2$ by letting $p_1 + p_2 = 1$ (Isaacs's model—the target is not allowed to remain ar rest), which requires a minimax solution over three polynomials $[P(-2), P(0), P(+2)]$ of the second order. It is easily shown that $p_1 = (\sqrt{5} - 1)/2 = 0.618 \cdots$ and the probabilities of arriving at the three possible points are

$$P(-2) = p_1^2 = 0.382$$

$$P(0) = p_2 = 0.382$$

$$P(+2) = p_1 p_2 = 0.236$$

For $n = 3$, we must achieve a minimax solution of seven polynomials of the third order—a prodigious task.

An optimal strategy for the attacking plane P cannot be formulated. Rather, for any $\varepsilon > 0$, there exists a strategy yielding a hit probability $\gamma - \varepsilon$, where γ is the value of the game, but no strategy assuring a hit probability of exactly γ. This type of strategy is referred to as a *near-optimal* or an ε *strategy*.

Hide-and-seek games

There are many versions of pursuit and evasion or hide-and-seek games that involve a statistical element. Illustrative of the genre is the game where the evader E hides in one of n cells while the pursuer P searches some given number of cells. The process is continued until either P locates E or some preselected number of cells m has been searched without success; the payoff is, accordingly, positive to P or E. Optimal strategies dictate that both players at each move choose randomly with equal probability from the complete set of n cells. If P pays E one unit unless capture is effected by m

moves, the value of the game to E is $(1 - 1/n)^m$. Usually, however, restrictions are placed on the behavior of either P or E, or both. For example, if P is enjoined to search without repetition (that is, he may not return to a cell previously examined), it can be shown that if the payoff to E is any increasing function of the number of cells searched before capture, then E's best strategy is also never to return to a cell previously occupied.

Hide-and-seek games in a plane are generally solvable only for simple geometric figures. Two players, P and E, each simultaneously select a point within the prescribed geometry; E escapes if his point lies more than a specified distance from P's point. For example, let the playing geometry be a circle of unit radius and let P win if the points chosen lie within $1/2$ unit of each other. We can solve the game by constructing the circles of Fig. 9-7.

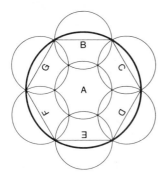

Fig. 9-7   Hide and seek in the unit circle

Within the circle of unit radius, a concentric circle of radius $1/2$ is drawn. The other six circles of radius $1/2$ are drawn with their centers on the midpoints of the chords of a hexagon inscribed within the unit circle. Evidently, if E plays by selecting at random one of the points $A, B, \ldots, G$, then P's best strategy is similarly to select one of these seven points at random. With these strategies, P will capture E with probability $1/7$.

If we define the game so that P is accorded a win if his point lies within a distance d of E's point, such that $1/2 \leq d < 1/\sqrt{2}$, then using the same strategies the value of the game to P is $(1 + \pi/\sin^{-1}d)^{-1}$.

A deceptively simple game of hide and seek, originally suggested by Melvin Dresher, has player A selecting an integer from the set of integers 1 to n (a region to hide) while player B guesses at A's integer. With each guess, B is given the information that the selected integer (if not guessed) is either higher or lower than the one guessed. The game continues until A's integer is identified by B, whence the payoff to A is one unit for each guess required minus the prize for guessing correctly.

Letting player A choose integer j, $1 \leq j \leq n$, with probability p_j, then a strategy for player B is an ordered set of the n integers denoted by $S_i = \{S_{ij}\}$, S_{ij} designating the number of the guess when j is selected. Determination of optimal strategies (that is, optimal probability distributions for player A and optimal search patterns for player B) involves highly complex procedures yet unsolved systematically by game theorists. However, Selmer Johnson has contributed several theorems relating to hiding and seeking strategies and has obtained solutions for $n \leq 11$.

It is evident that A's strategy should select integers close to the end points (1 and n) with greater frequency than integers near the center of the interval. Also, the probability distribution chosen by A is symmetrical about the center. That is,

$$p_j = p_{n-j+1}$$

For B's strategy, Johnson has proved two guiding theorems: (1) At each play B should guess an integer located inside the middle third of A's probability distribution on the current interval of uncertainty. (2) If, at a given play, B has located A's integer within the interval $k \leq j \leq m$ and strategy S_i dictates the next guess at r, below the median of A's frequency distribution on this interval, and if r is too small, a succeeding guess at $s > r$, then a necessary condition for the optimality of S_i is that

$$\sum_{k \leq j \leq r} p_j \leq \sum_{s \leq j \leq m} p_j$$

Some of the solutions computed by Johnson are presented as follows:

		p_1	p_2
$n = 2$:	S_1	1	2
	S_1	2	1

In this trivial example, $\{p_j\} = \{0.5, 0.5\}$ and there exists only a single strategy S_1 for B (in general, we designate a strategy S_i' to be that symmetric about the center to S_i; both are played with equal probability). The value of the game, and hence the equitable prize awarded to B for a correct guess, is 1.5 units (A receives one unit for each guess by B).

		p_1	p_2	p_1
$n = 3$:	S_1	2	1	2
	S_2	1	3	2

For this case, $\{p_j\} = \{0.4, 0.2, 0.4\}$, while B plays

$$\begin{pmatrix} S_1 & S_2 \\ 0.6 & 0.4 \end{pmatrix}$$

Thus B selects strategy S_1 with probability 0.6 (that is, B guesses the integer 2; if too high, he guesses 1, and if too low, 3). Since S_2 is not symmetrical, B actually plays S_2 with probability 0.2 and S_2' (2 3 1) with probability 0.2. The remaining two possible strategies (1 2 3) and (3 2 1) are dominated—we present here only undominated and nonzero-probability strategies. Value of the game is 1.8.

$n = 4$:

	p_1	p_2	p_2	p_1
S_1	2	1	3	2

Here $\{p_j\} = \{0.25, 0.25, 0.25, 0.25\}$. B, of course, plays S_1 with probability 0.5 and S_1' with probability 0.5. Value of the game is 2.

$n = 5$:

	p_1	p_2	p_3	p_2	p_1
S_1	2	3	1	3	2
S_2	2	1	3	2	3
S_3	2	1	4	3	2

Now A employs the probability distribution $\{p_j\} = \{5/18, 1/6, 1/9, 1/6, 5/18\}$ while B plays

$$\begin{pmatrix} S_1 & S_2 & S_3 \\ 4/9 & 4/9 & 1/9 \end{pmatrix}$$

Strategies S_2 and S_3 are shared with S_2' and S_3'. Value of the game is 20/9.

At the present time, solutions have not been computed for games with $n \geq 12$. The difficulties can be appreciated from the fact that the number of B's pure strategies for $n = 12$ is 208,012 (the great majority of which are dominated).

A variant of this hide-and-seek game permits player A to change his selected integer just prior to B's forthcoming guess, remaining, of course, within the bounds defined by B's previous guesses. Player B's strategy in this game is equivalent to the case wherein A's chosen integer remains unchanged. Another variant permits A to move his integer after B's guess.

Such a game is trivial: B guesses so as to bisect, as nearly as possible, the region containing A's integer. The value of this game is $1 + \lceil \log_2 n \rceil$, where $\lceil x \rceil$ defines the smallest integer not less than x.

A lexicographic adaptation of the hide-and-seek principle is the word game, Convergence in Webster.[†] Player A constructs an English sentence of four words, which must be structurally (albeit not necessarily semantically) sound. Player B then composes four-word trial sentences as guesses. Following a guess, A informs B whether each trial word is correct or whether it should be moved forward or backward in lexicographic order to approach the correct corresponding word. The payoff to A is the number of guesses required to determine all four words. Because of the interdependence of the four words, an average game entails 13 or 14 guesses.

Dueling

Dueling games, a subset of those games whose key element is timing, constitute another category with interesting ramifications; such games were first conceived and analyzed by Blackwell and Girschick. Duels can be either *noisy* or *silent*. In the former case, a player is aware of the moment his opponent has fired. Duels can also be characterized by the number of bullets each player has at his disposal and the constraints, if any, on the firing rate. Further, the bullets may exist only in a probabilistic sense.

NOISY DUEL, SINGLE BULLET EACH

In its simplest form, a duel consists of two players, A and B, who face each other at a distance X_0 at time t_0 and approach each other at a linear rate until $X = 0$ at time t_f. Each player possesses a single bullet and an accuracy $p(t)$; that is, $p_a(t)$ and $p_b(t)$ are the probabilities that A and B, respectively, will hit his opponent when firing at time t. It is presumed that $p(t)$ is monotonically increasing to a value of unity at t_f. Thus, if one player fires at his opponent at time $t < t_f$ and misses, the opponent's best course is then to wait until time t_f, thereby securing a sure kill. In general, if player A fires at time $t_a, t_0 \leq t_a \leq t_f$, and B fires at time $t_b, t_0 \leq t_b \leq t_f$, the payoff to A, $f(T)$, can be written in the form

$$f(T) = \begin{cases} p_a(T) - [1 - p_a(T)] = 2p_a(T) - 1, & \text{if } T = t_a < t_b \\ -p_b(T) + [1 - p_b(T)] = 1 - 2p_b(T), & \text{if } T = t_b < t_a \\ p_a(T) - p_b(T), & \text{if } T = t_a = t_b \end{cases} \qquad 9\text{-}17$$

[†] In his article "Games of Identification or Convergence," E. N. Gilbert attributes the invention of Convergence in Webster to Hassler Whitney.

where $T = \min(t_a, t_b)$. It is simple to show that the three forms of Eq. 9-17 take on equal values when

$$p_a(T) + p_b(T) = 1 \qquad\qquad 9\text{-}18$$

Hence, Eq. 9-18 describes a minimax solution to the duel, and both players should fire simultaneously at this value of t (it is assumed that the value of killing an opponent is unity while the value of being killed is -1). The value γ of the game is given by

$$\gamma = p_a(T) - p_b(T)$$

If the two duellists are equally skilled, they should fire when their accuracies reach 0.5; the value of such a game is, of course, zero.

A generalization of the simple duel described by Blackwell involves accuracy functions $p(t)$ not necessarily monotonic. If we denote the maximum value of the accuracy functions in the interval (T, t_f) as

$$m_a(T) = \max p_a(T), \qquad T \leq t \leq t_f$$

$$m_b(T) = \max p_b(T), \qquad T \leq t \leq \ \leq t_f$$

the payoff to A assumes the form

$$f(T) = \begin{cases} p_a(T) - [1 - p_a(T)]m_b(T), & \text{if } T = t_a < t_b \\ -p_b(T) + [1 - p_b(T)]m_a(T), & \text{if } T = t_b < t_a \\ p_a(T) - p_b(T), & \text{if } T = t_a = t_b \end{cases}$$

General solutions ensuring the game value can be computed. Because of the nonmonotonic character of $p(t)$, however, the corresponding strategies are not necessarily optimum if the opponent deviates from his indicated strategy.

NOISY DUEL, MANY BULLETS; PROBABILISTIC BULLETS

If the two duellists possess equal accuracy functions $p(t)$, but a different number of bullets, their optimal strategies are immediately apparent. Specifically, if player A is equipped with $b_a(t)$ bullets and player B with $b_b(t) \leq b_a(t)$ bullets, an optimal strategy for A (and also for B, if his number of bullets matches that of A) consists of firing a bullet when

$$p(t) = [b_a(t) + b_b(t)]^{-1} \qquad\qquad 9\text{-}19$$

If B is accorded fewer bullets, he should shoot only after A's first firing time and then only if A has not fired. The value γ of the game is expressed by

$$\gamma = \frac{b_a(t_0) - b_b(t_0)}{b_a(t_0) + b_b(t_0)} \qquad\qquad 9\text{-}20$$

where t_0 designates the starting time of the duel.

As an example, if A is initially furnished three bullets and B two bullets, then A should pull the trigger once when the accuracy function reaches the value $p(t) = 1/5$, as indicated by Eq. 9-19. If A misses, then both A and B fire one shot when $p(t) = 1/4$, and if both miss, the last bullets should be discharged simultaneously when $p(t) = 1/2$. Value of the game, from Eq. 9-20, is 1/5 to player A.

Blackwell and Girschick have considered the case of two duellists with equal accuracy, where each has only a probability of possessing a bullet. If P_1 is the probability that player A possesses a bullet and P_2 the probability that B possesses a bullet, they have shown that, for $P_1 > P_2$, player A should fire with the density

$$f(T) = \frac{1 - P_2}{2P_2[(2T/t_f) - 1]^{\frac{3}{2}}}, \qquad \frac{(1 + P_2^2)t_f}{(1 + P_2)^2} \le T \le t_f$$

a fraction Γ of the time and should fire at time t_f the remaining fraction $1 - \Gamma$ of the time, where

$$\Gamma = \frac{P_2(1 + P_1)}{P_1(1 + P_2)}$$

It should be noted that the moment at which A fires is a function only of his opponent's probability of possessing a bullet, while the percentage of the time that he fires at that moment is a function of both P_1 and P_2. To obtain the optimum strategy for the case where $P_2 > P_1$, we simply interchange P_1 and P_2. The value of the game to player A is

$$\frac{P_1 - P_2}{1 + \min(P_1, P_2)}$$

SILENT DUELS

In the duels described above, each player is immediately informed of the event that his opponent has fired. Such duels are characterized as *noisy*. An alternative is to equip each gun with a silencer so that neither player is aware of his opponent's moment of firing (unless, of course, the opponent is successful, in which case the game is over and the information academic). Such duels are characterized as *silent*. In a silent duel, if players A and B possess, respectively, accuracy functions p_a and p_b, monotonically increasing from zero to unity over the interval t_0 to t_f, and if player A chooses to fire at time t_a while B elects to fire at time t_b, the value of the game is given by

$$\gamma(t_a, t_b) = p_a(t_a) - p_b(t_b) + \delta p_a(t_a)p_b(t_b) \qquad\qquad 9\text{-}21$$

where

$$\delta = \begin{cases} 1, & \text{if } t_a < t_b \\ -1, & \text{if } t_b < t_a \\ 0, & \text{if } t_a = t_b \end{cases} \qquad\qquad 9\text{-}22$$

From Eqs. 9-21 and 9-22 we can derive optimal strategies for the two duellists. Assuming that A and B employ firing densities $f(t_a)$ and $f(t_b)$, respectively, such that $mt_f \leq t_a, t_b \leq t_f$, where m is a positive number less than unity, we can show that

$$f(t_a) = \left[\frac{1}{p_a(mt_f)} + \frac{1}{p_a(t_f)}\right]\frac{dp_b(t_a)/dt_a}{p_b^2(t_a)p_a(t_a)} \qquad\qquad 9\text{-}23$$

and

$$f(t_b) = \left[\frac{1}{p_a(mt_f)} + \frac{1}{p_a(t_f)}\right]\frac{dp_a(t_b)/dt_b}{p_a^2(t_b)p_b(t_b)} \qquad\qquad 9\text{-}24$$

The equations

$$\phi(mt_f) = \frac{1}{p_b(mt_f)} + \frac{1}{p_b(t_f)}$$

and

$$\theta(mt_f) = \frac{1}{p_a(mt_f)} + \frac{1}{p_a(t_f)}$$

exhibit unique solutions $m_1 t_f$ and $m_2 t_f$, where $0 \leq m_1, m_2 \leq 1$. For the case $m_1 = m_2$, the optimal strategy for player A is to apply the firing density $f(t_a)$ specified by Eq. 9-23, $m_1 t_f \leq t_a \leq t_f$, while player B should follow the density $f(t_b)$ indicated by Eq. 9-24, $m_1 t_f \leq t_b \leq t_f$. For $m_1 > m_2$, the optimal strategy dictates that A employs the density $f(t_a)$, $m_1 t_f \leq t_a \leq t_f$, and B employs the density $f(t_b)$ a fraction Γ of the time and fires at t_f the remaining fraction $1 - \Gamma$ of the time, where

$$\Gamma = \left\{ 1 - \frac{p_a(t_f)p_a(m_1 t_f)\,\theta(m_1 t_f) - p_a(m_1 t_f) - p_a(t_f)}{p_a(t_f)p_a(m_1 t_f)\,\theta(m_1 t_f)[p_b(t_f) + 1]} \right\}^{-1}$$

Finally, for $m_2 > m_1$, the optimal strategy for player B is to subscribe steadfastly to the density $f(t_b)$, $m_2 t_f \le t_b \le t_f$, while A should employ $f(t_a)$, $m_2 t_f \le t_a \le t_f$, a fraction Γ of the time and should fire at t_f the remaining fraction $1 - \Gamma$ of the time, where

$$\Gamma = \left\{ 1 + \frac{p_b(t_f) + p_b(m_2 t_f) - p_b(t_f)p_b(m_2 t_f)\,\phi(m_2 t_f)}{p_b(t_f)p_b(m_2 t_f)\,\phi(m_2 t_f)[p_a(t_f) + 1]} \right\}^{-1}$$

The value γ of the game is given by

$$\gamma = \begin{cases} \dfrac{p_b(t_f) - p_b(m_1 t_f) - 2p_b(t_f)p_b(m_1 t_f)}{p_b(t_f) + p_b(m_1 t_f)}, & \text{if } m_1 > m_2 \\[2ex] \dfrac{p_a(m_2 t_f) - p_a(t_f) + 2p_a(t_f)p_a(m_2 t_f)}{p_a(t_f) + p_a(m_2 t_f)}, & \text{if } m_2 > m_1 \end{cases}$$

There are other variants of dueling games that can be explored. For example, we might assign a probability that a hit is not lethal, but merely incapacitates the opponent so that his firing power is reduced; we might mix live ammunition with blanks, according to some probability distribution; we might allow several opponents, each concerned with his own survival or as a selfless member of a team (in the general multiple duel, m contestants on one side face n on the other—the winning side is that which has eliminated all opposition); or we might hamper one player by forcing him to play a silent duel while his opponent is accorded the ears to play a noisy duel.

Recent studies of dueling games have considered the case where one contestant is supplied with both noisy and silent bullets which are fired in a prescribed order. Several extensions of this type of duel are immediately apparent. An interesting variant, neither noisy nor silent, is the machine-gun duel, a game that introduces the notion of firing rate. Two players are planted a fixed distance apart and are supplied with machine guns. The weapon assigned to player A possesses a single-shot hit probability of P_A and fires at a rate of R_A shots per unit time; that accorded player B is characterized by a single-shot effectiveness P_B and a firing rate of R_B

shots per unit time. Such a duel has been analyzed by A. D. Groves. A game that we propose to the interested reader is the "Fire and Flee" duel. In this version each player is given n bullets, and after observing that some fraction of them have been discharged without felling his opponent, he may exercise the option to flee the scene, thereby altering his opponent's monotonic accuracy function and combining the duel with elements of a pursuit game.

TRUELS

The field of three-person games has only recently been explored by game theorists because of the inordinate complexities that usually arise. Certain "trueling" games, however, are amenable to at least partial analysis. Consider, for example, the simple truel (we herewith coin the obvious nomenclature) with three players A, B, and C, each equipped with a pistol and an arbitrarily large supply of ammunition. For his turn, each player may fire one bullet at either of his opponents (if two are yet alive) or into the air. The game proceeds until either a single truelist remains or three successive shots are fired into the air. Initially, the players select their own accuracy functions, a, b, and c, respectively, which are announced simultaneously. An equitable random device is then used to determine a revolving order of firing. We assign a game value of $+1$, which is awarded to the survivor (if all the truelists survive, each receives $1/3$).

With no loss of generality, we can designate player A as the owner of the highest accuracy function, B as the second most skilled player, and C as the least skilled, so that $a \geq b \geq c$. Assuming that no player selects an accuracy less than 0.5, it is apparent that player C never fires at either opponent if both remain (it is to C's advantage to fire into the air until one adversary eliminates the other, thereby affording C first shot in the resulting duel). Thus, of the six possible firing echelons, only two are distinct: that in which A precedes B and that in which B precedes A. In either case, A fires at B (no one fires at C first, since he poses the lesser threat) if his mathematical expectation therewith produces a value of $1/3$ or greater; otherwise, he fires into the air. Player B must inquire as to A's expectation from firing (when A precedes B) and if it exceeds $1/3$, B fires at A regardless of his own expectation. The winner of the A versus B duel, if it occurs, then engages player C to resolve the truel.

The expectation $E(A)$ of player A equals the probability $P(A)$ of that player surviving, which equals the probability $P(A \rightarrow B)$ that A kills B times the probability $P(A \rightarrow C | A \rightarrow B)$ that A kills C, given that A has first dispatched B. We can readily formulate these values. If A precedes B in the order of firing,

$$E(A) = P(A) = P(A \to B)P(A \to C|A \to B)$$

$$= a \sum_{i=0}^{\infty} [(1 - a)(1 - c)]^i \cdot a(1 - c) \sum_{i=0}^{\infty} [(1 - a)(1 - c)]^i$$

$$= \frac{a}{a + b - ab} \cdot \frac{a(1 - c)}{a + c - ac} = \frac{a^2(1 - c)}{(a + b - ab)(a + c - ac)} \qquad 9\text{-}25$$

Similarly,

$$E(B) = P(B) = P(B \to A)P(B \to C|B \to A)$$

$$= \frac{b^2(1 - a)(1 - c)}{(a + b - ab)(b + c - bc)} \qquad 9\text{-}26$$

$$E(C) = P(C) = P(C \to A|A \to B) + P(C \to B|B \to A)$$

$$= \frac{ac}{(a + c - ac)(a + b - ab)} + \frac{bc(1 - a)}{(a + b - ab)(b + c - bc)} \qquad 9\text{-}27$$

If B precedes A in the order of firing,

$$E(A) = P(A) = \frac{a^2(1 - b)(1 - c)}{(a + b - ab)(a + c - ac)} \qquad 9\text{-}28$$

$$E(B) = P(B) = \frac{b^2(1 - c)}{(a + b - ab)(b + c - bc)} \qquad 9\text{-}29$$

$$E(C) = P(C) = \frac{bc}{(a + b - ab)(b + c - bc)}$$

$$+ \frac{ac(1 - b)}{(a + b - ab)(a + c - ac)} \qquad 9\text{-}30$$

Initially, player A's game expectation is given by the average of Eqs. 9-25 and 9-28, B's expectation by the average of Eqs. 9-26 and 9-29, and C's expectation by the average of Eqs. 9-27 and 9-30. App. Table L tabulates these a priori expectations for values of a, b, and c between 0.50 and 1.00 (quantized to 0.05 steps) such that the truel is active; for those values not listed, all three players fire into the air and the game is a draw—of value 1/3 to each truelist.

It is apparent from Table L that player B finds himself in the most unenviable position. Each player strives to choose an accuracy function that is (1) the highest possible lowest value of the three accuracies, or (2) the highest accuracy—that is, 1.00. To be caught in the middle is anathema. As an illustration, let the three players select accuracies $a = 1.00$, $b = 0.75$, and $c = 0.50$, respectively. If A wins a shooting position prior to B's, he eliminates B with unity probability and then is shot at by C; if C misses (probability $1/2$), A dispatches C on the next round. Hence $P(A) = 0.50$, $P(B) = 0$, and $P(C) = 0.50$. If B is selected to shoot first, he calculates $P(A)$ as 0.50, given A's turn; hence he must fire at A although his expectation remains less than $1/3$. If he is successful, he competes with C until but one player survives, with C shooting first; if he misses (probability $1/4$), he is eliminated by A, who then engages C to resolve the truel. Player C, if awarded first shot, sends it into the air, thereby guaranteeing himself the first opportunity to eliminate the survivor of the A versus B contest. Equations 9-28, 9-29, and 9-30 yield $P(A) = 1/8$, $P(B) = 9/28$, and $P(C) = 31/56$. Thus, the a priori expectations of the three players with these accuracy functions are

$$E(A) = \frac{(1/2 + 1/8)}{2} = \frac{5}{16}$$

$$E(B) = \frac{(0 + 9/28)}{2} = \frac{9}{56}$$

$$E(C) = \frac{(1/2 + 31/56)}{2} = \frac{59}{112}$$

Even for this elementary truel, to compute the optimal mixed strategies from the array of expectations shown in Table L involves overwhelming difficulties. Further, the definition of rational behavior is not immediately apparent in this type of 3-sided competition and thus "optimal" strategy is not clearly defined. As with most multiperson multimove games, this truel may not enjoy a unique, noncooperative equilibrium point (see Chapter 2). We therefore introduce two simplifications, which permit a complete description of the ensuing game: (1) each player is supplied with but a single bullet, which he may fire at another player or into the air; (2) the order of firing is announced *before* the accuracy functions are chosen. It is now more convenient to designate the notation A, B, and C as defining the players in their order of firing (rather than by accuracy functions); thus A fires first, B second, and C third. Evidently, if A fires at either adversary he selects as his target B or C, as $b > c$ or $c > b$. Player B always shoots at C if the latter still survives or at A otherwise. Player C, if not eliminated before his turn, fires at A or B equiprobably if both remain

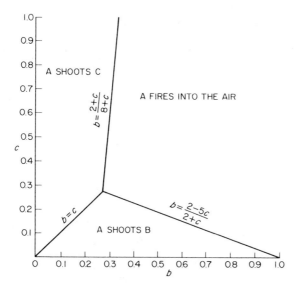

Fig. 9-8   A truel firing diagram

(independent of their accuracy functions) or at A if B has been killed.

It is apparent that player A always adopts the role of a perfect marksman ($a = 1.00$). By killing B or C, his expectation $E_s(A)$ becomes

$$E_s(A) = \frac{1}{2}\max(1 - b, 1 - c)$$

since his game value is 1/2 if the remaining player misses and 0 otherwise [probability $\min(b, c)$]. By shooting into the air, A receives value 1/2 with probability $b + (c/2)(1 - b)$, value 0 with probability $(c/2)(1 - b)$, and value 1/3 with probability $(1 - b)(1 - c)$. His expectation $E_n(A)$ in this case is therefore given by

$$E_n(A) = \frac{1}{12}(2b - c + bc + 4)$$

(we assume that C holds no grudges in deciding at whom he shoots). Thus, A eliminates that opponent owning the higher accuracy function whenever $E_s(A) > E_n(A)$. The values of b and c whereby this condition holds are indicated in Fig. 9-8.

The overriding consideration for both B and C is that each wishes to select an accuracy function smaller than the other, thus diverting the fire of A if (b, c) lies within A's firing region. From C's viewpoint, lesser accuracies are even more attractive, since he must still worry over B's shot if A fires into the air. Payoffs and conditional expectations for each action are shown in Table 9-3—the notation A↑ signifies that A fires into the air and B × C denotes that B shoots at but misses C. From this figure we can write for $E(B|A\uparrow)$, B's expectation, given that A fires into the air,

$$E(B|A\uparrow) = \frac{1}{12}(4b + c - bc + 2) \qquad\qquad 9\text{-}31$$

Also

$$E(C|A\uparrow) = \frac{1}{6}(2c - b - 2bc + 1) \qquad\qquad 9\text{-}32$$

If collusion were permitted, or were mutually advantageous, between B and C, Eqs. 9-31 and 9-32 indicate that $b = 1/3$ and $c = 1.00$ result in an equitable game $[E(A) = E(B) = E(C)]$. However, the point $(b, c) = (1/3, 1)$ does not represent an equilibrium point, since if either B or C deviates from this point by lowering his accuracy, the concomitant expectation increases (since A then fires at the other player). Consequently, the only "stable" point for players B and C arises from the selection $b = c = 0$. Thus, B and C declare themselves totally ineffective and the value of the truel is 1/2 to A and 1/4 to B and C. This solution does not preclude the existence of other equilibrium points (for example, those involving "bluffing" or "deterring"). Since it is possible here for two players to gain even by nonexplicit cooperation and lose by individual action, this truel constitutes a nonzero-sum game. The theory of games has yet to develop a completely satisfactory methodology for the solution of cooperative games.

To effect a yet more complex and challenging truel, we can void the simplification that each player knows his order of firing *ab initio*.

Truels constitute a unique set of games in that all participants in the truel may maximize their expected payoffs by not firing. This situation does not pertain in duels—where one person's gain is another's loss—or in polyuels with four or more persons. In the latter instances, persons can always be eliminated with advantage until the game is reduced to a truel.

Miscellaneous statistical games

PARKING-PLACE PROBLEMS

Consider that we are driving our one-dimensional automobile along a line toward a goal G. The line is divided uniformly into parking places, which we are allowed to examine, in sequence, for a possible vacancy. Empty spaces occur independently with probability p, and upon accepting one, we

TABLE 9-3 Truel Payoffs and Conditional Expectations

Actions	Payoffs A	B	C	Conditional (to A's action) Probability of Occurrence	$E(A)$	Conditional Expectations $E(B)$	$E(C)$
A↑ B↑C	$\frac{1}{2}$	$\frac{1}{2}$	0	b	$b/2$	$b/2$	0
A↑ B×C C↑→A	0	$\frac{1}{2}$	$\frac{1}{2}$	$(c/2)(1-b)$	0	$(c/4)(1-b)$	$(c/4)(1-b)$
A↑ B×C C×→A or C×B	$\frac{1}{3}$	$\frac{1}{3}$	$\frac{1}{3}$	$(1/2)(1-b)(1-c)$	$(1/6)(1-b)(1-c)$	$(1/6)(1-b)(1-c)$	$(1/6)(1-b)(1-c)$
A↑ B×C↑→B	$\frac{1}{2}$	0	$\frac{1}{2}$	$(c/2)(1-b)$	$(c/4)(1-b)$	0	$(c/4)(1-b)$
A→B C↑→A	0	0	1	c	0	0	c
A→B C×→A	$\frac{1}{2}$	0	$\frac{1}{2}$	$1-c$	$(1/2)(1-c)$	0	$(1/2)(1-c)$
A→C B↑→A	0	1	0	b	0	b	0
A→C B×→A	$\frac{1}{2}$	$\frac{1}{2}$	0	$1-b$	$(1/2)(1-b)$	$(1/2)(1-b)$	0

are penalized k units, where there are k parking places remaining to the goal. If we reach the goal without having parked, we are penalized a total of N units. Thus, as we drive along and observe an empty spot $k + 1$ places from G, we may accept it with a payment k or continue closer to G with an expected payment E of

$$
\begin{aligned}
E &= \sum_{i=1}^{k} p(1 - p)^{k-i}(i - 1) + (1 - p)^k N \\
&= \frac{kp - 1 + (1 - p)^k}{p} + (1 - p)^k N
\end{aligned}
\qquad 9\text{-}33
$$

The critical value of k, designated by k_c, occurs for $E = k$; that is,

$$
k_c = \frac{-\log(1 + pN)}{\log(1 - p)}
$$

We accept a parking spot whenever $k < k_c$; otherwise, we continue driving toward G. As a numerical example, if $p = 1/10$ and $N = 100$, then $k_c = 22.3$. We would, accordingly, accept the first empty spot within 23 places of the goal.

In general, if empty spaces occur according to some probability distribution p_i as a function of their distance from the goal (rather than independently with constant probability), the expected payment from a strategy of rejecting the $(k + 1)$st place and accepting the next available one is

$$
E = \sum_{i=1}^{k} p_i(i - 1) \prod_{j=1}^{k-i} (1 - p_{i+j}) + \prod_{j=1}^{k} (1 - p_j)N
\qquad 9\text{-}34
$$

Equation 9-34 reduces to Eq. 9-33 when all values of p_i are equated.

Another facet of one-dimensional parking lots is the expected number of cars $E(n)$ of unit length that can be parked in a lot of length n if the cars are parked randomly (with uniform distribution) in the available space. To formulate $E(n)$, we observe that the probability that the rear end of the first car to be parked lies in the interval $(t, t + dt)$ is $dt/(n - 1)$ for $0 \leq t \leq n - 1$. The length of the parking lot can thence be decomposed into the two intervals $(0, t)$ and $(t + 1, n)$, in which the expected number of cars are designated by $E(t)$ and $E(n - t - 1)$, respectively. Integrating t over $(0, n - 1)$ results in the equation

$$
E(n) = 1 + \frac{2}{n - 1} \int_0^{n-1} E(t)\, dt, \qquad n > 1
$$

We would expect intuitively that $E(n)$ is directly proportional to n, and indeed it can be shown that $E(n) \sim cn$ as $n \to \infty$, where

$$c = \int_0^\infty \exp\left\{-2\int_0^t \frac{1 - e^{-u}}{u} \, du\right\} dt = 0.748 \cdots$$

Thus, approximately 1/4 of the lot is wasted with random parking.

ELIMINATION AND ROUND-ROBIN TOURNAMENTS

Of the various procedures for selecting a winner from among many contestants, perhaps the most common is the single elimination, or knock-out, tournament. The players are matched pairwise for a single game and only the winners of each round advance to the succeeding round. A particular configuration for matching the contestants is known as a draw. With 2^n players in the tournament, there are $\binom{2^n}{2^{n-1}}/2$ ways of setting up the first round and the total number of draws is, therefore,

$$\prod_{i=2}^n \left[\frac{\binom{2^i}{2^{i-1}}}{2}\right]^{n-i+1} = \frac{2^n!}{2^{2^n-1}}$$

The tournament comprises $2^n - 1$ games with 2^{2^n-1} possible outcomes for each draw (total number of outcomes for all draws is, of course, $2^n!$).

The probability that a given player wins the tournament following a random draw is simply his probability of winning n matches in succession averaged over all possible draws. Let p_{ij} be the pairwise win probability that the ith player defeats the jth player in a single trial and as an illustration consider a tournament of eight players ($n = 3$) possessing the set of pairwise win probabilities shown in Table 9–4. Averaging over the 315 draws, we

TABLE 9-4   Illustrative Set of Pairwise Win Probabilities

		\$j\$th player						
		1	2	3	4	5	6	7	8
---	---	---	---	---	---	---	---	---	---
	1		0.55	0.60	0.65	0.70	0.75	0.80	0.85
	2	0.45		0.55	0.60	0.65	0.70	0.75	0.80
	3	0.40	0.45		0.55	0.60	0.65	0.70	0.75
ith player	4	0.35	0.40	0.45		0.55	0.60	0.65	0.70
	5	0.30	0.35	0.40	0.45		0.55	0.60	0.65
	6	0.25	0.30	0.35	0.40	0.45		0.55	0.60
	7	0.20	0.25	0.30	0.35	0.40	0.45		0.55
	8	0.15	0.20	0.25	0.30	0.35	0.40	0.45	

compute the probabilities $P(i)$ that the ith player wins the tournament:

$$P_i = \frac{1}{315} \sum_{\substack{j \\ i \neq j \neq k \neq m}} \sum_{k < m} \left[p_{ij}(p_{ik}p_{km} + p_{im}p_{mk}) \sum_{\substack{n \\ n \neq r \neq s \neq t \\ \neq i \neq j \neq k \neq m}} \sum_{r} \sum_{s < t} p_{in}p_{nr}(p_{ns}p_{st} + p_{nt}p_{ts}) \right]$$

9-35

Evaluating Eq. 9-35 for each i, using the sample pairwise win probabilities, the results are listed in the first column of Table 9-5.

TABLE 9-5   Probability of a Tournament Win

	Single Elimination Random Draw	Single Elimination Seeded Draw	Single Elimination With Replication Random Draw
$P(1)$	0.307	0.351	0.388
$P(2)$	0.226	0.240	0.255
$P(3)$	0.164	0.160	0.161
$P(4)$	0.116	0.103	0.097
$P(5)$	0.081	0.066	0.055
$P(6)$	0.054	0.042	0.027
$P(7)$	0.034	0.025	0.013
$P(8)$	0.020	0.013	0.005

More often, the draw for a tournament is not selected at random but is designed to favor the better players. Such an arrangement, known as a *seeded* draw, is sketched in Fig. 9-9. With the same set of pairwise win probabilities, the probabilities $P(i)$ that the ith player emerges victorious become those shown in the second column of Table 9-5. As expected, the better players gain increased chances of winning and the poorer players decreased chances.

Fig. 9-9   The seeded draw.

We can also compute the probability of the two best players entering the finals as 0.128 for a random draw and 0.258 for the seeded draw. This difference accounts for the attractiveness of the seeded draw in many professional sports (such as tennis).

If the number of players in a tournament is not exactly 2^n, then a filling number of pseudo players are designated and awarded win probabilities of zero. Any real player is given a win probability of unity against a pseudo player and is said to have a "bye." When i and j are both pseudo players, $p_{ij} = p_{ji} = 0$ (thus all "byes" are confined to the first round).

One method of improving the single elimination tournament (insofar as favoring the better players) consists of adding replication to each match. With this procedure each pair of players competes until one has won m games out of a possible $2m - 1$. If p_{ij} is the probability that i defeats j in a single contest, the probability q_{ij} that i wins the best m out of a possible $2m - 1$ is

$$q_{ij} = p_{ij}^m \sum_{k=0}^{m-1} \binom{n + k - 1}{k} p_{ji}^k$$

This type of tournament affords yet further advantage to the better players since we can show that, for $p_{ij} \geq 1/2$, $q_{ij} \geq p_{ij}$. Letting each competition be resolved by the best two out of three matches, and with our illustrative set of (single-trial) pairwise win probabilities (Table 9-4), the distribution of final win probabilities for each player is that of the third column of Table 9-5. The extent to which superior players are favored by replication (or seeded draws) is, of course, strongly dependent upon the particular pairwise win probabilities of the competing players.

Double elimination, or double knockout, tournaments also constitute a common format for handling a large number of competitors. These tournaments are usually arranged so that 1/4 of the contestants are eliminated at each round following the first.

Another format is the serial elimination tournament—characterized as a single elimination tournament with 2^n players followed by a second single elimination playoff among the winner and those n players beaten by the winner. If the winner does not also win the playoff, an additional game between the original winner and the playoff winner determines the ultimate victor. Serial elimination tournaments with replication can, of course, also be conducted. These tournaments have been investigated by D. T. Searls and by W. A. Glenn.

Round-robin procedures (each player vies against every other player a fixed number of times) are not generally applicable as elimination tournaments. However, the round-robin does exhibit some elimination characteristics. For example, in a tournament of four players wherein each player contends once against each adversary, six games are held with four possible outcomes of the final standings:

| | Games won by player | | | |
	A	B	C	D
1.	3	2	1	0
2.	3	1	1	1
3.	2	2	2	0
4.	2	2	1	1

Outcomes

The first two outcomes declare player A the winner; the third and fourth outcomes eliminate one and two players, respectively, and require further competition. With five players, a single round-robin procedure may produce any of nine outcomes, five of which uniquely proclaim a winner; with six players, 13 of a possible 22 outcomes designate a winner; a round-robin of seven players admits of 59 possible outcomes, 35 of which specify a winner; and with eight players, there are 100 such outcomes of a possible 167.

Obviously the probability of each outcome is a function of the players' pairwise win probabilities. If $p_{ij} = p_{ji} = 1/2$ for all i and j, the single round-robin tournament with four players has the following distribution of outcomes:

P(Outcome 1) $= 3/8$

P(Outcome 2) $= 1/8$

P(Outcome 3) $= 1/8$

P(Outcome 4) $= 3/8$

Hence the probability p of determining a winner in this four-player tournament is 0.5; with five players, $p = 0.586$; with six players, $p = 0.627$; a seven-player round-robin is uniquely resolved with probability $p = 0.581$; and with eight evenly matched players, $p = 0.634$. As the number of players increases indefinitely, the probability of obtaining a unique outcome approaches unity.

If one player has a high win probability against each of his adversaries, his probability of winning the tournament is generally greater from a round-robin than from a single elimination procedure.

Inquizition

Solutions to the following statistical problems are perched beyond the reaches of all but the most agile game theorists. In each case, only partial analysis can be readily achieved.

1. *The Harem-staffing Problem.* From a supply of n candidates, the Sultan wishes to select m girls for his harem. The n aspirants are paraded one by one before the Sultan, each being either selected or rejected. Once rejected, a girl cannot be recalled. Since m nymphs *must* be chosen, the final few may be forced upon the Sultan to complete the seraglio complement. A preference ordering of the girls is assumed, although not known a priori. What function of the girls' desirability should the Sultan adopt as his objective, and what is his concomitant strategy? Note: For $m = 1$, assuming that the Sultan wishes to maximize his probability of engaging the best maiden—he assigns a utility of 1 to this girl and 0 to all others—show that his optimal strategy consists of rejecting the first n/e candidates (for large n) and then selecting the first girl who exceeds the best of that sample; if no better one appears, he is stuck with the final girl. Show also that his expected utility for this objective is approximately e^{-1} for large n.

Rather than maximizing the probability of acquiring the best girl(s) regardless of the consequences, the Sultan may elect to minimize the absolute rank(s) of the girl(s) he chooses. Show that for any n however large and $m = 1$, a strategy exists for which the expected absolute rank of the girl chosen is less than 4.

2. *Goofspiel or GOPS* (Game Of Pure Strategy). Each of two players is given a set of integers 1 through N (let $N = 13$ for mechanization with playing cards). A third set of integers 1 through N constitutes the game objective. For a move, an integer from the game set is exposed, and the players bid for its capture by simultaneously playing one of the (remaining) integers from their personal sets, the higher number played winning the exposed integer; the event of a tie is resolved by the subsequent move. Show that if one player adopts the strategy of selecting his playing integer according to a uniform distribution, the second player can achieve a positive expectation.

3. *Three-Person Battle.* Each of three players is given a set of integers 1 through N. For a move, each player selects one of his (remaining) integers, and plays it simultaneously. If two players tie (by exposing identical integers), the third player wins that move and captures those numbers played by his two adversaries; if all three players tie, that tie is resolved by the subsequent move. After all N moves, that player whose collection of integers totals the greatest number [of $3N(N + 1)/2$] wins the game. What strategic principle should be followed by the players?

4. *Martini Golf.* The object of the game of golf is to impel a small white ball into a slightly larger hole with a minimum number of strokes delivered by means of a set of specialized clubs. We designate by $p_a(n)$ the probability that player A requires n strokes for a given hole; $p_b(n)$ represents player B's probability distribution for scoring n strokes. Whenever a player wins a hole (by using less strokes than his opponent), he must consume one martini. After j martinis, player A's probability distribution $p_a^j(n)$ of holing out in n strokes becomes

$$p_a^j(n) = p_a(n - j)$$

and, similarly,

$$p_b^j(n) = p_b(n - j)$$

Compute the probability that player A has taken less strokes after a round of 18 holes. If one player is permitted to add strokes deliberately, and the lower score on each hole wins one unit while the lower final score wins m units, what strategy should he follow to maximize his expected gain?

Suggested references

ALEXANDER, S. S., "Price Movements in Speculative Markets: Trends or Random Walks," *Industrial Management Rev.*, **2** (1961).

ANCKER, C. J., "Stochastic Duels With Limited Ammunition Supply," *Operations Research*, **12**, No. 1 (January–February, 1964), pp. 38–50.

ANTOSIEWICZ, H. A., "Analytic Study of War Games," *Naval Research Logistics Quarterly*, **2**, No. 3 (September, 1955), pp. 181–208.

ARVESEN, JAMES N., and BERNARD ROSNER, "Optimal Pari-Mutuel Wagering," Mimeograph Series # 250, Dep. of Statistics, Purdue Univ., Indiana, February, 1971.

BACHELIER, LOUIS, *Théorie de la Spéculation*, Gauthier-Villars, Paris, 1900.

BLACK, F., and M. SCHOLES, "The Pricing of Options and Corporate Liabilities," *J. Political Economy* (May–June, 1973), pp. 637–654.

BLACK, F., and M. SCHOLES, "The Valuation of Option Contracts and a Test of Market Efficiency," *J. Finance* (May, 1972), pp. 399–417.

BLACKETT, D. W., "Some Blotto Games," *Naval Research Logistics Quarterly*, 1, No. 1 (March, 1954), pp. 55–60.

BLACKWELL, DAVID, "On Multi-Component Attrition Games," *Naval Research Logistics Quarterly*, 1, No. 3 (September, 1954), pp. 210–216.

BLACKWELL, DAVID, and M. A. GIRSHICK, "A Loud Duel With Equal Accuracy Where Each Duellist Has Only a Probability of Possessing a Bullet," Research Memorandum RM-219, The RAND Corporation, Santa Monica, California, Aug. 18, 1949.

BOREL, EMILE, *Les Probabilités et la Vie*, Presses Universitaires de France, Paris, 1943.

BROWN, RICHARD H., "A Stochastic Analysis of Lanchester's Theory of Combat," Technical Memorandum ORD-T-323, Operations Research Office, The Johns Hopkins University, Baltimore, Maryland, AD-82944, December, 1955.

BROWN, RICHARD H., "Theory of Combat: The Probability of Winning," *Operations Research*, 11, No. 3 (May–June, 1963), pp. 418–425.

COOTNER, P. H., "Stock Prices: Random Versus Systematic Changes," *Industrial Management Rev.*, 3, (1962), pp. 24–25.

COOTNER, PAUL H. (ed.), *The Random Character of Stock Market Prices*, Massachusetts Institute of Technology Press, Cambridge, Mass., 1964.

COWLES, III, ALFRED, "Can Stock Market Forecasters Forecast?," *Econometrica*, 1, (1933), pp. 309–324.

DASILVA, E. R., and ROY M. DORCUS, *Science in Betting*, Harper & Brothers, 1961.

DAVID, H. A., "Tournaments and Paired Comparisons," *Biometrika*, 46, (1959), pp. 139–149.

DORFMAN, ROBERT, PAUL A. SAMUELSON, and ROBERT M. SOLOW, *Linear Programming and Economic Analysis*, McGraw-Hill Book Company, Inc., New York, 1958.

DRESHER, MELVIN, *Games of Strategy—Theory and Applications*, Prentice-Hall, Inc., Englewood Cliffs, New Jersey, 1961.

EFRON, BRADLEY, "Optimum Evasion vs. Systematic Search," Rand Memorandum RM-3582-ARPA, The RAND Corporation, Santa Monica, California, April, 1963.

EISENBERG, EDMUND, and DAVID GALE, "Consensus of Subjective Probabilities: The Pari-Mutuel Method," *Ann. Math. Statistics*, 39, No. 1 (March, 1959).

FAMA, E. F., "The Distribution of the Daily First Differences of Stock Prices: A Test of Mandelbrot's Stable Paretian Hypothesis," Doctoral Dissertation, University of Chicago, 1963.

FAMA, EUGENE F., and MARSHALL E. BLUME, "Filter Rules and Stock-Market Trading," *The Journal of Business of the University of Chicago*, 39, No. 1, Pt. 2 (January, 1966), pp. 226–241.

FISHER, LAWRENCE, "Outcomes for 'Random' Investments In Common Stocks Listed on the New York Stock Exchange," *The Journal of Business of the University of Chicago*, 38, No. 2 (April, 1965).

FISHER, LAWRENCE, and JAMES H. LORIE, "Rates of Return on Investments In Common Stocks," *The Journal of Business of the University of Chicago*, 37, No. 1 (January, 1964).

GILBERT, E. N., "Games of Identification or Convergence," *SIAM Rev.*, 4, No. 1 (January, 1962), pp. 16–24.

GIRSHICK, M. A., "A Generalization of the Silent Duel, Two Opponents, One Bullet Each, Arbitrary Accuracy," Research Memorandum RM-206, The RAND Corporation, Santa Monica, California, 1 August, 1949.

GLENN, W. A., "A Comparison of the Effectiveness of Tournaments," *Biometrika*, **47** (1960), pp. 253–262.

GODFREY, M. D., C. W. J. GRANGER and O. MORGENSTERN, "The Random Walk Hypothesis of Stock Market Behavior," *Kylos*, **17** (1964), pp. 22–30.

GRANGER, C. W. J., and OSKAR MORGENSTERN, " Spectral Analysis of New York Stock Exchange Prices," *Kylos*, **16** (1963), pp. 1–27.

GRANVILLE, JOSEPH E., *A Strategy of Daily Stock Market Timing for Maximum Profit*, Prentice-Hall, Inc., Englewood Cliffs, New Jersey, 1960.

GROVES, ARTHUR D., "The Mathematical Analysis of a Simple Duel," Ballistic Research Laboratories, Report No. 1261, Aberdeen, Maryland, August, 1964.

ISAACS, RUFUS, "The Problem of Aiming and Evasion," *Naval Research Logistics Quarterly*, **2**, Nos. 1 and 2 (March–June, 1955), pp. 47–67.

ISAACS, RUFUS P., "Optimal Horse Race Bets," *Am. Math. Monthly*, **60**, No. 5 (May, 1953), pp. 310–315.

JACKSON, J. T. ROSS, "Some Speculative Strategies in the Stock Market," Doctoral Dissertation, Case Institute of Technology, Cleveland, Ohio, 1964.

JOHNSON, SELMER M., "A Search Game," *Advances in Game Theory*, edited by M. Dresher, L. S. Shapley, and A. W. Tucker, *Ann. Mathematics Studies* No. 52, Princeton University Press, Princeton, New Jersey, 1964, pp. 39–48.

KAHN, HERMAN, and IRWIN MANN, "Game Theory," RAND Report P-1166, The RAND Corporation, Santa Monica, Calif., July 30, 1957.

KASSOUF, SHEEN, T., "An Econometric Model for Option Price with Implications for Investors' Expectations and Audacity," *Econometrica*, **37**, No. 4 (1969), pp. 685–694.

KEMENY, JOHN G., and GERALD L. THOMPSON, "The Effect of Psychological Attitudes on the Outcomes of Games," *Contributions to the Theory of Games*, **3**, pp. 273–298; *Ann. Mathematics Studies*, No. 39, Princeton University Press, Princeton, New Jersey, 1957.

KENDALL, M. G., "The Analysis of Economic Time Series—I: Prices," *J. Roy. Statist. Soc.*, **116** (1953), pp. 11–25.

KENDALL, M. G., "Further Contributions to the Theory of Paired Comparisons," *Biometrics*, **11**, No. 1 (March, 1955), pp. 43–62.

KLAMKIN, M. S., D. J. NEWMAN, and L. SHEPP (Solution by Alan G. Konheim and Leopold Flatto), "Problem 60-11, A Parking Problem," *SIAM Rev.*, **4**, No. 3 (July, 1962), pp. 257–258.

KLEIN, LAWRENCE R., *A Textbook of Econometrics*, Row, Peterson and Co., White Plains, New York, 1953.

KNUTH, DONALD F., "The Triel: A New Solution," *J. Recreational Math.*, **6**, No. 1 (Winter, 1973), pp. 1–7.

KONHEIM, ALAN G., "The Number of Bisecting Strategies for the Game Γ (N)," *SIAM Rev.*, **4**, No. 4 (October, 1962), pp. 379–384.

KÖNIG, DENES, "Theorie der Endlichen und Undendlichen Graphen," *Akademische Verlagsgesellschaft*, Leipzig, 1936.

LANCHESTER, F. W., *Aircraft in Modern Warfare: The Dawn of the Fourth Arm*, Constable and Co., London, 1916.

LARSON, H. D. (Solution by Leo Moser), "A Dart Game," *Am. Math. Monthly*, **55**, No. 10 (Dec., 1948), pp. 640–641.

MANDELBROT, BENOIT, "The Variation of Certain Speculative Prices," *J. Business* (October, 1963).

MILNOR, JOHN, "Sums of Positional Games," *Contributions to the Theory of Games*, **2**, Ann. *Mathematics Study* No. 28, Princeton University Press, Princeton, New Jersey, 1953, pp. 291–301.

MOORE, A., "A Statistical Analysis of Common Stock Prices," Doctoral Dissertation, University of Chicago, 1962.

MORSE, PHILIP M., and GEORGE E. KIMBALL, *Methods of Operations Research*, The Technology Press of Massachusetts Institute of Technology and John Wiley & Sons, Inc., 1st ed. (rev.), 1951.

MURPHY, JR., ROY E., *Adaptive Processes in Economic Systems*, Academic Press, Inc., New York, 1965.

NÄSLUND, BERTIL, "Decisions Under Risk—Economic Applications of Chance-Constrained Programming," ONR Research Memorandum No. 134, Graduate School of Industrial Administration, Carnegie Institute of Technology, Pittsburgh, Pennsylvania, November, 1964.

NIEDERHOFFER, VICTOR, "Clustering of Stock Prices," *Operations Research*, Vol. 13, No. 2 (March–April, 1965), pp. 258–265.

OSBORNE, M. F. M., "Periodic Structure in the Brownian Motion of Stock Prices," *Operations Research*, **10** (1960), pp. 345–379.

PARETO, VILFREDO, "Manuel d'Economie Politique," Giard et Brière, Paris, 1927.

RAPOPORT, ANATOL, *Fights, Games, and Debates*, The University of Michigan Press, Ann Arbor, 1960.

ROSENFELD, JACK LEE, "Adaptive Competitive Decision," *Advances in Game Theory*, edited by M. Dresher, L. S. Shapley, and A. W. Tucker; Ann. Mathematics Study No. 52, Princeton University Press, Princeton, New Jersey, 1964, pp. 69–83.

SAKAGUCHI, MINORU, "Topics in Information and Decision Processes," Statistics Department, The George Washington University, 1964–1965.

SAMUELSON, PAUL A., "International Price Equilibrium: A Prologue of the Theory of Speculation," *Weltwirtschaftliches Archiv*, **79** (1957), pp. 181–221.

SAMUELSON, PAUL A., "Rational Theory of Warrant Pricing," *Industrial Management Rev.*, **6**, No. 2 (1965), pp. 13–31.

SAMUELSON, PAUL A., and ROBERT C. MERTON, "A Complete Model of Warrant Pricing that Maximizes Utility," *Industrial Management Rev.*, **10**, No. 2 (1969), pp. 17–46.

SCHLAIFER, ROBERT, *Probability and Statistics for Business Decisions*, McGraw-Hill Book Company, New York, 1959.

SEARLS, DONALD T., "On the Probability of Winning with Different Tournament Procedures," *J. Amer. Statistical Assoc.*, **58** (Dec., 1963), pp. 1064–1081.

SHAPLEY, LLOYD S., "Some Topics in Two-Person Games," RAND Memorandum RM-3672-1-PR, The RAND Corp., Santa Monica, Calif., October, 1963.

SHAPLEY, LLOYD S., "Values of Large Games, III: A Corporation With Two Large Stockholders," RAND Memorandum RM-2650-PR, The RAND Corp., Santa Monica, Calif., December, 1961.

SHUBIK, MARTIN, *Strategy and Market Structure*, John Wiley & Sons, Inc., New York, 1959.

SHUBIK, MARTIN, "Does the Fittest Necessarily Survive?", Chapter 5 of *Readings in Game Theory and Political Behavior*, edited by Martin Shubik, Doubleday & Co., Inc., Garden City, New York, 1954.

SMITH, GERALD, "A Duel With Silent Noisy Gun Versus Noisy Gun," University of California, Department of Mathematics, June, 1965.

THORP, EDWARD O., and SHEEN T. KASSOUF, *Beat the Market*, Random House, New York, 1967.

THORP, EDWARD O., "Extensions of the Black-Scholes Option Model," pp. 1029–1036, 39th Session of the International Statistical Institute, Vienna, Austria, August, 1973.

THORP, EDWARD O. "Portfolio Choice and the Kelly Criterion," pp. 599–619, in Ziemba, W. T., and Vickson, R. G., *Stochastic Optimization Models in Finance*, Academic Press, 1975.

THORP, EDWARD O. "Options in Institutional Portfolios: Theory and Practice," pp. 229–251, *Proceedings of the Seminar on the Analysis of Security Prices, Center for Research in Security Prices*, Univ. of Chicago, May, 1975.

TINTNER, GERHARD, *Econometrics*, John Wiley & Sons, Inc., New York, 1952.

WEINER, M. G., "An Introduction to War Games," RAND Report P-1773, The RAND Corp., Santa Monica, Calif., Aug. 17, 1959.

CHAPTER TEN

GAMES OF PURE SKILL AND COMPETITIVE COMPUTERS

Games of pure skill

We define games of pure skill to be devoid of all probabilistic elements. Such games are not often associated with monetary wagers, although formal admonishments against so profiting from a skill are not proclaimed in most cultures. From a rational standpoint, it might be expected that man should be far more willing to express financial confidence in his skills rather than risking his earnings on the mindless meanderings of chance. Experience, however, has strongly indicated the reverse proposition to hold true.

TIC-TAC-TOE

Possibly the oldest and simplest of the games of pure skill is Tic-Tac-Toe (the name itself apparently derives from an old English nursery rhyme). With many variations in spelling and pronunciation, its recorded history extends back to about 3500 B.C.—according to tomb paintings from Egyptian pyramids of that era.

In its usual form, Tic-Tac-Toe is played on a 3×3 matrix, as drawn in Fig. 10-1, with two players alternately occupying an empty square with a personal mark; conventionally, $\times$'s and O's are used for the first and second player, respectively. Winner of the game is that player placing three of his marks along a line, diagonally, horizontally, or vertically. In the event that

Fig. 10-1   The Tic-Tac-Toe matrix

neither player succeeds in obtaining three colinear marks, the game is a draw.

There are approximately 5000 distinct games of Tic-Tac-Toe (a large number of symmetrical patterns exist of the 9! moves associated with nine cells). About 30 percent of these games end with a drawn position and, with rational play on the part of both players, no other conclusion will be reached.[†] The opening move must be one of three: center (cell 5), corner (cells 1, 3, 7 or 9), or side (cells 2, 4, 6, or 8). Correct response to a center opening is placement of a mark in a corner cell (responding in a side cell lead to a loss). Correct response to a corner opening is occupying the center. To a side opening, the correct response is the center, adjoining corner, or far side. Additional counterresponses to a total of nine moves are readily obtained from only casual study.

A simple but fundamental proof by contradiction demonstrates that Tic-Tac-Toe constitutes a tie or a win for the first player. Let us suppose that the game is a win for the second player. Then let the first player select any first move at random and thereafter play in accordance with the presumed winning strategy of the second player. Since the cell initially marked by the first player cannot act to his detriment and since he has available to him the alleged winning strategy of the second player, we have a logical contradiction, and the game cannot be a win for the second player.

Variants of Tic-Tac-Toe extend back several millenia. A form popular in ancient China, Greece, and Rome comprised two players, each with three personal counters. The players alternately place a counter in a vacant cell of the 3 × 3 matrix until all six counters have been played. If neither player has succeeded in achieving a colinear arrangement of his three counters, the game proceeds by moving at each turn a personal counter to any empty cell adjacent orthogonally. The first player has a forced win by occupying

---

[†] The basic strategy is sufficiently simple that bright chimpanzees have been trained to play with creditable performance.

the center cell as his opening move. Other versions, which result in a draw from rational play, permit diagonal moves or moves to any vacant cell. Moving-counter Tic-Tac-Toe has also been proposed for 4 × 4 and 5 × 5 matrices. The latter example was invented by John Scarne and called "Teeko." Two players alternately place four personal counters on the board followed by alternating one-unit moves in any direction. The objective is to maneuver to a configuration of four personal counters, either colinear or in a square formation on four adjacent cells.

A modern variant of Tic-Tac-Toe permits either player to place either mark (× or O) at each move. This game offers limited appeal, since the first player has a forced win by placing a mark (say ×) in the center cell. If the second player responds with an O in a corner cell (an × anywhere obviously loses), the first player locates an O in the opposite corner and is thence presented with a winning opportunity by any move open to his opponent. If the second player responds to the center opening by occupying a side cell with an O, the first player places an O in the opposite side cell. Thence, the second player is forced to mark an O in one of the two vacant side cells; the first player follows with either an × or O in the remaining side cell. Now any move by the second player leads to an immediate win for his opponent.

More sophisticated Tic-Tac-Toe addicts prefer a version known as Tandem Tic-Tac-Toe. Each player possesses a conventional 3 × 3 cellular matrix, which he labels with the nine integers 1, 2, . . . , 9, each cell being marked with a distinct integer. The marking process occurs one cell at a time—as a concealed move each player selects a cell and a correlative integer; the move is thence exposed and, with the information obtained, a second cell of each array is marked secretly, then revealed, etc., until all nine cells of the matrices are numbered. For the second phase of the game, player A places an × in each of the two Tic-Tac-Toe arrays in such a manner that the numbers of the two cells occupied by the × 's are identical. Player B then selects two matching cells for his two O's. This procedure continues with the usual objective of obtaining three colinear personal symbols. If a win is achieved in one matrix, the game continues in conventional fashion in the other matrix until it terminates. Clearly, both players strive for two wins or a single win and a tie. Player B's evident strategy is to avoid matching of the center and corner cells between the two matrices.

Yet other variants of the basic game that we can recommend are Kit-Kat-Oat, wherein each participant plays his opponent's personal mark; Toe-Tac-Tic, wherein the first player to obtain three colinear marks *loses*; and Kriegspiel Tic-Tac-Toe. In Kit-Kat-Oat, the disadvantage lies with the first player; he can achieve a draw, however, by placing his opponent's mark in the center cell as his first move and thereafter playing symmetrically about the center to his opponent's previous move. In Kriegspiel Tic-Tac-Toe, each of the two players is accorded a personal 3×3 matrix, which he marks privately. A referee superimposes the two matrices and ensures that corresponding cells are marked on only one matrix by rejecting any moves to the contrary. As usual, the player who places three colinear personal marks wins. Since the first player possesses a pronounced advantage, we suggest that he be handicapped by losing a move upon receiving a rejection from the referee. Imposition of this handicap reduces, but does not eliminate, his advantage. Played with 4×4 matrices, Kriegspiel Tic-Tac-Toe appears to offer the first player a slight edge, although his rejected moves are lost while the second player is guaranteed a legal move at each turn. The reader is encouraged to ascertain the size of the matrix whereby, under the handicap rule, Kriegspiel Tic-Tac-Toe becomes a "fair" game.

Since two-dimensional Tic-Tac-Toe exists logically for two players, we might infer that three- and four-dimensional Tic-Tac-Toe can be constructed for three and four players, respectively. In n dimensions, a player can achieve a configuration with n potential wins so that the $n - 1$ succeeding players cannot block all the means to a win.

Two-person, n-dimensional Tic-Tac-Toe offers some mathematical facets. Played in a hypercube of side k, the second player can force a tie if $k \geq 3^n - 1$ (k odd) or $k \geq 2^{n+1} - 2$ (k even). However, for each k there exists an n_k such that for $n \geq n_k$, the first player can win. In the 3^3 game, the first player has a simple forced win and the game cannot be drawn since it is impossible to select 14 of the 27 cells without some 3 being colinear, either orthogonally or diagonally. Three-dimensional Tic-Tac-Toe is usually played with $k = 4$. Another class of Tic-Tac-Toe, largely unexplored, is the n-dimensional moving-counter game.

Computers programmed to play Tic-Tac-Toe have been commonplace for several years; one of the earliest schemes was devised by W. Kirster about 1940. A straightforward format consists of classifying the nine cells in order of decreasing strategic desirability. The computer investigates those classes successively until it encounters an empty cell, which it then occupies. This type of simple device can be constructed with relays alone. The Brainiac, a kit produced by Berkeley Associates, is a computer of this type. A device that converges to an optimal Tic-Tac-Toe strategy through a learning process is MENACE (Matchbox Educable Noughts And Crosses Engine), a "computer" constructed by Donald Michie from about 300 matchboxes and a number of variously colored small glass beads (beads are added to or deleted from different matchboxes as the machine wins or loses against different lines of play, thus weighting the preferred lines). Following an "experience" session of 150 plays, MENACE is capable of coping (that is, drawing) with an adversary's optimal play.

[An alternative to the pure-strategy forms of Tic-Tac-Toe consists of marking the cells of the 3 × 3 matrix in accordance with numbers drawn (at random and without replacement) from the set of integers, 1, 2, ..., 9. Enumeration of all patterns shows that the first player wins with probability 0.585 and the second with probability 0.288.]

MILL

A game similar to Tic-Tac-Toe is that of Mill (sometimes referred to as "Nine Men's Morris"). Played on a board of 24 points, Mill comprises two contending players, each equipped with nine personal chips that are placed and possibly moved on points of the board. The Mill board is formed by three concentric squares and four transversals, as illustrated in Fig. 10-2. The players alternately place their chips on one of the points

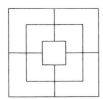

Fig. 10-2   The Mill board

until the 18 chips are exhausted; then each in turn moves one of his chips to an adjacent point defined along any line on which it stands. Whenever a player establishes three chips on a line, this formation being known as a "mill," he is entitled to remove an opposing chip from the board, with the proviso that it may not be a member of an adverse "mill." (An established "mill" may be "opened" by moving one chip off the common line; it can then be "closed" by moving the chip back, whence the formation is credited as a new "mill.") The object of the game is to reduce the number of chips at the opponent's command to two. A player also loses if, after placing all nine chips, he is blocked from making a move.

Popular in Germany and the Scandinavian countries, Mill offers a degree of skill well above that of Tic-Tac-Toe without the enormous number of possible strategies associated with conventional board games such as Chess or Checkers. An analysis of Mill strategies has not been published; however, it would appear that a forced draw should result in a contest between two intelligent players.

NIM AND ITS VARIATIONS; TSYAN/SHI/DZI; TAC TIX

Another simple two-person game of pure skill is Nim. It is dubiously reputed to be of Chinese origin, possibly because it reflects the simplicity in structure combined with subtle strategic moves (at least to the mathematically unanointed) ascribed to Oriental games or possibly because it was known as Fan-Tan (although unrelated either to the mod 4 Chinese counter game or the elimination card game) among American college students toward the end of the nineteenth century. Actually, the word Nim (presumably from *niman*, an archaic Anglo-Saxon verb meaning to take away or steal) was appended by Charles Leonard Bouton, a mathematics professor at Harvard, who published the first analysis of the game in 1901. In the simplest and most conventional form of Nim, an arbitrary number of chips is apportioned into an arbitrary number of piles, with any distribution whatever. Each player, in his turn, removes any number of chips one or greater from any pile, but only from one pile. The player removing the final chip wins the game.

In the terminology of Professor Bouton, each configuration of the piles is designated as a "safe" or "unsafe" combination. Let the number of chips in each pile be represented in binary notation; then a particular configuration is uniquely "safe" if the mod 2 addition of these binary representations (each column being added independently) is zero; this form of addition is known as the *digital sum* and is designated by the symbol $\dotplus$. For example, three piles consisting of 8, 7, and 15 chips are represented as follows:

$$
\begin{aligned}
8 &= 1000 \\
7 &= 111 \\
15 &= 1111 \\
\hline
\text{Digital sum} &= 0000
\end{aligned}
$$

and constitute a "safe" combination. Similarly, the digital sum of 4 and 7 and 2 is 1 ($100 \dotplus 111 \dotplus 10 = 1$); three piles of 4, 7, and 2 chips thus define an "unsafe" configuration.

It is easily demonstrated that if the first player removes a number of chips from one pile so that a "safe" combination remains, then the second player cannot do likewise. He can change only one pile and he must change one. Since, when the numbers in all but one of the piles are given, the final pile is uniquely determined (for the digital sum of the numbers to be zero), and since the first player governs the number in that pile (that is, the pile from which the second player draws), the second player cannot leave that number. It also follows, with the same reasoning, that if the first player leaves a "safe" combination and the second player diminishes one of the piles, the first player can always diminish one of the remaining piles and thereby regain a "safe" combination. Clearly, if the initial configuration is "safe," the second player wins the game by returning the pattern to a "safe" one at each move. Otherwise, the first player wins.

Illustratively, beginning with three piles of four, five, and six chips, the first player performs a parity check on the columns:

$$
\begin{aligned}
4 &= 100 \\
5 &= 101 \\
6 &= \underline{110} \\
\text{Digital sum} &= 111
\end{aligned}
$$

He observes that removing one chip from the pile of four, or three chips from the pile of five, or five chips from the pile of six produces even parity (a zero digital sum, a "safe" position) and leads to a winning conclusion. Observe that from an "unsafe" position, the move to a "safe" one is not necessarily unique.

Sometimes a modified version of Nim is conducted under the rule that the player removing the last chip *loses*. The basic strategy remains unaltered, except that the configuration $1, 1, 0, 0, \ldots, 0$ is "unsafe" and $1, 0, 0, \ldots, 0$ is "safe."

If the number of counters initially in each pile is selected at random, allowing a maximum of 2^{m-1} chips per pile, the possible number of different configurations N with k piles is determined by

$$
N = \binom{2^m + k - 2}{k}
$$

Frequently Nim is played with three piles, whence

$$
N = \frac{(2^m + 1)(2^m)(2^m - 1)}{6} = \frac{2^{m-1}(2^{2m} - 1)}{3}
$$

The number of "safe" combinations N_s in this case is

$$N_s = \frac{(2^{m-1} - 1)(2^m - 1)}{3}$$

Thus, the probability P_s of creating a "safe" combination initially is given by

$$P_s = \frac{N_s}{N} = \frac{2^{m-1} - 1}{2^{m-1}(2^m + 1)}$$

which is the probability that the second player wins the game, assuming that he conforms to the correct strategy.

A generalization of Nim proposed by E. H. Moore allows the players to remove any number of chips (one or greater) from any number of piles (one or greater) but not exceeding k. Evidently, if the first player leaves fewer than $k + 1$ piles following his move, the second player wins by removing all the remaining chips. Such a configuration is an "unsafe" combination in generalized Nim. Since the basic theorems regarding "safe" and "unsafe" patterns are still valid, a player can continue with the normal strategy, mod $(k + 1)$, until the number of piles is diminished to less than $k + 1$, whence he wins the game. To derive the general formula for "safe" combinations, let the n piles contain, respectively, $c_1, c_2, \ldots, c_n$ chips. In the binary scale of notation,[†] each number c_i is represented as $c_i = c_{i0} + c_{i1}2^1 + c_{i2}2^2 + \cdots + c_{ij}2^j$. The integers c_{ij} are either zero or 1 and are uniquely determinable. The combination is "safe" if and only if

$$\sum_{i=1}^{n} c_{ij} = 0, \mathrm{mod}\,(k + 1), \quad j = 0, 1, 2, \ldots$$

that is, if and only if for every place j, the sum of the n digits c_{ij} is exactly divisible by $k + 1$.

Moore's generalization is referred to as Nim_k. Professor Bouton's game thus becomes Nim_1 and provides a specific example wherein the column addition of the chips in each pile is performed mod 2.

Another generalization, termed Matrix Nim and designated by Nim^k (this nomenclature was applied by John C. Holladay to distinguish the game from Moore's version), consists of arranging the k piles of chips into an $m \times n$ rectangular array. For a move in this game, the player removes

---

[†] It is also possible to develop the theory with a quaternary representation of the numbers. Such a procedure, although less familiar than binary representation, involves fewer terms.

any number of chips (one or greater) from any nonempty set of piles, providing they are in the same row or in the same column, with the proviso that at least one column remains untouched. The game concludes when all the piles are reduced to zero, the player taking the final chip being the winner. Nim^k with $k = 1$ becomes, as with Moore's generalization, the ordinary form of Nim.

A "safe" position in Nim^k occurs if the sum of the chips in any column is equal to the sum of the chips in any other column and if the set of piles defined by selecting the smallest pile from each row constitutes a "safe" position in conventional Nim.

A variation proposed by Claude Shannon is the playing of Nim_1 with the restriction that only a prime number of chips may be removed from the pile. Since this game differs from Nim_1 only for those instances of four or more chips in a pile, a "safe" combination is defined when the last two digits of the binary representations of the number of chips in each pile sum to zero, mod 2. For example, a three-pile game of Nim_1 with 32, 19, and 15 chips provides a "safe" configuration in Dr. Shannon's version, although not in the conventional game. This situation is illustrated as follows:

$$
\begin{array}{rl}
15 = & 1111 \\
19 = & 10011 \\
32 = & 100000 \\
\hline
\text{Digital sum} = & 111100
\end{array}
$$

It should be noted that the basic theorems of "safe" and "unsafe" combinations do not hold for prime-number Nim_1.

Obviously, we can impose arbitrary restrictions for other variants of Nim. For example, a limit can be imposed on the number of chips removed or that number can be limited to multiples (or some other relationship) of another number. A more clever version, due to W. A. Wythoff,[†] restricts the game to two piles, each with an arbitrary number of chips. A player may remove chips from either or both piles, but if from both, the same number of chips must be taken from each pile. The "safe" combinations are the Fibonacci pairs: $(1, 2), (3, 5), (4, 7), (6, 10), (8, 13), (9, 15), (11, 18), (12, 20), \ldots$. The rth "safe" pair is $([r\tau], [r\tau^2])$, where $\tau = (1 + \sqrt{5})/2$ and $[x]$ is defined as the greatest integer not exceeding x. It should be noted that every integer in the number scale appears once and only once. Although evidently unknown to Wythoff, the Chinese had long been playing the identical game under the name of Tsyan/shi/dzi (picking stones).

[†] In the Nieuw Archief voor Wiskunde, 1907.

Another ingenious Nim variation, which opens up an entire new class, was proposed by Piet Hein[†] under the name Tac Tix (known as Bulo in Denmark). In Tac Tix, which follows logically from Matrix Nim, the chips are arranged in an $n \times m$ array. The two players alternately remove any number of chips either from any row or from any column, with the sole proviso that all chips taken on a given move be adjoining. Tac Tix must be played under the rule that the losing player is the one removing the final chip. Otherwise, there exists a simple strategy that renders the game trivial: The second player wins by playing symmetrically to the first player unless the matrix has an odd number of chips in each row and column, in which case the first player wins by removing the center chip on his first move and thereafter playing symmetrically to his opponent. No strategy is known for the general form of Tac Tix, except for a 3×3 game wherein the first player can always win with proper play (his first move should take the center or corner chip or the entire central row or column). As a practical game between sophisticated game theorists, the 6×6 board is recommended.

A Nim-type game proposed by David Gale (and dubbed "Chomp" by Martin Gardner) is also played with mn chips in an $m \times n$ array. Letting (i, j) denote the chip in the ith row and jth column of the array, the first player selects chip (i_1, j_1) and thereby removes all chips for which $i \geq i_1$ and $j \geq j_1$. The second player then chooses chip (i_2, j_2) from those remaining, thereby removing all chips for which $i \geq i_2$ and $j \geq j_2$. Play continues, alternating between players in this fashion, until that player removing chip $(1, 1)$ loses.

Gale's "auto-proof" that the game is a win for the first player for all m and n proceeds as follows: Either the first player has a winning strategy in which his first move is (m, n) or he loses by the selection of (m, n). In the latter instance, there must exist a response (i_2, j_2) that wins for the second player. But since the first player could have selected (i_2, j_2), the second player has no winning move exclusively available to him. The game is thus a win for the first player.

Numerous games have been proposed whose solutions become apparent once their Nim-like structures are revealed. Two such examples are Northcott's Nim and Stepine's game. Northcott's Nim is played on any $n \times m$ checkerboard. In each row of the board is placed a white piece and a black piece. For his turn White may move any one of his pieces along its row, in either direction, as far as the empty squares allow. Black then moves any

---

[†] A Copenhagen resident of Dutch ancestry, Herre Hein is also the creator of Hex.

one of his pieces under the same rules. The game proceeds in this manner until one player cannot move—and thereby loses.

Northcott's Nim is equivalent to Nim_1 with a pile of chips for each row. The number of chips in a particular pile is equivalent to the number of squares between the black and white pieces in the corresponding row. (Each player's prerogative to increase the space between black and white pieces does not alter the character of the game or its ultimate convergence.)

Stepine's game is played with n coins and a gold-piece arrayed at intervals along a line whose left-hand side terminates in a moneybag (illustrated in Fig. 10-3 for six coins and the gold-piece). A move (by each of two players in successive turns) consists of shifting any coin or the gold-piece any number of empty spaces (one or more) leftward. When a coin is moved to the leftmost space, it falls into the moneybag. That player who deposits the gold-piece in the moneybag is the winner.

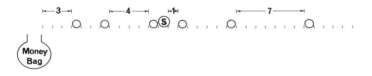

Fig. 10-3   Stepine's game.

Again, the resolution of Stepine's game lies in recognizing its Nim-like structure. Accordingly, the coins (and gold-piece) should be considered pairwise beginning at the right. The number of pairs corresponds to the number of piles and the number of spaces within each pair to the number of chips in that pile in the Nim_1 equivalency. If a coin is left unpaired, the winning strategy includes the moneybag space if the gold-piece forms the left side of a pair and excludes the moneybag space if it forms the right side of a pair (if the gold-piece is leftmost, it can be moved directly into the moneybag). In the example shown in Fig. 10-3, we compute the digital sum of 3, 4, 1, and 7—which is nonzero. A winning move consists of reducing the 3, 1, or 7 interval by one.

For the reader who wishes to perform original research in the area of Nim strategies, we commend the following variants of the basic rules for which optimal strategies have not yet been formulated.

    1. Nim_k played under the restriction that chips may be removed only from a prime number of piles.

2. Nim_k or Nim^k played with the imposition of limits on the number of chips removed; that is, at least a_i and no more than b_i chips may be taken from the ith pile (or row or column) at each move.
3. Tsyan/shi/dzi played with the option of removing simultaneously from the two piles an arbitrary ratio $a:b$ of chips (rather than an equal number).
4. Tsyan/shi/dzi played with three or more piles, where the player is awarded the option of removing the same number of chips simultaneously from each pile (≥ 3).
5. Tac Tix played with upper and lower limits placed on the number of chips that may be removed at each move.
6. Tac Tix played under the option of removing the same number of chips in both directions from a row-column intersection.

A Nim_1-playing computer should logically be a relatively simple device due to the binary nature of the strategy. The first such computer was the Nimatron, patented in 1940 by Dr. Edward U. Condon, former director of the National Bureau of Standards. Built by the Westinghouse Electric Corporation, Nimatron was exhibited at the New York World's Fair, where it played 100,000 games, winning about 90,000 (most of its defeats were administered by attendants demonstrating that possibility). At present it reposes in the scientific collection of the Buhl planetarium in Pittsburgh. One year later a vastly improved machine was designed by Raymond M. Redheffer. Both the Redheffer and Condon computer programs were devised for play with four piles, each containing up to seven chips. Subsequently, a Nim_1-playing device named Nimrod was exhibited at the 1951 Festival of Britain and later at the Berlin Trade Fair. A different approach to Nim was expressed through a simple relay computer developed at the Research Institute of Mathematical Machines (Prague) in 1960. The machine, programmed with a knowledge of the optimal strategy, is pitted against a mathematical neophyte. The designated objective is to achieve a victory while disclosing as little information as possible regarding the correct game algorithm. Hence the computer applies its knowledge sparingly as a function of its opponent's analytic prowess.

SINGLE-PILE COUNTDOWN GAMES

Although not linked by firm evidence, it is likely that Nim is related to a game described by Bachet de Mésiriac in the early seventeenth century. From a single pile comprising an arbitrary number of chips, each of two players alternately removes one or more, but not more than a, chips. The winner is that player who reduces the pile to zero. Thus, a "safe" position in

Bachet's game occurs when the number of chips in the pile totals 0, mod $(1 + a)$.

Single-pile games[†] can be formulated by specifying any restricted set of integers $S = \{n_1, n_2, \ldots\}$ that prescribe the number of chips that may be taken from the pile at each move. For each such set of integers, there exist positions (states) of the pile that are winning, losing, or tying for the player confronted with a move. Designating the winning and losing states by $W(S)$ and $L(S)$, respectively, we observe that

$$W(S) \cup L(S) = \text{the set of all integers} \geq 0$$

and

$$W(S) \cap L(S) = \varnothing$$

that is, the union of the winning and losing sets includes all nonnegative integers while the intersection of these sets is empty, under the assumption that the set of tying positions $T(S)$ is empty. The assumption that $T(S) = \varnothing$ is valid if and only if zero is not a member of the subtractive set S and if unity is a member of S. For greater harmony, it is always advisable to include the number 1 in the subtractive set and to designate the winner as that player reducing the pile to zero.

As in the various Nim games, every member of S added to a member of $L(S)$ results in a member of $W(S)$. Thus, a losing or "safe" position is always attainable from a winning or "unsafe" position, but not from another "safe" position.

Two subtractive sets S_1 and S_2 are characterized as *game isomorphic* if they define games with identical losing states. For example, the set of all positive powers of two $S_1 = \{1, 2, 4, 8, \ldots\}$ is game isomorphic to $S_2 = \{1, 2\}$ since

$$L(S_1) = L(S_2) = \{0, \text{ mod } 3\}$$

(no power of 2 is a multiple of 3) and the set of primes $S_1 = \{1, 2, 3, 5, 7, \ldots\}$ is game isomorphic to $S_2 = \{1, 2, 3\}$, since

$$L(S_1) = L(S_2) = \{0, \text{mod } 4\}$$

(no prime is a multiple of 4). Thus, a single-pile countdown game where only a prime number of chips may be subtracted can be won by the first player to reduce the pile to a multiple of 4.

It can be demonstrated that game isomorphism is closed under union, but not under intersection. For example, consider the two subtractive sets $S_1 = \{1, 4, 5\}$ and $S_2 = \{1, 3, 4, 7\}$. We compute $L(S_1)$ by the paradigm

---

[†] The succeeding analysis of single-pile games was first outlined in a USC lecture by Professor Solomon Golomb.

TABLE 10-1   Computation of Losing States $L(S_1)$

$L(S_1)$	S_1 1	S_1 4	S_1 5
0	1	4	5
2	3	6	7
8	9	12	13
10	11	14	15
16	17	20	21
18	19	22	23
24	25	28	29
26			

shown in Table 10-1. The sequence of $L(S_1)$ is determined by entering in the $L(S_1)$ column the lowest integer not previously represented; that integer is then added to 1, 4, and 5, respectively, and the sum entered in the corresponding column, etc. Evidently, $L(S_1) = \{0, 2, \bmod 8\}$. By the same technique, we can also calculate $L(S_2) = \{0, 2, \bmod 8\}$ and show that $L(S_1 \cup S_2) = \{0, 2, \bmod 8\}$, whereas $L(S_1 \cap S_2) = \{0, 2, \bmod 5\}$.

To complete our understanding of the sets that exhibit game isomorphism, we introduce the states $\lambda(S)$ as all the nonnegative first differences of $L(S)$. We can prove that $\lambda(S)$ cannot intersect S—that is,

$$\lambda(S) \cap S = \varnothing$$

and the converse statement that any number not in $\lambda(S)$ can be adjoined into S. Illustratively, consider the set $S = \{1, 4\}$ which generates the set of losing positions $L(S) = \{0, 2, \bmod 5\}$. In this instance, the numbers 3, mod 5, are obtained by first differences of the other members of $L(S)$, so that $\lambda(S) = \{0, 2, 3, \bmod 5\}$. All remaining numbers (1, mod 5, and 4, mod 5) can be adjoined to S:

$$S \cup \{1, \bmod 5, \quad 4, \bmod 5\} \equiv S^*$$

Thus, any set S^* is game isomorphic to S. For example, the game played with $S = \{1, 4\}$ is equivalent (in the sense of identical losing positions) to that played with $S^* = \{1, 4, 9, 16\}$.

Given a particular subtractive set, it is not always possible to find another set with the property of game isomorphism. For example, consider the game whereby, from an initial pile of m chips, each player alternately subtracts a perfect square number of chips, $S = \{1, 4, 9, 16, \ldots\}$, with the usual objective of removing the final chip to score a win. It is not apparent that a simple formula exists which determines the "safe" positions $L(S)$ for this game. However, as demonstrated by Professor Golomb, it can be shown that the sequence of "safe" positions is generated by an appropriately constructed shift register.

A binary shift register is a simple multistage device whereby, in a given configuration, each stage exhibits either a 1 or a 0. At prescribed intervals the output of each stage of the register assumes the value represented by the output of the previous stage over the previous interval. The outputs from one or more stages are operated upon in some fashion and fed back into the first stage. For the single-pile countdown game with $S = \{1, 4, 9, 16, \ldots\}$, the appropriate shift register is of semi-infinite length, since the perfect squares form an infinite series. The outputs of stages 1, 4, 9, 16, ... are delivered to a NOR gate and thence returned to the first stage. Figure 10-4 indicates the perfect-square shift register. Initially, the first stage is loaded with a 1 and the remaining stages with 0's. If at least one 1 enters the NOR gate, it feeds back a 0 to the first stage as the register shifts; otherwise, a 1 is fed back. The continuing output of the shift register designates the "safe" and "unsafe" positions, with 1 representing "safe" and 0 "unsafe." Table 10-2 illustrates the shift-register performance. According to the output sequence, positions 2, 5, and 7 (of the first 8) are "safe"; that is, if a player reduces the pile of chips to 2, 5, or 7, he possesses a winning game, since his opponent can achieve only an "unsafe" position.

Allowing the perfect-square shift register to run for 1000 shifts produces 1's at the positions shown in Table 10-3. Thus, beginning with a pile of 1000 or less, the player who reduces the pile to any of the positions shown in Table 10-3 can achieve a win.

There are 114 "safe" positions for a pile of 1000 chips, 578 "safe" positions for a pile of 10,000 chips, and 910 "safe" positions for a pile of 20,000 chips. Evidently as the number of initial chips m increases, the percentage of "safe" positions decreases. The totality of "safe" positions is infinite, however, as $m \to \infty$ (there exists no largest "safe" position).

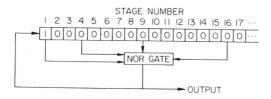

Fig. 10-4   The perfect-square shift register

TABLE 10-2   The Perfect-Square Shift Register Output

Number of Shifts, t	Shift Register Contents after t Shifts	Output Symbol after tth Shift
1	1 0 0 0 0 0 0 0 0 0 . . .	0
2	0 1 0 0 0 0 0 0 0 0 . . .	1
3	1 0 1 0 0 0 0 0 0 0 . . .	0
4	0 1 0 1 0 0 0 0 0 0 . . .	0
5	0 0 1 0 1 0 0 0 0 0 . . .	1
6	1 0 0 1 0 1 0 0 0 0 . . .	0
7	0 1 0 0 1 0 1 0 0 0 . . .	1
8	1 0 1 0 0 1 0 1 0 0 . . .	0
.		.
.		.
.		.

A great number of interesting forms of single-pile countdown games can be invented. For example, we can regulate each player to subtract a perfect cube number of chips. For this game, the semi-infinite shift register of Fig. 10-4 is rearranged with the outputs of stages 1, 8, 27, 64, . . . fed to the NOR gate. The output of such a shift register indicates "safe" positions at 2, 4, 6, 9, 11, 13, 15, 18, 20, 22, 24, 34, 37, 39, 41, 43, 46, 48, 50, 52, 55, 57, 59, 62, 69, 71, 74, 76, 78, 80, 83, 85, 87, 90, 92, 94, 97, 99, ...

The shift register method can also be utilized to solve more elementary countdown games. For example, consider Bachet's game with $a = 4$— that is, $S = \{1, 2, 3, 4\}$. In this instance we construct a finite four-stage shift register (the number of stages required is specified by the largest member of S) with the outputs of all four stages connected to the NOR gate, as shown in Fig. 10-5. Inserting a 1 into the first stage and 0's into the

TABLE 10-3   The "Safe" Positions for the Perfect-Square Game

2	5	7	10	12	15	17	20	22	34	39	44	52	57
62	65	67	72	85	95	109	119	124	127	130	132	137	142
147	150	170	177	180	182	187	192	197	204	210	215	238	243
249	255	257	260	262	267	272	275	312	317	322	327	332	335
340	345	350	369	377	390	392	397	425	430	437	442	447	449
464	502	507	510	512	515	517	520	522	554	572	589	595	600
613	619	652	663	665	680	702	704	707	724	770	787	793	827
850	855	860	862	865	867	872	894	918	923	928	935	940	979
990	997												

remaining stages and permitting the shift register to run, results in the output sequence 00001000010000100.... Thus, as we would expect, the "safe" positions occur at 0, mod 5.

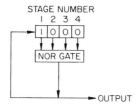

Fig. 10-5   Shift register for Bachet's game

Many extensions of Bachet's game are worthy of note. For example, we might impose the additional constraint that each player must remove at least b chips (but no more than $a > b$) at each move. A win is awarded to that player reducing the pile to $b - 1$ or less chips. The "safe" positions for this game are $0, 1, 2, \ldots b - 1, \mod(b + a)$. If different limits are assigned to each player, the possessor of the larger limit can secure the winning strategy.

Another, more interesting, variation of Bachet's game arises from the prohibition that the same number of chips (of the set $S = \{1, 2, \ldots, a\}$) cannot be subtracted twice in succession.[†] If a is even, no change is effected by this rule: $L(S) = \{0, \mod(a + 1)\}$. If a is odd, correct strategy alters in certain critical positions; for example, if $a = 5$ and there are six chips remaining, the winning move consists of subtracting three chips, since the opponent cannot repeat the subtraction of 3. Specifically, for $a = 5$, $L(S) = \{0, 7, \mod 13\}$. For any odd value of a, except 1 and 3, $L(S) = \{0, a + 2, \mod(2a + 3)\}$; for $a = 3$, $L(S) = \{0, \mod 4\}$.

The following variants of the basic theme are recommended to the addicted reader.

1. A single-pile countdown game played under a rule constraining one player to remove a number of chips defined by one set of integers while the second player may remove a number of chips described by a different set of integers. Note that "safe" and "unsafe" positions are not mutually exclusive in this game.

[†] This version, as well as several other restricted countdown games, was suggested to the author by David L. Silverman of the Hughes Aircraft Company Advanced Projects Laboratory.

2. A single-pile game played under the rule that each member of the subtractive set $S = \{n_1, n_2, \ldots,\}$ can be used only once. Clearly, the initial number of chips m must be chosen less than or equal to the sum of the set of numbers $n_1 + n_2 + \cdots$.

3. A single-pile game wherein for his moves, each player is given the choice of subtracting or adding the largest perfect square (or cube or other function) number of chips contained in the current pile. Evidently the number of chips in the pile can be increased indefinitely under the rules of this game; it is also evident that certain positions lead to a draw—for example, with a pile of two chips, a player will add one, whereas with a pile of three chips, he will subtract one; thus if the pile ever contains two or three chips, the game is drawn. Every drawn state less than 20,000 is reducible to the 2-3 loop except for the loop 37, 73, 137, 258, 514, 998, 37, . . . , wherein only one player has the option of transferring to the 2-3 oscillation. Some of the winning, losing, and tying states are listed in Table 10-4.

TABLE 10-4   The Game of Add or Subtract a Square: Winning, Losing, and Tying Positions

$L(S)$	$W(S)$	$T(S)$
5, 20, 29, 45, 80, 101, 116, 135, 145, 165, 173, 236	1, 4, 9, 11, 14, 16, 21, 25, 30, 36, 41, 44, 49, 52, 54, 64, 69, 81, 86, 92, 100, 105, 120, 121, 126, 144	2, 3, 7, 8, 12, 26, 27, 37, 51, 73, 137, 258

THE GRUNDY FUNCTION; KAYLES

Single-pile and other countdown games, such as Nim and Tac-Tix, are susceptible to analysis through certain powerful techniques developed by the theory of graphs. According to that theory, we have a *graph* whenever there exists (1) a set X and (2) a function Γ mapping X into X. Each element of X is called a *vertex* and can be equated to what we have termed a position, or state, of a game. For a finite graph (X, Γ), we can define a function g that associates an integer $g(x) \geq 0$ with every vertex x. Specifically, $g(x)$ denotes a *Grundy function* on the graph if, for every vertex x, $g(x)$ is the smallest nonnegative integer (not necessarily unique) not in the set

$$g(\Gamma x) = \{g(y)|y \in \Gamma x\}$$

It follows that $g(x) = 0$ if $\Gamma x = \varnothing$.

Since, in graph representation of a countdown game, each vertex represents a state of the game, and since we conventionally define the winner as that player who leaves the zero state for his opponent, the zero Grundy function is associated with a winning vertex. From all other vertices, there always exists a path to a vertex with a zero Grundy function and from a zero Grundy function vertex there are connections only to vertices with nonzero Grundy functions (this statement is equivalent to the theorem of "safe" and "unsafe" positions at Nim). Letting the initial state in a countdown game be represented by x_0, the first player moves by selecting a vertex x_1 from the set Γx_0; then his opponent selects a vertex x_2 from the set Γx_1; the first player moves again by selecting a vertex x_3 from the set Γx_2, etc. That player who selects a vertex x_k such that $\Gamma x_k = \varnothing$ is the winner. Analogous to the countdown games discussed previously, there is a collection of winning positions (vertices) that lead to a winning position irrespective of the opponent's responses. Specifically, the "safe" positions $L(S)$ with which a player wishes to confront his adversary are those whereby the digital sum of the individual Grundy functions is zero.

As an example, let us consider a simplified form of Tac Tix, embodying n distinct row of chips, with no more than m chips in any row. A legal move consists of removing any integer number of adjoining chips from 1 to j, where $1 \leq j \leq m$. If chips are removed from other than a row end, the consequence is the creation of an additional row (since the chips removed must be adjoining). Two players alternate moves and that player removing the final chip is declared the winner. For $j = 2$, the game is known as Kayles.

To compute the Grundy functions for Kayles, we begin with $g(0) = 0$; thence $g(1) = 1$, $g(2) = 2$, and $g(3) = 3$, since the two previous Grundy functions cannot be repeated. For $g(4)$, we observe that a row of four chips can be reduced to a row of three, a row of two, a row of two and a row of one, or two rows of one; the respective Grundy functions are 3, 2, the digital sum of 2 and 1 (that is, 3), and the digital sum of 1 and 1 (that is, 0). Hence, the vertex associated with a row of four counters is connected to other vertices with Grundy functions of 3, 2, 3, and 0. The smallest integer not represented is 1 and therefore $g(4) = 1$. Table 10-5 presents a tabulation of the Grundy functions for Kayles.

As seen from Table 10-5, the Grundy functions for Kayles are almost periodic for smaller values of x and become perfectly periodic with period 12 for $x \geq 71$. We are consequently led to inquire as to the type of games associated with periodic Grundy functions. R. K. Guy and C. A. B. Smith have delineated a classification system that can distinguish those games

TABLE 10-5   Grundy Functions for Kayles

x	$g(x)$	x	$g(x)$	x	$g(x)$	x	$g(x)$	x	$g(x)$	x	$g(x)$	x	$g(x)$
0	0	12	4	24	4	36	4	48	4	60	4	72	4
1	1	13	1	25	1	37	1	49	1	61	1	73	1
2	2	14	2	26	2	38	2	50	2	62	2	74	2
3	3	15	7	27	8	39	3	51	8	63	8	75	8
4	1	16	1	28	5	40	1	52	1	64	1	76	1
5	4	17	4	29	4	41	4	53	4	65	4	77	4
6	3	18	3	30	7	42	7	54	7	66	7	78	7
7	2	19	2	31	2	43	2	55	2	67	2	79	2
8	1	20	1	32	1	44	1	56	1	68	1	80	1
9	4	21	4	33	8	45	8	57	4	69	8	81	8
10	2	22	6	34	6	46	2	58	2	70	6	82	2
11	6	23	7	35	7	47	7	59	7	71	7	83	7

whose Grundy functions are ultimately periodic. They define a sequence of numerals $\alpha_1\alpha_2\alpha_3\cdots, 0 \le \alpha_j \le 7$ for all values of j, such that the jth numeral α_j symbolizes the conditions under which a block of j consecutive chips can be removed from one of the rows of a configuration of chips. These conditions are listed in Table 10-6. A particular sequence of α_j's defines the rules of a particular game.

TABLE 10-6   The Classification System For Periodic Grundy Functions

α_j	Conditions for Removal of a Block of j Chips
0	Not permitted
1	If the block constitutes the complete row
2	If the block lies at either end of the row, but does not constitute the complete row
3	Either 1 or 2
4	If the block lies strictly within the row
5	Either 1 or 4 (but not 2)
6	Either 2 or 4 (but not 1)
7	Always permitted (either 1 or 2 or 4)

Thus, Kayles is represented by 77 and Nim by 333 .... The Guy and Smith rule states that if a game is defined by a finite number N of α_j's and if positive integers y and p exist (that is, can be found empirically) such that

$$g(x + p) = g(x)$$

holds true for all values of x in the range $y \leq x < 2y + p + N$, then it holds true for all $x \geq y$, so that the Grundy function has ultimate period p.

Illustratively, consider the game of Kayles played with an initial configuration of three rows of 8, 9, and 10 chips. Referring to Table 10-5, the binary representations of the appropriate Grundy functions are displayed in the form

$$
\begin{aligned}
g(8) &= 1 \\
g(9) &= 100 \\
g(10) &= 10 \\
\hline
\text{Digital sum} &= 111
\end{aligned}
$$

Thus, the vertex $x_0 = (8, 9, 10)$ is not a member of $L(S)$ and hence constitutes a winning position. One winning move consists of removing a single chip from the row of 8 in a manner that leaves a row of 2 and a row of 5. The opponent is then faced with $x_1 = (2, 5, 9, 10)$ and a zero Grundy function: $g(2) \dotplus g(5) \dotplus g(9) \dotplus g(10) = 10 \dotplus 100 \dotplus 100 \dotplus 10 = 0$. He cannot, of course, find a move that maintains the even parity on the digital sum of the resulting Grundy functions.

Simplified forms of Tac Tix (where the mapping function Γ is restricted to rows only) can be played with values of $j > 2$. Table 10-7 tabulates the Grundy functions up to $g(10)$ for $3 \leq j \leq 7$. The game defined by $j = 4$ is known as Double Kayles (or 7777 in the Guy–Smith classification system);

TABLE 10-7   Grundy Functions for Simplified Tac Tix

Grundys	$j = 3$	$j = 4$	$j = 5$	$j = 6$	$j = 7$
$g(0)$	0	0	0	0	0
$g(1)$	1	1	1	1	1
$g(2)$	2	2	2	2	2
$g(3)$	3	3	3	3	3
$g(4)$	4	4	4	4	4
$g(5)$	1	5	5	5	5
$g(6)$	6	6	6	6	6
$g(7)$	3	7	7	7	7
$g(8)$	2	3	8	8	8
$g(9)$	1	2	3	9	9
$g(10)$	6	8	2	3	10

its Grundy functions exhibit an ultimate period of 24. In general, for $j = 2^i$, the resulting Kayles-like games have Grundy functions that ultimately repeat with period $6j$. Many other games with ultimately periodic

TABLE 10-8 Some Games with Ultimately Periodic Grundy Functions

Game (Guy–Smith Classification System)	Grundy Functions $g(0), g(1), \ldots$	Period
03	$00\overline{11}$	4
12	$01\overline{001}$	4
13	$\overline{0110}$	4
15	$01\overline{1011221 22}$	10
303030 ⋯	$\overline{01}$	2
(Nim with $S = \{2i + 1, \ i = 0, 1, \ldots\}$)		
31	$012\overline{01}$	2
32	$0\overline{102}$	3
33030003 ⋯	$\overline{012}$	3
(Nim with $S = \{2^i, \ i = 1, 2, \ldots\}$)		
34	$010120\overline{103121203}$	8
35	$0\overline{120102}$	6
52	$0102\overline{2103}$	4
53	$0112210224\overline{0122112241}$	9
54	$010\overline{1222411}$	7
57	$0\overline{1122}$	4
71	$012\overline{10}$	2
72	$01\overline{023}$	4

Grundy functions are suggested by the Guy–Smith classification system. For example, game 31 (where $\alpha_1 = 3$, $\alpha_2 = 1$) specifies the rule that one chip may be removed if it constitutes a complete row or if it lies at either end of a row without being a complete row, while a block of two chips may be removed only if it constitutes a complete row. Some of these games are listed in Table 10-8. The overlined numbers refer to the periodic component of the Grundy functions.

Nim and its variations, as discussed in the previous section, can also be analyzed with the theory of graphs. If the initial configuration in Nim₁, say, consists of n piles of chips, the corresponding graph requires an n-dimensional representation such that the vertex $(x_1, x_2, \ldots, x_n)$ defines the number of chips x_1 in the first pile, x_2 in the second pile, etc. Allowable moves permit a vertex to be altered by any amount one unit or more in a direction orthogonal to an axis. The Grundy function of the number of chips in each pile equals that number—that is, $g(x) = x$; thus, the Grundy function of each vertex is simply $g(x_1) \dotplus g(x_2) \dotplus \cdots \dotplus g(x_n)$. The members of $L(S)$ are those vertices labeled with a zero Grundy function; the game winner is that player who reaches the vertex $(0, 0, \ldots, 0)$.

It is simpler to demonstrate these statements by considering a two-pile game such as Tsyan/shi/dzi. In this instance, the rules (Γ) permit each player to move one or more units along a line orthogonally toward either axis and also one or more units inward along the diagonal (corresponding to the removal of an equal number of chips from both piles). Grundy functions for the vertices of a Tsyan/shi/dzi game are readily calculated.

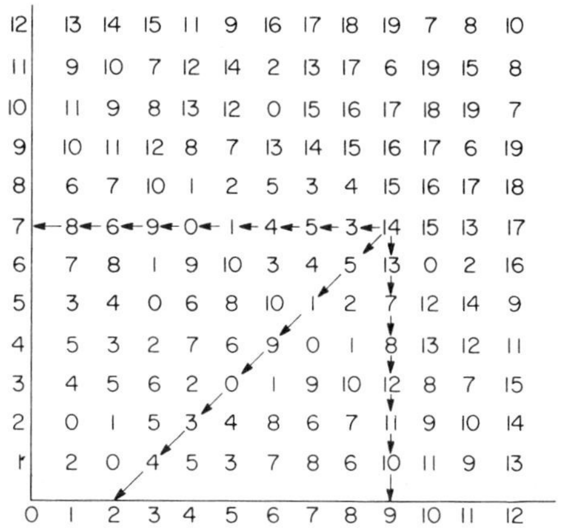

```
12│ 13  14  15  11   9  16  17  18  19   7   8  10

11│  9  10   7  12  14   2  13  17   6  19  15   8

10│ 11   9   8  13  12   0  15  16  17  18  19   7

 9│ 10  11  12   8   7  13  14  15  16  17   6  19

 8│  6   7  10   1   2   5   3   4  15  16  17  18

 7│◄─8◄─6◄─9◄─0◄─1◄─4◄─5◄─3◄─14  15  13  17

 6│  7   8   1   9  10   3   4   5  13   0   2  16

 5│  3   4   0   6   8  10   1   2   7  12  14   9

 4│  5   3   2   7   6   9   0   1   8  13  12  11

 3│  4   5   6   2   0   1   9  10  12   8   7  15

 2│  0   1   5   3   4   8   6   7  11   9  10  14

 1│  2   0   4   5   3   7   8   6  10  11   9  13
  └──────────────────────────────────────────────
    0   1   2   3   4   5   6   7   8   9  10  11  12
```

Fig. 10-6   Grundy functions for Tsyan/shi/dzi

The vertex (0, 0) is labeled with a zero, since it terminates the game; Grundy functions along the two axes increase by one with each outgoing vertex, since connecting paths are allowed to vertices of all lower values. The remaining assignments of Grundy functions follow the definition that a vertex is labeled with the smallest integer not represented by those vertices it is connected to by the mapping function Γ. Values of the graph to (12, 12) are shown in Fig. 10-6. From the vertex (9, 7), for example, the mapping function permits moves to any of the positions along the three lines indicated. Those vertices with zero Grundy functions are, of course, the members of $L(S)$ and constitute the "safe" positions: the Fibonacci pairs $([r\tau], [r\tau^2])$, $r = 1, 2, 3, \ldots$, where $\tau = (1 + \sqrt{5})/2$ and the brackets define the greatest integer not exceeding the enclosed quantity.

DISTICH; EVEN WINS

Countdown games can be distinguished by the position that designates the winner. In the game of "Distich," for example, two players alternately divide a pile of chips, selected from a group of n piles, into two unequal piles.[†] The last player who can perform this division is declared the winner. Strategy for the play of Distich evidently follows the rule of determining those vertices with a zero Grundy function, thus specifying the "safe" positions $L(S)$. The Grundy function for a configuration of n piles is simply the digital sum of the Grundy functions of each pile. Since a pile of one or two chips cannot be divided into two unequal parts, we have $g(1) = g(2) = 0$. For a pile of three chips, $g(3) = 1$, as 3 can be split only into 2 and 1; the digital sum of the Grundy functions of 2 and 1 is 0, and 1 is thus the smallest integer not connected to the vertex (3). Table 10-9 tabulates the Grundy functions for Distich up to $g(100)$. We should note that for Distich, as well as for Tsyan/shi/dzi and Nim, the Grundy functions are unbounded, although high values of $g(x)$ occur only for extremely high values of x. The "safe" positions for Distich are $L(S) = \{1, 2, 4, 7, 10, 20, 23, 26, 50, 53, 270, 273, 276, 282, 285, 288, 316, 334, 337, 340, 346, 359, 362, 365, 386, 389, 392, 566, \ldots\}$.

As a numerical example, we initiate a Distich game with three piles of

TABLE 10-9   Grundy Functions for Distich

x	$g(x)$	x	$g(x)$	x	$g(x)$	x	$g(x)$	x	$g(x)$
1	0	21	4	41	5	61	1	81	2
2	0	22	3	42	4	62	3	82	4
3	1	23	0	43	1	63	2	83	5
4	0	24	4	44	5	64	4	84	2
5	2	25	3	45	4	65	3	85	4
6	1	26	0	46	1	66	2	86	3
7	0	27	4	47	5	67	4	87	7
8	2	28	1	48	4	68	3	88	4
9	1	29	2	49	1	69	2	89	3
10	0	30	3	50	0	70	4	90	7
11	2	31	1	51	2	71	3	91	4
12	1	32	2	52	1	72	2	92	3
13	3	33	4	53	0	73	4	93	7
14	2	34	1	54	2	74	3	94	4
15	1	35	2	55	1	75	2	95	3
16	3	36	4	56	5	76	4	96	5
17	2	37	1	57	2	77	3	97	2
18	4	38	2	58	1	78	2	98	3
19	3	39	4	59	3	79	4	99	5
20	0	40	1	60	2	80	5	100	2

[†] Initially proposed by P. M. Grundy.

10, 15, and 20 chips. The corresponding Grundy functions are 0, 1, and 0, respectively, and their digital sum is 1; thus, for the vertex (10, 15, 20), the Grundy function is 1. A winning move is to split the pile of 10 into two piles of 3 and 7; the digital sum of the four Grundy functions associated with 3, 7, 15, and 20 is zero. The first player should be the winner of this particular game of Distich.

A modification of Distich allows a pile to be divided into any number of unequal parts. For this game, the Grundy functions $g(1)$, $g(2)$, $g(3)$, ... take the values 0, 0, 1, 0, 2, 3, 4, 0, 5, 6, 7, 8, 9, 10, 11, 0, 12, ...—that is, the sequence of positive integers spaced by the values $g(2^i) = 0$, $i = 0, 1, 2, \ldots$.

A game of Russian origin bearing a kindred structure with other countdown games is that of "Even Wins." In the original version, two players alternately remove from one to four chips from a single pile initially composed of 27 chips. When the final chip has been removed, one player will have taken an even number and the other an odd number; that player with the even number of chips is declared the winner. Correct strategy consists of reducing the pile to a number of chips equal to 1, mod 6, if the opponent has taken an even number of chips, and to 0 or 5, mod 6, if the opponent has an odd number of chips. The theorems of Nim with regard to "safe" and "unsafe" positions apply directly. All positions of the pile 1, mod 6, are "safe." Since 27 is equivalent to 3, mod 6, the first player can secure the win.

In more general form, "Even Wins" can be initiated with a pile of any odd number of chips from which the players alternately remove from 1 to n chips. Again, that player owning an even number of chips when the pile is depleted wins the game. The winning strategies are as follows: If n is even and the opponent has an even number of chips, $L(S) = \{1, \mod(n + 2)\}$; if the opponent has an odd number of chips, $L(S) = \{0, n + 1, \mod(n + 2)\}$. For odd n, winning strategy is defined by $L(S) = \{1, n + 1, \mod(2n + 2)\}$ if the opponent has an even number of chips and $L(S) = \{0, n + 2, \mod(2n + 2)\}$ if the opponent has an odd number. If a random odd number of chips is selected to comprise the pile initially, the first player possesses the win with probability $n/(n + 2)$, n even, and probability $(n - 1)/(n + 1)$, n odd.

The type of recursive analysis presented in this section is also applicable, in theory, to such "take-away" games as Tic-Tac-Toe, Pursuit games, Chess, Hex, and Pentominoes, and in general, to any competitive attrition game. Beyond the field of countdown games, more extensive applications of Grundy functions are implied by the theory of graphs. A potential area of considerable interest encompasses solutions for the dual control of finite-state games. A variant of such games is the "rendezvous" problem where the dual control reflects a cooperative nature. Other examples will likely arise in abundance as Grundy functions become more widely used.

POLYOMINOES

A fascinating class of games can be derived by manipulation of polyominoes on a chessboard (the term *polyomino* was devised in 1953 by Dr. Solomon W. Golomb, then a graduate student at Harvard University). By definition, an *n*-omino covers a rookwise-connected set of *n* squares of the chessboard. Several examples of polyominoes from $n = 1$ to $n = 4$ are pictured in Fig. 10-7. From the figure we can observe that monominoes and dominoes have unique configurations, the tromino can assume one of two forms, and the tetromino any of five. Asymmetrical pieces turned over are not regarded as constituting distinct forms.

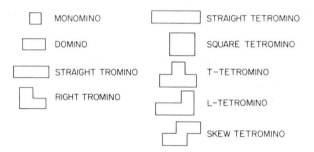

Fig. 10-7. Monominoes, dominoes, trominoes, and tetrominoes (*Permission—Joseph S. Madachy*)

The general properties of polyominoes have been extensively investigated by Golomb. He has proved a number of theorems, some of which we state here without repeating the proofs.

    I. The chessboard can be completely covered by 21 straight trominoes and a single monomino if and only if the monomino is located at one of the four squares shown in Fig. 10-8.

    II. Regardless of the placement of the monomino, the remaining 63 squares of the chessboard can be covered with 21 right trominoes.

    III. The chessboard can be completely covered by 16 straight, square, T-, or L-tetrominoes, but not by 16 skew tetrominoes (in fact, not even a single edge can be completely covered).

    IV. It is impossible to cover the chessboard with 15 T-tetrominoes and one square tetromino, nor can coverage be achieved with 15 L-tetrominoes and one square tetromino, nor with 15 straight or skew tetrominoes (in any combination) and one square tetromino.

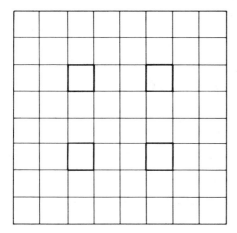

Fig. 10-8 Monomino placement (*Permission—Joseph S. Madachy*)

    V. The five distinct tetrominoes cannot be grouped together so as to form an unbroken rectangle.

    Proofs of these theorems, which lie in the domain of *combinatorial geometry*, are in general based on establishing certain coloring patterns for the chessboard squares and thence determining whether or not each color is blanketed by the various polyominoes. For example, to demonstrate the negative sense of Theorem I, we can paint the chessboard in the tricolored pattern of Fig. 10-9. With this scheme there are 22 red squares, 21 white

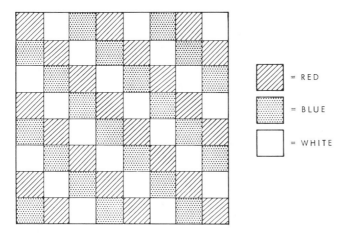

    = RED

    = BLUE

    = WHITE

Fig. 10-9. Straight tromino coverage (*Permission—Joseph S. Madachy*)

squares, and 21 blue squares. Placing the monomino on the lower left-hand corner leaves 22 red, 21 white, and 20 blue squares. Since a straight tromino, however situated, covers one red, one white, and one blue, it is obvious that 21 straight trominoes cannot cover the remaining 63 squares. It is equally obvious that to achieve complete coverage, the monomino must be located on a red square (in particular, reasons of symmetry dictate one of the four squares shown in Fig. 10-8).

There exist 12 distinct pentominoes and, from a recreational standpoint, their properties are more compelling than those of the other polyominoes. Golomb recommends the letter appellations indicated in Fig. 10-10 to describe the 12 shapes. It can be shown that the distinct pentominoes, which together overlay a total of 60 squares, may be grouped to

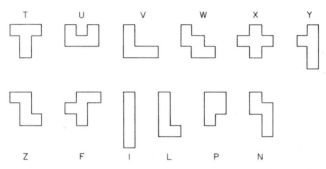

Fig. 10-10   The 12 pentominoes (*Permission—Joseph S. Madachy*)

form such patterns as a 3 × 20 rectangle, a 4 × 15 rectangle, a 5 × 12 rectangle, and a 6 × 10 rectangle. In the latter instance, Professor C. B. Haselgrove of Manchester University, England, programmed a computer to find the total number of basically distinct ways (excluding rotations and reflections) of filling the rectangle. The result was a total of 2339 patterns. On the other hand, there are but two unique solutions for the 3 × 20 rectangle, one of which is illustrated in Fig. 10-11. A verification of the uniqueness of the two solutions was obtained in 1958 by Dana S. Scott of Princeton University with a program for the MANIAC computer. It

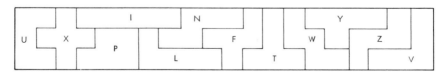

Fig. 10-11   Pentominoes on a 3 × 20 rectangle

should be observed that either side of a pentomino may be used in accommodating it into the rectangle.

A similar type of "jigsaw" puzzle involves arranging the 12 pentominoes on a chessboard, leaving a 2 × 2 hole (a square tetromino). If the 2 × 2 hole is placed in the center of the board, there are 65 basically different solutions (determined by Scott with MANIAC). One example is shown in Fig. 10-12.[†] Actually, the four uncovered squares can be distributed in arbitrary fashion about the board.

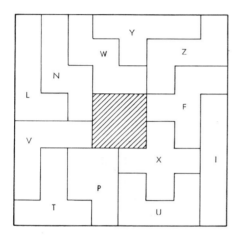

Fig. 10-12   Pentominoes on a chessboard

Of the various ways in which some of the above characteristics might be implemented in game form, perhaps that combining the simplest format with the most subtle complications is the Pentomino Game suggested by Golomb. In this game, two players alternately fit onto the chessboard one of the set of 12 distinct pentominoes until either no pieces remain or none of those remaining will fit on the board. The player unable to place a piece is declared to be the loser.

Maximum duration of the Pentomino Game is clearly 12 moves—when each of the 12 pieces has been played. A maximal game is highly improbable. Minimum duration is five moves; an example of a minimal game is shown in Fig. 10-13. None of the remaining seven pentominoes can be placed on the board.

A game-theoretic solution of the Pentomino Game has not been achieved and likely will not be without a significant advancement in compu-

---

[†] The first published solution of the 12 distinct pentominoes and a square tetromino covering the chessboard is credited to Henry Dudeney (*The Canterbury Puzzles*, 1907).

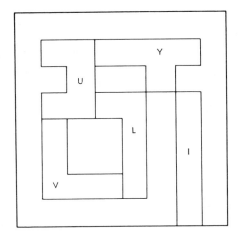

Fig. 10-13.   A minimal pentomino game

ter technology. However, it is self-evident that a win must occur for one of the two players. Golomb, a black-belt master of mathematical judo, offers two basic strategic principles:

1. Try to move in such a way that there will be room for an even number of pieces.
2. If you cannot analyze the situation, do something to complicate the position, so that the opponent will have even greater difficulty in analyzing it.

A typical game described by Golomb is pictured in Fig. 10-14. For the first move, player A places the X pentomino near the center, thereby preventing his opponent from splitting the board. Player B then places the U contiguous to the X, which also avoids splitting the board. Maintaining the theme of central placement, A locates the L as centrally as possible for the third move. Selecting the V, player B places it in a strategically poor fashion, which permits A to achieve a favorable split of the board. For the fifth move, A takes advantage of B's blunder by adroitly applying the W to split the board into two identical regions. Thus, his strategy is thenceforth to move in one region as his opponent does in the other. Player B situates the I in the lower left-hand area, leaving the P as the only remaining piece that could fit that region. Player A then performs the seventh and final move by preempting the P and placing it in the upper right-hand area. B cannot fit one of the remaining five pentominoes on the board and A therefore wins the game.

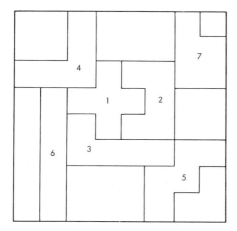

Fig. 10-14   Sample pentomino game

Several variations of the basic game have also been suggested by Golomb. In Choose-Up Pentominoes, the two players alternately select a piece from the set of 12 pentominoes until each has six; the game then proceeds in the normal manner, each player allowed to place only a member of his own set on the board. The player choosing first plays second to compensate for the advantage of first choice. Strategy for Choose-Up Pentominoes differs from that of the standard game in that instead of attempting to leave an even number of moves following his own move, the player strives to leave as many moves for his own pieces and as few moves as possible for his opponent's pieces. An approximate preference ordering of the values of the 12 pentominoes is $PNUYLVITZFWX$ (as a convenient mnemonic device, we suggest the sentence, "Pentominoes Need Understanding; You Lose Victory In The Zone Filled With Xenon"). In other variations of the basic game, the pentominoes can be distributed at random between the two players, more than one set of the 12 distinct pieces can be used, more than two players can participate, and boards other than the 8×8 chessboard can be introduced. For applied gamesters, colored plastic pentominoes were marketed in 1957 under the trade name Hexed,[†] and previously, under the commercial name Pan-Kai.

Of the higher order n-ominoes, the number and complexity increases exponentially with n, rendering them generally unsuitable for game applications. There are, for example, 35 hexominoes and 108 heptominoes, one of

† Tyrne Products, Inc., 233 Broadway, New York, N.Y.

the latter being nonsimply connected; that is, a hole is contained within that particular heptomino configuration. Further, there are 363 octominoes plus 6 with holes; 1248 enneominoes[†] plus 37 with holes; and 4460 decominoes plus 195 with holes. A total of 17,073 hendecominoes[†] and 63,000 dodecominoes exist, including those multiply-connected.[‡] The question of determining the number of distinct n-ominoes as a function of n is identical to a classical unsolved cell growth problem. We consider a one-celled animal of square shape, which can grow in the plane by adding a cell to any of its four sides; we then inquire as to how many distinct connected n-celled animals are possible under isomorphism. Stein, Walden, and Williamson of the Los Alamos Scientific Laboratory have programmed a computer to generate the isomorphism classes of such animals.

Although no computer program has yet been written for polyomino play, it should not be difficult to devise a competent program employing a variety of heuristics. The principal heuristics might be consideration of the symmetry of the pieces, possible use of board and piece coloring, optimal selection of the place on the board to fit the next piece, the optimal piece to select at each step, and the number and kinds of pieces eliminated from use by possible placements. Similar programs have been written for synthesizing a chessboard from a number of irregular components in the manner of a jigsaw puzzle.

Instead of constructing rookwise-connected sets of squares, we can effect the edgewise union of sets of equilateral triangles or of hexagons (only such sets of these three regular polygons can fill a plane). The sets of equilateral triangles, known as polyiamonds, were first explored by T. H. O'Beirne. For a given number of cells, fewer distinct shapes are possible than with polyominoes: moniamonds, diamonds, and triamonds can assume only one shape; there are three different-shaped tetriamonds four pentiamonds, 12 hexiamonds, and 24 heptiamonds.

Solid polyominoes have also been investigated by Golomb and R. K. Guy. Known as "Soma Cubes," they were invented by the prolific Piet Hein, who conceived the first pertinent theorem: The one irregular solid tromino and the six irregular solid tetrominoes (irregular in that the figure somewhere contains a corner) can be joined together to fashion a $3 \times 3 \times 3$

[†] Although "polyominoes" constitutes a false etymology from "dominoes," we advocate the pure approach of applying strictly Greek-root prefixes rather than the usual deplorable practice of successively mixing Greek and Latin roots.

[‡] The n-ominoes for $n = 11$ and 12 were enumerated on a CDC-1604 computer by Thomas R. Parkin of Aerospace Corporation.

cube. These seven solid polyominoes comprise a "Soma set," which can be used to devise a multitude of entertaining constructions. Additionally, we suggest an investigation into the properties of "polyominoids": two-dimensional squares in three-space. An n-ominoid contains n coplanar or orthogonal squares, thus resembling the floors, walls, and ceilings of a pathological office building. There exist 2 distinct dominoids (one coplanar domino plus one in three-space) and 10 distinct trominoids (2 trominoes plus 8 in three-space). The number of n-ominoids rises precipitously with increasing n.

The inventor of Tac Tix and Soma Cubes, Piet Hein, is also the creator of another fascinating mathematical game: Hex. Originated in 1942 while Hein was attending the Niels Bohr Institute for Theoretical Physics in Copenhagen, it was invented independently in 1948 by John F. Nash, then a graduate student at Princeton University. Hex is played on a rhombic-shaped board composed of hexagons. Conventionally, the Hex board has 11 hexagons along each edge, as shown in Fig. 10-15, although any reasonable number can be used (because of the resemblance of the Hex board to the tiles found on bathroom floors, the game is sometimes known as "John"). Two opposite sides of the rhombic are labeled the A sides, while the other two sides are designated as B's; hexagons at the corners of the board

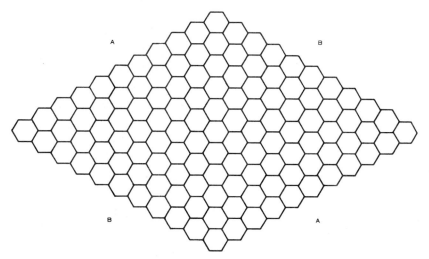

Fig. 10-15   The Hex board

represent joint property. Players A and B alternately place personal chips (usually black and white) on any unoccupied hexagon. The objective for each competitor is to complete a continuous path of personal chips between his two assigned sides of the board.

It is self-apparent that Hex cannot end in a draw, since a player can block his opponent only by completing his own path across the board. There exists a *reductio ad absurdum* existence proof—similar to that for Tic-Tac-Toe and Gale's Nim game—that the first player always possesses a win, although for boards 7 × 7 or greater, no winning strategy has been developed. For Reverse Hex (the player who forms a chain across the board *loses*), it can be shown that the first player has a winning strategy on an $n \times n$ board when n is even and the second player can win when n is odd.

An interesting analog mechanism to play Hex (although the game obviously involves digital processes) was designed by Claude Shannon and E. F. Moore. The basic apparatus establishes a two-dimensional potential field corresponding to the Hex board, with A's counters as positive charges and B's counters as negative charges. A's sides of the board are charged positively and the two other sides (B's) are charged negatively. An analog device with appropriate resistance networks and other circuitry was constructed to locate the saddle points, it being theorized that certain saddle points should correspond to advantageous moves. Shannon reports that the machine won about 70 percent of its games against human opposition when awarded the first move. As second player, the machine triumphed about 50 percent of the time. Its positional judgment proved satisfactory although it exhibited weakness in end-game combinatorial play.

Superficially similar to Hex is the game of Bridg-it,[†] created by David Gale. The Bridg-it board, shown in Fig. 10-16, comprises an $n \times (n + 1)$ rectangular array of dot marks embedded in a similar $n \times (n + 1)$ rectangular array of square marks. In turn, player A connects two adjacent dot marks with an a-colored bridge and player B connects two adjacent square marks with a b-colored bridge. The winner is the first player to complete an unbroken line between his two sides of the board.

As for Hex, the existence of the first player's winning strategy is readily proven for Bridg-it. Since the nature of this strategy was not immediately apparent, several Bridg-it-playing machines were constructed that performed with moderate success. Then, Oliver Gross of the RAND Corp. devised the general winning strategy illustrated by the dotted lines in Fig. 10-16. Player A begins by playing the bridge indicated in the figure; there-

---

[†] A trade name. It is marketed by Hasenfield Bros., Inc., Central Falls, Rhode Island.

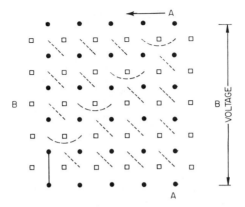

Fig. 10-16   The Bridg-it board and Oliver Gross's solution.

after, whenever a bridge by B crosses the end of a dotted line, A plays by crossing the other end of the same line. This pairing strategy—which can be extended to a Bridg-it board of any size—guarantees a win for A.

An unsolved variation of the Bridg-it game restricts each player to *m* bridges. If neither player has won after the 2*m* bridges have been placed, the game proceeds by shifting a bridge to a new position at each move.

PURSUIT GAMES

Another rich vein attractive to game theorists is that category termed Games of Pursuit. We distinguish between general games involving a pursuer and an evading target as mentioned previously and Games of Pursuit in that the latter do not involve probabilistic elements. In the generic model of a pursuit game, a pursuer P attempts capture of an evader E within some specified spacial enclosure (usually two-dimensional, for simplicity); the evader, of course, has the objective of avoiding or delaying capture, either indefinitely or over a specified time interval. Either P or E, or both, may be constrained in motion by bounds on speed, acceleration, direction, etc.

As a subset of the field known as "differential games" (motions of bodies treated as vectors in the playing space), pursuit games have been investigated most thoroughly by Rufus Isaacs, who is responsible for the initial concepts and terminology. Two examples contributed by Isaacs are (repeating his phraseology) "The Homicidal Chauffeur" and "The Hamstrung Squad Car." In the first example, P and E move in a common plane with respective speeds v_p and v_e, where $v_p > v_e$ (no loss of generality ensues from the assumption that P and E are always moving at maximum speed); the restriction is placed on P's path, which is not permitted a radius of curvature less than a fixed value R. The payoff is the time required for P to capture E, where the capture region is defined as a circle of radius ρ fixed about P; the game concludes when E is maneuvered within this region. The evident analogy is that of an automobile intent upon running down a fleeing pedestrian caught in an unobstructed area.

If P and E are initially close together, E can avoid capture by maneuvering within P's circle of maximum curvature. Thus, qualitatively, P's optimal strategy is to recede from E to where he can turn at a radius of curvature R to be facing directly at E. From E's standpoint, it is advisable to pursue P in order to delay P's attaining adequate separation; thence, as P begins his turn, E should flee directly away until captured. Figure 10-17 depicts these strategies. Initial positions for P and E are P_0 and E_0, respectively. As P recedes, E follows to E_1, then turns (while P is turning) and flees, succumbing to P's greater speed at E_2.

If P's radius of curvature is sufficiently large, E can evade capture indefinitely by sidestepping as P approaches. Specifically, it can be shown that capture can be evaded under the condition

$$\frac{\rho}{R} < \sqrt{1 - \left(\frac{v_e}{v_p}\right)^2} + \sin^{-1}\left(\frac{v_e}{v_p}\right) - 1$$

Conversely, capture is always possible when this inequality is reversed.

In the example of "The Hamstrung Squad Car," the chase occurs along the grid lines of an infinite square lattice—pictorially, the parallel and orthogonal streets of a large city. A fugitive pedestrian E is fleeing from a squad car P, and while E can move in any direction, P must conform to traffic rules prohibiting left turns and U-turns. Discretizing the model, we constrain P and E to one of the vertices of the lattice. At each instant, E may move one space to any of the four adjoining points; P may move two spaces, but only in a direction coinciding with or to the right of his previous move. Capture occurs when both participants occupy the same or adjacent points on the grid. The payoff is the number of moves required for capture.

With respect to P's initial position P_0, the problem is to label each vertex with a value representing the number of moves required for capture, assuming E begins at that point, with optimal play on the part of both P and E. Conventionally, the first move is awarded to P. The origin (P_0) and its eight adjoining points (the capture region about the origin) are

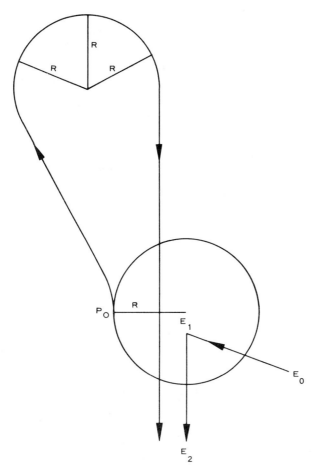

Fig. 10-17 Qualitative pursuit and evasion strategies
(*Permission—RAND Corporation*)

immediately labeled 0. And, since P moves first, the points on which E is captured by P's first move are evident and are labeled 1—we assume a direction for P's previous move. To determine those points on which capture occurs in two moves, we note the set of points completely surrounded (in the four directions allowable) by 0's and 1's, with at least one 1 included in the palisade ; if a move by P translates an unmarked point into such an enclosed point (the translation occurs in a manner always leaving P at the origin and its direction of motion fixed straight ahead), then the former is labeled 2. In general, if a move by P translates an unmarked point onto one completely surrounded by four points previously marked with 0's, 1's, 2's, ..., or n's, with at least one n included, then that point is labeled $n + 1$.

Table 10-10 illustrates the entire numbered lattice, assuming P's previous move as shown. After the points marked 11 are located, no further points can be found satisfying the specified construction procedure. If E is initially located at a point labeled $n \leq 11$, he can, with optimal play, be captured in n moves under the stated constraints. If E begins at an unmarked point, then, exercising proper tactics, he is never subject to capture. E's optimal strategy is to move to the highest label possible with respect to P's

TABLE 10-10   A Pursuit Problem With Directional Constraints

			8	11					
			5	8					
		3	4	7	10				
		2	3	4	7				
	1	1	1	3	6	9			
	1	1	1	2	3	6			
	0	0	0	1	1	5	8		
	0	0 P_0	0	1	1	2	3		
9	0	0 ↑	0	1	1	3	4	5	8
	7	4	3	2	3	4	7	8	11
10	7	4	3	6	7	10			
		8	5	6	9				
		11	8						

(Permission—RAND Corporation)

position and direction of motion. If possible, E should move to an unlabeled point; it can be demonstrated that, beginning on an unlabeled point, E is always offered the possibility of moving to another unlabeled point following his translation in the coordinate system engendered by P's move (thus he perpetually evades capture).

More complex games are generated by increasing P's speed advantage to three or more moves to 1 and by considering triangular or polygonal lattices for the field of play with corresponding constraints on P's motion.

Optimal pursuit strategies have found a multitude of engineering applications. In their general form, they are related to the "proportional navigation" law utilized in many missile guidance systems. A treasury of fascinating pursuit lore is available in Rufus Isaacs's excellent book on differential games.

Computer programs for board games

Of those pandemic pastimes of pure skill that have retained their popularity under the contemporary sophisticated view of competitive events, the majority offer a complexity that precludes a complete solution for a best strategy, even with the aid of high-speed digital computers. Most of these surviving games of skill are board games. Generally, they are either *capture* games, such as Checkers, Reversi, Chess, and the multitudinous forms of Fairy Chess, where the objective is to capture all or certain critical elements of the opponent's forces (sometimes, as in the game of Kalah, the pieces are not identified—except by temporary location—as property of a particular team); *control* games, such as Go,[†] where the objective is to control territory by surrounding sections of the playing field (in Go, the capture of the opponent's stones is merely a means toward acquiring territory); or *blockade* games, such as Do-guti, where the objective is to confine the adversary to a particular portion of the playing area, or Dama, where the objective is to acquire a particular portion of the board while blocking an adversary from acquisition of a similar area.

Generally, these pastimes exhibit a structure in addition to that necessary to define their game-theoretic properties. For every position, a set of possible moves is defined for each player. Further, there is a finite set P of possible positions and a particular initial position $P_0 \in P$. At each position there also exists a set of possible moves $M_a(p)$ for player A and $M_b(p)$ for player B. The condition of finiteness then states that successive positions $p_1, p_2, p_3, \ldots$ are such that

$$p_{j+1} \in M_a(p_j) \cup M_b(p_j), \qquad j = 1, 2, 3, \ldots$$

must terminate. In theory, games conforming to this condition can be solved completely by computer programming. In practice, the move tree connecting the positions has such an astronomical number of branches that even a high-speed digital computer could investigate only a small percentage of the branches within a reasonable time period. The game theorist is consequently confronted with the perennial problem of establishing the relative values of tangible versus intangibles—of material versus time, space, and mobility. And since every position may be specifically distinct, general principles can be applied only as a guide, not as gospel.

[†] Go-Moku, despite the association implied by its name, is not a control game, but a game of alignment. Played on a Go board, it is merely a form of super Tic-Tac-Toe, with the objective of achieving a colinear configuration of five (and only five) adjoining stones.

Historically, attempts to construct game-playing computers extend back to 1769 when the Hungarian inventor Baron Wolfgang von Kempelen astounded Europe with a device known as the Maelzel Chess Automaton (so named because it was exhibited and exploited by M. Maelzel). Despite several learned papers purporting to analyze its method of operation, the Automaton was actually controlled by a Chess-skilled dwarf. The deception was exposed when, during a match, someone shouted "Fire," thereby inducing paroxysms of panic in the machine.

An honest attempt at designing a Chess-playing machine was made by the Spaniard L. Torres y Quevado at the end of the nineteenth century. Señor Torres's device, a relatively simple switching circuit, was designed to play an end game whereby a King and Rook could, within a few moves, force a checkmate against an opponent possessing only a King.

To play a "perfect" Chess strategy, a computer composed of high-speed conventional switching circuits would require aeons of analytic effort. At each instant of play, a Chess situation offers an average of about 32 possible moves with about 32 possible replies for each move. Thus, for a game lasting 40 moves (by each of the two adversaries), there are approximately $(32 \times 32)^{40} \simeq 10^{120}$ variations to consider. A computer capable of evaluating one variation per microsecond would calculate for more than 10^{93} centuries to select its first move.

It is evident, therefore, that for the nontrivial games of pure skill, we cannot with present techniques design a computer to play a "best" strategy —contrary to the situation for the games of Nim and Tic-Tac-Toe, for example, where a computer can be constructed to play a "perfect" game (where a win is possible, the computer will always win). Instead, we must compromise by programming a computer to achieve a reasonably skillful game by following certain general principles of play or maxims of sound strategy. These strategic principles can be evolved empirically or can be derived by the computer itself through its own experience of playing games by trial and error, by self-analysis of failures, or by other means that improve its playing skill.

CHESS

Most of the current game-playing computer programs are based upon techniques adumbrated in 1948 by Claude Shannon. Confining his analysis to the game of Chess, Shannon proposed creating a playing strategy governed by an evaluation function (encompassing three factors: material, Pawn structure, and mobility). Any position P is evaluated in the following manner:

$$E(P) = 200(\Delta K) + 9(\Delta Q) + 5(\Delta R) + 3(\Delta B + \Delta N) + \Delta P$$
$$- 0.5(\Delta D + \Delta S + \Delta I) + 0.1(\Delta M)$$

where ΔK, ΔQ, ΔR, ΔB, ΔN, and ΔP are the differences in the number of Kings, Queens, Rooks, Bishops, Knights, and Pawns possessed by White over those remaining to Black; ΔD, ΔS, and ΔI represent the differences in doubled Pawns, backward Pawns, and isolated Pawns, respectively; ΔM is the difference in the number of legal moves available. If $E(P)$ is positive the position is evaluated as advantageous to White. Other, more intricate evaluation functions have been devised. All such functions, Shannon indicated, can claim only "statistical validity."

White plays to create positions that maximize $E(P)$, while Black counters by seeking positions that lead to minimum values of $E(P)$—so that a minimax solution is ultimately obtained.

Evaluating functions according to prescribed principles of play (these principles generally differ greatly when applied to the opening, middle, or end game) and to a fixed depth of the move tree is designated by Shannon as following a type A strategy. Such a strategy is relatively slow and has proved ineffectual in competition against high-caliber players. To consider variations over a six-move (or six-"ply") future—that is, three moves by each player—involves about 10^9 evaluations, a task requiring several days of computer time with current technology. Consequently, Shannon has proposed a type B strategy, which screens the variations to be evaluated according to some selection function and which then examines these significant variations over as many future moves as practical and only at positions reflecting a degree of stability.

Following a type A or type B strategy, the computer would always recommend the same move in the same position. It is possible to avoid this *idée fixe* by introducing a statistical element so that if two or more moves are of nearly equal value, one is selected at random. The principal weakness of a program for a type A or B strategy is the inability of the computer to learn from the consequences of inferior play.

The first Chess-playing program translated into practice was designed by the eminent British theoretician A. M. Turing in 1951 for the MADAM computer. Pursuing an essentially type B strategy, the machine played at a low-level of competence, usually resigning after a series of tactical blunders.

Several attempts were launched toward gaining an insight into Chess-programming techniques by designing a simplified Chess model. One of the few fruitful miniatures was designed at the Los Alamos Scientific Laboratory in 1956 for the MANIAC I computer. The Chess model comprised a 6 × 6 board with the Bishops removed from the conventional array of pieces, castling disallowed, and the initial Pawn move restricted to one square. Computer time to evaluate variations over two full moves into the future averaged 12 minutes per move. Evaluation of position was defined as the sum of material advantage (derived by evaluating capture and recapture possibilities) and mobility (the number of legal moves available to the player following each possible future move). The machine played a weak game, exhibiting a mortal fear of checks, and therefore tending to sacrifice material to avoid checks.

A complete Chess program (searching the move tree to a four-ply depth) was written in 1957 for an IBM 704 computer by Bernstein, Roberts, Arbuckle, and Belsky of the IBM Corporation. The program posed eight questions to be answered at each move:

1. Has check been announced, and if so, can the checking piece be captured, or a piece interposed, or can the King be moved away?
2. Are any exchanges possible, and if so, can material be gained by entering upon the exchange, or should the piece be moved away?
3. Is castling possible if not previously performed?
4. Can a minor piece be developed?
5. Can an open file be occupied?
6. Is there a piece that can be placed on the critical squares created by Pawn chains?
7. Can a Pawn move be made?
8. Can a piece move be made?

From the answers to these questions, the program selects only the seven most logical moves in each position for further analysis (this technique is known as "forward pruning"). Each variation is evaluated by four considerations: material gain, King defense, piece mobility, and control of important squares. Approximately 2800 positions are evaluated to select a move, the process requiring an average of 8 minutes and a computer program of 7000 words. In its play, the computer was rated as amateur caliber. Its strategy was weak in the end game and it appeared biased toward moving pieces under attack rather than defending them.

A more sophisticated, albeit slower, Chess program was realized in 1958 by Newell, Shaw, and Simon, using the RAND JOHNNIAC computer. The basic format of the program involved goals, move generation, evaluation, and final choice. The more important goals considered were King safety, material balance, center control, development, King-side attack, and Pawn promotion. Goals can be added to or deleted from the program independently. A weighted list of goals controls the subsequent processing leading to a final choice of move.

Representing a deliberate simulation of the human thought process, Newell, Shaw, and Simon instituted into the Chess program an information processing language (IPL) that offers the significant advantage of interpretative programming over direct machine-coding techniques. Being task-oriented, a source language is effective as a means of performing continuous changes. Fundamentally, an IPL is designed to manipulate lists, permitting the execution of programs involving highly complicated list structures without attendant overwhelming problems of memory assignment and program planning. There are about 100 terms in the Chess vocabulary, which enables the computer to express essentially all the significant considerations leading to selection of a move.

More recently (in 1961) Niessen, Lieberman, and Kotok at M.I.T. Computation Center developed a Chess program for the IBM 709 computer using a variable-depth search and terminating each variation investigated either at an arbitrary maximum or at a position of approximate stability. Evaluation was then performed at those points of the move tree. The criteria controlling the evaluation were a weighted sum of material balance, center control, Pawn structure, "tempo" advantage, and development. Material values employed were Pawn 1, Knight and Bishop 3, Rook 5, Queen 9, and King 1000, these values being multiplied by 60 when combined with the other evaluating functions. If, during the game, the computer achieved a four-point lead, the material multiplying factor was adjusted so that equal trades appear advantageous. While it is not immediately feasible to achieve, a more advanced program might vary the material advantage as a function of the position and remaining pieces. Center-control points were designated as worth 1/60 of a Pawn, a maximum of eight such points being awarded for control of a particular center square. Development points were weighted as 1/15 of material points, with one point given for Pawn development and three to four points for piece development. Points for the Pawn structure function were weighted as 1/20 of material points. An open file was accorded eight points and a passed Pawn, ten points. Isolated Pawns, backward Pawns, and doubled Pawns were penalized by minus one, minus five, and minus three points, respectively. With these criteria, the machine was capable of a skill on the level of an intelligent amateur with about 100 games' experience.

Depending on the positional complexity, from 5 to 20 minutes were required by the IBM 709 to reach a choice of move. Since the machine was investigating many irrelevant positions, it was decided to prune the move tree of obviously inferior branches. An interesting scheme for this purpose, designated the "alpha-beta" heuristic, was proposed by Prof. John Mc-Carthy, currently at Stanford University. Alpha is a number representing the value of the best position that White can achieve by some future number of moves under a pessimistic evaluation criterion. Beta is a numeric describing the best position that White can achieve under an optimistic evaluation. At each level, optimistic and pessimistic evaluations are performed. If a possible White move is optimistically less than alpha or pessimistically greater than beta, it is discarded, since White has a better alternative in the first instance and Black has a better alternative in the second. The reverse strategy is applicable for Black.

A significant improvement in computer Chess was achieved in 1967 with the MacHack VI program written by Richard Greenblatt for the M.I.T. PDP-6 computer. MacHack VI, designed in accordance with Shannon's type B strategy with extensive forward pruning, can search enormously large trees. Its evaluation function is composed of five factors: material, material ratio, Pawn structure, King safety, and center control. About 50 heuristics are used to determine the plausibility of a given move.

In recent years, these Chess programs have been modified and improved in degree, but not in kind. Mostly, the programs have followed Shannon's type B strategy (J. Biit, COKO III, SCHACH, and OSTRICH, *inter alia*). One exception is the TECH program developed by James Gillogly of the Carnegie-Mellon University. TECH (written for a PDP-10 computer) generates all legal moves to a fixed depth (five-ply in the middle game). It achieves greater speed than other "brute force" programs by using a simpler evaluation function which expresses the difference in material owned by Black and White.

Beginning in 1966 with a U.S. versus U.S.S.R. match, computer Chess tournaments have been held at frequent intervals. The Russian programs have generally demonstrated superiority [in the 1966 match, the Soviet ITEK (Institute of Theoretical and Experimental Physics in Moscow) beat a Stanford University IBM 7000 programmed by Alan Kotok and John McCarthy by a score of 3 to 1]. The first World Computer Chess Championship was held at Stockholm in August, 1974. KAISSA (the Russian program) finished first, winning all four of its games. Second and third places were earned by U.S. and Canadian programs: CHESS 4.0 (written for the Northwestern University CDC-6600) and RIBBIT (written for the University of Waterloo Honeywell 6060). KAISSA's unique feature was a multidomain search wherein each successive domain examines a subset of moves that were admissible in the preceding domain. Both KAISSA and CHESS 4.0

constitute amalgams of type A and type B strategies. Compared to human players, these programs are competitive on a "B" level.

At present, it appears that Chess programs are improving asymptotically. With greater speed, the move tree can be searched to greater depths, but not deep enough to formulate the long-range plans conceivable by a human player. Although evaluation functions can be ever refined, no function has produced stable and unique values for every possible position under evaluation. A major advance would be development of an evaluation process which, *sui generis*, leads to the "best" move without the time-consuming drawback of exhaustive tree searching.

For play between humans, the principal controversy of recent years concerns the manner of crediting draw games in resolving the matches for the world Chess championship. It is customary for a championship match to consist of $2n$ games ($n = 12$) with 1 point awarded for a win, 1/2 point for a draw, and 0 for a loss. The champion requires a score of n points to retain his title; the challenger needs $n + \frac{1}{2}$ to supersede him.

If champion and challenger are of equal skill, the probability of either winning a single game is $\frac{1}{2}(1 - r)$, where r is the probability of a draw—and R_n is the probability that both score n points in a match of 2^n games, then the champion will retain his title with probability P_n given by

$$P_n(r) = R_n + \tfrac{1}{2}(1 - R_n) = \tfrac{1}{2}(1 + R_n) \qquad\qquad 10\text{-}1$$

The probability $Q_n(r)$ that the match will result in k wins by the champion, k wins by the challenger, and $2n - 2k$ draws is the multinomial distribution (Eq. 2-16),

$$Q_n(r) = \frac{(2n)!}{(k!)^2(2n - 2k)!} \left(\frac{1 - r}{2}\right)^{2k} r^{2n - 2k}$$

and

$$R_n(r) = \sum_{k=0}^{n} Q_n(r)$$

For $n = 1$, Eq. 10-1 yields

$$P_1(r) = \tfrac{1}{4}(3r^2 - 2r + 3)$$

which is minimized for $r = 1/3$: $P_1(1/3) = 2/3$. For $n = 2$,

$$P_2(r) = \frac{35}{16} r^4 - \frac{15}{4} r^3 + \frac{21}{8} r^2 - \frac{3}{4} r + \frac{11}{16}$$

which is minimized for $r = 0.253$: $P_2(0.253) = 0.614$. For $n = 12$, as in championship matches, $P_{12}(r)$ is minimized with $r = 0.087$: $P_{12}(0.087) = 0.543$. The minimizing value of r approaches 0 for large n.

For moderate values of n, the champion is accorded a substantial advantage by the system that registers draw games as value $1/2$; the figures support those who contend that draws should not play a strategic role in championship play. Equation 10-1 advises the champion to play conservatively—that is, to adopt a strategy leading to large values of r—and urges the challenger to seek wins even at considerable risk. In grandmaster play, $r \sim 2/3$; illustratively, $P_{12}(2/3) = 0.571$, $P_{12}(0.9) = 0.635$, $P_{12}(1/2) = 0.557$, $P_{12}(0) = 0.581$.

The preceding analysis errs slightly in that champion and challenger can be considered of equal ability only in paired games with each playing White and Black in turn.

Compilations of recent international tournaments indicate that White's win probability is 0.31 while Black's win probability is 0.22. The probability of a draw is 0.47. These data suggest an equitable scoring system of 1 and 0 points to either player for a win and loss, respectively, while White receives 0 and Black receives $1/4$ point for the draw. Thus, over a series of games, the assignment of the White and Black pieces becomes theoretically irrelevant. For world championship play, drawn games should either be discounted or scored as $1/8$ for Black.

CHECKERS (DRAUGHTS)

Virtually all game-theoretic problems posed by Checkers have been solved except for a complete catalogue of strategies. Seven possible alternatives exist for Black's opening move with seven alternative ways of responding. Of the 49 two-move openings, 45 lead to draws and 4 to losses (with "correct" play). There are at least 142 distinct three-move openings that lead to draws. In major tournaments, players are not allowed to choose opening moves, but are assigned one of the 142 openings selected at random. The preponderant number of games in expert play are drawn.

Of the moderate number of computer programs for the game of Checkers, that designed in 1959 by Dr. Arthur L. Samuel of IBM for the IBM 704 has proved to be the most effective (C. S. Strachey's earlier program for a large-scale computer is worthy of note). The principal feature of Samuel's program is the introduction of a learning technique enabling the machine to improve its skill with playing experience. Move selection is accomplished by the computer by investigating several moves into the future along the branches of the move tree and evaluating the resulting board position by means of a linear polynomial. The individual terms of this polynomial are numerical measures of the various properties of the board positions; an appropriate coefficient defining the relative importance of each term is entered as a multiplicative factor and the complete terms summed linearly to form the evaluation polynomial. Typical terms relate to such concepts as mobility, control of diagonals, capture possibilities, and number and location of Kings; a total of 16 terms comprise the polynomial.

To effect the learning procedure, the computer is programmed to act as two different players, Alpha and Beta. Following each move, Alpha generalizes on its experience by adjusting the coefficients of its evaluation polynomial and replacing those terms that appear to be unimportant with new parameters drawn from a reserve pool. Beta, on the other hand, retains the same polynomial throughout the game. Subsequent to a period of self-play, a neutral portion of the program compares the relative playing abilities of Alpha and Beta. If Alpha has won a majority of the games, its current method of evaluation is transferred to Beta, whereas if Beta has won a majority, Alpha is penalized with one demerit. After Alpha has accumulated a given number of demerits, a drastic alteration of its evaluation polynomial is executed by reducing the coefficient of its dominant term to zero. The move-by-move evaluation on the part of Alpha avoids penalizing the superior moves in a game that is subsequently lost, owing to one cataclysmic blunder. The drastic alteration in Alpha's polynomial is occasionally required to extricate the learning process from a localized trap on a secondary maximum in the evaluation space. Generally, Alpha wins a large percentage of games at the beginning of a series. Then, as learning proceeds, it becomes increasingly difficult for Alpha to achieve an improvement in its skill, and its win percentage decreases with time.

Computer time necessitated by Samuel's program is held to 30 seconds per move by means of an elaborate table of past games from which information can be swiftly searched, sorted, and extracted. Thus a large number of games can be self-played by the computer, allowing considerable development of the learning process. The machine is capable, ultimately, of a caliber of play exceeding the capability of the best human Checker connoisseur.

Checker variants have not, at this writing, been subjected to computer analysis. Other than the standard American Checkers, or English Draughts, the more popular forms include le Jeu des Dames (the French Checkers game), Polish Checkers (a French invention played with 20 pieces per side on a 10 × 10 board), German Checkers, or Damenspiel, Turkish Checkers (played with 16 men per side on a conventional 8 × 8 board), and Poddavki, a Russian view of Checkers in which the object is to lose all one's pieces. In le Jeu des Dames, a piece, upon reaching the eighth row, is transformed into a Queen (rather than a King). A Queen may move as far as desired along any diagonal over any number of opposition pieces, capturing all those in its wake. Curiously, the greater prowess of the Queen weakens her force against other Queens. Whereas two Kings can always capture an opposition King, four Queens may be required to eliminate an opposing Queen when the latter is situated on the long diagonal (otherwise three Queens are sufficient). A Checkers-like game amenable to computer logic is "Fox and Geese." It is played with four checkers moving only in the forward direction attempting to entrap the solitary King checker manipulated by the opponent.

DAMA

The game of Dama is played on a checkerboard with eight pieces per side located initially on the first and last two ranks of the board. Although the pieces move in a Checkers-like fashion, the strategy of Dama is distinct from that of Checkers, the character of the game falling into a *blockade* format. The objective of the game is to move the eight pieces constituting one team from their initial two ranks across the board to the opposite pair of ranks while preventing the opponent from fulfilling the corresponding objective. If a player causes a blocked position whereby his opponent retains no legal move, the game is declared to be won by the opponent. Each piece moves diagonally forward by single step or can jump one or more pieces, as in conventional Checkers. The pieces jumped can be members of either side and are not removed from the board after being jumped. There are $56! \times 10^9$ ways, without considering jumps, that a player's pieces can reach the desired final configuration. Thus, analysis is accomplished by establishing an evaluation polynomial comprising a linear combination of figures of merit. Using this technique, Dama has been programmed by N. V. Findler for SILLIAC, the electronic computer of the Adolph Basser Computing Laboratory.

GO

In contrast to the "artificial" rules that govern Chess and Checkers play—in the sense that these rules (such as those specifying the movements of the pieces) can be altered in many ways without altering the strategic format—the game of Go[†] exhibits a "natural" legalistic structure. It has survived for centuries without change. Played by setting black and white stones on the intersections of a 19×19 square array, the deceptively simple objective of Go is (for Black and for White) to surround as great an area of the playing field as possible. Stones of the same color form chains if rookwise connected. A vacant point orthogonally adjoining a chain is a *degree of freedom*; chains or single stones left with no degrees of freedom are removed from the board and added to the opponent's score at the conclusion of the contest. Final scoring is the sum of stones captured and vacant points of territory surrounded.

There can occur $3^{19 \times 19} \simeq 10^{172}$ possible board positions during the course of a Go match. No mathematical theory of the game is known or is within the technical horizon.

The first significant effort at machine simulation of Go is due to H. Remus, using an IBM 704 computer. As a simplification, the program was written for a reduced field of size 11×11, thereby yielding $3^{11 \times 11} \simeq 10^{57}$ possible board positions. A lexicon of certain position classes that have been proved successful from past games is continuously compiled (retaining only those moves showing a maximum ratio of success.) When it is the computer's move, its first action is to search the lexicon for a possible successful move in the current position. If no such move is available, a selection of another move is achieved by examining a linear combination of weighted criteria applied to the concomitant position. These criteria include the possible number of degrees of freedom of chains, number of stones captured, distance from the last stone set by the opponent, and number and loyalty of stones in certain areas. After completion of each game, its experience is evaluated and culled for the lexicon. Thus, as its learning progresses, the computer should find the lexicon supplying an increasing percentage of its moves.

An alternative approach to computer Go is to combine positional evaluation and tree searching as is practiced with Chess. Thorp and Walden have produced such programs to play Go on $M \times N$ boards for small values of M and N. For the full 19×19 board, the number of game tree branches

---

[†] Although usually credited to the Japanese (who can rightfully claim greatest proficiency), Go is of Chinese origin, probably about the beginning of the third millenium B.C. It is known as Wei-ch'i (envelopment game) in Chinese and was not introduced into Japan until A.D. 754, when the Japanese ambassador to China, Kibidaijin, returned home to spread the word. The idea of capturing pieces by surrounding them originated with the ancient Egyptian game of Senat (the modern version, Seega, is still played); in this game, pieces were captured by colinear straddling moves.

to investigate is more than 75 orders of magnitude greater than that associated with Chess. Further, Go reflects a greater number of ranks in the hierarchy of skilled players, suggesting that it demands greater levels of skill in determining "best" strategic moves.

THOUGHTS ON COMPUTERS

It is clear that the games of pure skill we have described pose problems of ultracomplexity to the present generation of computers. A staggering amount of computing power is demanded for a machine to play such games with even mediocre proficiency. However, the ability of the computer to modify its own instructions is the greatest single faculty suggesting that in the near future, probably within ten years, machines will be able to defeat decisively any grand-master player of any currently known game. In the case of Chess, it being an historically evolved conventional system with emotional appeal, there are many master players who resent the intrusion of a computer into what they consider to be an artistic domain. Michael Botvinnik, an electrical engineer as well as a former world Chess champion, although defending his "Persian poetry" as an art with science playing a subsidiary role, yet predicts the imminence of super machine play. Perhaps, in a mechanomorphic future, Chess tournaments will be restricted to android competitors and machines awarded ratings in a national Chess organization.

The probable nature of the logical structure of such machines is difficult to forecast. At present, the trend is toward an imitation of the human brain structure. Yet a human brain contains approximately ten billion neurons, logic and memory units, and possesses the capabilities of instinct, intuition, and imagination, which permit intelligent, adaptive, and creative behavior. A contemporary computer, by comparison, encompasses the equivalent of about 100,000 neurons; it cannot act intuitively by the accepted meaning of intuition.[†] Human Chess players employ a qualitative and functional analysis; computers might be well advised to seek a different *modus operandi*. There is no profound reason why the ultimate format of game-playing computers should resemble a human counterpart any more than interplanetary rockets should adhere to aviary principles. Whatever the course of development, the limits of computers with respect to human functions have yet to be seen.

[†] Nor can it dream.

Two board problems

The reader is invited to test his ingenuity in the following games of pure skill.

1. *Quadraphage.* As its name implies, the Quadraphage is a Chess-like piece that "eats away" any square it is placed upon. For a move the Quadraphage may leap to any unoccupied square. With a Chess King and a Quadraphage situated on an infinite Chessboard and alternating moves, show that it is possible for the Quadraphage to entrap the King. (Specifically, if the King begins at the center of a 34 × 34 board, he cannot escape the board against a Quadraphage using optimum strategy.)

2. *Mini-Chess.* Each of two players is given a King, a Rook, and a Pawn. White places one of his three pieces on the board. Black then places one of his pieces on any (legal) square. White places his second piece, then Black, and White and Black again. From the configuration now established, White moves first and the play proceeds in the conventional manner of a Chess end game. What principles should each player follow for the place-ment of his pieces?

Suggested references

ALONSO, J. "Blanco o Negro" *Ajedrez Canario*, October, 1974.

BELLMAN, RICHARD, "System Identification, Pattern Recognition and Dynamic Programming," Hughes Aircraft Co., Research Report No. 327, December, 1964.

BERGE, CLAUDE, *The Theory of Graphs*, John Wiley & Sons, Inc., New York, 1962.

BERGE, CLAUDE, and A. GHOUILA-HOURI, *Programming, Games and Transportation Networks*, Methuen & Co., Ltd., London, 1965.

BERLINER, HANS J., "Some Necessary Conditions for a Master Chess Program," *Proc. Third Internat. Joint Conf. Artificial Intelligence*, pp. 77–85, Stanford, California, 1973.

BERNSTEIN, ALEX, and MICHAEL DE V. ROBERTS, "Computer vs. Chess Player," *Scientific American*, Vol. 198 (June, 1958).

BERNSTEIN, ALEX, MICHAEL DE V. ROBERTS, T. ARBUCKLE, and M. A. BELSKY, "A Chess Playing Program for the IBM 704," Proc. Western Joint Computer Conference, May 6–8, 1958, at Los Angeles, California, pp. 157–159. Published by AIEE, New York, March, 1961.

BLOCK, H. D., "Learning in Some Simple Non-biological Systems," *Amer. Scientist.* **53**, No. 1 (Spring, 1955), pp. 59–79.

BOTVINNIK, MIKHAIL, "Men and Machines at the Chessboard," *The Soviet Review*, **55**, No. 2, Pt. 1 (March, 1961), pp. 55–59.

BOUTON, CHARLES, "Nim, A Game With a Complete Mathematical Theory," *Ann. Math.*, **3**, Series 2 (1901), pp. 35–39.

BOUWKAMP, C. J., "Catalogues of Solutions of the Rectangular $3 \times 4 \times 5$ Solid Pentomino Problem," Technische Hogeschool, Eindhoven, Netherlands, Dept. of Mathematics, July, 1967.

BYARD, STANLEY, "Robots Which Play Games," *Science News*, No. 16, (1950), pp. 65–77.

CLUFF, MILON H., "A Survey of Game Playing on Digital Computers." Unpublished Memorandum of the IBM Corp.

CONDON, EDWARD V., "The Nimatron," *Am. Math. Monthly*, **49**, No. 5 (May, 1942), pp. 330–332.

DAVIES, D. W., "A Theory of Chess and Noughts and Crosses," *Science News*, No. 16 (1950), pp. 40–64.

DOMORYAD, A. P., *Matematicheskiye Igri i Razvlecheniya* (Mathematical Games and Pastimes), Fizmatgiz, Moscow, 1961.

EVANS, RONALD, "A Winning Opening in Reverse Hex," *J. Recreational Math.*, **7**, No. 3 (Summer, 1974), pp. 189–192.

FINDLER, N. V., "Some Remarks on the Game 'Dama' Which Can Be Played on a Digital Computer," *The Computer J.*, **3**, No. 1 (April, 1960), pp. 40–44.

GALE, DAVID, "A Curious Nim-Type Game," *Amer. Math. Monthly*, **81**, No. 8 (October, 1974), pp. 876–879.

GARDNER, MARTIN, *The Scientific American Book of Mathematical Puzzles and Diversions*, Simon and Shuster, New York, 1959.

GARDNER, MARTIN, *The Second Scientific American Book of Mathematical Puzzles and Diversions*, Simon and Shuster, New York, 1961.

GARDNER, MARTIN, "Mathematical Games," *Scientific American*, **199**, No. 3 (September, 1958), pp. 182–188.

GARDNER, MARTIN, "Mathematical Games," *Sci. Amer.*, **228**, No. 1 (January, 1973), pp. 111–113.

GILLOGLY, JAMES J., "The Technology Chess Program," *Artificial Intelligence*, **3** (1972), pp. 145–163.

GOLOMB, SOLOMON W., *Polyominoes*, Charles Scribner's Sons, New York, 1964.

GOLOMB, SOLOMON W., "Checker Boards and Polyominoes," *Am. Math. Monthly*, **LXI**, No. 10 (December, 1954), pp. 675–682.

GOLOMB, SOLOMON W., "Part I—Dominoes, Pentominoes and Checker Boards," *Recreational Math. Mag.* (August, 1961), pp. 3–11.

GOLOMB, SOLOMON W., "Part II—Patterns and Polyominoes," *Recreational Math. Mag.*, (Oct., 1961), pp. 3–12.

GOLOMB, SOLOMON W., "Part III—Where Pentominoes Will Not Fit," *Recreational Math. Mag.* (Dec., 1961), pp. 3–22.

GOLOMB, SOLOMON W., "Part IV—Extensions of Polyominoes," *Recreational Math. Mag.* (April, 1962), pp. 7–17.

GOLOMB, SOLOMON W., "A Mathematical Investigation of Games of 'Take-Away'," *J. Combinat. Theory*, **1**, No. 4 (December, 1966), pp. 443–458.

GREENBLATT, R. D., D. E. EASTLAKE, and S. D. CROCKER, "The Greenblatt Chess Program," *Proc. Fall Joint Computer Conf., 1967*, pp. 801–810, AFIPS Press, Montvale, New Jersey, 1967.

GROSSMAN, H. D., and DAVID KRAMER, "A New Match-Game," *Am. Math. Monthly*, **52** (October, 1945), pp. 441–443.

GRUNDY, P. M., "Mathematics and Games," *Eureka*, **2** (1939), pp. 6–8.

GRUNDY, P. M., and CEDRIC A. B. SMITH, "Disjunctive Games With the Last Player Losing," *Proc. Cambridge Phil. Soc.*, **52**, Part 3 (July, 1956), pp. 527–533.

GUY, RICHARD K., "Some Additional Recreations, I," *NABLA*, The Bulletin of the Malayan Mathematical Society, 7, No. 3 (October, 1960), pp. 97–106.

GUY, RICHARD K., and CEDRIC A. B. SMITH, "The G-Values of Various Games," *Proc. Cambridge Phil. Soc.*, **52**, Part 3 (July, 1956), pp. 514–526.

HALES, A. W., and R. I. JEWETT, "Regularity and Positional Games," *Trans. Amer. Math. Soc.*, **106**, No. 2 (February, 1963), pp. 222–229.

HANSEN, GILBERT J., "A Heuristic Approach to Solution of Checkerboard Puzzles," Systems Research Center, Document 49-A-64-16, Case Institute of Technology, 1964.

HARARY, FRANK, "Unsolved Problems in the Enumeration of Graphs," Publication of the Mathematics Institute of the Hungarian Academy of Science, No. 5, 1960, pp. 63–95.

HO, YU-CHI, A. E. BRYSON, JR., and S. BARON, "Differential Games and Optimal Pursuit-Evasion Strategies," Cruft Laboratory Technical Report No. 457, Harvard University, Cambridge, Mass., Nov. 4, 1964.

HOLLADAY, JOHN C., "Matrix Nim," *Am. Math. Monthly*, **65**, No. 2 (January, 1958), pp. 107–109.

HOLLADAY, JOHN C., "Cartesian Products of Termination Games," *Contributions to the Theory of Games*, Vol. 3, Study No. 39. Princeton University Press, Princeton, New Jersey, 1957, pp. 189–200.

ISAACS, RUFUS P., "Games of Pursuit," Report P-257, The RAND Corp., Santa Monica, Calif., Nov. 17, 1951.

ISAACS, RUFUS P., *Differential Games*, John Wiley & Sons, Inc., New York, 1965.

KALME, CHARLES, "Bobby Fischer: An Era Denied," *Chess Life Rev.*, **30**, No. 11 (November, 1975), pp. 717–729.

KENYON, J. C., "Nim-like Games and the Sprague–Grundy Theory" (Masters Thesis), Dep. Mathematics, Univ. of Calgary, Alberta, Canada, April, 1967.

KOTOK, A., "A Chess Playing Program," Memorandum No. 41 of the RLE and MIT Computation Center, 1962.

MCINTYRE, D. P., "A New System for Playing the Game of Nim," *Am. Math. Monthly*, **49**, No. 1 (January, 1942), pp. 44–46.

MADACHY, JOSEPH, "Pentominoes—Some Solved and Unsolved Problems," *J. Recreational Math.*, **2**, No. 3 (July, 1969), pp. 181–188.

MARTENS, HENRIK H., "Two Notes on Machine Learning," *Information and Control*, **2**, (December, 1959), pp. 364–379.

MICHIE, DONALD, "Trial and Error," *Penguin Science Survey*, Part 2 (1961), pp. 129–145.

MOORE, ELIAKIM H., "A Generalization of the Game Called Nim," *Ann. Math.* **11**, Series 2 (1910), pp. 93–94.

MOTT-SMITH, GEOFFREY, *Mathematical Puzzles*, Dover Publications, Inc., 2nd ed., rev., 1954.

MURRAY, H. J. R., *A History of Board Games Other Than Chess*, Oxford at the Clarendon Press, 1952.

NEWBORN, MONROE, *Computer Chess*, Academic Press, New York, 1975.

NEWELL, ALLEN, J. C. SHAW, and H. A. SIMON, "Chess Playing Programs and the Problem of Complexity," *IBM J. Research and Development*, **2**, No. 4 (October, 1958), pp. 320–335.

NEWELL, ALLEN, J. C. SHAW, and H. A. SIMON, "Report on a General Problem Solving Program," *Proc. Internl. Conf. Information Processing*, UNESCO, Paris (June, 1959), pp. 256–264.

PELIKÁN, PAVEL, "Machine Performing the Game Nim," *Stroje na Zpracování Informací*, No. 8 (1962), pp. 163–169.

READ, R. C., "Contributions to the Cell Growth Problem," *Canadian Math. J.*, **14**, No. 1 (1962), pp. 1–20.

REDHEFFER, RAYMOND, "A Machine for Playing the Game Nim," *Am. Math. Monthly*, **55**, No. 6 (June–July, 1948), pp. 343–350.

REMUS, H., "Simulation of a Learning Machine for Playing Go," *Proc. Internl. Fed. Information Processing Congress* 62, Munich, (September, 1962), pp. 192–194. No. Holland Publishing Co., Amsterdam, 1962.

RYLL-NARDZEWSKI, C., "A Theory of Pursuit and Evasion," Report P-2606, The RAND Corp., Santa Monica, Calif., August, 1962.

SAMUEL, ARTHUR L., "Some Studies in Machine Learning, Using the Game of Checkers," *IBM J. Research and Development*, **3** (July, 1959), pp. 210–229.

SHANNON, CLAUDE E., "Game-Playing Machines," *J. Franklin Inst.*, **260**, No. 6 (December, 1955), pp. 447–453.

SHANNON, CLAUDE E., "Computers and Automata," *Proc. IRE*, **41**, No. 10 (October, 1953), pp. 1234–1241.

SLAGLE, JAMES, *Artificial Intelligence, the Heuristic Programming Approach*, McGraw-Hill, New York, 1971.

SLAGLE, J. R., and J. K. DIXON, "Experiments with Some Programs that Search Game Trees," *J. Assoc. Comput. Machine.*, **16**, No. 2 (April, 1969), pp. 189–207.

SMITH, CEDRIC A. B., "Compound Games with Counters," *J. Recreational Math.*, **1**, No. 2 (April, 1968), pp. 67–77.

STEIN, P., and S. ULAM, "A Study of Certain Combinatorial Problems Through Experiments on Computing Machines," *Proc. High Speed Computer Conference*, Louisiana State University, 1955, pp. 101–106.

STEVENS, ARTHUR A., *Bluebook of Charts to Winning Chess*, A. S. Barnes & Co., New York, 1969.

THORP, EDWARD O., and WILLIAM E. WALDEN, "A Computer Assisted Study of Go on $M \times N$ Boards," *Informat. Sci.*, **4**, No. 1 (January, 1972), pp. 1–33.

WALKER, R. J., "An Enumerative Technique for a Class of Combinatorial Problems," *Proc. Symposia in Appl. Math.*, Vol. X (Combinatorial Analysis), American Mathematical Society, Providence, Rhode Island, 1960, pp. 91–94.

WICHMANN, HANS and SIEGFRIED, *Chess. The Story of Chesspieces from Antiquity to Modern Times*, Paul Hamlyn, London, 1965.

ZOBRIST, A., "A Model of Visual Organization for the Game of Go," *Spring Joint Computer Conf.*, 1970.

CHAPTER ELEVEN

FALLACIES AND SOPHISTRIES

Psychology and psilosophy

To Alice's insistence that "one *can't* believe impossible things," the White Queen demurred: "I daresay you haven't had much practice. When I was your age, I always did it for half-an-hour a day. Why, sometimes I've believed as many as six impossible things before breakfast."

The White Queen's sophistry is particularly applicable to gambling for, as we have remarked in the Preface, the phenomenon of gambling continues to be associated with superstition and metaphysics. Anthropologists have often commented on the striking resemblance between the uneducated gambler and the primitive. Before declaring war, the primitive consults his crystal ball, tea leaves, buzzard entrails, or other divination media, and if the gods signify success, war follows simply as an administrative action. If, subsequently, the war becomes a losing cause and he flees the battlefield, it is not from cowardice but rather because the "signs" have been erroneously read or interpreted and the gods really favored the opposition. Thus his losses are due to "fate"—an inexorable decision from which there is no appeal. Similarly, a gambler assigns his successes to a combination of "luck" and prowess and his failures to the adversity of the gods of chance. Such a belief is an apparently ineradicable irrationality of the unenlightened gambler.

The ubiquitous belief in "luck" and numerology has not been confined to the unsophisticated gambler. There has been no lack of eminent geniuses who, in senility or in moments of sad aberration, succumb to the irrationalities that beset frailer men.[†] Huygen's faith in "six" as the perfect number led him to the conviction that the planet Saturn could possess but a single moon. His belief is no more preposterous than Hobbes's geometry which "plussed or minused you to heaven or hell," the efforts of Leibnitz to apply geometrical principles to ethics and politics or his attempts to determine by geometry the selection of the King of Poland and the deployment of the French army (for Louis XIV), John Craig's "Mathematical Principle of Christian Theology," or Sir James Jeans's conviction that the cosmos was the creation of a divine mathematician. Some of these creeds arise directly from supernaturalism and others from the more sophisticated appeal of the Cartesian image of an Admirable Science of Numbers which would solve all human problems, a doctrine that yet finds ardent devotees in contemporary psychology.

There have been many attempts to establish axiomatic principles for intuitive mathematics. Perhaps the first such effort arose through the concept of "moral" expectation as opposed to mathematical expectation. Buffon held that the "moral" value of any sum varies inversely with the total wealth of the individual who acquires it. Cramer considered it to vary as the square root of total wealth. D. Bernoulli maintained that the "moral" value of a fortune varies as the logarithm of its magnitude: that is, the personal value of any small monetary increment dx is inversely proportional to the total sum x in the possession of the individual (this idea is familiar to psychophysicists in the form of Fechner's law).

We have emphasized the advantages of the objective utility function and objective probability for gambling phenomena. The introduction of "intuition" and "morality" into the workings of gambling theory is but another trap for the unwary set by the unenlightened.

FALLACIES

Without mathematical context, we shall list some of the fallacies prevalent in gambling as a result of psychological influences. The uneducated gambler exemplifies, par excellence, the processes of intuitive logic. He is often charged with emotion and directed by passionate, primitive beliefs; thus his acts may often contrast with the dictates of his objective knowledge. He injects a personal element into an impersonal situation.

[†] Apropos is the comment of Frederick the Great, writing of Prince Eugen and Marlborough: "What a humbling reflection for our vanity (when) the greatest geniuses end up as imbeciles . . .".

Culled from many observations and laboratory experiments,[†] the following 12 fallacies appear to be most prevalent and most injurious (in terms of profit and loss) to the susceptible gambler:

1. A tendency to overvalue wagers involving a low probability of a high gain and undervalue wagers involving a relatively high probability of low gain. This tendency accounts for some of the "long-shot" betting at race tracks.
2. A tendency to interpret the probability of successive independent events as additive rather than multiplicative. Thus the chance of throwing a given number on a die is considered twice as large with two throws of the die as it is with a single throw.
3. After a run of successes a failure is inevitable, and vice versa (the Monte Carlo fallacy).
4. The psychological probability of the occurrence of an event exceeds the mathematical probability if the event is favorable and conversely. For example, the probability of success of drawing the winning ticket in a lottery and the probability of being killed during the next year in an automobile accident may both be one chance in 10,000; yet the former is considered much more probable from a personal viewpoint.
5. The prediction of an event cannot be detached from the outcomes of similar events in the past, despite mathematical independence.
6. When a choice is offered between a single large chance and several small chances whose sum is equal to the single chance, the single large chance is preferred when the multiple chances consist of repeated attempts to obtain the winning selection from the same source (with replacement); however, when there is a different source for each of the multiple chances, they are preferred.
7. The value of the probability of a multiple additive choice tends to be underestimated and the value of a multiplicative probability tends to be overestimated.
8. When a person observes a series of randomly generated events of different kinds with an interest in the frequency with which each kind of event occurs, he tends to overestimate the frequency of occurrence of infrequent events and to underestimate that of comparatively frequent ones. Thus one remembers the "streaks"

[†] A large percentage of these experiments were conducted, strangely, with children. Is it the wage scale or the naïveté of juveniles that accounts for this situation?

in a long series of wins and losses and tends to minimize the number
of short-term runs.

9. A tendency to overestimate the degree of skill involved in a gambling
situation involving both skill and chance.

10. A strong tendency to overvalue the significance of a limited sample
selected from a relatively large population.

11. The concept of "luck" is conceived as a quantity stored in a
warehouse, to be conserved or depleted. A law of conservation
of "luck" is implied, and often "systems" are devised to distribute
the available "luck" in a fortuitous manner. Objectively, "luck"
is merely an illusion of the mind.

12. The sample space of "unusual" events is confused with that of
low-probability events. For one example, the remarkable feature
of a bridge hand of 13 Spades is its apparent regularity, not its
rarity (all hands are equally probable). For another, if one holds a
number close to the winning number in a lottery, one tends to feel
that a terribly bad stroke of misfortune has caused one *just* to
miss the prize. Bertrand Russell's remark that we encounter a
miracle every time we read the license number of a passing automobile is encompassed by this fallacy. The probability of an
"unusual" occurrence should be equated to the ratio of the number
of unusual (by virtue of symmetry or other aesthetic criteria) events
to the total number of events.

In addition to those enumerated above, there exist other fallacies
more directly associated with superstition than with intuitive logic. For
example, there is the belief that the gambler's "attitude" affects the results
of a chance event—a pessimistic frame of mind (I'm going to lose $X) biases
the outcome against the gambler. Another example is attributing animistic
behavior to inanimate objects: "the dice are hot." Of course the concept
of "luck" permeates and pervades the experience of the superstitious gambler. He has lucky days,[†] lucky numbers, lucky clothes (worn during
previous winning sessions), and lucky associates (he firmly believes that
certain individuals are inherently more "lucky" than others and are more
likely to achieve gambling success or, perhaps, to contaminate others with
their power). He believes in a "sixth sense" which anticipates or compels the
direction to success. And, he may carry amulets, talismans, fascina, charms,

---

[†] Indeed, our modern calendar was preceded (before 2000 B.C.) by an astrological list of
lucky and unlucky days to mark the occurrence of noteworthy events.

or mascots, consult *sortes* or oracles, and avoid black cats, ladders, or turning his back to the moon while gambling.

It is peculiar that our modern society, having consigned its seers, witches, water diviners, graphologists, geomancers, anthroposophists, astrologers, spiritualists, phrenologists, and pendulum swingers to the dark intellectual limbo, yet preserves a medieval approach to the laws of chance. With the gambler resides the last vestige of codified superstition.

Paranormal phenomena

Throughout our cultural development there have been no known groups that have failed to reveal a body of beliefs and actions that transcend ordinary experience. The type of noumenon currently fashionable is that encompassed by the field of parapsychology. To its adherents, parapsychology offers the fervor and personal involvement of mysticism and fundamentalist religion; to its detractors it is a brilliant beacon for those who prefer certainty to truth, for those prone to consult supernatural powers for the resolution of uncertainties, and for those ignorant of cause-and-effect relationships. Satisfying the Spinozistic yearning for an extra-human quality, it clearly fulfills a need. As Voltaire might have said, "if parapsychology did not exist, it would have been necessary to invent it."

Various forms of ostensibly paranormal activity have been recorded over many centuries. Fire walking, water divining, lycanthropy, shamanism, spiritualism, poltergeists, levitation, "materialization," faith healing, and oriental thaumaturgy have each experienced times of popular appeal. In the seventeenth century, animism was a prevalent doctrine; doctors proclaimed a belief in "animal spirits" as the motive force of blood circulating in the human body. In the Victorian era, psychical "research" emphasized communication with the dead. Nonphysical communication between living persons was a logical extension, and in 1882 the term *telepathy* was coined by F. W. H. Myers (about seven years earlier Mark Twain proposed the phrase *mental telegraphy*). The foundation was laid for contemporary parapsychology theory.

Gamblers were now offered the dream of "beating the game" through the exercise of personal, psychic powers. Cards could be read from the back, Roulette numbers predicted, and dice levitated to produce the desired outcome. Fortunes were available to those who possessed the "gift"; the "mind" could now conquer the universe.

THE STATISTICAL APPROACH

Perhaps the most significant turn in parapsychology investigation was the introduction of the statistical approach. While no reason exists to assume that paranormal phenomena admit of statistical measures, this approach has its ingenious qualities. The obliging nature of the random number tables is well proven. And the field of statistics bows to no master for ability to furnish subterfuge, confusion, and obscuration.

The first modern statistical experiments to test the existence of telepathic communication were performed in 1912 by J. E. Coover at Stanford University. About 100 students were induced to endure 14,000 trials of guessing cards drawn from conventional 52-card decks. The results of the poorly controlled experiments were slightly above expectations due to chance alone, although Dr. Coover denied any significance implied by the experiments. A similar series of card-guessing trials, sponsored by the Society for Psychical Research, was undertaken by Ina Jephson in London in 1929. Sir Ronald Fisher was consulted to establish the scale of probability for partial successes (for example, guessing the Ace of Spades instead of the Ace of Clubs). Each day, for a total of five days, 240 people guessed a card at random from a pack of 52 cards and then, following a shuffling operation, guessed again, the operation being performed five times. Of the 6000 guesses, 245 were correct (chance expectation = 115.4) in addition to many partial successes. Later repeated under more rigidly controlled conditions, the experiments exhibited no obvious paranormality.

In the United States, the first university experiments attempting telepathic communication by the guessing of playing cards were initiated by Dr. G. H. Eastabrooks of Harvard in 1926. A total of 1660 trials was performed wherein card color was conjectured; 938 successes resulted (expectation = 830). Dr. and Mrs. J. B. Rhine commenced their experiments in 1927 at the Psychology Laboratory of Duke University. The Rhines replaced the conventional 52-card pack with the 25 Zener cards; five kinds of cards comprise the deck, as illustrated in Fig. 11-1, and there are five of each kind. With these cards, Dr. Rhine has conducted or supervised a truly formidable number of experiments (over 10,000 cases) involving telepathy, clairvoyance (knowledge of events at a distance), precognition (divination of the future), and psychokinesis or PK (mental control over physical objects).

Dr. Rhine has coined the term extrasensory perception, or ESP, which subsumes telepathy, clairvoyance, and precognition. Head of the Duke Parapsychology Laboratory since 1940 (it was founded in 1935), he is the leading American advocate of the existence of paranormal phenomena.

Fig. 11-1   The Zener cards

His experiments generally consist of an "agent" who notes each of the 25 Zener cards sequentially and transmits telepathically to a "percipient" who records his "received signal." Subsequently, the recorded version of the percipient is compared with the actual order of the cards. Sometimes the agent and percipient are in the same room and can communicate verbally; in other experiments they are separated and communicate by lights or buzzers. The guesses have been attempted with and without the presence of observers, at distances from a few feet to across continents, and with delays ranging up to several years. The same set of cards has been utilized for the investigation of precognition and postcognition by examining the guesses for a possible forward or backward displacement (that is, the percipient may be guessing one card ahead or one behind the actual card in the sequency being transmitted). Another area attended by Rhine is that of psychokinesis, whereby the success of mental attempts to influence the rolls of a die is measured statistically.

In England, the leading investigator of ESP phenomena has been Dr. S. G. Soal of London University. By virtue of his mathematical background and efforts to maintain elaborate safeguards against fraud and subconscious deception, Dr. Soal has achieved a higher reputation for the veracity of his experiments than that generally accorded the American parapsychologists. Further, his investigations have frequently uncovered no evidence of ESP and he has reported such negative results in appropriate publicaticns. To date, all his experiments with clairvoyance or psychokinesis have concluded with negative results. It is interesting to note that the first four years (1935–1939) of his experimentation, conducted with 160 subjects recording 128,000 guesses, produced only results that were well within the predictions due to chance occurrence. Subsequently, following the suggestion of another ESP experimenter, Whately Carington, Dr. Soal rechecked his records for evidence of displacement and apparently found significant indication of precognition and postcognition.

There are many other ESP experimenters now extant, from those working under standards suitable for parlor games to others equipped with highly complex (and expensive) laboratory equipment. Dr. Andrija Puharich operates a laboratory in Maine where he has attempted to analyze the nature of telepathic communication by measuring the interference pattern between electric or magnetic fields and ESP waves (the agent or percipient is seated in a Faraday cage!). The Communications Science Laboratory of AFCRL (Air Force Cambridge Research Laboratories) at Hanscom Field, Massachusetts, conducts a government-sponsored program for investigating ESP phenomena. Westinghouse, Bell Telephone Laboratories, General Electric, and the RAND Corporation have invested efforts in parapsychology. In the Soviet Union, the subject is titled "Biological Radio Communication"; laboratories devoted to its existence and exploitation are operating in Moscow, Leningrad, and Omsk (naturally, the results are classified Secret). The world's first chair of parapsychology was established at the University of Utrecht (first occupant of the chair: Professor Tenhaeff) after the Netherlands Ministry of Education had officially recognized the subject as a branch of psychology. International meetings of parapsychologists have been held regularly since 1952. Possibly there exist hundreds of small concentrations of ESP experimenters, each guessing the unseen series of Zener cards, each rolling dice while concentrating, muscles taut, on directing the outcome, and each publishing their results in the available journals with such embarrassing exuberance.

ATTITUDES TO ESP

What reasonable position can we assume in the face of this overwhelming mass of "evidence"? To dismiss it out of hand would be unobjective, although we cannot accept it comfortably. As Aristotle declared, in speaking of oracular dreams, "It is neither easy to despise such things, nor yet to believe them." Yet we suspect that, were there any real evidence for the existence of extrasensory perception, scores of reputable scientists would then leap into such a fascinating field. For the existence of ESP would revolutionize our understanding of the physical universe and would demand a drastic overhaul of modern philosophy. But scientists and philosophers unquestionably retain a negative view of ESP, many with such intensity that they find it difficult to repress a Nietzschean outburst against the determined believers. Very likely, their reasoning is similar to Hume's in his argument regarding miracles[†]: "A miracle is a violation of the laws of nature; and as a firm and unalterable experience has established these laws, the proof against a miracle, from the very nature of the fact, is as

[†] In *An Enquiry Concerning Human Understanding.*

entire as any argument from experience can possibly be imagined ... no testimony is sufficient to establish a miracle unless the testimony be of such a kind that its falsehood would be more miraculous than the fact which it endeavors to establish ...". Are the miracles of Rhine, Soal, *et al.*, less miraculous than the possibility of fraud, self-deception, or error?

William James once remarked that "the limits of the powers of the human mind are unknown." Thus we cannot stand obdurate in denying that ESP may exist. We can, however, assume a strongly negative posture until shown credible evidence. None such has been forthcoming.

MATHEMATICAL CRITIQUES OF ESP EXPERIMENTS

We cannot, of course, skewer the subject with mere rejection of the auspicious data accumulated. Critique or reinterpretation of the data is indicated or, in some instances, results may be ascribed to a cause other than the one claimed. Generally, criticism is directed at the method of statistical analysis, the standards of the experiment itself, or the integrity and sophistication of the individuals supervising the experiments.

In the 1930's and 1940's, a considerable amount of criticism was expressed over the methods of statistical evaluation employed by Dr. Rhine and other ESP investigators. Virtually all this criticism was invalid, ill-considered, and crushingly refuted. Indisputably, the statistical evaluations of ESP experiments have been of a quality far beyond the standards of the experiments themselves. As a consequence, the mathematical soundness of the analysis of the ESP and PK experiments has been declared to prove the soundness of the experimental procedures (*ignoratio elenchi*). In addition to the fact that one rigorous element of a structure does not automatically imply a totally sound structure, there yet remain certain mathematical fallacies to which ESP experimenters are prone.

The first problem in examining the existence of ESP by telepathic transmission of card symbols is to distinguish between prediction and guessing. A scale must be established which measures the results in terms of their departure from chance occurrences. Following a technique used by psychometrists, the ESP investigators have adopted the term *critical ratio*, which provides a numerical evaluation of the significance of a series of "guesses" in terms of the number of standard deviations above (or below) the expectation due to chance. That is,

$$\text{Critical ratio} = \frac{\text{observed deviation from chance expectation}}{\text{one standard deviation}}$$

(Initially, probable error was used instead of standard deviation; thus the critical ratio would be increased by 0.6745.) This definition is a convenient and sensible one, particularly if the probability of the various correct "guesses" follows a binomial distribution, for then the probability that the results are due solely to chance is obtainable directly from tables of the probability integral. Indeed, a binomial distribution is assumed in the evaluation of ESP experiments with card guessing.

Consider a "percipient" guessing cards drawn (without replacement) from a deck of N cards composed of N/M kinds. Then an implicit assumption in application of the binomial distribution is that each kind may be represented in the deck by any number from zero to N. If there are M cards of each kind comprising the deck and this information is available to the "percipient," it is highly probable that his guesses will closely correspond to the composition of the deck; that is, he will tend to guess N/M kinds of cards and M of each kind. The probability of n correct guesses is then expressed by

$$P(n) = \binom{N}{n} \frac{M^n}{N^n} \left(\frac{N-M}{N}\right)^{N-n}, \quad = \binom{N}{n} \frac{M^n(N-M)^{N-n}}{N^n} \qquad 11\text{-}1$$

With a knowledge of the deck structure, the probability distribution of guesses can be derived as

$$P(n) = \sum_{m=0}^{N-n} (-1)^m \binom{n+m}{n} S_{n+m} \qquad 11\text{-}2$$

where

$$S_n = \sum \left(\frac{M^k}{k_1!(N-1)_{n-1}} \prod_{j=1}^{k-1} (N-jM) \prod_{i=1}^{n-1} \frac{1}{k_{i+1}!} \left\{ \frac{[(M-1)_i]^2}{(i+1)!} \right\}^{k_{i+1}} \right) \qquad 11\text{-}3$$

$$k = \sum_{i=1}^{n} k_i \quad \text{and} \quad n = \sum_{i=1}^{n} i k_i$$

The summation in Eq. 11-3 is over those partitions of n restricted by

$$k \le \frac{N}{M} \quad \text{and} \quad i \le M$$

Equations 11-1 and 11-2 are evaluated for the Zener pack of cards—that is, for $N = 25$ and $M = 5$. The results are tabulated in Table 11-1.

TABLE 11-1   Probabilities for Guessing Zener Cards

No. of Correct Guesses	Probability Due to Chance (Binomial Distribution)	Probability Due to Chance (Exact Distribution)
0	3.778×10^{-3}	4.286×10^{-3}
1	2.361×10^{-2}	2.545×10^{-2}
2	7.084×10^{-2}	7.336×10^{-2}
3	1.358×10^{-1}	1.366×10^{-1}
4	1.867×10^{-1}	1.843×10^{-1}
5	1.960×10^{-1}	1.919×10^{-1}
6	1.633×10^{-1}	1.603×10^{-1}
7	1.108×10^{-1}	1.101×10^{-1}
8	6.235×10^{-2}	6.331×10^{-2}
9	2.944×10^{-2}	3.090×10^{-2}
10	1.178×10^{-2}	1.291×10^{-2}
11	4.015×10^{-3}	4.654×10^{-3}
12	1.171×10^{-3}	1.453×10^{-3}
13	2.928×10^{-4}	3.942×10^{-4}
14	6.273×10^{-5}	9.310×10^{-5}
15	1.150×10^{-5}	1.914×10^{-5}
16	1.797×10^{-6}	3.423×10^{-6}
17	2.378×10^{-7}	5.312×10^{-7}
18	2.643×10^{-8}	7.115×10^{-8}
19	2.434×10^{-9}	8.247×10^{-9}
20	1.826×10^{-10}	7.981×10^{-10}
21	1.087×10^{-11}	7.079×10^{-11}
22	4.939×10^{-13}	4.011×10^{-12}
23	1.611×10^{-14}	4.011×10^{-13}
24	3.355×10^{-16}	0
25	3.355×10^{-18}	1.604×10^{-15}

The difference between the two distributions is not excessive, the exact distribution being skewed slightly toward the extreme values. Assigning a binomial distribution to card-guessing phenomena results in a platykurtic bias of the probabilities. The binomial distribution, for the Zener deck, is characterized by a standard deviation of

$$\sigma = \sqrt{Npq} = \sqrt{25(1/5)(4/5)} = 2.000$$

where $p = 1/5$ is the probability of a correct guess and $q = 1 - p$. For the exact distribution of guesses (knowing the composition of the Zener pack), the standard deviation is computed numerically as

$$\sigma = 2.041$$

Thus, the assumption of a binomial distribution in connection with guessing cards from the Zener pack causes an error of 2 percent in the critical ratio, favoring the existence of ESP.

R. C. Read has examined that ESP experiment wherein each card is exposed to view following the attempt by the "percipient" to guess its symbol. Under this rule, an intelligent guessing strategy is to select for the next unexposed card that symbol (not necessarily unique) which occurs most frequently among the remaining unexposed cards. If we are using an $n \times n$ deck (n kinds of cards with n of each kind), the expected number of correct guesses can be derived as

$$E = \frac{1}{n^2} \sum_{m=1}^{n^2} \frac{A_m}{\binom{n^2 - 1}{m - 1}} \qquad \textit{11-4}$$

where A_m is the coefficient of t^m in the expression

$$n(1 + t)^{n^2} - \sum_{s=0}^{n-1} \sum_{r=0}^{s} \left[\binom{n}{r} t^r \right]^n$$

For the Zener deck, $n = 5$, and Eq. 11-4 results in

$$E = 8.647$$

an expectation considerably greater than that (five) obtained without the sequential exposure of each card.

Another source of error arises from incorrect treatment of the forward or backward displacement of the guesses. Rigorous experimental technique dictates that the object of a series of guesses be established a priori. If the series of trials is sufficiently long, it becomes more feasible to permit a posteriori decisions as to the object of the experiment. However, in a relatively short sequence of guesses, the expectation of the number of correct guesses increases with the flexibility of the a posteriori decisions. For example, a series of 25 guesses with the Zener cards, the guessing occurring with zero displacement, yields an expectation of

$$E = \sum_{i=0}^{25} ip(i) = 5$$

for the number of matches |with either the binomial or exact distribution used for $p(i)$, the probability of guessing exactly i cards correctly|. Now, if we are allowed to decide a posteriori that we will search the recorded data for evidence of a forward displacement of one card (precognition), no displacement (telepathy), or a backward displacement of one card (postcognition) and select that which is maximum, the expected number of correct guesses is expressed by

$$E = \sum_{i=0}^{25} \sum_{j=0}^{i} \sum_{k=0}^{j} ip(i)\,p(j)\,p(k)\lambda_{ijk} = 6.740$$

where

$$\lambda_{ijk} = \begin{cases} 6 & \text{for } i \neq j \neq k \\ 3 & \text{for } i \neq j = k \quad \text{or} \quad i = j \neq k \\ 1 & \text{for } i = j = k \end{cases}$$

and the exact probability distribution of Table 11-1 is used for $p(i)$, $p(j)$, and $p(k)$. Obviously, if displacements greater than plus or minus one card are allowed, the expected number of correct guesses increases further. On the other hand, as the length of the series of trials increases, the expectation decreases, approaching the value (5) obtained by establishing the data analysis procedure a priori.

Inadequate shuffling of the Zener cards is yet another potential source of higher scores in telepathic experiments. From the analysis presented in Chapter 6, we can note that more shuffles are required to randomize odd-numbered deck lengths than a deck of $2n$ cards. Thus, special precautions are indicated when employing a 25-card deck. Although the mental feat of predicting cards by estimating the shifts in position due to shuffling is a prodigious one, it is not above the ability of some practiced individuals. Further, only a limited success is required to provide a significant improvement in the results.

Another error common in ESP experimentation arises when the number of trials of card guessing is not established a priori. With the trials concluded at the option of the experimenter (usually when the "percipient" becomes "tired" and his success rate declines; this circumstance is referred to as the "headache phenomenon"), unusual results can be guaranteed. To illustrate this concept, let us examine the null hypothesis H_0 that the mean number of correct guesses in a series of trials is that due chance expectation, as opposed to the hypothesis H_1 that the mean number of guesses is greater (say) than chance expectation. Then, if it is assumed that the series of guesses is normally distributed, the conventional statistical test based on a sample of fixed size—n trials—dictates that we must reject H_0 in favor of H_1 if and only if the number of correct guesses S_n is such that

$$S_n - np > Cn^{1/2} \hspace{4cm} \textit{11-5}$$

where p is the chance probability of achieving a correct guess and C is some constant. The probability $P(C)$ of rejecting H_0 despite its truth is

$$P(C) = 1 - \frac{1}{\sqrt{2\pi}} \int_{-\infty}^{C} e^{-x^2/2} \, dx$$

By selecting a suitably large value of C, $P(C)$ can be rendered as small as desired.

Now it follows from the law of the iterated logarithm that with unity probability the inequality of Eq. 11-5 is valid for infinitely many values of n if the sampling is continued indefinitely, regardless of the extent to which $P(C)$ is decreased. Thus, the experimenter must eventually encounter a value of n whereby the inequality of Eq. 11-5 holds; terminating the experiment at that point compels us to reject the null hypothesis H_0, despite its truth. It is evident that when optional stopping is permitted, the usual statistical procedures for hypothesis testing cannot be applied. We are advised to insist on establishing beforehand the sample size or, at least, of restraining it to be within reasonable limits. With the flexibility inherent in the ability to alter at will the number of trials, it is not surprising that ESP is described (by parapsychologists) as a phenomenon visited upon some people sometimes.

We should note that consequences of optional stopping are not relevant in games of known probability, as discussed in Chapter 3. In those instances it is not a statistical hypothesis under examination, but the running sum of a binary sequence, which is automatically concluded if at any time it reaches some preestablished value.

OTHER CRITICISMS

It is sometimes difficult to understand how the elementary points expressed above can be ignored by ESP investigators. The accusation of fraud has been raised, most notably by Dr. George Price in *Science* magazine; and, for certain graduate students participating in the experiments, certain *soi-disant* "psychics," and certain individuals with vested interests in the existence of ESP, the perpetration of outright fraud likely explains many outstanding results. Several examples of collusion have been uncovered by statistical analyses of the series of correct "guesses" that detected significant periodicities, indicating a high probability of prearranged "guesses" at predetermined positions on a printed form. Subconsciously motivated scoring errors in favor of the basic premise have been detected by hidden cameras. However, in many instances, the unquestionable sincerity and stature of the experimenters must render the possibility of duplicity exceedingly small. Without impugning an experimenter's integrity, we would be well advised to recall Dicey's dictum that men's interests give a bias to their judgments far oftener than they corrupt their hearts. This bias, which can descend to the level of blatant axe grinding, is often accompanied by incredible naïveté concerning the safeguards necessary to ensure a controlled experiment.

Finally, it should be noted that the existence of telepathic ability would enable reliable communication links without transfer of energy (thereby violating the Heisenberg principle). Information theory is unequivocal in demonstrating that any system providing a finite capacity for transmitting information can, with appropriate coding, transmit with any desired degree of accuracy. According to Shannon's mathematical theory of communication, the capacity C, in bits per trial, of a communication system composed of telepathic transmissions of the five Zener symbols is

$$C = \log_2 5 + \frac{n}{25} \log_2 \left(\frac{n}{25} \right) + \frac{25 - n}{25} \log_2 \left(\frac{25 - n}{100} \right)$$

where $n \, (\geq 5)$ is the mean number of correct guesses per 25 trials (the formula applies only for equiprobability in selecting any of the five symbols). With six correct guesses per 25 trials, $C \simeq 0.0069$ bits per trial, and for $n = 7$, $C \simeq 0.026$ bits per trial. We could consequently effect a communication system with a data rate of several bits per hour—adequate for communicating with submerged Polaris submarines, for example. If the principles of communication theory are admitted, we could increase the data rate by an array of ESP "transmitters" connected for simultaneous emission.

Although but one of the many exercises in futility in the search for certainty, ESP has perhaps developed the most convoluted and elaborate illogic.[†] The common technique of ESP practitioners, contrary to scientific tradition, is to concoct a speculative thesis and then attempt to confirm its truth. For example, one such hypothesis, propounded to mollify those with a rudimentary knowledge of physical phenomena, is that highly complex organisms (the human brain) do not obey the known laws of physics. The prodigious amount of data accumulated in the pursuit of such specula-

---

[†] An interesting featherweight contender to ESP is the "science" of *pataphysics*. Its adherents, including Eugène Ionesco and Raymond Queneau, founded a society, the College of Pataphysics, in Paris. As defined by its creator Alfred Jarry: "Pataphysics is the science of imaginary solutions."

tive knowledge serves to demonstrate what sumptuous logical super-structures the human mind can build upon inadequate bases.

SOME ADDITIONAL ESP EXPERIMENTS

A limited series of ESP and PK experiments was supervised by the author and a small group of associates.[†] Insofar as possible a dispassionate inquiry into the existence of ESP and PK was launched with *tabula rasa* objectivity; the viewpoint was neither credulous nor incredulous. We were, however, unable to devise a satisfactory methodology for mounting a rational assault on the irrational. Equipment from accessible engineering laboratories was utilized, as well as a polygraph and an EEG. Since interpretation of results obtained through the latter two instruments is not rigidly deterministic, their indications were not accepted without supporting evidence. No religious, psychological, or preternatural overtones were permitted gratuitously in the hypotheses. Those experiments involving statistical elements were checked for possible sources of biased mechanization—in Chapter 5 we have seen the "significant" deviations from chance occurring from poor quality dice (cf. Wolf's and Weldon's dice data).

The statistical experiments in telepathy and clairvoyance, conducted with the "percipient" in complete isolation (a soundproof and lightproof chamber was used), produced results well within one standard deviation of chance expectation. Telepathic trials with the "agent" and "percipient" in the same room communicating orally (to signal each card in sequence) yielded, especially with pairs that had worked together for long periods, increasing success with a decreasing number of symbols. That is, binary choices (guessing the color of cards in a conventional deck) were extremely successful, five-level choices (the Zener pack) considerably less so, and 26-level and 52-level choices produced only chance results. Of course, as the number of choices increases, the amount of information required from sensory cues increases correspondingly; and it is likely that the subconscious transmission and reception of sensory cues is more efficient when given an established rapport between two individuals closely associated.

For the PK experiments, a cesium-beam atomic clock was used. By concentrating on the molecular streams, various individuals attempted to change the resonant frequency by altering the vibration of only a few molecules. The results were negative.

[†] The group is continuing its activities and has been formally constituted as the Yoknapa-tawpha Martini and Metaphysical Society.

Suggested references

ABRAMOWSKI, E., *Le Subconscient Normal*, Paris, 1914.

BERGLER, EDMUND, *The Psychology of Gambling*, Hill and Wang, New York, 1957.

BROAD, C. D., *Lectures on Psychical Research*, Routledge and Kegan Paul, London, 1962.

CARRINGTON, W. WHATELY, *Telepathy. An Outline of Its Facts, Theory, and Implication*, London, 1945.

COHEN, JOHN, "The Psychology of Luck," *The Advancement of Science*, **16** (December, 1959), pp. 197–204.

COHEN, JOHN, *Chance, Skill, and Luck*, Penguin Books Ltd., England, 1960.

COHEN, JOHN, E. J. DEARNALEY, and C. E. M. HANSEL, "The Addition of Subjective Probabilities," *Acta Psychologica*, **12**, No. 5/6 (1956), pp. 371–380.

COHEN, JOHN, and C. E. M. HANSEL, "The Nature of Decisions in Gambling," *Acta Psychologica*, **13**, No. 5 (1958), pp. 357–370.

COHEN, JOHN, and C. E. M. HANSEL, "The Idea of a Distribution," *British J. Psych.*, **46**, Part 2 (May, 1955), pp. 111–121.

COHEN, JOHN, and C. E. M. HANSEL, "The Idea of Independence," *British J. Psych.*, **46**, Part 3 (August, 1955), pp. 178–190.

COHEN, JOHN, and C. E. M. HANSEL, *Risk and Gambling*, Philosophical Library Inc., New York, 1956.

COHEN, JOHN, and C. E. M. HANSEL, "Preference for Different Combinations of Chance and Skill in Gambling," *Nature*, **183**, Part 1 (Mar. 21, 1959), pp. 841–842.

COOVER, J. E., "Experiments in Psychical Research at Leland Stanford Junior University," Stanford University, Calif., 1917.

DALE, H. C. A., "A Priori Probability in Gambling," *Nature*, **183**, Part 1 (Mar. 21, 1959), pp. 842–843.

DURAND, GILBERT, *et al.*, *Encyclopédia de la Divination*, Paris-Tchou, France, 1965.

EPSTEIN, RICHARD A., "Displacement in Telepathy Experiments," Hughes Aircraft Co., Report TP-64-19-12, OP-67, July, 1964.

EPSTEIN, RICHARD A., "Probability Distributions in Card Guessing Experiments," Hughes Aircraft Co., Report TP-64-19-13, OP-66, July, 1964.

GARDNER, MARTIN, *Fads and Fallacies in the Name of Science*, Dover Publications, Inc., New York, 1952.

GREENWOOD, JOSEPH A., and T. N. E. GREVILLE, "On the Probability of Attaining a Given Standard Deviation Ratio in an Infinite Series of Trials," *Ann. Math. Statistics*, **10** (1939), pp. 297–298.

GRUENBERGER, FRED J., "A Measure for Crackpots," *Science*, (Sept. 25, 1964), pp. 1413–1415.

HANSEL, C. E. M., "Experimental Evidence for ESP," *Nature*, **184**, Part 2 (Nov. 7, 1959), pp. 1515–1516.

HEINLEIN, C. P., and J. H. HEINLEIN, "Critique of the Premises and Statistical Methodology of Parapsychology," *J. Psych.*, **5** (1938), pp. 135–148.

HELMER, OLAF, and NICOLAS RESCHER, "On the Epistemology of the Inexact Sciences," The RAND Corporation, Report R-353, Santa Monica, Calif., February, 1960.

HERR, D. L., "A Mathematical Analysis of the Experiments in Extra-Sensory Perception," *J. Exptl. Psych.*, **22** (1938), pp. 491–495.

HOPP, M., *Uber Hellsehen*, Berlin, 1916.

HUIZINGA, JOHAN, *Homo Ludens: A Study of the Play Element in Culture*, The Beacon Press, paperback ed., 1955.

KOOPMAN, B. O., "The Axioms and Algebra of Intuitive Probability," *Ann. Math.*, **41**, 2nd Series (1940), pp. 269–292.

MACDOUGALL, WILLIAM, *The Frontiers of Psychology*, London, 1934.

MURPHY, GARDNER, and ROBERT O. BALLOU (eds.), *William James on Psychical Research*, Chatto and Windus, London, 1962.

PRICE, GEORGE R., "Science and the Supernatural," *Science*, **122**, No. 3165, (Aug. 26, 1955), pp. 359–367.

RAWCLIFFE, D. H., *Illusions and Delusions of the Supernatural and the Occult*, Dover Publications, Inc., New York, 1959.

READ, RONALD C., "Card-Guessing With Information—A Problem in Probability," *Am. Math. Monthly*, **69**, No. 6 (June–July, 1962), pp. 506–511.

RHINE, JOSEPH B., *Extra-Sensory Perception*, Bruce Humphries, Boston, 1934.

RHINE, JOSEPH B., *New World of the Mind*, William Sloane Associates, New York, 1953.

ROBBINS, HERBERT, "Some Aspects of the Sequential Design of Experiments," *Bull. Am. Math. Soc.*, **58**, No. 5 (September, 1952), pp. 527–535.

ROGOSIN, H., "An Evaluation of Extra-Sensory Perception," *J. Gen. Psych.*, **21** (1939), pp. 203–217.

ROGOSIN, H., "Probability Theory and Extra-Sensory Perception," *J. Psych.*, **5**, (1938), pp. 265–270.

SMITH, ALSON, *The Psychic Source Book*, Creative Age Press, New York, 1951.

SOAL, S. G., and F. BATEMAN, *Modern Experiments in Telepathy*, Yale University Press, 1954.

SOAL, S. G., J. B. RHINE, P. E. MEEHL, and M. SCRIVEN, and P. W. BRIDGEMAN, "Comments on Science and the Supernatural," *Science*, **123**, No. 3184 (Jan. 6, 1956), pp. 9–19.

THOULESS, ROBERT H., *Experimental Psychical Research*, A Pelican Original, 1964.

WEST, D. J., *Psychical Research Today*, A Pelican Book, rev. ed., 1962.

General references

Proceedings and Journals of the Society for Psychical Research (London), 1882– .

Journal of Parapsychology (Duke University Press), 1937– .

Journal of the American Society for Psychical Research, 1940– .

EPILOGUE

A well-known short story by Robert Coates describes the incredibly chaotic events transpiring from suspension of the law of averages.[†] We have demonstrated—convincingly, we hope—that the law of averages, or the central limit theorem, or the law of large numbers, etc., can be relied upon in dealing with the phenomena of gambling. We can, in fact, and with a modicum of smugness do, advise: You can bet on it.

In order to synthesize even an elementary framework of gambling theory, we have resorted to the disciplines of probability theory, statistics, and game theory as well as sampling occasional fruits from other branches of mathematics. With these analytic tools, it is possible to evolve the basic principles of gambling theory and thence to derive optimum game strategies and optimal courses of action for individual participation in gambling situations as functions of initial bankroll, objective, etc. As a caveat, it should be stated that the theorems proved herein refer to numbers—that is, abstract quantities; applications to dice, coins, cards, etc., are entirely adventitious.

The games considered in this book range from the simplest strategic

[†] Robert M. Coates, "The Law," *New Yorker*, Vol. 23, Part 4 (Nov. 29, 1947), pp. 41–43. (All car owners in the Greater New York area decide simultaneously upon an evening's excursion over the Triborough Bridge; restaurants find only a single item on the menu being ordered; a small notions store is inundated by hundreds of customers, each in single-minded search of a spool of pink thread. Eventually, by legislating human behavior, Congress amends the oversight of never having had incorporated the law of averages into the body of federal jurisprudence.)

contests, such as coin matching, to intricate nonstrategic games of skill, such as Chess, or the extreme complexity of social phenomena, as represented by economic conflict. Elementary coin, wheel, and dice games, *inter alia*, have been analyzed completely and their strategies specified. In general, however, games whose outcomes depend not merely on natural statistical fluctuations, but on the actions of other players and wherein a player must select from among relatively complex strategies, pose mathematical problems yet unsolved. Poker (a strategic game based on imperfect information and inverted signaling) and Bridge (a strategic game involving information exchange) provide two examples where detailed optimum strategies cannot be enumerated because of the astronomical amount of attendant computation.

We have also considered games of pure chance, where the opponent is an impartial, godlike statistician, games of mixed chance and skill, such as Blackjack, where the dependence between plays suggests the value of a memory, games of pure skill, such as Nim and Pentominoes, where the opponent is another player, and games involving nonstationary statistics, such as horse racing or stock market speculation. Gambling on games of pure skill is comparatively rare at present (although it was common in past eras), possibly because a hierarchy of the participants is soon established in a closed community. It would appear that gambling on outcomes determined solely by chance, or on judgments of which horse or dog is the speediest, offers greater appeal. While these categories are not presumed to exhaust the subject, they do comprise a substantive encapsulation of most gambling phenomena.

The subjective element often inherent in games, particularly in those of an economic nature, is considered by means of the fundamental concept of utility functions. Yet the extent to which utility theory describes actual human behavior is debatable. The assumption that individuals act objectively in accordance with purely mathematical dictates to maximize their gain or utility cannot be sustained by empirical observation. Indeed, people more often appear to be influenced by the skewness of the probability distribution; hence the popularity of lotteries and football pools with highly negative mathematical expectations. Perhaps the nature of human preference precludes a normative theory of utility.

An alternate lens through which we can scrutinize the subject of gambling is that constructed by the parapsychologists. We have reviewed the evidence for extrasensory perception and have classified the phenomenon as a *trompe l'oeil*. Similarly, we have dismissed as fantasy the value of propitiating the gods of fortune through esoteric rituals.

"Gambling," said Dr. Theodore Reik, "is a sort of question addressed to destiny." To answer the question requires a hazardous ascent up the slippery ladder of probability, gambling theory and statistical logic. What treasures await the successful climber, we will not speculate. Information, as we have shown, can only enhance our expectation.

Rien ne va plus.

APPENDIX TABLES

TABLE A(1)   Dealer's Up-Card = Ace

Expectation By Drawing Minus Expectation By Standing

Player's Cards ↓ / →	A	2	3	4	5	6	7	8	9	10
A	(16)[17]									
2	(16)[17]	(16)[17]								
3	(16)[17]	(16)[17]	(16)[17]							
4	(16)[17]	(16)[17]	(16)	(16)						
5	(16)[17]	(16)	(16)	(16)	(16)					
6	0.2829[18]	(16)	(16)	(16)	(16)	0.2308(16)	0.1358(16)			
7	−0.0076	(16)	(16)	(16)	(16)	0.1804(16)	0.1815(16)	0.1486		
8	−0.3033	(16)	(16)	0.2734(16)	0.2638(16)	0.1770(16)	0.1477	−0.0919	−0.5697	
9	−0.6141	(16)	0.2821(16)	0.2714(16)	0.2142(16)	0.1410(16)	−0.0876	−0.5509	−1.0505	−1.5334
BJ		0.3239(16)	0.2797(16)	0.2252(16)	0.2122(16)	0.1705(16)	0.1441			

( ) = t′, Maximum Hard Drawing Number
[ ] = t″, Maximum Soft Drawing Number

Doubling Down Expectations

	A	2	3	4	5	6	7
A	−0.5855	−1.3201					
2	−0.5846	−1.3188	−1.2979				
3	−0.5898	−1.2953	−1.1267				
4	−0.6164	−1.1259	−0.7977	−0.7999			
5	−0.6543	−0.8026	−0.4104	−0.4051	0.0378		
6	−0.5253	−0.4114	−0.0235	0.0319	**0.2402**	−0.8329	
7	−0.3610	0.0087	**0.2057**	**0.2220**	−0.8337	−0.9379	−1.0308
8	−0.2011	**0.1889**	0.2057	−0.8425	−0.9299	−0.9432	−0.9291
9	−0.0563	−0.8538	−0.8370	−0.9208	−1.0092	−0.9898	
10	0.1879	−0.8056	−0.8571	−0.9310	−1.0120	−1.0176	−1.1093

Expectations By Splitting Pairs

	A	2	3	4	5	6	7	8	9	10
A	**0.2239**									
2		−0.4212								
3			−0.4651							
4				−0.5278						
5					−0.6137					
6						−0.6176				
7							−0.6151			
8								**−0.3649**		
9									−0.1139	
10										0.0978

Expectations From Optimal Strategy

	A	2	3	4	5	6	7	8	9	10
A	0.2239s									
2	−0.0678h	−0.2589h								
3	−0.1006h	−0.2916h	−0.3340h							
4	−0.1539h	−0.3349h	−0.3450h	−0.2090h						
5	−0.2061h	−0.3311h	−0.2171h	−0.0702h	0.0906h					
6	−0.1999h	−0.2258h	−0.0785h	0.0815h	0.2402d	−0.3862h				
7	−0.1010	−0.0828h	0.0868h	0.2220d	−0.3768h	−0.4434h	−0.4947h			
8	0.2897	0.0864h	0.2057d	−0.3749h	−0.4330h	−0.4534h	−0.4557h	−0.3649s		
9	0.6807	0.1889d	−0.3745h	−0.3831h	−0.4412h	−0.4958h	−0.4955h	−0.4519h	−0.0552	
10	1.5000	−0.3489h	−0.3925h	−0.4450h	−0.4987h	−0.5088h	−0.4670h	−0.0820h	0.3077	0.6501

d = double down
s = split
h = hit (draw)

Player's Expectation = −0.3604
Player's Conditional Expectation (No Dealer BJ) = −0.0846

TABLE A(2) Dealer's Up-Card = 10

( ) = t*, Maximum Hard Drawing Number
[ ] = t*₅, Maximum Soft Drawing Number

d = double down
s = split
h = hit (draw)

Expectation By Drawing Minus Expectation By Standing

Player's Cards	A	2	3	4	5	6	7	8	9	10
A	(15)[18]	(15)[18]	(15)[17]							
2	(15)[18]	(15)[17]	(15)[18]							
3	(15)[18]	(15)[17]	(15)							
4	(15)[18]	(15)[18]	(16)	(15)						
5	(15)[18]	(15)[18]	(15)	(15)	(15)					
6	0.2291[18]	(16)	(15)	(16)	(15)	0.1656(16)				
7	0.0475	(16)	(15)	(15)	0.1418(15)	0.0807(16)	-0.0076			
8	-0.1522	(16)	(15)	0.1457(15)	0.0843(15)	0.0704(16)	0.0392	0.0065		
9	-0.5424	(15)	0.1468(15)	0.1369(15)	0.0816(15)	0.0294(16)	0.0060	-0.1659	-0.4907	
10	BJ	0.1930(15)	0.1459(15)	0.0935(15)	0.0373	0.0361	-0.1429	-0.4672	-0.8126	-1.4201

Doubling Down Expectations

Player's Cards	A	2	3	4	5	6	7	8	9	10
A	-0.4614									
2	-0.4755	-1.0943								
3	-0.4793	-1.0928	-1.0709							
4	-0.4987	-1.0728	-0.9571	-0.7457						
5	-0.5369	-0.9567	-0.7447	-0.4514	0.0190					
6	-0.4355	-0.7520	-0.4578	0.0119	**0.1707**	-0.7955				
7	-0.3290	-0.4481	0.0151	**0.1710**	-0.7831	-0.9028	-1.0307			
8	-0.2383	0.0066	**0.1623**	-0.7981	-0.9039	-0.9320	-0.9462	-1.0196		
9	-0.0518	**0.1428**	-0.8131	-0.8133	-0.9070	-1.0201	-1.0201	-1.1131	-1.2479	
10	0.1556	-0.7317	-0.8061	-0.8958	-0.9991	-1.0138	-1.1105	-1.2448	-1.4201	-1.6739

Expectations By Splitting Pairs

Player's Cards	A	2	3	4	5	6	7	8	9	10
	0.1942	-0.4415	-0.4858	-0.5447	-0.6339	-0.6315	-0.6031	**-0.4481**	-0.2607	0.0368

Expectations From Optimal Strategy

Player's Cards	A	2	3	4	5	6	7	8	9	10
A	**0.19442s**									
2	-0.08889h	-0.27756h								
3	-0.1236h	-0.3078h	-0.3436h							
4	-0.1704h	-0.3090h	-0.3348h	-0.2410h						
5	-0.22234h	-0.3451h	-0.2509h	-0.1381h	0.0378h					
6	-0.18887h	-0.2503h	-0.1411h	0.0344h	**0.1707d**	-0.3866h				
7	-0.13887h	-0.1541h	0.0296h	**0.1710d**	-0.3846h	-0.4503h	-0.5097h			
8	0.0643	0.0305h	**0.1623d**	-0.3859h	-0.4464h	-0.4648h	-0.4748h	**-0.4481s**		
9	0.5546	**0.1428d**	-0.3885h	-0.3987h	-0.4531h	-0.5098h	-0.5120h	-0.3907h	-0.1333	
10	1.5000	-0.3466h	-0.3931h	-0.4458h	-0.5011h	-0.5069h	-0.4123h	-0.1552h	0.1025	0.5832

Player's Expectation = -0.1693

Player's Conditional Expectation (No Dealer B.J.) = -0.1017

TABLE A(3)   Dealer's Up-Card = 9

Legend:

( ) = r'. Maximum Hard Drawing Number
[ ] = r'. Maximum Soft Drawing Number
d = double down
s = split
h = hit (draw)

Expectation By Drawing Minus Expectation By Standing

Player's Cards →	A	2	3	4	5	6	7	8	9	10
A	(16)[18]									
2	(16)[18]	(16)[18]								
3	(16)[18]	(16)[18]	(16)[18]							
4	(15)[18]	(16)[18]	(16)[18]	(16)[18]						
5	(16)[18]	(15)[18]	(15)[18]	(15)[18]	(15)					
6	0.2724[18]	(16)	(15)	(15)[19]	(16)	0.1623(16)				
7	0.0918	(16)	(16)	(16)	0.1591(16)	0.1326(16)	0.0808(16)			
8	-0.2797	(16)	(16)	(16)	0.1141(16)	0.0944(16)	0.0927(16)	0.0293		
9	-0.6598	(16)	0.1412(16)	0.1342(16)	0.1055(16)	0.0558(16)	0.0578	-0.1212	-0.4010	
10	BJ	0.1831(16)	0.1775(16)	0.1224(16)	0.0598(16)	0.0599	-0.1116	-0.3998	-0.9636	-1.5859

Doubling Down Expectations

Player's Cards →	A	2	3	4	5	6	7	8	9	10
A	-0.4195									
2	-0.3743	-1.0469								
3	-0.3978	-1.0659	-1.0653							
4	-0.4242	-1.0454	-0.9490	-0.7105						
5	-0.4529	-0.9291	-0.7122	-0.2763	0.1746					
6	-0.3493	-0.7009	-0.2869	0.1646	0.2399	-0.8149				
7	-0.2656	-0.2715	0.1537	0.2247	-0.8233	-0.8682	-0.9779			
8	-0.0582	0.1844	0.2152	-0.8315	-0.8471	-0.8880	-0.8939	-0.9746		
9	0.1228	0.2138	-0.8386	-0.7588	-0.8608	-0.9678	-0.9647	-1.0657	-1.1947	
10	0.2025	-0.7444	-0.7528	-0.8411	-0.9535	-0.9586	-1.0555	-1.1919	-1.3987	-1.6838

Expectations By Splitting Pairs

	A	2	3	4	5	6	7	8	9	10
	0.2898	-0.3704	-0.3917	-0.4562	-0.5571	-0.5394	-0.5315	**-0.3833**	**-0.0929**	0.1723

Expectations From Optimal Strategy

Player's Cards →	A	2	3	4	5	6	7	8	9	10
A	0.2898s									
2	-0.0141h	-0.2225h								
3	-0.0600h	-0.2625h	-0.3100h							
4	-0.1134h	-0.3046h	-0.3039h	-0.2044h						
5	-0.1668h	-0.2840h	-0.2171h	-0.0511h	0.1746d					
6	-0.1347h	-0.2084h	-0.0511h	0.1646d	0.2399d	-0.3862h				
7	-0.0870h	0.0524h	0.1537d	0.2247d	-0.3896h	-0.4185h	-0.4746h			
8	0.2880	0.1844d	0.2152d	-0.3949h	-0.4134h	-0.4372h	-0.4432h	-0.3833s		
9	0.7656	0.2138d	-0.3922h	-0.3652h	-0.4259h	-0.4797h	-0.4820h	-0.4116h	-0.0929s	
10	1.5000	0.3444h	-0.3588h	-0.4135h	-0.4753h	-0.4793h	-0.4161h	-0.1961h	0.2643	0.7440

Player's Expectation = -0.0432

TABLE A(4) Dealer's Up-Card = 8

( ) = t', Maximum Hard Drawing Number
[ ] = t'', Maximum Soft Drawing Number

Expectation By Drawing Minus Expectation By Standing

Player's Cards	A	2	3	4	5	6	7	8	9	10
A	(16)[17]									
2	(16)[17]	(16)[17]								
3	(16)[17]	(16)[17]	(16)[17]							
4	(16)[17]	(16)[17]	(16)[17]	(16)						
5	(16)[17]	(16)[17]	(16)	(16)	(16)					
6	0.3203	(16)	(16)	(16)	(16)	0.2141(16)				
7	-0.0707	(16)	(16)	(16)	0.2147(16)	0.1439(16)	0.1314(16)			
8	-0.4420	(16)	(16)	0.2220(16)	0.1547(16)	0.1735(16)	0.1657(16)	0.1250		
9	-0.6080	(16)	0.1952(16)	0.1819(16)	0.1502(16)	0.1024(16)	0.0980	-0.0637	-0.6326	
10	BJ	0.2028(16)	0.1870(16)	0.1664(16)	0.1062(16)	0.1022	-0.0828	-0.6625	-1.2739	-1.6259

Doubling Down Expectations

Player's Cards	A	2	3	4	5	6	7	8	9	10
A	-0.2994									
2	-0.3187	-1.0298								
3	-0.2594	-1.0255	-0.9998							
4	-0.3175	-1.0233	-0.8528	-0.4418						
5	-0.3350	-0.8577	-0.4229	0.0147	**0.3229**					
6	-0.2359	-0.4318	0.0281	**0.3172**	**0.3657**	-0.7129				
7	-0.0105	0.0213	**0.3269**	**0.3402**	-0.7127	-0.8454	-0.8609			
8	0.2036	**0.2945**	**0.3300**	-0.7214	-0.8324	-0.7783	-0.7809	-0.8567		
9	0.2357	**0.3277**	-0.7070	-0.7287	-0.7667	-0.8602	-0.8602	-0.9572	-1.1362	
10	0.3126	-0.6290	-0.7103	-0.7444	-0.8488	-0.8496	-0.9542	-1.1339	-1.3941	-1.6854

Expectations By Splitting Pairs

	A	2	3	4	5	6	7	8	9	10
	0.4065	-0.1909	-0.2432	-0.2897	-0.3895	-0.3715	**-0.3776**	**-0.0591**	**0.2070**	**0.3446**

Expectations From Optimal Strategy

d = double down
s = split
h = hit (draw)

Player's Cards	A	2	3	4	5	6	7	8	9	10
A	0.4065s									
2	0.0391h	-0.1410h								
3	0.0350h	-0.1808h	-0.2311h							
4	-0.0355h	-0.2342h	-0.2284h	-0.0548h						
5	-0.0843h	-0.2178h	-0.0570h	0.1081h	0.3229d					
6	-0.0649h	-0.0559h	0.1175h	0.3172d	0.3657d	-0.3217h				
7	0.1209	0.1076h	0.3269d	0.3402d	-0.3210h	-0.3944h	-0.3776s			
8	0.6078	0.2945d	0.3300d	-0.3192h	-0.3868h	-0.3691h	-0.3691h	-0.0591s		
9	0.7848	0.3277d	-0.3161h	-0.3389h	-0.3701h	-0.4207h	-0.4278h	-0.4149	0.2070s	
10	1.5000	-0.2745h	-0.3282h	-0.3574h	-0.4180h	-0.4248h	-0.3942	0.0955	0.5768	0.7832

Player's Expectation = 0.0541

TABLE A(5) Dealer's Up-Card = 7

( ) = t*, Maximum Hard Drawing Number
[ ] = t*s, Maximum Soft Drawing Number

Expectation By Drawing Minus Expectation By Standing

Player's Cards	A	2	3	4	5	6	7	8	9	10
A	(16)[17]									
2	(16)[17]	(16)[17]								
3	(16)[17]	(16)[17]	(16)[17]							
4	(16)[17]	(16)[17]	(16)[17]	(16)						
5	(16)[17]	(16)	(16)	(16)	(16)					
6	0.1492	(16)	(16)	(16)	(16)	0.2286(16)				
7	−0.2300	(16)	(16)	(16)	0.2349(16)	0.1669(16)	0.1128(16)			
8	−0.3884	(16)	(16)	0.2380(16)	0.1664(16)	0.1501(16)	0.1773(16)	0.1289		
9	−0.5281	(16)	0.2445(16)	0.2152(16)	0.1517(16)	0.1396(16)	0.1323	−0.3277	−0.9665	
10	BJ	0.2608(16)	0.2007(16)	0.1267(16)	0.1140(16)	0.1071	−0.3322	−0.9553	−1.3084	−1.6076

Doubling Down Expectations

Player's Cards	A	2	3	4	5	6	7	8	9	10
A	−0.1458									
2	−0.1643	−0.9421								
3	−0.1807	−0.9378	−0.8722							
4	−0.1460	−0.8713	−0.5342	−0.0943						
5	−0.1922	−0.5588	−0.1182	0.1976	**0.4663**					
6	0.0238	−0.1339	0.1829	**0.4754**	**0.5005**	−0.6040				
7	0.2557	0.1668	**0.4447**	**0.4874**	−0.5914	−0.7212	−0.8318			
8	0.3326	**0.4166**	**0.4726**	−0.5707	−0.7141	−0.7433	−0.6756	−0.7565		
9	0.3532	**0.4554**	−0.5858	−0.6081	−0.7363	−0.7535	−0.7585	−0.9012	−1.1308	
10	0.4254	−0.5033	−0.5916	−0.7161	−0.7457	−0.7524	−0.9070	−1.1331	−1.3965	−1.6859

Expectations By Splitting Pairs

Player's Cards	A	2	3	4	5	6	7	8	9	10
Pair	**0.5407**	**−0.0058**	**−0.0684**	**−0.1666**	**−0.2317**	**−0.2077**	**−0.0560**	**0.2586**	**0.3611**	**0.4774**

Expectations From Optimal Strategy

d = double down
s = split
h = hit (draw)

Player's Cards	A	2	3	4	5	6	7	8	9	10
A	**0.5407s**									
2	0.1073h	**−0.0058s**								
3	0.0604h	−0.1192h	**−0.0684s**							
4	0.0337h	−0.1639h	0.0706h	0.1106h						
5	−0.0238h	−0.0674h	0.0926h	0.2013h	0.4663d					
6	0.0596h	0.0918h	0.1977h	0.4754d	0.5005d	**−0.2077s**				
7	0.4120h	0.1836h	0.4447d	0.4874d	−0.2582h	−0.3307h	**−0.0560s**			
8	0.6145h	0.4166d	0.4726d	−0.2456h	−0.3275h	−0.3485h	−0.3241h	**0.2586s**		
9	0.7732h	0.4554d	−0.2471h	−0.2741h	−0.3480h	−0.3632h	−0.3750h	−0.1229	0.4011	
10	1.5000	−0.2120h	−0.2704h	−0.3422h	−0.3645h	−0.3762h	−0.1213	0.3887	0.6101	0.7647

Player's Expectation = 0.1445

TABLE A(6) Dealer's Up-Card = 6

( ) = t', Maximum Hard Drawing Number
[ ] = t's, Maximum Soft Drawing Number

Expectation By Drawing Minus Expectation By Standing

Player's Cards ↓ \ →	A	2	3	4	5	6	7	8	9	10
A	(11)[17]									
2	(11)[17]	(11)[17]								
3	(11)[17]	(11)[17]	(11)[17]							
4	(11)[17]	(11)[17]	(11)	(11)						
5	(11)[17]	(11)	(11)	(11)	(11)					
6	0.1228	(11)	(11)	(11)	(11)	-0.0369				
7	-0.0669	(11)	(11)	(11)	-0.0440	-0.1203	-0.2022			
8	-0.2420	(11)	(11)	-0.0454	-0.1307	-0.1602	-0.1941	-0.2213		
9	-0.4184	(11)	-0.0486	-0.0859	-0.1676	-0.2331	-0.2203	-0.4698	-0.8505	
10	BJ	-0.0075	-0.0802	-0.1617	-0.2416	-0.2198	-0.4696	-0.8528	-1.1905	-1.5423

Doubling Down Expectations

Player's Cards ↓ \ →	A	2	3	4	5	6	7	8	9	10
A	0.2440									
2	0.2302	-0.2490								
3	0.2218	-0.2438	-0.2106							
4	0.2007	-0.2111	-0.0522	0.1932						
5	0.2167	-0.0563	0.1899	0.4433	0.7236					
6	0.2665	0.1237	0.3792	0.6633	0.7614	-0.4041				
7	0.3849	0.3574	0.6361	0.7315	-0.3750	-0.5799	-0.7528			
8	0.4808	0.6151	0.7122	-0.3853	-0.5534	-0.6650	-0.7422	-0.7989		
9	0.5515	0.6916	-0.4046	-0.4744	-0.6354	-0.8193	-0.8000	-0.9625	-1.1706	
10	0.6399	-0.3357	-0.4759	-0.6341	-0.7916	-0.7976	-0.9617	-1.1695	-1.4128	-1.6898

Expectations By Splitting Pairs

	A	2	3	4	5	6	7	8	9	10
	0.7583	**0.2401**	**0.2196**	**0.1806**	**0.1297**	**0.1513**	**0.2204**	**0.3563**	**0.4369**	**0.5421**

Expectations From Optimal Strategy

d = double down
s = split
h = hit (draw)

Player's Cards ↓ \ →	A	2	3	4	5	6	7	8	9	10
A	0.7583s									
2	0.2302d	0.2401s								
3	0.2218d	0.0192h	0.2196s							
4	0.2007d	0.0141h	0.0592h	0.1932d						
5	0.2167d	0.0696h	0.1899d	0.4433d	0.7236d					
6	0.2665d	0.1321h	0.3792d	0.6633d	0.7614d	0.1513s				
7	0.3849d	0.3574d	0.6361d	0.7315d	-0.1435	-0.1697	0.2204s			
8	0.4824	0.6151d	0.7122d	-0.1473	-0.1460	-0.1723	-0.1770	0.3563s		
9	0.6942	0.6916d	-0.1538	-0.1514	-0.1501	-0.1765	-0.1796	-0.0114	0.4369s	
10	1.5000	-0.1604	-0.1578	-0.1554	-0.1542	-0.1790	-0.0113	0.2681	0.4841	0.6974

Player's Expectation = 0.2415

TABLE A(7) Dealer's Up-Card = 5

( ) = $\hat{r}$, Maximum Hard Drawing Number
[ ] = $\tilde{r}$, Maximum Soft Drawing Number

Expectation By Drawing Minus Expectation By Standing

Player's Cards →	A	2	3	4	5	6	7	8	9	10
A	(11)[17]									
2	(11)[17]	(11)[17]								
3	(11)[17]	(11)[17]	(11)[17]							
4	(11)[17]	(11)[17]	(11)	(11)						
5	(11)[17]	(11)	(11)	(11)	(11)					
6	0.1354	(11)	(11)	(11)	(11)	−0.0697				
7	−0.0461	(11)	(11)	(11)	−0.0633	−0.1497	−0.2241			
8	−0.2363	(11)	(11)	−0.0645	−0.1509	−0.1927	−0.2172	−0.2865		
9	−0.4194	(11)	−0.0683	−0.1070	−0.1913	−0.2699	−0.2876	−0.4470	−0.7928	
10	BJ	−0.0280	−0.1028	−0.1850	−0.2681	−0.3025	−0.4481	−0.7927	−1.1565	−1.5193

Doubling Down Expectations

Player's Cards →	A	2	3	4	5	6	7	8	9	10
A	0.2108									
2	**0.2123**	−0.2140								
3	**0.2036**	−0.2085	−0.1837							
4	**0.1750**	−0.1852	−0.0619	0.1592						
5	**0.1482**	−0.0712	0.1550	0.4150	**0.6947**					
6	**0.2800**	0.1306	0.3916	0.6776	**0.7873**	−0.3437				
7	**0.3491**	0.3321	0.6150	0.7234	−0.3734	−0.5571	−0.7593			
8	**0.4489**	0.5920	0.6991	−0.3906	−0.5583	−0.6530	−0.7553	−0.9039		
9	**0.5253**	0.6796	−0.4103	−0.4817	−0.6454	−0.8135	−0.9023	−0.9827	−1.1799	
10	**0.6312**	−0.3441	−0.4880	−0.6463	−0.8076	−0.8874	−0.9825	−1.1807	−1.4174	−1.6912

Expectations By Splitting Pairs

A	2	3	4	5	6	7	8	9	10
0.7322	**0.2386**	**0.2283**	**0.1967**	**0.1302**	**0.1722**	**0.1998**	**0.3123**	**0.4147**	**0.5208**

Expectations From Optimal Strategy

d = double down s = split h = hit (draw)

Player's Cards →	A	2	3	4	5	6	7	8	9	10
A	0.7322s									
2	0.2123d	0.2386s								
3	0.2036d	0.0215h	0.2283s							
4	0.1750d	0.0089h	0.0490h	0.1967s						
5	0.1482d	0.0568h	0.1550d	0.4150d	0.6947d					
6	0.2800d	0.1306h	0.3916d	0.6776d	0.7873d	0.1722s				
7	0.3491d	0.3321d	0.6150d	0.7234d	−0.1288	−0.1338	0.1998s			
8	0.4608	0.5920d	0.6991d	−0.1234	−0.1314	−0.1369	−0.1605	0.3123s		
9	0.6821	0.6796d	−0.1308	−0.1283	−0.1357	−0.1412	−0.1636	−0.0444	0.4147s	
10	1.5000	−0.1441	−0.1368	−0.1339	−0.1382	−0.1412	−0.0432	0.2023	0.4478	0.6737

Player's Expectation = 0.2355

TABLE A(8)   Dealer's Up-Card = 4

Player's Cards →

( ) = t′. Maximum Hard Drawing Number
[ ] = t′ₛ Maximum Soft Drawing Number

Expectation By Drawing Minus Expectation By Standing

Player's Cards	A	2	3	4	5	6	7	8	9	10
A	(11)[17]	(11)[17]	(11)[17]							
2	(11)[17]	(11)[17]	(11)[17]							
3	(11)[17]	(11)[17]	(11)[17]							
4	(11)[17]	(11)[17]	(11)	(11)						
5	(11)[17]	(11)[17]	(11)	(11)						
6	0.1140					-0.0475				
7	-0.0479				-0.0465	-0.1281	-0.2104			
8	-0.2329			-0.0399	-0.1198	-0.1586	-0.1907	-0.2446		
9	-0.4298		-0.0426	-0.0746	-0.1546	-0.2310	-0.2578	-0.4556	-0.7637	
10	BJ	0.0179	-0.0693	-0.1477	-0.2272	-0.2600	-0.4699	-0.7613	-1.1159	-1.4912

Doubling Down Expectations

Player's Cards	A	2	3	4	5	6	7	8	9	10
A	0.1324									
2	**0.1151**	-0.3840								
3	**0.1091**	-0.3517	-0.3017							
4	**0.0849**	-0.3235	-0.1784	0.0394						
5	**0.0626**	-0.1955	0.0367	**0.2970**	**0.5898**					
6	**0.1545**	0.0190	**0.2896**	**0.5855**	**0.7039**	-0.3988				
7	**0.3127**	**0.2718**	**0.5704**	**0.6851**	-0.4022	-0.5730	-0.7488			
8	0.3652	**0.5049**	**0.6252**	-0.4456	-0.6021	-0.6854	-0.7606	-0.9197		
9	0.4482	**0.6001**	-0.4677	-0.5262	-0.6810	-0.8394	-0.9040	-1.0801	-1.1934	
10	0.5629	-0.4048	-0.5328	-0.6822	-0.8358	-0.9069	-1.0685	-1.1941	-1.4237	-1.6927

Expectations By Splitting Pairs

Player's Cards	A	2	3	4	5	6	7	8	9	10
	0.6686	**0.1121**	**0.1019**	0.0720	0.0094	0.0469	**0.1032**	**0.2152**	**0.3197**	0.4431

Expectations From Optimal Strategy

Player's Cards	A	2	3	4	5	6	7	8	9	10
A	0.6686s									
2	0.1151d	0.1121s								
3	0.1091d	-0.0410h	0.1019s							
4	0.0849d	-0.0552h	-0.0166h	0.0978h						
5	0.0626d	-0.0103h	0.0866h	0.2970d	0.5898d					
6	0.1545d	0.0811h	0.2896d	0.5855d	0.7039d	0.0469s				
7	0.3127d	0.2718d	0.5704d	0.6851d	-0.1546	-0.1584	0.1032s			
8	0.4155	0.5049d	0.6252d	-0.1829	-0.1813	-0.1841	-0.1896	0.2152s		
9	0.6539	0.6001d	-0.1913h	-0.1885	-0.1859	-0.1886	-0.1942	-0.0844	0.3197s	
10	1.5000	-0.1940h	-0.1971h	-0.1934	-0.1907	-0.1935	-0.0644	0.1642	0.4041	0.6448

d = double down
s = split
h = hit (draw)

Player's Expectation = 0.1826

TABLE A(9) Dealer's Up-Card = 3

Legend:

( ) = $\bar{t}$, Maximum Hard Drawing Number
[ ] = $\bar{t}'$, Maximum Soft Drawing Number

d = double down
s = split
h = hit (draw)

Expectation By Drawing Minus Expectation By Standing

Player's Cards →	A	2	3	4	5	6	7	8	9	10
A	(12)[17]									
2	(12)[17]	(12)[17]								
3	(11)[17]	(12)[17]	(12)[17]							
4	(11)[17]	(11)[17]	(11)[17]	(11)						
5	(11)[17]	(11)[17]	(11)	(11)						
6	0.1301	(11)	(11)			−0.0202				
7	−0.0741	(12)			−0.0186	−0.0945	−0.1695			
8	−0.2505			−0.0186	−0.0941	−0.1274	−0.1574	−0.2215		
9	−0.4533		−0.0025	−0.0392	−0.1125	−0.1858	−0.2088	−0.4146	−0.7609	
10	BJ	0.0486	−0.0220	−0.1048	−0.1818	−0.2109	−0.4171	−0.7783	−1.0963	−1.4825

Doubling Down Expectations

Player's Cards →	A	2	3	4	5	6
A	0.0503					
2	0.0345	−0.5015				
3	0.0245	−0.4970	−0.4722			
4	0.0138	−0.4452	−0.3252	−0.0875		
5	−0.0110	−0.3116	−0.0877	0.1956	**0.5096**	
6	0.0739	−0.0822	0.1892	0.5009	**0.6294**	−0.4624
7	0.1889	0.1946	0.4921	0.6111	−0.4620	−0.6186
8	0.3386	0.4825	0.5904	−0.4776	−0.6218	−0.6953
9	0.3817	0.5380	−0.5288	−0.5705	−0.7122	−0.8636
10	0.4961	−0.4555	−0.5754	−0.7114	−0.8583	−0.9215

Expectations By Splitting Pairs

Player's Cards →	A	2	3	4	5	6	7	8	9	10
	0.6128	0.0245	−0.0314	−0.0528	−0.1077	**−0.0686**	**−0.0205**	**0.1317**	**0.2416**	0.3823

Expectations From Optimal Strategy

Player's Cards →	A	2	3	4	5	6	7	8	9	10
A	0.6128s									
2	0.0705h	0.0245s								
3	0.0442h	−0.0983h	−0.0314s							
4	0.0234h	−0.1062h	−0.0815h	−0.0528						
5	−0.0019h	−0.0615h	0.0194h	0.1956d	0.5096d					
6	0.0739d	0.0238h	0.1892d	0.5009d	0.6294d	−0.0686				
7	0.1889d	0.1946d	0.4921d	0.6111d			−0.0205			
8	0.4198	0.4825d	0.5904d			−0.2148	−0.2239	0.1317		
9	0.6441	0.5380d	−0.2557	−0.2460	−0.2167	−0.2202	−0.2497	−0.1207	0.2416	
10	1.5000	−0.2193h	−0.2657	−0.2509	−0.2474	−0.2499	−0.1190	0.1444	0.3835	0.6361

Player's Expectation: 0.1354

TABLE A(10)   Dealer's Up-Card = 2

( ) = t^*, Maximum Hard Drawing Number
[ ] = t'_c, Maximum Soft Drawing Number

Expectation By Drawing Minus Expectation By Standing

Player's Cards →	A	2	3	4	5	6	7	8	9	10
A	(12)[17]	(12)[17]	(12)[17]	(12)	(12)	(12)				
2	(12)[17]	(12)[17]	(12)[17]	(12)	(12)	(12)				
3	(12)[17]	(12)[17]	(12)[17]	(12)	(12)	(12)				
4	(12)[17]	(12)	(12)	(12)	(12)	(12)				
5	(12)[17]	(12)	(12)	(12)	(12)	(12)				
6	0.1389	(12)	(12)	(12)	(12)	0.0090				
7	-0.0718	(12)	(12)	(12)	0.0095	-0.0676	-0.1386			
8	-0.2849	(12)	(12)	0.0215	-0.0669	-0.0953	-0.1190	-0.1794		
9	-0.4702	(12)	0.0217	-0.0076	-0.0900	-0.1576	-0.1795	-0.3936	-0.7649	
10	BJ	0.0676(13)	0.0082	-0.0584	-0.1416	-0.1674	-0.3799	-0.7515	-1.1348	-1.4739

Doubling Down Expectations

Player's Cards →	A	2	3	4	5	6	7	8	9	10
A	-0.0150									
2	-0.0304	-0.5816								
3	-0.0373	-0.5866	-0.5672							
4	-0.0632	-0.5600	-0.4302	-0.1890						
5	-0.0768	-0.4028	-0.1723	**0.1135**	**0.4464**					
6	**0.0133**	-0.1670	**0.1118**	**0.4322**	**0.5672**	-0.5154				
7	0.1245	**0.1174**	**0.4260**	**0.5417**	-0.5152	-0.6654	-0.8139			
8	0.2302	**0.4245**	**0.5336**	-0.5293	-0.6638	-0.7263	-0.7823	-0.9086		
9	0.3693	**0.5248**	-0.5426	-0.5868	-0.7188	-0.8620	-0.9123	-1.0604	-1.2559	
10	0.5168	-0.4956	-0.6083	-0.7371	-0.8729	-0.9302	-1.0762	-1.2653	-1.5000	-1.6935

Expectations By Splitting Pairs

Player's Cards →	A	2	3	4	5	6	7	8	9	10
	0.5657	**-0.0474**	**-0.1158**	**-0.1617**	**-0.1992**	**-0.1647**	**-0.1050**	**0.0637**	**0.1876**	**0.3307**

Expectations From Optimal Strategy

Player's Cards →	A	2	3	4	5	6	7	8	9	10
A	**0.5657**s									
2	0.03392h	**-0.0474**s								
3	0.0169h	-0.1314h	**-0.1158**s							
4	-0.0117h	-0.1507h	-0.1230h	-0.0126						
5	-0.00317h	-0.0994h	-0.0165h	0.1135d	0.4464d					
6	0.0133d	-0.0130h	0.1118d	0.4322d	0.5672d	**-0.1647**s				
7	0.1358	0.1174d	0.4260d	0.5417d	-0.2526h	-0.2651	**-0.1050**s			
8	0.4016	0.4245d	0.5336d	-0.2598h	-0.2650	-0.2679	-0.2721	**0.0637**s		
9	0.6559	0.5248d	-0.2663h	-0.2858	-0.2694	-0.2734	-0.2766	-0.1366	**0.1876**s	
10	1.5000	-0.2434h	-0.3042h	-0.3102	-0.2948	-0.2977	-0.1582	0.1188	0.3848	0.6272

d = double down
s = split
h = hit (draw)

Player's Expectation = 0.0989

Table B   Player's Exact Expectation When Holding 16 vs. a 10

	Player's Cards	Expectation by Drawing	Expectation by Standing	Gain by Drawing over standing
2-Card Holding	6, 10	−0.5069	−0.5430	0.0360
	8, 8	−0.5118	−0.5183	0.0065
	7, 9	−0.5120	−0.5180	0.0060
3-Card Holding	6, 9, A	−0.5117	−0.5374	0.0257
	6, 6, 4	−0.5368	−0.5597	0.0229
	2, 6, 8	−0.5215	−0.5425	0.0211
	3, 6, 7	−0.5291	−0.5374	0.0083
	3, 3, 10	−0.5444	−0.5439	−0.0005
	2, 4, 10	−0.5491	−0.5448	−0.0043
	7, 8, A	−0.5172	−0.5116	−0.0057
	2, 7, 7	−0.5265	−0.5159	−0.0106
	5, 10, A	−0.5496	−0.5360	−0.0136
	3, 4, 9	−0.5557	−0.5415	−0.0142
	2, 5, 9	−0.5595	−0.5422	−0.0174
	3, 5, 8	−0.5665	−0.5372	−0.0292
	5, 5, 6	−0.5859	−0.5560	−0.0299
	4, 4, 8	−0.5683	−0.5375	−0.0308
	4, 5, 7	−0.5797	−0.5330	−0.0467
4-Card Holding	4, 10, A, A	−0.5453	−0.5348	−0.0106
	2, 3, 10, A	−0.5423	−0.5422	−0.0001
	2, 2, 2, 10	−0.5438	−0.5513	0.0075
	5, 9, A, A	−0.5556	−0.5298	−0.0259
	2, 4, 9, A	−0.5547	−0.5395	−0.0153
	3, 3, 9, A	−0.5491	−0.5375	−0.0117
	2, 2, 3, 9	−0.5519	−0.5483	−0.0036
	6, 8, A, A	−0.5171	−0.5314	0.0144
	2, 5, 8, A	−0.5653	−0.5355	−0.0298
	3, 4, 8, A	−0.5618	−0.5358	−0.0260
	2, 2, 4, 8	−0.5639	−0.5443	−0.0196
	2, 3, 3, 8	−0.5583	−0.5442	−0.0141
	7, 7, A, A	−0.5222	−0.5048	−0.0174
	2, 6, 7, A	−0.5262	−0.5362	0.0101
	3, 5, 7, A	−0.5728	−0.5302	−0.0425
	4, 4, 7, A	−0.5752	−0.5326	−0.0427
	2, 2, 5, 7	−0.5743	−0.5414	−0.0329
	2, 3, 4, 7	−0.5715	−0.5412	−0.0303
	3, 3, 3, 7	−0.5659	−0.5389	−0.0270
	3, 6, 6, A	−0.5289	−0.5583	0.0294
	2, 2, 6, 6	−0.5309	−0.5693	0.0384
	4, 5, 6, A	−0.5813	−0.5552	−0.0261
	2, 3, 5, 6	−0.5780	−0.5659	−0.0121
	2, 4, 4, 6	−0.5802	−0.5658	−0.0144
	3, 3, 4, 6	−0.5745	−0.5662	−0.0083
	5, 5, 5, A	−0.6309	−0.5489	−0.0820
	2, 4, 5, 5	−0.6296	−0.5616	−0.0681
	3, 3, 5, 5	−0.6242	−0.5605	−0.0637
	3, 4, 4, 5	−0.6262	−0.5632	−0.0630
	4, 4, 4, 4	−0.6284	−0.5645	−0.0638

TABLE C(1)   Drawing Strategy for Depleted Decks

Depleted Deck	Dealer's Up-Card									
	A	2	3	4	5	6	7	8	9	10
$Q(A) = 0$		(12)	(11)	(11)	(11)	(11)	(15)	(16)	(15)	(15)
$Q(2) = 0$	(16) 17		(12) 17	(11) 17	(11) 17	(11) 17	(15) 17	(16) 17	(15) 18	(15) 17
$Q(3) = 0$	(16) 17	(12) 17		(11) 17	(11) 17	(11) 17	(15) 17	(15) 17	(15) 18	(15) 17
$Q(4) = 0$	(16) 18	(12) 17	(11) 17		(11) 17	(11) 17	(15) 17	(15) 17	(15) 18	(15) 18
$Q(5) = 0$	(16) 17	(11) 17	(11) 17	(11) 17		(11) 17	(15) 17	(15) 17	(14) 18	(14) 18
$Q(6) = 0$	(14) 18	(11) 17	(11) 17	(11) 17	(11) 17		(16) 17	(16) 17	(14) 18	(14) 18
$Q(7) = 0$	(16) 17	(11) 17	(11) 17	(11) 17	(11) 17	(11) 17		(16) 17	(16) 18	(12) 18
$Q(8) = 0$	(16) 17	(11) 17	(11) 17	(11) 17	(11) 17	(11) 17	(16) 17		(16) 18	(16) 18
$Q(9) = 0$	(16) 17	(11) 17	(11) 17	(11) 17	(11) 17	(11) 17	(16) 17	(16) 18		(16) 18
$Q(10) = 0$	(17) 18	(17) 18	(17) 18	(17) 18	(17) 18	(17) 18	(17) 18	(17) 18	(17) 18	

( ) = t^*, maximum hard drawing number.

no paren. = t_s^*, maximum soft drawing number.

TABLE C(2) Doubling-Down Strategy for Depleted Decks†

	A	2	3	4	5	6	7	8	9	10
Q(A) = 0	10, 11		9, 10, 11	9, 10, 11	9, 10, 11	8, 9, 10, 11	10, 11	10, 11	10, 11	11
Q(2) = 0	10, 11	10, 11	9, 10, 11, 14	9, 10, 11, 14, 15, 16, 17, 18	9, 10, 11, 14, 15, 16, 17, 18	8, 9, 10, 11, 14, 15, 16, 17, 18	9, 10, 11	9, 10, 11	10, 11	10, 11
Q(3) = 0	10, 11	9, 10, 11		8, 9, 10, 11, 13, 15, 16, 17, 18, 19	7, 8, 9, 10, 11, 13, 15, 16, 17, 18, 19	7, 8, 9, 10, 11, 13, 15, 16, 17, 18, 19, 20	9, 10, 11	9, 10, 11	10, 11	10, 11
Q(4) = 0	10, 11	9, 10, 11, 18	9, 10, 11, 13, 14, 18, 19		7, 8, 9, 10, 11, 13, 14, 16, 17, 18, 19, 20	7, 8, 9, 10, 11, 13, 14, 16, 17, 18, 19, 20	9, 10, 11	10, 11	10, 11	10, 11
Q(5) = 0	10, 11	9, 10, 11, 17, 18	9, 10, 11, 13, 14, 15, 17, 18, 19	8, 9, 10, 11, 13, 14, 15, 17, 18, 19		8, 9, 10, 11, 13, 14, 15, 17, 18, 19, 20	9, 10, 11, 17	10, 11	10, 11	10, 11
Q(6) = 0	10, 11	9, 10, 11, 16, 18	9, 10, 11, 16, 18, 19	8, 9, 10, 11, 13, 14, 15, 16, 18, 19	8, 9, 10, 11, 13, 14, 15, 16, 18, 19, 20		9, 10, 11	10, 11	10, 11	10, 11
Q(7) = 0	10, 11	9, 10, 11, 15, 16, 17	9, 10, 11, 15, 16, 17, 19	8, 9, 10, 11, 13, 14, 15, 16, 17, 19	9, 10, 11, 15, 16, 17, 19	9, 10, 11, 15, 16, 17, 19	9, 10, 11	10, 11	10, 11	10, 11
Q(8) = 0	11	9, 10, 11, 14, 15, 16, 17, 18	9, 10, 11, 14, 15, 16, 17, 18	9, 10, 11, 15, 16, 17, 18	9, 10, 11, 14, 15, 16, 17, 18	9, 10, 11, 14, 15, 16, 17, 18	10, 11			10, 11
Q(9) = 0	11	9, 10, 11, 15, 16, 17, 18	10, 11, 17	9, 10, 11, 15, 16, 17, 18	9, 10, 11, 13, 14, 15, 16, 17, 18	9, 10, 11, 13, 14, 15, 16, 17, 18	10, 11	10, 11		11
Q(10) = 0									11	

†Values greater than 11 refer to soft totals.

TABLE C(3) Splitting Pairs Strategy for Depleted Decks

	A	2	3	4	5	6	7	8	9	10
Q(A) = 0		2, 3, 6, 7, 8, 9	2, 3, 6, 7, 8, 9	2, 3, 4, 6, 7, 8, 9	2, 3, 4, 6, 7, 8, 9	2, 3, 4, 6, 7, 8, 9	2, 3, 6, 7, 8	7, 8, 9	8, 9	8
Q(2) = 0	A, 8		A, 3, 6, 7, 8, 9	A, 3, 4, 6, 7, 8, 9	A, 3, 4, 6, 7, 8, 9	A, 3, 4, 6, 7, 8, 9	A, 3, 6, 7, 8	A, 3, 7, 8, 9	A, 8, 9	A, 8
Q(3) = 0	A, 8	A, 2, 6, 7, 8, 9		A, 2, 4, 6, 7, 8, 9	A, 2, 4, 6, 7, 8	A, 2, 4, 6, 7, 8, 9, 10	A, 2, 7, 8, 9, 10	A, 2, 8, 9	A, 8, 9	A
Q(4) = 0	A, 8	A, 2, 3, 6, 7, 8, 9	A, 2, 3, 6, 7, 8, 9		A, 2, 3, 6, 7, 8, 9, 10	A, 2, 3, 6, 7, 8, 9, 10	A, 2, 3, 7, 8, 9	A, 2, 3, 8, 9	A, 3, 8, 9	A, 8
Q(5) = 0	A, 8	A, 2, 3, 6, 7, 8, 9	A, 2, 3, 6, 7, 8, 9	A, 2, 3, 6, 7, 8, 9		A, 2, 3, 6, 7, 8, 9, 10	A, 2, 3, 7, 8, 9	A, 2, 3, 7, 8, 9	A, 7, 8, 9	A, 8
Q(6) = 0	A, 8, 9	A, 2, 3, 7, 8, 9	A, 2, 3, 7, 8, 9	A, 2, 3, 7, 8, 9	A, 2, 3, 7, 8, 9, 10		A, 2, 3, 7, 8, 9	A, 7, 8, 9	A, 7, 8, 9	A, 8
Q(7) = 0	A, 8	A, 2, 6, 8, 9	A, 2, 3, 6, 8, 9	A, 2, 3, 6, 8, 9	A, 2, 3, 6, 7, 9	A, 2, 3, 6, 8, 9		A, 6, 8, 9	A, 8, 9	A
Q(8) = 0	A	A, 6, 7, 9	A, 2, 3, 4, 6, 7, 9	A, 6, 7, 9	A, 2, 3, 6, 7, 9	A, 2, 3, 6, 7, 9	A, 6, 7		A, 8, 9	A
Q(9) = 0	A, 8, 9	A, 3, 6, 7, 8,	A, 3, 6, 7, 8	A, 3, 6, 7, 8	A, 2, 3, 6, 7, 8	A, 2, 3, 6, 7, 8	A, 3, 6, 7, 8	A, 3, 6, 8	A, 9	A, 8
Q(10) = 0	4, 8, 9	3, 4, 7, 8	3, 4, 7, 8	3, 4, 7, 8	3, 4, 7, 8	2, 3, 4, 7, 8	2, 3, 4, 7, 8, 9	2, 3, 4, 7, 8, 9	2, 3, 4, 7, 8, 9	2, 3, 4, 7, 8, 9

TABLE D Relative Frequency of Occurrence of *T* Ratios

T-Ratio Range	Relative Frequency of Occurrence	Relative Frequency of Double Down	Relative Frequency of Pair Splitting ($\times 10^{-4}$)	Relative Gain ($\times 10^{-4}$)	Relative Frequency of Insurance ($\times 10^{-4}$)	Relative Insurance Gain ($\times 10^{-4}$)	Expectation $\left(\dfrac{\text{Total Gain}}{\text{Total Bet}}\right)$
0.0 to 0.1	0.0000	0.0000	0.0	0.0	0.0	0.0	0.0000
0.1 to 0.2	0.0002	0.0000	0.2	0.1	0.0	0.1	0.0045
0.2 to 0.3	0.0001	0.0000	0.0	0.1	0.0	0.0	0.0931
0.3 to 0.4	0.0006	0.0000	0.7	1.8	0.2	0.3	0.1438
0.4 to 0.5	0.0018	0.0000	1.8	0.0	0.6	0.9	0.0220
0.5 to 0.6	0.0013	0.0000	1.3	2.8	0.6	0.6	0.1165
0.6 to 0.7	0.0010	0.0000	1.0	2.6	0.4	0.4	0.1296
0.7 to 0.8	0.0048	0.0002	4.3	7.1	2.4	2.3	0.0847
0.8 to 0.9	0.0030	0.0002	2.7	6.1	1.5	1.3	0.1038
0.9 to 1.0	0.0147	0.0009	8.9	18.5	7.7	5.5	0.0715
1.0 to 1.1	0.0012	0.0001	1.0	1.9	0.7	0.4	0.0828
1.1 to 1.2	0.0108	0.0009	7.4	14.5	6.6	3.1	0.0688
1.2 to 1.3	0.0121	0.0011	5.9	16.4	7.0	3.1	0.0691
1.3 to 1.4	0.0206	0.0019	6.5	20.5	12.0	5.1	0.0538
1.4 to 1.5	0.0239	0.0026	6.7	21.7	14.7	4.5	0.0472
1.5 to 1.6	0.0200	0.0022	4.1	17.5	13.0	3.4	0.0449
1.6 to 1.7	0.0311	0.0036	4.6	22.7	19.8	4.2	0.0372
1.7 to 1.8	0.0419	0.0051	6.8	22.8	26.4	4.6	0.0290
1.8 to 1.9	0.0438	0.0053	7.5	19.7	27.9	2.6	0.0217
1.9 to 2.0	0.0941	0.0119	16.6	36.5	34.8	6.0	0.0194
2.0 to 2.1	0.0379	0.0042	7.1	9.7	12.8	0.4	0.0116
2.1 to 2.2	0.0680	0.0076	12.9	10.9	21.4	1.2	0.0078
2.2 to 2.3	0.2133	0.0159	28.4	16.2	7.0	0.3	0.0035
2.3 to 2.4	0.0640	0.0072	12.8	9.8	5.5	1.1	0.0075
2.4 to 2.5	0.0645	0.0069	13.4	1.0	4.5	1.2	0.0014
2.5 to 2.6	0.0304	0.0029	6.4	-3.7			-0.0055
2.6 to 2.7	0.0350	0.0047	7.4	-4.1	2.0	0.5	-0.0043
2.7 to 2.8	0.0282	0.0027	6.3	-4.2			-0.0067
2.8 to 2.9	0.0190	0.0017	4.2	-4.4			-0.0103
2.9 to 3.0	0.0374	0.0037	8.2	0.1	2.7	0.5	0.0007

3.0 to 3.1	0.0011	0.0001	0.2	−0.2			−0.0102
3.1 to 3.2	0.0145	0.0011	3.1	−3.5			−0.0111
3.2 to 3.3	0.0086	0.0007	1.8	−2.6			−0.0139
3.3 to 3.4	0.0115	0.0010	2.5	−3.2			−0.0127
3.4 to 3.5	0.0140	0.0013	3.1	−3.0			−0.0096
3.5 to 3.6	0.0036	0.0003	0.7	−1.7			−0.0437
3.6 to 3.7	0.0064	0.0005	1.4	−1.9			−0.0136
3.7 to 3.8	0.0058	0.0004	1.2	−2.1			−0.0168
3.8 to 3.9	0.0013	0.0001	0.3	−1.2			−0.0432
3.9 to 4.0	0.0131	0.0011	2.9	−2.2			−0.0075
4.0 to 4.1	0.0000	0.0000	0.0	−0.0			−0.0000
4.1 to 4.2	0.0020	0.0002	0.4	−1.5			−0.0336
4.2 to 4.3	0.0020	0.0002	0.5	−0.5			−0.0116
4.3 to 4.4	0.0040	0.0003	0.8	−0.8			−0.0094
4.4 to 4.5	0.0054	0.0004	1.2	−1.2			−0.0104
4.5 to 4.6	0.0005	0.0000	0.1	−0.3			−0.0252
4.6 to 4.7	0.0019	0.0001	0.4	−0.9			−0.0222
4.7 to 4.8	0.0010	0.0001	0.2	−0.8			−0.0375
4.8 to 4.9	0.0000	0.0000	0.0	−0.1			−0.0847
4.9 to 5.0	0.0107	0.0013	2.6	−4.5			−0.0184
5.0 to 5.1	0.0000	0.0000	0.0	−0.0			−0.0000
5.1 to 5.2	0.0001	0.0000	0.0	0.0			0.0033
5.2 to 5.3	0.0004	0.0000	0.1	−0.2			−0.0253
5.3 to 5.4	0.0012	0.0002	0.3	−0.4			−0.0163
5.4 to 5.5	0.0026	0.0000	0.6	−0.3			−0.0045
5.5 to 5.6	0.0000	0.0000	0.0	0.1			0.0694
5.6 to 5.7	0.0009	0.0000	0.2	0.3			0.0165
5.7 to 5.8	0.0003	0.0000	0.1	−0.0			−0.0059
5.8 to 5.9	0.0000	0.0000	0.0	−0.0			−0.0000
5.9 to 6.0	0.0071	0.0005	1.7	0.3			0.0017
6.0 to 6.1	0.0000	0.0000	0.0	−0.0			−0.0000
6.1 to 6.2	0.0000	0.0000	0.0	−0.0			−0.2857
6.2 to 6.3	0.0000	0.0000	0.0	−0.1			−0.0829
6.3 to 6.4	0.0004	0.0000	0.1	−0.2			−0.0298
6.4 to 6.5	0.0014	0.0000	0.4	−0.8			−0.0253
6.5 to 6.6	0.0000	0.0000	0.0	−0.0			−0.0000
6.6 to 6.7	0.0002	0.0000	0.0	−0.1			−0.0125
6.7 to 6.8	0.0000	0.0000	0.0	−0.0			−0.0126
over 6.8	0.0210	0.0013	5.8	6.8			−0.0147
Total	1.0000	0.0876	0.0228	+0.0226	0.0232	+0.0053	+0.0123

Note: Probability of Tie = 0.0832.

TABLE E Optimal Strategy for All Cards Exposed

	Total	Cards	Maximum Drawing Numbers t^*	t^*_c	Doubling Down Hard	Soft	Splits
	4	2, 2	13	17	10, 11	17, 18	A, 7, 8
	5	2, 3	12	17	10, 11	13, 14, 15, 16, 17, 18, 19,	A, 2, 3, 6, 7, 8, 9
	6	2, 4	11	17	9, 10, 11		A, 2, 3, 6, 7, 8, 9
		3, 3	11	17	8, 9, 10, 11		A, 2, 3, 4, 6, 7, 8, 9
	7	2, 5	16	17	10, 11		A, 2, 3, 7, 8
		3, 4	16	17	9, 10, 11		A, 2, 3, 7, 8
Dealer's Hard Hand	8	2, 6	16	17	10, 11		A, 7, 8, 9
		3, 5 or 4, 4	16	17	10, 11		A, 2, 3, 7, 8, 9
	9	2, 7 or 3, 6	16	18	10, 11		A, 8, 9
		4, 5	15	18	10, 11		A, 8, 9
	10	2, 8	15	18	11		A, 8
		3, 7 or 5, 5	15	18	11		A
		4, 6	16	18	11		A
	11	2, 9	15	17			A
		3, 8	14	17			A
		4, 7	13	17			A
		5, 6	13	18			A
	12	2, 10					
		3, 9 or 4, 8	11	17	8, 9, 10, 11	13, 14, 15, 16, 17, 18, 19	A, 2, 3, 4, 6, 7, 8, 9, 10
		5, 7 or 6, 6	11	17	8, 9, 10, 11	13, 14, 15, 16, 17, 18, 19, 20	A, 2, 3, 4, 6, 7, 8, 9, 10
	13		11	17	7, 8, 9, 10, 11	13, 14, 15, 16, 17, 18, 19, 20	A, 2, 3, 4, 6, 7, 8, 9, 10
	14		11	17	5, 6, 7, 8, 9, 10, 11	13, 14, 15, 16, 17, 18, 19, 20	A, 2, 3, 4, 6, 7, 8, 9, 10
Dealer's Hard Hand	15		11	17	5, 6, 7, 8, 9, 10, 11	13, 14, 15, 16, 17, 18, 19, 20	A, 2, 3, 4, 6, 7, 8, 9, 10
	16		11	17	5, 6, 7, 8, 9, 10, 11	13, 14, 15, 16, 17, 18, 19, 20	A, 2, 3, 4, 6, 7, 8, 9, 10
	17		16	17			2, 3, 6, 7, 8
	18	8, 10	17	18			2, 3, 7, 8, 9
		9, 9	17	18			3, 6, 7, 8, 9
	19	9, 10	18	18			9
	20	10, 10	19	19			
		A, A	15	17	11		A, 8
		A, 2	14	17	10, 11		A, 7, 8
		A, 3	13	17	10, 11		A, 7, 8
Dealer's Soft Hand		A, 4	12	17	10, 11		A, 2, 6, 7, 8, 9
		A, 5	12	17	9, 10, 11	17, 18	A, 2, 3, 6, 7, 8, 9
		A, 6	16	17			A, 2, 3, 6, 7, 8
		A, 7	17	18			2, 3, 7, 8, 9
		A, 8	18	18			9
		A, 9	19	19			

TABLE F Optimal Zero-Memory Strategy for Zweikartenspiel

	Total	Cards	Maximum Drawing Numbers t^*	t^*_s	Double Down Hard	Soft	Split
	4	2, 2	12	17	10, 11		A, 8
	5	2, 3	11	17	10, 11		A, 8
	6	2, 4	11	18	10, 11	18	A, 2, 3, 6, 7, 8, 9
		3, 3	11	17	9, 10, 11	13, 14, 15, 16, 17, 18	A, 2, 3, 4, 6, 7, 8, 9
	7	2, 5	15	17	10, 11		A, 8
		3, 4	14	17	10, 11		A, 2, 3, 7, 8
Dealer's Hard Hand	8	2, 6 or 4, 4	14	18	10, 11		A, 8, 9
		3, 5	15	18	10, 11		A, 8, 9
	9	2, 7	15	18	10, 11		A
		3, 6 or 4, 5	14	18	10, 11		A
	10	2, 8	14	18	11		A
		4, 6	14	18			A
		3, 7 or 4, 5	13	18			A
	11	2, 9	13	17			
		3, 8 or 4, 7	12	17			
		5, 6	12	18			
	12	2, 10 or 3, 9	11	17	8, 9, 10, 11	13, 14, 15, 16, 17, 18, 19	A, 2, 3, 4, 6, 7, 8, 9
		4, 8	11	18	8, 9, 10, 11	13, 14, 15, 16, 17, 18, 19	A, 2, 3, 4, 6, 7, 8, 9
		5, 7	11	18	8, 9, 10, 11	13, 14, 15, 16, 17, 18, 19, 20	A, 2, 3, 4, 6, 7, 8, 9, 10
		6, 6	11	17	8, 9, 10, 11	13, 14, 15, 16, 17, 18, 19, 20	A, 2, 3, 4, 6, 7, 8, 9, 10
	13	3, 10	11	17	8, 9, 10, 11	13, 14, 15, 16, 17, 18, 19	A, 2, 3, 4, 6, 7, 8, 9
		4, 9	11	18	7, 8, 9, 10, 11	13, 14, 15, 16, 17, 18, 19, 20	A, 2, 3, 4, 6, 7, 8, 9, 10
		5, 8 or 6, 7	11	17	6, 7, 8, 9, 10, 11	13, 14, 15, 16, 17, 18, 19, 20	A, 2, 3, 4, 6, 7, 8, 9, 10
	14	4, 10 or 5, 9 or 6, 8	11	17	5, 6, 7, 8, 9, 10, 11	13, 14, 15, 16, 17, 18, 19, 20	A, 2, 3, 4, 6, 7, 8, 9, 10
		7, 7	11	18	5, 6, 7, 8, 9, 10, 11	13, 14, 15, 16, 17, 18, 19, 20	A, 2, 3, 4, 6, 7, 8, 9, 10
Dealer's Hard Hand	15	5, 10	11	17	5, 6, 7, 8, 9, 10, 11	13, 14, 15, 16, 17, 18, 19, 20	A, 2, 3, 4, 6, 7, 8, 9, 10
		6, 9 or 7, 8	11	18	5, 6, 7, 8, 9, 10, 11	13, 14, 15, 16, 17, 18, 19, 20	A, 2, 3, 4, 6, 7, 8, 9, 10
	16	6, 10	11	17	5, 6, 7, 8, 9, 10, 11	13, 14, 15, 16, 17, 18, 19, 20	A, 2, 3, 4, 6, 7, 8, 9, 10
		7, 9 or 8, 8	11	18	5, 6, 7, 8, 9, 10, 11	13, 14, 15, 16, 17, 18, 19, 20	A, 2, 3, 4, 6, 7, 8, 9, 10
	17		17	17			2, 3, 6, 7, 8
	18	8, 10	18	18			8, 9
		9, 9	18	18			3, 8, 9
	19	9, 10	19	19			
	20	10, 10	20	20			
Dealer's Soft Hand		A, A	14	17	11		A
		A, 2	13	17	11		A
		A, 3	12	17	10, 11		A
		A, 4	11	17	10, 11		A, 8
		A, 5	11	18	10, 11		A, 6, 7, 8, 9
		A, 6	17	17			A, 2, 3, 6, 7, 8
		A, 7	18	18			9
		A, 8	19	19			
		A, 9	20	20			

TABLE G Mathematical Expectations as a Function of the Dealer's Cards

Dealer's Cards →	A	2	3	4	5	6	7	8	9	10
A	−0.1201									
2	−0.0560	0.0185								
3	−0.0166	0.0776	0.2744							
4	0.0411	0.1455	0.1682	0.0662						
5	0.1064	0.0637	0.0741	−0.0325	−0.1613					
6	0.3068	0.0147	−0.0350	−0.1657	−0.2141	0.3693				
7	0.1020	−0.0299	−0.1660	−0.2156	0.3691	0.4571	0.5376			
8	−0.1344	−0.1153	−0.2159	0.3483	0.4549	0.4817	0.5034	0.5733		
9	−0.4593	−0.2142	0.3451	0.3915	0.4815	0.5574	0.5734	0.3214	0.1155	
10	−0.9633	0.2911	0.3659	0.4685	0.5546	0.5687	0.3309	0.1244	−0.1153	−0.4377

TABLE H Mathematical Expectations for Zweikartenspiel

Dealer's Cards →	A	2	3	4	5	6	7	8	9	10
A	−0.2138									
2	−0.1426	−0.0599								
3	−0.0932	0.0097	0.2088							
4	−0.0309	0.0819	0.0689	−0.0322						
5	0.0388	−0.0409	−0.0256	−0.1353	−0.2660					
6	0.2490	−0.0900	−0.1423	−0.2705	−0.2809	0.3095				
7	0.0237	−0.1333	−0.2673	−0.2819	0.3106	0.4203	0.4864			
8	−0.2456	−0.2240	−0.2856	0.2914	0.3987	0.4287	0.4533	0.5268		
9	−0.6475	−0.2861	0.2857	0.3341	0.4279	0.5071	0.5267	0.2694	0.0390	
10	−1.0000	0.2303	0.3090	0.4153	0.5047	0.5205	0.2827	0.0563		−0.6077

TABLE I   Probability Distributions of the Suits In a Coalition

Distribution (e-f-g-h)	Probability of Occurrence P_u (Suits Unspecified)	Probability of Occurrence P_s (Suits Specified)
8-7-6-5*	0.23604	0.00984
7-7-6-6*	0.10491	0.01749
9-7-6-4*	0.07285	0.00304
8-7-7-4	0.06557	0.00546
9-6-6-5	0.06557	0.00546
7-7-7-5	0.05245	0.01311
8-6-6-6	0.05245	0.01311
8-8-6-4	0.04918	0.00410
9-7-5-5	0.04918	0.00410
9-8-5-4*	0.04098	0.00171
8-8-5-5*	0.03319	0.00553
9-8-6-3	0.02186	0.00091
10-7-5-4	0.02186	0.00091
8-8-7-3	0.01967	0.00164
10-6-5-5	0.01967	0.00164
9-7-7-3	0.01457	0.00121
10-6-6-4	0.01457	0.00121
10-7-6-3*	0.01166	0.00049
10-8-5-3*	0.00656	0.00027
9-8-7-2	0.00596	0.00025
11-6-5-4	0.00596	0.00025
9-9-5-3	0.00455	0.00038
10-8-4-4	0.00455	0.00038
9-9-4-4*	0.00316	0.00053
10-8-6-2	0.00238	0.00010
11-7-5-3	0.00238	0.00010
10-9-4-3*	0.00202	0.00008
9-9-6-2	0.00166	0.00014
11-7-4-4	0.00166	0.00014
10-7-7-2	0.00159	0.00016
11-6-6-3	0.00159	0.00016
8-8-8-2	0.00134	0.00034
11-5-5-5	0.00134	0.00034

TABLE J Three-Hand Residue Distributions

No. of Cards of a Particular Suit in South Hand	Distribution of the Residue (from 13) Among Other Three Players in a Specified Order								
0	5-4-4 0.08100	5-5-3 0.05832	6-4-3 0.04320	6-5-2 0.02121	7-3-3 0.01728	7-4-2 0.01178	6-6-1 0.00471	8-3-2 0.00353	7-5-1 0.00353
	8-4-1 0.00147	9-2-2 0.00054	7-6-0 0.00036	9-3-1 0.00033	8-5-0 0.00020	9-4-0 6.3×10^{-5}	10-2-1 3.6×10^{-5}	10-3-0 1.0×10^{-5}	11-1-1 1.6×10^{-6}
	11-2-0 7.5×10^{-7}	12-1-0 2.1×10^{-8}	13-0-0 1.3×10^{-10}						
1	4-4-4 0.09347	5-4-3 0.06730	6-3-3 0.03589	5-5-2 0.03304	6-4-2 0.02447	7-3-2 0.00979	6-5-1 0.00734	7-4-1 0.00408	8-2-2 0.00200
	8-3-1 0.00122	6-6-0 0.00074	7-5-0 0.00057	8-4-0 0.00025	9-2-1 0.00019	9-3-0 5.3×10^{-5}	10-1-1 1.2×10^{-5}	10-2-0 5.8×10^{-6}	11-1-0 2.8×10^{-7}
	12-0-0 3.4×10^{-9}								
2	4-4-3 0.08723	5-3-3 0.06281	5-4-2 0.04282	6-3-2 0.02284	5-5-1 0.01285	6-4-1 0.00952	7-2-2 0.00623	7-3-1 0.00381	6-5-0 0.00132
	8-2-1 0.00078	7-4-0 0.00073	8-3-0 0.00026	9-1-1 7.3×10^{-5}	9-2-0 3.4×10^{-5}	10-1-0 2.2×10^{-6}	11-0-0 4.7×10^{-8}		
3	4-3-3 0.09199	4-4-2 0.06272	5-3-2 0.04516	5-4-1 0.01882	6-2-2 0.01642	6-3-1 0.01004	7-2-1 0.00274	5-5-0 0.00261	6-4-0 0.00193
	7-3-0 0.00077	8-1-1 0.00035	8-2-0 0.00019	9-1-0 1.5×10^{-5}	10-0-0 4.5×10^{-7}				
4	3-3-3 0.11039	4-3-2 0.07527	5-2-2 0.03695	4-4-1 0.03136	5-3-1 0.02258	6-2-1 0.00821	5-4-0 0.00434	6-3-0 0.00232	7-1-1 0.00137
	7-2-0 0.00063	8-1-0 7.8×10^{-5}	9-0-0 3.4×10^{-6}						
5	3-3-2 0.10370	4-2-2 0.07071	4-3-1 0.04321	5-2-1 0.02121	4-4-0 0.00831	5-3-0 0.00598	6-1-1 0.00471	6-2-0 0.00218	7-1-0 0.00044
	8-0-0 2.1×10^{-5}								
6	3-2-2 0.11313	3-3-1 0.06913	4-2-1 0.04714	5-1-1 0.01414	4-3-0 0.01330	5-2-0 0.00653	6-1-0 0.00145	7-0-0 0.00011	
7	2-2-2 0.14545	3-2-1 0.08889	4-1-1 0.03704	3-3-0 0.02507	4-2-0 0.01709	5-1-0 0.00513	6-0-0 0.00053		
8	2-2-1 0.13737	3-1-1 0.08395	3-2-0 0.03875	4-1-0 0.01614	5-0-0 0.00224				
9	2-1-1 0.16027	2-2-0 0.07397	3-1-0 0.04520	4-0-0 0.00869					
10	1-1-1 0.24040	2-1-0 0.11095	3-0-0 0.03129						
11	1-1-0 0.22807	2-0-0 0.10526							
12	1-0-0 0.33333								

TABLE K(1)   Two-Hand Residue Probabilities—13 Cards

Residue	Partition	Probability	Residue	Partition	Probability
13	7-6 or 6-7	0.56625	8	5-3 or 3-5	0.47121
	8-5 or 5-8	0.31851		4-4	0.32723
	9-4 or 4-9	0.09831		6-2 or 2-6	0.17135
	10-1 or 3-10	0.01573		7-1 or 1-7	0.02856
	11-2 or 2-11	0.00117		8-0 or 0-8	0.00165
	12-1 or 1-12	3.2×10^{-5}	7	4-3 or 3-4	0.62174
	13-0 or 0-13	1.9×10^{-7}		5-2 or 2-5	0.30522
12	7-5 or 5-7	0.45735		6-1 or 1-6	0.06783
	6-6	0.30490		7-0 or 0-7	0.00522
	8-4 or 4-8	0.19056	6	4-2 or 2-4	0.48447
	9-3 or 3-9	0.04235		3-3	0.35528
	10-2 or 2-10	0.00462		5-1 or 1-5	0.14534
	11-1 or 1-11	0.00021		6-0 or 0-6	0.01491
	12-0 or 0-12	2.7×10^{-6}	5	3-2 or 2-3	0.67826
11	6-5 or 5-6	0.57169		4-1 or 1-4	0.28261
	7-4 or 4-7	0.31761		5-0 or 0-5	0.03913
	8-3 or 3-8	0.09528	4	3-1 or 1-3	0.49739
	9-2 or 2-9	0.01444		2-2	0.40696
	10-1 or 1-10	0.00096		4-0 or 0-4	0.09565
	11-0 or 0-11	2.0×10^{-5}	3	2-1 or 1-2	0.78000
10	6-4 or 4-6	0.46197		3-0 or 0-3	0.22000
	5-5	0.31183	2	1-1	0.52000
	7-3 or 3-7	0.18479		2-0 or 0-2	0.48000
	8-2 or 2-8	0.03780			
	9-1 or 1-9	0.00350			
	10-0 or 0-10	0.00011			
9	5-4 or 4-5	0.58902			
	6-3 or 3-6	0.31414			
	7-2 or 2-7	0.08567			
	8-1 or 1-8	0.01071			
	9-0 or 0-9	0.00046			

TABLE K(2)   Two-Hand Residue Probabilities—12 Cards

Residue	Partition	Probability	Residue	Partition	Probability
13	7-6 or 6-7	0.58635	8	5-3 or 3-5	0.47382
	8-5 or 5-8	0.31412		4-4	0.33315
	9-4 or 4-9	0.08725		6-2 or 2-6	0.16584
	10-3 or 3-10	0.01163		7-1 or 1-7	0.02584
	11-2 or 2-11	0.00063		8-0 or 0-8	0.00135
	12-1 or 1-12	9.6×10^{-6}	7	4-3 or 3-4	0.62929
12	7-5 or 5-7	0.46393		5-2 or 2-5	0.30206
	6-6	0.31573		6-1 or 1-6	0.06407
	8-4 or 4-8	0.18122		7-0 or 0-7	0.00458
	9-3 or 3-9	0.03580	6	4-2 or 2-4	0.48547
	10-2 or 2-10	0.00322		3-3	0.35961
	11-1 or 1-11	0.00011		5-1 or 1-5	0.14123
	12-0 or 0-12	7.4×10^{-7}		6-0 or 0-6	0.01373
11	6-5 or 5-6	0.58635	5	3-2 or 2-3	0.68323
	7-4 or 4-7	0.31412		4-1 or 1-4	0.27950
	8-3 or 3-8	0.08725		5-0 or 0-5	0.03727
	9-2 or 2-9	0.01163	4	3-1 or 1-3	0.49689
	10-1 or 1-10	0.00063		2-2	0.40994
	11-0 or 0-11	9.6×10^{-6}		4-0 or 0-4	0.09317
10	6-4 or 4-6	0.46642	3	2-1 or 1-2	0.78261
	5-5	0.31983		3-0 or 0-3	0.21739
	7-3 or 3-7	0.17768	2	1-1	0.52174
	8-2 or 2-8	0.03332		2-0 or 0-2	0.47826
	9-1 or 1-9	0.00269			
	10-0 or 0-10	6.7×10^{-5}			
9	5-4 or 4-5	0.59968			
	6-3 or 3-6	0.31094			
	7-2 or 2-7	0.07996			
	8-1 or 1-8	0.00909			
	9-0 or 0-9	0.00034			

TABLE K(3)   Two-Hand Residue Probabilities—11 Cards

Residue	Partition	Probability	Residue	Partition	Probability
13	7-6 or 6-7	0.61300	8	5-3 or 3-5	0.47678
	8-5 or 5-8	0.30650		4-4	0.34056
	9-4 or 4-9	0.07298		6-2 or 2-6	0.15893
	10-3 or 3-10	0.00730		7-1 or 1-7	0.02270
	11-2 or 2-11	0.00022		8-0 or 0-8	0.00103
12	7-5 or 5-7	0.47154	7	4-3 or 3-4	0.63854
	6-6	0.33008		5-2 or 2-5	0.29799
	8-4 or 4-8	0.16841		6-1 or 1-6	0.05960
	9-3 or 3-9	0.02807		7-0 or 0-7	0.00387
	10-2 or 2-10	0.00187	6	4-2 or 2-4	0.48651
	11-1 or 1-11	3.4×10^{-5}		3-3	0.36488
11	6-5 or 5-6	0.60514		5-1 or 1-5	0.13622
	7-4 or 4-7	0.30875		6-0 or 0-6	0.01238
	8-3 or 3-8	0.07719	5	3-2 or 2-3	0.68922
	9-2 or 2-9	0.00858		4-1 or 1-4	0.27569
	10-1 or 1-10	0.00034		5-0 or 0-5	0.03509
	11-0 or 0-11	2.8×10^{-6}	4	3-1 or 1-3	0.49624
10	6-4 or 4-6	0.47154		2-2	0.41353
	5-5	0.33008		4-0 or 0-4	0.09023
	7-3 or 3-7	0.16841	3	2-1 or 1-2	0.78571
	8-2 or 2-8	0.02807		3-0 or 0-3	0.21429
	9-1 or 1-9	0.00187	2	1-1	0.52381
	10-0 or 0-10	3.4×10^{-5}		2-0 or 0-2	0.47619
9	5-4 or 4-5	0.61300			
	6-3 or 3-6	0.30650			
	7-2 or 2-7	0.07298			
	8-1 or 1-8	0.00730			
	9-0 or 0-9	0.00022			

TABLE K(4)   Two-Hand Residue Probabilities—10 Cards

Residue	Partition	Probability	Residue	Partition	Probability
13	7-6 or 6-7	0.65015	8	5-3 or 3-5	0.48011
	8-5 or 5-8	0.29257		4-4	0.35008
	9-4 or 4-9	0.05418		6-2 or 2-6	0.15004
	10-3 or 3-10	0.00310		7-1 or 1-7	0.01905
12	7-5 or 5-7	0.48011		8-0 or 0-8	0.00072
	6-6	0.35008	7	4-3 or 3-4	0.65015
	8-4 or 4-8	0.15004		5-2 or 2-5	0.29257
	9-3 or 3-9	0.01905		6-1 or 1-6	0.05418
	10-2 or 2-10	0.00072		7-0 or 0-7	0.00310
11	6-5 or 5-6	0.63015	6	4-2 or 2-4	0.48762
	7-4 or 4-7	0.30007		3-3	0.37152
	8-3 or 3-8	0.06430		5-1 or 1-5	0.13003
	9-2 or 2-9	0.00536		6-0 or 0-6	0.01083
	10-1 or 1-10	0.00012	5	3-2 or 2-3	0.69659
10	6-4 or 4-6	0.47739		4-1 or 1-4	0.27090
	5-5	0.34372		5-0 or 0-5	0.03251
	7-3 or 3-7	0.15588	4	3-1 or 1-3	0.49536
	8-2 or 2-8	0.02192		2-2	0.41796
	9-1 or 1-9	0.00108		4-0 or 0-4	0.08669
	10-0 or 0-10	1.1×10^{-5}	3	2-1 or 1-2	0.78947
9	5-4 or 4-5	0.63015		3-0 or 0-3	0.21053
	6-3 or 3-6	0.30007	2	1-1	0.52632
	7-2 or 2-7	0.06430		2-0 or 0-2	0.47368
	8-1 or 1-8	0.00536			
	9-0 or 0-9	0.00012			

TABLE K(5)   Two-Hand Residue Probabilities—9 Cards

Residue	Partition	Probability	Residue	Partition	Probability
13	7-6 or 6-7	0.70588	7	4-3 or 3-4	0.66515
	8-5 or 5-8	0.26471		5-2 or 2-5	0.28506
	9-4 or 4-9	0.02941		6-1 or 1-6	0.04751
12	7-5 or 5-7	0.48869		7-0 or 0-7	0.00226
	6-6	0.38009	6	4-2 or 2-4	0.48869
	8-4 or 4-8	0.12217		3-3	0.38009
	9-3 or 3-9	0.00905		5-1 or 1-5	0.12217
11	6-5 or 5-6	0.66515		6-0 or 0-6	0.00905
	7-4 or 4-7	0.28506	5	3-2 or 2-3	0.70588
	8-3 or 3-8	0.04751		4-1 or 1-4	0.26471
	9-2 or 2-9	0.00226		5-0 or 0-5	0.02941
10	6-4 or 4-6	0.48375	4	3-1 or 1-3	0.49411
	5-5	0.36281		2-2	0.42353
	7-3 or 3-7	0.13822		4-0 or 0-4	0.08235
	8-2 or 2-8	0.01481	3	2-1 or 1-2	0.79412
	9-1 or 1-9	0.00041		3-0 or 0-3	0.20588
9	5-4 or 4-5	0.65307	2	1-1	0.52941
	6-3 or 3-6	0.29025		2-0 or 0-2	0.47059
	7-2 or 2-7	0.05331			
	8-1 or 1-8	0.00333			
	9-0 or 0-9	4.1 × 10			
8	5-3 or 3-5	0.48375			
	4-4	0.36281			
	6-2 or 2-6	0.13822			
	7-1 or 1-7	0.01481			
	8-0 or 0-8	0.00041			

TABLE K(6)   Two-Hand Residue Probabilities—8 Cards

Residue	Partition	Probability	Residue	Partition	Probability
13	7-6 or 6-7	0.80000	7	4-3 or 3-4	0.68531
	8-5 or 5-8	0.20000		5-2 or 2-5	0.27413
12	7-5 or 5-7	0.49231		6-1 or 1-6	0.03916
	6-6	0.43077		7-0 or 0-7	0.00140
	8-4 or 4-8	0.07692	6	4-2 or 2-4	0.48951
11	6-5 or 5-6	0.71797		3-3	0.39161
	7-4 or 4-7	0.25641		5-1 or 1-5	0.11189
	8-3 or 3-8	0.02564		6-0 or 0-6	0.00699
10	6-4 or 4-6	0.48951	5	3-2 or 2-3	0.71797
	5-5	0.39161		4-1 or 1-4	0.25641
	7-3 or 3-7	0.11189		5-0 or 0-5	0.02564
	8-2 or 2-8	0.00699	4	3-1 or 1-3	0.49231
9	5-4 or 4-5	0.68531		2-2	0.43077
	6-3 or 3-6	0.27413		4-0 or 0-4	0.07692
	7-2 or 2-7	0.03916	3	2-1 or 1-2	0.80000
	8-1 or 1-8	0.00140		3-0 or 0-3	0.20000
8	5-3 or 3-5	0.48733	2	1-1	0.53333
	4-4	0.38073		2-0 or 0-2	0.46667
	6-2 or 2-6	0.12183			
	7-1 or 1-7	0.00995			
	8-0 or 0-8	0.00016			

TABLE K(7)   Two-Hand Residue Probabilities—7 Cards

Residue	Partition	Probability	Residue	Partition	Probability
12	6-6	0.53846	6	4-2 or 2-4	0.48951
	7-5 or 5-7	0.46154		3-3	0.40793
11	6-5 or 5-6	0.80769		5-1 or 1-5	0.09790
	7-4 or 4-7	0.19231		6-0 or 0-6	0.00466
10	6-4 or 4-6	0.48951	5	3-2 or 2-3	0.73427
	5-5	0.44056		4-1 or 1-4	0.24476
	7-3 or 3-7	0.06993		5-0 or 0-5	0.02098
9	5-4 or 4-5	0.73427	4	3-1 or 1-3	0.48951
	6-3 or 3-6	0.24476		2-2	0.44056
	7-2 or 2-7	0.20098		4-0 or 0-4	0.06993
8	5-3 or 3-5	0.48951	3	2-1 or 1-2	0.80769
	4-4	0.40793		3-0 or 0-3	0.19231
	6-2 or 2-6	0.09790	2	1-1	0.53846
	7-1 or 1-7	0.00466		2-0 or 0-2	0.46154
7	4-3 or 3-4	0.71387			
	5-2 or 2-5	0.25699			
	6-1 or 1-6	0.02856			
	7-0 or 0-7	0.00058			

TABLE K(8)   Two-Hand Residue Probabilities—6 Cards

Residue	Partition	Probability	Residue	Partition	Probability
10	5-5	0.54545	5	3-2 or 2-3	0.75758
	6-4 or 4-6	0.45455		4-1 or 1-4	0.22727
9	5-4 or 4-5	0.81818		5-0 or 0-5	0.01515
	6-3 or 3-6	0.18182	4	3-1 or 1-3	0.48485
8	5-3 or 3-5	0.48485		2-2	0.45455
	4-4	0.45455		4-0 or 0-4	0.06061
	6-2 or 2-6	0.06061	3	2-1 or 1-2	0.81818
7	4-3 or 3-4	0.75758		3-0 or 0-3	0.18182
	5-2 or 2-5	0.22727	2	1-1	0.54545
	6-1 or 1-6	0.01515		2-0 or 0-2	0.45455
6	4-2 or 2-4	0.48701			
	3-3	0.43290			
	5-1 or 1-5	0.07792			
	6-0 or 0-6	0.00217			

TABLE K(9)   Two-Hand Residue Probabilities—5 Cards

Residue	Partition	Probability	Residue	Partition	Probability
8	4-4	0.55555	4	3-1 or 1-3	0.47619
	5-3 or 3-5	0.44444		2-2	0.47619
7	4-3 or 3-4	0.83333		4-0 or 0-4	0.04762
	5-2 or 2-5	0.16667	3	2-1 or 1-2	0.83333
6	4-2 or 2-4	0.47619		3-0 or 0-3	0.16667
	3-3	0.47619	2	1-1	0.55555
	5-1 or 1-5	0.04762		2-0 or 0-2	0.44444
5	3-2 or 2-3	0.79365			
	4-1 or 1-4	0.19841			
	5-0 or 0-5	0.00794			

TABLE K(10)   Two-Hand Residue Probabilities—4 Cards

Residue	Partition	Probability	Residue	Partition	Probability
6	3-3	0.57143	3	2-1 or 1-2	0.85714
	4-2 or 2-4	0.42857		3-0 or 0-3	0.14286
5	3-2 or 2-3	0.85714	2	1-1	0.57143
	4-1 or 1-4	0.14286		2-0 or 0-2	0.42857
4	2-2	0.51429			
	3-1 or 1-3	0.45714			
	4-0 or 0-4	0.02857			

TABLE K(11)   Two-Hand Residue Probabilities—3 Cards

Residue	Partition	Probability	Residue	Partition	Probability
4	2-2	0.60000	2	1-1	0.60000
	3-1 or 1-3	0.40000		2-0 or 0-2	0.40000
3	2-1 or 1-2	0.90000			
	3-0 or 0-3	0.10000			

TABLE K(12)   Two-Hand Residue
Probabilities—2 Cards

Residue	Partition	Probability
2	1-1	0.66667
	2-0 or 0-2	0.33333

TABLE L   Game Expectations for a Simple Truel

| Accuracy Functions | | | Game Expectations | | | Accuracy Functions | | | Game Expectations | | |
a	b	c	E(A)	E(B)	E(C)	a	b	c	E(A)	E(B)	E(C)
1.00	1.00	0.65	0.18	0.18	0.65	0.95	0.55	0.55	0.31	0.09	0.60
1.00	1.00	0.60	0.20	0.20	0.60	0.95	0.55	0.50	0.34	0.10	0.55
1.00	1.00	0.55	0.23	0.23	0.55	0.95	0.50	0.50	0.36	0.09	0.55
1.00	1.00	0.50	0.25	0.25	0.50	0.90	0.90	0.60	0.19	0.19	0.62
1.00	0.95	0.65	0.18	0.16	0.66	0.90	0.90	0.55	0.21	0.21	0.58
1.00	0.95	0.60	0.21	0.18	0.61	0.90	0.90	0.50	0.24	0.24	0.53
1.00	0.95	0.55	0.24	0.21	0.56	0.90	0.85	0.60	0.20	0.17	0.63
1.00	0.95	0.50	0.26	0.23	0.51	0.90	0.85	0.55	0.22	0.19	0.58
1.00	0.90	0.65	0.19	0.15	0.66	0.90	0.85	0.50	0.25	0.22	0.53
1.00	0.90	0.60	0.22	0.17	0.61	0.90	0.80	0.60	0.21	0.16	0.64
1.00	0.90	0.55	0.25	0.19	0.56	0.90	0.80	0.55	0.23	0.18	0.59
1.00	0.90	0.50	0.28	0.21	0.51	0.90	0.80	0.50	0.26	0.20	0.54
1.00	0.85	0.65	0.20	0.13	0.67	0.90	0.75	0.60	0.22	0.14	0.64
1.00	0.85	0.60	0.23	0.15	0.62	0.90	0.75	0.55	0.24	0.16	0.59
1.00	0.85	0.55	0.26	0.17	0.57	0.90	0.75	0.50	0.27	0.18	0.55
1.00	0.85	0.50	0.29	0.20	0.52	0.90	0.70	0.60	0.23	0.13	0.65
1.00	0.80	0.65	0.21	0.12	0.67	0.90	0.70	0.55	0.26	0.14	0.60
1.00	0.80	0.60	0.24	0.14	0.62	0.90	0.70	0.50	0.29	0.16	0.55
1.00	0.80	0.55	0.27	0.16	0.57	0.90	0.65	0.60	0.24	0.11	0.65
1.00	0.80	0.50	0.30	0.18	0.52	0.90	0.65	0.55	0.27	0.13	0.60
1.00	0.75	0.65	0.22	0.11	0.67	0.90	0.65	0.50	0.30	0.15	0.56
1.00	0.75	0.60	0.25	0.13	0.62	0.90	0.60	0.60	0.25	0.10	0.66
1.00	0.75	0.55	0.28	0.14	0.58	0.90	0.60	0.55	0.28	0.11	0.61
1.00	0.75	0.50	0.31	0.16	0.53	0.90	0.60	0.50	0.31	0.13	0.56
1.00	0.70	0.65	0.23	0.10	0.68	0.90	0.55	0.55	0.29	0.10	0.61
1.00	0.70	0.60	0.26	0.11	0.63	0.90	0.55	0.50	0.32	0.11	0.56
1.00	0.70	0.55	0.29	0.13	0.58	0.90	0.50	0.50	0.34	0.10	0.57
1.00	0.70	0.50	0.33	0.14	0.53	0.85	0.85	0.55	0.21	0.21	0.59
1.00	0.65	0.65	0.24	0.08	0.68	0.85	0.85	0.50	0.23	0.23	0.54
1.00	0.65	0.60	0.27	0.10	0.63	0.85	0.80	0.55	0.22	0.19	0.60
1.00	0.65	0.55	0.30	0.11	0.58	0.85	0.80	0.50	0.24	0.21	0.55
1.00	0.65	0.50	0.34	0.13	0.53	0.85	0.75	0.55	0.23	0.17	0.60
1.00	0.60	0.60	0.28	0.09	0.63	0.85	0.75	0.50	0.25	0.19	0.55
1.00	0.60	0.55	0.32	0.10	0.59	0.85	0.70	0.55	0.24	0.15	0.61
1.00	0.60	0.50	0.35	0.11	0.54	0.85	0.70	0.50	0.27	0.17	0.56
1.00	0.55	0.55	0.33	0.09	0.59	0.85	0.65	0.55	0.25	0.14	0.61
1.00	0.55	0.50	0.36	0.10	0.54	0.85	0.65	0.50	0.28	0.16	0.57
1.00	0.50	0.50	0.38	0.08	0.54	0.85	0.60	0.55	0.26	0.12	0.62
0.95	0.95	0.60	0.19	0.19	0.61	0.85	0.60	0.50	0.29	0.14	0.57
0.95	0.95	0.55	0.22	0.22	0.56	0.85	0.55	0.55	0.27	0.11	0.62
0.95	0.95	0.50	0.24	0.24	0.51	0.85	0.55	0.50	0.30	0.12	0.58
0.95	0.90	0.60	0.20	0.18	0.62	0.85	0.50	0.50	0.32	0.10	0.58
0.95	0.90	0.55	0.23	0.20	0.57	0.80	0.80	0.50	0.22	0.22	0.56
0.95	0.90	0.50	0.26	0.22	0.52	0.80	0.75	0.55	0.21	0.18	0.61
0.95	0.85	0.60	0.21	0.16	0.62	0.80	0.75	0.50	0.23	0.20	0.56
0.95	0.85	0.55	0.24	0.18	0.57	0.80	0.70	0.55	0.22	0.16	0.62
0.95	0.85	0.50	0.27	0.21	0.53	0.80	0.70	0.50	0.25	0.18	0.57
0.95	0.80	0.60	0.22	0.15	0.63	0.80	0.65	0.55	0.23	0.15	0.62
0.95	0.80	0.55	0.25	0.17	0.58	0.80	0.65	0.50	0.26	0.17	0.58
0.95	0.80	0.50	0.28	0.19	0.53	0.80	0.60	0.55	0.24	0.13	0.63
0.95	0.75	0.60	0.23	0.13	0.63	0.80	0.60	0.50	0.27	0.15	0.58
0.95	0.75	0.55	0.26	0.15	0.59	0.80	0.55	0.55	0.25	0.11	0.64
0.95	0.75	0.50	0.29	0.17	0.54	0.80	0.55	0.50	0.28	0.13	0.59
0.95	0.70	0.60	0.24	0.12	0.64	0.80	0.50	0.50	0.30	0.11	0.59
0.95	0.70	0.55	0.27	0.14	0.59	0.75	0.75	0.50	0.21	0.21	0.57
0.95	0.70	0.50	0.31	0.15	0.54	0.75	0.70	0.50	0.23	0.19	0.58
0.95	0.65	0.60	0.25	0.11	0.64	0.75	0.65	0.50	0.24	0.18	0.59
0.95	0.65	0.55	0.29	0.12	0.59	0.75	0.60	0.50	0.25	0.16	0.59
0.95	0.65	0.50	0.32	0.14	0.55	0.75	0.55	0.50	0.26	0.14	0.60
0.95	0.60	0.60	0.26	0.09	0.65	0.75	0.50	0.50	0.26	0.12	0.61
0.95	0.60	0.55	0.30	0.11	0.60	0.70	0.55	0.50	0.24	0.15	0.61
0.95	0.60	0.50	0.33	0.12	0.55	0.70	0.50	0.50	0.25	0.13	0.62

AUTHOR INDEX

SUBJECT INDEX